D0931099

Vagrant Nation

Vagrant Nation

Police Power, Constitutional Change, and the Making of the 1960s

RISA GOLUBOFF

OXFORD
UNIVERSITY PRESS

OXFORD
UNIVERSITY PRESS

Oxford University Press is a department of the University of Oxford. It furthers
the University's objective of excellence in research, scholarship, and education
by publishing worldwide. Oxford is a registered trade mark of Oxford University
Press in the UK and certain other countries.

Published in the United States of America by Oxford University Press
198 Madison Avenue, New York, NY 10016, United States of America.

Library of Congress Cataloging-in-Publication Data
Names: Goluboff, Risa Lauren, 1971– author.
Title: Vagrant nation : police power, constitutional change, and the making
of the 1960s / Risa Goluboff.
Description: New York : Oxford University Press, 2016. | Includes
bibliographical references and index.
Identifiers: LCCN 2015028972 | ISBN 978-0-19-976844-8 (hardback)
Subjects: LCSH: Vagrancy—Law and legislation—United States—History. |
BISAC: HISTORY / United States / 20th Century. | HISTORY / Social History.
| LAW / Legal History.
Classification: LCC KF9450 .G65 2016 | DDC 345.73/0248—dc23 LC record available
at http://lccn.loc.gov/2015028972

1 3 5 7 9 8 6 4 2
Printed by Sheridan, USA

Cover Image: Police arrest a Vietnam War protestor on the steps
of the Supreme Court in April 1971.

For Rich, Ellie, and Solly

CONTENTS

Introduction

In 1949 Los Angeles, a police officer arrested Isidore Edelman as he spoke from a park bench in Pershing Square. Twenty years later, an officer in Jacksonville, Florida, arrested Margaret "Lorraine" Papachristou when she was out for a night on the town.

Edelman and Papachristou had very little in common. Edelman was a middle-aged, Russian-born, communist-inclined soapbox orator. Papachristou was blond, statuesque, twenty-three, and a Jacksonville native. The circumstances of their arrests were different, too. It was Edelman's strident and offensive speeches that caught the attention of the police—his politics were just too inflammatory for the early Cold War. For Papachristou, it was her choice of companions—she and her equally blonde friend had been out with two African American men in a southern city not quite transformed by the civil rights era.[1]

What Edelman and Papachristou shared despite their differences was the crime for which they were arrested: vagrancy. California law made a vagrant of everyone from wanderers and prostitutes to the willfully unemployed and the lewd. Edelman's earlier arrests off the soapbox had made him "dissolute" and therefore a vagrant under the law. Papachristou was arrested under a Jacksonville ordinance that criminalized some twenty different types of vagrants, including "rogues and vagabonds, or dissolute persons who go about begging, . . . persons who use juggling or unlawful games or plays, common drunkards, . . . common railers and brawlers, persons wandering or strolling around from place to place without any lawful purpose or object, habitual loafers, disorderly persons." Such a law, noted a judge in 1970, sounded like "a casting advertisement in an Elizabethan newspaper for the street scene in a drama of that era." To the police, the listed categories did not even exhaust the law's possibilities. They noted that Papachristou and her companions were vagrants for an improvised and far more modern reason: "prowling by auto."[2]

As the evocative language of these laws suggests, the crime of vagrancy had long historical roots. William Blackstone, the doyen of eighteenth-century English legal commentators, noted that "idleness" was "a high offense against the public oeconomy" not only in England but in China and ancient Athens as well. Modern American lawyers liked to highlight vagrancy laws' obsolescence by tracing the laws to the medieval English Statutes of Labourers of the fourteenth century. Their more direct roots, scholars would have scolded them, hailed (merely) from the sixteenth century. Together with sumptuary laws that told the English who could wear what—making one's rank instantly apparent—and "poor laws" that supervised and supported the needy, vagrancy laws were built for hierarchy and social order. Despite much-touted myths of American upward and outward mobility, the laws proliferated along with English colonists on this side of the Atlantic too.[3]

Indeed, when Edelman was arrested in 1949, vagrancy was a crime in every state and the District of Columbia. It was the basis for hundreds of thousands of arrests every year, not including arrests for related crimes like loitering and being a suspicious person. With a few exceptions, and despite the many varieties of vagrancy laws, scattered challenges to the laws' constitutionality prior to the 1950s failed. A prominent 1946 treatise captured prevailing sentiment when it concluded that vagrancy laws' legality "cannot be doubted." Four hundred years on the books were decisive evidence of their legitimacy.[4]

Two features of vagrancy laws made them especially attractive. First, the laws' breadth and ambiguity gave the police virtually unlimited discretion. It was the officer on the beat who determined in the first instance—and often, as it turned out, the last—what it meant to loiter, to lack a lawful purpose, to be dissolute or suspicious. Because it was almost always possible to justify a vagrancy arrest, the laws provided what one critic called "an escape hatch" from the Fourth Amendment's protections against arrest without probable cause. As one Supreme Court justice would write in 1965, vagrancy-related laws made it legal to stand on a street corner "only at the whim of any police officer."[5]

Second, vagrancy laws made it a crime to be a certain type of person—anyone who fit the description of one of those colorful Elizabethan characters. Where most American laws required people to *do* something criminal before they could be arrested, vagrancy laws emphatically did not. "The purpose of vagrancy laws is to subject persons, whose habits of life are such as to make them objectionable members of society, to police regulations promotive of the safety or good order of the community in which they are found," a popular 1955 legal treatise observed. The goal was "to prevent crimes which may likely flow from a vagrant's mode of life, by cutting out at the roots breeding places of many crimes offensive to the personal well-being of many citizens. . . . Such preventive purpose wholly fails if a law enforcement officer must wait until a crime is committed."[6]

Armed with this roving license to arrest, officials employed vagrancy laws for a breath-taking array of purposes: to force the local poor to work or suffer for their support; to keep out poor or suspicious strangers; to suppress differences that might be dangerous; to stop crimes before they were committed; to keep racial minorities, political troublemakers, and nonconforming rebels at bay. As these uses suggest, vagrancy laws were linked to a conception of postwar American society—as they had been linked to a conception of sixteenth-century English society—in which everyone had a proper place. The vagrancy law was often the go-to response against anyone who threatened, as many described it during vagrancy laws' heyday, to move "out of place" socially, culturally, politically, racially, sexually, economically, or spatially. Over time, states and localities deployed and retooled vagrancy laws for use against almost any—real or perceived, old or new—threat to public order and safety.[7]

The officer on the beat in the 1950s and 1960s saw such threats everywhere, in the "queer," the "Commie," the "uppity" black man, the "scruffy" young white one. It was his job to see these threats, to determine who was "legitimate" and who not. He was trained to see difference as dangerous, to see the unusual as criminal. That was what not only his superiors but also the upstanding taxpayers wanted, expected him to do. When he walked the streets questioning and arresting the scum, the flamboyant, the detritus, and the apostate, he brought vagrancy laws with him, and he did his job.[8]

Between Edelman's arrest and Papachristou's twenty years later, literally millions of people shared their vagrancy fates. Some of those arrested comported with the usual image of the vagrant. Sam Thompson, for example, was an underemployed handyman and alcoholic arrested some fifty-five times in Louisville, Kentucky, in the 1950s. But many, like Edelman and Papachristou, are more suprising. The police arrested for loitering the Reverend Fred Shuttlesworth, co-founder with Martin Luther King Jr. of the Southern Christian Leadership Conference, when he spoke briefly with colleagues on a Birmingham street corner during a 1962 department store boycott. It was vagrancy the police used when they could not get Tulane law student Stephen Wainwright to cooperate with a murder investigation in New Orleans' French Quarter in 1964. It was vagrancy as well that justified the 1966 arrest of Martin Hirshhorn, a young cross-dressing hair stylist arrested in his hotel room in Manhattan wearing only a half-slip and brassiere. Police turned to vagrancy in 1967 when they arrested Joy Kelley in the "crash pad" she had rented for herself and her hippie friends in Charlotte, North Carolina. And they used it again when they mistook Dorothy Ann Kirkwood for a prostitute when she was on her way to meet her boyfriend on Memphis's famous Beale Street in 1968.[9]

These and other vagrancy suspects were white and black, male and female, straight and gay, urban and rural, southern, northern, western, and midwestern. They had money or needed it, defied authority or tried to comply with it. They were arrested on public streets and in their own homes; as locals or strangers; for political protests or seeming like a murderer; for their race, their sexuality, their poverty, or their lifestyle.

Vagrancy laws were thus not only a fact of the legal landscape in the middle of the twentieth century. They were also a fact of life for countless Americans. Working-class immigrant families warned their maturing children not to leave home without money that could inoculate them from vagrancy arrests. Early "homophile" organizations educated their gay and lesbian members about "lewd vagrancy" arrests and how to avoid them—"wear at least three items of clothing of your own sex" was a common refrain. Black newspapers warned their readers that vagrancy arrests were a likely consequence of any racially presumptuous behavior. Civil rights organizations tried to head off seemingly inevitable vagrancy arrests of workers heading south by providing "vagrancy forms" that attested to the workers' standing as "reputable member[s] of the community."[10]

The vagrancy law regime, then, regulated so much more than what is generally considered "vagrancy." Vagrancy laws were as versatile as they were common and legally valid. They represented an approach to policing, a vision of society, and, for many, an inescapable vulnerability.

That was all about to change. The case that followed Edelman's 1949 arrest marked a new era in the history of vagrancy laws. Though Edelman himself did not emerge victorious, his case both signaled and set in motion a process of rapid and fundamental legal transformation. Laws on the books for four centuries were now, suddenly, on the constitutional defensive. Over the next twenty years, alleged vagrants and their lawyers, social reformers, activists, the media, state legislators, state and lower federal courts, and, somewhat belatedly, the Supreme Court condemned vagrancy laws and their uses. Even the laws' fiercest defenders—the police who relied on them—substantially narrowed their justifications for the laws' legitimacy. In a trio of cases in 1971 and 1972, including Papachristou's own, the Court announced that vagrancy, loitering, and suspicious persons laws were unconstitutional.[11]

This book shows how that change happened. It asks how a category of laws that had been ubiquitous and presumptively legitimate for centuries lost its constitutional validity over the course of just twenty years.

The answer to that question can be found in the major upheavals that convulsed American legal, social, intellectual, cultural, and political life between the 1950s and the 1970s. Those who had long lacked social and political power began to organize, march, and protest; stand fast before fire hoses and riot gear; hire lawyers and bring appeals. In doing so, they projected a new image of American society in which vagrancy policing was anathema. To them, the cop on the street—with the vagrancy law tucked away in his pocket—was the "pig," the "Man," the "Establishment." The language of equality and nonconformity became a mantra, the image of the respected and fulfilled individual, the Holy Grail.

Telling the history of vagrancy laws' demise thus means telling a legal history of the 1960s writ large. As may already be apparent, the age-old crime of vagrancy became a flashpoint in virtually every great cultural controversy of the time. From sexual freedom to civil rights, from poverty to the politics of criminal justice, from the Beats to the hippies, from communism to the Vietnam War, the great issues of the day all collided with the category of the vagrant. Vagrancy, police power, and the Constitution met on streets and parade grounds, skid rows and lunch counters, at polite sit-ins, militant protests, and outright riots. Wherever the sixties happened, vagrancy law was there.

Indeed, legal challenges to vagrancy laws were made both necessary and possible by other changes in American law and society between the mid-1950s and the early 1970s. Because vagrancy laws had been a key way of keeping people in place, they presented obstacles to the other goals (of racial equality, sexual freedom, political protest) of their usual targets. Local officials and low-level judges armed with discretion-licensing vagrancy laws could, and did, thwart those goals just as Jim Crow, the draft board, and the welfare agency did. Though the vagrancy law challenge claimed only a limited immunity from arrest on sight, that immunity was crucial to all kinds of other ambitions. Because any right would be hard to vindicate if a person could not walk down the street without being arrested for who he or she was, alleged vagrants began to insist on their right to make their own place in the world, the faultiness of the whole idea of place, or both.

These claims went to the heart of the pressing questions of the era. When was difference dangerous? How could law enforcers identify such danger? To what extent and under what parameters could the law safely embrace the challenge to the status quo, especially at a moment of deep anxiety about crime, violence, and disorder? The undoing of vagrancy laws long used to neutralize any threat was thus an integral part of the making of the 1960s because it had to be.

The profound upheavals of the period made the dramatic change in vagrancy laws' fortunes not only necessary but also possible. Many of vagrancy laws' targets were now organized, assertive, and—this is key—represented by lawyers. Given that vagrancy cases promised neither glory nor money, people arrested for vagrancy had had little luck finding legal counsel even a generation earlier. During the 1960s, however, some of the best educated, most pedigreed lawyers actively sought out vagrancy clients. Louis Lusky, first in his class at Columbia Law School, former Supreme Court law clerk, and later an eminent scholar at his alma mater, pursued Sam Thompson's case all the way to the Supreme Court. Anthony Amsterdam, first in *his* class at the University of Pennsylvania Law School, former Supreme Court clerk, and eminent scholar at *his* alma mater (as well as at Stanford and New York University law schools), helped shepherd Fred Shuttlesworth's case to the same court and many other cases through the state and lower federal courts. As these and other lawyers joined the growing staffs of the American Civil Liberties Union (ACLU) or the NAACP Legal Defense Fund (LDF), or brand new legal aid and public defender offices, they knew they were not their fathers' lawyers. They saw themselves as part of a self-conscious social and professional network very different from the Wall Street firms for which they had been trained.[12]

To these lawyers, cases that had always been dismissed as involving the most trivial of charges suddenly seemed full of possibility. Conceived for a very different time and place, vagrancy laws no longer served their original purposes. Whether one took as the lodestar an expanding welfare state that deemed the poor worthy of support or a free-wheeling market economy that deemed them an unavoidable reality, criminalizing poverty was simply incongruous. So too was criminalizing difference, as the premises underlying vagrancy laws' many other functions also came under attack. Reform movements were claiming, and courts were increasingly offering, constitutional protection for new people and new rights—the rights of racial minorities and the poor, or rights to free speech, nonconformity, and privacy. Legal professionals questioned the fundamental basis of the criminal law, asking whether it should—as vagrancy laws did—regulate either public or private morality. The Warren Court's bevy of emerging rules for the police and the courts were dubbed nothing less than a "criminal procedure revolution."

These changes of the 1960s made the largely hidden, centuries-old practices of vagrancy law governance visible and visibly problematic. Law enforcement officers did what they had always done with vagrancy laws. But as new groups linked their own claims against the laws to those of other groups, a full picture of the vagrancy law regime began to materialize. Each new arrest revealed deep tensions between vagrancy laws and developing, if contested, tenets of criminal law and procedure and emerging, if contested, ideas of constitutional rights to freedom and equality.

Prior to the 1960s, the Constitution had endorsed, or at least tolerated, vagrancy laws—capacious grants of discretion to arrest people on sight. After that time, it did not. Though the Supreme Court did not vindicate every claim of every vagrancy law challenger, its rejection of vagrancy laws marked a fundamentally new constitutional orientation toward people out of place. The history of vagrancy laws' fall from constitutional grace is thus a history not only of how a legal regime lost its legitimacy, how the rules of policing shifted, or how "the sixties" came to be. It is also a story of how the meaning of the Constitution itself changed.

Telling that story requires leaving behind preconceptions about how constitutional change happens. A conventional approach would likely place Supreme Court Justice William O. Douglas at the center. The story would begin with Douglas telling (possibly apocryphal) tales of a youth spent riding the rails and bedding down with hoboes. It would detail Douglas's abiding condemnation of vagrancy laws and his ultimate success authoring their invalidation in *Papachristou v. Jacksonville*. The story would close with Douglas's death and *Papachristou* as the opinion he wanted read at his funeral. The lesson would be simple: Douglas was a man with a vision and the power to make it happen.

That story is not this book. Constitutional change does not begin and end at the Supreme Court, with the decisions or biographies of the justices. It does not even begin with some heroic lawyer or organization identifying an obvious constitutional issue and crafting a strategy to address it. The story told here bears little resemblance, for example, to the usual history of the NAACP "on the road" to *Brown v. Board of Education*.[13]

Against what has become the standard model of the organized, straight-ahead legal campaign, the vagrancy law challenge may seem at first glance like no model of constitutional change at all. To be sure, organizations like the ACLU and the NAACP LDF were repeat players and organizational hubs for information and publicity. But the lawyers and clients who propelled the challenge were not their minions, dispatched from New York or Washington, DC. Nor did vagrancy law challengers have any unified theory of attack for some time.

The many, often barely visible, uses of vagrancy laws made a full picture of the regime long difficult to discern. It was only through a process of discovery and publicity, borrowing and adapting, that litigants, lawyers, and judges could even begin to map out the extensive terrain of vagrancy laws' reign. At first, it was not clear that vagrancy laws themselves would be the target. Law enforcers—the beat officers, police brass, prosecutors, and local judges who exercised vagrancy law discretion—seemed at least equally responsible for the injuries to person, dignity, and future prospects that the regime inflicted. That lawyers and clients settled on constitutional challenges to vagrancy laws resulted more from convergence than coordination.

But one can hardly dismiss a free-wheeling constitutional challenge that produced some two hundred fifty published cases over a twenty-year period. Improvisational, cumulative, and only loosely networked, the challenge was irrepressible because vagrancy law represented a legal obstacle so pervasive and so intrusive that every social movement of the era ran smack into it and tried to push it over. The vagrancy law challenge offers a model of constitutional change that very much began "from below" but did not remain there. It moved from the lived experiences of people like Edelman and Papachristou into the formal processes of "the law." Cases kept coming not in one place or as a result of one group or one set of lawyers. They kept coming because the laws were critical to the maintenance of an increasingly contested order and hierarchy in American society.

The vagrancy law challenge thus produces a new image of legal and constitutional change. One might liken the litigation strategies with which we have become familiar to the 1950s high school prom—organized, fixed, and known, even if contingent in many of its particulars. By contrast, one might think of the vagrancy law challenge as a groovy 1960s "happening"—no one really planned it; the guest list was unwritten; the entertainment self-created; the location, duration, and content relatively spontaneous and open. Vagrancy cases shared certain constraints and opportunities, characteristics and approaches, but each case grew out of its own social world and took on its own shape.

Constructing and relating this diffuse and improvised history requires its own kind of orchestrated improvisation. The chapters highlight different areas of social life—from skid rows to hippie communes to gay bars—and different areas of legal doctrine—from free speech to criminal law and procedure to civil rights. Some chapters begin with the Supreme Court, others with lawyers, and still others with "vagrants" themselves. Some focus tightly on the vagrancy law challenge itself, while others extend to the developments that made that challenge possible or appealing. Some explore the lost world of vagrancy policing, while others assess the legal doctrines deployed to destroy it. Like vagrancy laws themselves, this story travels the entire country, from rural Louisiana to big city California. It takes account of vagrancy law defendants and their lawyers, social movement organizations, legislators and other politicians, lower court judges, legal scholars, and the media as well as the police officers, prosecutors, and other local officials responsible for vagrancy enforcement. Whatever person, place, or moment serves as the starting point, the story moves not only forward in time as the challenge gains adherents and momentum but also up and down the legal process, from litigant to lawyer to judge and back again.

This book thus shows the real work of legal and constitutional change. It shows how vagrancy laws' fall was both shockingly quick—twenty years is a metaphorical blink of an eye given a four-hundred-year-old regime—and slowly elaborated. It is difficult for a regular person to decide to fight a law. It takes knowledge and consciousness, financial resources and human ones. Even once a person has decided to fight and gotten a lawyer, it is hard to get a case to court in a posture, and with the right kinds of facts, that allows a court to answer a legal question crafted so as to produce the effect lawyers and clients desire. There are the obstructionist police officers who drop cases whose outcomes they fear and the well-meaning prosecutors who do so when they think the police were out of line; the reluctant judges who don't want to go out on a limb and the Supreme Court justices who often have their eyes on larger stakes or some other case that term. The process by which judges, and especially Supreme Court justices like

William O. Douglas, came to see vagrancy laws as a problem is an important part of the story. But so are the many arrests that never became convictions, the cases courts never saw, those they never decided, and even those in which they utterly failed to deal with what often seemed an intractable problem. History is full of such false starts and meandering paths, of successes and failures, of conflict seen and not seen, of ideas on the table and those that fall off of it. This is that kind of history, the messy kind, the human kind. It tries to understand how change happens in a complex world, and what it means when it does.

Reconstructing vagrancy laws' downfall as a legal history of the 1960s is a hard story to contain. First, there is the problem of defining the subject. Vagrancy laws were not a clearly delineated category. They were derivative, sprawling, and overlapping. Sometimes they included loitering or being a suspicious person. Sometimes those crimes were separate. Sometimes they included drunkenness or prostitution, but just as often those too were separate. Some states considered vagrancy to be a more serious charge than disorderly conduct or breach of the peace. Some less. Moreover, it was not that vagrancy laws served as the sole law enforcement tool against any particular threat. For the political dissident, vagrancy shared law enforcement space with sedition; for the gay man, it was sodomy; and for the street protestor, breach of the peace or disorderly conduct. As a result, what follows necessarily includes not only vagrancy laws themselves but also the various legal, and extralegal, constellations of which they were a part. It includes the laws and the criminal justice apparatus that enforced them. It details arrests and the brutality that sometimes accompanied them. The shifting scope of inquiry is determined by the particular social world from which the case emerged as well as from the regulatory landscape, the practices of police departments and officers, the acts of suspects, the strategies of lawyers, and the framings of judges.[14]

Still, the focus of this story always remains vagrancy laws and their challengers. This is a story about the use and abuse of law, rather than the use and abuse of force. Moreover, in keeping the focus on vagrancy-related laws, rather than their close relations, it follows the lead of many at the time who viewed vagrancy, loitering, and often suspicious persons laws as different in kind from most other laws. One prominent lawyer singled them out as "the paradigmatic harassment statutes." A Supreme Court justice put vagrancy laws "in a class by themselves."[15]

Second, there is the problem of when to begin the story of vagrancy laws' decline. Because people have always chafed under the laws' strictures, the story could begin as far back as defiance to the 1349 Statutes of Labourers or the various Tudor vagabonds acts, or with early efforts to evade and defy vagrancy enforcement on these shores. Or it might begin in the Depression Era of the 1930s, when poverty took on new meaning in the United States, and the

Supreme Court decided a handful of cases that began to undermine some of the basic assumptions buttressing vagrancy laws. These cases would become staples in the vagrancy law challenge a few decades later, but when they were decided, they were scattershot and disconnected. For the most part, vagrancy laws survived not only the Depression but the war that followed. The developments of the 1930s are thus better understood as resources for, and precursors to, the vagrancy law challenge of the 1960s than the beginning of the story itself.[16]

Third, it is difficult to maintain focus on vagrancy laws against the vast sweep of the 1960s. As shown here, that era will be both familiar and unfamiliar. As history does not usually proceed in neatly bounded decades, this book covers a rather "long 1960s." It begins in the early 1950s, when Edelman challenged his arrest, the civil rights movement entered a new phase, the Beats arrived on the cultural scene, the first gay and lesbian organizations emerged, and lawyers began to recognize vagrancy law as a constitutional problem. It ends in the early 1970s, with *Papachristou v. Jacksonville* crystallizing the claims of the prior twenty years.

Within that period, there is no one-to-one correlation between the events that dominate conventional histories of the era and the events that become visible through the vagrancy law lens. Though international developments come into view, the campaign's focus on changing the U.S. Constitution makes this a national, rather than global, story. Within that national frame, some movements of the long 1960s did not significantly partake of the vagrancy law challenge, and some left less of an imprint on the law books than those emphasized here. Because the vagrancy harassment of African Americans was so critical to the growing consensus against vagrancy laws, for example, they are the racial minority most visible here. Moreover, though women enter the story to fight vagrancy laws that interfered with their sexual autonomy, there is little sustained discussion of Second Wave feminist vagrancy law challenges. That absence is due partially to the fact that the protests of the women's movement postdated the heyday of the vagrancy law regime. In part, however, vagrancy laws had long applied differently to women, and during the long 1960s, the state often preferred other legal methods of regulating women. The rise of conservatism at the very moment left and liberal social movements were staking their claims also appears here only obliquely. Conservative activists are not present as vagrancy challengers because they did not, so far as the historical record reveals, tend to get arrested for vagrancy. Where the ideas and institutions undergirding the rise of conservatism informed the views of vagrancy laws' defenders, however, they are frequently, if implicitly, in evidence. Whether on the left or the right, not every iconic person, place, or incident of the 1960s can be found in these pages. The history of the vagrancy law challenge thus produces *a*, not *the*, legal history of the sixties.[17]

Finally, containing the story of vagrancy laws' aftermath is even more challenging than containing the story of its demise. For the story—like the institutional incentives for the police to engage in social control— continues today and, no doubt, tomorrow. It is not just that the present repeatedly butts into the past, as aspects of the vagrancy law regime call to mind current problems of police power, social control, and constitutional interpretation. It is also that the story does not end in 1971 and 1972, when the Supreme Court struck down vagrancy, loitering, and suspicious persons laws.

The Court's declaration that vagrancy laws as they were written were incompatible with the Constitution was important. It suggested that the Constitution might embody some fundamental ideas that had come out of the social, political, cultural, and legal battles of the previous decades. But it was not everything. For one, the Court invalidated vagrancy laws only after it had created other methods of authorizing police discretion. It hoped that methods like stop and frisk would be more congruent with contemporary ideas about criminal justice and constitutional rights. For another, the justices who ultimately disposed of vagrancy laws stopped short of a wholesale validation of the individual rights claims that the vagrancy law challenge inspired.

Most fundamentally, the end of the vagrancy law story is unruly because there can be no definitive ending. The Court is not the only or the final arbiter of the legitimacy of any law. The moment when the Supreme Court and the Constitution (belatedly) joined the fray is as good a moment to pause as any. That vagrancy laws—long considered among the most trivial of violations—had constitutional dimensions suggested that nothing was now too small for constitutional consideration. What is more, the Constitution had taken the side of vagrancy laws' challengers. We should not mistake, however, a moment of punctuation for resolution. The Supreme Court's interventions fundamentally transformed, rather than ended, the war between order and disorder, control and freedom. The battles that would follow, battles that would remain profoundly contested and fundamentally constitutive of the fabric of American law and society, would be shaped indelibly by the one set in motion with Isidore Edelman's arrest in the fall of 1949.

1

From the Soapbox to the Courthouse

As he did most days, on September 22, 1949, Isidore Edelman left his apartment in the Happy Valley neighborhood of Los Angeles and trekked five miles downtown. His destination was Pershing Square. His plan was to spend the day talking.

Even among the many characters the park had on frequent display, this soapbox orator stood out. Perhaps it was his presence. Though he was a small, balding, middle-aged man, Edelman's eyes were wide awake, and his smile had more than a little mischief in it. Perhaps it was his perseverance. Day in and day out, parkgoers could count on Edelman for education, provocation, and entertainment.

Most likely, though, Edelman's fame was due to what he said there in the park at the beginning of the Cold War. Edelman had come to the United States from Russia in 1910, when he was eleven years old. During the early New Deal, he worked for the federal theater project of the Works Progress Administration (WPA). Later, he described himself as a "freelance pamphleteer." Edelman joined the Communist Party in 1936, but he was expelled in 1947 because, in his words, "I criticized its leadership for waging relentless war against right and left deviationists in its ranks." That said, Edelman acknowledged that he remained "Communist in his thinking."[1]

For a year and a half, Edelman had taken his place in the square without incident. For a year and a half, he had preached his personal brand of left politics to warm, or at worst indifferent, reception. Then trouble began. Whether those who caused that trouble did so because they deemed Edelman a buffoon, an irritant, or a threat, they were not alone in worrying that views like Edelman's could destroy the nation's moral fabric and political security. Edelman's radical notions put many Americans in mind of Soviet power and the Soviets' recent explosion of their first atomic bomb. Who knew what fanatics like Edelman might do? In fact, a year after Edelman's arrest, Julius and Ethel Rosenberg would be arrested, and eventually executed, for spying for the Soviets.

Figure 1.1 Isidore Edelman, a left-wing soapbox orator in Los Angeles' Pershing Square in 1949. Edelman was one of many unpopular free speakers arrested for vagrancy. Though the Supreme Court ultimately dismissed his case, the fact that the Court even considered Edelman's plight marked a new era of vagrancy law vulnerability. UCLA Library Special Collections, Charles E. Young Research Library.

Doing their part to preserve the nation, self-described patriots began harassing Edelman. They heckled him. They held a red flag over his head while he talked, warning his audience of his political views. They dunked him in the park's fountain. Nearby police officers did not respond.[2]

Had the officers merely ignored Edelman, he probably would have counted himself lucky. But they went after him, arresting him sixty-three times in quick succession. Sometimes they brought him to the park office or the central police station only to let him go. That cut short his speeches and added to his arrest record, but at least there wasn't more. Other times, though, he was charged with, and convicted of, begging, soliciting funds, distributing handbills. One charge was for defacing a park bench (of the thick concrete type) by standing on it to make himself heard. Then things got worse, not least because Edelman had begun to rail against the officers themselves. One told him, "Lay off the police and the police will lay off you."[3]

That was not Isidore Edelman's way. He was an inveigher against injustice, and inveigh he did. So when, on that hot fall Thursday in September, he made his way to Pershing Square, the police again arrested him. This time, the charge was vagrancy. Among the many sections of the California vagrancy law criminalizing wanderers, beggars, drunkards, and the like, was subdivision five, section 647 of the California Penal Code, which made a vagrant of anyone who was "lewd or dissolute." The police defined dissolute as lawless. Since Edelman had been arrested before, they deemed him lawless, dissolute, and guilty of vagrancy. [4]

The trial that followed was either a paragon of justice or a three-ring circus, depending on one's perspective. For the charge of vagrancy, which carried a maximum penalty of $500 or six months in prison, the State of California hosted a nine-day jury trial. Across the witness stand paraded a cast of Pershing Square characters—the hecklers and the police officers, the other orators and the sympathetic listeners who had stopped visiting the park for fear of arrest themselves. They testified to hearing Edelman speak for hours on end. Some had heard him as many as eight hundred times. They praised him and condemned him. They displayed politics both petty and grand. [5]

In hearing all that testimony, the judge had in mind a trial that would determine the very essence of Edelman's character: was he or was he not "dissolute"? Edelman, the judge told the jury, was "not charged in this case with any violation of any particular act, but he is charged with being a person of a certain status, or a person being in a certain condition." Edelman's "character" was "the ultimate question." Though the judge warned the jury that Edelman's political beliefs were not at issue, much of the testimony apparently attempted to establish Edelman's character by way of his politics. [6]

It was the politics of Edelman's arrest that mobilized lawyers to his cause—good lawyers, lawyers who had been battling vagrancy laws on behalf of political rabble-rousers for decades. Much had changed since the vagrancy criminalization of poverty had begun to look anachronistic during the Great Depression of the 1930s. With the rise of the American Civil Liberties Union (ACLU) during and after World War I, institutional and doctrinal support for free speech had exploded. Though the Supreme Court had only danced around the edges of vagrancy laws themselves, the resulting sea change in First Amendment doctrine made it possible to conceive of Edelman's injuries as constitutional harms.

All of Edelman's lawyers circulated within this relatively new civil-liberties-labor milieu. His trial lawyer was the noted radical, frequent hothead, and former ACLU lawyer Leo Gallagher. His appellate lawyers were A. L. Wirin and Emmanuel Redfield, both established vagrancy law foes affiliated with the ACLU. Though Gallagher had initially focused his ire on what he viewed as a politically motivated arrest (which happened to be for vagrancy), eventually the vagrancy law itself (which lent itself to such political arrests) came into focus. As the case drew attention to the political uses of vagrancy laws and the stigma they imposed, it suggested that laws previously too trivial or too entrenched for constitutional scrutiny were now vulnerable to attack.

Workers, Wobblies, and Radicals

When Leo Gallagher condemned Isidore Edelman's arrest as political persecution, he knew of what he spoke. Los Angeles police were following the lead of government officials who had long used vagrancy laws against workers, radicals, and other political dissidents. To lawyers like Gallagher, this history made it clear that Edelman's arrest was not the idiosyncratic response of a few fed-up police officers on the Pershing Square beat. Rather, it represented the continuation of a well-established, and often explicit, vagrancy law response to political threats.

Edelman's arrest can be traced back to the very beginning of Anglo-American vagrancy laws. Because the English Statutes of Laborers had aimed to ensure that after the Black Death of the mid-fourteenth century everyone who could work did, they were frequently identified as the progenitors of the American criminalization of unemployment. The more direct antecedents of laws like California's were the English vagrancy laws of the sixteenth and seventeenth centuries, passed alongside laws instituting new methods of poor relief, erecting houses of correction, and controlling wages. Though such laws were primarily economically motivated—untethered workers could exact exorbitant wages in a tight labor market and the wandering unemployed could try to obtain relief from local governments not obligated to support them—they served critical political purposes as well. The "sturdy rogues" and "masterless men" of the Elizabethan era, for example, were a problem for governance as well as economy.[7]

Vast differences in demographic, political, and economic context notwithstanding, the American colonies and then the states continued to use vagrancy laws to control workers' economic and political power in a changing political economy. As aspiration if not reality, the description of one nineteenth-century English historian would have struck a chord on both sides of the Atlantic: "A man must work where he happened to be, and must take the wages offered to him on the spot, and if he went about, even to look for work, he became a vagrant and was regarded as a criminal."[8]

By the end of the nineteenth century, the threat of menacing new classes of wandering American men, mostly black in the South and white in the North, West, and Midwest, called forth an avalanche of vagrancy and related laws. In the South, vagrancy laws were directed at the mobility—physical, political, economic, and social—of newly freed slaves. Every state in the former Confederacy passed sweeping new vagrancy laws after the Civil War. Outside the South, reformers and their legislative allies used vagrancy laws to discipline those who might, by begging or shunning regular work, flout the wage labor system the war had been partially fought to preserve.[9]

As the problem of the transient unemployed exploded with the industrial revolution, the perceived moral failings of men marked by indolence, filled with radical ideas, or bitten by the bug of "the hobo life" captured the public imagination. Hoboes were politically volatile, economically unstable, physically threatening, and culturally transgressive. Structural economic explanations for unemployment—like the disappearance of arable land and the appearance of periodic depressions—fell comparatively flat. The able-bodied young man who roamed the country in search of work became a "tramp"—a threat, a menace, an outrage. Vagrancy laws and tramp acts—which imposed harsher penalties against those unemployed who wandered too far from home—made work by those who could work the legal norm. And though hoboes often managed to honor these laws in the breach, they made any form of unemployment— whether willful or involuntary—legally unacceptable.[10]

As these laws proliferated, so too did their uses. Tramps were often not only would-be workers; they were increasingly union men as well. With the spread of labor unions, it became more apparent that workers posed political as well economic threats, and that their speech as well as their wandering idleness required containment. Even when the union men were not tramps, employers and their allies called striking men "tramps, bummers, and vagrants." Union men protested, but vagrancy and tramp laws proved powerful weapons of "the employing class." From the mines of Telluride, Colorado, to the textile mills of South Carolina, the police used vagrancy laws to suppress both labor organizing and the free speech such organizing required.[11]

During the early twentieth century, the Industrial Workers of the World, known as the IWW or the Wobblies, were a prime target of this use of vagrancy laws. Unlike most unions at the time, the radical labor activists, anarchists, and socialists who founded the IWW let in everyone who wanted to join—native-borns and immigrants, whites and blacks, men and women, those with jobs and those without. Many Wobblies were transient, and the IWW soon became identified with the hoboes who rode the rails and haunted the highways for work. The Wobblies also became known for their syndicalism—their belief that workers themselves should own the means of production—their in-your-face tactics, and their rhetoric of class warfare, sabotage, and revolution. At its height in the 1910s, the IWW claimed around 100,000 members and could call on twice that number for support. "Quit your job. Go to Missoula. Fight with the Lumber Jacks for Free Speech. . . . [D]efy the police, the courts and the people who live off the wages of prostitution," urged the *Industrial Worker* in the fall of 1909.[12]

When hundreds of poor, obstreperous Wobblies calling for revolt "invaded," local authorities reacted aggressively to the threat such "trouble makers," "malcontents," and "agitators" posed to economic order and political stability. City officials would find additional monies, swear in extra peace officers, pass new laws prohibiting vagrancy (or disorderly conduct, breach of peace, or incitement to riot), and literally stake out city boundaries. Sometimes officers

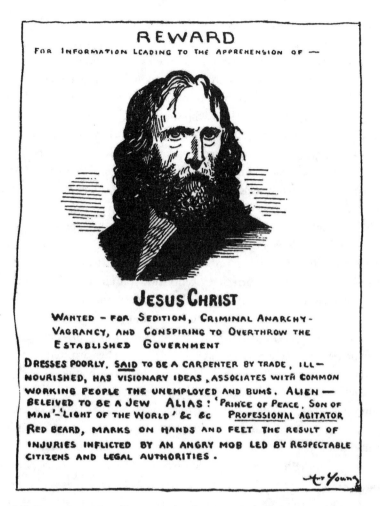

Figure 1.2 Poster from 1917 illustrating the close association between radical speech and vagrancy arrests in the first decades of the twentieth century. The lesson: Jesus was as seditious as the Wobblies and the Socialists, and he would have been equally subject to vagrancy arrest. Art Young.

would travel to the next railroad stop up the line to keep Wobblies at a distance. Because of the wandering nature of the Wobbly beast, such incidents were of more than local interest. Vagrancy arrests in Butte, Montana, were announced in the *Chicago Tribune* and the *Duluth* (Minnesota) *News-Tribune*. *The Oregonian* reported the interception of workers on their way from Arizona to California.[13]

Even if the Wobblies managed to breach these defenses, vagrancy laws still proved useful. Police departments in Fargo and Minot, North Dakota, for example, advertised themselves as essentially operating "free employment bureaus." According to a Minot newspaper, farmers should "call the police station by phone and the number of men desired . . . will be sent to them." Officers then arrested rank-and-file workers in large numbers. Two hundred fifty arrested here, sixty-seven arrested there. The police often instituted a "48 hour unemployment rule," in which those not working within two days would be arrested for vagrancy or issued what were called "work-or-get-out-of-town" orders. At other times, offi-cers "worked all day arresting IWW who were vags as per orders," and judges set the conditions for freedom. Judges offered "floaters," which suspended sentences just long enough for the Wobbly to either get a job or leave town. The Wobblies did not always cooperate. Convening meetings in jail cells, they sometimes took a principled stand to refuse floaters, finding themselves instead sentenced to the rock pile.[14]

Police sometimes turned to vagrancy arrests more to suppress IWW orga-nizers as political threats than to utilize IWW workers as economic resources. At one point, *The Oregonian* reported, "I.W.W. so Quiet Coup Is Feared," and, just to be safe, the police arrested twenty-two "on charges of being vagrants and on suspicion of being IWW." Law enforcement officers raided and closed IWW headquarters, seized books, and arrested anyone present. To justify the arrests, news reports emphasized the lack of funds found on "snared agitators" or highlighted their refusal to accept available work when arrested on a "techni-cal charge of vagrancy." Others noted that the alleged unlawfulness of the IWW itself could make an IWW organizer a vagrant for lacking a "lawful calling" or for "promoting, advocating, and inducing the commission of criminal syndicalism." A Kansas City, Missouri, ordinance from World War I explicitly expanded the definition of a vagrant to include anyone who was a member of any organiza-tion or association that "utter[ed] seditious sentiments against the United States government."[15]

Indeed, the IWW's signature tactic for years—what it called the "free speech fight"—aggressively invited such political vagrancy arrests. Modeled after ear-lier socialist protests, Wobblies set up soapboxes—literally the wooden crates in which soap and other dry goods were typically shipped—to sell the orga-nization's brand of radicalism in deliberately provocative language. Until the Wobblies moved away from free speech fights in 1913, officers on the Wobbly beat spent their days removing one "soapboxer" after another from his or her perch, often arresting them for vagrancy.[16]

With the outbreak of World War I and the subsequent shock of the Russian Revolution, fear of revolt and disloyalty at home intensified, and the legal weap-ons available for combating Wobblies and other political radicals proliferated. Congress passed the Espionage Act of 1917 and the Sedition Act of 1918. In the states, "red flag laws" made it a felony to display the symbol of communism. Permit laws gave local officials unfettered discretion to decide who could, and who could not, speak in public. A rash of state criminal syndicalism laws made it a felony to advocate violence as a way of "accomplishing a change in industrial ownership or control or effecting any political changes." Whereas in the past, one California official commented, "the police could only conduct raids, make arrests and prefer the futile charges of vagrancy or disturbing the peace," the state finally had legislation that could lead to convictions and substantial sentences. The official predicted "an aggressive enforcement of the new law against the IWW's."[17]

The existence of laws specifically aimed at subversives did not obviate the need for vagrancy laws. Because of the relative ease of vagrancy prosecutions, what ended up as criminal syndicalism charges often began with vagrancy arrests. In Butte, Montana, in 1918, police held forty-one alleged Wobblies "on charges of vagrancy pending investigation" of five suitcases filled with literature that might justify more serious federal charges. During a strike in Texas a few years later, police arrested miners on vagrancy charges and transported them one hundred miles to Fort Worth for federal questioning. When the men were released after twenty-four hours without food, they had to find their own way home. [18]

As the IWW lost steam after Espionage Act convictions of one hundred of its leaders in 1918, local officials continued to make political vagrancy arrests of other radicals, organizers, radical organizers, and radicals and organizers together—it was not always clear where the one group ended and the other began, and officials did not always care—not to mention rank-and-file workers, strikers, and picketers. Across the country in coal mines, on docks, and in every labor context in between, the police used vagrancy laws—as well as laws prohibiting loitering, obstructing traffic, holding parades, and making loud noise—"to break strikes," as one labor newspaper put it. They locked up communists. They ran organizers and agitators out of town. Twenty-three mine workers arrested for vagrancy here. Four communists arrested there. One hundred union men arrested somewhere else.[19]

The California vagrancy law that would snare Isidore Edelman some twenty years later was prized by officials across the state in the 1920s and 1930s. Employing the old anti-Wobbly techniques, government agents, ranchers, and farmers would alert the next town about the possible arrival of communist agitators, and police would promptly arrest them. One organizer in the California fields was taken into custody twenty-five times between 1929 and 1936. Prosecutors sometimes acknowledged that they "didn't have any case against" striking workers, but law enforcement officers arrested them anyway, offered them "floaters," held them for a few hours, never brought them before a court, and finally released them. Though judges set bail for most vagrancy defendants at very low levels—still usually beyond the actual vagrant's means—radicals and workers charged under the same law were required to post an outsized bail of $1,000, in what became known as "$1,000 vagrancy."[20]

Like the Wobblies, Depression-era workers and activists did not accept these arrests without a fight. In the late 1930s, the Senate's LaFollette Committee on Civil Liberties was charged with investigating labor-related civil liberties violations. During one hearing, a witness recounted that a worker had asked his arresting officer for the basis of his arrest. The officer answered, "You have heard of vagrancy, haven't you?" The worker replied, "You have heard of the suit for false arrest, haven't you?" Communists in Los Angeles in 1930 took such complaints to the streets. They protested "police brutality" toward the working class. "Down with the vagrancy laws," their placards declared. Because of the political uses of vagrancy laws, free speakers who had originally focused on worker organization or higher wages were now using their soapboxes to denounce the police and the laws themselves. [21]

Civil Liberties Lawyers, Civil Liberties Law

Both political vagrancy arrests and protests against them continued into the Depression decade, but things had changed all around them. Most critically, political vagrancy defendants began to find new allies: lawyers willing to take their cases. The IWW had had some legal help in the early 1900s but nothing like this, nothing like the cadre of attorneys—increasingly armed with legal precedents and sympathetic popular opinion—prepared to make a federal case out of a thirty-day vagrancy sentence.[22]

This was nowhere more apparent than in Southern California, where Isidore Edelman's trial lawyer, Leo Gallagher, was present at the birth of the ACLU's very first local affiliate. The creation and growth of the ACLU fundamentally transformed the legal and political landscape by creating the will, institutional support, and personnel to bring constitutional challenges on behalf of labor activists and radicals. Organized during World War I to defend conscientious objectors, the national ACLU consolidated as political persecution escalated, rather than receded, with the end of the war. For its part, the Southern California ACLU (SCACLU) emerged out of an IWW-led 1923 Los Angeles dock strike in which Gallagher had been involved. The arrest of four hundred Wobblies on vagrancy and other charges—and of muckraker Upton Sinclair for trying to read the Constitution aloud—highlighted the need for civil liberties protection in southern California.[23]

Gallagher came to the IWW via a conservative Catholic family and Yale Law School, after flirtations with philosophy and the priesthood, service in World War I, and a few years as a "fruit tramp." Law school had trained him for commercial, rather than subversive, law practice, but he found that the ACLU and the Communist-affiliated International Labor Defense (ILD) offered more appealing alternatives. In a 1935 profile in *The Nation*, SCACLU colleague Carey McWilliams described Gallagher as "slight of figure, shiny and academic in manner, [giving] the impression of being a mistreated gnome, whose sorrowful study-weakened eyes, beneath close-cropped gray hair, gaze from thick lenses at a world that is unsatisfactory, disheartening, and uncivilized. . . . No blatant ranter, he can be violently indignant." This indignance, plus a hot temper and a lack of faith in the judicial process, perhaps accounted for what McWilliams called the "terrifying" "Leo Gallagher legend"—that Gallagher was "a blasphemous and illiterate shyster who receives fabulous sums of money from Moscow to besmirch the sacred tables of the law." According to one client, Gallagher "was thrown out of more courtrooms than anyone else I ever saw or heard of."[24]

Edelman's second lawyer, Abraham Lincoln Wirin, shared some of Gallagher's views. He, Gallagher, and their sometime law partner Grover Johnson were referred to as "the radical triumvirate" of the SCACLU, which was itself at the radical edge of the national ACLU. Some thirteen years younger than Gallagher, Wirin was born in Russia and grew up in Boston. Though he eschewed his illustrious name for the more pedestrian "Al," Wirin honed his sense of injustice early—he was first arrested for political protest as a teenager. While a scholarship student at Harvard, he was active in the Socialist Party and in the defense of anarchists Sacco and Vanzetti. Like Gallagher, Wirin quickly tired of commercial and bankruptcy law practice in Los Angeles after law school at Boston University. He became the ACLU's first full-time lawyer. Where Gallagher and Johnson tacked toward the ILD, Wirin moved between the ACLU and the labor-friendly agencies of the federal government. Such crossing of ideological and institutional lines was possible during the Popular Front era of the 1930s—when the Communist Party was open to cooperation with liberals and other lefties and vice versa. What ultimately split Wirin and Gallagher apart was less the politics of the left than the politics of World War II. When the two decided that the ACLU should defend Japanese Americans from exclusion and internment, some of their more nationalistic labor union clients objected. Gallagher stuck with the unions, Wirin with the increasingly anti-communist ACLU. One of Gallagher's other law partners described Wirin as someone who always advertised his opposition to communism. "I want the court to know I am not a Communist," he would announce. "And I absolutely disagree with them, but the worst people are entitled to the protection of the Constitution." Wirin's penchant for distancing himself from his clients went beyond politics. When representing a rock concert promoter later in life, Wirin described himself as "strictly a Beethoven man."[25]

Nevertheless, some still found Wirin too far to the left. Ernest Besig, a New York lawyer with a Cornell law degree who started out in the SCACLU but was dispatched to grow the San Francisco ACLU in the mid-1930s, commented in 1934, "We [the ACLU] are not an agency that seeks to bring about a workers' and farmers' revolution. In that matter I feel that Al takes the wrong position. [He thinks that] the purpose of the Civil Liberties Union is to advance the revolution. . . . I am not ready to take that position; I am not a Communist. . . . I am willing, however, to protect the constitutional rights of all groups by constitutional and legal means." With the passage of an anti-communist resolution by the national ACLU in 1940, and the deepening of the Cold War in the late 1940s, the left-leaning tendencies of the SCACLU increased tension with the national organization. According to Carey McWilliams, his good friend Wirin "was a jump or two ahead of us. He would get into cases before the board had authorized it or had known much about it." Wirin not only acted fast, he also thought fast. ACLU colleagues described him as "the mastermind of [the SCACLU's] legal program."[26]

These lawyers, Gallagher and Wirin and their colleagues, were instrumental in vagrancy cases starting in the early 1930s, through Edelman's case in the early 1950s, and beyond. Wirin's law partner, Fred Okrand, was still bringing vagrancy-related cases to the Supreme Court as late as 1983. Even so, these men would not have identified themselves as vagrancy lawyers. They would not have advertised a "vagrancy law practice." One might say that one of the costs of doing business as a radical or labor activist in the 1930s was the vagrancy arrest. Thus part of the business of labor lawyers, radical lawyers, and civil liberties lawyers was finding ways to stop such arrests, defend against them, or invalidate the laws on which they were based. When Mexicans and Filipinos, Californians and "Okies" were arrested anywhere in the state of California, the ACLU and the ILD were there. Gallagher, Wirin, and others went to court, sought injunctions, issued press releases, and published articles.[27]

Being a lawyer for striking workers, ILD activists, and Communist Party members was no sidelines job in 1930s California. These were no "parlor pinks," no "limousine liberals." When the lawyers tried to talk with workers, the police usually tried to thwart them. Some officials even arrested the lawyers for vagrancy, a practice the LaFollette Committee condemned as "a prostitution of the State vagrancy law." Law enforcement also either purposefully ignored or actively participated in vigilante violence against lawyers. When Wirin succeeded in getting an injunction against police interference with a planned meeting with Imperial Valley farmworkers in early 1934, the police held to their word. They refused to interfere when anti-labor vigilantes kidnapped Wirin, beat and robbed him, and left him stranded in the desert barefoot. The police then offered their services, making a deal with Wirin that they would see him to safety so long as he left the valley altogether. Wirin accepted. A few months later, Grover Johnson was beaten on the El Centro courthouse steps after obtaining the release of several strike leaders. A county official hit Johnson on the head and yelled, "You red son of a bitch, arguing constitutional law. We'll give you a taste of our constitutional law!" A few months after that, it was Ernest Besig's turn. He had gone to the Imperial Valley to investigate the detention of seven union men who were held for twenty-two days before being convicted and sentenced to four months for vagrancy. While waiting for a train home, Besig was assaulted. His assailant yelled, "This will teach you to keep out of the Valley."[28]

Later that same year, and despite these attacks, the lawyers launched their most substantial anti-vagrancy law effort of the decade. They had known Emma Cutler, a twenty-six-year-old self-professed communist working with the ILD, for some time. Both Gallagher and Wirin had previously represented her, and she and Wirin had together defended beet workers charged with vagrancy and other crimes. Just hours after Cutler arrived in the Valley in 1934, police arrested her for vagrancy. It took Grover Johnson and the district attorney eight days, a record for the usually low-stakes justices' court, to seat a jury. The prosecution argued that the ILD was part of the Communist Party and wanted to overthrow the government. Johnson responded that the political party had rights like any other. The jury deliberated for twenty-three hours before convicting Cutler. Although a federal investigator criticized the conviction, the trial judge stood by it: "Miss Cutler was convicted by a jury on the basis of past association with five Communists who were sentenced from Imperial Valley in 1930." Cutler's political views, in other words, made her a vagrant.[29]

A bevy of SCACLU lawyers joined Grover Johnson in fighting Cutler's conviction. They made numerous arguments in support of her release. The judge rejected every one. But unlike previous political vagrancy arrests, this one left a mark. *Ex parte Cutler* made it into the law books. Its very presence raised the profile of political vagrancy arrests and augured changes to come.[30]

It was not just the availability of lawyers that was new in the 1930s. It was also the legal context in which they operated. When Isidore Edelman arrived in the United States in 1910 just as the IWW was gaining real infamy, it was hardly conceivable that the Supreme Court would ever give much consideration to protecting free speech. By the time Edelman brought his case to the Court forty years later, the First Amendment had been fundamentally transformed.

For almost one hundred fifty years after its ratification, the Constitution protected free speech in theory more than practice. As a general matter, the broad "police power" of state governments to protect the health, welfare, and morals of their citizens was commonly thought to justify a wide array of restrictions on free speech. Moreover, it was not easy to find a way to bring the Constitution to bear given that federal violations were rare and state violations considered immune from constitutional oversight. From the perspective of many radicals, the paper guarantee of the First Amendment of the United States Constitution was just that—words on an aging piece of paper. Neither radicals nor many of their lawyers had faith in the law's supposed majesty. Especially as judges rejected most of their constitutional claims, they viewed trials more as stages for political argumentation than legitimate forums for determining their rights.[31]

By the time Edelman's case came to the Supreme Court in 1952, however, the justices, with help from lawyers for the ACLU, the Jehovah's Witnesses, and other dissident groups, had been chipping away for thirty years at state and federal interference with free speech, especially unpopular speech in public spaces. When Congress passed the 1917 Espionage Act and the 1918 Sedition Act, it generated not only authority for the aggressive regulation of speech but also big targets for federal First Amendment challenges. By 1919, responding to arguments by the ACLU and other civil libertarians, Justices Oliver Wendell Holmes and Louis Brandeis began to suggest that the Constitution should provide greater protection for free speech. In a case in which he agreed with the validity of a federal Espionage Act conviction, Holmes nonetheless suggested that only speech that presented a "clear and present danger" could be prohibited. That same year, both Holmes and Brandeis dissented from the Court's affirmance of another conviction under the same law. By 1925, the Court as a whole had begun both to take federal restrictions on free speech more seriously and to assume that the states were equally bound to respect some constitutional limits. In 1927, the ACLU convinced the Court to reverse the insufficiently substantiated criminal syndicalism conviction of an IWW organizer. When Leo Gallagher challenged California's "red flag law" in 1931, the Court for the first time invalidated a law on First Amendment grounds.[32]

Just as suppression of labor organizing and suppression of free speech had gone hand in hand for decades, protection of labor unions and protection of free speech now ascended together. As both Congress and the executive came to embrace organized labor as part of the New Deal, so too the Supreme Court frequently protected free speech rights in the 1930s precisely because the speech was about labor. Two such cases in the 1940s, *Thornhill v. Alabama* and *Carlson v. California*, addressed the constitutionality of loitering laws retooled specifically to prevent labor organizing. The *Thornhill* Court pointed out that the law "readily [lent] itself to harsh and discriminatory enforcement by local prosecuting officials, against particular groups deemed to merit their displeasure." The problem was not just that these loitering laws generically hindered free speech on the streets. It was that the laws hindered the free speech of labor organizers, which was "indispensable to the effective and intelligent use of the processes of popular government to shape the destiny of modern industrial society." According to the La Follette Committee, "The effect of these decisions seems to destroy one of the most effective weapons of repression in the hands of the employers' associations particularly in rural California. . . . [I]n effect the court said that if disorder was the concern of legislative body, ordinances should be drafted to deal with disorder, without including free speech within their prohibitions."[33]

Indeed, over the course of the 1930s and 1940s, the Court increasingly attempted to distinguish "disorder" from free speech, to protect speech whose value seemed somehow greater than its portent of danger. In a host of cases and circumstances, the Court deemed communists, the Congress of Industrial Organizations (CIO), the ACLU, and Jehovah's Witnesses more deserving of a platform than an arrest. By 1943, the Supreme Court announced that the First Amendment occupied a "preferred position" of constitutional importance. The protection of free speech became a fundamental way in which the United States, at war with Nazi Germany and fascist Italy, could distinguish its democratic system of government from their totalitarian ones.[34]

Both the increased presence of civil liberties lawyers and this sea change in the Court's willingness to protect unpopular speakers transformed the context of political vagrancy arrests in the fifteen years before Edelman's case. These arrests continued as local officials tried to suppress radical ideologies—from the Back to Nature Party to Sinn Fein—in Nashville, Tampa, and Miami; Pittsburgh, Milwaukee, and Schenectady; Baltimore, Washington, and Guilford County, North Carolina. Now, however, police and prosecutors using vagrancy laws to protect their communities from subversion and possible revolution more often had to defend their position.

It is perhaps no surprise that many who appeared before the La Follette Committee were among the attackers. The civil liberties stalwarts on the committee were a promising audience for arguments that the California vagrancy law should be redefined so that it could not "be used as a pretext for arresting persons unemployed by virtue of a labor dispute or otherwise" and that loitering laws should be amended to eliminate liability for people who attended public gatherings to hear what was said. Vagrancy laws were more diffuse and multifaceted than the usual law silencing unpopular speech, but government officials often wielded them for similar reasons. If vagrancy laws could fill the protected spaces for free speech that advocates and judges had recently worked so hard to create, then such laws might need to be reined in as well.[35]

Law enforcement officers soon found themselves at odds not only with overzealous civil libertarian lawyers and progressive politicians but also with appellate judges and a growing, if still limited, swath of mainstream public opinion. Consider the *New York Times*. It gave prime coverage to an ACLU protest letter "signed by more than a score of leading members of the American Bar" that described "civil liberties" as "in danger in California" during the 1934 San Francisco general strike. After noting that the police had seized papers and closed meeting places, the statement observed, "Vagrants do not have meeting places to be closed. Vagrancy does not call for lawless seizure of papers. The police have imprisoned these men for their political views. The police have imprisoned 300 men on American soil, in defiance of the American Constitution." Written by ACLU leaders Wirin, Morris L. Ernst, and Arthur Garfield Hays, it was signed by eminent liberal legal scholars like Zechariah Chafee, Karl Llewellyn, and Herbert Wechsler; African American civil rights activist Charles H. Houston; and a long list of other lawyers, academics, former judges, and government officials.[36]

Wide-scale condemnation followed other political uses of vagrancy law as well. When prominent socialist organizers traveled to Terre Haute, Indiana, to join a picket line in the fall of 1936, for example, they were all arrested for vagrancy. A month later, local police again turned to vagrancy to arrest Communist Party presidential candidate Earl Browder and others in order to prevent Browder from giving a speech. Both the *New York Times* and the *Washington Post* covered the story on the front page in sympathetic terms, going so far as to place "vagrants" in quotation marks. The *Times* editorialized that "to arrest [the men] on sight on a trumped-up charge, or to forbid them to meet and to speak, is . . . hostile to our institutions." "It is to be hoped," the *Times* quipped with northeastern, big-city chauvinism, "that few of us are ready to submit meekly to the haughty rule of even so majestic an official as the Chief of Police of Terre Haute, Ind."[37]

In Birmingham, Alabama, police, prosecutors, and trial court judges clashed with appellate judges for more than a decade over the propriety of political vagrancy arrests. In 1930, police arrested Angelo Herndon, a black communist, and Joseph Carr, a white one, for vagrancy. The two men were fined $500 and sentenced to twelve months at hard labor, but appeals courts reversed the convictions. Undeterred, the Birmingham police repeatedly turned the vagrancy law against communists in the 1930s and 1940s. Jack Barton understood well both why he was arrested for vagrancy and why the trial judge dismissed the charges. "You see, while I am being held for investigation I am not allowed to communicate with anyone, but when the 72 hours are up the police must either turn me loose or put charge against me. . . . [T]hey placed this charge of vagrancy against me, and I got in touch with a lawyer. . . . I proved that . . . at the time I was arrested I had $35 in my possession and was receiving a salary of $10 a week from the Communist Party. This, of course, meant that . . . the judge threw the case out."[38]

More than a decade later, the Birmingham police were still fighting communists with vagrancy laws, despite such judicial resistance. Bull Connor, the police commissioner who would make his name brutalizing African American civil rights protestors in the 1960s, was already adept at using vagrancy law to political advantage. In 1948, Connor declared, "There's not enough room in town for Bull and the Commies." Two years later, he announced a mop up of "every known communist in Birmingham." He started by arresting Sam Hall Jr.,

Alabama Communist Party chairman and southern editor for the *Daily Worker*, in his own home. Hall had the good fortune to hire attorney Morel Montgomery, who had learned the vagrancy ropes defending Al Capone's southern colleagues against their own Birmingham vagrancy charges. Arguing that Hall was employed (albeit by the Communist Party and the *Daily Worker*) and had an income, owned a Chevrolet and a home, Montgomery succeeded in getting the conviction reversed. Once again, a court disagreed with the police about what made a man a vagrant, even if he was a communist. The judicial resistance Bull Connor encountered suggested that the rules might be changing for the kinds of dissidents officials had long arrested for vagrancy—in other words, for people like Isidore Edelman.[39]

A Radical in Court in the Early Cold War

Edelman's trial took place in late October 1949. Prosecutor Richard Hayden and defense lawyer Leo Gallagher had very different ideas about what the nine days of testimony were intended to prove. Hayden, himself a liberal Democrat and later member of the National Association for the Advancement of Colored People (NAACP) and the ACLU, understood his goal as proving Edelman a vagrant by showing that he was "dissolute." As Judge Byron J. Walters charged the jury, "Vagrancy is a status or a condition and it is not an act. . . . One is guilty of being a vagrant at any time and place where he is found . . . although then and there innocent of any act demonstrating his character."[40]

In describing vagrancy as a crime of status or condition, Judge Walters was distinguishing it from the usual type of crime, the crime of "conduct." What had become known as the "status/conduct distinction" was not a distinction that would have made sense to those who had passed or enforced the early English vagrancy laws. By the time Edelman's case arrived at the Supreme Court, however, and indeed for some time before then, the distinction between status and conduct had become a common one. Where most criminal laws required that a person commit certain acts, vagrancy laws criminalized the people themselves. And where most criminal laws required some kind of intent to commit a crime, vagrancy liability followed simply from being a particular type of person, regardless of mental state. In other words, vagrancy laws lacked both what the criminal law called *actus reus*, a guilty act, and *mens rea*, a guilty mind.[41]

Different though vagrancy was from most criminal law, police departments, prosecutors, judges, and legal scholars had never found the category particularly problematic. Throughout the nineteenth century, courts were forthright about the fact that vagrancy law properly regulated status rather than conduct. In part, this was because they did not really think of vagrancy laws as criminal laws. Despite the criminal penalties they carried, legal professionals and government officials viewed the laws as quintessential "police power regulations"—regulations that inhered in the state's comprehensive power to enforce order, eliminate danger, and protect the public welfare and morals. As such, prohibitions on vagrancy were subject to fewer (or no) constitutional constraints and fewer procedural protections than were "criminal laws." As one South Carolina judge mused in 1837, "I think it is not the main purpose of [vagrancy laws], to proceed by way of punishing for an offence; for vagrancy, in itself, can hardly be deemed a distinct offence." In language that would become a veritable mantra about vagrancy laws, a New York judge concluded some twenty years later, "These statutes—declaring a certain class or description of persons vagrants . . . are in fact rather of the nature of public regulations to prevent crime and public charges and burdens, than of the nature of ordinary criminal laws prohibiting and punishing an act or acts as a crime or crimes." And twenty years after that, the Supreme Court of Ohio reasoned, "It is a mistake to suppose that offenses must be confined to specific acts of commission or omission." Where the public welfare was threatened, "the offense does not consist of particular acts, but in the mode of life, the habits and practices of the accused in respect to the character or traits which it is the object of the statute creating the offense to suppress."[42]

A few equivocal critiques surfaced in the twentieth century, but most courts and commentators continued to defend vagrancy laws. According to the well-known treatise *Corpus Juris* in 1934, vagrancy laws were not intended "to punish [vagrants] for the doing of specific overt acts." Or as the Virginia Supreme Court put it: "The offense does not consist in particular affirmative acts of a person but of his mode of life, habits, and character." Into mid-century, judges upheld convictions on the basis that vagrancy laws were not subject to the usual conduct requirements, and treatises explained the legitimacy of such laws. The unusual form of vagrancy laws was simply not a problem for the common law, for political legitimacy, for doctrinal frameworks, or for the constitutional community. Venerated for their longevity and their flexibility, vagrancy laws' exceptionalism was precisely their advantage.[43]

Under the California vagrancy law, then, prosecutor Hayden's job was to prove Edelman dissolute. To that end, Hayden called fourteen witnesses who waxed eloquent about Edelman's radical ideas and anti-establishment rants. The witnesses accused Edelman of verbally attacking men in uniform, calling people liars, condemning the police and the mayor, and trying to foment revolution. Because Hayden was unsure of how closely "dissolute" would align with "immoral," he also had witnesses recall Edelman's speeches condemning American men who bathed women in wine—which Edelman defended as showing the depravity of the national culture—and prostitution—which Edelman used to contrast an idealized socialist society with the problems of the commodified family under capitalism. If the court defined dissolute as lewd or immoral, the government wanted to have such statements in the record.[44]

To Gallagher and Edelman, the case was not about character. It was about politics. Indeed, it was most likely politics that had brought lawyer and client together. Gallagher had been challenging vagrancy laws on behalf of radicals like Edelman for at least fifteen years; he specialized in defending communists, in taking on "political cases," especially after he loosened his ties to the SCACLU during World War II. For Gallagher, Edelman was no doubt an equally attractive client: a radical persecuted by the police for his politics, another example of bias in the system. One can imagine that Edelman and Gallagher each saw the other as a kindred spirit. They seemed to agree with much of what the Communist Party had to say. They were both indignant and irascible, quick to point out injustices, and fearless in shouting them from whatever perch they could claim—the park bench for Edelman, the courtroom for Gallagher.[45]

Most of Gallagher's strategy at trial was to prove that the police and the prosecutors were targeting Edelman for his politics. He hoped the judge would rein in the discriminatory exercise of law enforcement discretion. Granted, Gallagher responded to the claims of lewdness and immorality. Edelman was "always a gentleman" with a "good" reputation as "a law-abiding citizen." But Gallagher spent far more energy characterizing Edelman as a persecuted free speaker and the case as a "frame-up" and a "fraud." He got one of the prosecution witnesses to admit that he had repeatedly shouted Edelman down when Edelman had tried to speak. Moreover, not to be outdone, Gallagher called eighteen defense witnesses who detailed Edelman's persecution at the hands of the "fascist element" and the police.[46]

To prove that the police arrested Edelman for his politics, Gallagher requested that the district attorney's office produce arrest records for the city of Los Angeles. He hoped to prove that Edelman's arrest was discriminatory, "that there are thousands and thousands of individuals in this city that are walking around but have committed many more offenses than this defendant that have never been charged with vagrancy." Though Gallagher never got his records, the city attorney acknowledged that of the 50,000 misdemeanor violations processed each month, vagrancy charges for repeat offenders were reserved for just a few thousand repeat gamblers, panhandlers, drunks, and prostitutes.[47]

Edelman claimed to fit into none of those categories. He was merely a radical and a contrarian. Edelman's arresting officer stated that Edelman "made work difficult for him." Another testified that when asked by Pershing Square regulars why he did not protect Edelman, he had replied that if Edelman "needed police protection he should not be in Pershing Square." A third was said to have told a restaurant manager, "While you and I are talking, there's a Commie being ducked in the Pershing Square fountain," but he denied it on the stand.[48]

The location of Edelman's arrest added to Gallagher's certainty that political bias was at work. Like London's Hyde Park and Chicago's Bughouse
Square, Pershing Square was a gathering place for soapbox orators of all types,
a crowded, buzzing hive of politics and humanity. At the turn of the twentieth century, "a hotbed of ranting and wailing from loafers who preached the
socialistic doctrine" pushed out the more respectable. After 1919, when the
Los Angeles police chief made it department policy to "stamp out I.W.W. movement" and "drive reds from the city," police arrested "spouters" in the square for
speeches and "disloyal conversations." When Earl Browder was arrested while
trying to speak there in the 1930s, the only thing he managed to get out before
the police took him away was, "We object to the suppression of speech in Los
Angeles!"[49]

For Gallagher and Edelman, the trial offered a platform not only for revealing
police suppression of radical speech but also for Edelman's radical speech itself.
Even in the "engrossed statement on appeal"—the detailed summary of the volu-
minous trial testimony that took two years for the lawyers to negotiate—one
can hear the tenor of Edelman's language, the cadence of his speech. While on
the stand over the course of three days, Edelman held forth about the meaning of religion and human progress, the "intellectual and moral bankruptcy of
our social order," the need to "cope with the problems of jobs, homes, health,
racial relations and peace," and the belief that "fascism was the dictatorship of
Big Business." And on. And on. Though Gallagher likely encouraged Edelman
to speak in such a register for the sake of the views themselves, it seems likely
that the prosecutor tolerated it and the judge allowed it because they viewed the
statements Edelman had made in Pershing Square as damning evidence of his
lawlessness.[50]

After nine days of parrying about what Edelman said and who he was, Judge
Walters charged the jury. His instructions, part boilerplate, part tailor-made
for Edelman, must have given Gallagher some satisfaction. The judge did state
that "a systematic discrimination against the defendant, or persons of his class"
could turn a constitutional law into a constitutional violation. In other respects
the instructions must have frustrated Gallagher. Judge Walters pointed out that
although "dissolute" often refers to lax morals, other types of "laxness and loose-
ness and lawlessness" could make one "a dissolute person in other respects." If
the jury found that Edelman had previously violated the law, it could deem him
dissolute and convict him as a vagrant.[51]

There was no one-to-one correlation between the acts and the character.
The jury might find that Edelman had violated the law but not find his character to be lawless and dissolute. Or it might find that even though Edelman
did not commit the legal violations alleged, he was nonetheless of a lawless and
dissolute character. Given that the judge had allowed both the prosecution and

the defense to offer extensive evidence of Edelman's political beliefs, he perhaps lacked credibility when he told the jury that "the defendant is not on trial for his political opinions."[52]

The jury took ten hours to convict. Walters sentenced Edelman to ninety days, and Edelman announced that he would appeal. Two weeks later, Fred Okrand, not Leo Gallagher, represented Edelman in court, and just after the new year, Okrand and his law partner, Al Wirin, officially became Edelman's attorneys. Unfortunately for Edelman, the notice that his appeal had been set for hearing erroneously went to Gallagher, who was no longer practicing with Wirin. Though Gallagher informed the court of the mistake, Wirin only found out by happenstance that he had missed his chance to argue the appeal. The appeals court summarily affirmed Edelman's conviction and refused to reconsider. Having pursued the case as far as he could in the state courts, Wirin sought review from a higher authority.[53]

As *Edelman v. California* wound its way through the courts, its focus began to shift. Gallagher had maintained that the import of the case lay in police discrimination against Edelman's speech. But both Edelman's new lawyers and the Supreme Court justices to whom they now turned gradually, if incompletely, began to view Edelman's problem as the law itself, rather than police enforcement of it.

Federal law required the Supreme Court to hear some types of cases, but Edelman's was not one of them. Instead, Edelman presented the Court with a petition for certiorari, or "cert" for short, which asked for discretionary review of his case. The Court had already rejected a petition from Edelman once before, and it initially seemed this time would be no different. Justices Hugo Black, William O. Douglas, and Felix Frankfurter fell one vote short of the four necessary to grant cert. Some of the other justices worried that because the state court had not passed on the federal questions (because Edelman's lawyers had missed the hearing), the Court might lack power to decide them.[54]

Black and Douglas were not happy. The Court's fiercest defenders of civil liberties at the time, both men were New Deal Democrats who owed their seats on the Court to President Franklin D. Roosevelt. Though Black and Douglas ended up in the same place by the 1930s, they had not started out that way. Black grew up poor in rural Alabama, attended the University of Alabama Law School, joined the Ku Klux Klan to forward his political career in Jim Crow Birmingham, and served as United States senator from Alabama. His support for civil rights and civil liberties as a justice came as a surprise to many. Douglas, a tall, lanky, misanthropic westerner, came to the Court via Columbia Law School (as a student), Yale Law School (as a professor), and the Securities and Exchange Commission (as commissioner). Their personalities were different too—Black the quiet diplomat, Douglas the difficult loner.[55]

Their differences notwithstanding, by the early 1950s Black and Douglas shared not only an identification with those living on the social and economic margins and a generally rights-protective outlook, but also considerable skepticism of vagrancy laws. At twenty-five, Black had been appointed to the Birmingham police court, where he witnessed the abusive arrests and summary justice that vagrancy laws occasioned. When he later ran successfully for solicitor of Jefferson County, Alabama, in 1914, he attacked the fee system by which jailors and sheriffs were paid for each day they held a person in custody. During the campaign, Black announced that the electorate was "tired of having hundreds of Negroes arrested for shooting craps on payday and crowding the jail with these petty offenders." After he took office, Black quickly released five hundred prisoners he deemed the system's victims.[56]

For his part, Douglas was personally invested in what he called in one interview "tolerance for minorities, for unorthodox points of view for all classes of thought and all races and religions and creeds." He peppered his many autobiographical writings with (possibly apocryphal) claims to a hobo past (among other embellishments and misstatements of fact). Douglas recalled how he worked the eastern Washington wheat harvest with the Industrial Workers of the World. He shared meals with the "vagabonds" who lived under the Yakima River railroad bridge. He rode the rails, jumped off freight trains to avoid the policing of railroad company "yard bulls," self-identified as a migrant worker, and preferred the vagrants' code of ethics to that of the "Establishment." However much the details of those stories might have lacked veracity, Douglas had grown up without money, and he had worked at jobs many of his colleagues would have found beneath them. Indeed, Douglas was certainly the only justice who would have cared to fabricate such a low-brow past. He was also the only one with an honorary membership in the "Hoboes of America," which regularly sent him correspondence and newsletters, and made him a "Knight of the Road" in 1939.[57]

Bringing these priors to *Edelman*, Black and Douglas threatened to publish a dissent from the denial of certiorari—an unusual step. They wanted the public to know that the Court had chosen to let stand Edelman's conviction and the California vagrancy law. They might have dug in their heels with extra force in *Edelman* because First Amendment cases involving defendants with similar politics had not been going their way lately. Though Chief Justice Earl Warren had proven far more liberal than Republican President Dwight D. Eisenhower had expected when he appointed him—leading a unanimous Court to invalidate school segregation in *Brown v. Board of Education*, for example—he and his fellow justices seemed to find less space for speech like Edelman's as the Cold War heightened national security concerns. When Joseph McCarthy snatched a senate seat from Robert M. LaFollette Jr. in 1946, it was probably impossible to predict the dire consequences of the shift from civil liberties-protecting Wisconsin progressive to communist-hunting Wisconsin demagogue. The day after Edelman's arrest, President Truman announced that the Soviet Union had the atomic bomb. The start of the Korean War a few months later heightened fears about both the Cold War and domestic communism. Influential political theorist Hannah Arendt argued that Stalin's communism had replaced Hitler's fascism as the prime totalitarian threat to individual liberty. Whether this changed political climate or doctrinal concerns in the cases themselves or both were the cause, the Court had recently eschewed protection for communists and fellow travelers. In case after case, Black and Douglas found themselves dissenting, sometimes alone.[58]

Black and Douglas's plan to publish their opinion made some justices uncomfortable—it seemed too much like the public airing of the Court's dirty laundry. The threatened dissent had its desired effect. A few days after Black circulated his draft, the Court granted Edelman's petition. Though it was not unusual to overlook procedural irregularities like the state court's failure to address the federal constitutional question, neither was it necessary. At least some justices wanted to get to vagrancy questions, even if it took some fancy procedural footwork.[59]

In their briefs to the Court before oral argument, Wirin, Okrand, and Abraham Gorenfeld—a Los Angeles labor and civil liberties lawyer who assisted on the brief—followed Gallagher's lead while somewhat expanding the scope of the case. Like Gallagher, Wirin and his colleagues emphasized that California's vagrancy prosecution of Edelman violated his freedom of speech. Wirin also followed Gallagher in leaving some First Amendment stones unturned. Most striking in light of both prior and subsequent developments was the absence of *Thornhill* and *Carson*, the cases in which the Court had invalidated labor-related loitering laws in 1940. Vagrancy and loitering laws shared deep historical roots, and they could often be found in a single grab-bag statute. Even when states or cities passed freestanding loitering laws, courts had occasionally considered them in connection with other types of vagrancy laws. But the *Edelman* brief revealed that even lawyers with decades of experience lacked any sense that vagrancy and loitering laws were of a piece, were a single problem that could be—or had to be—addressed together. It was not until after *Edelman*, as commentators identified commonalities across cases and lawyers and judges increasingly made such connections, that *Thornhill* would come to join the vagrancy law canon.[60]

In other respects, Wirin and Okrand began to branch out from Gallagher's emphasis on the politically motivated arrest and prosecution to attack vagrancy laws themselves. They claimed that the law was unconstitutionally "void for vagueness" because both "lawless" and "dissolute" were impossible to define—as evidenced by the uncertainty at trial about whether the prosecution had to prove that Edelman was immoral. Under the due process clause of the Fourteenth Amendment, an unduly vague law was unconstitutional because it failed to provide "ascertainable standards of guilt." The lawyers also argued that despite the long legitimate and exceptional character of vagrancy laws, under both the California Penal Code and "the basic theory of American criminal law," "crimes must be based on overt acts or omissions, not on guilty intentions." In other words, they took issue with the fact that the law created a status crime.[61]

The lawyers had good reason to think that the justices would welcome these anti-vagrancy law arguments. In 1939, in *Lanzetta v. New Jersey*, the Court had reviewed a law stating that "any person not engaged in any lawful occupation, known to be a member of any gang consisting of two or more persons, who has been convicted at least three times of being a disorderly person, or who has been convicted of any crime . . . is declared to be a gangster." Though the law did not speak of vagrancy per se—*Edelman* would mark the first occasion on which the Supreme Court considered a traditional "vagrancy law"—the case was closely related. *Lanzetta*'s law grew out of widespread attempts in the 1930s by state and local legislatures to apply vagrancy laws to gangsters, organized criminals, and other "public enemies." Moreover, its constitutional infirmities were the same ones the Court would later find in vagrancy laws. Though one might have read the law as both fairly specific and requiring some past conduct, the Court concluded that it was vague and "condemn[ed] no act or omission." The justices did not clarify, however, whether the fact that the law created a status crime—declaring anyone who fit its definition "to be a gangster"—was part or all of what made the law vague or whether it represented a separate constitutional infirmity of its own. If the latter, the Court made no mention of what precisely in the Constitution prohibited the creation of a status crime.[62]

A decade later, and just a few years before *Edelman*, Justice Frankfurter made the link between *Lanzetta* and vagrancy laws even clearer. The Court's only Jewish justice at the time, and, like Edelman, an immigrant (from Austria), Frankfurter-the-justice had proved something of a disappointment to liberal friends and colleagues who had known him as an advisor to both the ACLU and the NAACP. Viewed as alternately pedantic and garrulous—in either version, always the combative law professor from his years teaching at Harvard Law School—Frankfurter's insistence that judges limit their constitutional interventions often put him at odds with Black and Douglas. On vagrancy, however, the three found common ground. In dissent in *Winters v. New York*, a case that also relied on vagueness, Frankfurter described *Lanzetta* as involving a law "of the type that seek[s] to control 'vagrancy.'" Such laws, he wrote in language that would be quoted over and over in the vagrancy law challenge, were "in a class by themselves, in view of the familiar abuses to which they are put." In vagrancy laws, "definiteness is designedly avoided so as to allow the net to be cast at large, to enable men to be caught who are vaguely undesirable in the eyes of police and prosecution, although not chargeable with any particular offense." Such laws, Frankfurther concluded, were "not fenced in by the text of the statute or by the subject matter so as to give notice of conduct to be avoided."[63]

Well before *Edelman* arrived at the Court, then, *Lanzetta* had made clear that a majority of the justices openly condemned both vague laws and laws that seemed to lack any requirement that a person do something—commit some act—before he could be arrested. Moreover, at least one justice—and not even one of the most liberal—had already explicitly declared that vagrancy laws raised such concerns in *Winters*.

Wirin and Okrand built upon these arguments in their briefs. In accordance with Supreme Court procedures, they might have extended their claims during oral argument at the Court. Whether due to Wirin's view of the merits of the case, the severity of the procedural problems, strapped resources, or low priority, however, Wirin and Okrand agreed with Los Angeles' lawyers to submit *Edelman* on the briefs alone. The decision "much concerned" ACLU national staff counsel Herbert Monte Levy. Levy had been aware of several affiliates' runins with vagrancy laws by 1952, and he had gone so far as to suggest to a recent Yale law graduate who had written a student note on vagrancy laws that he draft a model ordinance. Levy had been excited not only to publicize that the ACLU had brought a vagrancy challenge to the high court, but also to make use of the organization's new Washington, DC, office to support *Edelman*.[64]

Not content to let the case rest on the briefs, Levy prevailed on Emanuel Redfield to argue the case. Born in New York City, Redfield held a bachelor's degree from New York University and a law degree from Fordham. Though he was practicing at a firm in the early 1950s, he spent much time on the business of the fledgling New York affiliate of the ACLU (NYCLU). He spent a good deal of that time on the vagrancy law issue. Redfield and his colleagues had lobbied for the repeal of New York's vagrancy law, and he had already filed a $50,000 false arrest suit challenging the law.[65]

Because of differences in the key provisions of the California and New York statutes, Redfield came to *Edelman* with a different set of critiques from Gallagher, Wirin, and Okrand. The New York law defined a vagrant as one who is "without employment and no means to maintain himself." As a result, Redfield was inclined to combine his vagueness arguments not with free speech arguments but with Thirteenth Amendment claims that the law violated prohibitions on involuntary servitude. Redfield's constitutional concerns went to the basic premises of vagrancy laws—that everyone who could work had to work—rather than the laws' ostensible abuse against political dissidents.[66]

Given Redfield's late entry into the case, and the fact that the only copy of the briefs was at the Supreme Court clerk's office, it was not clear that Redfield would get the chance to read the briefs before he had to stand up before nine justices on Edelman's behalf. Despite the lack of preparation, Redfield later reported to Okrand that he thought he had gotten "along quite well in the vagrancy argument." He nonetheless found the immediate future bleak. The fact that the highest California court to review the case had neither considered nor decided the federal question seemed an insurmountable obstacle. Redfield predicted that the Supreme Court would either reverse because Edelman had been denied an opportunity to appeal or else "dismiss the writ as improvidently granted."[67]

Redfield had higher hopes for the vagrancy law challenge more generally, a challenge that in his view hinged on the status crime problem. Redfield told Okrand that it was "advisable to search out and press the point of due process of the prosecution of a person based on his character (as this case is). . . . I believe it is the right of every free man to be 'unrestrained' and 'unashamed.'" He was convinced that "the issue of vagrancy will and should be kept alive." Indeed, he continued to pursue it himself.[68]

Redfield was right on both counts. Even with the benefit of oral argument, the justices turned out not to be as committed to deciding the case as Black and Douglas might have hoped. They alone voted against dismissing the writ as improvidently granted during the justices' conference after oral argument. While "DIGs," as were they were known, were not unheard of, neither were they common. The Court had made a mistake in granting review, such a dismissal said, and the justices admitted it publicly. The Court would continue to DIG vagrancy cases with disproportionate frequency over the next twenty years, as it repeatedly tried, and repeatedly failed, to answer the vagrancy question.[69]

Redfield was also right that the vagrancy law challenge was far from dead. Indeed, the opinions eventually published in *Edelman* propelled the issue forward even as they killed the case itself. The Court's opinion dismissing the case made clear that though Black and Douglas were alone in wanting to decide the case, they were not alone in worrying about the law's constitutionality. Though the majority opinion explained the procedural questions that prevented the Court from deciding the case, it also acknowledged that the Court had granted certiorari in the first place "because of serious constitutional questions" as to "whether the vagrancy statute is invalid under the Fourteenth Amendment."[70]

Like Wirin, Black and Douglas did not cite *Thornhill* or *Carlson*, but they did broaden the lawyers' First Amendment argument considerably in their dissent. Committed free speech defenders, they contended that Edelman's vagrancy conviction "was based primarily on what he had said in public speeches made in a Los Angeles park" and that the "free speech question was . . . obviously involved in this vagrancy prosecution." Citing *Winters*, Black and Douglas found the law so "vague and indefinite . . . as to permit within the scope of its language the punishment of incidents fairly within the protection of the guarantee of free speech." They also embraced the more general due process arguments Wirin had made, finding California's law "too vague to meet the safeguarding standards of due process of law in this country." They quoted at length from the jury instructions describing vagrancy as "a continuing offense" that involved Edelman's "character" and "status" rather than any particular conduct. They cited *Lanzetta* as precedent.[71]

The relative weight of, and relationship between, the various arguments against Edelman's conviction—that the police had targeted Edelman as a political dissident, that the law was vague, and that it created a status offense—remained shifting and uncertain in the opinion. In their original draft dissent from the denial of certiorari, Black and Douglas had focused more on the status/conduct distinction. They had complained that "such statutes . . . can be used as dragnets to convict *unorthodox and unpopular persons* against whom no specific crimes can be proven." In the final draft, however, the free speech issues took precedence, as when Black described the law as "dragnet legislation used to abridge *public discussion* of 'views on political, social or economic questions.'" The speech, not the people, were the real concern. As *Edelman* brought new attention to the vagrancy law regime, the use of the laws to suppress free speech came most readily into focus. The case—and the crux of the vagrancy law problem—remained closely tied to the political context that had created it.[72]

Edelman's status as a free speaker might have influenced Black and Douglas throughout the case, but *Edelman* also increased attention to the vagrancy law itself. That attention cost Edelman. As he continued to find trouble in the months after the Supreme Court dismissed his case, observers repeatedly harped on Edelman's inferior status as a vagrant. To many, vagrants and free speakers were mutually exclusive categories. To be a vagrant was to be an outcast, a nobody, a criminal. To be a free speaker was to be potentially constitutionally protected and politically salient. No doubt, Edelman's conviction was for vagrancy, and it was likely to haunt him regardless of the arguments his lawyers made on his behalf. But the fact that the case shifted his image from "free speaker wrongly arrested (for vagrancy)" to "alleged vagrant challenging vagrancy law (who happened to be a free speaker)" highlighted the nature of the conviction and changed Edelman's perceived cultural and constitutional position.

The stigma of Edelman's status as a vagrant became particularly apparent the next time Edelman brought a case to the Supreme Court. Edelman had long been the kind of joiner organizations were eager to expel. As the *Los Angeles Times* put it, for decades, Edelman had "bounced energetically into leftist organizations—and then been bounced unceremoniously by the groups who found his radicalism extending to themselves." Right around the time of Edelman's own criminal appeals, his new passion became the National

Committee to Secure Justice in the Rosenberg Case. Though avowed communists Julius and Ethel Rosenberg had been convicted of conspiring to commit
espionage, the committee—and many left-leaning Americans—maintained
their innocence. Convinced that the committee pursued its strategy at the possible expense of the Rosenbergs' lives, Edelman once again found himself at
odds with colleagues. The Los Angeles chapter informed him that "by the action
of the full committee at its regular meeting"—to which Edelman had somehow
not been invited—"you have been expelled." Edelman then found two attorneys
willing to represent him as a "next friend" of the Rosenbergs even though he had
never even met the couple.[73]

In mid-June of 1953, six months after the dismissal of Edelman's vagrancy
case and just as the justices were scattering across the country for their summer
recess, Edelman appealed directly to Justice Douglas as the Rosenbergs' "next
friend." With the guilt or innocence of the Rosenbergs—and the process of their
condemnation—a national preoccupation for more than two years, Douglas
had previously denied a variety of Rosenberg petitions. He now granted a stay
of execution, issued an opinion sending the case back to the district court, and
promptly departed for his summer home and nature refuge in Goose Prairie,
Washington. When he had almost made it through Pennsylvania, he heard a
radio report that Chief Justice Vinson had called an immediate special session
to dispose of the issues raised in Douglas's opinion. Furious that he had been
purposefully excluded, Douglas turned around and headed back to the capital.[74]

When the Court convened the next day, some of the justices were impatient
and nervous. They had been avoiding the Rosenbergs for years. Douglas's interest in the case at this late date seemed, in Frankfurter's words, a "grandstand play."
Any petitioner would have found a less than ready welcome, but Edelman's was
downright hostile. Justice Jackson questioned Edelman's standing as next friend,
describing his entry into the case an "intrusion" and a "disorderly intervention . . .
more likely to prejudice than to help the representation of the accused persons
in highly publicized cases." When Daniel Marshall, one of Edelman's lawyers,
began to speak, Jackson asked him who his client was. The question was clearly
rhetorical. Before Edelman's name was out of Marshall's mouth, Jackson replied,
"Was he the Edelman who was before this Court last year in a vagrancy case?"
Angry, Marshall answered, "Let's get this straight. It was a free speech case. It is
improper to call it vagrancy." Chief Justice Vinson warned Marshall not to let
his "temperature rise." Jackson was not ready to let the point rest. He raised it
again in his published opinion in the case, which was joined by all of his brethren
save Black, Douglas, and Frankfurter. Jackson wrote, "Edelman is a stranger to
the Rosenbergs and to their case. . . . What may be Edelman's purpose in getting himself into this litigation is not explained. . . . It does not appear that his
own record is entirely clear or that he would be a helpful or chosen champion."

He cited *Edelman v. California*. What better proof of Edelman's bad motives and besmirched record than a conviction finding him, as a person, dissolute? The justice thus disparaged Edelman's Rosenberg theory by denigrating the theorist as a vagrant.[75]

But Marshall's response was key: the justice had misunderstood the case. Edelman's lawyer argued that *Edelman* was not really a vagrancy case, and Edelman was not a vagrant. It was a free speech case, and Edelman was due constitutional protections for his speech, whatever its content. One of Edelman's vagrancy lawyers remembered the case the same way. In an oral history many years later, Fred Okrand recalled that Edelman had been arrested more than once. He remembered that a Los Angeles provision against speaking without a permit in public had been declared unconstitutional in one of Edelman's cases. He nowhere mentioned that Edelman's Supreme Court case had been for a vagrancy conviction or had failed to overturn the law. In Okrand's mind too, then, many years later, the heart of the Edelman case was free speech and not vagrancy.[76]

Indicting and stigmatizing Edelman as a vagrant was not limited to the Supreme Court. Though press reports often referred to Edelman's free speech efforts—the *Los Angeles Times* called him "a one-track-minded little soapbox orator from Los Angeles' Pershing Square"—they more often highlighted the vagrancy issue. The *Chicago Daily Tribune* referred to Edelman as "an ex-convict described as the condemned atom spies' 'next friend,'" and it noted that Justice Douglas had supported Edelman's defense in "a criminal case" six months prior. Like Justice Jackson, the paper used Edelman's arrests as a form of impeachment—the vagrancy conviction was intended to impugn Edelman's character, and it had done just that. Edelman "admitted he has been arrested 12 or 15 times by Los Angeles police as a beggar and dissolute vagrant, has served time in jail and still faces trial on one of the vagrancy charges." Even as his lawyers and two Supreme Court justices held him up as a protectable free speaker, to much of the world, Edelman remained merely a convicted vagrant.[77]

The increased emphasis in *Edelman* on the vagrancy law itself might not have done much for Edelman's reputation, but it wasn't bad for his ongoing legal woes or for the incipient vagrancy law challenge more generally. Even as the justices deliberated about Edelman's plight, another challenge to the very same "lewd or dissolute" subsection of the California vagrancy law arrived at the Court. This case too was riddled with procedural difficulties. Even so, when the Court denied certiorari in the case a week after dismissing Edelman, Black and Douglas noted publicly that they would have heard the case. They were clearly still looking for an opportunity to invalidate California's vagrancy law.[78]

Moreover, the opinions that came out of *Edelman* signaled to lawyers, scholars, and judges that there might really be a constitutional problem with vagrancy laws. The Court's hints about the constitutional vulnerability of the California law began bearing fruit for Edelman himself almost immediately. Police arrested Edelman at least four more times in the two years following his Supreme Court case. One arrest was a direct consequence of his defeat at the high court. After the Court had dismissed his case, Edelman served forty-six days of his ninety-day vagrancy sentence. (The ACLU viewed Edelman's early release as an attempt to "forestall a test case" of the "speech right.") California law also required Edelman to register as a convicted vagrant and dissolute person once his appeals to the Supreme Court had been exhausted. He did not. At his trial for failure to register, his attorney, the same Dan Marshall who had represented him in *Rosenberg*, "hinted darkly at a connection between Edelman's part in the Rosenberg case and his local court difficulty." In Marshall's view, this new charge, like the original vagrancy charge, was just another instance of political persecution by law enforcement. Edelman was convicted and given forty-eight hours to register and receive a suspended ninety-day sentence.[79]

In a surprise move that seemed clearly influenced by the justices' constitutional intimations in *Edelman*, the California appeals court reversed Edelman's conviction for failing to register. The registration law generally targeted sex offenders, which led the court to conclude that for a vagrancy conviction to lead to a registration requirement, "dissolute" had to mean "lewd." Despite half-hearted prosecution efforts to show otherwise, Edelman's brand of dissoluteness had not been lewd. The reversal on registration did not formally reverse Edelman's vagrancy conviction, but the decision called that conviction's foundation deeply into doubt. Indeed, though it is unclear what part *Edelman* itself played, a few months later, another California appellate court struck down the section of the vagrancy law making vagrants of those who associated with known thieves.[80]

Beyond Edelman's case and the California courts, a variety of other lawyers and scholars took note of *Edelman* as a signal of the possible invalidity of vagrancy laws. A note in the *Harvard Law Review* just a few months later used *Edelman* to build an argument against status crimes. The Mattachine Society, a pioneering organization in what was then called the "homophile" movement, reprinted another article that used *Edelman* to condemn the routine arrests of gay men in allegedly compromising circumstances. It was hardly surprising that Mattachine looked to *Edelman* with hope: it was under the same subsection of the California vagrancy law—making a vagrant of any "lewd or dissolute" person—that police officers arrested gay men for "vag lewd," as it was commonly called. The article was optimistic that *Edelman* "may lead to an entire reevaluation of the vagrancy law by the California State Courts." Yet another article, this one in the left-leaning *Lawyers Guild Review*, invoked Edelman in its condemnation of the vagrancy law as "the most time-honored foe of due process." Just as *Edelman* had stimulated a variety of arguments by those directly involved in the case, then, it also led outside observers to see in it multiple possibilities: for undermining status crimes, stopping the harassment of sexual minorities, and condemning dubious police practices.[81]

Such optimism notwithstanding, the rest of the decade would pass before the Supreme Court returned to the question of vagrancy law. As would happen repeatedly over the course of the vagrancy law challenge, the justices had balked when they had an opportunity to act. In the meantime, the anti-vagrancy law efforts of scholars, legislators, defendants, and their lawyers began to expand public and professional understanding of the scope of the vagrancy law regime beyond *Edelman's* close alignment with political protest and free speech. One such early advocate was Ernest Besig, the ACLU lawyer who had left the Southern California agricultural fights to defend civil liberties during the San Francisco general strike of 1934. Though Besig's encounters with the California vagrancy law emerged out of very different contexts and pushed him in very different directions from *Edelman*, Black and Douglas's dissent was one of the first resources to which he would turn.

2

The Vagrancy Law Education
of Ernest Besig

Here is how it began, the vagrancy law education of Ernest Besig: with a file with the words "Victimless Crimes" and "Vagrancy" scrawled across the lip; a list of cases in that file, handwritten and growing, that included *Edelman v. California*; and a police raid on a black Bay Area neighborhood in the winter of 1954.

Here is how it ended, or at least came to partial and temporary repose: with the 1962 repeal of the California vagrancy law and the passage of a new disorderly conduct statute. Between the raid and the repeal, developments in California and across the country made laws and law enforcement methods that had previously seemed almost unassailable begin to look vulnerable. As Besig homed in on repeal, he described it as "the most important civil liberties legislation adopted by the California legislature in [his] memory."[1]

Besig was no vagrancy neophyte when he began his crusade in earnest in 1954. Twenty years earlier, he had been among the vanguard of lawyers encountering vagrancy laws while defending the civil liberties of farmworkers for the Southern California ACLU (SCACLU)—and getting assaulted in the process. When ACLU founder and director Roger Baldwin dispatched Besig to San Francisco in response to the general strike there in 1934, Besig again encountered the vagrancy law. Twenty-five years later, he reflected that "the Vagrancy Law has been one of our constant concerns." Between the mid-1950s and the early 1960s, Besig and his Northern California ACLU (NCACLU) were "overwhelmed with complaints about improper application of this law" from African Americans, gay men and lesbians, the Beats, "suspicious" persons, and others. The scope of the vagrancy law problem had grown to such proportions that Besig concluded that the NCACLU "could devote [its] entire energies to problems arising under this law and still not make much of a dent on the problem."[2]

Day in and day out, the people of Northern California told their vagrancy law stories to Besig. Some of the details he documented were human details, details of shame or worry, of fear or anger or wonderment. Accused vagrants complained that the police questioned them in the rain. They had been to a museum with a companion, who was a painter and loved museums. Other details went to the charges themselves—whether someone was well dressed, or had a job, was a longtime resident of the city, or was intoxicated, or was a Ph.D. student carrying Latin books. Frequently, the details the targets thought were important were beside the point of the particular provision under which they had been arrested. They assumed a stereotyped definition of vagrancy that required, depended on, their poverty. They emphasized that they had shown the police their money, that they had been out shopping and spent large sums. But when the vagrancy charge was being lewd or wandering about, being a common drunk or prostitute, their proof was inapposite. Such people might not have been vagrants in the traditional sense, but they were nonetheless, and quite clearly, vagrants under California law. With twelve separate sections, the century-old law that had brought down Isidor Edelman could do almost anything. Besig discovered that the police used it so that it did.

The range of Besig's vagrancy law encounters highlighted the complexities involved in defining and diagnosing the problem. Did the problem inhere in the law or police enforcement of it, the wording of the statute or its substance, policing for conformity or policing for public safety? Leo Gallagher had emphasized enforcement in *Edelman*, but Al Wirin, Emanuel Redfield, and the justices of the Supreme Court had moved toward the law itself. Besig came to see a law easy to abuse and police officers—whether trying to prevent crime or venting bigotry or both—inclined to abuse it. The breadth of the law and the proclivities of the police reinforced one another and left uncertain the best method of redress.

Besig's files offer a unique window into the process by which vagrancy enforcement looked increasingly illegitimate in the late 1950s and early 1960s. As Besig knew, however, he was hardly alone. Other ACLU lawyers, including but not limited to Wirin to the south and Redfield to the east, had already begun targeting vagrancy laws. Moreover, at both the professional and the grassroots level, the police practices that supported and benefited from those laws were also coming under fire in the 1950s. So was the whole notion of criminalizing morality. The hundreds of pages of notes, newspaper clippings, and records Besig accumulated in the eight years after the 1954 North Richmond raid reveal not only the many uses to which the police put the vagrancy law but also how much changed in the perception of vagrancy laws during a decade known more for stasis than transformation.

When the California legislature repealed the vagrancy law in 1962, Besig called it a victory. Repeal had been unthinkable in California eight years earlier and stymied just three years before it succeeded. The victory was fundamentally incomplete, however. Even as Besig achieved some resolution in the early 1960s, both the nature of the problem and how much had truly been resolved remained deeply uncertain.

The Many Faces of Vagrancy Law
in 1950s San Francisco

The first incident in Besig's "Vagrancy" file, the one that likely sparked its creation and the one that reveals Besig's initial instincts and uncertainties, was a 1954 vice raid on the black neighborhood of North Richmond. According to the Contra Costa County sheriff, the area was a magnet for "hoodlums"—prostitutes, gamblers, and drug dealers. The sheriff had more than one hundred law enforcement officers set up street blockades, enter every bar, restaurant, and café, and order patrons—watching floor shows, eating chicken dinners, or having a drink—to raise their hands over their heads and submit to searches. Once the officers had decided against arresting a given person, he or she was given proof of clearance to display to those manning the blockades outside. Anyone who protested was threatened with violence or arrest. When a disabled veteran said he could not raise his hands over his head, an officer stated, "If you act like an ass, we'll treat you like an ass." Despite the aggressive police action, the "hoodlums"—perhaps tipped off beforehand—had all decided to stay home that particular night. The officers interrogated around four hundred people. They took seventy into custody. Failing to find evidence of gambling, prostitution, or narcotics, they booked three African Americans "for investigation" and forty-three for vagrancy.[3]

Both the raids and the vagrancy charges raised the NCACLU's ire. Besig complained that the police had lacked warrants and probable cause for the raids. "They invaded the privacy of persons by unlawful searches and seizures." That problem was compounded by the obvious racial element. Complaints about police harassment of, and discrimination against, African Americans were already prominent in many cities, and Besig applied them readily. "Mass Arrests of Negroes in Lawless Raid," announced the ACLU newspaper. Where law enforcement presented itself as fighting vice and petty crime that happened to be in a black neighborhood, the NCACLU saw racial prejudice "against a seemingly helpless minority." Despite his Cornell law degree, Besig never took the California bar—and so could not practice as a lawyer in the state— so staff attorney Lawrence Speiser, a recent graduate of Hastings College of Law, took over the cases. Speiser managed to get dismissals for a number of defendants and acquittals for some of those who went to trial. The NCACLU also helped file twenty false arrest claims totaling $305,000 against government officials.[4]

Besig was less clear about how to attack the vagrancy law itself. There was no set canon of vagrancy cases to cite, no obvious theory of why laws like California's were problematic. There were, however, scattered resources. Scrawling "Vagrancy Law" across the top of a legal pad just after the arrests, Besig collected a hodge-podge of decisions, theories, and definitions of vagrancy, touching on loitering and unemployment, idleness, the status-conduct distinction, and vagueness. He catalogued Supreme Court cases, lower court cases, and treatises. In addition to *Edelman*, Besig identified as useful Al Wirin's communist vagrancy case of *In re Cutler*, Justice Felix Frankfurter's dissent in *Winters v. New York*, and the gangster case of *Lanzetta v. New Jersey*. As an afterthought, crowded between two lines already filled with writing, he added the labor loitering case of *Thornhill v. Alabama*. Though *Thornhill* had not seemed relevant to anyone during the Edelman litigation, Besig began to assimilate it into the vagrancy law canon.[5]

Part of Besig's problem was a basic lack of clarity about what made those arrested "vagrants." Besig initially amassed evidence to prove that they were not vagrants in the traditional sense of subdivision one of the California law, which made it a crime to lack "visible means of living," not "seek employment," and refuse labor when offered despite having "the physical ability to work." His notes emphasized the financial and employment status of those arrested. "Tucker picked up vagrancy even though had check for $155 last week," he wrote about one person. About others, he noted, "Job," "Unemployment," "Dis Able [*sic*] Veteran," and "being supported." Besig's assumption was that subdivision one arrests made some sense. Cases in Illinois, Alabama, and elsewhere had attempted to equate those who had only illegitimate means of support—like gamblers and prostitutes—with those who lacked visible means. Subdivision one was also most familiar to Besig from the SCACLU's Depression-era vagrancy battles on behalf of farmworkers. Indeed, Besig would continue to encounter subdivision one enforcement of the classic vagrancy concept into the mid-1950s. A year after North Richmond, newspapers reported that police in the Central Valley were assisting ranchers by arresting for subdivision one vagrancy potential farmhands who "suddenly became criminal vagrants" when they refused low pay. Though the men clearly fit the legal category, Besig and the NCACLU protested their arrests anyway.[6]

As it turned out, the police had not even considered subdivision one for the North Richmond raids. Besig was planning to defend against charges not contemplated. Some of the police complaints initially charged Edelman's subdivision five, making every "lewd or dissolute person" a vagrant. Someone had subsequently crossed out that charge. In its place, was subdivision three, describing the defendant as one "who roams about from place to place without any lawful business."[7]

These three different aspects of the vagrancy law—the willfully unemployed, the lewd and dissolute, and the loiterer—potentially applied to very different types of people. They would later occasion different constitutional critiques and different law enforcement defenses. Yet here both lawyers preparing for a defense and those preparing for a prosecution were unsure of which to apply. The "catchall" of vagrancy masked the law's many guises, obviated law enforcement's need to clarify the nature of the crime, and left Besig unclear about how to articulate a challenge to the law itself.

The vagrancy law problem came into sharper focus two years after North Richmond with another police raid. The target in 1956 was Hazel's Inn, a gay bar in Sharp Park, just south of San Francisco. Thirty-five officers entered the bar, announcing, "This is a raid." They arrested seventy-seven men, ten women, and three teenagers. Many were arrested on "vag lewd" charges brought under subdivision five's criminalization of any "lewd or dissolute person." The San Mateo County sheriff announced that the "purpose of the raid was to make it clear to these people that we won't put up with this sort of thing." He had another goal too: to prove that Hazel's Inn was used as a "resort" by "sex perverts." Such use was justification for revoking a liquor license—a fate to which several of the Bay Area's thirty-odd gay bars had already succumbed after fights in the press, the courts, and the legislature. Indeed, a year after the raids, the state revoked Hazel Nickola's liquor license.[8]

If the raid in North Richmond had revealed an implicit conflict between law enforcement officers who saw threats to the social fabric and Besig who saw discrimination, Hazel's Inn made the conflict undeniable. In the years after World War II, government repression of "sexual perverts," "sexual deviates," and "sexual psychopaths" was the driving force behind a moral panic that led to government commissions, new laws, and more aggressive law enforcement. According to politicians, mental health professionals, religious leaders, and law enforcement experts, homosexuals posed threats to the moral wellbeing of the nation and the psychic health of American children. They could not be trusted in many types of public or private employment, they undermined the effectiveness of the military, and they were not allowed to immigrate to the United States. In the midst of Cold War anti-communism, both the presumed psychological defects of homosexuals and their vulnerability to blackmail made them a national security threat that had to be neutralized. In what has since been dubbed the "Lavender Scare" that accompanied the "Red Scare," politicians forced thousands of "lavender lads" out of the federal government. Sometimes the condemnation of homosexuality required "treatment" and "conversion" to heterosexuality. More often, surveillance, quarantine, and criminal suppression were used to contain the perceived harms of homosexuality and its possible spread.[9]

The sentiments of the San Mateo sheriff thus reflected a standard law enforcement position, especially in areas with rapidly growing and increasingly visible gay populations in the 1950s. One police chief candidly announced in 1959,

"We want to drive out the homosexuals who crowd in here and outrage every-one. 90% of the men who bother people in bars are not from Marin County." He warned that he would use the law—including vagrancy arrests—to push them out. In the early 1960s, the police chief of Los Angeles worried about "the rising menace of the vagrant lewd situation" as the city seemed "a mecca for homosexu-als." On the other side of the continent, Philadelphia's Mayor Dilworth wrote an ACLU leader in 1959 that "places where queers congregate raise the devil with a neighborhood in very short order, and it is very difficult to break up such groups without some violation of civil rights. . . . [W]hile they are relatively harmless by themselves, when they get to running in packs they can be really vicious, and louse up a neighborhood in no time flat."[10]

San Mateo's turn to vagrancy arrests of gay men and lesbians was equally stan-dard. Sodomy laws were universal, but the crime was difficult to prove because it occurred in private. California's sodomy law dated back to 1850. As early as 1914, Long Beach had paid vice specialists by the arrest to entice gay men with sexual advances. But such mandates and the indignities they involved—the peeping into public toilets or trolling of public parks—caused both anxiety and eviden-tiary difficulties. Departments often turned instead to vagrancy, disorderly con-duct, public lewdness, or solicitation laws—none of which required proof of an actual sex act. New York's police in the 1950s, for example, repurposed a law that made a vagrant of anyone disguised "in a manner calculated to prevent his being identified" that had originally responded to rebellious nineteenth-century farm-ers disguised as Native Americans. Now they applied it to men who presented themselves as women. Police in California, St. Louis, Philadelphia, Toronto, Chicago, Portland, and Washington, DC, used arrests of what were sometimes called "social vagrants" to keep sexual deviants under wraps.[11]

Gay men were more frequent targets of "vag lewd" arrests than lesbians, as the police often found them liaising in public spaces—bars, parks, beaches, public restrooms, transportation depots. But women too were charged with vagrancy. Women reported that in early 1950s Los Angeles, they risked arrest simply when standing in front of a lesbian bar or by dressing or "looking too masculine." In Tampa, Florida, in June 1957, police arrested twelve women for their "man-nish" dress. "We always heard the story that you had to wear at least three items of clothing of your own sex, and it does seem that the police were concerned about cross-dressing, that that was a big thing," recalled early lesbian activist Del Martin. "I guess that was the way they could identify us, you know. And that's how we could identify ourselves."[12]

These charges had debilitating and frequently very public consequences, as newspapers reported names, home addresses, and occupations of those arrested. In 1955, the *Los Angeles Times* found it newsworthy that national civil rights leader Bayard Rustin had been arrested on suspicion of lewd vagrancy

Figure 2.1 Arrest of a gay man at a Mardi Gras Ball in northern California in 1965. Because the crime of sodomy was difficult to detect and prove, the police often turned instead to vagrancy arrests—otherwise known as "vag lewd." The public shaming that accompanied such arrests is apparent in this suspect's attempt to shield his face and identity. Evander Smith—California Hall Papers (GLC 46), Gay & Lesbian Center, San Francisco Public Library.

after giving a speech about world peace. Convictions—and sometimes even just arrests—meant losing jobs teaching in the public schools, jeopardizing professional licenses and certifications, or being court-martialed out of the military or expelled from public office. Those arrested more than once for public sexual behavior could be involuntarily committed as "sexual psychopaths." In 1947, as Isidore Edelman well knew, California became the first state to require anyone convicted of immoral conduct, including vag lewd, to register as a sex offender. Unsurprisingly, those arrested for vag lewd usually pled guilty, ideally to lesser—non-sex-based—charges that avoided such collateral consequences.[13]

Not everyone avoided confrontation over vag lewd arrests. An unintended effect of the increased repression of homosexuality during and after World War II was that gay men and lesbians became more visible to one another and better able to organize. At the grassroots level, an incipient "homophile" movement tried to increase toleration for gay men and lesbians. The pioneering Mattachine Society, established in Los Angeles in 1951, initially modeled itself after the Communist Party, with "cells," assumed names, and security measures taken to protect the identity of their members. "We decided to call ourselves Mattachine after . . . medieval peasant monks who wore masks. . . . We too were forced to wear masks on the job and elsewhere." The Daughters of Bilitis, named to honor Sappho, followed in 1955, aiming to educate the public "to accept the Lesbian as an individual and eliminate the prejudice which places oppressive limitations on her." [14]

Vag lewd quickly became an issue for Mattachine when co-founder Dale Jennings decided to fight his arrest in 1952. Jennings hired George Shibley, a progressive lawyer with a penchant for representing unpopular defendants. (He would later defend Robert F. Kennedy's assassin Sirhan Sirhan.) During the trial, Jennings took the unusual step of publicly embracing his homosexuality, but he denied the sexually provocative behavior alleged by an undercover officer. He also welcomed, rather than shied from, publicity. His fellow Mattachine Society members formed the Citizens' Committee to Outlaw Entrapment, raised money for the trial, and distributed leaflets. The leaflets likened "the homosexual minority" to "Minorities in general" in a rhetorical effort to transform the group from reviled deviants to protected victims. When Jennings's trial ended in a hung jury—with only one juror holding out for conviction—prosecutors decided not to retry the case. This was viewed as a victory for gay men and lesbians in California, and Mattachine grew in its wake. [15]

Meanwhile, scientific and legal professionals were beginning to rethink homosexuality. In 1948 and 1953, Alfred Kinsey published two controversial but best-selling reports on human sexuality that contended that homosexuality, as well as other "taboo" sexual practices, was far more common than previously thought. With support from some in the ACLU, Kinsey used his scientific work to promote legal change. [16]

Indeed, the idea that homosexuality more properly belonged to the realm of private choice than public concern found its way into a burgeoning debate about the role the criminal law should play in regulating morality generally. John Stuart Mill first suggested in 1859 that what would become known as "victimless crimes"—crimes with moral, rather than concrete, harms to third parties—should not be penalized. Right around the time of the Hazel's Inn raid in 1956, discussion of the subject intensified, with sodomy as a prime example. A year before Hazel's Inn, the elite, politically mainstream lawyers and legal scholars in the American Law Institute (ALI) had eliminated sodomy laws from the Institute's draft Model Penal Code (MPC). "The Code does not attempt to use the power of the state to enforce purely moral or religious standards," the drafters explained. "We deem it inappropriate for the government to attempt to control behavior that has no substantial significance except as to the morality of the actor. Such matters are best left to religious, educational and other social influences." The Model Code excluded "from the criminal law all sexual practices not involving force, adult corruption of minors, or public offense" because "no harm to the secular interests of the community is involved in atypical sex practice in private between consenting adult partners." A few months after the raid, the Wolfenden Report in Great Britain agreed: "It is not, in our view, the function of the law to intervene in the private lives of citizens, or to seek to enforce any particular pattern of behavior." It was convinced that "there must remain a realm of private morality and immorality which is, in brief and crude terms, not the law's business."[17]

Change was coming, but it hardly made a challenge to vag lewd either easy or obvious. Indeed, despite the fact that vag lewd arrests often stood in for sodomy prosecutions, the MPC left vag lewd intact. On one level, vag lewd laws might have seemed more problematic than the sodomy laws the MPC condemned. Sodomy laws at least pretended to regulate conduct, whereas vag lewd made no such pretense. Vagrancy laws criminalized the status of being lewd, and law enforcement officials understood homosexuality, by definition, to be lewd. This made gay men and lesbians vagrants, and that made them criminals. Supreme Court justices had already expressed concerns about status crimes in *Lanzetta*, *Winters*, and *Edelman*. Though the contexts were different, the same criticisms seemed to apply.[18]

Few people applied them, however. In the mid-1950s, the main concern among those in the vanguard of decriminalizing victimless crime was less the status-conduct distinction than the difference between public and private conduct. The kind of sodomy thought most protectable was the kind that took place in private. Though vag lewd arrests often occurred in private places, the association of the crime with public displays of sexuality made it more legally justifiable.[19]

Whether the charge was vagrancy or sodomy, change was slow in coming in part because lawyers were in short supply. The rare lawyer willing to represent the rare defendant willing to risk the publicity of a trial made clear that high fees had to compensate for the risk to the lawyers' reputations. Said one about a vag lewd arrest, "I'll take care of it. It ain't cheap, but I'll take care of it." According to another, "The police didn't have to deal with any trials from these cases because the clients were too embarrassed to be subjected to a jury trial, and the attorneys were too embarrassed to defend them." The result was that "they would either plead guilty and pay a fine or they'd waive a jury trial . . . [and] most often be convicted by the judge, pay a fine, and be left with a police record."[20]

Even the civil-liberties-minded ACLU shied away. A year after Hazel's Inn, Speiser contacted national ACLU staff counsel Rowland Watts about pursuing cases stemming from the raid. "In the light of Justices Black's and Douglas' dissent in Edelman vs. California . . . it would appear that the question of the constitutionality of the vagrancy law is one which should be challenged." Though Watts left the ultimate decision to Speiser, he cautioned that "we [the national ACLU] are not enthusiastic about the value of this case in challenging the outrageous import of the vagrancy laws in various parts of the country." It was thus not that the national lawyers were opposed to challenging vagrancy laws. In fact, around the same time, Watts actively encouraged other affiliates to pursue vagrancy challenges. Rather, something about Speiser's case seemed problematic. Watts might have viewed vag lewd as peripheral to the central problems of vagrancy laws, whatever he perceived those to be. Or perhaps the problem was the Northern California branch itself, which had long proven a thorn in the national office's side.[21]

The more likely problem was that the case involved both sexual orientation generally and gay sexual conduct in public specifically. Since at least the alliance with Alfred Kinsey, some within the ACLU had viewed repression of gay men and lesbians as problematic. Watts himself cared about the issue. But the organization as a whole was, as one closeted member of the national board later put it, at best "notably silent" on the rights of homosexuals. Earlier in 1957, the board had concluded that it was "not within the province of the Union to evaluate the social validity of laws" that criminalized homosexuality. Although the board condemned police entrapment and sex offender registration, it found "no constitutional right to practice homosexual acts." It concluded that "behavior," "as distinguished from belief and speech protected by the Constitution," could "be regulated or prohibited." With its anti-communist policy dating from 1940, the ACLU considered homosexuality, unlike race or religion, a legitimate risk factor for national security purposes. The national board would not repeal its 1957 statement until 1964. It would not formally endorse gay rights until 1966. Even those lawyers who would become the vanguard allies of gay men and lesbians within ACLU affiliates—like Frank Kameny in DC, Fred Okrand in Southern California, and a few others—did not begin their efforts in earnest until years after the NCACLU's first attempts. Watts's lukewarm response to Speiser might have put a damper on the Hazel's Inn lawsuits. There is no evidence in the record that Besig and Speiser ever managed to file them.[22]

That said, Besig and Speiser defended gay men and lesbians against criminal prosecution earlier and more vigorously than other civil liberties-minded lawyers in the 1950s. It seems likely that their vagrancy framework led them to view vag lewd as part of a broader conflict over the criminal regulation of morality and vagrancy laws' role in imposing it. Besig's linkage of vagrancy with "victimless crimes" long before the term entered common parlance in either legal scholarship or judicial opinions made clear that he was sympathetic to the kinds of

arguments made in the MPC and the Wolfenden Report. The increasing organization of gay men and lesbians in California also likely influenced how Besig
understood such arrests and enabled him to identify similarities between the
arrests in North Richmond and those in Sharp Park. He announced, "The raid is
similar to one in North Richmond a couple of years ago. Only, in that case, the
victims were a minority race—Negroes." At least in part because of the central
role of California's vagrancy law in policing, Besig was uniquely positioned to
see the connection between North Richmond and Hazel's Inn, between police
repression of racial minorities and sexual ones.[23]

By the late 1950s, Besig was well versed in vagrancy law enforcement against
farmworkers, African Americans, and gay men and lesbians. Still, his vagrancy
law education was far from over. As yet another unpopular force invaded the Bay
Area, the police response again highlighted both the apparently infinite flexibility of the vagrancy law and commonalities among its targets.

Born and nurtured on the campuses and streets of New York City, the Beat
Generation and many of its most prominent members began moving west in
the 1950s. It was in San Francisco that the police confiscated Allen Ginsburg's
controversial poem *Howl*, the state put bookstore owner Lawrence Ferlinghetti
on trial for selling such obscene literature, and the ACLU's Lawrence Speiser
and others defended Ferlinghetti. The case put San Francisco on the map as the
cultural center of the new Beat phenomenon. Though the historically Italian
American North Beach area had long been a gathering place for bohemians and
artists, it now seemed virtually overrun with men in beards and turtlenecks and
women in flowing skirts and hair. A police sergeant noted that approximately
two hundred North Beach residents had signed a petition protesting "the activities of these people." The press viewed the Beats as so foreign that North Beach
was often referred to in the news as "Beatland," "Beatnikstan," or "Beatnikland."
The neighborhood was poised for conflict between old-timers and new arrivals,
conflict in which neither the police nor the vagrancy law would remain neutral.[24]

The problem the Beats posed for the police was not entirely novel. The Beats
understood themselves as inheriting both the physical and spiritual mantle of
hoboes, bums, and the wandering life. It was not just that the Beats rejected Cold
War America, with its suffocating anti-communist politics and suburban culture.
It was also that they embraced, and tried to rehabilitate through imitation, what
Jack Kerouac called "the vanishing American hobo." Moreover, given both realities and stereotypes of Beat culture, the police viewed the Beats as criminal drug
users (like the North Richmond African Americans) *and* sexual deviants (like
the Hazel's Inn homosexuals). As one officer put it, "These North Beach bums!
These Beatniks! . . . They stand around drinking and throwing bottles on the
pavement, and they sit on the curbs—dirty, unsightly and using bad language.

. . . We get complaints." San Francisco Mayor George Christopher announced, "I don't care what they call people—Beatniks, eatniks or deadbeats—you can't excuse narcotics addiction or prostitution just because someone calls himself an artist or writer. The orders are out to give no special favors to the beats."[25]

The Beats posed threats not only to public safety but also to mainstream sensibilities. On the surface, the self-image of many Americans in the 1950s—and the dominant image in popular culture—was of family-oriented, dad-in-charge, white-bread, Ozzie-and-Harriet orthodoxy. What one prominent intellectual called "the vital center" prized consensus to ward off the dangers of communism and other un-Americanisms. Beneath that smooth surface conformity, however, new impulses toward religious liberalism, psychological fulfillment, and identification with outsiders roiled. James Dean was a "Rebel without a Cause" and Marlon Brando was "The Wild One," while Jackson Pollock made art that did not look like art and Thelonious Monk and Miles Davis made music that broke all the usual rules.[26]

Everything about the Beats—their dress, their language, their sex lives, their drug use, their work, art, music, and literature—challenged the image of American complaisance. Similarities between Beats and so-called sexual deviants especially provoked police harassment. North Beach was home to both popular gay bars and Beat hangouts. Moreover, both gay men and lesbians and the Beats were engaged, to greater or lesser degrees, and with more or less self-consciousness, in a rebellion against the traditional, heterosexual, monogamous, nuclear family. Given Allen Ginsberg's high-profile gay imagery in *Howl* and a Beat subculture that was often, though not always, welcoming to gays and lesbians, both law enforcement and mainstream Americans frequently linked and equated the two subcultures.[27]

In key ways, however, the two groups generated different policing problems. Where many gay men and lesbians remained closeted in order to protect themselves from an outcast status—thus requiring undercover work and surveillance for enforcement—the Beats provocatively publicized their rejection of mainstream American culture. They took a more combative stance toward "the Establishment" generally and the "Beatnik patrol" in particular. Complained one officer, "These Beatniks argue with the officer. They're always arguing with the officer."[28]

As police surveillance of North Beach tripled, Jack Kerouac found himself "genuinely actually no shit afraid of walking down North Beach," given that it was "absolutely silly with cops." With support from police chiefs Francis Ahern and Thomas Cahill, the police went after party pads that lacked liquor licenses, littering outside Beat hangouts, and the like. From the Tea Room to Eric's Party Pad to the Cellar, the police were everywhere the Beats wanted to be. Jay Hoppe, the twenty-nine-year-old owner of the Co-Existence Bagel Shop, often called a

Beat "rendezvous," charged the police with "systematically attempting to ruin [his] business." He described how groups of three or four officers would enter his shop between six and eight times a day and leave a parked patrol wagon out front. Hoppe's attorney said he had "never seen such deliberate malice by a government." Even the lawyers who defended the Beats found themselves arrested on petty charges. When Cahill advised police officers not to harass men with beards in anticipation of residents of Calaveras County visiting San Francisco for "Pioneer Days," the clear implication, as several news articles noted, was that the police had previously harassed men just for wearing beards.[29]

No single clause of the vagrancy law was as apt for Beat arrests as vag lewd was for arresting gay men in public, but that detail proved no obstacle to "vagging" the Beats. Threats of vagrancy arrests were a frequent refrain of Officer William Bigarani, a second-generation Italian American San Franciscan and Korean War veteran who understood himself as engaged in an ongoing battle with the Beats. Defining a "beatnik" as "a slight bit lower than a Bohemian," he kept a collection of dossiers on his charges. According to one Beat poet, Bigarani "had a real hatred for Beatniks," and he often warned them away from North Beach. "If I see you around after midnight, I'll run you in for vag," he would say. Bigarani arrested black Beat poet Bob Kaufman so often—over twenty times in two years—that there could usually be found a "Bob Kaufman Can" by the door of the Co-Existence Bagel shop for bail donations. Bigarani also repeatedly arrested William Bosia, a North Beach artist. Though on one occasion Bosia had sold a painting for $200 and was expecting a commission on another, Bigarani and another officer arrested him for vagrancy. An officer allegedly told Bosia, "We're going to get you every week until you get a haircut, shave and put on a suit and tie."[30]

The Beats' racial breaches provoked the police as much as their aesthetics did. Besig fielded numerous complaints from female Beats about harassment for the race of their companions. According to one North Beach bookstore owner, Bigarani was incensed by white women and black men together, what he called "Fillmore Pioneers," after an integrating San Francisco neighborhood. Commented a store owner, "When Big B saw black and white he couldn't contain himself; . . . [h]e'd stop the couple, accuse the chick of being a hustler and the dude of being a pimp and threaten to run them in the next time he saw them on the street." Bigarani told two white women out with a black man that the man "was a bad person and that we should not be with him and further that we had no business being in this area and then he ordered us to go home." He threatened to arrest one of the women for prostitution, and he explained "the shocking and embarrassing things that would happen to me if I were arrested for such an offense"—including a thirty-hour surveillance and a medical examination for venereal disease. Bigarani ordered the man to leave the area, and on subsequent nights, in the man's words, he said "that I should not be around this area for if I were I would be locked up on a 'Vag' charge if nothing else." One officer told another woman that so long as she "live[d] in this beatnik area," she "would be stopped." She wrote Besig: "My feeling is that I do not wish to be persecuted because of my interacial [sic] friends. I'm a working, single-parent mother and an upstanding citizen of my community. It is emotionally upsetting, frightening [sic], humiliating and annoying to be treated in such an unjustifiable mannor [sic] and to be told I may not go where I choose to go."[31]

To Besig and the NCACLU, complaints like these reinforced the already obvious conclusion that the police were using the same vagrancy laws it used against racial and sexual minorities against "artists and non-conformists whom the press has loosely lumped together as 'beatniks.'" In an ongoing epistolary campaign, Besig complained to Police Chief Cahill about Bosia specifically, Bigarani generally, and vag threats writ large. He asked Cahill whether the police were enforcing an unofficial curfew in North Beach, as the ACLU would "be glad to test the matter in court." Though the case never materialized, Besig was not the only one questioning the legitimacy of vagrancy law as social control. The *San Francisco Chronicle* asked, "Are Beatniks Being Pushed Around Because They Are Nonconformists?"[32]

If a fair bit of Besig's vagrancy law education resulted from the use of the vagrancy law against vice and petty crime—which Besig viewed as trying to maintain racial, sexual, and cultural control—an equally important part of his curriculum concerned the use of the law against violent and property crime. Such crime was on the rise in 1950s San Francisco—everything from run-of-the-mill purse snatchings and muggings to more sensational and sensationalized crimes in which old men were "savagely beaten" by "groups of young thugs." One newspaper editorialized, "It is a sobering fact that law-abiding San Franciscans no longer can walk the streets of their city at night with the sense of safety they felt a decade ago. In some neighborhoods the defense was to not walk the streets at all after nightfall." Tensions increased with the crime rate, and the pressure was on for the police to do something about it.[33]

That something was frequently a vagrancy arrest. Though many of those who went to Besig for assistance were white and lived relatively conventional lives, they had somehow roused the suspicions of the police. When the police used the vagrancy law to arrest these suspects—whether to prevent future crimes, investigate past crimes, or incapacitate potential criminals—they often noted vagrancy "1, 5, 6" or "1, 3, 6." That common police notation suggested that such vagrants might be criminals because they had no legitimate means of support (1), were wandering about suspiciously (3, 6), or were outright dissolute (5). The police apparently overlooked a 1951 case that had concluded that one person could

not simultaneously be convicted on two counts of vagrancy for being two different types of vagrants.[34]

Whatever the technical charge, two distinct rationales supported vagrancy
arrests for crime control purposes. Police officers, judges, and other legal professionals had long argued that vagrants—who by traditional definition lacked a
lawful means of a livelihood—would be forced into a life of crime to support
themselves. In his influential 1886 treatise, University of Missouri law professor Christopher G. Tiedeman wrote, "The vagrant has been very appropriately
described as the chrysalis of every species of criminal. A wanderer through the
land, without home ties, idle, and without apparent means of support, what but
criminality is to be expected from such a person?" Tiedeman was optimistic that
if "vagrancy could be successfully combated, if every one was engaged in some
lawful calling, the infractions of the law would be reduced to a surprisingly small
number." That was why vagrancy laws were preventive regulations, rather than
"ordinary criminal laws" that only operated after criminal acts had been committed. The idea that the unemployed were a threat to public order as much as to
the public fisc had deep roots in the assumption that vagrancy would lead to ever
more serious criminal activity.[35]

The second rationale was more strategic—vagrancy arrests could loosen
legal and constitutional constraints on the police. The dominant judicial view
that the Fourth Amendment to the Constitution prohibited "searches and seizures"—including "seizures" of people, or arrests—without "probable cause"
appeared to sanction only two realistic police responses to suspicious activity
or a suspicious-looking person: either wait for probable cause to search or arrest
or do nothing. As police officers sought alternatives to that unsatisfying choice,
they found that they were often able to arrest suspicious persons under vagrancy
laws where they would have been stymied by procedural restraints from arresting them for other crimes. Vagrancy laws, then, were what law professor Caleb
Foote called "an escape hatch" to the Fourth Amendment, whether the goal was
investigation of an earlier crime or prevention of a forthcoming one.[36]

The breadth and ambiguity of vagrancy laws made finding—or
constructing—a violation easy. A police officer involved in a 1907 California
case explained the practice in a precedent judges and scholars would repeatedly
cite. Describing why he had arrested two men for vagrancy when he actually
suspected them of an assault he had not witnessed and for which he lacked a
warrant, the officer testified, "I says: 'Well, the only thing we can do—we didn't
see it—we will go and vag them.'" For decades, police officers, legislators, and
judges unabashedly espoused this use of vagrancy laws against assorted "hoodlums," "gangsters," "mobsters," "criminal characters," "habitual criminals," and
"public enemies." A New York Law Revision Commission Report reviewing (but
leaving intact) that state's vagrancy law in 1935 put it bluntly, "The underlying

purpose [of the vagrancy laws] is to relieve the police of the necessity of proving that criminals have committed or are planning to commit specific crimes."[37]

By the time San Francisco faced its postwar crime wave, the high-profile use of vagrancy laws against high-profile mobsters had made the crime control vagrancy arrest highly visible and easily imitated. Mobsters were notoriously difficult to catch actually committing the crimes that made them so infamous—murder, extortion, and the like. Just as tax evasion felled some gangsters, vagrancy arrests nabbed others. Some jurisdictions passed new vagrancy-like laws specifically tailored to gangsters—such as the statute struck down in 1939 in *Lanzetta v. New Jersey*. Others applied existing vagrancy laws. As early as 1915, Chicago and Illinois officials pointed out that vagrancy laws making it a crime to have "no lawful means of support" could apply to notorious criminals. By the 1940s, such arrests frequently made headlines and prompted early vagrancy concern in organizations like the ACLU. "Owney Madden Seized at Garden, Held as Vagrant," ran the *Post* in 1940 about the former head of Hell's Kitchen's Gopher Gang. "Waxey Gordon, Picked Up as Vagrant, Is Told by Police to Stay Out of New York," announced another headline. "Johnny Torrio Arrested Here as Undesirable."[38]

The equally high-profile defenses to the application of "the vagrancy law to the modern type of moneyed hoodlums," as the *Chicago Tribune* put it, publicized the tactic even more widely. Unlike the usual vagrant, these vagrants had money. They also had lawyers. The legendary Clarence Darrow, who had defended the teaching of evolution (The Scopes "Monkey" Trial), saved murderers from execution (Leopold and Loeb), and defeated murder charges against black men who had killed a white one (Ossian Sweet), told the press, "I broke my resolve to keep out of criminal practice because I feel that this vagrancy campaign is outrageous. If authorities wish to harass the lawless, they should indict them and try them on charges of which they are guilty." As Darrow suggested, the use of vagrancy laws against mobsters was less to procure convictions—with their meager sentences—than to get criminals out of circulation, create an opportunity to investigate them for other crimes while in jail, and pressure them into relocating. Vagrancy arrests accompanied by bail amounts in the tens of thousands of dollars were thus intended to serve as punishment in their own right. Though appeals courts sometimes lowered bail and dismissed charges, trial judges stated explicitly that if they thought a gangster would get out on $50,000, "I would make it more."[39]

Such practices made vagrancy arrests a highly visible strategy for combating crime. Indeed, the California case in which the Supreme Court had denied certiorari, over Douglas and Black's objections, a week after dismissing *Edelman v. California* in 1953 involved the vagrancy conviction of Los Angeles mobster Jack Dragna. Though Dragna had been arrested some eight times before 1950, the authorities had never managed to convict him. For months, they kept him under around-the-clock surveillance and wiretapped both his own home and the "love nest" he shared with his mistress. When, according to the prosecution, the wiretaps captured "sexual intercourse and acts of sex perversion" with a person not Dragna's wife, the police arrested Dragna for vagrancy as a "dissolute" person under the same subdivision five as Edelman. Because Dragna was reputed to be the "top man" in the Los Angeles Sicilian Black Hand Society, as well as a rival and colleague of mobster Mickey Cohen, Dragna's vagrancy arrest and conviction made frequent and prominent news. When Dragna died of a heart attack in early 1956, front-page coverage again highlighted his "vagrant" status.[40]

If cases like Dragna's served as the model, rising crime rates and new judicial rules governing police behavior served as the impetus for more aggressive crime control vagrancy enforcement by the mid-1950s. Police felt especially cramped by the unexpected 1955 California Supreme Court reversal of established doctrine in *People v. Cahan*. In a precursor to the national "exclusionary rule" the United States Supreme Court would adopt six years later, *Cahan* announced that if an officer performed a search that was not backed by probable cause, any resulting evidence would be excluded from consideration of the defendant's guilt. To the police, this rule felt like an insult both to their skills—even when they lacked probable cause, they had good instincts about crime, instincts that judges should not second guess—and to their law enforcement goals—guilty people were set free as a direct result of the rule. Los Angeles police chief William H. Parker repeatedly blamed *Cahan* for a 37.5 percent increase in major crimes in the mid-1950s.[41]

A new series of raids and "blitzes" against "thugs," "hoodlums," "undesirables," and "narcotics addicts" in early 1957 San Francisco—all of whom were, or could be made into, vagrants—both embodied this approach and led to criticism of it. "We'd like to remove all those who have an aptitude for crimes," said one police official. Another announced, "As long as strong-armed crime continues here, the unannounced roundups will continue." Even when few arrests followed, the police announced victory. "We may not come up with much, but if by clearing the streets we can prevent crimes from being committed we will have accomplished something." Indeed, by the fall of 1957, both officials and the media were pleased. Opined the *San Francisco Examiner*, "San Franciscans walk their streets at night with a greater sense of personal safety since the police began sweeping up undesirables in areas of strong arm robberies and purse snatchings."[42]

Besig's experiences with the vagrancy arrests of African Americans, gay men and lesbians, and Beats made him skeptical that the law really performed the crime control function these officials claimed for it. He criticized the law as a "catch-all" and rejected the characterization of those arrested as probable, potential, or actual criminals. Whether Besig was right that vagrancy prosecutions did little to reduce serious crime mattered less to him, however, than the fact that any crime reduction that resulted came at far too high a cost. He lamented that the vagrancy law "alone has given arrest and criminal records to thousands of law-abiding California citizens who were either too friendless or too poor to protect themselves." As he fielded complaints from so many different types of people in so many different types of circumstances, Besig was not inclined to concede any legitimate uses of the vagrancy law. Nor was he inclined to give the police the benefit of the doubt.[43]

Constructing the Vagrancy Law Problem

The initial notes Besig took when he opened his file in 1954 depict a lawyer confronting a problem with few legal resources at hand. Though he identified a smattering of relevant cases, he noted only one law review article—from 1935. The files give the impression that Besig was intellectually on his own.[44]

Not for long. During the 1950s, challenges to, and scholarly critiques of, vagrancy laws increased in scope and frequency. Much of this early anti-vagrancy law energy came from other ACLU affiliates. Emanuel Redfield was still on his hunt for the ideal case to challenge New York's vagrancy law into the 1960s. By the end of the 1950s, ACLU lawyer Louis Lusky was busy challenging vagrancy and loitering laws in Louisville, Kentucky. Anti-vagrancy-law sentiment was hardly limited to the ACLU. Opinion pieces in Florida and bar association committees in Louisiana expressed growing concern about the "abuses and misuses" of vagrancy laws.[45]

As a trickle of law review articles about vagrancy became a steadier stream in the 1950s, some scholars maintained that "the vagrancy law is one of the most effective weapons in the arsenal of law enforcement, and if the officer's use of this weapon should be seriously impaired the security of the citizen would be grievously weakened." They found it both "utopian" and illogical to expect the police "to voluntarily give up one of their prime weapons" in fighting crime.[46]

An increasing number of scholars, however, challenged such arguments. Where an individual was arrested for vagrancy in lieu of some other crime of which he was suspected, one scholar argued, "if the ground of suspicion is a reasonable one, detention in most cases is possible on charges other than vagrancy; if a vagrancy charge is used, it suggests that the grounds of suspicion are not reasonable and that traditional safeguards are being circumvented." Professor Caleb Foote of the University of Pennsylvania Law School, writing what was to become the flagship article on vagrancy law in 1956, thought it difficult to tell whether the defects police officers identified in criminal law and procedure were "real or imagined." Data were hard to come by. Most police departments did not record those vagrancy arrests that were replaced by more serious charges. Indeed, Foote and others thought the advantage of the vagrancy arrest "illusory" because "the substitution of harassment for the more difficult job of obtaining the evidence necessary to convict criminals of the substantive offenses of which they are guilty encourages superficial and inefficient police work." Foote argued that vagrancy arrests for investigation were especially ineffective, as real criminals with real money would find counsel (Clarence Darrow!) and quickly evade the charge. It was only the true vagrants—who, he assumed, had committed no worse crime than their indigence—who would remain locked up for any length of time. Other scholars followed his lead, voicing skepticism about police needs and determining that vagrancy law was not the answer.[47]

Judges questioning vagrancy laws also grew more numerous over the course of the 1950s. There was certainly no shortage of courts happy to restate that vagrancy laws were legitimate exceptions to the usual limitations on the criminal law, especially in crime control cases. In response to a defendant's claim that an arresting officer had not witnessed the defendant in any criminal act, one court responded: "This argument overlooks the nature of vagrancy statutes. They are designed to prevent crime and if the officer must wait until a crime is committed, the preventive purposes of the statute wholly fail." Another quoted the standard line: "'A vagrant is a probable criminal; and the purpose of the statute is to prevent crimes which may likely flow from his mode of life.'" Indeed, the court noted that even "attitudes" could place one in the "class of persons" subject to vagrancy laws.[48]

Other courts resisted these traditional ways of thinking about vagrancy laws. Some were skeptical of vagrancy arrests as pretexts for other criminal charges where probable cause was lacking. One court rejected what it described as "a good example of over-zealous law enforcement" when a vagrancy arrest "was an obvious subterfuge to try and secure evidence of bookmaking." Other courts alluded to "formidable" constitutional issues, reversed vagrancy convictions for a lack of evidence, and began describing vagrancy and related charges as "anachronistic." A California court described subdivision 1 as "apparently based on the outdated concept that it is a criminal offense not to work." A 1958 false arrest suit brought as a test case of Wisconsin's vagrancy law resulted in an $11,000 judgment—including punitive damages—for a woman against three police officers.[49]

Even the Supreme Court got into the act. Though the Court would not reenter the vagrancy arena itself until 1960, a 1957 case augured well for the challenge. In *Lambert v. California*, the Court struck down a Los Angeles criminal registration ordinance. The law made it an offense for one convicted of a crime not to register with the police. Registration laws, commentators observed, "operate[d] in much the same fashion as vagrancy and prostitution laws where the personal condition of those affected determine the coverage of the ordinance." Critics suspected that registration laws, like vagrancy laws, were used by police to arrest people on suspicion of other crimes, and they criticized them for characterizing the offense "in terms of *being* rather than in terms of *acting*." Though the justices had trouble pinpointing the exact constitutional problem with the law, *Lambert* made clear that the questions *Edelman* had raised, questions with which Besig was struggling, were still very much on the table.[50]

At the same time that new intellectual resources encouraged constitutional challenges to the law, concern about police conduct also grew: the law was enforced by people, and those people might be part of the problem. Though police abuses were nothing new, the widespread and organized condemnation of police power took new form in the 1950s. Nationally, Besig followed the critiques and proposals of police practices committees proliferating in ACLU affiliates in the late 1940s. The committees recommended the creation of civilian complaint review boards and aggressive citizen education about individual rights during encounters with the police.[51]

Organizing closer at hand also exposed Besig to the problem of abusive police power. The publicity that attended both vagrancy arrests and police abuse made people rethink their own police experiences. The isolation and shame of arrest were at least complemented, if not replaced, by the realization of a systematic problem. Just the act of writing down or speaking the facts of an arrest—at times in lengthy, handwritten letters to Besig—could be empowering. Other victims took more public but still haphazard actions. A young couple who lived in the racially diverse Fillmore district of San Francisco printed their own handbills protesting 1958 police rousts. "POLICEMEN HARASSED, INTERROGATED and INTIMIDATED scores of people at RANDOM," the handbill charged. It called on readers to "STOP ARBITRARY POLICE METHODS" and "POLICE DISCRIMINATION." It identified for particular concern the problem of arresting people for " 'looks', not 'acts'." For their troubles, the couple found themselves arrested: they had not obtained the required permit to distribute their handbill.[52]

More organized grassroots challenges by each of the marginalized groups who complained to Besig characterized the dual problems of law and law enforcement somewhat differently. Dale Jennings's arrest, and Mattachine's organizing against it, illustrated that vagrancy laws were an obvious problem for gay men in the Bay Area. The Daughters of Bilitis also publicized what Besig called "clear abuses of the vagrancy law" when three female college students "were arrested in a bar and charged with wearing men's clothes—slacks." That the problem extended beyond the laws themselves was apparent in the main argument of the Mattachine Society's Citizens' Committee to Outlaw Entrapment defense of Jennings in 1952, for example. The claim that the undercover officer had entrapped Jennings, not that the law was unconstitutional, shifted the emphasis of the trial from Jennings's conduct to that of the officer, and the emphasis of the critique from the law itself to police misconduct. Jennings and Mattachine tried to transfer public sympathy for the increasingly visible (straight) victims of police misconduct to gay victims by describing themselves as "in full sympathy with the spirit of rebellion in our community concerning police brutality against Minorities in general." That "the special police brutality against the homosexual minority" extended beyond vagrancy laws was apparent as well in so-called "gay-ola" scandals, in which police extortion of gay bars for protection of their liquor licenses became the subject of intense public scrutiny. When a 1959 mayoral candidate charged that Mayor Christopher and Chief Cahill had allowed San Francisco to become "the national headquarters of the organized homosexuals in the United States," Christopher announced—and subsequently enforced—"a vigorous new campaign" against gay bars and their patrons.[53]

Indignation about police practices, both generally and with regard to vagrancy enforcement, peaked in 1959 with the creation of two new citizens groups representing Besig's other two main vagrancy constituencies. The Fillmore Citizens Committee emphasized race discrimination in policing, police misconduct, and brutality, with the discriminatory use of the vagrancy law a less prominent complaint. The committee, spearheaded by the city's first African American judge, John W. Bussey, and local NAACP president Granville Jackson, reflected ongoing debates about whether the community suffered because it was full of crime but lacking adequate police protection or full of police in search of fabricated crime. Did the fact that African Americans comprised 7 percent of the population but 35 percent of arrests reflect discrimination or good police work in response to a rising black crime rate? The committee largely embraced the former position, the police the latter. Jackson stated, "We probably handle more complaints against the police department than any other organization in San Francisco. Members of minority groups should have protection no matter who they are."[54]

Nearby, the North Beach Citizens Committee was also forming in the spring of 1959, and it too emphasized prejudice—against the Beats—as a central motivator of police conduct. Reverend Pierre Delattre, a twenty-eight-year-old Congregational minister provided a meeting place in his storefront Bread and Wine Mission—so-called for the victuals offered on a nightly basis. With his all-American good looks, his pectoral cross worn over a hooded sweatshirt, and his fancy degree from the University of Chicago Divinity School, Delattre the "beatnik priest" also lent the claims of his flock gravitas. The North Beach Citizens Committee charged the police with harassment, "nuisance arrests," vilification, and "endless questioning." Delattre emphasized that he and his colleagues were "not out to get the police"; they just wanted to "encourage proper law enforcement." He thought that it was "no secret that some of the merchants and old families and the small North Beach paper are trying to drive us out." He emphasized police bias. "People always feel a threat from nonconformist groups, and the police are no different."[55]

As Delattre and his committee determined to "fight for our civil liberties," their tactics were characteristically unconventional. At one point, they proposed a resolution that the "loitering law be applied to police." They also posted poetry mocking and condemning the police, and Officer Bigarani in particular, in the window of the Co-Existence Bagel Shop. "One day Adolf Hitler had nothing to do. . . . So he moved to San Francisco and became an ordinary Policeman, devoted to stamping out Beatniks." The poems cursed the officers: "May their eyes bulge from their paperbag heads . . . may their rotting souls disintegrate among their rancid fetid nightstick bones." Proclaiming, "After all, I do have feelings," Bigarani marched into the shop and tore down the poems. In the brouhaha that followed, police officials defended Bigarani—"A police officer has a duty to confiscate material offensive to the public"—and the ACLU defended the Beats—"This looks like a clear free speech violation." Speiser told the Beats to write more poems and post them all over town. The poets were hoping to get arrested, but they did not. "Isn't that the way?" one complained. "You never can find a policeman when you want one."[56]

As these various grassroots organizations called on Besig and the NCACLU for support, they revealed that the problem involved more than legislative drafting. The growing anti-vagrancy law literature condemned such laws as too vague, broad, and flexible to be a meaningful check on official authority. But these protests offered an alternative explanation: the police themselves might be the problem. Regardless of the law's construction, lawless police officers would not follow it anyway.

To put the issue that way—as a black-and-white choice between blaming laws and blaming law enforcers—is too stark. Besig viewed the vagrancy law as both a serious problem in itself and a relatively discrete and identifiable way of solving part of the larger problem of police power. Where Besig labeled his initial folder "Victimless Crimes" and "Vagrancy," he now added to that title "Due Process, Police Practices, Prostitution, etc." The question thus became what should be done about the intimately related problems of a discretion-granting vagrancy law and a discretion-abusing police force.[57]

Solving the Vagrancy Law Problem

Besig answered that question in the multiple. In part, this was because constitutional litigation against vagrancy laws was elusive. The frequent dismissal of vagrancy cases made challenging the constitutionality of the law as a defense to criminal charges difficult. In one North Beach cause célèbre in which Bigarani arrested "petite, 20-year-old 'blonde beatnik" Wendy Murphy, ACLU lawyer Albert Bendich saw an opportunity to stop the beatnik patrol's "indiscriminate arrests." After all the testimony was in, however, the judge agreed with Bendich that the prosecution had not proved the vagrancy charge. Though Murphy was convicted on other charges—she had scuffled with the "burly" Bigarani and even thrown office supplies at him in the police station—the case offered no opportunity to challenge the vagrancy law on appeal.[58]

Besig and his lawyers tried to find other ways to get the constitutional question into the courts. The NCACLU filed false arrest suits—on behalf of a student booked on a "$1,000 vag" charge upon leaving a restaurant and a postal worker arrested while walking down the street, both in the early hours of the morning. Besig also initiated a taxpayer lawsuit that sought an injunction to stop the police department from making such widespread vagrancy arrests. The complaint charged the city and county with engaging "upon a course of arrests and detentions of persons lawfully and quietly entering or leaving public vehicles of transportation, public places of entertainment and restaurants, and persons lawfully and quietly walking on the streets at night in route from said public establishments to their homes." Because such arrests were made "without any probable cause, and without any justification or authority of law," the ACLU lawyers charged that using taxpayer funds to support the arrests was unlawful. The strategy built on the lead of none other than Besig's Southern California colleague Al Wirin. Almost a decade earlier, in 1948, Wirin had succeeded in bringing a taxpayer suit against Los Angeles, and he was at that moment in the midst of winning his second.[59]

Constitutional challenges were only the beginning. The NCACLU's Police Practices Committee reported in the late 1950s that its members "did not feel there was any single answer to the problem" of "lawless police activity in San Francisco . . . which involves particularly the vagging of persons in North Beach and other areas." In addition to litigation, the committee's nine-point program included a study of the problem by Boalt Law School for which they were seeking foundation support; a leaflet about individual rights during police encounters; discussion of the problem with the police chief, mayor, and police commission; support from the NAACP and other interested groups; cooperation with the North Beach Citizens Committee; possible changes in the law; exploration of a citizens complaint board; and publicity. Besig rounded the list out to ten points with the late addition of "Bail money."[60]

Besig attempted several of these strategies. He tried to influence police policy directly, constantly corresponding with police department officials over both specific vagrancy arrests and more general crime-fighting strategies that relied on vagrancy enforcement. Besig also appealed to the mayor. "During the past two years we've repeatedly called attention to Dragnet methods of law enforcement which have resulted in hundreds of arrests of law-abiding citizens," he wrote George Christopher toward the end of 1958. "Our protests thus far have been unavailing and any complaints that have been filed have been whitewashed."[61]

Besig's most substantial efforts were against the vagrancy law itself, though in the political rather than litigative arena. He joined in a frontal legislative assault on the law. The moment was auspicious for such an attack. Democrat Edmund G. "Pat" Brown won the 1958 governor's race in a landslide, and Democrats took control of both houses of the California legislature for the first time in the twentieth century. Regulation of the police had been a key issue for both parties in the recent election, and the reformist *San Francisco Chronicle* was growing in circulation and influence daily. In July of 1958, liberal San Francisco assemblyman John A. O'Connell chaired two days of hearings on police practices and laws relating to arrest for the Interim Subcommittee on Constitutional Rights. According to the Daughters of Bilitis's *The Ladder*, O'Connell charged that vagrancy was being used to "circumvent the State Supreme Court ban on illegally obtained evidence."[62]

Everyone who was anyone in vagrancy law protests was at the hearing. If it had not been previously apparent that the vagrancy law had many uses for many kinds of people out of place, the array of folks at the hearing made it undeniable. In its detailed coverage of the hearings, *The Ladder* reported that "Big Daddy" Nord, a "bearded character" fresh from his own battles with the police was there to "plead . . . the cause of the Beat Generation." Gregory Stout, a local attorney, made the case for those—mostly gay men—arrested under the "vag-lewd" clause. African American deputy public defender Joseph G. Kennedy and lawyer Terry Francois of the local NAACP identified racial discrimination in the enforcement of the vagrancy laws. John McFeeley, a lawyer on the NAACP's legal redress committee, offered evidence that 866 of 1,575 people arrested as "$1,000 vags" were black, even though the ratio of whites to blacks among ordinary vagrancy and other arrests (except drunkenness) was five to one. Mexican Americans represented by Ralph Guzman of the Los Angeles ACLU complained of the "'sidewalk justice'" dispensed by police officers "in the form of unprovoked beatings in the city's big Mexican colony." A member of the state bar's criminal law and procedure committee reported that in the previous year the Los Angeles police had arrested 15,000 people and released them after taking fingerprints and mug shots. Representing the NCACLU, Speiser emphasized the procedural problems with vagrancy arrests—the lack of effective legal remedies or legal guidance on booking procedures, a code of conduct for the police, or the rights of those arrested. Pulling many of the complaints together, the *San Francisco Examiner* described testimony about "mass arrests in trouble spot districts" and "charges against discrimination against racial minority groups and 'Beatniks.' "[63]

As some law enforcement officials also criticized California's vagrancy law, a rift surfaced between the police and prosecutors. District Attorney Thomas Lynch was already on record as skeptical of police use of the law in 1957. So was then-attorney general, soon-to-be-governor, Pat Brown. Both Lynch and Brown agreed, as the San Francisco News reported, that "police shouldn't overwork the law, just to bring in persons for questioning." During the hearing itself in 1958, Lynch went further in his criticisms than he had in the past. He deemed the law "very archaic" and "entirely inadequate to meet modern conditions." He explained that he had instructed his deputies to dismiss charges—which he acknowledged it did in some 70 percent of vagrancy cases—unless the arresting officer appeared in court with convincing proof. The California Democratic Party piled on. Its platform that summer called for "drastic overhaul of vagrancy laws."[64]

Several members of the law enforcement establishment did defend themselves, however. Though Brown, who was still attorney general at the time of the hearings in July 1958, acknowledged that "people are literally kicked around by some police officers," he saw such incidents as the exception. He was as quick to criticize "zealot[s]" whose protests against the police aided criminals as police abuse itself. Police officials took a similar stance. For years, Police Chief Ahern had recognized "the growing hostility to arrests for vagrancy" and admitted that "on occasions the vagrancy laws may have been abused." But he insisted that the law was "being enforced strictly according to [its] meaning" and that "the utilization of such laws have on innumerable occasions resulted in the prevention of many serious crimes." Though acknowledging potential abuse, the president of the Police Commission agreed that "the police are justified in their intensified vagrancy arrests, where persons are picked up on suspicion." After all, "A policeman has the security of the city in his hands."[65]

Alfred Arnaud, the police department's top legal officer, explained that roundups were instituted only after investigation revealed particular neighborhoods as hotbeds of criminal activity. But he had only feeble response to apparently damning statistics, like the dismissal of 71.4 percent of 4,229 cases in 1957. His answers to committee members' questions about $1,000 vagrancy arrests were similarly unsatisfying. In 1957, police arrested 2,547 as "$1,000 vags," and prosecutors dismissed all but 333 cases. When asked what statutes authorized $1,000 vag, Arnaud replied, "Well, there is no authorization."[66]

Even as these officials defended their vagrancy enforcement, they did seem to hear at least some of the criticisms raised at the hearings. The following fall, Chief Cahill announced the end of $1,000 vag arrests. He claimed that the police were "not losing anything. . . . Hereafter, if a man is a vagrant, he will be charged with being a vagrant. If he is more than a vag, then we should charge him with what we think he is." The *Examiner* announced, "Cahill Ends '$1000 Vag' Arrest Policy." The *Chronicle* reported, "The unique—and probably illegal—arrest charge of $1000 vagrancy used by San Francisco police for perhaps a century was scrapped by Chief Tom Cahill yesterday." The paper matter-of-factly reported what Besig had long argued: "The charge was a catch-all used as a holding booking against prostitutes, gamblers and anybody else whom police suspected of wrongdoing but against whom they had no hard evidence." Besig was pleased, and he told Cahill so—in the context of filing yet another vagrancy complaint against the police. For there was the rub: even with a change in official policy, vagrancy arrests did not abate.[67]

Indeed, the November after the hearings, the conflict between Besig and Cahill made front-page news when the two clashed at a conference on civil liberties and law enforcement. Besig charged the police with following "a very dangerous policy" of "abusing the vagrancy and drunk laws." He claimed that "hundreds of persons have been picked up for no reason. We've gotten literally scores of these complaints." An assistant district attorney responded that "a great deal of the criticism undoubtedly is true," but he defended the police. Cahill said unequivocally, "We do not make illegal arrests. . . . [T]he vagrancy law is certainly not being abused; that is a false accusation." He went on the offense, asking, "What answer do these people have to the rise in crime and viciousness? Should we stop making arrests?" It appeared that Cahill's efforts were having some effect on crime. After topping the state charts in the first half of 1958, the San Francisco crime rate had finally begun to fall by December. Cahill took credit, and the newspapers gave it to him. By February, major crime was down 15.9 percent.[68]

The more substantial result of the 1958 hearings was that Assemblyman O'Connell called upon Berkeley law professor Arthur Sherry to draft new vagrancy legislation. A former lawyer in both the district attorney's and the attorney general's offices, Sherry called the current law "completely indefensible." But he also believed that vagrancy laws "serve a necessary purpose and remain an essential means by which law enforcement agencies discharge their primary function of preserving law and order and preventing the commission of crime." In the bill he drafted, Sherry attempted to "harmonize" the vagrancy concept "with notions of a decent, fair and just administration of criminal justice . . . which will at the same time make it possible for police departments to discharge their responsibilities in a straightforward manner without the evasions and hypocrisies which so many of our procedural rules force upon them." His goal was to emphasize conduct over status and precision over "the hazy penumbra of medieval ideas of social control characteristic of existing law."[69]

The resulting bill retained a fair bit of the old law in modern form. The most substantial, and least controversial, substantive change was the wholesale elimination of the crime of being idle and poor. More cosmetically, Sherry changed the title from "vagrancy" to "disorderly conduct," and the language from "every person who. . . [is a certain way or engages in a certain course of conduct is] a vagrant" to "every person who commits any of the following acts shall be guilty of disorderly conduct." In salvaging the vagrancy law as a useful tool for crime control, Sherry also replaced the two outdated and vague loitering provisions with a misdemeanor punishing anyone who "loiters or wanders upon the streets or from place to place without apparent reason or business and who refuses to identify himself and to account for his presence when requested by any peace officer to do so." Though he believed it "probably impossible" to state "the terms of police authority in such a way as to minimize abuse without impairing the ability to take necessary action," he rejected that difficulty as "a valid argument for simply denying the polic[e] power to take any action with respect to the 'suspicious person.'" Even if some abuse was inevitable, limiting and licensing discretion seemed better than the alternative.[70]

Almost a year after the initial hearings, O'Connell and two other assemblymen introduced a bill to repeal and replace the California vagrancy law. Though the bill was essentially Sherry's, it differed in one fundamental way: it omitted the loitering provision altogether. Both that omission and the greater police tolerance of nonconformity and disorder that the bill seemed to require provoked opposition. One Republican state senator called it "the Beatnik's bill of rights" and complained that it "gives social status to those who are now vagrants. The police should have the right to pick up known criminals who are just wandering around."[71]

Even so, both Democrat-dominated houses passed the bill, and press coverage generally adopted the conclusions of the many groups who had testified at O'Connell's hearings. "The Bill, in effect, requires police to place a specific charge against a person, rather than allowing the old method of booking a man for 'vagrancy' and then, at leisure, searching a dozen subsections of law for the kind of vagrancy." It "eliminates vagrancy as a condition or status and makes commission of an act the standard of arrest." The *San Francisco News* predicted that the new law would "be a model for the country."[72]

At O'Connell's urging, Besig wrote Pat Brown, the former attorney general who was now governor, to encourage him to sign the law. "In my estimation," Besig wrote, "outside the racial field, the most important civil liberties legislation adopted by the legislature in my memory is John O'Connell's A.B. 2712, Prof. Sherry's excellent revision of the Vagrancy Law. In fact, I would rank it in importance with the [Fair Employment Practices Committee] and the Housing bill." Emphasizing how the existing vagrancy law had been one of his "constant concerns," he thought it obvious that "the law has no proper place on our books in this day and age." He concluded, "I am sure I speak for the entire membership of our Board of Directors in urging you most strongly to sign this bill into law in the interest of civil liberties."[73]

Much to Besig's consternation, Brown vetoed the bill. Brown seemed generally convinced by the vagrancy law critique. He told the press that the bill had a "laudable purpose in eliminating certain status classifications presently punishable as vagrancy." Because Brown thought "it removed from police control certain conduct which was dangerous to the security of the public," however, it went "too far in its sweeping limitations." In other words, status crimes could go, but suspicious loitering had to stay. A Democrat remembered as a liberal, Brown had announced a tough anti-crime program even before taking office. His veto confirmed that stance, suggesting to Besig that "in the due process field [Brown's] position will be a conservative one—indeed, much more so than that of the legislature itself."[74]

Besig pressed Brown for an explanation. "We are extremely concerned about your veto and we would like to know the basis for your action," Besig wrote. "We know, of course, that police chiefs in the state and, possibly, district attorneys exerted great pressure upon you to veto this measure, but we are reluctant to believe that you acted on grounds of political expediency." Besig sought guidance for the future: "Certainly you will agree that the vagrancy law as it presently stands lends itself to many abuses and the record shows that there are wholesale violations of civil liberties as a result of the enforcement of this law. . . . [W]e would like to know what you would propose in place of the O'Connell Bill." [75]

Brown made clear that his objection to the new vagrancy law was its unnecessary limitation of crime control authority. He stated that although he was "sympathetic to the overall purpose of the bill which was to punish individuals only for wrongful actions and not simply because of their status," he worried that it "unfortunately removed from police control certain dangerous conduct, regulation of which is necessary in the public interest." He also noted in a handwritten postscript that Sherry himself had asked him to veto the law because of the absence of just such a loitering provision. There might have been political will, and even gubernatorial support, to modernize and streamline the vagrancy law, but withdrawal of police authority to use the new law to combat crime had gone too far even for the bill's drafter. Though Besig had predicted that the law might not pass the legislature, it was disappointing that it had failed instead on the desk of a Democratic governor.[76]

Assemblyman O'Connell had just reached out to Besig to restart efforts to repeal the law in February of 1960 when the courts gave his efforts an unexpected boost. A month after O'Connell's second set of hearings—attended by many of

the same advocates as the first—jails across California suddenly emptied themselves of "common drunkards." While Besig had sought in vain for the vagrancy
case that could support a constitutional challenge, appointed defense counsel in
Long Beach had more luck. It was criminal defense lawyers, after all, who represented those more frequently and successfully prosecuted for vagrancy—the
drunks and the prostitutes—rather than those, like the Beats, whose cases
usually led nowhere. In *In re Newbern*, lawyer Ernest L. Graves convinced the
California Supreme Court to strike down the common drunkard clause of the
state's vagrancy law as void for vagueness. In addition to Emery T. Newbern himself (previously arrested nearly 200 times), hundreds were released. By noon,
the papers noted, some were already back in jail, booked under city ordinances
for drunkenness in public view.[77]

The legal impact of the case promised to be more enduring. According to
Sherry, prior to 1960, "the cases reflect an attitude of almost unquestioning
acceptance of the theory and application of the vagrancy law." Just a year before
Newbern, one California court had gone to great lengths to uphold the common
drunkard clause. *Newbern* thus represented "a clear break with traditional judicial tolerance of the propositions that it is permissible for vagrancy to differ from
other crimes, that one who comes within its categories acquires a continuing
status as a petty criminal and that, for this offense, the otherwise indispensable
elements of a crime, act and intent, need not apply."[78]

Newbern brought new energy to vagrancy law challenges. In reporting on the
invalidation, the press noted that "various section[s] of the vagrancy law . . .
have been assailed as relics of the Dark Ages." A month after the decision, the *San
Francisco Examiner* titled an article on a challenge to the vagrancy law's prostitution subdivision, " 'Common? I'm No Such Thing.' " If the common drunk clause
was too vague, an alleged prostitute argued, then so was the common prostitute
clause.[79]

With *Newbern* fresh in his mind, Arthur Sherry renewed his calls for a revised
law in the *California Law Review* in October of 1960. Sherry still hoped to find the
fine line between constraining the police and empowering them, between critics who lambasted law enforcement and supporters who defended it, between
retaining the law for crime control while blunting its use against minorities and
nonconformists. Sherry complained that despite his best efforts, the earlier bill
"did not face up to the problem of defining law enforcement authority with
respect to the person whose conduct is strongly suggestive of incipient criminality." He reminded the legislature that in eliminating "antique" vagrancy statutes
"it is not necessary to sacrifice tools that are essential to the proper enforcement
of the law nor to remove existing controls over conduct that threatens the public
safety." Sherry accordingly resurrected the provision that anyone who "loiters
or wanders upon the streets or from place to place without apparent reason or

business and who refuses to identify himself and to account for his presence when requested by any peace officer to do so" was guilty of disorderly conduct.[80]

Once again the legislature balked at the open-endedness of Sherry's loitering provision. This time, perhaps with Governor Brown's veto in mind, they made it more stringent rather than omitting it altogether. In the end, the law provided for a loitering arrest only "if the surrounding circumstances are such as to indicate to a reasonable man that the public safety demands such identification." This time, there was only a single dissenter in the state senate, and Governor Brown seemed more amenable. Not only was the bill itself different, but the courts had now indicated a new stance toward the vagrancy law. If the law was going to fail, Brown might have thought, better to salvage a suspicious loitering provision, capitalize on political will, and take credit himself. When he had announced his 1961 legislative program, he had acknowledged, "We are . . . going to have to do something about the vagrancy laws." So Brown signed O'Connell's bill, announcing, "Our vagrancy laws were, without doubt, the most often abused and at the same time the most difficult ones with which to obtain a conviction in court." With Brown's signature, California proved itself far ahead of the national vagrancy curve. As one paper put it, the state had "blazed a path other states should follow." With litigation challenging the constitutionality of vagrancy laws still in its infancy, a coalition of African Americans, Mexican Americans, Beats, gay men and lesbians, and civil libertarians had seized a propitious moment and succeeded in repealing California's hundred-year-old vagrancy law.[81]

Besig's vagrancy files end with coverage of the bill's passage. That silence, after a long campaign, could easily indicate that Besig thought his job was done. Repeal had solved the problem Besig had faced for the prior eight years. The vagrancy law, as such, was no more. Its shift from status to conduct meant that it no longer criminalized people themselves. The law withdrew from the police explicit authority to arrest people for who they were and licensed people to think differently about their rights vis-à-vis the police. More specifically, the law removed any trace of the original justification for vagrancy laws—the criminalization of idle poverty—and the most capacious and catch-all loitering provisions. In place of the latter was a self-consciously narrower and intentionally discretion-constraining crime of what would eventually be called "suspicious loitering." The *Sacramento Bee* crowed, "The new law lays the principle that men cannot be thrown in jail or run out of the county because the enforcement officers do not like their looks or dress. It underwrites the principle that in America a man has to commit an actual crime before breaking the law."[82]

The repeal's transformation was far more equivocal and partial than such pronouncements made it seem. On the broadest level, Besig had never conceived of the problem as solely involving the language of the law. Even as the law itself changed, the challenge of policing remained. Whether changing the language from status to conduct would change police practices depended in part on one's view of the police, and Besig's was rather dim. Moreover, the law still gave the police plenty of room to maneuver. Though disorderly conduct might require more conduct than vagrancy, if certain people were likely to engage in those disorderly activities, then they were still likely to be arrested. The distinction between status and conduct was thus not necessarily as sharp as legal scholars or advocates might have liked to believe. This was most apparent with regard to homosexuality, where it was not clear how much the change from "lewd" persons to "lewd and dissolute conduct" actually changed liability or enforcement.[83]

It was also unclear how effectively the new suspicious loitering provision would constrain the police. That provision was key to the repeal—Brown and Sherry insisted it was necessary for crime control even as they seemed to reject the kind of policing of African Americans, Beats, and gay men and lesbians that had drawn so much fire. The idea was to differentiate between legitimate and illegitimate uses of vagrancy law, between real danger and mere difference. Neither side was happy with the compromise embodied in the new law. The police had defended the law wholesale. Though crime control rationales were most prominent, the police had never entirely forsaken the law's other benefits. Indeed, even as Brown touted the new bill as saying "it is what a man does, not who or where he is that defines the crime," he also made it clear that he did not think the police had relinquished all authority to maintain social order. "The new law will make it possible for the police in California to make valid arrests to protect the public from vagrants who live on the fringes of our society."[84]

For his part, Besig had condemned the vagrancy law categorically. It was not merely the social control arrests that he opposed. It was virtually all of them. He rejected even police claims that they used the law for legitimate control of crime. Though Besig was pleased by the changes to the law, calling them "a big improvement," he complained that the loitering provision gave back some of the authority the repeal had intended to withdraw. Though the new law ended the status nature of the crime, it could still be used for so-called victimless crimes and for the harassment of minorities and nonconformists.

The new law thus recast, but did not eliminate, the conflict between Besig's view of the criminal law as an inappropriate tool for enforcing morals and the police view that vice and disorder had to be controlled. The vagrancy section of a 1963 report on the activities of the NCACLU indicated that the conflict resumed almost immediately. Shortly after the bill's passage, the San Francisco police put the new law to use against some North Beach residents lounging in a public park in the middle of the day. Besig and the ACLU intervened with another constitutional challenge, which at least one trial judge embraced. Indeed, the problems that Besig had identified beginning with North Richmond in 1954, problems that continued to dog him even with his legislative success, would provoke legal challenges for decades to come. Some thirty years later, Fred Okrand—the SCACLU lawyer who had joined Al Wirin in representing Isidor Edelman—would still be challenging police use of the new disorderly conduct law in the Supreme Court.[85]

Even as the disorderly conduct law replaced some of the authority of the vagrancy laws, both sides of this political battle understood that something big was at stake. To opponents and defenders, vagrancy laws represented an opaque and limitless reservoir of police authority. Though vagrancy laws did not exhaust that authority, they were its emblem, its easiest access point, its most prominent manifestation. The simultaneous police use of the California vagrancy law against so many groups—and the increasing organization and assertiveness of those groups—had made far more of the vagrancy law regime's operation visible, salient, and open to further attack.

3

Shuffling Sam Thompson
and the Liberty End Café

In January of 1959, Sam Thompson's main goal was staying away from Union Bus Station in Louisville, Kentucky. This was not an easy task. Thompson lived out of town and the bus was his ride home. But it seemed that whenever Thompson went to the station, the Louisville police arrested him. So his lawyer told him to stay away.

Thompson looked like the kind of man police arrested often—poor, black, with no steady job, and what appeared to be a drinking problem and a penchant for "perversion." From Thompson's point of view, such attention was misplaced. Sure, he drank, sometimes in public, but he was no vagrant. He worked odd jobs as a "Man Friday," he had a place to live, and his modest income easily covered his modest lifestyle. Nonetheless, Thompson's interactions with the police in many ways epitomized the use of vagrancy laws for their most essential and long-standing function: policing the visibly poor and underemployed.[1]

Ideas about why and how to police such people, like ideas about policing non-conformity, were increasingly open to question in the 1950s. The problem was not just abuse of the laws but their essential purposes—their regulation of the idle and economically displaced, from tramps to hoboes to skid row vagrants. Even as many government officials maintained traditional attitudes about such policing, two separate critiques gained prominence. Some judges, social workers, and other reformers became convinced that the penal model of punishing the poor and the alcoholic was ill conceived. Alcoholism, this welfarist approach argued, was a disease rather than a sin or a crime. From that vantage point, the whole system needed to be reoriented from punishment to treatment and rehabilitation.

For civil libertarians like Thompson's lawyer, Louis Lusky, the issue was less with *whether* the criminal justice system punished people like Sam Thompson than *how* it did so. If punishment it was to be, then such punishment should be imposed only after fair and just process. Like Ernest Besig in San Francisco,

Lusky could see both vagrancy laws and their enforcement as problematic, and he initially attacked the problem through both the courts and police and judicial reform efforts. Where Besig's most significant successes came in the legislative arena, Sam Thompson gave Lusky a way to bring skid row policing into Supreme Court litigation. As Lusky constructed a constitutional case out of Thompson's predicament, he again departed from Besig's holistic approach: he emphasized the defects of law enforcement over those of the laws themselves. Lusky's litigation strategy left vagrancy and loitering laws intact, but it pointed the way toward judicial supervision of local law enforcement. It also gave the Supreme Court, and the nation, a glimpse into the kind of policing that men like Sam Thompson endured every day.

The Police as Peacekeeper

It was chilly the Saturday night in January 1959 that Thompson was arrested despite his avoidance of the bus station. In order to stay warm while he waited for his bus, Thompson went to a black bar at the corner of Liberty and West streets. The Liberty End Café was a few blocks from Union Station, just past the heart of the black business district on Walnut Street. Even as this border city haltingly desegregated, Walnut Street remained home to the best black hotels, restaurants, and nightclubs; the best shopping, doctors, and lawyers. As one black Louisvillian put it, "You could find *everything* you wanted on that street. You could get entertained, get embalmed and get fed." But the neighborhood around Walnut Street also had its seedy side. A 1948 study described it as an area "of blight with numerous beer taverns, clubs and cheap rooming houses, [and] overcrowding."[2]

Thompson was familiar with the area. The youngest of Harry and Liza Thompson's five children, Sam had spent his whole life in Louisville. Most of his family worked in service jobs, some in private homes and some in restaurants. As early as seventeen, Thompson described himself as doing "house work." Thirty years later, he was still a sometime handyman and junk collector who owned three lots given to him by his mother and lived rent-free as an "up-keeper" of an adjacent house.[3]

A reporter would later describe Thompson as "slim, dignified with direct eyes." Perhaps that dignity was the origin of his nickname of "Preacher." Though Thompson was only forty-seven years old when his case went to the Supreme Court, observers referred to him as "an old man" and an "elderly Negro." (Lusky, Thompson's lawyer, was only a year or so younger, but no one described him as old.) Perhaps people portrayed Thompson as old because it made him seem less threatening than a young African American man, the kind increasingly presumed to be a dangerous criminal. Or perhaps years of hard living had made Thompson old beyond his years—the life expectancy for alcoholics was dramatically lower than for the population at large.[4]

In any event, the name of the Liberty End Café would turn out to be prophetic for Thompson. He arrived there around 7 PM, and it was already crowded. Thompson was shuffling his feet to the jukebox—maybe the song was "Rockin' Robin" or "Splish Splash"—and chatting with various people in the booths when two white Louisville police officers walked in. Whether they were on a "routine check," making sure all was in order, or looking specifically for Thompson would become a matter of some dispute. Regardless, Officers Randall H. Barnett, a relatively new member of the force, and William Lacefield, with almost twenty years of experience, began asking the manager questions about Thompson. The manager said that Thompson had been there around half an hour and that he had not purchased anything. The officers then approached Thompson and asked what he was doing there. They were skeptical when he told them that he was waiting for the bus to Buechel, the Louisville suburb where he lived. After all, there was no bus stop out front, and Thompson did not have a bus ticket on him. Lacefield and Barnett took Thompson outside and told him he was under arrest. Thompson asked why, and according to one of the officers, he became "very argumentative." So the police added a disorderly conduct charge to the original loitering charge.[5]

Such arrests were old news to Thompson. Over the years he had been arrested more than fifty times for loitering, vagrancy, disorderly conduct, public drunkenness, and "perversion." In fact, in the weeks before this most recent encounter, Thompson had been arrested twice and tried once. The first arrest had occurred exactly two weeks before at the Louisville Haymarket, where police were always on the lookout for petty crime. According to Thompson, he had accidentally brushed against another pedestrian. When he realized that the man had stabbed him in the arm, Thompson asked nearby Officer Ford Clayton Fletcher for help. Fletcher brought Thompson to a hospital. He had Thompson's wound cared for, but then he arrested Thompson for public drunkenness and disorderly conduct. Fletcher never pursued the man who had stabbed Thompson.[6]

Frustrated, angry, and convinced that he had been wrongly arrested, Thompson called Dr. Wynant Dean, an eye surgeon in the city. Thompson had been a handyman for Dean and Dean's father for thirty years. Dean's son would later describe how every Thursday, "Thompson would stop by to wax the floor or rake and burn the leaves in the autumn." Every Thursday, Dean paid Thompson $12—basically his entire income.[7]

Luckily for Thompson, Dean was not only a doctor. He was also a member of the board of the Kentucky Civil Liberties Union (KCLU)—a local ACLU affiliate established four years earlier. Dean called KCLU-affiliated lawyers Marvin

Morse and Louis Lusky for help. A native of Westchester, New York, and graduate of Colgate University and Yale Law School, Morse had served as a judge advocate at Fort Knox during the Korean War. Like many another northern lawyer or doctor stationed there, Morse married a local and settled in Louisville after the war. He joined Lusky in Louisville's Jewish community. Lusky took the younger lawyer under his wing, and the two began sharing office space and cases.[8]

When Dean called, Morse went down to the jail to see what the problem was. With Morse by his side, Thompson pleaded not guilty and demanded a trial on the charges stemming from the Haymarket incident. One can imagine the surprise of both the police court judge and the police officers ready for an open-and-shut case involving a repeat offender and habitual drunk when Thompson showed up in court with an Ivy League-educated lawyer and started asking for some real legal process. That was not common practice in the Louisville Police Court in 1959.[9]

Four days later, released on bond and awaiting his trial, Thompson was arrested again. This time, he had come into town to sell "some old junk." He was at the bus station, sitting on a bench in the designated black waiting room in the late afternoon. (Though the bus station had officially desegregated after a sit-in in 1954, Jim Crow signs remained, and almost everyone involved in Thompson's case still regularly referred to the "colored waiting room.") Officer J. S. Suter and the same Officer Fletcher who had arrested Thompson at the Haymarket later claimed they had been making a "routine check" of the station when the dispatcher told the officers that "some colored men were in the waiting room drinking." Suter smelled alcohol on Thompson's breath, and he did not believe that Thompson was waiting for a bus. Suter asked Thompson for social security and pay receipts, but Thompson did not have them. Suter later testified, "I charged Thompson with vagrancy and loitering because he didn't give me any proof as to working anywhere."[10]

According to Thompson, after the officers arrested him at the bus station, and while they were taking him to police headquarters, one of the officers said, "I ought to whip your ass," and "pulled [Thompson's] hat roughly down over his face." This led Thompson and Morse to conclude that the bus station arrest was retaliation for Thompson's retaining counsel, pleading not guilty, and insisting on a trial for his Haymarket disorderly conduct charge. Morse drove straight from meeting with Thompson to discuss the case with Louis Lusky.[11]

Raised in Louisville, Lusky had graduated first in the Columbia Law School class of 1937. Following the conventional path of the top graduates of the top law schools, Lusky served as the law clerk to Supreme Court Chief Justice Harlan Fiske Stone and then joined a big New York City law firm. At Root, Clark, Buckner & Ballantine, he had the good fortune to work on a number of influential First Amendment cases with Grenville Clark, the first chairman of the American Bar Association's Bill of Rights Committee.[12]

By 1959, when Sam Thompson retained Morse and Lusky for his defense, Lusky had been practicing law in Louisville for years. He was also, and here is where he departed from the usual professional narrative, a founder and active member of the KCLU. The affiliate had emerged in 1955 out of Lusky's defense of a man charged with sedition after he and his wife had purchased a home for a black family in a white neighborhood. The case cost Lusky some paying clients. He mused to Grenville Clark, "I don't mean to suggest that people here in Louisville think I am disloyal. Their attitude is, rather, that I am rather peculiar and that it may be better to put their affairs in the hands of a more normal sort of person."[13]

Lusky was not deterred. It was not just that he was deeply committed and that the KCLU provided him with an institutional home and a network of like-minded civil libertarians. He was also, as Columbia Law School colleague and NAACP LDF legal director Jack Greenberg later put it, "a stubborn guy." If Lusky had pre-ordered peanut chicken for dinner on an airplane (in the days when airplanes still served pre-ordered dinner, or dinner of any kind) and was given cashews instead, he put up a fuss at 30,000 feet. From Bill of Rights violations to parking tickets to the minutiae of academic bureaucracy, Lusky challenged injustice—on his own behalf and that of secretaries, students, maintenance workers, and others. One colleague called him a "curmudgeon" who nonetheless "could not conceal his concern for the welfare of individuals and his devotion to principle." As one KCLU member said, Lusky defended "nonconformism," including Sam Thompson's brand of nonconformity, as "an essential part of American life."[14]

For some time before Lusky and Morse took on Thompson's case, public and professional appetites for information about vagrants and vagrancy had been voracious. Police journals, newspapers, and both academic and popular presses published hundreds of exposés, studies, and policy prescriptions in the postwar decades. When the *Chicago Daily News* ran a twelve-part series on skid row in 1949, for example, the newspaper gained as many as 20,000 new readers a day.[15]

This landslide of publications tended to fixate on identifiable skid rows in major cities. With almost 400,000 people, Louisville was the thirty-first most populous city in the country. Its problem with drunks and vagrants was hardly on the same scale as the Bowery in New York or South of Market Street in San Francisco. The difference, however, was largely of degree. As one commentator put it in 1955, "In cities and towns which are too small to support a full-blown skid row, simpler substitutes are found: perhaps only one block, or the town square, or the county courthouse; but always there is a place—that place where [petty offenders] gather, and where the police and other authorities know they can be located at any hour in any season."[16]

Louisville had its share of such places, and the bus station was one. For years, it had required constant policing and counted more arrests than all the other transportation depots in the city combined. The kind of attention the police gave the bus station and the men who frequented it was the kind of attention police had long given vagrants everywhere.[17]

Once upon a time, the story usually went, in the forty years around the turn of the twentieth century, young, energetic men out to see the world inhabited marginal urban areas known as the "main stem." Frequently at, if not over, the edge of legality, they epitomized the need for vagrancy laws. These "men on the move" were condemned as successors to the tramps of an earlier era—dangerous threats who rejected the American work ethic and the American family. Other contemporaries, however, accepted tramping for work as a common life phase for young men before domesticity settled in. Some even celebrated the hobo as emancipated and countercultural, as rejecting the strictures of middle-class modernization and civilization for a renewal of the American frontier. That kind of hobo, the kind Jack London personified in his tramping memoir *The Road*, was widely seen as the progenitor of the Beats—creative, restless, and fiercely independent. "I became a tramp," London wrote, "because of the life that was in me, of the wanderlust in my blood that would not let me rest." Alternatively, an economic, labor-based interpretation viewed the men as true American heroes greasing the seasonal wheels of the national economy. Still others viewed hoboes as political creatures, radicalized by "hobo colleges" and the International Workers of the World, stirring up revolution for good or for ill, providing a critique, not a bulwark, of American capitalism. These views all reflected some aspect of reality, as those who moved through the main stem were truly a diverse lot. They represented the very best of America—its frontier spirit and quest for adventure—and its very worst—the potential for sin and debauchery, the proximity of violence, the penchant for lawlessness among the mobile and the unattached.[18]

By 1929, the main stem had begun to lose what one observer called its "picturesque wickedness." A drastic reduction in the need for the seasonal labor of the men of the main stem resulted from a number of developments: the rise of welfare capitalism; the mechanization of agriculture, industry, and lumber; a reduction in railroad construction; the rise of the automobile; and an increasingly racially and ethnically diverse field of agricultural laborers with more local, family-based migration patterns. The Depression of the 1930s, in turn, vastly increased both the numbers and transiency of the American unemployed. As Franklin Roosevelt's New Deal partly nationalized prior state and local responsibility for the poor, the unemployed turned to new transient camps, housing developments, and forms of welfare, and the main stem population periodically mushroomed and contracted. Even with the migration of whole families—like John Steinbeck's Joads in *The Grapes of Wrath*—the lone male hobo still captured some vital American identity. John Dos Passos closed his three-volume great American *U.S.A.* trilogy in 1936 with a vignette called "Vag," about one such itinerant.[19]

By the 1940s, the area that had once been the main stem would have been pretty much unrecognizable to "a man of the open road" from the late nineteenth century. In its place, often literally, was "skid row," whose very different inhabitants were equally ripe for vagrancy arrests. Many of the entertainments and services that had made the main stem vibrant—the hobo colleges, the movie houses, the burlesque theaters—had disappeared. Where the main stem was imagined as a place of danger and exoticism, with people literally going places (from the "stem"), skid row was imagined as depressed and depressing (a confined and confining "row"). It was the last place anyone went, and where they stayed because they had no place else to go.[20]

The physical plant of the main stem became home to what contemporaries described as a new type of unattached man: sedentary rather than dynamic, old rather than young, often ill (mentally or physically), moving in and out of work on a daily or weekly rather than seasonal basis. A few observers, especially in later years, found some hope on skid row—attachments and community among the inhabitants—as well as less distance between skid rowers and other poor and working-class Americans. The vast majority of studies in the 1950s and 1960s, however, presented skid rowers as "disaffiliated," without ties or employment, often alcoholics, sometimes veterans, often surviving on meager forms of public assistance. Where the men of the main stem had shared dormitory rooms on a way station to someplace else, the skid row vagrant had his own isolated cubicle in a "cage hotel" as a semi-permanent residence.[21]

That said, there were continuities between skid row and the main stem. Both were largely male spaces marked by heavy drinking. Both were filled with poor people, misfits of various types, the disabled. The main stem had always had its share of "the home guard"—those who never wandered too far, those for whom the absence of a stable job, family, and home had become more a way of life than a way station. But the home guard had previously been overwhelmed by a diversity of livelier, more mobile, and more self-consciously rebellious or countercultural types. The home guard dominated the declining skid row population from the 1940s until the 1970s, when most cities eliminated the neighborhoods completely in pursuit of "urban renewal."[22]

Observers also identified skid row, like the main stem before it, as a place where one particular type of male interaction flourished: sex. Since at least the turn of the twentieth century, mobile men had been associated with homosexuality. As Nels Anderson, a former hobo and sociologist who pioneered the serious study of hoboes, put it, "I knew . . . that Hobohemia had its homos." Everyone from police officers to scholars thought the same of skid row, though estimates of what percentage of men on skid row had same-sex encounters ranged wildly (the former said 80 percent, the latter 10 percent). More fundamentally, observers disagreed about whether the men's sexual behavior was the cause or effect of their presence on the row.[23]

The men of skid row were viewed, then, as objects of study, pity, and disgust. They evoked a lexicon of disease and deviance. Some thought of skid row "as a kind of social sewer through which the dregs of society flow on their way to alcoholic oblivion," others as "a gangrenous and costly boil on society's neck."[24]

Whatever the metaphor of choice, the men of skid row, like the men of the main stem, were undeniably charges of the local police. They were at best eyesores, at worst imminent felons, and at all times "undesirables." It was hard to deal with such men once and for all. Because they were locals, the "floater," that sentence that gave a transient arrested for vagrancy his freedom so long as he immediately left town, was unworkable. And unlike "real" criminals, whose serious crimes carried serious sentences, imprisonment could not incapacitate skid rowers for long. They had to be managed, day in and day out.

Vagrancy laws were crucial to that process. From their origins, vagrancy and loitering laws had targeted those who failed to work, who failed to remain in their prescribed place in the economic order. In the heyday of tramps and hoboes, the presumed immorality of idle poverty that had undergirded vagrancy from its origins was still deeply ingrained within the law. From 1837 on, the Supreme Court had given its imprimatur to such a view. In *New York v. Miln*, the Court had stated, "We think it as competent and as necessary for a state to provide precautionary measures against the moral pestilence of paupers, vagabonds, and possibly convicts as it is to guard against the physical pestilence [of] infectious disease." In the late nineteenth and early twentieth century, the Progressive movement took a new, "social crime," approach that viewed crime as a symptom of other social problems and criminal law as a tool for social engineering. Prominent legal scholar Roscoe Pound, settlement house leader Jane Addams, and other Progressives joined police officials, lawyers, and judges in embracing vagrancy and similar laws because they thought, in Pound's words, that "preventive justice [was] the most effective agency of social control."[25]

By the 1950s, the legal assumption that idle poverty was inherently immoral, dangerous, and appropriately criminal had been declining for some time. In part, this change was due to the prevalence of forced joblessness during the Depression of the 1930s. The 1941 case of *Edwards v. California* reflected the new trend. When the Supreme Court struck down a law that made it a crime to bring an indigent person into California, it announced that "the theory of the

Elizabethan poor laws no longer fits the facts." The Court explicitly rejected the reasoning in *Miln*: "Whatever may have been the notion then prevailing, we do not think that it will now be seriously contended that, because a person is without employment and without funds, he constitutes a 'moral pestilence.' Poverty and immorality are not synonymous."[26]

Edwards did not involve a vagrancy law, though its rupture of centuries-old jurisprudential assumptions about regulating the poor readily applied to the vagrancy law context. If poverty resulted from large-scale structural economic issues rather than the moral failings of individuals, punishment seemed anachronistic and unjust. A 1935 law review article that would become a popular citation in later years commented that "vagrancy laws were no longer fitted to social conditions. Today joblessness and wandering are largely the derivatives of objective, not subjective conditions." This was especially the case after the late 1940s, when efforts to guarantee full employment failed to gain political traction. By 1960, the same Arthur Sherry who had been instrumental in "modernizing" California's vagrancy law noted the incongruity that such laws could coexist with "the complex of labor legislation found in every state." Indeed, despite all the hubbub that accompanied the California vagrancy law repeal, the removal of the prohibition on idle poverty barely registered.[27]

That the old rationales for arresting the unemployed poor had somewhat eroded led less to the discontinuation of such arrests than to new rationales for them. Still the essential reservoir of police power, vagrancy and loitering laws came to enable, rather than justify, not only arrests of Beats or gay men but even of vagrants themselves. According to Egon Bittner, a sociologist at the University of California Medical School and later Brandeis University, men like Sam Thompson were "perceived by the police as producing a special problem that necessitates continuous attention and the use of special procedures." Based on fieldwork and police interviews, Bittner's influential 1967 study revealed the symbiotic relationship between what Bittner called skid row "peacekeeping" and both old and new justifications for the vagrancy arrests on which peacekeepers frequently relied.[28]

Bittner's basic argument was that police work on skid row was fundamentally different from "law enforcement." Where "law officers" generally convicted those arrested in courts of law, "peace officers" operated largely outside of the formal structures of arrest, detention, and conviction. They used their authority to "direct, aid, inform, pacify, warn, discipline, roust, and do whatever else they do without making arrests." In other words, these officers exercised the police power in the traditional sense of the term—to keep order.[29]

Decades before Bittner wrote, these peacekeeping activities had become something of an ugly secret within police departments. Both before and after the advent of professional policing in the early nineteenth century, local officials had been tasked with generally keeping the peace, which included neutralizing the threat of poor and idle people. Such policing had been a key part of the Progressive project around the turn of the century. In the early decades of the twentieth century, however, police reformers self-consciously began to transform policing. Departments gained autonomy from party politics. They hired better-educated men and trained them more extensively. A new image of the police as professional crime fighters enforcing the law pushed skid row peacekeeping out of the core of the police mission.[30]

That said, managing vagrants remained a central and costly, if unsung, part of the job of the postwar police. In 1946, San Francisco spent approximately 30 percent of its budget on the arrest and jailing of drunks. In 1957, vagrancy and other public order offenses on skid row comprised around half of all arrests in Minneapolis. In Chicago in the early 1960s, one-quarter of all arrests took place on skid row, and the city spent $5,000,000 per year policing it. It spent an estimated 112 man-hours per day simply processing drunks at the police station.[31]

Contrary to the centralizing tendencies of police departments, Bittner showed, special "bum squads" worked with a "virtual absence of disciplinary control" and with almost complete "discretionary freedom." Politics and top-down policy intruded only occasionally, as when city bigwigs ordered round-ups in advance of important local events. Peacekeepers used their discretion to achieve two distinct goals: to contain skid row spatially and maintain peace on skid row itself. The isolation and relative invisibility of skid row created space for deviance. Once outside of the informal but identifiable boundaries of skid row or its equivalent, though, vagrants were out of place—a threat to both safety and sensibilities—and subject to arrest. As long as vagrants remained in place, politicians, and much of the public, were happy. John Murtagh, who served as chief magistrate in New York City between 1950 and 1960, believed that such "wholesale arrests" were "what the public wants"—they were a way "to keep depravity from becoming too assertively public."[32]

Staying within the confines of skid row, however, hardly meant insulation from the police. As Bittner showed, maintaining peace on skid row entailed a combination of surveillance, coercion, and protection. Officers turned not only to arrests but also to alternative sanctions like warnings, direct discipline, and reparations.[33]

Authorized in part by status-based vagrancy and habitual drunkenness laws, the relationship between illegal conduct and arrest on skid row was rarely one to one. As Bittner put it, the officer gave "the consideration of strict culpability a subordinate status among grounds for remedial sanction," or "the association between delict and sanction is distinctly occasional." In other words, officers on skid row rarely arrested all those who had engaged in illegal conduct and often arrested those who had not. The law alone was not a reason to arrest but a resource to be used in resolving problems on the street. "To arrest someone *merely* because he committed some minor offense ... is perceived as containing elements of injustice." On the flip side, those the police arrested did not always conform precisely to the requirements of the law the police invoked. Perhaps they were not yet drunk, or had not been publicly disorderly, or had money in their pockets, or had been working a job. The officers asked themselves not whether any particular person should be arrested for a particular violation but what violation should be used to address the problems caused by the particular person. Despite the fact that the officers knew by 1967 that their conduct was "difficult to reconcile with the doctrines of civil liberties," they defended it as acceptable on skid row.[34]

Within this context, vagrancy laws justified such police practices and were in turn justified by them. If peacekeeping was at heart a "police power" endeavor, the vagrancy law, a "police power regulation," was its ideal instrument. Both peacekeeping and vagrancy law enforcement relied less on specific illegal conduct than on the past acts and known status of the vagrant. Vagrancy laws presumed that one's status as a vagrant continued until the vagrant had "reformed." Presence on skid row was proof that one had not yet reformed.[35]

The key to such skid row policing, then, was an officer's efforts to have "an immensely detailed factual knowledge of [his] beat," which in turn required familiarity and trust. "The conversational style," Bittner observed, "is casual to an extent that by non-skid-row standards might suggest intimacy." Once this "intricately limited privilege" was exceeded, however, once a vagrant challenged the officer's "right to ask questions and issue commands," the officer felt he had to reassert—usually through arrest, though also perhaps through violence—his ultimate authority.[36]

Even the fact of periodic arrests did not seem, to the police at least, to interfere too much with these relationships. As Bittner described, "Patrolmen find that disciplinary and coercive actions apparently do not affect their friendly relations with the persons against whom these actions are taken. Those who greet and chat with them are the very same men who have been disciplined, arrested, and ordered around in the past, and who expect to be thus treated again in the future." The police thought most skid rowers believed that "the police [were] just doing their job," though a "vociferous minority" did resist arrests.[37]

Peacekeepers armed with vagrancy and loitering laws were thus part of the social order and social life of the vagrant. According to one observer, "the law occupies the very center of the skid rower's life. Arrest, or at least its possibility, is no further away than the policeman on the beat." The skid row officer had the discretion to determine when to intervene, when to make an arrest, whom to arrest, and for what offense. At its worst, such discretion could mean indifference, arbitrariness, abuse, brutality, and corruption. Some officers shook down poor men regularly on the day they received their welfare money. Others arrested skid row drunks just to make their quotas with easy prey.[38]

At best, the peace officer on skid row used his discretion to protect, as much as control, his charges. The idea that police power regulations like vagrancy laws were intended paternalistically to benefit their objects had a long pedigree. "These men are like children," explained one officer. "We have to look out for them." As the police notation "Drunk-Safekeeping" indicated, some arrests were intended, in Bittner's words "to keep skid-row inhabitants from sinking deeper into the misery they already experience."[39]

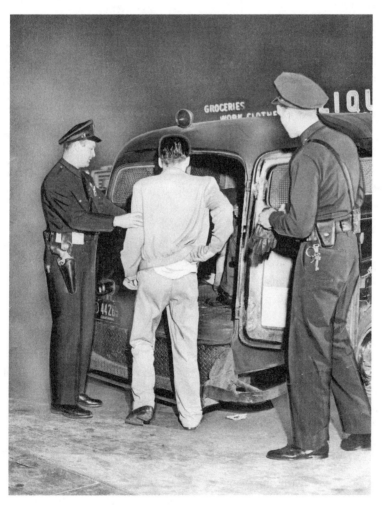

Figure 3.1 Arrest of a man on Los Angeles' skid row in 1955. Arrests for vagrancy and loitering, as well as disorderly conduct and public drunkenness, were so frequent that critics in the 1950s began to condemn the "revolving door" of arrest and the summary procedures of "assembly-line justice" that followed. Herald-Examiner Collection, Los Angeles Public Library.

The assumption that periodic arrests and short jail sentences were appropriate, sufficient, or all that was possible no longer reigned by the time Sam
Thompson faced down the Louisville police in 1959. Reformist policymakers, judges, lawyers, social workers, and scholars were increasingly arguing
that the criminal justice system might not be the right institution for vagrants
at all. Not only did cyclical economic realities make labor surpluses inevitable, but moral condemnation for the "bum" had been partially replaced by
a view of alcoholism as "a social disease which must be treated." The question
was whether vagrants belonged in a jail, a shelter, a hospital, or Alcoholics
Anonymous.[40]

Judges like New York City's John Murtagh advocated such welfare-ori-
ented reform. Having attended Harvard Law School and Yale's Summer
School of Alcohol Studies—a leader in the movement to recognize alcoholism as a major public health problem—Murtagh liked to "boast I got my law
at Harvard, my alcohol at Yale." All joking aside, Murtagh was disturbed by
what he saw on the Bowery and in his own courtroom. Reflecting the views
of a growing number of reformers, Murtagh wrote, "Incarceration never
cured a derelict. . . . The problem of the skid-row derelict is basically social,
medical, and spiritual in nature." He thus supported New York's policy of
arresting only those who were disorderly or dangerous and taking those
who required safekeeping to a municipal shelter rather than jail. That shift
was part of what came to be called "penal welfarism," a reform policy that
preferred rehabilitation to punishment. As early as 1961, some observers
claimed that the punitive "approach to the problems of the skid row drinker
[had] been abandoned."[41]

Such predictions turned out to be premature. Among urban policymakers,
the concern was more often with eliminating skid rows through urban renewal
than with finding ways to assist the people who lived there. Even within academic
circles, conflict was far from over. The drafters of the Model Penal Code, for
example, clashed with the broader membership of the American Law Institute
over this very issue. Some cities also flouted the prediction of consensus, preferring to continue the traditional pattern of arrests in the late 1950s and early
1960s. Though New York's policy led to only 15,000 skid row arrests per year,
Chicago reported 50,000, and Los Angeles approached 100,000. Los Angeles
Police Chief William Parker defended the aggressive policing of vagrants, sometimes condemning the "New York system" as one in which "drunks are left to lie
in the gutter."[42]

Like other police departments, Louisville had professionalized in recent
years—taking advantage of new technology, improving the quality of recruits,
changing the way it did business. (In 1956, it built a $2,000,000 police head-
quarters it claimed was second only to that of Los Angeles.) Even so, the

discretionary policing of places like the bus station remained largely unchanged. Though Louisville had first hired African American officers in the 1920s and surrounding Jefferson County in the late 1940s, white officers still far outnumbered their black coworkers. Even to a white, middle-class high school student at the time, "The police were God. You just didn't mess with them. . . . You just stayed out of their way."[43]

That no doubt went doubly for the poor, alcoholic African American—except that it was not usually possible for him to avoid the police. For when the police saw Sam Thompson, they did not just see Sam Thompson. Though Thompson had a home and a small but regular income, he seemed to share much—idleness, indigence, alcoholism, perhaps "perversion"—with the skid row habitués who had become so visible. They saw not just a man but a problem. In line with the tenets of peacekeeping, their interactions with Thompson were routine and frequent—one need look no further than Thompson's more than fifty arrests. Indeed, Thompson's answer to a question at one of his trials reveals how quotidian his police encounters had become. Asked how often he was arrested at the bus station, Thompson replied matter-of-factly, "Well, [Officer] Suter always arrests me when I go there to catch the bus to go to Buechel."[44]

The fact that Thompson sought out a police officer to complain about his stabbing in the Louisville Haymarket indicates that his relationship with the police had previously been much like the relationships described in the contemporary literature. Despite his many prior arrests, or perhaps because of some of them, Thompson thought the police would protect him when he needed protection.

He might, then, have viewed his arrest after the Haymarket incident as a violation of that norm. He did not accept the police assessment of the situation. He had been harmed. He had complained. Yet he had been arrested. When things did not turn out as Thompson thought they should, it was then his turn to violate the norms. He resisted the penalty the police had identified as appropriate by showing up in police court with Marvin Morse by his side.

Perhaps by the lights of skid row policing, Thompson's Haymarket arrest had made sense. The determination to take Thompson into custody brought him first to the hospital, getting him needed medical attention. The arrest that followed might have resulted from Officer Fletcher's sense that Thompson was drunk and could use some time to dry out; or that hurt as he was, he was vulnerable to further violence, and jail would be a safe place to heal; or that exercised as he was, he was a potential harm to his aggressor or to others, and jail would be a safe place to cool off. Of course, the intention might have been less charitable, might have resulted from annoyance at having to deal with Thompson yet again.

It was perhaps not until after Thompson turned to the KCLU, not until he betrayed the rules of peacekeeping by denying the officer his authority and forcing him to testify in court, that his relationship with the police turned. From then on, as Lusky and Morse would repeatedly argue, any protective aspect of Thompson's relationship with the police deteriorated. It was replaced with an adversarial one.

A Federal Case at the Louisville
Police Court, Winter 1959

If adversarial it was to be, then principled and curmudgeonly Louis Lusky was the man for the job. Lusky's work with the KCLU had acquainted him with many of the less savory, and in Lusky's view less constitutional, aspects of Kentucky criminal law and procedure. Thompson's case promised to crack wide open some Louisville police and judicial practices that Lusky deemed overdue for correction.[45]

As Lusky and Morse propelled Thompson through the Louisville court system and beyond, the arguments they made were not Judge Murtagh's welfarist arguments. Their question was not how best to help men like Thompson but how to stop law enforcers from violating Thompson's constitutional rights. Lusky and Morse, like their ACLU colleagues elsewhere, saw the problems of the police and the police court less through a therapeutic or sociological lens and more through a civil liberties one. With both the Model Penal Code and the Wolfenden Report suggesting a more limited role for the criminal law in regulating morality and so-called victimless crimes, and the ACLU increasingly concerned with faulty and unjust criminal procedures, it was no longer clear that the law should be able to do with vagrants what it would.[46]

The civil libertarian and welfarist approaches thus shared a common target: the "revolving door" of vagrancy and other petty arrests and the "assembly-line justice" that followed. But they diverged in their prescriptions for change. Murtagh's welfarist vision could allow, and might even require, heightened coercive paternalism of the type Progressives had embraced in the early twentieth century and Bittner observed into the 1960s. To save a vagrant from himself might mean authorizing even greater police authority than simply punishing him, briefly and intermittently, for his failings. It might require long-term and involuntary commitment and rehabilitation. On the other hand, Lusky and Morse's concern with the civil liberties of people like Sam Thompson could easily vindicate their rights without meaningfully improving their welfare.[47]

As social reformers and civil libertarians pondered what to do with or for the many Sam Thompsons who came through local courtrooms, the Police Court of Louisville, like the Louisville police, hardly noticed. If Isidor Edelman's nine-day trial in California seemed out of all proportion to the lowly crime of vagrancy, the Louisville police court procedures proved the more common opposite extreme more disturbing. First established in the early nineteenth century, urban police courts—like their close counterparts municipal courts, mayor's courts, magistrate's courts, recorder's courts, and justices' courts—had from the beginning handled large volumes of petty offenses. When the police "pinched" Jack London for vagrancy in Niagara Falls in the 1890s, his "trial" experience gave his "patriotic American citizenship . . . a shock from which it has never fully recovered." Having watched the vagrants before him processed "fifteen seconds to a hobo—and thirty days," he determined to stand up for the "liberty" his ancestors had bequeathed him. When he tried to interject, the judge cut him off, giving him thirty days in fifteen seconds, just like the rest.[48]

Much to Lusky's chagrin, many of the procedures London described remained the same some sixty years later. The Louisville police court processed some 25,000 cases like Thompson's every year. It did so largely on the testimony of the arresting police officer, and largely without jury trials, appeals, counsel for defendants, or transcripts of the proceedings.[49]

Some things had changed by the 1950s, however. According to local lore, the Louisville police court judge in the 1930s and 1940s would regularly interrupt proceedings by leaning over his desk to spit tobacco juice into an old brass cuspidor. That no longer happened in 1959.

More important, scholars began to scrutinize and condemn these police court procedures. Born in Cambridge and educated in economics at Harvard, Caleb Foote was a Quaker who spent a year and a half in prison as a conscientious objector during World War II before attending law school at the University of Pennsylvania. As a law professor at his alma mater, Foote was troubled by, and wrote extensively about, the injustices policing and low-level criminal procedure visited upon the poor.[50]

For his flagship 1956 article on vagrancy law and enforcement, Foote followed the lead of scholars who called themselves legal realists—researching not the "law on the books" but the "law in action." He watched justice dispensed in thousands of vagrancy and drunkenness cases in Philadelphia's low-level courts. Foote's observations might have been amusing if they were not so chilling. The courts he described were marked by the same extreme informality, impatience, and imprecision that had "dazed" Jack London. From his more scholarly perch, Foote watched groups of fifty or sixty men brought into the courtroom. Together they would stand, as the magistrate surveyed them, asking a question here or making an observation there. In some instances, the magistrate would call out a name, look at whoever responded, and pronounce sentence. "You look like [a vagrant], three months," a magistrate declared. Another stated, "Some people, you look at them, you know they're lying." With no colloquy, no lawyer, no opportunity for the defendant to contest the charge in a substantial way, the magistrate would rapidly convict and sentence—one magistrate disposed of fifty-five cases in a fifteen-minute period. Once convicted, defendants often served short sentences before their appeals could be perfected. Even when appeals were legally available, the lack of written records rendered them largely ineffective.[51]

Just as the goal of peacekeeping was not the enforcement of the law, the goal of these summary proceedings rarely seemed to be the adjudication of guilt. Though defendants were sometimes discharged, innocence rarely seemed the reason. "Guilt is always presumed from the derelict's presence in court," noted one observer. Judge Murtagh reflected this assumption as well. He recounted that on his first night presiding over New York City's night court, he had "followed the traditional sentencing policy that if a drunk is not too seedy and says he has a job, he is given a suspended sentence; otherwise, he is given fifteen or thirty days, depending on his condition." No one, it would appear, was actually acquitted.[52]

So inevitable was conviction that at least some defendants saw protest as futile. One middle-aged man picked up for drunkenness claimed he couldn't have been drunk when arrested because he had only been out for an hour, and he "couldn't get drunk in an hour." When asked how he pleaded, however, he said, "Guilty." The police court judge asked why. According to an observer, the defendant "shrug[ged] his shoulders and mumble[d], 'Get it over with.'"[53]

In fact, given the status nature of the vagrancy concept, guilt often had little to do with evidence of a particular crime at a particular moment. It was at best a function of prior conduct and more commonly a function of one's status. The clerk of some police courts would routinely read out not only the charge but also how often the defendant had been in court earlier that year and even in years past. "Twice before in court this year, 140 times other years." Or the judge would state the record before pronouncing sentence. "This is the sixth time you have been in here this year. Ninety days."[54]

Neither the police nor the magistrates seemed much concerned with technical requirements of due process. In part, this might have resulted from the historical view of vagrancy as a police power regulation that did not require the same protections as a criminal offense. In part, it may have been due to the fact that police officers and judges often shared similar views of the project at hand, and the judges felt they had to support the police: "There is cooperation up and down the line," said a Chicago municipal judge. The lack of process may also have stemmed from sheer volume, or from the fact that the officials adjudicating these cases were, as one law review note put it, "usually educationally unqualified to do legal research." Whether ignorant of the required elements of vagrancy or simply uncaring, it seemed to Foote at least that the magistrates "never applied them." The specific charge was not even read to the defendant in front of the magistrate. Indeed, Foote pointed out that in 1950 there were only 1,241 arrests for vagrancy but 1,430 commitments of vagrants to the Philadelphia House of Correction.[55]

The demographic realities of vagrancy defendants further compounded these procedural laxities. Most vagrancy defendants were too poor to hire lawyers, and few states in 1959 provided counsel for misdemeanor charges. Serving out sentences was cheaper than the cost of an appeal. The "utter impotence" of the defendants immunized the police use of vagrancy and related laws from meaningful oversight. When the police failed to offer vagrants and drunks the possibility of bail or the phone call that other arrestees customarily received, they may have assumed, perhaps rightly, that the defendants could afford no bail and knew no one who could.[56]

With Lusky leading the charge, the KCLU had been attacking these procedural defects in the Louisville Police Court and the Jefferson County Quarterly Court for some years before Thompson's arrest. Lusky pursued cases, proposed studies, and lobbied the legislature. As chair of the KCLU's Criminal Code Committee, he compiled a thirty-page report of problematic incidents. After many fits and starts, and much political wrangling, Kentucky finally incorporated some of the KCLU's proposed reforms in a Criminal Code Revision in 1962.[57]

When Lusky distributed his report across the country, a copy fell into the hands of Louis B. Schwartz, a professor at the University of Pennsylvania Law School. Schwartz was at that very moment reviewing the section of the American Law Institute's Model Penal Code proposal on "Disorderly Conduct." (He would later spearhead sections on vagrancy and loitering as well.) The section produced no small amount of difficulty for Schwartz for precisely the reasons that had motivated Lusky's investigation. Schwartz called the report a "world beater" and a very effective way of articulating the problems with low-level criminal procedures.[58]

After all was said and done, one local practice especially bothered Lusky: "filing away charges with leave to redocket." Something less than conviction but short of dismissal, filing away left the defendant vulnerable to future prosecution and precluded malicious prosecution suits against government officials. In 1957, the *Louisville Courier-Journal* ran two long stories—entitled "Are 'Vagrancy' and 'Filed Away' Acceptable Police Tools as Used Here?" and " 'Vagrancy' and 'Filed Away' Can Hurt a Man's Job's Chances"—quite critical both of using vagrancy and loitering laws to hold suspects for investigation and of filing away. Lusky, "a Louisville attorney interested in civil liberties matters," figured prominently among the critics, while the city's police chief and the Commonwealth's attorney defended the need to hold potential suspects. The following year, the KCLU had some judicial success in the Kentucky Court of Appeals in challenging filing away, and state senators introduced a bill aimed at curbing the practice. Though it passed the Senate, the House eventually buried it, and, appellate warnings aside, police courts continued to file away charges undeterred.[59]

Thompson's two trials—the first over the bus station arrest, followed two weeks later by the Liberty End Café charges—initiated a new phase in Lusky's battle with the Louisville police and court system. The other players in this new phase were also Louisville locals, but they took very different views of the situation. Judge Hugo Taustine circulated in the same general social networks as Lusky and Morse. He was a World War I veteran, a 1922 graduate of the University of Louisville Law School, a Democrat, a mason, a shriner, and a prominent member of Louisville's Jewish community. Prosecutor John Dougherty had been five years behind Taustine as a Louisville law student, and he had spent his career in Louisville, at times in practice with his wife, at other times in the employ of the government.[60]

When the trial for Thompson's arrest at the bus station came up, Lusky made himself a nuisance right from the start. Four men—who the police assumed were sharing a bottle—had been arrested together that January day in the black waiting room. The plan was to try all four together. Yet when the case was called, Lusky insisted on a separate trial for his client. One can almost hear the annoyance in Taustine's voice when he finally gave in, "All right, we will try Sam Thompson first."[61]

The trial involved two overlapping charges that illustrate the overlapping relationship between "vagrancy" and "loitering." The city loitering ordinance combined traditional vagrancy and loitering prohibitions. It made it unlawful for anyone "without visible means of support, or who cannot give a satisfactory account of himself . . . to loaf, congregate, or loiter upon" public streets or to "sleep, lie, loaf, or trespass" in private premises without consent. The state vagrancy law criminalized any "able-bodied male person who habitually loiters or rambles about without means to support himself, and who has no occupation at which to earn an honest livelihood" and any "able-bodied person without visible means of support who habitually refuses to work, and who habitually loiters on the streets or public places of any city." The vagrancy charges thus required both habitual loitering and indigence, whereas the loitering ordinance disaggregated poverty and the failure to account for oneself, and only one or the other was required for conviction.[62]

Lusky accordingly needed a "satisfactory account" of Thompson's presence at the bus station to counter the loitering charge and proof of Thompson's "visible means of support" to counter both loitering and vagrancy. As to the "satisfactory account," Lusky argued that Officer Suter had not even tried to ascertain whether Thompson intended to catch a bus, whether he had a bus schedule on him, whether his bus left from that station, and whether there was one leaving soon. Where Suter saw a drunk black troublemaker sharing a bottle with other black men at the bus station, Lusky and Thompson painted a picture of a law-abiding man waiting for a bus to take him home. Thompson had not spoken to the other men but instead had talked with the only woman present. Unlike the men, "Miss Alma Ford," as the record referred to her, was respectable. She was a domestic, a neighbor, and a friend of Thompson's mother.[63]

To counter the lack of livelihood claims, Lusky called Dr. Wynant Dean to testify that Thompson worked for him. He also took Thompson through his day to show just how much money he had on him as he went about selling junk, settling debts, buying a soft drink, and preparing to ride the bus. Convinced that he had disproven both the vagrancy and the loitering charge, Lusky moved for dismissal. No go.

Prosecutor Dougherty had an altogether different view of the case. He was trying to show that Thompson knew the other men, that on all days but Thursday—his one day of work for the Deans—he could be found at the bus station, and perhaps—by referencing "winos who make dates" and the "perverts that hang around" there—that he was homosexual. Over Lusky's objections, Dougherty and Taustine tried to get Thompson to admit to his frequent presence at the station and resulting arrests.[64]

As the three men went around in circles, Lusky's temper rose. It seemed increasingly clear to him that the evidence he had put on meant nothing to either the prosecutor or the judge. He was simply speaking past them. Lusky was trying to show that Thompson had money and a job and therefore was not a vagrant; and that he was at the bus station to catch a bus and was therefore not loitering.

The judge and prosecutor were not talking about specific acts or testimony or facts. They were talking about Thompson. At one point, Officer Suter suggested that Thompson had not only a long record of misdemeanors—which he certainly had—but also a felony record. It took Lusky quite a bit of effort to convince the judge that the two Sam Thompsons were not the same. Without Lusky, Thompson would not have had a chance.

Even so, Thompson did have a record, and everyone knew it.

As the trial wore on, it became clear to Lusky that Thompson's record, and Officer Suter's general knowledge of Thompson's history, whereabouts, and activities, were the main evidence for conviction. "I have arrested him before and I know him," Suter testified. At another point, Prosecutor Dougherty said, "This man has a long record of arrests and has been charged with perversion." Lusky retorted, "I am not running him for public office; I am just defending him here on these charges and claim he is not guilty of this crime."[65]

Lusky's challenge went to the very legitimacy of skid row policing—that combination of vagrancy laws, peacekeeping policing, and summary police court procedures. In all three aspects of such policing, past conduct or a person's status overshadowed evidence about what the person had done most recently. The officer's legitimacy as peacekeeper came from his personal knowledge of local vagrants and his authority to arrest them regardless of whether their most recent conduct was actually illegal. For a vagrancy conviction, it did not matter whether Thompson had been without funds or employment at the time of this particular arrest. Typically, once determined to be a vagrant, one was criminally liable "at any time before he reform[ed]."[66]

Judge Taustine was not inclined to embrace Lusky's view of substantive law, policing, or his own authority. If Lusky was channeling an implicit and growing national civil liberties critique of skid row policing, Taustine and Dougherty were offering a common defense of the same. At one point, Taustine announced, "The officer has testified he has arrested this man before on similar charges and I am basing my decision on that."[67]

When all the testimony was in, and conviction loomed, Judge Taustine asked Lusky if he wanted "an appealable fine." If not, Taustine would impose the minimum—$10. But if Lusky wanted to appeal, then Taustine would fine Thompson $20, the minimum amount appealable to any state court under Kentucky law. Lusky replied, "If there is going to be a fine I would like for it to be an appealable fine, but first, I would like to file a brief after I get this transcript." The judge suggested that he fine Thompson $10 on the loitering charge and "file away with leave to redocket" the vagrancy charge. Not surprisingly, Lusky objected. He wanted either dismissals or appealable sentences. He was so persistent that the judge ended up insisting that he had "a right" to sentence Thompson according to the law, and the prosecutor claimed that Lusky was just "trying to intimidate the [police] officer."[68]

Without Thompson's own voice in the record, it is hard to know what he would have wanted. Perhaps he would have preferred the lesser fine, perhaps even filing away. The latter would have left him with the most money in his pocket, even if it meant forgoing the option of appeal or a lawsuit against the officer. The fact that Thompson had reached out to Wynant Dean suggested that he wanted to fight the charges, and perhaps Lusky knew that. Or perhaps Lusky's arguments about appealable fines were not in his client's best interests. Either way, the situation reveals a potential tension between not only defense lawyers and government officials but also defense lawyers and their clients.

In the end, Taustine refused to dismiss the charges or grant a new trial, but he did give Thompson appealable sentences: $20 for loitering and thirty days in jail for vagrancy. Dougherty's response to Lusky's efforts on this front was straight out of the best book of legal clichés: "We have thousands of cases here and every time this gentleman comes in with a case he wants to make a federal case out of it and this is nothing but a two-bit case."[69]

It was at this point that Lusky instructed Thompson to stay away from the bus station. Neither man thought the retaliation was over, especially after the fireworks of the police court trial. It was not. When Thompson avoided the bus station by waiting for his bus in the Liberty End Café, the police arrested him again.[70]

The trial that followed the Liberty End Café arrest was reminiscent of the previous one. The players were mostly the same: Lusky for Thompson, Dougherty as prosecutor, and Taustine as judge. There were Lusky's motions and objections and constitutional arguments. There was resistance and annoyance from both judge and prosecutor. Though this case lacked a vagrancy charge—it concerned Thompson's alleged loitering in the Liberty End Café and his alleged disorderly conduct upon being forcibly removed—the vagrancy elements in the loitering law kept the same issues in play.

The basis of the state's case was that Thompson had been hanging around the tavern for more than half an hour without ordering anything. Plus, he had been dancing illegally in a bar without a dance hall license. Thompson's argument was that he had ordered food and drink, he was welcomed by the manager, he was waiting for a bus, and he was merely shuffling his feet to the music. Lusky also claimed that the police had been looking for Thompson, as evidenced by Officer Barnett mentioning to the manager that Thompson "had been in something down at the bus station." As for the disorderly conduct charge, the officers saw Thompson as "belligerent" and "argumentative," whereas Thompson claimed he had merely preserved his rights by asking for the basis of the arrest. Under Kentucky law, anyone who did not immediately question an arrest waived his right to be told of the charges against him.[71]

There was much wrangling about the admissibility of Thompson's record, about whether these particular officers knew about the bus station arrest days before, about bus schedules and bus stops—it turned out that Thompson's bus stopped just half a block down from the Liberty End Café and he frequently waited at the café—and about whether he could, as he claimed, have bought some macaroni and beer from a waitress without the manager noticing. Though the charges did not include a lack of visible means of support, Taustine nevertheless offered, "He has to buy his clothing and pay for drugs and his beer and whiskey—I know he drinks that because I can—I have judicial knowledge of that from the fact he comes in here so often." Lusky, unsurprisingly, objected to such judicial knowledge, but Taustine just considered them "facts."[72]

When Lusky again sought dismissal of the charges, Dougherty again fell back on Thompson's past rather than his specific illegal conduct at the Liberty End

Café that cold January night. Dougherty objected, "This man has a long record and every time Mr. Lusky comes into this court he wants to make a big case out of a minor one."[73]

This time, Taustine imposed a $10, non-appealable fine on each charge.

Lusky asked Thompson how they should proceed. Lusky said, "If it's necessary, I'll go to the limit—to the U.S. Supreme Court. Are you agreeable?" Thompson was. Thompson later said to the press, "If you are being continually beaten on the shoulder..., that shoulder gets tired after a while. I felt something should be done about it."[74]

It was a good thing that Thompson was willing to take the case all the way to the Supreme Court, as Lusky probably already knew when he asked the question that the high court would be their target sooner rather than later. Jurisdictional rules specified that the Supreme Court would hear a case only after the highest state court had ruled. Because Lusky could not appeal Thompson's convictions in any state court, the highest court authorized to hear his case was also the lowest: the Louisville Police Court was his one and only shot at justice in the Kentucky courts. It had just missed. The Supreme Court was thus not only the last place Lusky could go, it was also the first.[75]

It would not have been crazy for Lusky to have stopped before then. A few years earlier another Kentucky lawyer had rebuffed pressure from the national ACLU to take a similar appeal on the ground that "I just think the Supreme Court would almost laugh at any effort made on our part to correct an injustice which cost two men $15 each." Though Thompson's total $20 fine was less than that, Lusky was convinced that the harm of the constitutional violation Thompson suffered was "not measurable in purely monetary terms." Rather, "It is the bald denial of *justice* which is the matter of constitutional concern." From Lusky's perspective, then, Taustine might have done him a favor by denying him an appeal in state court. Though the unappealable fine meant to prevent appeals altogether, Lusky used it to vault straight to the top of the American judicial pyramid.[76]

Before Lusky could get to the high court, however, he had to solve the problem of mootness. Courts could only review judgments in cases where their intervention still mattered. Once Thompson paid his two $10 fines or served them out in jail at $2 per day, the law deemed his case "moot." There would be no point to reviewing it. Because of the small amount of money at stake, and the few days it would take to serve the sentences, Lusky imagined that police officers could keep arresting Thompson, the police court could keep punishing him, and Thompson would keep serving his sentences without ever—no matter how often this happened—having an opportunity for some other court to examine the law, the charges, or the proceedings. Lusky thus asked Taustine for a stay so that he could bring an appeal before Thompson had finished working out his sentence. Under Kentucky law, Taustine was authorized to suspend judgment for only twenty-four hours. Lusky asked for that, and Taustine gave it to him.[77]

Lusky and Morse then applied for a suspension of sentence in the Jefferson County Circuit Court. They recognized that although Kentucky law authorized no such suspension, the Supreme Court would want to see that they had least made a respectful effort in the state courts. Judge Lawrence S. Grauman ran in many of the same circles as Taustine, Morse, and Lusky—he was a Jewish Democratic mason and shriner. He was also already on record in the *Louisville Courier-Journal* as critical of both expansive police use of vagrancy and loitering laws and the practice of filing away charges instead of dismissing them. Grauman granted a ninety-day stay in light of Thompson's "Federal Constitutional right . . . to be allowed an opportunity to present his claims to the only court which has the jurisdiction to entertain them—the United States Supreme Court." He set bail at $35—the total amount in Lusky's pocket.[78]

The city appealed to the Kentucky Court of Appeals, then the highest court in the state. That court held, not unexpectedly, that the circuit court had not had the power to grant a stay. But it then took what the Supreme Court would later call "the extraordinary step" of granting a stay of its own, even though Lusky had not petitioned for one. The court concluded that Thompson "appears to have a real question as to whether he has been denied due process," and only a stay would make it possible to answer that question.[79]

Louis Lusky's Litigation Strategy

Now that Lusky had safely navigated the state courts, in what his future Columbia Law School colleague Jack Greenberg called "a procedural tour de force," he and his co-counsel turned to their Supreme Court petition for certiorari ("cert"). If Lusky had guessed that his own stature would get Thompson's petition at least a more careful look than most cases brought by poor alcoholic vagrants, he would have been right. Though "cert memos" from law clerks to justices assessing petitions for certiorari rarely mentioned lawyers, the very first sentence in the cert memo a clerk wrote to Justice John Marshall Harlan II noted, "This is an unusual petition, filed by Louis Lusky."[80]

In the petition and throughout the Supreme Court case that followed, Lusky made a strategic decision. Like Besig half a continent away, Lusky believed that both the laws and the law enforcers were problematic. As a result, Lusky might have challenged the entirety of skid row policing. He did not. He explicitly chose to focus on the procedures of the Louisville police and police court, and the specifics of Thompson's arrests and convictions, to the exclusion of the laws themselves.

Lusky's central argument was that Thompson's arrest at the Liberty End Café violated the due process clause of the Fourteenth Amendment to the Constitution because "there was *no* evidence that [Thompson] was guilty." At first glance, the argument looks rather narrow—a complaint about the decisions of these police officers on this single occasion. In keeping with that claim, the two sides dueled over what Thompson was doing in the tavern that night, and whether there was specific evidence on which the police could have arrested, and the police court convicted, him for loitering. All those competing details might have seemed small bore. But given the long acceptance of virtually unbridled police discretion, asking for federal judicial oversight of such a decision was in fact quite ambitious. Moreover, though the argument was a sound one as a matter of common sense, it was a novel one as a matter of precedent. Lusky cited no case directly on point.[81]

On closer inspection, Lusky's argument was even more radical. Lusky's apparently narrow "no evidence" argument managed to incorporate an attack on peacekeeping policing and the summary justice that accompanied it. By no evidence, Lusky meant not just that the events at the Liberty End Café did not support a loitering conviction. He meant that the type of evidence the government really thought mattered—evidence of who Thompson was and had been—was utterly illegitimate.

The crux of Thompson's problem, Lusky explained, was that because of how the police viewed him—whether as a needy vagrant or a rights-asserting troublemaker—Thompson could not "walk the streets of Louisville, or even innocently wait for a bus to his home, without being arrested on sight." Convictions followed arrests, and more arrests followed convictions. At best, charges were "filed away." Because police officers were immunized from malicious prosecution claims without a dismissal or acquittal, Thompson was "subjected to the unrestrained and arbitrary will of the Louisville police. . . [and] a virtual sentence of outlawry." The problem was not only Thompson's. "The real question is whether anyone in Kentucky [or any similar state] can incur the personal displeasure of the police without subjecting himself to a course of harassment for which there is no remedy." Indeed, the "fair check" or "routine check" procedures that the police claimed had led to Thompson's two arrests after Haymarket authorized officers to enter public places and require "whomever they please to account for their presence, show proof of employment, and otherwise explain their circumstances. If the explanation is unsatisfactory to the arresting officer an arrest is made and petty charges filed." Implicitly contrasting the United States to the totalitarian Soviet Union in the midst of the Cold War,

Lusky described such practices as "alien to our institutions" and constituting "a standing threat to the freedom and privacy of all."[82]

The problem, Lusky argued, was not just the police. It was also the police court. The summary nature of police court proceedings, the apparent nonexistence of acquittals (rendering malicious prosecution or false imprisonment suits unavailable), and the prohibitions on appeal to higher state courts for many convictions "vest[ed] the Louisville Police Court judge with absolute and arbitrary power."[83]

Embedded within Lusky's attack on Louisville law enforcement was an implicit critique of the third pillar of skid row policing: status crimes themselves. Lusky argued that it was only after Officer Suter mentioned that he had arrested Thompson in the past that Judge Taustine's "mind had frozen" against Thompson and Taustine presumed Thompson's guilt. Lusky claimed that the judge was "applying a *rule*—a rule that no defendant who has an arrest record will be acquitted." Such convictions were based "not [on] what petitioner has *done*, but what kind of man the police think he *is*." Though Lusky acted as if following that "rule" was itself unlawful, he was well aware that such a rule was at the heart not only of peacekeeping policing and summary justice, but of vagrancy and loitering laws themselves.[84]

That said, Lusky refrained from attacking the Louisville loitering ordinance. It was not that he liked vagrancy and loitering laws—he called them "broad and vaguely worded legislative prohibitions." But throughout the *Thompson* litigation, he assumed, "without conceding," the validity of the laws under which Thompson had been convicted. Lusky did not cite *Edelman v. California* or California's efforts to amend its vagrancy law. He did not cite the small but growing number of articles and cases that suggested something fundamentally wrong with vagrancy and loitering laws.[85]

Some at the Court were puzzled by Lusky's decision to stake his claim on the novel (and legally unsupported) claim of "no evidence" rather than to challenge laws that *Edelman* and other cases had already made somewhat vulnerable. At oral argument, Justice Frankfurter, whose own interest in vagrancy and loitering laws dated back to his call to arms in 1948's *Winters v. New York*, asked whether Lusky was also attacking the loitering law's constitutionality. Lusky answered in the negative. The law clerk who had been so impressed with Lusky's eminence was more openly critical. "I am not sure that Lusky has not hacked up irremedially [*sic*] by not challenging the statute as applied, since there was obviously 'evidence' in the case and the real question is whether a conviction for anything on the particular evidence is a violation of due process, a contention not made." In recommending that the Court deny certiorari, he mused, "Had Lusky directly attacked the loitering statute as applied I think the case might be certworthy, but this sloppy business about convicting on 'no evidence' when the question is 'evidence of what?' to me pretty well forecloses him."[86]

Why did Lusky not attack the loitering law? In part, Lusky did not think the law was the real problem for Thompson. "The essential issue in the present case is not the validity of the ordinances under which petitioner has been prosecuted, but the arbitrariness of the judgments. It actually makes no difference at all what ordinance or statute the petitioner is accused of violating," he wrote. "So long as his arrest record rather than his conduct is the basis of his convictions, little can be accomplished by an attack on the particular ordinance or statute which is the formal but not the actual reason for the prosecution. There would always be another ordinance or statute which could be made the excuse for a new criminal charge." During oral argument, Lusky suggested that if nothing else sufficed, the police would find a way to arrest Thompson for "eating a cream puff with the wrong expression on his face." In other words, the laws were not the problem. The police were.[87]

Lusky's views of legal doctrine likely weighed as heavily in his decision. As a law clerk to Chief Justice Stone in the 1937 Supreme Court term, Lusky had participated in one of the great doctrinal transformations of the twentieth century. In the 1905 case of *Lochner v. New York*, the Court had found that an individual's right to contract prevented a state from setting maximum hours of work in a bakery. The Court located that right in the Fourteenth Amendment's prohibition on depriving any person of "life, liberty, or property" without due process of law. Though that clause seemed only to ensure proper legal process before the deprivation of a right, in *Lochner* and other cases, the Court interpreted it as precluding certain government regulations that interfered with the right to contract. Around the time of Lusky's clerkship, the Court rejected this doctrine and began showing greater deference to legislatures' social and economic policies. The question that arose was whether the Court should ever protect individual rights now that the theory posthumously dubbed "substantive due process" was no longer viable. Were there any freedoms that could resist democratic legislation to the contrary?[88]

In tentative answer to that question, Lusky authored what became the most famous footnote in American constitutional history. Footnote four of *United States v. Carolene Products* identified specific circumstances under which courts should invalidate governmental actions as unconstitutional, even though they should generally refrain from scrutinizing run-of-the-mill laws too carefully. Lusky tried to skirt the problem of substantive due process by locating new freedoms in the text of the Constitution and in the supervision of the political processes that justified democratic rule and the minorities who most often suffered under it. The footnote eventually proved highly influential, and it continued to inform Lusky's approach to constitutional law and the judicial role for the rest of his life. Even when many of Lusky's former *Lochner* foes embraced a new set of substantive due process rights to privacy, sexual autonomy, and reproduction in cases like *Roe v. Wade* in the 1970s, Lusky remained staunchly opposed.[89]

Lusky's views on substantive due process might have colored his decision about the best way to litigate Thompson's case. By 1959, the most commonly raised criticisms of vagrancy laws was that they punished status and were void for vagueness in violation of the Fourteenth Amendment's Due Process Clause. Such arguments might have seemed too closely tied to doctrines Lusky had long abhorred. As legal scholar Anthony Amsterdam would point out in a law review note just a few months after the Supreme Court decided *Thompson*, void for vagueness had often stood in for substantive due process during the *Lochner* Era. Moreover, the 1939 gangster case of *Lanzetta v. New Jersey* and 1957's criminal registration case of *Lambert v. California* evinced confusion about where procedural due process ended, substantive due process began, and how both the status/conduct distinction and the void-for-vagueness doctrine fit within the two.[90]

Shortly after the Court decided *Thompson*, its invalidation of a law that criminalized being a narcotics addict in *Robinson v. California* confirmed such anxieties and ambiguities. Though the Court condemned the law specifically because it was a status crime, it avoided both procedural and substantive due process by basing the decision on the Eighth Amendment's prohibition on "cruel and unusual punishment." This was a highly unusual application of an amendment that had previously proscribed particular punishments rather than particular crimes. Few were fooled that substantive due process had not been the decision's real basis. In dissent, Justice Byron White wrote: "If this case involved economic regulation, the present Court's allergy to substantive due process would surely save the statute and prevent the Court from imposing its own philosophical predilictions upon state legislatures or Congress. I fail to see why the Court deems it more appropriate to write into the Constitution its own abstract notions of how best to handle the narcotics problem." Scholars described the Eighth Amendment basis in *Robinson* as a "euphemism" for substantive due process, the "more candid view" of the case.[91]

Lusky's avoidance of this doctrinal morass by arguing the absence of evidence—and the defects of law enforcement—rather than the deficiencies of the law is apparent in the decidedly *procedural* due process lexicon Lusky used. His was a language that pitted unconstrained power against "the impartiality of the law" more than the rights of individuals. The police court judge, Lusky contended, had granted the police "a hunting license," giving the police "arbitrary power." Words like "hurt," "harm," and "injustice" predominated over any implication of substantive due process or individual "rights."[92]

Whatever the reasons for his choice, Lusky was convinced that forgoing an attack on the laws themselves made his case more, not less, ambitious.

The police court's immense docket meant that "the present case cannot be regarded as an isolated phenomenon. The brand of 'justice' accorded to petitioner must also be meted out in a very large number of other cases." How else could the court process so many cases if it did not rely on prior guilt to prove present guilt? "The picture of the [Police] Court which thus emerges is a more chilling one than if the record disclosed downright sadism or neurotic caprice. It is the picture not of an evil court, but of a court confident that its motives and methods are in conformity with the desires, or at least the best interests, of the community." Lusky pointedly distanced policing in a modern liberal state from the Elizabethan England of the original vagrancy laws and the dystopia imagined by English writer and sometime tramp George Orwell. "The year is now 1960. It is not 1600; nor, if we may be permitted to say so, is it 1984."[93]

Lawyers for Louisville and Kentucky understood just how deep Lusky's challenge went. They did, as they had to, defend the evidence in Thompson's specific case. Assistant Louisville Director of Law (and Lusky's former University of Louisville classmate) Herman Frick found ample evidence on which Judge Taustine could have based Thompson's convictions. The city also offered a new defense of its prosecution: even if Thompson actually could support himself, such support was not a defense to loitering because it was not "visible." So long as Thompson worked only one day a week and "*appear[ed]* to have no financial responsibility whatsoever," he could be found guilty of loitering.[94]

But the city also defended itself against Lusky's deeper claims. As to the police court itself, more formal procedures were "utopian" and would only "result in a 'leaden-footed' judicial administration." Frick both downplayed the harm of "speedy justice" and recast it as a benefit to defendants. "Of course, expediency should not be permitted to result in great injustice, but in the case of a petty offense with a small punishment, the injustice is not great."[95]

Frick also justified the notion of the police as peacekeeper. For Lusky and Thompson, the recurring arrests, and the officers' and the judge's invocation of their prior knowledge of Thompson as justification for both arrests and convictions, was a problem. Not so for the city and state. "Past experience is, for the law enforcement officer, an indispensable aid for evaluating the actions of certain individuals who are frequent violators." The city thus justified the officer's knowledge and the utility and legitimacy of that knowledge for the law and the public peace. It was a defense of long-standing and still robust deference to local practices and norms.[96]

Finally, Frick argued that the officer's prior knowledge was especially valuable for the "somewhat anomalous categories" of "loitering, vagrancy, and 'suspicious persons' laws." Even though Lusky had not directly attacked the laws, Frick understood their crucial role in the skid row policing he was defending.

Describing "the regulation of loitering and vagrancy in public places" as a "common practice" with ample judicial support, he concluded that such laws "are not susceptible to the same tangible modes of proof that disclose most offenses." It was not only that the officers had sufficient proof of the usual kind to arrest Thompson on January 24 at the Liberty End Café, then. It was also that such arrests should not even require that kind of proof. "One characteristic common to such offenses is that they arise more from a course of conduct or a manner of life than from an isolated act." It would be silly to require "conscientious policem[e]n" to "turn their heads to await only the most pronounced evidence." By arresting those like Thompson—repeat and always incipient criminals—for crimes like vagrancy and loitering, "many major crimes have been nipped in the bud."[97]

When Lusky filed his Supreme Court reply brief, Thompson was back in jail. In fact, Thompson had already been arrested a dozen more times for various combinations of drunkenness in a public place, loitering, and disorderly conduct.[98]

Thompson was in jail yet again when Lusky and Frick trekked to Washington for oral argument at the Supreme Court in early 1960. In Thompson's $20 loitering case, the argument ran over time, and the justices reconvened the following day. The press found the extra time especially amusing. Lowly Sam Thompson had displaced "frock-coated Attorney General William P. Rogers"—he waited for almost an hour to be heard.[99]

During argument, the justices were generally sympathetic to Lusky and his client. One commentary described Frick as taking "quite a verbal beating from the Bench." Another stated that the justices "devoted an hour Tuesday to expressing their amazement at some of the operations of the Louisville Police Department and the City's Police Court." Justice Charles Whittaker asked, "Is it a violation of an ordinance of the City of Louisville for an old colored man to go into a grill and tap his foot to music while waiting for a bus on a cold night?" Justice Felix Frankfurter asked if it was illegal to "shuffle" in Louisville. The *New York Times* noted, "Behind this humor was the question of the use of loitering and vagrancy statutes by the police to jail those whom they regard as undesirables. This is a common practice all over the country, and the justices were obviously concerned about it."[100]

The opinion Justice Black wrote for the Court vindicated Lusky's claim that "it is a violation of due process to convict and punish a man without evidence of his guilt" and hewed closely to the facts surrounding Thompson's loitering arrest at the Liberty End Café. The case thus reflected a one-off victory. Without a direct attack on the loitering law itself, the Court left the ordinance intact. Moreover, future lawyers hoping to use the doctrine would have to engage in the same case-by-case factual analysis Lusky had. The bar for future no-evidence claims was high. Though the case was the Court's only unanimous constitutional law opinion of the 1959 Term, Justice Harlan's vote had come with some suggested revisions. A child of privilege educated at Princeton and Oxford who had served in several law enforcement jobs before joining the Court, Harlan was less enthused than many of the justices of the liberal Warren Court about federal judicial interference with state policies. He worried that the new no-evidence doctrine would become too elastic. He wanted the opinion to say that the record was "completely devoid" of evidence, or something along those lines, "to fend against the future use of this opinion" for run-of-the mill insufficiency of the evidence claims. Black adopted Harlan's suggested language verbatim.[101]

The opinion was less narrow than it first appeared, however. First, that the Court did interfere with the prerogatives of local police and police courts, even on a retail basis, was notable. *Thompson* represented an early example of increasingly intrusive Supreme Court oversight of state criminal justice procedures. Indeed, Black tried to disclaim such federal intrusion. By emphasizing the Kentucky Court of Appeals' "extraordinary stay," the Court indicated that this was not a case in which the United States Supreme Court was imposing its own—elite, northern, national—norms on long-standing local ones. It was a case in which the state's highest court had virtually invited the Supreme Court to help it discipline inferior courts and law enforcement officers over whom it had inadequate control.[102]

Second, though most of the brief opinion attended to the shuffle-dance and macaroni ordering at the Liberty End Café—the narrow form of the no-evidence claim—the opinion hinted at Lusky's arguments about the deeper problems of skid row policing. Lusky's descriptions must have resonated with Black's own experiences as a young police court judge in Birmingham, experiences he described throughout his life as formative of his constitutional views. Scattered through the brief opinion are mentions of police "reprisals" and "baseless" charges, "routine check[s]," officers "accost[ing]" Thompson, and possible confinement in "the workhouse."[103]

The effect of Lusky's overall critique of skid row policing was even more apparent outside the four corners of the opinion. On March 15, 1960, just days before the Court handed down *Thompson v. Louisville*, Justice Douglas gave a lecture on "Vagrancy and Arrest on Suspicion" at the University of New Mexico School of Law (later published in the *Yale Law Journal*). The timing of the lecture hardly seems coincidental. Douglas was thinking about vagrancy laws, about transients and the poor, about the injustices and procedural problems of magistrates' courts. Though he did not mention *Thompson* by name, as the Court had not yet announced the decision, the speech bears the hallmarks of Shuffling Sam. Douglas exhorted lawyers to challenge the problematic procedures Foote had identified. He also went where Lusky had not—to the "real nest of problems for the lawyer in these vagrancy statutes."[104]

Douglas had been contemplating vagrancy laws himself long before *Thompson*. As his dissent in *Edelman* had suggested, Douglas's self-mythology as an erstwhile vagrant and membership in the "Hoboes of America" was accompanied by a sincere interest in the constitutional defects of vagrancy laws. Douglas was the only member of the Court to maintain a subject file on "vagrancy" between the late 1950s and the late 1960s. Indeed, just a few months after his vagrancy speech, the sixty-two-year-old Douglas was himself mistaken for a "tramp." Douglas and two other Washington luminaries had led an annual hike along the district's C&O Canal in support of designating the area a national park. Caught in the rain, the trio had stopped at a nearby inn, dripping wet, only to be told by the innkeeper, "I run this place to make money, not to serve tramps." Douglas must have been delighted by the front-page news story that confirmed his hobo bona fides.[105]

In his pre-*Thompson* speech, then, Douglas argued that the laws were "too vague to satisfy constitutional tests"; they infringed on the right to travel; they were status crimes; and they threatened double jeopardy by allowing for successive prosecutions for the same conduct. Vagrancy laws, he lamented, were used "as a cloak . . . for arresting and convicting people for some other crime that cannot be proved or for conduct that is not a crime." They provided an "easy way of making arrests on suspicion" especially of poor people or "minority groups who are not sufficiently vocal to protect themselves."[106]

Douglas was not the only one to note the larger implications of *Thompson* for skid row policing. *Time* magazine surmised that "the court's unusual policing of police-court proceedings flashed a warning that convictions for loitering and disorderly conduct, often based on flimsy evidence or none at all, might now be toppled wholesale." *Reader's Digest* described the decision as an "acknowledgment of a growing problem in many parts of the country where police use the disorderly conduct, loitering and vagrancy laws to arrest persons, not for breaking the law, but simply for being a minor nuisance." *Thompson's* story might have been unusual in reaching the Supreme Court. But it was all too usual in other respects.[107]

Much of the commentary on the decision—widespread, front-page, and very favorable—focused less on the injustice the police court meted out to "Shuffling Sam" and more on the justice the Supreme Court offered. One paper summarized the dispute this way: Thompson's "lawyer says the Louisville officers are picking on him. Maybe they are, and then maybe he's a no-good bum." It went on, "But whatever he is, old Sam Thompson is entitled to the full protection of the laws of the United States, and the supreme court [*sic*] stands ready to see that he gets that protection, whether they like it in Louisville or not. And that is the

Inn Snubs 'Tramps': Udall and 2 Douglases

Sodden Hikers Given Scant Welcome by Proprietor's Wife

By The Associated Press.
WASHINGTON, May 7—"I run this place to make money, not to serve tramps!"

That was the forthright summary a woman innkeeper hurled at a bunch of drenched hikers yesterday—and her targets included Supreme Court Justice William O. Douglas, Senator Paul H. Douglas, Democrat of Illinois, and Secretary of the Interior Stewart L. Udall.

The hikers, about 170 strong, were nearing the end of a sodden, sixteen-mile course along the old C. & O. Canal route from Seneca, Md., to Washington when they stopped at the Old Anglers Inn near the Great Falls of the Potomac.

Justice Douglas and Mrs. Douglas were among the first arrivals and Senator Douglas led another group in a little later. Soon the inn was packed with dripping nature-lovers, many unwrapping lunches and ordering beverages.

Mrs. John T. Reges, wife of the proprietor, came down the stairs and expressed her general position. Then she leveled a finger at Senator Douglas and cried "Get off that rug! Get over there with the rest of the wet ones." The tall, gray-haired Senator meekly complied.

When told whom she had been Continued on Page 31, Column 4

Justice William O. Douglas, left, Secretary of the Interior Stewart L. Udall, center, and Senator Paul H. Douglas of Illinois pause during hike along the old C. & O. Canal.

United Press International Radiophoto

Figure 3.2 Headline and photo in the *Washington Post* of an innkeeper calling Supreme Court Justice William O. Douglas a "tramp" when he approached her inn during a rainy hike along the C&O Canal. The story played nicely into both Justice Douglas's self-mythology as a one-time hobo and his abiding constitutional concerns about vagrancy laws. He was the only justice with an honorary membership in the "Hoboes of America" and the only one who kept a file specifically on "vagrancy." Associated Press/*New York Times*/United Press International.

grand thing about this country's system of justice; it is just as concerned over an old man's shuffling in a tavern as it is over legal problems affecting billion-dollar corporations." The *Boston Herald* joined the patriotic self-congratulations: "We are, in a manner of speaking, shuffling our feet in rhythm to a great and pervading melody to be heard about this land."[108]

Lusky and his KCLU were also valorized. The *Louisville Courier-Journal* ran a piece entitled "Louis Lusky: Defender of Civil Liberties," complete with a detailed biography and a photo. "One of the glories of the law as we know it," the paper intoned, was "the willingness of well-known and well-to-do lawyers to fight a seemingly losing battle for the friendless and the penniless if they feel injustice is being done." In recognition of what Lusky later recalled as "more than 850 hours of professional time spent in seven court proceedings, various court papers and a real-estate problem involving Thompson's home," the editorial page "saluted" Lusky. So did legal luminaries across the country. Louis B. Schwartz, University of Pennsylvania law professor and drafter of more limited vagrancy, loitering, and disorderly conduct provisions for the ALI's Model Penal Code, sent Lusky and Morse a note complimenting them and predicting that the case "will generate waves of liberty for a long time."[109]

Yes and no. The celebratory tone of these articles was tempered by the recognition that, as stirring as *Thompson* was, it would not itself fix the problems in Louisville or anywhere else. Locally, though the *Courier-Journal* predicted that the case "may mean much to future Sam Thompsons, who never again will be quite as defenseless before hasty policemen and indifferent prosecutors as they have been heretofore," the reaction was mixed. For his part, Kentucky Commonwealth's Attorney Laurence Higgins looked forward to change. He hoped that "all of the efforts made and money spent by the Kentucky Civil Liberties Union will not have been in vain if, by reading the opinion, the judges and prosecutors in lower courts face up squarely to the proposition that under the law a person is not to be convicted solely because he has been arrested, or solely because a person has a prior criminal record, without regard to the legally admissible evidence of his guilt." Easy for him to say. As his statement revealed, he disavowed either power or responsibility. Both, in his view, seemed to lie with lower level officials.[110]

For their part, those officials were not so convinced of their own wrongdoing. The city's mayor, police chief, safety director, and Herman Frick himself did not seem to think the Supreme Court's decision would change their procedures much. Taustine dismissed a few arrests for vagrancy, loitering, and disorderly conduct that resembled *Thompson*. He nonetheless continued to file away vagrancy and loitering charges, even against one man who received publicity for being a "Second Sam" just weeks after the Supreme Court's decision.[111]

Whether a challenge to the laws themselves would have done more to rein in local officials is hard to say. Equally unclear is whether such a challenge would have met with success at the Supreme Court. Would the justices have gone for it in 1960? They had not in *Edelman* seven years earlier. Moreover, like Lusky, both Black and Douglas—New Dealers deeply opposed to economic substantive due process—might have worried about the constitutional basis for an invalidation. The narcotics addiction case of *Robinson v. California*, decided two years after *Thompson*, provides equivocal evidence. On the one hand, a challenge to the status nature of the crime there succeeded, and the Court found a way to avoid substantive due process. On the other hand, several justices intimated that they were willing to invalidate the addiction law partly because they felt it was distinguishable from vagrancy laws, which they deemed constitutional.[112]

It is also unclear what Sam Thompson made of his victory. The *Reader's Digest* quoted Thompson as responding to news of the Court's decision with the following: "It just made me feel good to know that my rights were being taken care of." The article concluded with Thompson saying, "When I see the police now, . . . we say hello to each other, and that's all." As *Time* magazine noted, however, when the case was decided, Thompson was once again in jail, this time serving a six-month sentence on four misdemeanor charges. Thompson's response to the Supreme Court's decision was less sanguine in reports by the *Louisville Courier-Journal*. When local reporters tracked Thompson down in the Jefferson County Jail to show him a story on the decision, he had two reactions. First, he was peeved that he had not had advance warning to clean himself up. "If I had been informed a couple days ahead of time I could have got a haircut and some 'John Doe' (civilian) clothes." Second, he was worried that the news coverage had been falsified. "That's no guarantee this is true," he said. "This is publicity." He was reluctant to talk with reporters because he still worried about reprisals.[113]

Lusky was less worried. Actually, he was downright proud. He mentioned (and sometimes detailed) his role in *Thompson v. Louisville* in a number of scholarly publications. His friends and colleagues discussed it prominently in their memorials after his death. Lusky also talked about it to decades of constitutional law students at Columbia Law School. As those students recall, Lusky described the case as supremely successful not only in legal outcome, but also in changing Sam Thompson's life. He told them that after the Supreme Court had decided the case, Thompson carried a copy of the opinion with him at all times. Though Thompson himself could not read, according to this story, he did not carry it for his own perusal. Rather, when a police officer would stop him, Thompson would show him the opinion. According to such lore, this display would have its intended effect: the officer would move on, and Sam Thompson would remain a free man. So far as the historical record is concerned, Thompson himself did not tell that story. In fact, other sources imply that the strategy was not as successful as Lusky suggested: Thompson was arrested five times in the three years after the Supreme Court's decision.[114]

As Lusky well knew, however, *Thompson's* major legacy came not in the form of police restraint with regard to Thompson himself, nor in the immediate disuse of vagrancy and loitering laws, nor in the passage of new procedural safeguards in low-level courts, nor in a wholesale revolution of skid row policing. Though Lusky's no-evidence rule would live on in everyday criminal cases, *Thompson's* most substantial legacy came from an unexpected corner: the civil rights movement.[115]

Lusky and Morse had avoided raising the race issue in *Thompson* because they did not think race was the issue. To the extent that Thompson was frequently arrested in "colored" spaces—the black bus station waiting room, a black bar—his poverty, his drunkenness, or his "perversion" might have seemed more salient than his race. Lusky later said in an interview that he had intentionally omitted "the racial issue from the record in order to present to the Supreme Court a clear case of arbitrary police action free from a question of racial discrimination. Insertion of the racial issue would probably have increased the chances for a grant of certiorari, but it would also probably have resulted in a narrower holding of less value to the civil rights movement."[116]

Just over a month before the Supreme Court decided the case, however, Thompson's race suddenly took on new import as the politics of civil rights in America changed. Dramatically. There had been public challenges to segregation and inequality before February 1, 1960. Lawyers had brought a series of cases in employment, labor unions, transportation, housing, voting, and education that had culminated in *Brown v. Board of Education*. There had been sit-ins and boycotts, protests and "journeys of reconciliation." In Louisville itself, members of the NAACP Youth Council had led sit-ins as early as 1956. By the time the Supreme Court heard Thompson's case, African American community leaders were pressing Louisville's mayor for an ordinance to end segregation in public accommodations.[117]

On February 1, 1960, students at North Carolina Agricultural and Technical College, a historically black college, unleashed a new energy in the civil rights movement when they sat in at a segregated lunch counter in the Greensboro Woolworth's. In city after city, chain store after chain store, lunch counter after library after bus depot, students and others exercised their rights or got arrested trying. Though their circumstances could hardly be compared with Sam Thompson's in most respects, they were arrested for many of the same kinds of petty offenses he had faced: disorderly conduct, breach of the peace, and yes, loitering and vagrancy.

As a result, when the Supreme Court decided Thompson's case, what many saw front and center was the race issue. Commentators then and now have transposed the timing so that it seemed that the Court knew when it took Thompson's case that such events were imminent. That seems unlikely, however, given the suddenness of the eruption of this new form of civil rights protest and the new legal issues it engendered. One example of how such events were unanticipated can be seen in the briefs of the city of Louisville. The city made much of the fact that the Liberty End Café was a "public" tavern because it was "situated at the side of . . . public ways" like streets and highways. The city clearly thought that categorizing the café as public would bring it more securely under the loitering ordinance (as the city would not then need to prove that Thompson lacked consent to be in the tavern). When the cases of civil rights protestors reached the courts a short time later, the states, the cities, and the proprietors of the sit-in establishments would fall all over themselves to prove that they were not "public." They had to be private so that the Fourteenth Amendment's Equal Protection Clause, which was interpreted to constrain only governmental actors, would not apply to them. Louisville's attorneys had no idea such arguments might be useful a few months hence, and they pushed in the other direction on the tricky issue of public versus private.[118]

It is difficult to say the extent to which the sit-ins influenced *Thompson*, given that they exploded after the Court's oral argument and initial deliberations in January but before the opinion was issued in March. With the sit-ins front page news, it would have been pretty impossible for the justices not to have known that the legal issues they raised would, sooner or later, make their way onto the Court's docket. The justices might eventually face hundreds of cases in which local law enforcement officers had arrested "undesirables" of a different sort for crimes they may, or may not, have committed, as a result, or not, of reprisal, under laws that may, or may not, have been too vague to stand constitutional scrutiny. Perhaps the new civil rights context accounted for Justice Harlan's concern that the standard set for a no-evidence claim be a rigorous one. Perhaps it was why the Court fashioned its decision as supportive, rather than critical, of state and local prerogatives—a concern that would grow in civil rights cases. Perhaps it was why the opinion focused tightly on the facts at the Liberty End Café rather than Lusky's condemnation of skid row policing generally. The scrutiny of the singular episode made the case more readily applicable to the very different social context of the coming civil rights cases. These tweaks, however, neither accounted for the Court's interest in the case nor pushed it toward an outcome in favor of *Thompson*. For the most part, from the first bench memo through the oral argument to the final disposition of the case, there was considerable consistency in the handling of the case—and that consistency sidelined its racial context.

None of the drivers of *Thompson* meant it to be a race or civil rights case, then, but that is what it became. Once the opinion came down, the possible connections were too tempting not to be made by both those defending the racial status quo and those attacking it. One white southerner sent Justice Black a Richmond *Times Dispatch* editorial entitled, "Precedent for Sitdowns?" The editors saw the unusual posture of the case as a statement about race and civil rights. "Were Sam Thompson white, with a police record of similar consistency, his name might never have made headlines." The paper speculated that the Court might have "intended to establish a precedent for the court in considering loitering and disorderly conduct cases arising from 'restaurant sit-downs' or other racial demonstrations."[119]

Jack Greenberg, longtime director-counsel of the NAACP's Legal Defense Fund (LDF), similarly infused the case with civil rights, though from a very different perspective. He later recalled, "As the sit-ins began, the Supreme Court had before it *Thompson v. City of Louisville*, which would affect the sit-in cases considerably—and the Court knew it." According to Greenberg, Justice Tom Clark had mentioned *Thompson* to James Nabrit Jr., a Howard University Law School professor and one of the LDF lawyers who represented the sit-in demonstrators. Clark had apparently said something along the lines of, "That takes care of your sit-in cases."[120]

From what is known today, and Lusky's lore aside, Thompson's life did not change dramatically after his Supreme Court case. He died twelve years later, in Louisville's General Hospital. Thompson donated his body to the University of Louisville Medical School, a decision that implied, despite his vagrant's status and long arrest record, that he still considered himself part of a larger human community.[121]

Thompson v. Louisville is a different matter. It has since lived several lives of its own. Though Lusky did not challenge, and the Court did not invalidate, the Louisville loitering ordinance, *Thompson* offered an alternative way of undermining the vagrancy regime: by closely supervising the local law enforcement apparatus with which the regime was symbiotically related. Moreover, despite Lusky's efforts to the contrary, Lusky helped set in motion the eventual revival of substantive due process. The "two-bit case" educated the Court about not only the power of the police and the workings of police courts but also the basic premises of vagrancy and loitering laws. Finally, as the LDF began representing scores of civil rights demonstrators, Greenberg later remembered, *Thompson* became "basic to the sit-in cases." The lawyers in the LDF and elsewhere would challenge civil rights convictions, sometimes for vagrancy and loitering, by claiming a due process violation due to lack of evidence. They called it "the Shuffling Sam Thompson approach."[122]

4

"For Integration? You're a Vagrant"

In the fall of 1958, three ministers from Montgomery, Alabama, traveled two hours to Birmingham to visit the Reverend Fred Shuttlesworth. Shuttlesworth, Martin Luther King Jr., and others had recently established the Southern Christian Leadership Conference. Shuttlesworth had also launched a new campaign against bus segregation in Birmingham that had left him and thirteen others in jail. King sent the Reverends Solomon S. Seay, Arthur W. Wilson, and Hannibal Hubbard—all of whom had helped spearhead their own city's bus boycott—to Birmingham for support.

Just after the ministers arrived at the Shuttlesworth home and sat down for lunch with Shuttlesworth's wife, Ruby, and some dozen others, two police officers arrived. The officers threatened to arrest the whole group unless the three strangers were identified. Acting on the personal orders of police chief Eugene "Bull" Connor, the officers accused the ministers of lacking "proper identification" and arrested them for vagrancy.

The Alabama vagrancy law listed thirteen types of vagrants, including anyone who "wanders or strolls about in idleness, or lives in idleness, who is able to work, and has no property sufficient for his support"; anyone "leading an idle, immoral, or profligate life," without support and work; loafers, drunkards, gamblers, beggars, prostitutes, traders in stolen goods, and those who do not support their families. Civil rights leaders and ministers were nowhere on the list, and which category purportedly included the three men, the police did not say. The penalties were serious—fines of up to $500 and hard labor of up to a year.[1]

The Birmingham police held the men for five hours. They released the ministers only after lecturing them at length and warning them against "agitating" in Birmingham. "We were treated like any common criminal," Wilson complained. "We were mugged [photographed], fingerprinted, and thrown into a cell with a lot of criminals." In Connor's view, that was what they were. "Those three Negroes . . . admittedly came here to aid in an unlawful boycott. . . . I ordered them arrested and will order anybody else arrested, white or black, who follows their foolish lead."[2]

The arrests were front page news in Atlanta, Washington, and Chicago as well as Birmingham and Montgomery—in white newspapers as well as black ones. What kept the story going was not only the arrests themselves but also the response they provoked. Civil rights and civil liberties organizations protested. They telegrammed state and national leaders to demand action. King—who had himself been arrested on a "trumped up charge" of loitering in Montgomery a month earlier—called the arrests "gestapo-like" and "a new low in the tactics that some southerners are willing to use to maintain the system of segregation." In a telegram to the U.S. attorney general, NAACP executive secretary Roy Wilkins called the arrests "a shocking abuse of police power and a flagrant violation of the ministers' constitutional rights." He noted Connor's "well known" "record of Negro persecution" and described the incident as part of "a reign of terror against Negro citizens" in Birmingham. The Justice Department had already started looking into the matter, but its investigation ultimately foundered on a combination of police stonewalling and judicial recalcitrance in impaneling a grand jury.[3]

The arrests of Seay, Hubbard, and Wilson were both remnants of the past and heralds of the future. As ecumenical as vagrancy laws seemed—offering almost inexhaustible and unreviewable discretion to contain any new problem that might arise—they had long held a special place for American blacks. Government surveillance of African Americans had always been a central aspect of Jim Crow, and vagrancy and loitering laws had always been a central aspect of that surveillance. Moreover, Seay, Hubbard, and Wilson were not just any African Americans. They were civil rights leaders. As such, Alabama officials thought they required not only racial regulation but also political suppression. Recall that vagrancy laws historically justified arrests of the political opposition of any stripe—Wobblies, farmworkers, leftists like Isidore Edelman—and Bull Connor himself had used Alabama's vagrancy law against everyone from communists to 1948 Progressive Party vice presidential candidate Glenn Taylor to irksome reporters. During the ministers' brouhaha, he boasted that Taylor still owed him jail time and a fine. This deeply rooted history of vagrancy regulation of both racial troublemakers and political agitators made it easy for Connor to choose vagrancy charges—as opposed to the many other crimes prohibited by the Alabama code—against the Montgomery ministers who had come to Birmingham.[4]

That choice, and the firestorm of protest that followed, would become a frequent refrain throughout the civil rights struggle. Everything about the incident was more exemplar than outlier: from Connor's view that the laws covered civil rights leaders to civil rights leaders' views that that coverage was illegitimate; from the lawyers' strategies to the prominent press coverage to the DOJ's failed investigation. Though southern law enforcement officials had, and used, myriad legal and extralegal resources to respond to the civil rights challenge, they regularly and routinely turned to vagrancy and loitering laws. They did so for similar reasons law enforcement officers everywhere did: the laws required little to no criminal conduct and no criminal intent; they rarely occasioned meaningful judicial oversight; and they had been used for so many purposes for so long that they just seemed more available than other laws. Southern officials accordingly turned vagrancy and loitering laws against leaders and rank-and-file demonstrators; against outsiders and locals; in public and in private; when the laws fit and when they did not. When police officers used the laws, movement targets and civil rights leaders publicly condemned the arrests at rallies, on speaking tours, in newspapers, and to the federal government.

The escalation of the civil rights struggle simultaneously clarified and publicized the illegitimacy of vagrancy enforcement. Revelations of this repressive use of vagrancy laws made undeniable what many African Americans had known for at least a century: that toppling Jim Crow required challenging not only segregation and inequality but also the laws that police used to defend and maintain the system. Vagrancy and loitering laws were not alone in buttressing that system, but the very public conflicts over the vagrancy arrests of movement actors made clear that buttressing it they were. Vagrancy law enforcement was not limited to vagrants like Sam Thompson or the stray radical like Isidor Edelman. The visibility of the laws' role in supporting Jim Crow and suppressing racial dissent revealed a vastly more extensive apparatus than many Americans had previously perceived.

If official use and civil rights protests of vagrancy arrests raised awareness of the extent of the vagrancy law regime, legal challenges generated new resources against it. As a growing army of lawyers went about defending movement activists, they saw the workings of vagrancy laws up close, and even in some instances experienced their power firsthand. Civil rights lawyers became foot soldiers in the fight against vagrancy laws, not necessarily for the laws' own sake but because of their deployment against the movement.

Never before had so many lawyers brought so many resources to bear on the vagrancy law problem. Though no avalanche of judicial invalidations followed immediately on the heels of civil rights vagrancy enforcement, movement-related lawyers propelled the challenge forward in two ways. First, the institutional realities of southern justice—dominated by whites, by people often intent on, or at least acquiescent in, maintaining Jim Crow—added a racial dimension to the charge that it was not only vague laws that made vagrancy regulation and repression possible, but also unconstrained police power and rigged judicial procedures. As lawyers moved from defending protestors in state and local courts to affirmatively suing police and other officials for declaratory judgments and injunctions in federal courts, they created new procedural mechanisms for use in future vagrancy cases. Second, lawyers defending civil rights clients against vagrancy and loitering charges began to think systematically about the constitutional problems with such laws. Their conclusions would define the contours of vagrancy law challenges far beyond the Jim Crow South.

Vagrancy Regulation as Racial Regulation

Race, racial identity, and a racialized sense of who was out of place had been part of vagrancy and related laws from their English origins. At times, vagrancy laws explicitly targeted certain groups. At other times, the laws were used, though not written, so as to target them. At various moments, the Irish, whom the English accused of loose morals, popery, and filth, and the Roma, then called gypsies or "Egyptians," who were itinerant and masterless, each came in for special attention. Many of the specific behaviors in the English vagrancy statutes, like prohibitions on "palmistry," originated in concerns about the Roma.[5]

In the New World as the old, colonies, and then states and localities, targeted religious and racial outliers. The Massachusetts Bay Colony enacted a special vagrancy law applicable only to Quakers in 1658, and the town of Salem excluded Indians after dark. Many states aggressively passed vagrancy laws regulating the whereabouts, livelihoods, and lives of their minority residents over the following centuries. So-called sundown towns excluded minorities not only with vagrancy laws but also with signs that read "Whites Only within City Limits after Dark," and "Nigger, Don't let the Sun Set ON YOU in ____." In the West and Southwest, Latinos, Chinese Americans, Japanese Americans, and Native Americans were targets; in Hawai'i, native Hawaiians and later Japanese Americans. (Through most of the twentieth century, "every person who practice[d] hoopiopio, hoounauna, hoomanamana, anaana or pretend[ed] to have the power of praying persons to death" was a "vagrant" in Hawai'i.)[6]

It was the South's treatment of African Americans that most deeply embedded vagrancy law within a system of racial subordination. In the South before 1865, slavery both regulated the mobility of most African Americans and privatized their support. Free, rather than enslaved, African Americans bore much of the brunt of vagrancy laws in the antebellum era. The free black was not only a potential ally for revolting or escaping slaves but also an oxymoron, a conceptual impossibility. Though slavery was far more porous in practice than in theory, it depended on the presumed equation of racial status with slave status. As a result, slave states placed restrictions on emancipated slaves remaining within the state, barred entry to free blacks from other states, and imposed penalties on those bringing free blacks into the state. Southern vagrancy laws often targeted only free blacks or imposed harsher punishments on them than on whites. In the

North, vagrancy laws supported localities that removed, "warned out," or denied
fiscal responsibility for blacks—and especially women of color—in disproportionate numbers. Other places kept a close eye on free blacks, whom they likened to "vagrants, . . . common prostitutes and other persons likely to become
chargeable," and some banned the entry of free blacks altogether.[7]

With the end of slavery, southern whites turned even more aggressively to
vagrancy laws as racial regulation. Even before the Civil War ended, union military officials put African American escaped slaves and war refugees back to work
in union areas under threat of vagrancy arrests. At war's end, the vagrancy laws
included in the so-called Black Codes of the South served at least two functions.
First, they regulated African American morality and social interactions with
whites. Among those whom the Mississippi vagrancy law classified as vagrants
were whites who associated with African Americans "on terms of equality" or
had sexual relations with them. Second, vagrancy laws, among others, were used
to return black Americans to a state as close to slavery as legally and practicably
possible.[8]

Northern criticism of the Black Codes emphasized these "odious vagrant
law[s]," as the *New York Times* called them. In part, such opprobrium stemmed
from the fact that all but North Carolina's new laws authorized the hiring out of
vagrancy convicts. Work as the remedy for idleness had become a central tenet
of penology before the war, and numerous colonies and states had set vagrants
to work. In the postbellum context, though, such provisions took on a new
and more ominous meaning. Selling the labor of newly freed slaves to private
employers smacked of slavery. Mississippi, for example, auctioned off vagrants
"at public outcry, to any white person."[9]

With the beginning of military reconstruction and the passage of federal legislation prohibiting explicit discrimination in 1866, southern states rewrote their
vagrancy laws in race-neutral terms. But race neutrality went only so far. Some
vagrancy laws applied only to counties with a majority black population. Most
were used predominantly against blacks. From citizen patrol to sheriff to jury to
judge, the whites who enforced vagrancy laws knew they were aimed at African
Americans. In a pattern that would continue into the civil rights era, officials
often used the laws most aggressively against African Americans who asserted
themselves. When thousands of blacks moved from Mississippi to Kansas in
1879, for example, the leaders of the exodus were arrested for vagrancy.[10]

Into the twentieth century, states and localities used vagrancy laws against
African Americans. As the system that came to be known as Jim Crow took
hold in the South, it became something of a regional pastime to enact vagrancy
laws with new provisions and stricter penalties. In part, such laws were intended
to keep African Americans in economic place—to thwart efforts to move out
of back-breaking and poorly paid agricultural work. The Atlanta *Constitution*

admonished the police, "Cotton is ripening. See that the 'vags' get busy." During one week in 1913, a cleanup of Birmingham's saloons resulted in some two hundred vagrancy arrests—almost entirely of African Americans—and city officials endorsed the slogan, "Go to work or go to jail." Even during World War II, officials continued to use vagrancy arrests to try to tether increasingly mobile African Americans to the agricultural workforce.[11]

Vagrancy laws also proved useful in keeping whites and minorities in prescribed social and cultural places. That meant apart, with whites on top. It was vagrancy for which an interracial couple was convicted in Denver in 1942 on the grounds that a state anti-miscegenation law made their relationship per se immoral. It was vagrancy and loitering that ensnared white women in black bars, or any whites in a black neighborhood, on the assumption that they were there only to engage in gambling, prostitution, or other vices. It was vagrancy and loitering that the police turned to when African Americans were found in white neighborhoods. That was the beauty of such laws—they were as flexible as necessary. Whether African Americans tried to challenge their prescribed place by moving farms, changing jobs, frequenting public places, or choosing sex partners, vagrancy charges seemed always an option.[12]

The rash of vagrancy laws passed in the early twentieth-century South remained largely unchanged into the post–World War II era. The context in which the laws operated, however, changed dramatically in the 1950s and 1960s. As long as many whites had tried to dominate African Americans, many African Americans had resisted. They used sabotage and foot-dragging; they escaped and revolted. As free people, they moved—North and West, or to the next farm over—to find better conditions, land worth owning, terms just a bit fairer. They organized to vote when they could, and they ran for office in the high times of Reconstruction. They married and kept families together. They joined churches, collected and disbursed money, and formed burial societies, self-help organizations, and women's clubs. They wrote letters to presidents, government agencies, and private organizations to ask for help. Though strategies changed across time and place, African Americans were always in struggle, and that struggle required whites interested in dominance always to struggle back.[13]

Black hopes rose during the 1930s, as President Franklin D. Roosevelt promised (partly hollowly, it turned out) more federal assistance than Washington had offered African Americans since the end of Reconstruction. World War II was even more revolutionary for black aspirations. African Americans entered the military, migrated for war-industry jobs, and joined unions, organizations like the NAACP, and political parties. They began voting Democratic in such numbers that they changed the party's entire political calculus by 1948. Even before the Supreme Court announced in *Brown v. Board of Education* that public school segregation violated the United States Constitution, boycotts, protests, and sit-ins began erupting sporadically across the country.

By the early 1960s, African American challenges to the status quo had escalated by several orders of magnitude. Within months of the first sit-ins in February 1960, an estimated 70,000 people had participated in demonstrations against segregation and discrimination. By March of 1961, the Congress of Racial Equality announced that 138 communities—mostly in the upper and middle South—had already integrated some of their facilities.[14]

In many places, however, especially in the Deep South, most whites met the civil rights challenge as they had long met African American resistance—with resistance of their own. When the battle moved from the courts and the schools into new arenas—streets, restaurants, and public buildings—many white southerners upped their game in the fight to retain Jim Crow, to retain the separation they understood as God-given, or economically expedient, or politically necessary. Some private white citizens took upon themselves the burden of maintaining their way of life. They harassed, beat, bombed, lynched, and murdered blacks and their white allies. They fired black employees, evicted black tenants, and revoked the professional licenses of those who pressed for change. Though the murders of civil rights workers James Chaney, Andrew Goodman, and Michael Schwerner in Philadelphia, Mississippi, represented the most famous incident of the summer of 1964, during that single season in that single state there were 1,000 arrests, 35 shootings, 30 bombings, 35 burned churches, 80 beatings, and at least 6 related murders.[15]

State and local officials sometimes took part in such violence. Even when they did not, they were often equally hostile. In response to the movement, state officials used police dogs, high-velocity water spray, and tear gas. They also relied on law. Those who engaged in marches, parades, sit-ins, stand-ins, swim-ins, read-ins, pray-ins, and lay-ins often violated one law or another. Even when they did not, arrests still followed. An Amnesty International Report estimated that officials arrested 20,000 people for civil rights activities in 1963 alone. Depending on the specifics of the situation, officers could and did use a multitude of laws already on the law books: vagrancy and loitering laws; disorderly conduct, breach of the peace, and disturbing the peace; parading without a permit, obstructing traffic, leafleting, and littering; criminal trespass and attempting to destroy state property; refusing to move on and failing to follow the command of a police officer. At times, the police moved slightly further afield to drunkenness, auto theft, shoplifting, or illegal possession of alcohol, and "the most imaginative variety of nonexistent traffic violations," as one observer put it. They even brought felony charges—invoking incitement to riot, conspiracy, and insurrection. Southern officials proved endlessly creative and entrepreneurial: officers in Mississippi arrested students who brought food and supplies to African Americans denied public assistance because of their support for civil rights. The charge was bringing narcotics—aspirin—across state lines.[16]

Even with the statute books chock full of arrest options for the vigilant and imaginative white official, states and localities responded much the same way the North Dakota mining towns had reacted to the Wobblies decades earlier: by passing tailor-made new laws. The prospect of 1,000 "invad[ing]" volunteers in the summer of 1964 prompted Mississippi to pass sixteen new laws, authorize local curfews, make it easier to transfer prisoners to the state prison farm at Parchman, and make it harder for out-of-state lawyers to practice law. Officials were taking no chances: according to press reports, they acquired "armored cars, manned with machine guns," and they compiled and distributed to sheriffs and police officers a list of laws that might be useful against civil rights workers.[17]

The array of possibilities for arresting activists and participants was dizzying. Some cities, like Atlanta, routinely used disorderly conduct, trespass, incitement to riot and insurrection, and breach of the peace laws. Other places, like Louisville, used loitering and disorderly conduct. The choice often depended on the particular legal cocktail available in a particular place. It also depended on context: police often invoked similar types of laws in similar circumstances. They arrested sit-in demonstrators on private property for trespass; where the nature of the property might be disputed, they would use disorderly conduct or breach of the peace; where marches or demonstrations on public streets were the problem, loitering and obstructing free passage were quite likely. There was sometimes a logical link between particular conduct and particular charges.[18]

Often, however, as for the skid row peacekeepers Egon Bittner described, the charging choice was underdetermined. The police first decided to arrest and only later decided the charge. There was much play in the joints of the law, much room for improvisation. In one trial, a defendant testified that he heard one officer ask another as he was being arrested, "What are you going to book him on?"[19]

Southern officials routinely and repeatedly answered that question with "vagrancy" or "loitering" or both. The passage of time has made it difficult to tease out exactly where or how often officials turned to vagrancy and loitering laws to suppress civil rights activity. Newspaper reports at the time and subsequent histories often reported movement arrests without saying what they were for. What for was always obvious: for challenging segregation, discrimination, and inequality. What for did not necessarily require an answer that cited a state law or a city ordinance. Though published opinions necessarily attended to such legal niceties, they often omitted the kind of information that would alert one to the civil rights context. Then there were all those arrests that never became prosecutions, and all those prosecutions that were never appealed, and all those appealed cases that were never published. It is thus difficult to say with certainty how often civil rights activists faced vagrancy and loitering charges.[20]

What is abundantly clear, however, is that southern officials did use vagrancy and loitering laws, both on their own and as entrées to more serious charges. Though officials sometimes seemed to link loitering more closely with public protests—where demonstrators were arguably idling about—they often viewed vagrancy and loitering charges as overlapping and interchangeable. More important, they viewed them as freely available and especially usable in the civil rights context, and they did not hesitate to say so. As Bull Connor put it in 1958: "We don't give a damn about the law. Down here we make our own law. . . . I had [the Montgomery ministers] picked up on a charge of vagrancy until we could find out what they were doing here. We're not going to have outsiders coming in and stirring up trouble. If they come here and do the wrong kind of talking, they'll see the inside of our jail."[21]

Other officials agreed. Just a few weeks before the ministers' Birmingham arrests, the Arkansas attorney general announced his plan to use vagrancy and inciting-to-riot laws against civil rights activists. One Georgia sheriff threatened workers for the Student Nonviolent Coordinating Committee (SNCC) that he would "get [them] for vagrancy or loitering." Another cavalierly answered the question of what charge justified his holding of civil rights workers in 1962, "Investigation, vagrancy, and all that crap."[22]

As such statements imply, the police did not always give much thought to the actual terms of the vagrancy or loitering laws. The laws were attractive precisely because their terms seemed rather forgiving, perhaps even optional, along several dimensions. In both Birmingham and elsewhere, officials made vagrancy arrests in private homes or other private spaces. In New Orleans in 1961, for example, police entered the home of a local African American without a knock or a warrant and arrested three white freedom riders for vagrancy. An even more prominent mismatch between the laws and the arrests involved the common requirement that vagrants and loiterers lack "visible means of support" or a "livelihood." Officers often ignored the pay stubs, letters of support from parents, employment contracts, and money that vagrancy suspects proffered.[23]

Take Hattiesburg, Mississippi. Sandra Adickes and William Jones, both New York City schoolteachers, spent part of the summer of 1964 at a Freedom School there working for the Council of Federated Organizations (COFO), a coalition of the state's major civil rights groups. Adickes and her students tried unsuccessfully to integrate the white library after passage of the Civil Rights Act of 1964—which mandated desegregation of such public facilities. Afterwards, they headed for lunch at S. H. Kress & Co. Adickes had heard that the store was willing to serve African Americans at its lunch counter and restaurant booths. She had heard partially right. The waitress told Adickes when refusing service,

"We have to serve the colored, but we're not serving white people who come in with them." As the still-hungry group left the store, a police car pulled up, and a police sergeant approached Adickes. She would later testify that he "put his hand around my arm and said, 'You're under arrest.' I asked on what charge. He said, '[V]agrancy.'" As she was booked at the police station, Adickes informed the officers that she was on her summer vacation from her $7,200-a-year teaching job. She "showed them that I had $20.08 in cash . . . , thirty dollars in travelers checks and a checkbook showing a balance of over $45.00 at the First National Bank of Hattiesburg." When Jones, Adickes's African American colleague, continued the library sit-in a few days later, the police again turned to vagrancy. When the police chief told Jones, "I am going to arrest you on vagrancy," Jones later testified, "I laughed, and he said, 'It's funny to you, isn't it?' and I answered, 'Yes, very funny. . . . Just how can you charge me with vagrancy when I am employed?'" [24]

That was not a question that bothered the police. Within the terms of the Hattiesburg vagrancy law—which made a vagrant of anyone "habitually loafing and loitering on the streets and avenues and in the public places of said City of Hattiesburg the greater portion of [his or her] time without regular employment or any visible means of support," Jones and Adickes were no vagrants. But as the arresting officer kept repeating to Adickes, he did not actually know why vagrancy was the charge. He just had "orders to pick [her] up." Either he or someone else thought that vagrancy was the way to do that. Even with the mismatch between the terms of the vagrancy law and the facts, such arrests seemed somehow more plausible, more defensible, more available, and more insulting than an arrest for, say, embezzlement. Or robbery.[25]

As local judges adjudicated such charges, they sometimes declined to follow the lead of the police. But many echoed the relatively cavalier attitude of law enforcement officers. A judge in Albany, Georgia, was unconvinced by a lack of vagrancy evidence for a group of northern and midwestern white women working for SNCC. Their lawyer, local civil rights legend-in-the-making Chevene Bowers "C. B." King, had a long history with vagrancy laws. King (no relation to Martin Luther Jr.) was "stocky, about six feet one inch tall, of a medium brown color with short curly hair, full features, . . . a mustache[,] . . . a deep, booming voice and . . . a precise, clipped manner" of speaking. King grew up poor in Albany, served in the Navy, and then attended Tuskegee Institute, Fisk University, and Case Western University Law School. He recalled in an interview that when a police officer came upon him and his friends playing in a playground when he was ten years old, "All of us little colored boys ran like chickens. . . . I hid under a building but some of the kids were arrested for 'vagrancy' or 'loitering.' Right then I felt that there was something wrong with the way the law operated in the Negro community. It was the symbol of the kind of force which I couldn't reconcile with what was right." [26]

In defending the SNCC workers against the same charges, King presented evidence that the women had told the arresting officers that they were employed by and received wages from SNCC and also received support from their parents. Several of the defendants' fathers backed up this claim by traveling to Georgia to attend their daughters' trials. With the middle-class fathers in the courtroom, the judge concluded that the women "were obviously nice girls from upstanding homes." He declared them vagrants anyway.[27]

The frequent disregard for evidence of vagrancy that would stand up in court suggests that officials were not always all that interested in courts, convictions, or judicially imposed punishments. The Birmingham police tactic of arresting the Montgomery ministers, holding them incommunicado for hours, and then releasing them repeated itself across the South in the 1960s. So did the use of inordinately high bail, meant either to incapacitate the activists indefinitely or to cripple the movement financially. As was the case with mobsters, political radicals, Beats, and skid row vagrants, when police only threatened arrests, or arrested folks but then dropped the charges, convictions were clearly not the goal.[28]

The goals of vagrancy arrests, rather, were to expel outsiders and thwart the movement. Law enforcement officers used the laws to rid their cities and towns of "invaders," "intruders," or "carpetbaggers"; "professional agitators," "trouble makers," "meddlers," "ideological manipulators," and "propagandists"; "civil rightsers," "communists," "left-wing agitators," "racial zealots," and "integrationists." The case of the white women working for SNCC in Albany, Georgia, is again illustrative. The judge suspended their sentences of probation on the condition that "they should go back home and not be with these bad associates in Albany." The next day, Charles Oldfather—father of one of the defendants and a "proper midwestern law professor"—tried to give another father-daughter pair a ride to the airport for their flight home. The police pulled Oldfather over for "driving with a defective muffler," searched him, cuffed his hands behind his back, and took him to the county jail, where he was informed that he would not be charged if he and his daughter left town. All four left immediately.[29]

Similar incidents occurred across the South. Officials echoed what Bull Connor told reporters in 1958: that Birmingham "does not need any outside agitators coming into our city and dabbling in our affairs." Others said: "If you come back to Smithville we'll have to arrest you for vagrancy." "I guess you'd better leave town now. You can leave town or take thirty days in jail." Sometimes, the activists rejected exit options and forced authorities to arrest them. Other times, the choice was a false one. When a Freedom Rider was released from the hospital in Birmingham in 1961—local Klansmen had been beaten him to a pulp—a patrolman threatened a vagrancy arrest if he "didn't get off the street." When the activist then tried to return to the safety of the hospital, a guard told him that "discharged patients were not permitted in the hospital."[30]

Vagrancy and loitering arrests were useful not only for expulsion but for disrupting protests and impeding organizing. Officers threatened and arrested movement activists with vagrancy or loitering arrests when they sat in at lunch counters and soda fountains, when they participated in boycotts and tried to integrate swimming pools, when they sold movement newspapers, when they canvassed black neighborhoods or college campuses, when they attempted to register to vote or to assist would-be voters, or even when they just walked down the street. As Dennis Roberts, a white Boalt Hall law student at Berkeley who served as C. B. King's first summer intern, put it, "It is obvious that the police intend to arrest every worker in [Albany] on any charge they can dream up when they see them." The arrests of twenty SNCC workers, most for vagrancy, crippled the remaining six—they took refuge for eight days in a church to avoid arrest and violence.[31]

What galled many local officials was not only that civil rights activists were demonstrating to change the status quo. It was also that they purported to live an alternative racial and cultural reality. The activists were too countercultural—some were called "lazy hippies," "CORE creeps," "weirdos," "beatnik sophomores," and a "flea-bitten crowd of white screwballs"—and too familiar with members of the other race. According to King and his female clients, the police called the Albany SNCC women "bleached n***s" and "Nigger sluts." One testified that when she asked her arresting officers why she looked suspicious, they replied that "any white girl in shorts, sleeveless sweater and open-toed shoes working in an all negro section of town was considered suspicious." White male activists also transgressed cultural norms by wearing T-shirts, blue jeans, and sneakers, and walking down public streets with black women. Explained one Louisiana police chief, "When you go in there in a mixed group, you are going to be arrested."[32]

As southern officials deployed vagrancy and loitering laws against the movement, African Americans and their white allies publicly, vehemently, and repeatedly charged that such arrests were fundamentally illegitimate bulwarks of Jim Crow. Activists and both the black and white press frequently referred to "fraudulent," "trumped-up," and "phony" vagrancy and loitering charges and those arrested as "so-called vagrants." The *Baltimore Afro-American* put it well in the title of one article: "For Integration? You're a Vagrant."[33]

The vagrancy threat to civil rights workers was so ubiquitous that it figured prominently in the training that civil rights organizations provided their non-southern staff and volunteers before they traveled south. In addition to advising workers to follow "strictly Puritan rules" like "no drinking, no smoking in public, no going bare foot, no wearing long hair down," and no going out with "any group that could possibly be construed as interracial dating," many organizations expected their volunteers to provide $500 in advance to pay for bail and other costs. Len Holt, an African American movement lawyer who worked with the Congress of Racial Equality (CORE) and the National Lawyers Guild, warned aspiring Freedom Riders: "You have no rights on this trip. You are a vagrant, an agitator—whatever they choose to call you. . . . This is Mississippi. You have no rights, nor does your lawyer have any rights."[34]

COFO issued special "vagrancy forms" that they hoped would shield their workers from arrest. When Jan Hillegas, a twenty-one-year-old white college graduate from Syracuse, New York, was arrested for vagrancy in Lowndes County, Mississippi, just after Christmas 1964, she and her companions each had a vagrancy form. It contained their names, physical descriptions, an assurance that COFO would provide board, lodging, salary, and necessaries to "maintain [them] as a reputable member of the community in Mississippi," the address of COFO's Jackson headquarters, and contact information for further questions. The forms, the money the workers had on them (ranging from $2 to $30), and evidence of parental support (including a telegram from Hillegas's mother) convinced neither the arresting officer nor the county attorney that vagrancy charges were inappropriate.[35]

When vagrancy arrests persisted despite these precautions, their targets articulated a deep sense of injury, a heightened sense of their own rights, and a vehement sense of outrage. Both the Montgomery ministers arrested in Birmingham in 1958 and Sandra Adickes arrested in Hattiesburg in 1964 lodged similar complaints: that they had been treated as a "common criminal." For African American professionals like the ministers, the vagrancy label was a class slur, a denigration of respectability as well as a criminal charge. For somewhat different reasons—having more to do with sexual purity than class position—the vagrancy convictions of the women working for SNCC in Albany, attorney King concluded, "would be defamation of character." As Isidor Edelman had made clear years earlier, vagrancy was not only a crime and a status; it was also an epithet.[36]

For others, the harm of the vagrancy arrest was less to their character than their rights. A frequent refrain of leaders from SNCC to SCLC to the National Urban League was that vagrancy arrests constituted, as one arrestee put it, a "violation of my civil rights." Such arrests were antithetical to the way "citizens" should be treated. Shortly after Alabama State College expelled Bernard Lee for leading a sitdown movement there, Lee was arrested for vagrancy. Though he had been active in the movement prior to his arrest, he reflected publicly that the vagrancy charge gave him an additional "will to fight. A desire for change."[37]

For white civil rights allies who were unaccustomed to the uses and abuses of vagrancy and loitering laws, seeing such arrests firsthand was revelatory. Charles Oldfather, the midwestern law professor and father of a SNCC worker, wrote in the *Harvard Law Record*, the magazine of his alma mater, " 'Vagrancy' in Albany, Georgia, consists of being white girls in the open company of Negroes." For him and his daughter, Patricia, "the rules were different. . . . [I]n the eyes of the rulers of Albany, we were at best Negroes, and, as we all know, the rules are different for Negroes." Boalt law student Dennis Roberts reflected at the end of his summer in Albany: "Things you never think about, just ordinary action such as walking down a street, takes on a whole new perspective. You have to wonder if you will be arrested for vagrancy or loitering." Roberts experienced the essence of the vagrancy threat in a way unusual for straight, educated white men. "It is very hard to verbalize the feeling of never being . . . sure that you are safe. . . . For the first time, the Constitution becomes immensely important and real to me: First Amendment guarantees that we constantly take for granted are here denied to the people, and you realize how vital and alive this document is and how unbelievable [sic] bad this country would be without it."[38]

The perceived outrageousness and illegitimacy of vagrancy arrests created focal points for protests and fundraising within the civil rights movement. One of the most prominent incidents began one Saturday in early 1962, when African American SNCC chairman Chuck McDew and Bob Zellner, SNCC's first white field secretary, stopped in Baton Rouge to check on Dion Diamond, a black field worker who had been imprisoned after leading student demonstrations at Southern University. Diamond was being held on $7,000 bail for trespassing, vagrancy, and disorderly conduct. When McDew and Zellner asked to visit Diamond, they were told that they would have to wait almost a week for "Colored day." Officials then arrested the two men for vagrancy despite their joint possession of over $100 and eventually charged them with criminal anarchy.[39]

The civil rights community swung into action, in part due to the severity and incongruity of the criminal anarchy charges. Because the original vagrancy arrests were a key part of the story that got told and retold as groups around the country mobilized, however, the uses of vagrancy laws to suppress civil rights activity became more visible to more people. In Columbus, Ohio, CORE held a round-the-clock vigil outside the state capitol. Comedian Dick Gregory protested the arrests at a New York rally. The Brotherhood of Sleeping Car Porters, CORE, the NAACP, and the National Urban League sent a flurry of telegrams to supporters noting the inapplicability of a vagrancy charge to men with over $100 and urging them to attend the men's hearing. The story of the Zellner and McDew vagrancy arrests and felony prosecution also figured prominently in testimony Eleanor Roosevelt and Norman Thomas heard during "a celebrity-studded" CORE panel on southern justice.[40]

The Baton Rouge incident was hardly the only one that led to publicity and protest. Indeed, multiple organizations concluded that tales of vagrancy arrests and their consequences made for excellent fundraising fodder in the North. The Committee to Defend Martin Luther King and the Struggle for Freedom, which included Nat King Cole, Harry Belafonte, Sidney Poitier, Shelley Winters, and A. Philip Randolph, sponsored a speaking tour on college campuses, at union meetings, and in churches for Bernard Lee, arrested for vagrancy after his expulsion from Alabama State College. Joni Rabinowitz, one of the white Albany SNCC workers and the daughter of a prominent civil rights lawyer, told her story of vagrancy arrest and imprisonment to multiple audiences in the New York area.[41]

Many of these denunciations included calls for federal action that foundered on local recalcitrance or federal reluctance. The FBI's investigation into the Birmingham arrests at the insistence of civil rights leaders initiated a periodic ritual of vagrancy arrest, movement condemnation, and failed federal intervention. CORE director James Farmer asked Attorney General Robert F. Kennedy to assist CORE members arrested for vagrancy. SNCC wired the Department of Justice to intervene on behalf of its members. In incident after incident, the FBI investigated whether the vagrancy arrests involved the violation of "civil liberties." When the Federal Civil Rights Commission planned an investigation of discrimination in the operations of criminal justice, it deemed vagrancy among its priorities.[42]

All of this protest, organization, and denunciation made the repressive use of vagrancy and loitering laws visible to an increasingly broad audience. The black press consistently reported on civil rights vagrancy and loitering arrests, often—at least fifty times—on the front page and always in harsh and condemnatory tones. Newspapers published prominent profiles of Bernard Lee and Charles McDew discussing their vagrancy arrests and confinement. Headlines, editorials, and articles referred to vagrancy arrests as a "reign of terror" and "a new low" for the "respect for the legal rights of Negro citizens." They stressed the "perverted justice" of such arrests and the notable and "unusual arrests" of ministers, students, CORE members, and "vote advocates" as vagrants. Papers asked, "What kind of justice is it that permits a Texas judge to levy a $400 fine on a white Baptist minister as a 'vagrant' for saying that he believed segregation violates God's ordinance?" They wondered whether vagrancy-wielding officials would "get away with" requiring defendants "to post shockingly high bail for a nonexistent offense." They criticized one city's police for making "no explanation as to why it took two days [of holding suspects for 'investigation'] to discover that those attending a church meeting were vagrants."[43]

Such denunciations were more frequent in the black press, but they appeared in white newspapers as well. The *New York Times* described how the Albany vagrancy ordinance was not only "frequently" used against SNCC, but how the judge "lashed out at . . . 'outside meddlers,'" and the police chief and his officers made racist and anti-Semitic comments. From the *Atlanta Daily World* and the *Chicago Daily Defender* to the *New York Times*, the *Washington Post*, and the *Harvard Law Record*, an increasingly wide swath of opinion leaders condemned the deployment of vagrancy and loitering laws to maintain white supremacy.[44]

An Accidental Army of Vagrancy Lawyers in the 1960s South

Vagrancy arrests of civil rights activists thus led to denunciations, rallies, investigations, and headlines that heightened public awareness. They also led to hearings, trials, and lawsuits that helped create new legal mechanisms for defending the movement and new legal arguments against vagrancy laws.

The very existence of lawyers willing to take civil rights cases was unprecedented in the 1960s. Within the South, the number of such lawyers was minuscule. Mississippi boasted four African American lawyers and 2,100 white ones, with almost all of the latter either staunchly opposed to defending civil rights protesters or fearing the consequences of doing so. Other southern bars were similarly, if not quite as starkly, situated. Before the late 1950s and early 1960s, the few sympathetic southern lawyers often cooperated with and received support from the NAACP and the NAACP Legal Defense Fund (LDF), which also fielded their own small groups of civil rights lawyers. A few other institutions—including the black National Bar Association (NBA), the Civil Rights Section and later Civil Rights Division of the United States Department of Justice, and the left-leaning National Lawyers' Guild (NLG)—also sometimes launched or supported civil rights challenges before the 1950s and 1960s. In contrast to the often massive state investment in defending Jim Crow, however, the number of lawyers willing and able to defend civil rights activists as thousands were arrested was tiny. Without additional legal support, the civil rights movement would quickly founder.[45]

After initial hesitation about the tactics—especially the civil disobedience— of the younger and more assertive generation of activists after 1960, the established, if small, civil rights bar organized to defend those arrested. Within a few years, a whole slew of organizations began hiring lawyers, establishing southern field offices, and serving as clearing houses for non-southern lawyers who volunteered across the region. Organizations ranged from the red-tinged NLG to the "establishment" Lawyers' Committee for Civil Rights under Law to the liberal standard-bearers of the NBA, the Law Students Civil Rights Research Council, and the Lawyers' Constitutional Defense Committee (LCDC)—spearheaded by the ACLU, CORE, the American Jewish Congress, the American Jewish Committee, the NAACP, and the LDF. Under the auspices of these many organizations, lawyers flew south or drove; stayed for a week or a month or several years; looked like "beatniks" or businessmen. They cooperated and squabbled. Despite their many differences, the lawyers shared social and professional networks, and they often collaborated on legal strategies and arguments. Like civil liberties and labor lawyers in 1930s California, these lawyers too faced beatings, as well as bombings, arrests, threats to their law licenses, and harassment at every turn.[46]

The existence of such an army of lawyers changed not only the civil rights conflict itself but also the face of legal challenges to the vagrancy regulation of race. If there had been relatively few resources for civil rights litigation in the South before 1960, the problem had been even more pronounced when it came to vagrancy arrests of African Americans. During the century after the Civil War, southern vagrancy prosecutions of African Americans faced few challenges of doctrinal note. African Americans resisted vagrancy enforcement—they attempted to evade arrest and defend themselves, they procured dismissals or acquittals, they worked off fines, and they served time as quickly as they could. A few managed to find a way to pay for legal representation or received it free of charge. But judicial opinions reveal almost none who succeeded in overturning their convictions, let alone the laws that justified those convictions. As late as the 1950s, published opinions addressing racially inflected vagrancy or loitering cases were a rarity. To the extent that courts were increasingly skeptical of vagrancy and loitering laws prior to the late 1950s, their skepticism emerged in cases almost entirely devoid of the role such laws played in the Jim Crow South.[47]

By the early 1960s, the new army of civil rights lawyers took up the legal defense of southern civil rights activists arrested on vagrancy charges. Though vagrancy and loitering laws were hardly the only, or even the central, targets of this army of lawyers, the fact that they were targets at all was transformative. Never before had so many lawyers experienced the deployment of such laws at such close range. Never before had so many lawyers spent so many hours thinking about the system that facilitated such arrests and the constitutional problems they posed.[48]

When Bull Connor's officers arrested Shuttlesworth's Montgomery associates in 1958, it was clear to almost everyone that Connor, as much as the Alabama vagrancy law, was a major part of the problem. Whatever effort it may have taken for lawyers like Ernest Besig, Caleb Foote, and Louis Lusky to discern the close relationship between vagrancy and loitering laws and the criminal justice processes that reinforced them in places like San Francisco, Philadelphia, and Louisville, no such effort was necessary in the Deep South.

Civil rights lawyers articulated a new gloss on the old insight about the relationship between laws and legal procedures. The laws were not only vague; many originated in discrimination. The police were not only powerful; they were almost entirely white, and they were largely devoted to upholding Jim Crow. The justice system did not uniformly deny due process; it was often rigged to the detriment of African Americans and their white allies. Recognition that, as one sympathetic federal judge put it in 1961, southern states were "marshall[ing] the full force of [their] criminal law to enforce [their] social philosophy through the policeman's club" was not especially novel by the 1960s. Police surveillance and brutality had always been a key part of Jim Crow and a frequent cause for African American grievances. As early as the 1930s, some of the racial injustices of the southern justice system had been apparent even to the rather distant Supreme Court.[49]

In the early 1960s, the constant friction of Jim Crow challenge and criminal justice reprisal made the relationship between the police, the courts, and African Americans an increasingly important part of civil rights protests. Many protests began with challenges to segregation and inequality. But many transformed into challenges to the very power of the police to arrest. After arrests at lunch counters, the locus of protest would shift to the courthouse, mayor's office, or police station. These protests then led to their own vagrancy or loitering arrests. An NAACP report in the spring of 1960 noted that although the movement had begun as a conflict between white and black citizens, the government's defense of segregation meant that the issue was "no longer between citizens, but has become a struggle between Negro citizens and state power." A sympathetic federal judge noted the criminal justice backstop to segregation in a case about the Jackson, Mississippi, bus station. The signs over station waiting rooms announcing which were for whites and which for "colored," added ominously, "By Order Police Department." To the judge, this meant that the "police add muscle, bone, and sinew to the signs."[50]

As civil rights lawyers were flooded with evidence of the systematic use of state and local criminal justice institutions to maintain and defend Jim Crow, they repeatedly noted the "totalitarian" nature of the system. For NAACP LDF lawyer Anthony Amsterdam, the detention of hundreds of demonstrators in Jackson, Mississippi, in 1965 at the state fairgrounds—which the National Council of Churches described as a "concentration camp" meant to "break the spirit, the will, the health and even the body of each individual"—was revelatory. The movement in the Deep South was "a war between the demonstrators on the one hand to clear an adequate space so they could demonstrate and the authorities who kept inventing new procedures and new laws and new concentration camps . . . to house them."[51]

Other lawyers put the same observation in different terms. Len Holt catalogued many of the complaints: "arrest without sworn warrants, search of attorney papers, armed atmosphere, no particulars, denial of jury trial, invalidity of the injunction, suspension of the rules of evidence, prejudgment of the cases, denial of the right to appeal by reason of the right to bail, and other diverse complaints." The overall effect, another lawyer concluded, was that "the state's legal process [had] become a sham, used not to grapple with tenacious questions of fact and law, guilt or innocence, but solely to maintain class and race power." With such observations in mind, the cadre of lawyers who had committed themselves to the civil rights movement tried, as one put it, to "neutraliz[e] white control of local justice systems" through either reform or avoidance.[52]

Many of the resulting strategies benefited the ongoing vagrancy law challenge. Take courts such as the one in which Sam Thompson was convicted in Louisville. Exposés like Caleb Foote's 1956 article and Supreme Court cases like Thompson's had raised the profile of such courts and their problematic procedures in recent years. Lawyers ready to take the petty cases these courts adjudicated, or defendants with the resources to hire them, however, were few and far between—until civil rights activists found themselves in the same tribunals. When movement participants began appearing in Hugo Taustine's Louisville police court and other courts like it, the deficiencies in such processes generated new opponents and increased visibility. Reports about the recorders' court in Albany, Georgia, for example, read like a racial variation of the quick magistrate court's judgments Foote had witnessed in Philadelphia. Dennis Roberts described how the court sentenced a black defendant—arrested while attending a mass meeting in a black housing project—to $200 and sixty days because he was known as a "bad nigra." Oldfather, the Harvard law grad and father of one of the vagrancy defendants in that same court, reported that what struck him "most vividly was the presumption of guilt which underlay the proceedings." The testimony of black witnesses was ignored; that of white police officers believed.[53]

Indeed, as civil rights lawyers began encountering such courts, Judge Taustine's Louisville Police Court began to look better by comparison. As one 1966 *Harper's* magazine article related, justices of the peace (JPs) "have little legal knowledge or training, often little formal education of any kind, and they hold court wherever they happen to be—in filling stations, stores, and schools. No trial record is kept." More to the constitutionally vulnerable point, courts in twenty-six states in the 1960s (including nine from the former Confederacy) employed a fee system in which either JPs personally or the system as a whole was financed by fees paid to them only when criminal defendants were convicted or civil defendants found liable. This led not only to a bias toward conviction but also, as Justice Hugo Black had noted when he ran for solicitor in Birmingham in 1914, to considerable mischief outside the courtroom: JPs had every reason to enlist peace officers to seek out and arrest potential "customers."[54]

The incentives were even better aligned when such arrests also served political purposes. As one movement lawyer commented, for a JP to find a civil rights defendant not guilty after the police had charged him "would be to make a mild declaration of war against those policemen, and that was asking for too big a donation of fairness and goodwill from a local justice of the peace who expected to continue living in Mississippi and holding political office." When a civil rights leader was arrested for reckless driving in Lowndes County, Alabama, a slew of NAACP LDF lawyers joined Montgomery lawyer Solomon Seay Jr.—son of the Reverend Seay arrested at Fred Shuttlesworth's home in 1958—in successfully arguing that the Alabama justice of the peace system was unconstitutional because JPs were paid only when they convicted.[55]

More important than lawyers' efforts to improve the hearings their clients would receive in local courts were their efforts to get out of such courts altogether. From the founding of the United States, the federal courts had been imagined as a forum devoid of the biases that presumptively afflicted not only fee-based courts but all state and local courts. It was not that federal courts welcomed civil rights defendants with open arms. Federal judges were white men from the same communities as their state court counterparts, subject to similar prejudices, pressures, and precedents. As lawyer Anthony Amsterdam later recalled, "When we entered the clerk's office in a Southern federal district court to file a lawsuit, we received treatment which, gauged by the standard scale for chilly receptions, amounted to the winter solstice in Antarctica." Federal officials in the South who bucked local custom often lived lonely, difficult, and endangered lives. There were those who did, however, and the lawyers of the civil rights movement took full advantage. Moreover, the interests of local and federal officials were not always aligned. Amsterdam gleefully remembered how different the reception was when he and other lawyers began challenging the JP procedures. "The deputy clerk at the desk skimmed my . . . complaint, broke into a beaming smile, and called out to the other deputies in the office: 'Hey, look at this here!' They, the chief clerk and several deputy marshals then crowded at the counter, skimmed our pleading, gave . . . a round of jubilant applause, and began regaling us with tales about the injustices they had suffered at the hands of j.p.'s when they tried to contest unfair traffic tickets. For a brief instant we were 'real folks,' made to feel welcome."[56]

During the summer of 1963, as some 250,000 Americans marched on Washington, civil rights lawyers across the South resurrected Reconstruction-era federal laws intended to protect freed slaves from state courts—and state vagrancy laws—by allowing them to shift their cases from state to federal courts under certain circumstances. Civil rights lawyers also expanded lower federal court jurisdiction over habeas corpus, which increased federal judicial power to release state prisoners or at least warn state courts not to delay proceedings for misdemeanor and petty charges. With some success, they argued against federal court "abstention"—claiming that federal courts could, and should, adjudicate federal constitutional rights even if that meant intervening into state law prosecutions or interpreting state laws before state courts had a chance to do so. Under nineteenth-century civil rights laws that the Supreme Court had recently resurrected, lawyers brought civil suits in federal court to enjoin government harassment and abuse.[57]

Such doctrine not only made it possible to bring constitutional challenges when officials dropped charges. It also transformed the optics of the cases. Civil rights activists came into court not as criminals appealing their convictions but as civil rights plaintiffs calling on the federal courts and the Constitution for affirmative protection against abuses of state power.

By the mid-1960s, civil rights lawyers had created a relatively coherent approach to the constant stream of arrestees that came through their offices. They had lists of local lawyers, volunteer law students, and lawyers ready to drop everything and head south at a moment's notice. They had form briefs, motions, and petitions; training seminars, conferences, and law review articles that offered doctrinal support. As Amsterdam later recalled, they used "wax stencil, crank operated, mimeograph machines which . . . turned out [forms] by the dozens and then when the demonstrators were busted, we just took all these down, filled in the names and filed them." In the words of prominent civil rights lawyer Arthur Kinoy, the movement soon had its "response to these mass arrests . . . down pat. File civil rights removal petitions in the federal court, yank the cases out of the state court, bail our people out on federal bail, and 'keep the movement moving.' "[58]

Vagrancy and loitering arrests both prompted and benefited from these innovations. Take habeas corpus. LDF lawyers worked with local Jackson, Mississippi, lawyer R. Jess Brown to try to release Jan Hillegas after her Lowndes County vagrancy arrest and before her trial in the justice of the peace court there. In addition to all of the usual arguments as to why the Mississippi vagrancy law and this particular conviction were unconstitutional, Brown, Amsterdam, and their colleagues tried to convince the federal courts to revisit a rule that required exhaustion of state remedies before federal habeas could be granted. After the lower federal courts denied the claims, the Supreme Court denied certiorari, though Justice Douglas was (characteristically) of the opinion that the Court should have granted. After the habeas effort failed, the lawyers immediately filed a removal petition as an alternate way of getting into federal court.[59]

In Hattiesburg, Mississippi, lawyers similarly deployed these new techniques. Adickes, Jones, and the other Freedom Project teachers who had been arrested for vagrancy were lucky that the Lawyers' Guild sent Eleanor Jackson Piel—the only woman graduate of Boalt Hall in 1943—to help them. Piel's mission was to remove the case so that other lawyers could pursue it. But Piel's involvement extended far beyond a single petition. The district court judge rejected Piel's attempt to remove. She had to go to the federal appeals court, which then agreed with her. "The utter baselessness of any conceivable contention that the vagrancy statutes prohibited any conduct in which these persons were engaged," the court concluded, demonstrated that the arrests had truly been intended to punish constitutionally protected conduct: integrating a public library. Even the one judge who partially dissented on the removal issue agreed that the "vagrancy charges against Miss Adickes were shown to be baseless and an unsophisticated subterfuge." Piel then proceeded to help Adickes bring a civil rights suit in federal court seeking $550,000 in damages.[60]

One consequence, then, of the massive state criminal law mobilization against the civil rights movement and the movement's massive response to the criminal charges was the creation of new strategies for reforming, avoiding, and overriding southern justice systems. Because vagrancy arrests were a common feature of the state response to civil rights challenges, those innovations grew in part out of the deployment of vagrancy laws against the movement. Even more important, those innovations benefited vagrancy law challenges. Most immediately, they benefited civil rights vagrancy cases like *Hillegas* and *Adickes*. In the longer term, they would be deployed as well in vagrancy cases that came out of wholly separate social contexts. Lawyers would apply these techniques aggressively, they would try to transform their clients from criminal vagrants to civil rights bearers, and they would sometimes even succeed.

For civil rights lawyers, the exposure to vagrancy and loitering arrests prompted not only new procedural strategizing but new substantive constitutional analysis as well. The effect of witnessing vagrancy laws in action in the South can be seen clearly in the evolving views of Anthony Amsterdam. Born and raised in Philadelphia, Amsterdam was a tall, thin, intense young man. The first time Amsterdam wrote about vagrancy laws was in the spring of 1960, as a law student at the University of Pennsylvania cramming to finish a required paper before graduation. In what became a published student note and one of the most-cited law review articles of all time, "The Void-for-Vagueness Doctrine in the Supreme Court," Amsterdam argued that vague laws were problematic because they failed to give both fair warning to potential violators and sufficient guidance to those tasked with enforcement. He also articulated what might have been behind Louis Lusky's worries about the relationship between void for vagueness and substantive due process: the Court had at times invoked vagueness to hide commitments to particular substantive values—to the right to contract during the Lochner Era or free speech in the late 1930s. A generation younger than Lusky, Amsterdam did not share Lusky's New Deal concerns about substantive rights.

If void for vagueness served substantive ends, Amsterdam was not appalled. Rather, he was open to what those ends might be.[61]

Amsterdam's interest in vagrancy laws in his 1960 note was both minimal and clearly written before the civil rights movement publicized race-related vagrancy enforcement. He relegated discussion of the laws to an extended footnote on *Edelman v. California*, which offered "a single disquieting image [of] all of the evils which justify the constitutional void-for-vagueness doctrine." Although the sit-ins had already begun by the time Amsterdam wrote, the civil rights

Figure 4.1 Anthony Amsterdam, a law professor and volunteer lawyer for the NAACP LDF and other organizations. Amsterdam was a frequent participant and key link in the vagrancy law challenge. He authored law review articles on the topic, wrote the briefs in two Supreme Court cases, and was involved in many more lower court cases. *The Pennsylvania Gazette.*

protestor was absent. Amsterdam's reference point remained the same "indigent defendant" as vagrancy foes before him. The first time Amsterdam wrote about vagrancy laws, then, the laws served as merely one of many examples of a larger doctrinal phenomenon in which he took a scholarly interest.[62]

The second time Amsterdam wrote about vagrancy laws could hardly have been more different. In 1967, Amsterdam published "Federal Constitutional Restrictions on the Punishment of Crimes of Status, Crimes of General Obnoxiousness, Crimes of Displeasing Police Officers, and the Like." As the title suggests, vagrancy and loitering laws were now the subject. Amsterdam viewed such laws as legal and constitutional problems to be dealt with in their own right. Void for vagueness was one way of attacking the problem of this category of laws rather than a problem for which this category of laws was one example. Amsterdam identified such laws as "the weapons of the establishment for keeping the untouchables in line" and part of the web of laws used as "catch-alls to stop . . . demonstrations."[63]

In the article, Amsterdam raised a panoply of constitutional objections to vagrancy and loitering laws. *Thompson v. Louisville*'s "Shuffling Sam Thompson approach"—that there was simply no evidence on which defendants might be convicted for the particular crime—was there. So too, following Amsterdam's note, was void for vagueness. Amsterdam also linked vagueness to the so-called overbreadth doctrine: where a vagrancy law threatened to inhibit conduct protected by the First Amendment—assembly, speech, and association of the kind civil rights protestors often engaged in—it could be challenged as not only vague, but as "overbroad." Amsterdam also drew on the right to travel interstate and to move more generally. He made claims about banishment constituting cruel and unusual punishment under the Eighth Amendment. He argued that vagrancy laws violated the prohibition on involuntary servitude under the Thirteenth Amendment, denied equal protection and substantive due process under the Fourteenth, and contravened the status crime prohibition of *Robinson v. California*. The laws also invaded various protections for criminal defendants, like the Fourth Amendment right not to be arrested on mere suspicion and the Fifth Amendment privilege against self-incrimination.[64]

Between 1960 and 1967, Amsterdam's vantage point on vagrancy and loitering laws had changed dramatically. In part, Amsterdam credited his Supreme Court clerkship with Felix Frankfurter for changing his perspective. Though Frankfurter was well known for his stated adherence to legal rules, he taught Amsterdam to think of the law in terms of human problems rather than intellectual ones.[65]

The more direct reason for Amsterdam's changing perspective was his involvement in the civil rights movement. Shortly after its publication, Amsterdam's note had come to the attention of Jack Greenberg, director-counsel of the LDF. The Brooklyn-born, two-time Columbia graduate and colleague of Louis Lusky had worked with Thurgood Marshall on *Brown v. Board of Education* and other landmark cases. When Marshall became a federal judge in 1961, Greenberg took over the leadership of the LDF. Though Amsterdam's note was signed only with his initials, within a year academics and judges were publicly crediting and citing him widely.[66]

Greenberg heard good things about both the note and its author. Amsterdam had been first in his class at Penn and the only non-Harvard graduate ever to merit a clerkship with Frankfurter. As early as 1965, *Time* magazine profiled Amsterdam in decidedly hagiographic terms. Stories about Amsterdam's genius and erudition—according to one judge, he was "the most dazzling person I have ever met"—would proliferate over the course of his career.[67]

More to the point, Greenberg saw how useful Amsterdam's vagueness arguments could be in challenging the elastic laws that authorized thousands of arrests against which LDF was suddenly defending civil rights protestors. He described Amsterdam's vagueness theory as "central" and "very important" to those challenges. Greenberg invited Amsterdam to one of the LDF's first Lawyers Training Institutes, where Amsterdam lectured the small group of African American and liberal white lawyers in the South willing to take on the cases of civil rights protestors. Indeed, Amsterdam's 1967 article began as a handout accompanying one such lecture. At Greenberg's request, Amsterdam thereafter became "essentially an unpaid staff member" and "a central part of the Legal Defense Fund," even though he also taught full-time at his alma mater, Penn Law School, and later at Stanford and New York University. Amsterdam was also a board member of the umbrella organization Lawyers' Constitutional Defense Committee, which meant he worked closely with other civil rights organizations and the ACLU.[68]

Over the next several years, Amsterdam became one of the growing army of lawyers who organically and responsively developed anti-vagrancy law arguments out of their defense of movement participants. Some lawyers, like C. B. King of Albany, Georgia, turned to the Fourteenth Amendment, while others invoked a long history of anti-slavery rights-consciousness in turning to the Thirteenth. When African American student CORE members were arrested in Shreveport for planning to boycott the state fair's "Negro Day," for example, their lawyer Jesse Stone contended that the vagrancy law's criminalization of being unemployed violated the Thirteenth Amendment's prohibition on involuntary servitude. "The attacks that we ended up making against those statutes just jumped out at you legally but it didn't start with some kind of legal concept or theory except to some very, very minor extent," Amsterdam recalled. Other than the "basic insight" of Amsterdam's note—that "the void for vagueness doctrine had a component that involved the protection of disfavored or unpopular people"—"everything else we learned, we learned in the field. And we just simply kept tailoring our legal theories to the different kinds of statutes."[69]

The title of a folder in which Amsterdam collected these litigation arguments encapsulates the effect of the civil rights movement on the vagrancy law challenge. Where Ernest Besig had scrawled "Victimless Crimes" across the lip of his own vagrancy folder some ten years earlier, Amsterdam now scrawled "Protection of Civil Rights Protestors and Demonstrators." Though Amsterdam mentioned vagrancy laws when he taught Criminal Law and Criminal Procedure to law students, he had no similar folder in his teaching files. It was his experiences as a civil rights lawyer witnessing the oppressive use of vagrancy and loitering laws firsthand, rather than his scholarly views about criminal law, that prompted Amsterdam to collect and develop the legal critiques that would become industry standard.[70]

Lessons from the Loitering Case of a "Notorious" Civil Rights Leader

As the lawyers constructed their legal theories against vagrancy and loitering laws, they tried them out in court. Some cases, like *Hillegas*, foundered on procedural obstacles. Others, like *Tinsley v. Richmond*, failed to convince the courts on the merits. Ruth E. Tinsley, a fifty-eight-year-old, middle-class, African American grandmother and leader of the Richmond and Virginia NAACPs, was arrested for loitering and failing to move on when ordered to do so by the police. Standing in front of a Thalheimer's Department Store in the midst of a boycott, she had been holding a leaflet that proclaimed, "Don't buy where you cannot eat, and turn your charge plate in." Perhaps her lawyer, Martin A. Martin, chose to describe Tinsley as an innocent bystander waiting for a friend because he thought she might have a better chance in the Virginia state courts that way. After the courts nonetheless upheld her conviction and the loitering law, Martin and LDF lawyers brought the case to the Supreme Court. They gave no indication that Tinsley was part of the civil rights movement. Perhaps the justices knew anyway. What would become an iconic photo of Tinsley had been splashed across the pages of national magazines. In the photo, two police officers drag a noncompliant but peaceful Tinsley between them, while one pulls along a German Shepherd with his other hand. Tinsley is well dressed, with a long coat, gloves, and a prim hat. She looks like what she was: a respected member of Richmond's black elite. Whether the justices knew Tinsley's real story or not, only Justice Douglas voted in favor of granting cert.[71]

The next time the NAACP LDF petitioned for certiorari in a loitering case, it placed the civil rights issue front and center. By the time Amsterdam wrote the brief in *Shuttlesworth v. Birmingham* in late 1964, Reverend Fred Shuttlesworth had already been bombed, beaten, and sprayed with fire hoses.

Figure 4.2 Arrest of NAACP leader Ruth Tinsley for loitering during a 1960 boycott of
a Richmond, Virginia, department store. Tinsley's was one of many civil rights-related
vagrancy and loitering arrests that brought attention and condemnation to the vagrancy
law regime. This photo epitomizing the injustice of arresting respectable citizens ran
in national magazines. Library of Congress, New York World-Telegram and the Sun Newspaper
Photograph Collection, Malcolm O. Carpenter.

He was no stranger to either vagrancy and loitering laws or the justices of
the Supreme Court. Shuttlesworth himself had already been arrested thirty-
five times, including at least once before for vagrancy, and the justices had
already considered his legal plight four times. Four years after Bull Connor
arrested the three Montgomery ministers for vagrancy in Shuttlesworth's
home, the Birmingham police arrested Shuttlesworth once again. It was the
spring of 1962, the charge was loitering, and this case too went up to the
high court.[72]

Accounts varied as to exactly what Shuttlesworth was doing to occasion this
particular loitering arrest. The arrest occurred during a selective buying campaign of Birmingham's downtown department stores. According to the city,
Shuttlesworth was arrested when he and some colleagues stopped to talk with
boycotters outside a store. He was part of a "crowd" of ten or twelve when the

police told them to move on. According to Shuttlesworth, he was on his way back from a federal court hearing on a previous arrest. As he and no more than four others slowed for a traffic light at an intersection, an officer blocked his path and told him to move on. In both versions, most of the group moved away and the officer repeated his order. Shuttlesworth replied, "You mean to say we can't stand here on the sidewalk?" After another order and challenge, the officer told Shuttlesworth he was under arrest. Shuttlesworth then said, "Well, I will go into the store," and though he started to, the officer arrested him. The facts were so complicated, and the accounts so varied, that Amsterdam's legal notes contained a diagram of the streets, where each of the protagonists was located, and what each knew.[73]

The day after the arrest, Shuttlesworth was tried in the Birmingham Recorders Court for violating two sections of the Birmingham city code. One section prohibited people from "stand[ing], loiter[ing] or walk[ing] upon any street or sidewalk in the city as to obstruct free passage" and refusing to move on. Another made it "unlawful for any person to refuse or fail to comply with any lawful order, signal or direction of a police officer." Shuttlesworth was found guilty and sentenced to 180 days of hard labor, a $100 fine, and costs. In a new trial on appeal to the circuit court, Shuttlesworth's local attorney, Peter A. Hall, tried to show that the police had targeted his client specifically because he was a civil rights leader. One officer claimed that he had not noticed the race of either Shuttlesworth or any of his companions. Others acknowledged noticing race but denied recognizing Shuttlesworth himself. The Alabama courts uniformly found testimony about the civil rights context "irrelevant and immaterial." All Shuttlesworth got out of his second trial was two months added to his sentence.[74]

Shuttlesworth was not an ideal Supreme Court vehicle: the evidence was too much in conflict, and the big issues—about race, loitering, and free speech—had been avoided in the state courts. It was narrow, raising only questions about what exactly the laws prohibited, whether they did so in precise enough language (the vagueness question), and whether there was any evidence that Shuttlesworth had contravened their prohibitions (the *Thompson* question). Though some of the justices' clerks despaired that there was "no solution to this case [that] seems truly satisfying"—one exclaimed, "What a mess"—the justices granted cert.[75]

Indeed, between 1958 and 1966, the Court heard oral argument in sixty-five cases involving sit-ins or other civil rights protests. It issued summary decisions in many more. The tenor of the cases, with a few exceptions in concurrences or dissents, was overwhelmingly sympathetic to the protestors. In every case through 1965, the Court found a way to vindicate the movement.[76]

As the Court did so, however, it generally avoided embracing the central constitutional claim of many of the demonstrations: that the segregation being protested was unconstitutional. The Court took the stance, as was a canon of its practice, that it would not reach constitutional issues unless necessary. Moreover, because many movement arrests occurred during protests of segregation in privately owned facilities, it was not clear that the Fourteenth Amendment, which prohibited "states" from denying equal protection, even applied. Though movement lawyers pushed the justices to decide the cases as violations of the Equal Protection Clause, and some justices were so inclined, they never managed to come together in a majority opinion.[77]

Rather than address the underlying challenges to Jim Crow itself, the justices relied on two alternative rationales to vindicate civil rights protestors, both of which prompted criticism. First, in cases stemming from street protests, they turned to the First Amendment—finding that public demonstrations were constitutionally protected speech, assembly, or association. As *Thornhill v. Alabama* had shown in the 1930s and 1940s, labor unions, political radicals, and Jehovah's Witnesses had seemed largely synonymous with First Amendment rights. Much to Edelman's misfortune, the Court was less protective of the First Amendment rights of communists and suspected communists in the 1950s. As southern states tried to suppress civil rights organizing late in that decade, the Supreme Court not only offered protection but expanded its conception of what the First Amendment protected. The question, according to legal scholar Harry Kalven in 1965, was whether "the citizen using the street as a forum and not as a passageway is making an anomalous use of it, and whether he is, in a sense, always out of place and out of order when he chooses the streets for his meeting place." Many of the justices answered those questions in the negative when it came to civil rights activists. The justices' willingness to decide cases on First Amendment grounds suggested that they had begun to view civil rights protestors as a new set of free speakers deserving of protection. Although some movement supporters bemoaned the deflection from racial equality to free speech, many saw it as salutary. Kalven commented, "We may come to see the Negro as winning back for us the freedoms the Communists seemed to have lost for us."[78]

The second alternate rationale came in for greater criticism. More commonly than using either equal protection or free speech arguments, the justices latched onto civil rights lawyers' secondary arguments for overturning convictions—arguments like the Sam Thompson no-evidence approach. In cases including both protests on the streets and sit-ins on private property, the Court would hold that protestors could not have breached the peace because they were peaceful; they could not have obstructed the sidewalk because they were walking only two abreast; they could not have loitered because they stopped only for a minute, or at a red light, or were purposefully heading to some destination. To arrest someone without any evidence was to violate their due process rights à la *Thompson v. Louisville*. The Court also accepted the vagueness arguments Amsterdam had articulated in his 1960 note. According to this approach, the laws southern officials used were unconstitutional because they failed to give notice to the defendant that what he or she was doing was potentially criminal. They also failed to provide the police and the courts standards to guide their discretion in identifying law violators. Such vagueness, like the lack of evidence in the *Thompson* approach, violated due process.[79]

Commentators both then and later lamented the Court's failure to take on the underlying challenges to Jim Crow in these cases. Using the *Thompson* no-evidence rule or void-for-vagueness were deemed narrow, small, ways of avoiding the "real" issue. The Sam Thompson approach required case-by-case analysis of whether evidence existed to support a particular arrest and conviction, and the void-for-vagueness approach addressed each law as sui generis. No doubt, the incremental, case-specific nature of these inquiries was appealing to some of the justices as a way to delay decisions about segregation in public accommodations and to give the political branches time to act.[80]

These approaches did not make the Court's decisions meaningless, however. Some of the justices worried that *Thompson* reasoning would actually be quite far-reaching. Justice Harlan had feared *Thompson*'s possible reach since the Court's original decision, and he had convinced Black to set a high bar for *Thompson* claims. *Thompson*, he continued to think almost two years later, was "bound to lead us into treacherous territory, unless we apply its teaching with the utmost circumspection, and with due sense of the limitations upon our reviewing authority." Harlan also feared that using *Thompson* and similar techniques to reverse convictions that in other contexts would go unnoticed would lead to "a body of 'Negro' law—something which would be *very* bad for the Court." As Jack Greenberg pointed out later in the decade, the Court's docket at the height of the civil rights movement looked quite odd if one thought of its cases merely as "so many trespass, breach of the peace, disorderly conduct and weight of evidence cases. It is unheard of for the Supreme Court, which can decide only a relatively small number of cases each term, to repeatedly take up such apparently minor matters." The cases made sense only in the context of changing American race relations, in the context of the Court's solicitousness of the civil rights movement, and in the ongoing challenges to petty laws that buttressed the police defense of segregation.[81]

More substantively, the Court's frequent reliance on *Thompson* and vagueness arguments set the stage for the vagrancy and loitering challenge. These cases did not challenge the aspect of Jim Crow some intended—segregation. That said, they most definitely interfered with a different aspect that the movement also challenged and that the Court had identified as problematic some thirty years earlier—the authority of police and the courts to arrest and convict at will, and the ability of the legislature to provide them with elastic laws with which to do so. Had the Court used equal protection in the sit-in cases, it would have made law with regard to segregation, but it would have done less to oversee police discretion to arrest, and especially to arrest free speakers. The approaches the Court chose instead constituted more direct—if never complete—regulation of the police. They removed tools that encouraged discriminatory and baseless arrests and reversed convictions that the Court deemed unsupportable. With its First Amendment analyses, the Court limited law enforcement interference with civil rights protestors understood as free speakers. With *Thompson*, the Court scolded the police for making arrests that had gone too far. With void for vagueness, the Court scolded not the police but the legislature, telling lawmakers to go back to the drawing board and make clearer precisely what behavior was criminal. Though such judicial invalidations were rarely the last word, they were at least a first.[82]

When Amsterdam wrote the brief challenging Shuttlesworth's loitering convictions, he drew on these themes, themes that had become prominent in both the Supreme Court's prior civil rights cases and in the movement's responses to vagrancy and loitering arrests. The brief depicted *Shuttlesworth* as a civil rights case, highlighted its rather tenuous free speech implications, and identified its similarity to loitering laws considered increasingly problematic in other contexts. (That trio of issues was not uncommon: a 1962 ACLU report described civil rights and civil liberties as a triangle consisting of free speech, due process, and equality.) Amsterdam spent considerable energy making race—Shuttlesworth's race, civil rights and race, Bull Connor's racism—part of the case. The brief mentioned all the racial evidence the trial courts had excluded. Amsterdam deemed it "inconceivable" that a person who had filled "half of the sidewalk for a minute and a half . . . would have been arrested and charged, and phantasmagoric that he would have been convicted and sentenced to almost eight months at hard labor" if he had not been "a Negro and a 'notorious' civil rights leader in Birmingham." James Nabrit III, son of a civil rights lawyer, Yale Law School graduate, and associate director-counsel at LDF (Greenberg's second-in-command), maintained this emphasis in the oral argument. He tried to equate Shuttlesworth and his rights with the entire civil rights movement. He showed how Connor used the law against Shuttlesworth because the latter was both racially and politically out of place.[83]

The LDF lawyers also capitalized on the recent equation of civil rights activists with First Amendment speakers. They argued that Shuttlesworth's conviction ran afoul of the amendment because the loitering ordinance was unconstitutionally vague and overbroad. They pointed out the many "classic" types of First Amendment protected speakers who would find themselves prohibited from expressing themselves under the Birmingham ordinance: "handbill distributors, soapbox speakers, peaceful demonstrators, religious evangelists requesting audience of passers-by." It did not matter that Shuttlesworth fell into none of those categories at the time of his arrest. The law could sweep such folks within its prohibitions, and the overbreadth doctrine enabled Shuttlesworth to make such claims on their behalf. Amsterdam argued that the Court should protect civil rights activists just as it had protected unionists against loitering laws that invited "arbitrary, autocratic and harassing uses by the police" in the 1940 case of *Thornhill v. Alabama*. If civil rights activists were the new free speakers, Amsterdam wanted to be sure that the justices counted Shuttlesworth among them.[84]

Finally, the LDF lawyers located *Shuttlesworth* in the larger context of problematic loitering laws. The brief noted that numerous courts had found laws criminalizing "loitering simplicter," loitering with no other—either obstructionist or criminal—element, constitutionally infirm. Amsterdam wrote, "Every court except the Supreme Court of Virginia which has considered the constitutionality of a proscription of loitering *simpliciter* has held such a proscription void for overbreadth and vagueness." (The Virginia case, of course, was that of Ruth Tinsley, whose appeal the Court had dismissed a few years earlier.) He also noted that though loitering *simpliciter* appeared to apply to everyone indiscriminately, it was often used "to suppress the members of an undesirable race." Where vagueness condemned both arbitrary and discriminatory enforcement, the latter was the bigger problem in *Shuttlesworth* and other race-based vagrancy cases. The problem with loitering, then, folded back onto Amsterdam's two other framings: loitering laws like this one could not stand because the discretion they gave police officers both licensed race discrimination and inhibited free speech.[85]

Justice Stewart wrote the Court's unanimous opinion reversing and remanding the case. Much of the opinion was technical. The Court reversed one of the counts on *Thompson* no-evidence grounds, as the state courts had only applied the ordinance to police orders of cars and trucks—a context not implicated. As for the other count, the Court acknowledged the constitutional problem with loitering *simpliciter*, but the Alabama Court of Appeals had clarified that loitering and refusing to move on did not alone violate the ordinance—it also required "a showing of the accused's blocking free passage." Because the Alabama court's decision came after Shuttlesworth's trial, it was unclear how the trial court had interpreted the law, and so the Court reversed and remanded. In concurrences, Brennan, Douglas, and Fortas to varying degrees all worried about what Alabama would do going forward and offered a variety of directions to the state courts.[86]

After the Court's remand, the state began, once again, to prosecute Shuttlesworth for the loitering charge. Amsterdam's efforts to remove the case to federal court failed. Three years after the Supreme Court's decision, and six years after the events that led to his loitering arrest, Shuttlesworth found himself back at the mercy of the Alabama state courts.[87]

Shuttlesworth v. Birmingham might have done little for Fred Shuttlesworth. But its various opinions did more for the ongoing vagrancy law challenge. Justice Fortas thought a lot about how to frame his concurring opinion. "The case can be reversed with or without reference to the [general] problem of loitering or the general right to use the sidewalks," he wrote to himself, "by reference to the realities of the situation—namely, the arrest was in the context of the boycott and was part of the general civil rights controversy." The real issue, in other words, was whether the case should "be reversed as *unconstitutional loitering statute* etc. or as *civil rights*." Amsterdam had amply prepared both options for him, but Fortas clearly wanted to choose one. Ultimately, he settled on civil rights. He emphasized the fact that the incident occurred during a boycott and that its victims were African American. Though the law seemed generally applicable, "Shuttlesworth's arrest was an incident in the tense racial conflict in Birmingham."[88]

Douglas considered joining Fortas's explicit acknowledgment of race, but he decided to link the case to the larger vagrancy and loitering context instead. Failing to obey the order of a police officer, "when one is not acting unlawfully, certainly cannot be made a crime in a country where freedom of locomotion is honored." Douglas's citation was to *Edwards v. California*, where he himself had first identified such a freedom as constitutionally grounded. Even if Shuttlesworth claimed only the freedom to pause on a street corner in his home city, Douglas, the mythical tramp and honorary Hobo of America, saw a connection to the most expansive themes of freedom of movement and the restless American spirit implicit in the vagrancy and loitering challenge.[89]

Notably, Stewart's majority opinion incorporated all of LDF's framings. Both the unanimity of the opinion and its author suggest how visibly problematic the use of vagrancy and loitering laws against the civil rights movement had become by 1965. Stewart was no wild-eyed liberal. Raised in Cincinnati but educated at a tony Connecticut boarding school and then Yale, Stewart spent his career before the judiciary in private practice and local Cincinnati politics. When President Eisenhower nominated Stewart to the Supreme Court in 1959, southern Democrats had worried that he would be too liberal on race. Stewart's pragmatic, unpretentious, and non-ideological approach to judging did not lead him in that direction. Rather, he became a swing vote on the Warren Court.[90]

Shuttlesworth was one of the cases where Stewart swung left. Taking language directly from the brief, Stewart concluded "that a person may stand on a public sidewalk in Birmingham only at the whim of any police officer of that city." Laws as broad as Birmingham's loitering ordinance, Stewart wrote, did "not provide for government by clearly defined laws, but rather for government by the moment-to-moment opinions of a policeman on his beat." The law bore "the hallmark of a police state," with its "potential for arbitrarily suppressing First

Amendment liberties." Stewart thus described a world in which loitering laws gave police officers too much discretion to suppress free speech by civil rights activists in a volatile racial environment.[91]

Because *Shuttlesworth* made visible the use of vagrancy laws to suppress free speech in the context of changing American race relations, it is not entirely clear which dog wagged which tail in the case. Perhaps the fact that this loitering challenge occurred in the context of racially charged and clearly harassing behavior of a civil rights leader made the Court more concerned about loitering. Perhaps the fact that this civil rights case involved loitering laws that were looking increasingly problematic across the board led the justices to take the civil rights case more seriously. Perhaps the abiding concern was free speech and tamping down police whimsy to arrest political dissenters at will. These questions were hard to disentangle, and each scenario, each possibility of causation, was perhaps simultaneously true.

These overlapping implications were visible to those outside the Court as well. When the *New York Times* reported on *Shuttlesworth*, it titled the article, "High Court Frees Rights Aide Again," and the caption under Shuttlesworth's photo read, "Conviction Reversed; The Rev. Fred L. Shuttlesworth, a Civil Rights Leader. Loitering Conviction Arising from Demonstration in Alabama in 1962 Was Dismissed by Supreme Court." That caption tells the whole story: this was a case about a civil rights leader. He was involved, though not at that moment, in a demonstration in Birmingham, known the nation over as "Bombingham." He was arrested for loitering. And he was freed, "again," by the Supreme Court.[92]

In the end, the *Shuttlesworth* victory, narrow as it was, reinforced and publicly broadcast the justices' views of civil rights activists as the new free speakers, their increasing disapproval of loitering laws and the broad police discretion they licensed, and the connections between them. Where Edelman had once stood on a park bench, a former communist cut off from his audience by Los Angeles police officers, now civil rights protestors stood. Though the claim could only be made obliquely on the facts of *Shuttlesworth* itself, everyone from Shuttlesworth to his lawyers to the clerks to the justices to the press knew that the very basis of First Amendment liberties was at stake in the civil rights struggle, at stake in the vagrancy and loitering cases that came out of it, at stake even where it didn't appear to be, in cases like *Shuttlesworth*, where the defendant was not addressing a crowd, or leading a march, or even holding a sign. Shuttlesworth, like Edelman, was the political opposition. And vagrancy and loitering laws were used against him. That was as clear to the Court and the press as it was to Bull Connor.

Shuttlesworth also made visible the problems, continuing and escalating, of racial regulation by vagrancy law. The case raised, for neither the first nor the last time, troubling issues about the relationship between the police and African

Americans who had become increasingly organized, assertive, and represented in challenging both white supremacy wholesale and the role of the police as its front-line defenders. The problem of police discretion generally and police discretion to harass, regulate, oppress, defame, and arrest African Americans on the street came up again and again in the civil rights struggles of the South. It came up again in different form in the late 1960s, as crime and crime control joined civil rights among the nation's most pressing problems. In this new context too, the justices would try to submerge the issue. But they would fail.

5

"Morals Are Flexible from One Generation . . . to Another"

When Anthony Amsterdam published "Federal Constitutional Restrictions on the Punishment of Crimes of Status, Crimes of General Obnoxiousness, Crimes of Displeasing Police Officers, and the Like" in May of 1967, he had already attacked such laws in the courts, mostly in the context of defending participants in the southern civil rights movement. In Amsterdam's view, the civil rights struggle was "the most important thing going on in this country, . . . this century's crisis of conscience." It was also, however, "but one battle in a larger war for social toleration of differences among men." It struck Amsterdam that "giving the text wider circulation would encourage a larger group of lawyers" to challenge such laws. In fact, he noted a few years later that even as the civil rights struggle provided the "context" for the vagrancy law challenge, the real "action" was challenging enforcement against "nonpolitical types who simply try to live their own life-styles on the streets of every city and town in the nation, and are subjected by these statutes to arrest, possible conviction, and imprisonment for violation of terms that are virtually impossible to understand."[1]

When the editors of the *Criminal Law Bulletin* came across the handout Amsterdam had prepared for the LDF Civil Rights Lawyers' Training Institute and asked if they could publish it, then, Amsterdam said yes. Though Amsterdam, like Ernest Besig and Louis Lusky, was as concerned with law enforcement abuse as with vagrancy laws themselves, this article addressed the latter. It was intended as a handbook for constitutional litigation against laws "designed and used practically exclusively to control undesirables."[2]

What was striking about this handbook was that it offered no example of a successful constitutional challenge. To be sure, Amsterdam cited cases for various propositions of legal doctrine. He mentioned the suggestive but not definitive Supreme Court cases on the subject—*Edelman v. California, Thompson v. Louisville*, his own *Shuttlesworth v. Birmingham*, and a 1966 case called *Hicks v. District of Columbia* that the Court had dismissed as improvidently granted over a heartfelt dissent by Justice William O. Douglas. But he included only a sin-gle citation to recent state and lower federal court vagrancy law activity: *Ricks v. District of Columbia*, in which an African American woman with prior arrests for prostitution and narcotics challenged a vagrancy law's constitutionality.[3]

Ricks was both a curious and a prescient choice. According to Amsterdam, Judge Harold Greene of the General Sessions Court had written a "brilliant" opinion indicating that "he would have held the District's vagrancy legislation unconstitutional." The use of the subjunctive was intriguing, but Amsterdam did not elaborate. "Would have" but for what, exactly? But for, Amsterdam did not say, too much damn precedent on the other side.[4]

By 1967, scholarly commentary condemning vagrancy laws abounded. Lawyers had been chipping away at the laws for years. A few legislatures had repealed or amended their laws. Judicial victories had been largely limited, how-ever, to trial court dismissals, *Thompson* no-evidence claims, and reversals on nonconstitutional grounds. The best Amsterdam could do, it seemed, was cite a judge who "would have" agreed with Amsterdam's arguments if he had been "free to do so." Despite the growing momentum, Amsterdam was not catalogu-ing a doctrinal movement that had already happened. He was providing a blue-print for cases that he himself and, he hoped, other lawyers would bring in the near future.[5]

Indeed, even as Amsterdam's article went to press in 1967, vagrancy chal-lenges were beginning to succeed. That same May, the Supreme Court of Nevada invalidated two status-based ordinances as violations of due process. Two months later the New York Court of Appeals struck down that state's vagrancy law. By the fall, the Supreme Judicial Court of Massachusetts and a federal court in Louisville, Kentucky, had done the same to other vagrancy-related laws. Over the following two years, anti-vagrancy law victories continued to accumulate.[6]

Amsterdam's prescience extended not only to the imminence of vagrancy invalidations but also to the types of newly proliferating cases. Amsterdam's invocation of *Ricks*—brought not by a famous civil rights leader but by a poor African American woman with a criminal record—presaged a new phase in the vagrancy law challenge. A dominant justification for vagrancy laws had always been explicitly moral: such laws were intended to eliminate, or at least suppress, vice—crimes of moral failing, crimes consisting more of violations of commu-nity norms than of direct and material harms to persons or property. Those fail-ings might be sexual or they might be pecuniary, but moral failings they were. According to both upstanding citizens and law enforcement officials, those engaged in vice were both moral and aesthetic hazards—potential dangers to themselves and others, nuisances to behold, and offenses to respectable sensibil-ities. They were, as one reporter put it, "a gallery of disagreeable figures, a study in depravities." It was one thing to condemn vagrancy laws because officials abused them against activists and ministers—because of the utter incongruity of the charges to the targets. It was an entirely different matter to argue what Louis Lusky had refrained from arguing outright in *Thompson*: that the laws were illegitimate even when used as intended against "unsavory types" like "drunks, junkies, drifters, homosexuals, . . . and prostitutes."[7]

That is precisely what the lawyers in *Ricks* and other cases now argued. Such arguments seemed newly available because the high-profile abuses of the laws in the civil rights movement cast doubt on these previously less controversial aspects of the vagrancy law regime and because the moral underpinnings of vagrancy laws no longer held. At least since the mid-1950s, when Ernest Besig labeled his vagrancy folder "Victimless Crimes," there had been dispute about whether prostitution, homosexuality, and idle poverty, as one scholar put it in 1965, "should be considered crimes, sins, vices, diseases, or simply . . . patterns of social deviance." When H. L. A. Hart staked out the position against criminal enforcement of morality in *Law, Liberty, and Morality* in 1963, and Lord Patrick Devlin took the opposite view with *The Enforcement of Morals*, an outpouring of books and articles followed. Scholars, judges, and even prosecutors lamented the "overcriminalization" that plagued American society, the energy improperly expended on "crimes without victims," and the inability of society to "coerce virtue." As those defending the criminalization of conventional morality spoke of danger, offense, disgust, and social breakdown, those inclined toward decriminalization or noncriminal regulation spoke of difference, freedom, privacy, and treatment. The latter rejected moral regulation through the criminal law and contended that ancillary harms, to the extent they existed, could and should be addressed through other means.[8]

These debates, and the changing social and cultural context in which they occurred, both propelled and reflected vagrancy challenges by the unemployed, prostitutes, and sexual minorities. Though always contested and incomplete, changing ideas about sexuality and sex equality, and social movements promoting those ideas, undermined many of the assumptions that justified arresting women like Hattie Mae Ricks—women who defied a conception of female sexuality that was increasingly in dispute. The same "sexual revolution," as well as a more assertive and self-conscious gay rights movement, brought into question the moral basis for criminalizing homosexual behavior that had stymied Ernest Besig in the 1950s. Indeed, as welfare activists, anti-poverty reformers, and government policies pushed toward a decoupling of poverty and immorality, even the most basic vagrancy concept—the immorality of idle poverty—became far more vulnerable than it had been less than ten years earlier when the Supreme Court decided *Thompson v. Louisville*.

The cases that followed illuminated tensions about the regulation of morality in public versus private, the regulation of status versus conduct, and the conceptualization of an issue as one of "vice" versus "victimless crimes." People the police saw as "undesirables" contended that they were worthy of constitutional protection. The question—asked slightly differently in the various contexts—was whether vagrancy laws would continue to serve as legitimate tools for regulating dangerous, uncomfortable, or offensive people and their vices or whether such laws had become constitutionally suspect because their erstwhile targets now had, as one scholar put it, "a right to be different."[9]

The Female Vagrant

Arrests of women for defying conventional mores of female sexuality, and for prostitution more specifically, were a mainstay of vagrancy enforcement for hundreds of years. In part because prostitution had not been a crime at common law, prostitutes had been treated as a kind of vagrant since the fifteenth century. One famous tract from 1566 described the female vagrant as a "cow . . . that goes to bull every moon, with what bull she cares not." By the early seventeenth century, the application of vagrancy laws to women leading a "lewd and idle" life was an established part of the vagrancy regulation that came to the New World with American colonists. Colonial anxiety about individual morality and colonial suppression of sexual deviance frequently manifested themselves in vagrancy prosecutions. As cities grew after independence, local officials tended to use vagrancy laws to maintain public order and morality more than to regulate private conduct. Because separate statutory prohibitions against prostitution per se remained almost nonexistent, officials used vagrancy and disorderly conduct laws with particular force against the increasingly public and increasingly commercial sex trade.[10]

Nineteenth-century vagrancy regulation of women was not confined to prostitutes. It bled over into regulation of women's sexuality and their use of public space more generally. Overlapping sets of cultural assumptions made women's presence in public inherently suspect. Victorian ideals deemed women passionless creatures who belonged in the privacy of the home rather than the rougher public spheres of street, politics, and market. To the extent that anyone actually lived such cloistered ideals, it was largely elite and middle-class women privileged and constrained to do so. Many working-class, ethnic, and minority women who neither subscribed to the chastity ideal nor had the luxury of staying out of public spaces found themselves policed by vagrancy laws. Even though the "separate spheres" of public and private were never vacuum sealed and were constantly renegotiated, these norms of passionlessness and seclusion led to the assumption that a woman in public—especially unaccompanied, at night, in "rough" areas or with "rough" men—was a problem that vagrancy laws could and should address.[11]

Both the continued use of vagrancy laws to regulate sexuality and this slippage between prostitutes and allegedly promiscuous women persisted deep into the twentieth century. Cases made clear that women could be deemed vagrants as prostitutes without money ever changing hands. A woman could find herself "dissolute" and therefore a vagrant because of a single instance of nude dancing at a "smoker." Another could find herself "lewd" because she "was roaming the country . . . with a man who was not her husband" and "dissolute" because the man was of "disreputable character." Associating with "women of bad character for chastity" in public or private or offering up one's body indiscriminately to men for intercourse were all that was necessary. As one 1943 case stated, "the law defines a prostitute to be a female given to indiscriminate lewdness."[12]

Such sentiments and such uses of vagrancy laws were still in evidence in the 1960s. Prostitution was not only a "departure from community mores"; it also caused "real" harms like the spread of venereal disease, organized crime, and extortion, as well as offense to the public. As a 1967 presidential task force report on the police commented, as late as 1965, women were arrested under an ordinance making it a crime simply for a " 'woman of notorious character' to walk or ride up 'the streets of this city.' " An amicus brief Anthony Amsterdam wrote for the LDF in the 1968 policing case of *Terry v. Ohio* contended that the police continued to stop "unescorted women or young girls in public places." That same year, the Minnesota Supreme Court found it reasonable to infer prostitution from "circumstances constituting a marked departure from community mores."[13]

Attitudes like these meant continued arrests, or at least harassment, of prostitutes, including for vagrancy. As was so often the case, the police turned to vagrancy laws, rather than the specially tailored prostitution laws that had emerged in the early twentieth century, for institutional and practical reasons. Institutionally, because prostitutes were a "vice" problem, they came within the purview of vice squad officers who frequently invoked multi-section vagrancy laws against a variety of petty criminals. One DC police officer defined a vagrant as an "undesirable" and an undesirable as "a prostitute, a junkie, a thief, a pervert, 'and what have you. The rest.' " It was not just that prostitutes were themselves a vice problem similar to other vice problems. It was also that they frequently engaged in, hung around, and were driven by or drawn to other vices as well. In 1971, police estimated that, like Ricks, half of the prostitutes in Washington, DC, used illegal drugs.[14]

As for the practicalities, vagrancy gave the police arrest options that were otherwise unavailable. The very "victimlessness" of prostitution—like many other crimes of "vice"—was partly why specially trained and tasked vice squads were necessary to ferret it out. Proving solicitation, for example, took undercover work, one-on-one work, time, energy, and resources. It also opened officers to

countercharges of entrapment. Moreover, once prostitutes recognized local officers, the latter could no longer make the undercover effort work at all. In many
cities, the police turned to vagrancy laws making a person a vagrant who was a
"night walker or common night walker," a "common prostitute," a "known prostitute," or just a "prostitute," all of which had the benefit of forgoing proof of the
actual underlying conduct. No theft was required to make a person a vagrant as a
common thief. No prostitution was required to make one a vagrant as a common
prostitute. Elsewhere, the lewd vagrancy laws that had been used for centuries
continued to suffice. In still other places, officials turned to laws prohibiting loitering for the purpose of soliciting prostitution. Officers would sometimes even
use generic vagrancy laws, much in the spirit such laws had been used against
mobsters some twenty or thirty years earlier. Women who sold themselves for
money had no "honest calling," no "legitimate means of support." After consult-
ing with a variety of local legal officials about what they could do to stop prostitution on Memphis's famous Beale Street, for example, that city's vice squad
officers began asking women in "unusually brief skirts, even by current miniskirt
standards" about their employment. If the women said they were unemployed,
the officers warned them. When the officers again encountered what one court
called "warned women," arrests for conventional vagrancy followed.[15]

As early as the 1930s, courts had occasionally upset vagrancy law prosecutions
of allegedly promiscuous women. Some cases held that one could not be proved
a vagrant by general reputation. Others suggested that a woman's bad character
or her walking in the company of a man was not enough to prove vagrancy. In
1932, the North Carolina Supreme Court invalidated an ordinance prohibiting
lewd women, regardless of purpose, from appearing in public places. It found
that "however much they may have offended against the decencies of society, or
run counter to the prevailing code of morals, or rendered themselves non grata
personae to the community, still they are human beings, citizens of a great commonwealth, and entitled to the equal protection of the laws." It concluded, "To
deny any one, not lawfully imprisoned, the right to travel the highways, to buy
goods, to eat bread, to attend divine worship, and the like, simply because he or
she happens, for the time being, to belong to an unfortunate class, is an unwarranted use of the police power."[16]

Even as prostitution-related vagrancy defendants successfully appealed their
convictions in the postwar years, courts largely confined themselves to nonconstitutional grounds. Though one case raised eleven different constitutional arguments against a vagrancy law, the court reversed for insufficient evidence against
the "sober, well-behaved and decently attired" defendant. Other nonconstitutional cases differed on whether the conduct supporting a prostitution-based
vagrancy or loitering conviction had to occur in public, and what that meant.

One case was skeptical that a woman could have loitered in her own home, while others accepted loitering in a hotel room and one's own office.[17]

By the late 1960s, judges were more skeptical about law enforcement's insistence that vagrancy laws were necessary to combat prostitution and promiscuity. As the New York City police tried to apply the lesson that street sweeps would more effectively rid Times Square of "brazen women" than "unprofitable and uneconomic" arrests for solicitation itself, they encountered a problem: the women did not readily fit under the terms of either the loitering or the disorderly conduct law. The police did not particularly mind. They were comfortable making arrests, having the district attorney's office dismiss the charges, and seeing the women released the next morning. That got the prostitutes off the streets during peak hours.[18]

Others did mind. One *New York Times* article stated that such arrests were made possible by "the combination of silence and a subtle double-play on the Constitution—making arrests on vague and indefinite grounds, which is a violation of due process, and on suspicion without probable cause, which contravenes the Fourth Amendment, and then dismissing the charges without trial." In the journalist's view, the practice was "about as constitutional as a mugging."[19]

Lawyer Burt Neuborne agreed, but finding a case to make the point was not easy. With recent degrees from Cornell and Harvard Law School, Neuborne had just recently left a private law firm to join the NYCLU staff. Attuned to the class politics of such arrests, he worried that a judge would see arrests of actual prostitutes as business as usual rather than as a violation of constitutional rights. That was how many prostitutes and their legal aid lawyers often understood them. "No one would listen on behalf of the working girls," Neuborne thought. So he made it known that he was looking for a middle-class defendant to illustrate the indiscriminate nature of the sweeps and to garner sympathy from a judge. If those arrested seemed independently worthy of constitutional rights, then the injustice of such arrests might become apparent for actual prostitutes as well. When two middle-aged, middle-class women waiting for their husbands were picked up in a sweep and brought in in the paddy wagon toward the end of the summer in 1967, Neuborne got a call. "What happened, of course, was that the charges against the two middle-class women got dismissed immediately," Neuborne later recalled. That left only likely prostitutes as defendants.[20]

Even so, Criminal Court Judge Amos Basel was sympathetic to named defendant Brandy Williams and the others. It was not that Basel approved prostitution. He described "these street girls [as] a health hazard" and defended the "right of the normal, decent citizen to go about the streets without affront to his or her sense of decency." He also understood the "tremendous" pressure on public officials by local business owners and business people. But Basel could not countenance this particular police response. He dismissed the cases and called them a "disgrace." After a long disquisition placing the prostitution challenge to New York's loitering law in the context of the larger vagrancy law challenge, Basel concluded that he need not determine the law's constitutionality. It was clearly misused in this instance. The law prohibited loitering while "engaged or about to engage in crime." Because prostitution was a "violation," not a crime, the loitering law did not apply. As Neuborne later recalled, the poor, African American women who had been jailed again and again with little recognition of their plight were "delirious" when the judge read "this wonderful opinion" from the bench. "No one had ever paid any attention to them before."[21]

That attention notwithstanding, the case neither invalidated the law nor ended the police practice. Two years later, Basel was still denouncing the same police approach to prostitution. "It's ridiculous," he said. "It's just harassment." Another two years later, the police were still trying to find that perfect yet elusive legal tool that was easier to prove than solicitation and more legally justifiable than loitering.[22]

As prostitution-related constitutional challenges to vagrancy laws became more prevalent, judges began to take the step Basel had deflected: invalidating prostitution-related vagrancy laws on constitutional grounds. It was one thing for courts to exempt specific individuals in specific circumstances from prosecution. But lawyers increasingly saw constitutional invalidation as the next necessary step. *Ricks*, the case Anthony Amsterdam described in his 1967 article, became the watershed case. That the case came out of the nation's capital was no surprise to observers of the anti-vagrancy law challenge. The DC law had lived a troubled life replete with saving constructions, presidential vetoes, and much handwringing. The law established eight different ways one could make oneself a vagrant. Although courts in many jurisdictions interpreted their status-based, continuing-offense vagrancy laws to license arrests with no proof of overt acts, by the mid-1950s, judicial supervision of vagrancy enforcement had led to fairly elaborate rules. The city's lawyers told police officers that in order to support a "daytime vagrancy case," they needed to make fourteen separate "observations" of a given individual. A nighttime case required seven. Different subsections came to have different requirements—"known pickpocket or thief" required only a single observation, whereas "leading an immoral or profligate life" required three. Each observation had to include an interview concerning the suspect's employment, address, and reason for being on the street. Because vagrants were unlikely to limit their wanderings to the boundaries of any given precinct, this interpretation required considerable cooperation in an age before widespread availability of computers. The saving grace was that it was not necessary for the same officer to make every observation of a given suspect.[23]

Following these instructions, the police vowed to combat vice with repeated arrests. "As soon as [an undesirable] gets back out on the street, we'll start a new file of observations." Officers recognized that they were "skirting close to the field of individual civil rights." With the "big enforcement club" of the vagrancy law, however, they were pleased to leave "the potential predator literally with no place to be unobtrusive." As the *Washington Post* reported, officials celebrated that "prostitutes and numbers writers are running at the sight of a uniformed man."[24]

With DC police not only aggressively using the vagrancy law but also bragging about it in the papers, lawyers had been trying to attack the law for years before *Ricks*. As early as 1960, the issue had caught the attention of George W. Shadoan, a graduate legal intern at Georgetown University Law Center. Shadoan asked the ACLU for assistance, but the organization's Washington office focused on legislation rather than litigation. Without a Washington affiliate or available volunteer attorneys, there was little to be done. Roland Watts, the legal director of the national ACLU in New York, told Shadoan that though "the ACLU is very much concerned with vagrancy legislation and its application in many localities," the office had largely been leaving such cases to the affiliates.[25]

A year later, the National Capital ACLU was established, and affiliated lawyers continued Shadoan's quest for a test case. By the time Hattie Mae Ricks came to the attention of affiliate chair Monroe Freedman, he had the institutional support he needed to take on the vagrancy laws. In Ricks he had found the client.

Ricks's story was a common one. She was African American, unemployed, born and bred in an area of the District police officers considered "a den of vice." After her first arrests for vagrancy and narcotics, it seemed to Ricks that she could never again escape the police. "I'm no angel," Ricks acknowledged. Even so, she found it upsetting and unfair that the police repeatedly accosted, questioned, and arrested her. They went so far as to follow her into a restaurant where she was eating. "It's embarrassing," she said. "Not everyone knows what I done. Why should they stop me all the time for just walking on the street?" From Ricks's perspective, the police harassed her as she simply tried to live her life.[26]

To the police, Ricks's presence in a high-crime neighborhood was not happenstance. It was causal. She was a junkie and a prostitute, even if she did not always happen to be using drugs or turning tricks when they saw her. When vice squad officers watched Ricks flag down cars, stand in front of a "known house of ill fame," or walk with a man toward such a destination, it was their job to observe, question, and regularly arrest her. It was their job to target neighborhoods like Ricks's, people like her, vices like hers.

And so they did. After Sol Rosen, a criminal defense lawyer Freedman knew, made the initial appearance in Ricks's case, he brought Freedman on board. He and Freedman hoped this would solve a perennial problem for challenging vagrancy laws: the fact that once a civil liberties or civil rights lawyer entered

an appearance in a vagrancy case, prosecutors would drop it to avoid constitutional challenge. Despite Freedman's late entry, the prosecutors still tried to get
rid of the case. At one point, they approached an incarcerated Ricks—without
Freedman or Rosen present. They told her that they would have her released
immediately if she agreed to allow the government to nolle pros the case—to
dismiss the charges while retaining the authority to bring them again later.[27]

When Freedman heard about the visit, he went to see Ricks. "It's an interesting problem for a legal ethics class," he later reflected. "I got into the case because
of the cause. But she was my client. I didn't want to overbear her will and persuade her not to [nolle pros], but at the same time I wanted to persuade her not
to do it. She had no education, but she was pretty smart. I explained to her that
if she agreed to [nolle pros], in a matter of weeks she'd be prosecuted all over
again. But if we went through with this, nobody would be prosecuted any more
for vagrancy or narcotics vagrancy. And she immediately agreed."[28]

As this statement reveals, by the late 1960s, Freedman and lawyers like him
saw themselves as part of a vagrancy law "cause." As a result, Freedman did
not limit his arguments to the facts of Ricks's situation. He understood the
case in the larger context of the cause. He suggested new interpretations, or at
least new applications, of a multitude of constitutional claims against vagrancy
laws. Freedman, Rosen, and Ralph Temple, also of the DC ACLU affiliate,
raised pretty much every claim they could think of: Fourth, Fifth, and Sixth
Amendment criminal procedure claims, void for vagueness, equal protection for
the poor, Robinson's Eighth Amendment cruel and unusual punishment theory,
and a due process freedom of movement claim. Moreover, the lawyers made it
clear that "these constitutional objections are not necessarily discrete. Rather,
they might more appropriately be viewed as integrally related aspects of what
is essentially a single major problem: that the Vagrancy Statute is phrased in
terms that are vague and that are dependent on socio-economic status, thereby
empowering the police to harass, arrest, and imprison citizens who appear to
them to be merely suspicious or vaguely 'undesirable.' "[29]

Freedman underscored his legal arguments with data about the realities of
vagrancy law enforcement. He cross-examined police officers to show that they
could not agree on a definition of loitering—it meant variously "standing around
in one spot not going anyplace," "walking back and forth from the corner," "flag-
ging automobiles," "standing idle in a doorway," and "hanging around on a street
corner" with "no apparent purpose or motive." Though Freedman's focus was
decisively on challenging the vagrancy law itself, following Besig and Lusky,
Freedman highlighted that the laws were so frequently used in part because of
the attitudes of law enforcement officers. Officers revealed the pretextual nature
of many vagrancy arrests when they testified that the reason to use vagrancy
rather than other laws was that the "person might be a real smooth operator and

I might not be able to catch them doing these other things." "In practical effect," testified one witness, "vagrancy is used as a charge or ground for arrest in cases where you feel there is prostitution or sodomy going on but you cannot make a case." More generally, the officers stated that at least one goal was to prevent future crimes. "If they are not out there, the crime can't be committed." The vagrancy law "helps to lower the crime rate of the precinct." "It is used to get the undesirables off the street."[30]

Freedman's efforts initially failed. As Amsterdam had noted in his article, General Sessions Judge Harold Greene felt hemmed in by precedent, found Ricks guilty, and upheld the law. Even as he resigned himself to his role, Greene predicted, in a part of the opinion Amsterdam did not mention, "I fully expect that eventually the D.C. vagrancy statute will be determined to be unconstitutional." A year and a half after Amsterdam's article, in the very case of *Ricks v. District of Columbia*, Greene's prediction came true. Spottswood Robinson III, a former NAACP LDF lawyer and the first African American appointed to the U.S. Court of Appeals for the District of Columbia Circuit, spoke for two other judges in striking down sections of the vagrancy law as void for vagueness. The provisions *Ricks* invalidated covered anyone "known to be a pickpocket, thief, burglar, confidence operator, or felon" as well as anyone "leading an immoral or profligate life" or anyone "who wanders about the streets at late or unusual hours of the night without any visible or lawful business and not giving a good account of himself." In other words, though the specific context was prostitution and the defendant a woman, Freedman had taken out one of the broadest, most commonly used sections of the vagrancy law of the nation's capital.[31]

Ricks may have been a pioneer, but it was not an outlier for long. Three months later, a federal district court in Memphis followed DC's lead. The case began with yet another African American woman suspected of prostitution, though Dorothy Kirkwood did not have the same history, record, or track marks as Hattie Mae Ricks. According to her lawyer, Kirkwood "was not charged with prostitution but like all other female blacks seen walking around, and doing nothing in particular, she was charged with vagrancy." It was clear that the Memphis Police Department "used vagrancy to take these women off the streets." Kirkwood claimed that she had been on her way to meet her boyfriend when a police officer got out of a squad car. Someone apparently shouted, "Run because he'll arrest you." Like other women in similar straits, she ran, and she was caught and arrested. At the time, Kirkwood was not working and she was living with relatives. She had never before been arrested for vagrancy or prostitution, and she denied any such activity. She and the officer disagreed about whether she had been previously "warned."[32]

Ronald Krelstein, a recent Vanderbilt Law School graduate, joined the vagrancy law cause on behalf of Kirkwood. With both the ACLU and the

NAACP LDF formally intervening at Krelstein's request, it was no surprise that many of the arguments in Krelstein's federal civil rights suit looked similar to those in other vagrancy cases. There were now templates, expertise. What might have been surprising was that Krelstein's arguments against racially discriminatory enforcement of the vagrancy law failed while his vagueness and overbreadth arguments on behalf of prostitutes succeeded. Lyndon B. Johnson appointee Robert M. McRae Jr. rejected the legitimacy of using vagrancy against prostitution when the women involved were "not on the street for criminal purposes." Even women who might be prostitutes had a right simply to be in public. *Kirkwood v. Ellington* struck down the Tennessee vagrancy law. Krelstein then filed a second case, and he won that too when the court invalidated the Memphis loitering and disorderly conduct ordinances.[33]

Like *Ricks*, Krelstein's challenges emerged out of the vagrancy regulation of prostitutes, and the judicial opinions they obtained validated their specific legal arguments. But also like *Ricks*, the lawyers understood themselves as part of a larger vagrancy cause, and they made arguments that ranged widely over constitutional claims and cited vagrancy-related cases from across a number of social contexts. These prostitution vagrancy cases invalidated laws that criminalized other types of vagrants too, and they created yet another generally applicable resource for the vagrancy "cause."[34]

That these victories came in the context of vagrancy regulation of women's sexuality was more than happenstance, however. At the very moment vagrancy laws were falling and their use against prostitutes was becoming visible and invalid, the whole landscape of American sexual and gender relations was shifting dramatically. What was moral and immoral, decent and indecent, was very much in flux.

What came to be called the postwar "sexual revolution" was initially most apparent on the cultural margins. Though both Beat and hippie sexual freedom applied to men more than women, to straights more than gay men and lesbians, the counterculture and a blossoming gay subculture visibly challenged conventional sexual mores. Both bohemians and homosexuals engaged in public "love-ins," sometimes just a few hundred yards apart at the same time. Moreover, as in San Francisco's North Beach, hippies and gay men and lesbians sometimes coexisted in the same neighborhoods, together establishing a visible, physical presence of what were increasingly called "alternative lifestyles." The hit 1967 musical *Hair*—which ran for almost 2,000 performances and four years—glorified free love, free sex, two men kissing, and the freely naked human form for the first time on a Broadway stage.

The sexual revolution wasn't just for those on the fringes, though, and it did not only occur in public. It took place among middle-class heterosexual people too, folks looking not for totally "free love" but perhaps freer love. Reports on sexuality among American men and women by Alfred Kinsey in the late 1940s and early 1950s revealed that mainstream American practices varied greatly from the myth of monogamous, heterosexual, missionary-position sex widely in circulation. Kinsey and others suggested that premarital sex, homosexuality, extramarital affairs, and sado-masochism were more common than generally understood. Beyond the specific findings, the Kinsey Reports and publications by sex researchers Masters and Johnson provoked national conversations about previously taboo sexual subjects. So did changing technology. Advances in contraception, and especially the advent of the birth control pill in 1960, created more space between sex and procreation. Contraception, and its more controversial cousin abortion, freed people—especially women—from the reproductive consequences of sex.[35]

As early as 1963, an article in the *Washington Post* commented, "Morals are flexible from one generation of women to another. At the turn of the century a woman who exposed the calf of her leg was considered to be a loose creature. Now the Bikini bathing suit adorns our landscape." The author found the signposts of both "female morality" and "sexual morals" "confusing." As men and women increasingly engaged in sex before marriage, sex outside of marriage, sex with multiple partners, sex with same-sex partners, large-scale demographic patterns began to shift. By 1971, surveys found that more than three-quarters of American adults thought premarital sex was okay. By the mid-1970s, a majority engaged in it. Marriage rates decreased, and divorce rates increased. People married later when they married at all. Abortion became a topic of public confession and debate. Activists in the ACLU, Planned Parenthood, and other organizations began attacking restrictive abortion laws in both courts and state legislatures.[36]

Deeply connected to these changing views of sexuality were new ideas about both relationships between men and women and the place of women in society. Women had entered the workforce in unprecedented numbers during World War II. Many had retreated, or had been forced to retreat, back into the home in the years after the war. Moreover, in the civil rights movement, among the Beats and then the hippies, in unions, and in left-leaning student movements, women found themselves simultaneously empowered and marginalized. In 1963, Betty Friedan published *The Feminine Mystique*, a bestselling book that galvanized women as critics of gender inequality and oppression. That same year, John F. Kennedy established the Presidential Commission on the Status of Women, and Congress passed the Equal Pay Act. The following year, Congress included discrimination on the basis of sex in employment among the prohibitions of the Civil Rights Act of 1964, and then Friedan helped organize the National Organization for Women to implement it. As women's groups sprouted up around the country, self-identified feminists fought for greater equality and freedom in the workplace and the family, and for more autonomy for their sex-ual, reproductive, and romantic decisions. More radical groups in the "women's liberation movement" went further, using language of "patriarchal domination." They argued for a more thoroughgoing revolution in gender relations.[37]

The undermining of traditional gender roles could be seen not only in life choices and political protests, but also in the physical appearance of young men and women. As one judge in a vagrancy case commented, "Today women are wearing their hair increasingly shorter, and men are wearing their hair increas-ingly longer. Facial make-up, hair dyeing and cosmetic treatment are no longer the exclusive province of women. Men's and women's clothing styles are becom-ing increasingly similar." The breakdown of assumptions of what aesthetic went with what gender meant that the personal was not only political; it was also sartorial.[38]

Women's liberation and sexual liberation sometimes came together in a redef-inition of female sexuality around women's own sexual desire. Feminists held a wide variety of views on sex, ranging from the idea that sex with men was inher-ently oppressive to a celebration of the liberatory potential of sex for women's self-fulfillment. Either way, sex and women's sexual freedom were entering a new era. New genres of sex-related self-help books—*Sex and the Single Girl* or *Women and Their Bodies*—previously either unthinkable, unpublishable, or unsellable, began to fill, and quickly fly off, bookstore shelves. As publications with far more explicit sexual content also began to be widely available—*Playboy* began pub-lishing in 1953 and opened its first club in 1960—debates about pornography grew heated. Whereas some feminists worried about the commodification and objectification of women, others reveled in pornography as a positive way for women to explore the erotic.[39]

These social transformations made halting and uneven inroads into legal doc-trine in the 1960s. Before the Supreme Court began to face cases about sexual freedom or sex equality, it heard cases about the cultural production of sex and things sexual. In 1957, the Court determined that obscene speech lay outside of First Amendment protection. What exactly constituted obscenity was a thorny question, however, one that left room for sexually explicit speech that was not utterly without social value. As the justices tried to identify the con-tours of obscenity, they had difficulty figuring out precisely what that would look like—leading Justice Stewart to announce, "I know it when I see it." What observers saw was that the Court would give a far wider berth to sexually explicit publications than ever before.[40]

Women made less headway with sex discrimination claims. As late as 1961, in a case upholding a Florida law that required men but not women to serve on juries, the Court stated, "Despite the enlightened emancipation of women from the restrictions and protections of bygone years, and their entry into many parts of community life formerly considered to be reserved to men, woman is still regarded as the center of home and family life." The Court thus validated, rather than undermined, the authority of sex stereotypes to justify legal discrimination.[41]

When it came to sexual freedom, the Warren Court was a bit more receptive. In the mid-1960s, the Court decided *Griswold v. Connecticut*, which again raised the question of unwritten or "substantive due process" rights that had occupied the Court during the *Lochner* era. Justice William J. Brennan Jr. suggested one way to invalidate Connecticut's law prohibiting the use of contraceptiveswithout adverting to substantive due process. When President Dwight D. Eisenhower had appointed Brennan in 1956 in an attempt to appeal to northeastern Catholic Democrats, he had not expected Brennan—one of eight children from an Irish immigrant family who had made his way to Harvard Law School—to become the intellectual leader of the Court's liberals. But that is precisely what happened when the unassuming but gregarious Brennan joined Black, Douglas, and Warren. In *Griswold*, Brennan's idea became Douglas's opinion for the Court. Douglas disclaimed substantive due process, preferring instead the "penumbras, formed by emanations" of the "specific guarantees in the Bill of Rights." These included marriage as "a relationship lying within the zone of privacy." Black was not convinced that this approach solved any constitutional problems. The case drove a wedge between him and Douglas—both anti-*Lochner* New Dealers—and Black dissented from what he described as "the same natural law due process philosophy found in *Lochner*."[42]

Douglas's constitutional innovation did not necessarily extend very far, however. The justices emphasized that Connecticut's law prohibited not just the sale but the actual use of contraceptives and that it applied to people who were married. Goldberg emphasized that the Court's decision in *Griswold* "in no way interferes with a State's proper regulation of sexual promiscuity or misconduct." Harlan described "adultery, homosexuality and the like" as "sexual intimacies which the State forbids." It seemed that the Court's willingness to decriminalize sexual practices might be limited to the private, the married, the straight, the conventional. [43]

At least some observers, however, thought the Court was on its way to approving the sexual revolution writ large. One *New York Times Magazine* story predicted "that the United States Supreme Court might render a decision declaring unconstitutional all state laws that attempt to regulate sexual behavior between consenting adults in private." A California appellate court expressed skepticism about the existence of any real consensus on sexual norms in striking down a law prohibiting "any act which openly outrages public decency." Modern America was simply too heterogeneous to assure the fairness of a jury's definitions. "When the statute speaks of 'public decency' does it presuppose some kind of consensus among the majority of the public as to what is and what is not 'decent' and, if that assumption is wrong, to which segment of the public is the trier to look?"[44]

Indeed, by the late 1960s, the criminal regulation of sexual morality had been one of the prime targets of the H. L. A. Hart conception of "victimless crime" for more than a decade. As with vagrancy and public drunkenness, where law enforcement saw criminal vice, civil libertarians saw adults making choices that at most harmed only themselves. The Wolfenden Report, the Model Penal Code, and many others had taken aim at fornication, prostitution, adultery, and other sex-related laws. Though many of the critiques of prostitution specifically acknowledged the need for some kind of regulation—often in light of concerns about venereal disease—they balked at the criminal regulation of prostitution for purely moral reasons.

By the early 1970s, the combination of women's rights and the sexual revolution would foster a prostitutes' rights movement that would bring together prostitutes and feminists in an uneasy coalition. Even before the founding of groups like COYOTE (Call Off Your Old Tired Ethics), changes in legal and cultural norms were evident in an increasingly strident strain of complaint in the vagrancy prostitution cases of the late 1960s and early 1970s: the injustice that female prostitutes were arrested and male johns walked away. This was an old complaint, but it was now drawing "the wrath of the women's liberation movement." Teenage girls and boys had long been subject to different rules, especially when it came to sexuality. Girls could be sent to reform school for promiscuous behavior at age sixteen in New York. Boys could not. The same discrepancies plagued adult women. In some states, it was not even clear at various moments whether male johns or male prostitutes had committed any criminal act at all. Moreover, women were generally subject to harsher criminal penalties. In New York, female vagrants were subject to indefinite commitment of up to three years; male vagrants to jail terms of up to three months. For prostitution, women could get three months; men, fifteen days. When law enforcement officers had to choose between going after a prostitute or a john, they would take the prostitute and the stiffer penalty. "Who's going to take the word of a prostitute?" one police officer added. Some men felt so immune from prosecution that they expected their money back when a law enforcement officer intervened before they received the services for which they had paid. As the ACLU's Norman Dorsen explained, "The legal concept of women . . . is essentially that they are children and wards of the state who can be punished for deviating from a strict moral code that is not applied to men."[45]

These changes in ideas about sex equality, sexual morality, and criminal regulation were neither unalloyed nor complete. Feminists fell short of many of their goals in the late 1960s and early 1970s. Increasingly organized

Criminal Court Judge Amos Basel presiding at a recent arraignment. "You've got to pay attention to them," he said, ". . . they're struggling in their way to cope with life."

Drawings for The New York Times by MANING

The presence of prostitutes is part of a ritual in which they are arrested, taken to the criminal courts building and then dismissed by the Judge when District Attorney's office refuses to press charges.

Figure 5.1 Illustrations for a *New York Times* article about New York City's criminal court. The captions reveal both the regular and ritual nature of prostitution arrests and Judge Amos Basel's weariness at failing to help the defendants brought before him. *New York Times*, Maning.

conservative activists defended the traditional family and gender roles. They eventually thwarted a proposed Equal Rights Amendment and many feminist reforms. Phyllis Schlafly, a prominent conservative leader, condemned feminists for "peddl[ing] the fiction that men are engaged in a vast conspiracy against women." She argued that the "ERA would take away legal rights that women possessed—*not* confer any new rights on women."[46]

Even so, the various changes of the era set the stage for the prostitution-related vagrancy challenges. Prosecutors and judges took a more lenient stance toward prostitutes and the vagrancy charges against them. One prosecutor commented that he did "not view it as evil in itself for a man to have sexual relations with a willing woman regardless of the paid situation." Even the police described how the dividing line between "good" and "bad" women had become more porous. When courts struck down vagrancy laws on behalf of Hattie Mae Ricks or Dorothy Kirkwood, then, they reflected changing ideas not only about vagrancy law, but also about vice and victimless crimes, sexual liberty, and sex equality.[47]

"Vag Lewd" and the Policing of Homosexuality (Continued)

This propitious combination of accumulating anti-vagrancy law resources, social movement momentum, and changing ideas about both the public and private spheres and the moral content of criminal regulation was equally clear to gay men and lesbians hoping to attack vagrancy and loitering laws. The arguments that were newly working for others all failed in 1960s sexuality vagrancy cases, however. Few litigants obtained individual relief; no headway was made in legal doctrine. The arguments the litigants made, and the reasons the courts rejected them, illuminate the boundaries and limitations of both the laws and the challenges to them.

The "police-vs.-homosexuals story," as one observer called it in 1967, was very much the same a decade after Ernest Besig encountered it in 1950s San Francisco. To many Americans, homosexuals remained as dangerous and offensive in the 1960s as they had been ten years earlier. Because laws targeted specifically at conduct in which gay men and women were likely to engage—law prohibiting sodomy, oral copulation, or solicitation of the same—were still hard to enforce, the police continued to use more readily available vagrancy laws. During raids in Boston, one woman recalled, "You had to show that you had money or you'd be picked up for vagrancy." These laws remained central to vice or morals squads' repression and harassment of gay men and lesbians in the 1960s, just as, and for many of the same reasons that, they justified prostitution arrests. Indeed, as states and cities turned "lewd vagrancy" and "loitering for solicitation" laws that had originally targeted prostitutes and lewd women against homosexuals, "vag lewd" came to be understood as almost exclusively referring to the latter.[48]

Notwithstanding the many obstacles that continued to impede those who would challenge vag lewd—difficulty finding counsel, fear of stigma, the likelihood of publicity, blackmail, and extortion that followed arrests—such challenges increased alongside changing self-conceptions of many gay men and lesbians and changing public perceptions of homosexuality. By the mid-1960s, more people had rejected the shame they were taught to feel about their "perversion" or "deviance" in favor of a gay "lifestyle" choice. More assertive and sometimes more rights-oriented organizations like the East Coast Homophile Organizations, the Society for Individual Rights, the Tavern Guild, and the Council on Religion and the Homosexual prompted more public and vociferous dissent. In 1964, when the Council hosted a New Year's Eve dance that provoked intense police surveillance and arrests, the latter were dismissed in response to political pressure. That same year, Frank Kameny—co-founder of both the East Coast Homophile Organizations and the Mattachine Society of Washington—convinced the Washington, DC, ACLU affiliate to condemn federal discrimination against homosexuality. Two years later, Kameny led the first public protests for gay rights in front of the White House and other federal buildings.[49]

A key galvanizing moment for the movement came in the winter of 1966. Two months earlier, police had interpreted the California gubernatorial election of conservative Ronald Reagan as a mandate for the suppression of homosexuality. The Los Angeles police deemed New Year's Eve an opportunity to put that mandate into practice. Just as midnight struck, patrons at the Black Cat Beer Bar on Sunset Boulevard—some of whom were in drag—sang "Auld Lang Syne" and performed the traditional midnight kiss. Undercover police officers then arrested six kissing men under California's 647(a)—soliciting or engaging in "lewd or dissolute conduct." The arrests sparked a riot, and later a picket and rally attended by some two hundred supporters. The incident both reflected and heralded major transformations in gay life, gay activism, and public opinion that would change the context in which sexuality related vagrancy cases would be brought and decided.[50]

An even more radical break came two and a half years later, when the New York City police conducted what they thought would be a routine bust of a gay bar in Greenwich Village. The raid on the Stonewall Inn turned into a riot that repeated itself for the next several nights. In the aftermath, fifty organizations exploded into eight hundred, including the Gay Liberation Front and the Gay Activists' Alliance, and gay activists instituted the tradition of gay pride marches. A few months later, the *Cleveland Plain Dealer* encapsulated some of the movement's new energy in an article entitled "Young Homosexual Women

Figure 5.2 Protests outside the Black Cat Beer Bar in Los Angeles in 1966. The protests were sparked by vagrancy arrests of gay men celebrating New Year's Eve with the traditional midnight kiss. The incident preceded the more famous Stonewall Rebellion by two and a half years and led to one of the most substantial, though still unsuccessful, cases challenging "vag lewd." ONE Archives at the USC Libraries.

Are Rebelling." It described how lesbians were "refusing to live with the limitations and restrictions imposed by society" and were instead "showing a sense of active resentment and rebellion." Stonewall became an origins story, a rallying cry, and an anniversary.[51]

The "homophile" movement thus gradually, and then rather suddenly, became a "gay liberation" or "gay rights" movement. It embraced gay identity and sought equal rights and public freedom rather than tolerance for a cramped closet. The movement adopted some of the tactics and rhetoric of the deepening militancy of the black freedom movement, the women's liberation movement, and the student New Left. Activists riffed on "Black Is Beautiful" and "Black Power" with "Gay Is Good" and "Gay Power."[52]

In tandem with changes in the self-concept and organization of gay men and lesbians, straight public opinion became somewhat less hostile to homosexuality in the late 1960s. Already a decade earlier, the Wolfenden Report, the Model Penal Code, and other professionals had recommended the decriminalization of sodomy, but they had been far out in front on the issue. As momentum for the sexual revolution merged with momentum against criminalizing victimless crimes and a growing gay rights movement, greater support for the decriminalization of sodomy followed. In 1964, the Ninth International Congress on Penal Law determined that homosexual behavior between consenting adults should not be criminalized. In 1967, the National Institute of Mental Health announced that it was forming a new task force on human sexuality that would focus on homosexuality. That same year, after three years of reconsidering its support for legal restrictions against homosexuality, the ACLU finally concluded that private consensual sex should not be illegal.[53]

New ideas about sexual morality also began to affect judicial views of sodomy laws. Wrote one appellate court in 1965 upon invalidating a law that criminalized "soliciting an unnatural sex act," "The sociological and biological range of sex acts is almost infinite. . . . [I]t is . . . apparent that many sex acts which may be logically classified as unnatural have widespread acceptance and frequent use." The Supreme Court of Alaska went further in finding void for vagueness a law prohibiting the "crime against nature." Clearly taking Hart's side in his debates with Devlin over the legitimacy of enforcing morality through the criminal law, the court noted the simultaneous "expansion of the concept of individual freedom" and the "corresponding decrease of religious beliefs as determinants of social and legal principles." The court explained, "The epochal work of Sigmund Freud, the taxonomic studies of Alfred Kinsey, and the work of countless others" have resulted in "a social and intellectual climate in which some of the revolutionary ideas of a generation ago have become the commonplaces of today. A reexamination of our entire regulation of sexual behavior by the criminal law may well be in order."[54]

At the level of policing, changes were afoot as well. Washington, DC, provides a case in point. In the early 1950s, arrests of gay men by police "decoys" were common. By the early 1960s, annual arrests on "homosexual charges" had dropped precipitously. On New Year's Day, 1966, the *Washington Post* praised the police for making half as many arrests in public places in 1965 as in 1964 for what it called "immoral behavior." The paper called "enlightened and eminently healthy reform" the decision to stop using decoys and instead to use twenty-four-hour uniformed police focused on complaints of solicitation or lewd conduct in public. It was not that the police had suddenly decided that homosexuality was a good thing. It was, rather, that they had decided to focus on its visible, public manifestations, the very kind most readily suppressed with vagrancy laws.[55]

In light of the increased vulnerability of vagrancy laws generally, the increased assertiveness of the gay rights movement, and changing public and legal opinion about victimless crimes and criminal sexual regulation, advocates began to attack sexuality related vagrancy and loitering enforcement. During the 1950s, Besig and his Northern California ACLU lawyers claimed that the "vag lewd" law was unconstitutional, but most other sexuality-related vagrancy cases made no such claims. Even as sexual minorities wrangled with police and prosecutors, they wrangled within relatively narrow confines. They claimed they were not what the law required them to be, they had not done what it required them to do. It was not until the mid-1960s that gay men and lesbians started to argue in earnest that lewd vagrancy laws, loitering laws, and other laws regulating gay sex were unconstitutional.[56]

The most developed challenges unsurprisingly emerged in New York and California, whose major cities hosted large gay communities and routine, if somewhat inconsistent, enforcement of vagrancy and loitering laws against them. Several cases concerned New York's section 887(7), which made a vagrant of anyone "who, having his face painted, discolored, covered or concealed, or being otherwise disguised, in a manner calculated to prevent his being identified, appears in a road or public highway, or in a field, lot, wood or inclosure." This "anti-masquerading" law dated back to 1845 and originally targeted rioting farmers who disguised themselves as Native Americans. By the mid-twentieth century, police had transformed the law into a prohibition against cross-dressers, "transvestites," and homosexuals. In 1964, defendants began arguing that the law was unconstitutionally vague and an arbitrary exercise of the police power. The New York courts definitively rejected such claims.[57]

Two years later, Martin Hirshhorn renewed the challenge. Since the age of seventeen, Hirshhorn had dressed as a woman. When arrested at twenty, he was working as a female hair stylist in Manhattan. His employer, his coworkers, his clients, and his friends knew he was biologically male. In February of 1965, two officers waited for Hirshhorn at the hotel where he lived ostensibly to investigate possible grand larceny. Hirshhorn walked right past them, dressed, as usual, as a woman. When the officers later knocked on the door of his hotel room—or, according to conflicting testimony, entered by breaking a lock—Hirshhorn was wearing only a half-slip and a brassiere. The officers searched the room without a warrant. They found some barbituates—on a shelf for all to see or in a box in a closet, depending again on conflicting testimony—and arrested Hirshhorn for the drugs and under the anti-masquerading vagrancy law. The detective did not arrest Hirshhorn for grand larceny, later testifying that, though that had been the asserted point of the visit, such a charge had not even occurred to him at the time. At trial, Hirshhorn argued that, among other things, 887(7) was unconstitutional. Calling Hirshhorn a "genuine transvestite," the trial judge convicted him but gave him a suspended sentence and a warning, and the appellate court affirmed.

Through the ACLU's Osmond K. Fraenkel and Stephen W. Stein, Hirshhorn petitioned the U.S. Supreme Court for certiorari ("cert"). In the petition, one can see how the various anti-vagrancy law arguments circulating at the time exacerbated a deep and long-standing tension about the nature of homosexuality and the best way for sexual minorities to advocate for themselves. The question was whether to embrace a homosexual or what would later be called a transgender identity or to claim a right to perform certain acts separate and apart from any identity. To fight only for the right to perform acts in private was to ask for much less than many wanted, much less than many considered their entitlement to full citizenship. That said, a homosexual identity was not obviously the better or more progressive choice. It had long been forced on gay men and lesbians by the medical, religious, legal, and governmental authorities that had constructed the category of the homosexual in order to regulate it. Indeed, it was not until 1965, and after long debate, that even Frank Kameny's Mattachine Society voted that "homosexuality is not a sickness."[58]

One readily available set of arguments based on *Robinson v. California* seemed to offer constitutional success at the possible cost of reinforcing this pathological view of homosexuality. The Supreme Court's opinion striking down California's law criminalizing narcotics addiction as cruel and unusual punishment under the Eighth Amendment could be read as prohibiting states from punishing three different things: an "illness," a "status," or a "condition." Hirshhorn's lawyers might have argued—as lawyers had in *Ricks*—that the vagrancy law unconstitutionally criminalized status in the sense of mere inaction. So conceived, the attack would not have played into the medicalized pathology of homosexuality. But that was not how Hirshhorn's lawyers used *Robinson*. Rather, the lawyers described transvestism as a "condition" and an "illness which is contracted involuntarily." Others took the same lesson from *Robinson* when it came to homosexuality. A law review note from 1967 discussed homosexuals in a section on "noncriminal treatment of other physical conditions" alongside narcotics addiction, alcoholism, and insanity.[59]

That said, one can see the beginnings of movement toward an affirmative identity-based sexuality in the *Hirshhorn* cert petition. The language of the statute helped. Building on the trial court's description of Hirshhorn as a "genuine transvestite," Hirshhorn's lawyers contended that Hirshhorn had only concealed his sex, not his identity. Because Hirshhorn "habitually wears female clothing, . . . [t]o do so is consistent with his identity and defines his identity. . . .

Petitioner would be concealing his identity only if he wore men's clothing." The lawyers thus suggested that Hirshhorn was enhancing—not disguising—his identity by presenting himself as a woman.[60]

The brief went one step further toward reconceiving Hirshhorn's behavior as protected nonconformity. Not only was Hirshhorn not concealing his identity—the problem the law intended to address—but he was only doing what everyone else was doing in the 1960s. "In this day and age, petitioner's conduct can hardly be said to offend public decency. Today's fashions result in long hair for men and cropped hair for girls; pants-suits, trousers and boots for girls and sequined evening coats for men." Though the argument did not go all the way toward suggesting that those like Hirshhorn—those who embraced a gender identity different from their biological sex—constituted an identifiable group entitled to constitutional protection, it nonetheless took two important steps. It recognized the identity component of Hirshhorn's actions, and it likened Hirshhorn to hippies and other young people who also wore unconventional clothing and engaged in nonconforming behavior.[61]

That was not how many of New York's prosecutors, police, and judges saw the issue. Manhattan District Attorney Frank Hogan argued that transvestites "directly offend and contradict the order of our contemporary culture." He fundamentally disagreed with the defense about the relationship between cross-dressing and disguised identity: "The dress of the opposite sex is potentially the most effective of all disguises because it is the most subtle. So basic is a person's sex to his identity, that in most cases law enforcement officers in search of a person initially narrow the scope of inquiry to 'male or female.' Transvestites are therefore as effectively disguised as if they were masked."[62]

As New York City police officers continued to enforce 887(7), and courts continued to validate convictions, even dissenting judges accepted the basic conclusion that transvestites—and the homosexuals with whom they were often equated—"offend[ed]" and "contradict[ed]." Justice Jacob Markowitz argued in one case that the law "in its present form" aimed to discourage "overt homosexuality in public places which is offensive to public morality." He dissented only because this particular offender seemed not to be homosexual but just a masquerade party attendee. Markowitz wanted to shield heterosexual and temporary gender nonconformists from a law intended to protect the public from the offense of overt homosexuality. "If appellant's conviction was correct then circus clowns, strangely attired 'hippies', flowing-haired 'yippies' and every person who would indulge in the Halloween tradition of 'Trick or Treat' ipso facto may be targets for criminal sanctions as vagrants." He worried that, "carrying the majority view to its logical conclusion, a young man or woman could possibly be convicted under this section as a vagrant merely for venturing into the street in his or her normal attire, which is otherwise acceptable in society today."[63]

Markowitz thus viewed 887(7) in the same context of the changing gender and cultural mores of the 1960s as Hirshhorn's lawyers, but he drew very different conclusions. Markowitz would have applied the law only to those who regularly concealed their identities in the service of "public homosexuality." Fraenkel and Stein argued that precisely because Hirshhorn was a transvestite, his gender bending was not identity-concealing but identity-enhancing. Where Fraenkel and Stein read the law as targeting "real" disguise, Markowitz read it as targeting "real" homosexuality. Markowitz and the Hirshhorn lawyers also disagreed about how to think about the relationship between gender-bending hippies and gender-bending homosexuals. Did the former pave the way for the latter, or delineate the outer edge of toleration? Hirshhorn's lawyers thought the first; Markowitz, the second. Judges often agreed with Markowitz, but distinctions could be difficult to make. A police officer on the Port Authority Bus Terminal beat said, "You've got to be careful. Just because a man has long hair, you don't go up and arrest him. He might be a concert pianist. Down here, if a man has pancake make-up on, it doesn't mean there's anything wrong. He might be a big Broadway actor. You have to watch and watch."[64]

These comparisons raised the larger question of where sexual minorities fit within the topography of those regulated by vagrancy law. Being categorized as a discriminated-against minority rather than a worthless undesirable was key to constitutional success. Litanies of "undesirables" targeted by vice and morals squads that included "homosexuals" or "perverts" alongside "dope addicts, pimps, [and] prostitutes" reinforced legal and popular ideas of the homosexual as both a criminal and a nuisance. Even as some of these groups were trying to remove themselves from the category of vice and immorality, claiming rights as a protection-deserving minority group was an uphill battle for those who called themselves "the homosexual minority." They argued that they were "a minority in no way different, as such, from other of our national minority groups."[65]

The issue came up explicitly in the defense of those arrested at the Black Cat Beer Bar on New Year's Eve 1967 under the lewd disorderly conduct law that had replaced California's vag lewd law. Charles W. Talley and Benny Norman Baker found legal counsel in Herbert Selwyn, a straight lawyer who often defended gay men and lesbians. (He commented that "there weren't any gay lawyers in those days who would admit it.") Selwyn's cert petition read more like a rehash of arguments in other types of vagrancy cases than it did like the somewhat apologetic and equivocal arguments offered in cases like *Hirshhorn*. Selwyn adapted void for vagueness and status crime arguments from vagrancy challenges to the new disorderly conduct context. He and Los Angeles City Attorney Roger Arnebergh battled over what exactly made the kisses in question lewd. According to Arnebergh, not all male-on-male kissing was lewd. "The president of France kissing a decorated hero, the premier of the Soviet Union kissing a returning cosmonaut, men from the 'old country' kissing a male relative or a father kissing a son—these acts engaged in a public place are not done in a lewd and dissolute manner." He claimed that a plethora of facts made the Black Cat kisses illegal: "the manner of the . . . kiss," "the gender of the parties," "the mode of dress," and "the place." Despite the fact that all this seemed to add up to these-were-gay-men-kissing-sexually-in-a-gay-bar, Arnebergh claimed that the convictions in no way punished the men's sexual status. Selwyn sought clearer standards for "how long a kiss may be prolonged with safety." Where did the law say that "kissing between non-related males in public for more than two seconds, provided neither party was the president of France nor the premier of the Soviet Union," was illegal?[66]

Selwyn emphasized his point by moving from vagueness under due process to discrimination under equal protection. The shift was important. Lawyers challenging sodomy and other sex crimes had largely relied on void for vagueness. In part, this was because language such as "crimes against nature" was antiquated and therefore potentially vague. In part, it was because many gay men and lesbians had not entirely embraced the idea of a homosexual identity that was a conceptual prerequisite for an equal protection claim. Even more important, whoever else might hope to find protection in a developing equal protection doctrine, homosexuals seemed highly unlikely to. Lawyers had been claiming discrimination on the basis of race and poverty in vagrancy cases for some time. But to contend, as Selwyn did, that the equal protection clause prevented selective enforcement against homosexuals of a law clearly intended to proscribe homosexual behavior was to inch out along a fragile limb of constitutional doctrine. "The simple fact of the matter," Selwyn argued, "is that on that festive occasion, no men in all Los Angeles County were arrested for kissing women in a lewd manner at any public place." Likening homosexuals to Chinese Americans and African Americans, he claimed the mantle of equal protection for his clients. "It took almost a century to grant the constitutional rights of our ethnic minorities in this country. Let us hope that the homophile minority will achieve its equal rights with more dispatch." If Eighth Amendment arguments under *Robinson* reinforced the image of homosexuals as sick or immoral, equal protection arguments tried to turn them into unconstitutionally oppressed rights-bearing citizens.[67]

The question that followed was how to describe the "rights" to which Selwyn thought his clients entitled. Indeed, the question of what conduct could be engaged in in public and what was reserved for private—as well as the related question of what could be prohibited even in private—was one of the most critical issues for gay and lesbian challenges to vagrancy and loitering laws. As a general matter, legal professionals seemed to agree that it was not formally illegal to be gay. That said, it seemed to many that the criminal prohibitions against sodomy and lewdness had the effect of criminalizing the status of homosexuality. Some courts thought that it could "not be doubted" that within legislative power to define vagrancy was the power to subject to police oversight "persons whose habits of life are such as to make them objectionable members of society." Even where the status of homosexuality was not explicitly the target, the eradication of homosexual behavior was. "The driving force" behind vagrancy and loitering laws, explained the *UCLA Law Review*, was "the suppression of sexual behavior, which by deviating from the societal norm, is deemed to be destructive per se of the moral fibre of society." Both Congress and the Supreme Court reinforced such ideas in the immigration context, where Congress decreed that the Immigration and Naturalization Service exclude homosexuals, and the Supreme Court validated the policy.[68]

Others thought that the real harm of homosexuality was less its existence than its public display. Though there was hardly agreement as to private, consensual, adult sodomy, *Griswold* in particular offered far more support for decriminalizing such hidden activities than for allowing homosexual behavior in public. One might countenance private homosexuality despite moral disapproval precisely because of its invisibility and victimlessness. Occasionally even those who vigorously policed public gay sex acknowledged that what was done in private was none of the law's business. As one vice control police veteran put it, "That's why I don't like anything public. Private, there is no problem." New York City's lawyers in *Hirshhorn* suggested that to the extent that transvestites had any rights, as the petition contended they did under *Griswold*, these rights applied only to the private sphere. Hirshhorn was "perfectly free to indulge his sartorial tastes in any private place, where it will not offend public order and decency." (No matter that the police had arrested Hirshhorn in his hotel room.)[69]

Whether the offense caused by otherwise harmless behavior in public view could constitute a criminally regulable harm was a point of more debate. Gay sex was one thing. But gay sex in public was a problem that had to be addressed. Because of this focus on sex in public, the arrests and the cases that followed more often involved gay men than lesbians. Few women were charged with vag lewd offenses because, as one morals division official put it, lesbians "don't troll like the men do." He said his division had wanted to assign a policewoman to investigate female homosexual activity but "she wasn't able to make any determination of anything going on." That said, police did arrest women in bars or just outside of them, when they thought the women "could stand a pinch."[70]

Just as law enforcement officers increasingly focused their energies on public acts rather than private ones, advocates for sexual decriminalization focused their challenges on private restrictions. They sometimes even agreed that public gay sex could be, perhaps even should be, regulated. When the

ACLU changed its policy on homosexuality, it only opposed laws penalizing private conduct. The sympathetic *UCLA Law Review* described "freedom from lewd public displays and freedom from bothersome sexual solicitations" as "legitimate public interests." To the extent that "the solicitation and consummation of homosexual acts in *public* becomes the only ground upon which the imposition of criminal sanctions is properly sustainable," it was far easier to launch constitutional attacks against privacy-intruding sodomy laws than public-regarding vagrancy laws.[71]

The Model Penal Code, which was at the cutting edge in recommending the elimination of laws criminalizing private consensual sodomy in 1955, reflected this same public/private-vagrancy/sodomy distinction. In addition to decriminalizing sodomy, the MPC also recommended eliminating generally applicable vagrancy laws. What the MPC did not recommend was the decriminalization of public solicitation for gay sex (though it did not criminalize similar heterosexual behavior), and the crimes of "flouting of decency" and "openly and notoriously maintain[ing] an illicit sexual relationship" proved difficult for the ALI to assess. Louis Schwartz, the main author of the sections of the MPC dealing with morals offenses, explained the distinction like this: "The target of this legislation is not private immorality but a kind of public 'nuisance' caused by congregation of homosexuals offensively flaunting their deviance from general norms of behavior." The point was not the behavior itself but the "outrage" the public would feel when confronted with it. Offense at "private debauchery" was not enough to justify criminalizing such private conduct. A California court encapsulated this distinction when it asked whether "an act which openly outrages public decency" referred "to conduct decent and moral when done in private, but not when in public; or conduct indecent or immoral, or both, even if private, which outrages the 'public', whether done in private or public? Finally, even if we decide which attitude of the public, the moral or the decorous, is the one which must be outraged, there is the question 'who is the public'?"[72]

Where the public/private line should be drawn was more complicated than might at first glance appear. On the one hand, the privacy interest that *Griswold* had identified might apply even in public spaces. In several cases, courts condemned as Fourth Amendment violations police surveillance of homosexual activity in places like public bathrooms. In addition, in a 1966 law review article criticizing police questioning of people on the street, Yale law professor Charles Reich (who later came out as gay) called for "protected crannies for the soul" on the public nighttime street. CORE General Counsel Carl Rachlin put it this way: "Privacy has been defended as to acts in our homes and in our bedrooms [*Griswold*]. Cannot one say that the citizen who commits no wrongful act should have at least a similar right to be free of the duty of explaining one's peaceful presence in a public place?" Though these commentators did not explicitly discuss homosexuality, their views called into question the sharp distinction between the private crime of sodomy—to which opposition was then growing—and the public crimes of vagrancy, loitering, and solicitation—which most favored retaining. Allowing expression of one's identity only in private might prove constitutionally inadequate to undermining vagrancy laws.[73]

On the other hand, dispute persisted over what would be considered private space immune from arrest. Law enforcement officers sometimes arrested gay men and lesbians in private places and charged them with lewd vagrancy and the like. *Hirshhorn* provides one example. In another instance, a man allegedly called the police during a party in his neighbor's home. He objected to the fact that the women were wearing pants. As in the Black Cat and Stonewall incidents, police and homosexuals battled over the public or private nature, and hence regulability, of gay bars as well. Gay groups contended that gay bars were a good thing— they kept gay men away from parks, restrooms, bus stations, and most pointedly, children. A New Orleans man wrote in 1960, "The idea [of raiding gay bars], I understand is to force the gay people out on the streets so they can be picked up for loitering, vagrancy, public display of homosexuality, etc." But he thought the policy counterproductive. "We gladly abandoned the streets. We gladly abandoned the parks. We gladly abandoned the museums and such. We had places we could go."[74]

Even the status of private gay clubs established for greater insulation from the "public" was uncertain. When one undercover officer joined such a club in Washington, DC, ultimately arresting the owner and three employees for operating a "disorderly house," jurors found the employees innocent and could come to no decision about the owner. Clearly, the jurors' sense of what was public and private, what was criminally disorderly and what not, differed more from the views of the police than from the views of the gay men operating the club. If the reason that gay sex, or even gay kissing, gay dancing, and gay hand-holding, was problematic was that they shocked the sensibilities of the regular, middle-class straight, then gay men and women who congregated in their own bars, clubs, or private homes could not seriously be taken to offend. Indeed, police must have found it frustrating when the signs they hung on gay bars announcing "Raided Premises" served only to titillate tourists who flocked to ogle.[75]

Into the early 1970s, sexuality related vagrancy challenges could tout the occasional grudging victory. In Washington, DC, after two remands, the second with quite specific instructions from the Court of Appeals for the District of Columbia Circuit, a trial court finally enjoined further police harassment. It declared, for the plaintiff only, the right to walk the streets without being questioned by law enforcement officers about his sexual orientation. Moreover, the very existence of debates about the criminalization of public versus private conduct shifted the defense of criminalization away from status altogether and toward some kind of concrete conduct.[76]

That said, status-based vag lewd laws remained on the books. "Vice" was to some extent morphing into "victimless crime," vagrants were vying for a new status as rights bearers, and courts and legislatures liberalized many aspects of sexuality regulation. But homosexuality remained a pariah status within much of the legal profession. The homosexual still seemed always out of place, everywhere (except perhaps in the closet). The vagrancy laws could legitimately try to lock up, commit, closet, or just plain harass him. The legal claim to rights-bearing status and especially the claim to be one's real self in public were difficult for sexual minorities to make. As lawyers and judges struggled to redraw the lines between public and private, between status and conduct, between the legitimate moral regulation of vice and the illegitimate moral regulation of victimless crimes, these cases showed how porous and indeterminate those categories were.[77]

The Criminalization of Idle Poverty

If changing ideas of sexual morality led to mixed results for sexuality-related vagrancy cases in the late 1960s, changing ideas about the moral valence of poverty had more definitive results. Like "perverts" and "prostitutes," the "drunks, junkies, drifters," and plain old idle unemployed offended both conventional moral tenets and mainstream sensibilities. As Sam Thompson well knew, the fundamental moral failing of idle poverty was a common justification for vice and morals squad vagrancy arrests. The criminalization of idle poverty had been the basic vagrancy concept for centuries.

That a practice that had routinely flown under the radar might no longer be constitutionally acceptable must have come as a surprise to men like Dunn, North Carolina, recorders' court judge Woodrow Hill. A few months after Anthony Amsterdam published his article in 1967, Hill initiated a widely publicized "crackdown" on vagrants that brought the LDF into a type of vagrancy case quite different from its usual civil rights arrest. "Farmers and businessmen are crying for help," Hill was quoted on the front page of the local paper. "They desperately need people to work and vagrancy isn't going to be tolerated in this town." Hill told the Dunn police chief that he wanted everyone loafing around without a job to be arrested and charged under a local ordinance that decreed, "Any and all tramps, vagrants, persons under suspicion who shall be found with no visible means of support, either male or female, shall not be allowed on the streets or other public place." The newspaper described Hill as "the leading

Knight" of the campaign and printed a few of the many letters of support he received in a column called "Dear Judge Hill."[78]

Judge Hill's crackdown was in many respects vagrancy business as usual. The legal response it generated was not. Though the "responsible citizens" of the area were pleased with Hill, Amsterdam, Greenberg, and their LDF colleagues joined Dunn civil rights lawyers J. Levonne Chambers and Samuel S. Mitchell to bring a groundbreaking federal civil rights suit. Using the procedural techniques that they and others had pioneered on behalf of the civil rights movement, lawyers transformed "apparent ne'er-do-wells" into rights-bearing contenders. Federal district court Judge Robert Hemphill, another recent Lyndon B. Johnson appointee, was no fire-eating liberal. By the time the LDF was done with him, though, he seemed to have drunk the vagrancy critique Kool-Aid. Echoing the LDF's brief, Hemphill concluded in the spring of 1968 that the ordinance was not only "vague and overly broad," but that it "restrain[ed] freedom of movement, subject[ed] persons to arrest and detention on suspicion, in effect require[d] a suspect to establish his own innocence, require[d] compulsory employment, create[d] a crime of the status of indigency and impose[d] sanctions upon poor people which [did] not apply to those with wealth in violation of a variety of provisions of the Constitution."[79]

Both the lawyers and the judge thus viewed *Smith v. Hill*, and the vagrancy problem it attacked, capaciously. They synthesized multiple frameworks of oppression and their constitutional counterparts. Hemphill extended *Robinson v. California*'s prohibition of criminalizing the status of narcotics addiction to the status of poverty. He articulated how race and class combined with the presumption of criminality to confer on city officials "dictatorial control over the streets and public places." The town might have been small (population 7,500) and the ordinance of only local significance, but the case, the decision, and the expansive opinion represented a broader shift in professional legal views of vagrancy laws and their constitutional infirmities.[80]

Since the Great Depression and the Supreme Court's pronouncement in *Edwards v. California* that "poverty and immorality are not synonymous," vagrancy law skepticism had been visible in a handful of judicial invalidations, a small burst of scholarly commentary, and *Thompson v. Louisville* and a few other Supreme Court decisions. Condemnation of discrimination against the poor, especially in the operation of criminal justice, continued in Supreme Court cases in the 1950s and 1960s. Cases analogized race and class, announcing that "a State can no more discriminate on account of poverty than on account of religion, race, or color." At moments, the Court seemed even on the verge of protecting positive rights to certain governmental goods or services, rather than only negative rights not to have the government discriminate. The states ratified an amendment to the federal constitution prohibiting poll taxes.[81]

Vagrancy laws nonetheless remained largely intact as the Depression receded. When President Franklin D. Roosevelt vetoed a vagrancy law for Washington, DC, in 1941, he was more concerned that the law might ensnare the "idle" children of the rich than that its criminalization of poverty was somehow wrong. Only once did the Court revisit the vagrancy criminalization of poverty between *Thompson* and the late 1960s. In the 1964 case of *Arceneaux v. Louisiana*, the Court considered the conviction of a white farmworker in Cajun country that recalled the use of vagrancy laws against African Americans on southern plantations from the previous century. After Sidney Arceneaux requested overdue wages, his landlord fired him and ordered him to leave the one-room shack he occupied as part of his compensation. Before Arceneaux could leave, sheriff's deputies (including the landlord's son) arrested him for vagrancy. After holding him partly incommunicado for several months, local officials released Arceneaux in a morass of procedural confusion. Though the Supreme Court granted certiorari and heard argument, the justices gave up trying to decipher what had happened and dismissed the case as improvidently granted. Even without resolution on the merits, at least some of the justices indicated that they found the case "outrageous." In an unusual move, Chief Justice Warren thanked Arceneaux's lawyer "for having carried the case of this prisoner to all the courts, and to this Court. . . . It is a public cause." While the Court was considering the case, Justice Arthur J. Goldberg, one of the more liberal of the Warren Court's generally liberal justices, mentioned vagrancy laws as an example of discrimination against the poor within the criminal justice system in a lecture at New York University Law School.[82]

By the late 1960s, the divergence between the immorality of poverty that predicated vagrancy laws and emerging ideas about poverty, work, and the labor market had grown even wider. Arresting people for unemployment seemed to some observers increasingly untenable given new cultural trends, grassroots efforts, reform movements, and governmental policies. The "discovery" of desperate white privation in Appalachia and elsewhere in books like Michael Harrington's 1962 *The Other America* not only put the many variants of American poverty on the national agenda but also suggested their deep incongruity and injustice. Indeed, if the structural nature of poverty had diminished the poverty-morality connection during times of hardship, the standard Keynesian presumption that a functioning economy required some small but significant level of unemployment—and the failure of full employment policy in the late 1940s—made it seem unfair that those deliberately, or at least knowingly, excluded from employment during boom times should be penalized. Justice Douglas commented in 1963, "The scientific revolution displaces men and substitutes the machine with the result that we have the promise of a permanent surplus of unemployed people." Was the sacrificial nonworker to be made a criminal on account of macroeconomic necessities? As ACLU-affiliated vagrancy lawyer Dan Struve put it on behalf of vagrancy clients in San Antonio, what justified vagrancy authority to arrest those "without visible means of support in a city that had been called "Poverty City, U.S.A.," listed at the bottom of metropolitan areas for family income?[83]

The civil rights struggle was at least equally responsible for changing ideas about poverty and unemployment. Economic justice had long been key to African Americans' goals. As it became apparent that the end of segregation laws left intact economic inequalities, organizations ranging ideologically from Martin Luther King Jr.'s Southern Christian Leadership Conference to the Black Panther Party explicitly linked poverty with racial injustice rather than immorality.[84]

The civil rights struggle also provided a launching pad for African American and Latina women who joined in a national welfare rights movement in the 1960s. Hundreds of local organizations and tens of thousands of women and their families joined together to try to transform the way Americans, and especially policymakers, thought about welfare and its recipients. They pressed for rights rather than a paternalistic charity that came with coercive strings and could be withdrawn without warning. They sought "fair hearings" for decisions regarding their welfare benefits, and they claimed respect for their dignity and autonomy in both the market and the home. Combining ideas from the civil rights movement with the burgeoning women's movement and the sexual revolution, they contested centuries of white efforts to control the sexuality of black women. In particular, they condemned unannounced midnight raids that conditioned welfare benefits on recipients' chastity and the absence of a "man in the house." Though courts did not validate all of the movement's claims, they did validate some. In one successful case, the Court self-consciously rejected earlier attitudes about the relationship between poverty and morality. "Federal welfare policy now rests on a basis considerably more sophisticated and enlightened than the 'worthy-person' concept of earlier times."[85]

The persistence of dire need among both whites and minorities inspired first John F. Kennedy and then Lyndon B. Johnson to formulate federal anti-poverty policies that rejected, if somewhat ambivalently, the assumption of the immorality of poverty. Johnson's "War on Poverty" became more urgent when violence repeatedly erupted in black neighborhoods between 1964 and 1968. This brought increased attention to inner-city "ghettos" and the structural economic problems they faced. Johnson's barrage of legislation created food stamps, Medicare and Medicaid, and reforms addressing education, jobs, voting, cities, and housing. It was intended to empower the poor in initiatives like the Economic

Opportunity Act's Community Action Program, Head Start, Neighborhood Development Centers, Job Corps, migrant worker programs, and local health care centers. With its emphasis on "maximum feasible participation" by poor people and providing a "hand up" rather than a "hand out," the most ambitious of these programs embodied a rights-bearing and effectual, rather than morally deficient and dependent, view of the poor. With its increased social welfare provision, it attenuated the historical assumption that the able-bodied must work for their subsistence. The welfare state required the decriminalization of poverty just as much as, if not more than, free market ideology did.[86]

These various developments never completely decoupled poverty and immorality. As welfare rights activists pointed out, many liberals supportive of a more generous welfare state continued to take a moralistic view of the poor. Moreover, many Americans, especially those in rapidly growing conservative organizations, resisted expanding "statism" and "welfarism"—in conservative political pioneer Barry Goldwater's words—and the moral claims of both welfare recipients and skid row drunks. To them, the new federal behemoth itself threatened to deny fundamental liberties, and the money it spent on the poor—and most controversially the minority poor—was destructive of market-based capitalism, the traditional family, and social order. Whether the police defended vagrancy laws because they subscribed to such views or because, as Egon Bittner suggested in his 1967 article, they appreciated any tool that would help them keep the peace and protect their vulnerable charges, one thing was clear: into the late 1960s, law enforcement continued to turn to vagrancy laws when faced with the poor, the unemployed, and the idle.[87]

A complete decoupling was not necessary to spur a new wave of vagrancy challenges. It was enough that someone like J. Skelly Wright—one of the nation's most prominent liberal federal appeals court judges—condemned vagrancy and similar laws for having "made it virtually a crime to be poor in public," which was not only "uncivilized" but also "futile and self-defeating." It was enough that the vagrancy law critique resonated simultaneously with the liberal welfare state and emerging, neo-liberal free market ideology. It was enough that Wright and others could conclude, as some had in the sexuality context, that vagrancy laws seemed to be more about obnoxious visibility than anything else. Vagrancy laws, he wrote, served "primarily the aesthetic function of removing from the sight of the establishment the wretchedly poor, whose condition we do nothing about but cannot bear to see. As one study points out, the only reason for many vagrancy arrests was apparently that 'the appearance of the victims was not attractive.' "[88]

Sentiments like these led to new vagrancy challenges not only because of changing ideas of poverty and the labor market but also because poor people had access to new resources. Though most states had already been providing some indigent criminal defendants with lawyers, the Supreme Court's 1963 case of *Gideon v. Wainwright* and those that followed made the requirement national, constitutional, and more expansive in declaring that the Sixth Amendment's guarantee of "the assistance of counsel" required states to provide free lawyers under certain circumstances. Around the same time, the War on Poverty created the Legal Services Corporation. With the rise of legal aid lawyers and public defenders, poor Americans had substantial access to legal representation for the first time in American history.[89]

The perception that poor people needed such legal assistance derived in part from concerns about procedural problems like those Louis Lusky and Caleb Foote had identified in the 1950s. Numerous organizations and agencies published reports about the many ways the administration of justice discriminated against the poor. Foote, father of modern anti-vagrancy law scholarship, published a whole series of articles—edited by his then-law student Anthony Amsterdam—on the need for bail reform. Others detailed the plight of vagrants and poor alcoholics who spent much of their lives entering and exiting the nation's jails in what was sometimes called "turnstile justice." The overall effect of discriminatory criminal justice practices, in the view of the critics, was to oppress and disempower the poor. In a 1969 article entitled, "The Courts Have Failed the Poor," Judge Wright lamented that the procedural deficiencies of the low-level courts with which the poor most frequently came into contact led them to see the law as "designed to keep them shackled to their poverty and imprisoned in the inner city."[90]

Taken together, social movement organization and critiques like Wright's spurred lawyers to bring a host of procedural and substantive challenges on behalf of the poor. The NAACP LDF challenge of Judge Hill's get-to-work crusade, for example, reflected just such an expansion for LDF. The lawyers of the LDF already perceived themselves as attacking poverty through their school desegregation and employment discrimination cases. But a grant from the Ford Foundation to create a National Office for the Rights of Indigent (NORI) gave their anti-poverty cases a new status and wider berth. The lawyers thought, in Amsterdam's words, that "it was important for us to challenge laws which oppressed poor people because they were poor as well as the traditional laws which oppressed people because they were black. [W]e began to make challenges to statutes on the economic discrimination ground as well as racial discrimination ground." LDF lawyers challenged eviction procedures, inferior government services, and a variety of anti-consumer practices that injured the poor. When Judge Hill gave them an opportunity to include a vagrancy challenge among these new efforts, they took it.[91]

The LDF was not alone. The changing poverty context also affected the ACLU's vagrancy docket and brought new ACLU vagrancy victories. Though in its early years the organization had defended the civil liberties of organizing workers, poverty and unemployment had never figured prominently among its priorities. By 1966, however, ACLU lawyers were asking, "What is happening to the civil liberties of the poor?" and "Is economic well-being a civil liberties concern?" The NYCLU's Paul Chevigny thought the answer to the latter was clearly yes. He argued that the ACLU "should more strongly push the idea of a right to a minimum income as a civil liberties issue." Though not everyone at the ACLU agreed, affiliated lawyers took on a number of poverty-related cases in the late 1960s and early 1970s, including both welfare rights cases and challenges to public drunkenness laws.[92]

As part of these efforts, ACLU lawyers brought constitutional litigation against vagrancy laws' criminalization of unemployment more self-consciously than they had in the past. The organization's affiliated lawyers had been battling vagrancy laws since Al Wirin's 1930s farmworker cases, but the 1960s witnessed a greater focus on the anachronism of criminalizing idle poverty. Emanuel Redfield needed no new impetus to challenge vagrancy laws. By the late 1960s, he had already argued one case—1953's *Edelman v. California*—to the Supreme Court and, as a 1964 *New York Times* article recounted, "had been searching for years for [a vagrancy] case on which to base an appeal." By 1964, Redfield was convinced that Charles Fenster was his man, if only he could find the right litigation strategy. The trick was that every time Fenster was arrested—as he was three times in three months—the courts acquitted him. That made it hard to challenge section 887(1)—making everyone a vagrant who "not having visible means to maintain himself, lives without employment"—even as the police continued to threaten Fenster with arrest. First Redfield lost in state court. Then he lost in federal court. On his third try, back in state court with a prayer for declaratory judgment, he finally won in the New York Court of Appeals in June of 1967. It had taken more than fifteen years for Redfield to overturn New York's vagrancy law.[93]

The case made headline news and became a staple citation in subsequent vagrancy cases. The key to *Fenster's* prominence was not only that it was pioneering, preceding LDF's *Smith v. Hill* by some nine months. It was also that the case explicitly undermined the basic premise of vagrancy laws. Throughout Redfield's crusade, he had challenged both the law's stated and historical purpose—to punish the poor and force them to work—and its more recent and strategic use—to prevent crime by evading the Fourth Amendment's probable cause requirement. Though the court ultimately referenced both problems, it put more emphasis on the problems with the law as conceived than abused. The court discussed how vagrancy laws implicated the Thirteenth Amendment's prohibition on involuntary servitude, the Fourteenth Amendment's application of equal protection of the law to the poor, and the Eighth Amendment's prohibition on crimes of status in *Robinson v. California*. The court found the law "defective on the ground that, whatever purpose and role it may or may not have served in an earlier day . . . in this era of widespread efforts to motivate and educate the poor toward economic betterment of themselves, of the 'War on Poverty' and all its varied programs, it is obvious to all that the vagrancy laws have been abandoned by our governmental authorities as a means of 'persuading' unemployed poor persons to seek work." Echoing the Hart position on victimless crimes, the court noted that "the only crime" of the skid row inhabitants who were the law's main victims was "against themselves." They were "more properly objects of the welfare laws and public health programs than of the criminal law."[94]

No one knew better than the legal aid lawyers and public defenders who regularly represented the poor that vagrancy laws were a problem. As a new segment of the bar, these lawyers did not have the kind of history with vagrancy laws that lawyers in the LDF and the ACLU did. But that did not dampen their enthusiasm once they began encountering vagrancy laws in the latter half of the 1960s. Many brought with them instructive experiences from previous social movement involvement.

Take Bruce Rogow. While attending the University of Florida Law School in 1961, he worked as a desk clerk at a motel in Gainesville. Rogow's response to the Florida law alums he encountered was, "This is what happens after 20 years. You wear orange pants and blue shirts and go to Florida football games." You become a real estate lawyer or insurance lawyer. "And I decided that I didn't want to be that kind of lawyer." At the same time, Rogow became friends with the motel's African American bellboy, who took him to his first NAACP meeting. After Rogow worked in Jackson, Mississippi, with Anthony Amsterdam and the Lawyers' Constitutional Defense Committee, he joined the staff of the Miami legal aid office, the first in the state.[95]

As Rogow transitioned from being a civil rights lawyer to a legal services lawyer, he applied lessons from Amsterdam about "using law in affirmative ways." When clients came to Rogow after vagrancy arrests, he saw the cases in the larger context of "low-level problems in the criminal law that affected poor people." Together with assistant and then public defender Philip Hubbart, Rogow successfully challenged a number of procedural practices that hurt poor defendants involving bail setting, probable cause hearings, prejudgment repossession of property (or replevin), and the right to counsel.[96]

When Rogow met Matthew Lazarus, he saw Lazarus's case and a challenge to the vagrancy laws under which Lazarus had been arrested as part of this larger "package" of cases he and Hubbart were bringing on behalf of poor people. In Rogow's recollection, "Matthew Lazarus was a white kid, kind of

scrawny, kind of homeless . . . and he did not fit in. He lived on the street off
and on." Perhaps Rogow also found appealing—and potentially constitutionally
salient—Lazarus's possible status as a free speaker, given what one law clerk later
referred to as Lazarus's "flamboyant Humphrey Muskie [presidential campaign]
attire."[97]

The case Rogow thought of as "Lazarus Rising" was ideal for a federal civil
rights suit because Lazarus had been arrested several times and continued to
be arrested even after the suit was filed. The arrests only stopped after a federal
judge issued a restraining order. Yet another recent Johnson appointee, federal
district judge Ted Cabot, fully adopted Rogow's arguments. The judge described
Lazarus as "a frequent winter visitor to Miami" who was unlike other tourists
only in that "his vacationlike attitude has resulted, on five occasions, in his arrest
and trial for violation of the state and city vagrancy laws." Cabot concluded that
"in a day when terms such as 'serfdom' and 'feudalism' are proper subjects for
grad school ancient history classes, we face a penal statute which historically
was designed as a substitute for serfdom." Cabot invalidated the law as vague
and overbroad. It was vague because, as anti-poverty activists had argued, it left
unanswered fundamental questions about the individual's relationship to the
labor market and subsistence. Cabot asked, "How is [the alleged vagrant] to
know how continuous his employment must be so as to satisfy the authorities?
What is sufficient property to sustain himself? For that matter, how well must
he sustain himself so as to protect him from being 'sustained' in the county jail?"
The law was overbroad because, as the victimless crime critique held, "it pun-
ishes conduct of an individual which in no way impinges on the rights or interests of others." Cabot called for a "modern" law that could both maintain order
and protect "citizens in the enjoyment of their constitutional rights."[98]

That *Fenster, Hill,* and *Lazarus* were brought suggests new lawyerly interest in and resources for vagrancy challenges to the criminalization of vagrancy
itself. That, and how, they succeeded suggests new judicial acceptance of changing constitutional ideas about poverty, immorality, and criminality. Indeed,
these cases provide only examples, if prominent examples, of such success. As a
result of LDF, ACLU, legal aid, and public defense efforts in the late 1960s, the
weight of judicial authority was shifting. Had Louis Lusky determined to challenge Louisville's vagrancy and loitering laws in 1960, he would have had few
precedents to cite. Less than a decade later, *Lazarus* relied on *Smith, Fenster,* and
other recent cases, noting that its conclusions were the same as "so many other
courts across the land," while a Georgia case upholding a vagrancy law relied on
two Missouri cases from 1911 and 1923. Invalidations made clear that courts
now found vagrancy laws problematic not only because they were improperly
used for crime control or harassing civil rights activists, Beats, or communists.
They were problematic because their very purpose was inimical to the modern

welfare state. Contemporary ideas about poverty, unemployment, and autonomy required new interpretations of the Constitution.[99]

Cases like *Ricks, Kirkwood, Fenster, Hill,* and *Lazarus* did not wholly transform the unemployed, the "promiscuous," or the "deviant" from vagrants to fully rights-bearing citizens, or vagrancy laws from entirely legitimate to entirely illegitimate. Some courts specifically reaffirmed the old chestnut that the vagrant was "the chrysalis of every species of criminal" and that the poor were "more likely to turn to crime to supply their bodily wants and needs." Most rejected the anti-vagrancy law claims of sexual minorities.[100]

Just a few years after Amsterdam published his training manual, however, vagrancy laws had become obvious targets for constitutional litigation. Lawyers in a host of different legal institutions representing a host of different types of vagrants were self-consciously making constitutional connections across social contexts. State and lower federal courts across the country were embracing their arguments. Momentum was growing.

"The Most Significant Criminal Case of the Year"

Stephen Wainwright's troubles began around midnight on October 12, 1964, when the white Tulane law student and Massachusetts native left his French Quarter apartment to get a bite to eat. He apparently resembled a murder suspect the New Orleans police were hunting. When a few officers approached him, Wainwright answered some basic questions. When the officers asked to see his forearm, where the murder suspect sported a "Born to Raise Hell" tattoo, he balked. The police eventually arrested him for "vagrancy by loitering" and resisting and reviling the police. Wainwright continued to refuse to bare his arm at the police station, and it was only after a scuffle with several officers that it became clear that Wainwright was not their man. When Wainwright wrote his own petition to the Supreme Court after a losing two-year battle in the state courts, the justices agreed to hear his case.[1]

The police officers who arrested Wainwright were not provoked by his relative poverty, his perceived immorality, his unpopular views. The police suspected Wainwright not of drunkenness or perversity. Rather, they thought he might have just committed murder. They had no real proof—in constitutional terms, no probable cause under the Fourth Amendment. Without that, it was difficult for the police to arrest Wainwright. So instead of letting Wainwright potentially get away with murder, they arrested him for vagrancy—investigatively, for questioning.

The justices of the Supreme Court seemed interested in *Wainwright v. New Orleans* for precisely that reason: it involved a pretextual arrest motivated by the suspicion that the defendant was involved in more serious crime. The justices could have taken other types of vagrancy cases in 1967. Around the same time, both Martin Hirshhorn, the "genuine transvestite," and Charles Fenster, among others, sought the Court's attention. The justices chose not to take those cases. Perhaps they were poor vehicles, or the issues were not yet ripe, or the outcomes—whether they struck down an idle-poverty vagrancy law or upheld a vag lewd one—were correct. Perhaps the justices thought the use of vagrancy laws in combating major, rather than petty, crime the more pressing policing issue. Or they thought the pretextual crime control application of vagrancy laws, rather than constitutional infirmities inherent in the laws, the more compelling constitutional one.[2]

That the justices were particularly interested in the ways vagrancy laws might license police discretion for crime control purposes was apparent not only from their choice of *Wainwright*. It was also clear in the justices' consideration of another case that involved police authority on the street: *Terry v. Ohio*. Granted four months after *Wainwright, Terry* raised the constitutionality of the police "stopping" and "frisking" suspects with less evidence than the probable cause they would need for "searches" and "seizures" under the Fourth Amendment.

By 1967, *Wainwright* and *Terry* raised rather urgent questions. Following the insights of Caleb Foote, Ernest Besig, Louis Lusky, and Anthony Amsterdam, a growing cadre of lawyers, activists, academics, and state and lower federal judges had concluded that both vagrancy laws and their enforcers were a problem. As the southern civil rights movement highlighted the role of law enforcement in racial inequality, and police abuse and brutality in non-southern cities sparked violence and riots, liberal lawyers and scholars began paying more attention to the issue of police discretion generally and vagrancy enforcement specifically. They called for both invalidation of vagrancy laws and increased supervision of the police.

As much, if not more, of the urgency about these issues came from the other side of the political spectrum, where the police and their allies complained that the new judicially imposed constitutional rules of the Warren Court's "criminal procedure revolution" prevented them from keeping order in disorderly times. According to statistics compiled by the FBI, the property crime rate increased by 73 percent and violent crime by 57 percent between 1960 and 1967. The latter doubled by 1969. Moreover, thanks to the (failed) 1964 presidential bid of conservative Barry Goldwater, crime and crime control had become national politics. Richard M. Nixon followed Goldwater's lead. He won the presidency in 1968 in part by blaming Lyndon B. Johnson, Democratic liberals, and the Supreme Court for "coddling criminals" in cases like *Miranda v. Arizona* and *Escobedo v. Illinois*. Linking street crime with social movement activism, riots, and assassinations—of the Kennedys, Malcom X, Martin Luther King Jr.— appealed to both a grassroots conservative movement that had been growing for years and to "the silent majority" of politically moderate Americans who found recent events deeply destabilizing.[3]

Within this context, law enforcement advocates clamored for more, not less, leeway for the police. In particular, states and cities tried to preserve some vagrancy-type authority in the crime control context and to increase police authority to stop, question, frisk, and detain people even when they lacked the probable cause that the Fourth Amendment seemed to require. By the late 1960s, as anti-vagrancy law sentiment became more widespread, law enforcement advocates were somewhat less inclined to defend the use of vagrancy laws to criminalize poverty, regulate morality, or defend white supremacy. They remained deeply committed, however, to the need for vagrancy law authority in crime control. In other words, even if some forms of difference were no longer so dangerous, some still were: the kinds of difference that meant that major crime was in progress.

Advocates and scholars on both sides of the debate considered vagrancy laws and stop and frisk authority together. On a conceptual level, both issues implicated the exercise of police discretion, highlighted the ways such discretion could harm civil rights and free speech, and exacerbated police-minority community tensions. On a practical level, vagrancy laws and stop and frisk authority seemed to offer alternative ways of giving police power on the streets. Vagrancy laws licensed police discretion through the substance of the criminal law. They provided a crime ill-defined enough to support almost any arrest. Stop and frisk did so by relaxing the procedural rules governing law enforcement officers and allowing them to investigate even without probable cause. Where vagrancy law challengers hoped the Court would both invalidate vagrancy laws and reject stop and frisk authority, law enforcement advocates hoped for both substantive and procedural laxity.

Taken together, then, *Wainwright* and *Terry* represented both sides of the vagrancy problem Besig had identified more than a decade earlier—the existence of possibly constitutionally infirm laws and possibly underconstrained and lawless enforcers—and put two sets of choices to the justices. First, the justices had to decide whether to expand police authority, restrict police authority, or maintain the status quo. Second, they had to decide whether they would act through the procedural rules that governed the police, the substantive laws that authorized arrests, neither, or both. In answering these questions, the justices would try to figure out how to grant discretion to nip "real" crime in the bud or apprehend "real" criminals while denying discretion to regulate people the Court increasingly refused to see as out of place.

The problem was that it was not always clear when officers made vagrancy arrests or stops and frisks because they suspected "real" crimes were afoot and when they did so to regulate, harass, and control minorities and other marginalized groups. It was not always clear when the police were regulating difference and when they were eliminating danger. Race and racial prejudice compounded the problem. Urban crime committed by young, black men had become almost inextricable from civil rights protest in the minds of many whites and government officials. It was not simply that the Court sought to enable police discretion to confront and detain some people and restrict it with regard to others. It was that, to some, the two groups were not always distinguishable.

As the Supreme Court's term began on the first Monday in October of 1967, anti-vagrancy law advocates were optimistic. Momentum against vagrancy laws had been growing, with a number of lower court invalidations and reversals of convictions in the summer and fall of 1967 alone. Several justices had already indicated their skepticism of vagrancy laws generally. The Court as a whole had sporadically hinted that pretextual uses of vagrancy laws in the service of more serious crime control might be problematic. Moreover, the Court's ongoing criminal procedure revolution reflected an ample judicial appetite for federal constitutional supervision of the police. According to the Supreme Court Preview in the *Congressional Quarterly Fact Sheet* (CQ), "Criminal law cases again lead the list of cases expected to make news this year." Noting that *Wainwright, Terry,* and a few additional stop and frisk cases would likely be treated "as a group," it speculated that the "most significant criminal case of the year could be *Wainwright v. City of New Orleans.*" It might even end up "a landmark decision."[4]

Law Student, Murder Suspect, Vagrant

As his law student status suggests, Stephen Wainwright was not your usual vagrant. From a family of musical Yankee lawyers in Massachusetts, Wainwright graduated from Wesleyan University in 1961, spent a year at Boston University Law School, and traveled around the country playing the banjo and singing folk songs. He became enamored with New Orleans and decided to continue law school at Tulane University. His New England father queried, "What's a Tulane?" Upon learning the answer, he opined, "That's a foreign country, they don't even use the British system of jurisprudence down there." Wainwright transferred nonetheless, and he even continued to play his banjo at a Bourbon Street bar as a law student.[5]

When Wainwright refused to show the police his arm, then, he was calling on his deeply ingrained legal pedigree and education. He told the police that he was a law student, announcing, "The law says I must only give you my name and address; that is all I am required to give you." The officer was skeptical, as he thought Wainwright "was not dressed as a law student." Rather, he looked a little Beat, in his denim jacket, T-shirt, and dress slacks. Wainwright also stood on his dignity. He had just the day before been to a doctor about "an unsightly skin disease on his arms and chest" that he did not want to reveal for the world to see. As he later put it in his Supreme Court petition, he told the police that he "refuse[d] to allow [himself] to be molested [and humiliated] by a bunch of cops here on the street." The police arrested Wainwright for vagrancy by loitering.

When he tried to walk away, they added resisting an officer. When he said in the patrol car, "All right, you stupid cops," they added "reviling the police."[6]

At the stationhouse, Wainwright continued to refuse to remove his jacket, in part because he had not been allowed to call his lawyer. The police were determined to get the jacket off to see whether he was their murder suspect. Wainwright and the police "danced" and "bounced" around the interrogation room until the police forcibly removed the jacket and discovered no tattoo. Wainwright was clearly "Born to Raise Hell," but he was not their man.[7]

After the tussle, Wainwright was finally allowed to call his lawyer, roommate and judicial clerk Dan A. Spencer. When Spencer arrived at the stationhouse at 1:45 AM, the police had moved Wainwright elsewhere. Spencer was not allowed to see him. When Spencer insisted, the police arrested him for (and he was later convicted of) reviling the police and vagrancy for refusing to move on. From where had he refused to move on? The police station. Spencer and Wainwright were both released a few hours later. They immediately sought medical care for injuries Wainwright complained the police had inflicted during the jacket scuffle.[8]

For eight months, Wainwright's case was repeatedly postponed and continued. Wainwright, like Sam Thompson, was convinced that this was in retaliation for his complaints of police brutality and false arrest. Wainwright criticized Judge Andrew Bucaro for the "lengths" to which he had gone "to protect the officers involved in this case." He alleged that Bucaro had stated that because a judge "could not be re-elected without the support of the New Orleans Police Department ... the Judges ... must, of necessity, support the policemen, whether they were right or wrong." Indeed, according to Spencer, the city attorney's office had said that its duty in municipal court cases was "as much to protect policemen from possible civil actions as it [was] to obtain convictions of guilty persons."[9]

By May of 1965, the original vagrancy and reviling the police charges were gone (though the record is unclear as to what exactly happened to them). In their place, prosecutors brought two charges of disturbing the peace by assault and one charge of resisting an officer. These grew out of the scuffle at the police station, not the initial street arrest. By the time a trial date was set, Wainwright had graduated from law school, and he had to travel back to New Orleans from his law practice outside Boston to attend. Though the resisting-an-officer conviction that followed was reversed on appeal, the other two convictions were affirmed. The appellate court described Wainwright as "belligerent" and suggested that "this entire episode could have been avoided if the defendant . . . had attempted to be more cooperative."[10]

Still not feeling particularly cooperative, Wainwright wrote his own petition to the Supreme Court. He found the task relatively easy because "Justice Douglas had written about things like this before. And he knew all about what happened when people got arrested for vagrancy when they hadn't been vagrants, so he probably was well aware of what happened to me." In the petition, Wainwright relied on Douglas's 1960 *Yale Law Journal* article on vagrancy laws and arrests on suspicion. That said, the vagrancy law itself did not figure prominently in Wainwright's understanding of the case. When Wainwright wrote in June of 1966, he preceded both Anthony Amsterdam's call to arms and the watershed lower-court vagrancy law invalidations that began accumulating in 1967. Instead, Wainwright framed his case in terms of unconstitutional police questioning, highlighting the injustice of the arrest and the indignity of the demand that he remove his jacket in public.[11]

The facts of the case nonetheless teed up both sides of the vagrancy law problem. It provided the justices opportunities to condemn the police questioning, Wainwright's vagrancy arrest, the vagrancy law itself, or some combination of all three. Much of the press coverage took Wainwright's side and reflected the multiple issues swirling about the case. One article predicted that police authority like that exercised in *Wainwright* would "come under close scrutiny." Mused a prominent columnist, "A petty case? Yes. But it presents, however ludicrously, a towering issue of constitutional law. Surely, in a free society, a man has every right to walk peacefully to a diner at midnight without being harassed by the cops." Asked another, "Can police arrest a man on a rigged 'vagrancy' charge, take him to headquarters and force him to disrobe because he resembles a composite drawing of the man they are looking for?"[12]

By the time his case came up for briefing in the fall of 1967, Wainwright was no longer its steward, and his priorities, though still present, had been integrated into the increasingly settled legal frameworks of vagrancy law and police discretion. When the Court agreed to hear the case, the vagrancy defendant had been, as the *New York Times* later reported, at Grenoble University in France. Worried that he would not have adequate access to American law books, and knowing from law school that the ACLU would take criminal cases with possible constitutional merit, Wainwright had asked the ACLU for help. Once the national office was sure that none of the relevant local affiliates wanted the case, *Wainwright* became the first vagrancy case the national ACLU represented directly. Under the supervision of acting legal director Marvin Karpatkin—legal director Mel Wulf was also in Europe—lawyers in and around the ACLU found *Wainwright* a promising case that would "make some much needed law." Many weighed in on the arguments. Karpatkin wrote Wainwright, "Because of the unusually important issues in this case, as well as my personal interest in these issues, I will personally involve myself in the preparation of the brief, and I expect to handle the oral argument as well."[13]

Wainwright's new lawyers brought to his case more than a decade of experience with vagrancy laws as well as a keen awareness of the growing scholarship on the relationship between such laws and police discretion. Paul Chevigny, the director of the NYCLU's Police Practices Project and the author of Wainwright's brief, was an elegant and erudite young lawyer with degrees from Yale and Harvard. Like many of his generation, he had begun his career at a Wall Street law firm and gone south during the civil rights movement. When he returned north, Wall Street no longer appealed, and he began working for a neighborhood legal services office in Harlem. Soon after that job exposed him to the widespread problem of police brutality, the NYCLU hired him to study the issue. Three years later, in 1969, his efforts culminated in *Police Power*, one of the first books systematically to expose police brutality.[14]

Chevigny thus had firsthand experience with police authority and its most violent abuses. He was also familiar with a recent and burgeoning literature about more banal exercises of police discretion and the enhancement of that discretion with vague vagrancy-type laws. Law enforcement officers had long acknowledged—and sometimes boasted about—using vagrancy arrests when probable cause was absent. Ernest Besig, Louis Lusky, Caleb Foote, and others publicized these pretextual uses of vagrancy laws in their various corners of the country in the 1950s. By 1967, novel and ambitious investigative studies—notably by the American Bar Foundation and the American Bar Association's Criminal Justice Standards Project—affirmed their observations on a massive and national scale. The "discovery" of police discretion—the freedom "to make a choice among possible courses of action or inaction" in the definitive words of scholar Kenneth Culp Davis—at the point of arrest drew particular attention. The traditional image the police officer tried to project was that he mechanically applied the law as written by the legislature. The resounding scholarly conclusion was the repudiation of that image, not just anecdotally, but social scientifically.[15]

The studies showed that law enforcement officers used vagrancy and related laws in particular "to justify detention and interrogation of persons suspected of more serious crimes," as well as "dragnets" or "roundups" of known criminals in the vicinity of a crime for which there were no apparent suspects. The vagrancy arrest could be made without a warrant; it would give the police the opportunity to search, fingerprint, investigate, identify, and interrogate those arrested; and the person could later be charged with another crime. Though some courts condemned such pretextual arrests, many facilitated them by validating both searches incident to vagrancy arrests without warrants and prosecutions of more serious crimes after vagrancy arrests. Officers assumed that even when they did not have adequate justification to charge a property crime or crime of violence, vagrancy laws were "intended primarily as aids to investigation" and provided a viable alternative. They remained within the boundaries of legality by using substantive law to evade a procedural obstacle.[16]

Even if such uses of vagrancy laws were technically legal, a growing number of scholars in the early 1960s deemed them problematic for the rule of law. Because legislatures could not know the substance of these "low visibility" decisions to arrest, they could not correct, clarify, or constrain the boundaries of criminal vagrancy. Because such arrests often resulted in dismissals, police behavior was immunized from judicial oversight as well. Releasing a defendant prior to any kind of judicial hearing meant that the defendant had no opportunity to defend himself against the charge, that his record of arrest stood, and that he became more vulnerable to future arrests as a result of that record. The arrest record served as "a self-fulfilling prophecy," and the arrest served as its own punishment.[17]

Indeed, the studies revealed that that the police often used their previously invisible discretion to apply vagrancy and other vague laws beyond the admittedly elastic and diaphanous boundaries of the law. Just as police officers regularly arrested people for vagrancy who did not fit the legislative definitions of the crime in the free speech, civil rights, sexuality, and skid row contexts, so too academic studies and reported cases revealed the same practice in crime control. The extent to which pretextual vagrancy arrests in any jurisdiction crossed the line into the abuse of vagrancy laws depended partly on the nature of particular laws. As is obvious by now, vagrancy laws were a motley and varied lot, and some types were more easily harnessed for crime control than others. Those laws that contained broad prohibitions on "wander[ing] about the streets at late or unusual hours of the night, without any visible or lawful business" or "being a suspicious person" readily lent themselves to the crime control function. Jurisdictions without such provisions had to work harder. Status-based laws that made a criminal of any "idle or dissolute person, without visible means of support, who is physically able to work but does not seek or accept employment," for example, were "ill-adapted to such police practices." If applied as written, these status-based vagrancy laws would not legitimately support many vagrancy arrests intended for preventive or investigatory policing. But then, the data showed that such laws were not always applied as written.[18]

So did the ACLU's own cases. When Wainwright appealed to the ACLU in 1966, the organization and its lawyers had been part of a loose but coordinated anti-vagrancy law network since the 1930s. In the mid-1960s, legal director Mel Wulf was regularly sharing vagrancy law information among lawyers in the organization's affiliates across the country. Just prior to *Wainwright*, two cases brought Wulf, Karpatkin, and Chevigny personally into contact with vagrancy and loitering laws. Wulf had been a key supporter when the ACLU's DC affiliate had taken the lead in the Dupont Circle guitar-player case of *Hicks v. District*

of Columbia. In addition, Chevigny filed and Karpatkin argued a federal civil
rights suit challenging "dragnet arrests" under a New York law that prohibited
narcotics-related loitering. Chevigny found it "very difficult to determine what
arrests, if any, constitute police abuses under such a statute, because it is difficult to tell what arrests are authorized." Though he conceived of the case as primarily about a "pattern of [police] abuse," it also educated him about vagrancy
and loitering laws, which he would later describe as "paradigmatic 'harassment
statutes.'"[19]

In *Wainwright,* Chevigny and the ACLU lawyers focused more on the "wholly
unrelated and spurious" vagrancy charge than the constitutional defects of the
law itself. The police had argued that the vagrancy charge had been justified by
the fact that Wainwright had stood still on the street for some five seconds, that
he was not carrying identification, and that he had "very little funds" on him. The
ACLU countered that the conviction was "so baseless it must fall as a matter of
due process." Just like *Shuttlesworth* and the other civil rights movement cases,
this one too cited *Thompson v. Louisville.*[20]

Wainwright and his lawyers underscored *Wainwright's* importance by linking this case about a potential murderer to the vagrancy and policing issues
to which the Court had already been exposed in civil rights cases and, even
earlier, labor rights cases. "It was 1964 when I got arrested and there was an
awful lot going on in the South," Wainwright reflected. Despite the absence of
free speech concerns in *Wainwright,* the ACLU lawyers wrote that "if the police
wish to disperse a group of people distributing leaflets in public, they need only
tell them to move on, under threat of arrest. If they refuse, they can be arrested,
whether constitutionally or not, and all physical refusals to move can be made
valid basis for conviction." The lawyers challenged the idea that allowing resistance would "encourage disrespect for the law" by insisting that it was the very
belief in the right to resist unlawful orders that made people willing to follow
lawful ones.[21]

New Orleans' response to *Wainwright* revealed both some newfound law enforcement acceptance of the vagrancy law critique and continued resistance to it. Just
as Wainwright's lawyers highlighted their client's similarities to Court-favored
civil rights protestors, the government highlighted the darker side of the social
movements of the 1960s: the disorder and violence that had only worsened
between the time the Court granted Wainwright in January of 1968 and oral
argument the following October. The summer that intervened had been dubbed
"The Long Hot Summer" for the 159 riots the nation had endured. New Orleans
Assistant District Attorney Richard Seither referred to "these troubled times
of demonstrations, riots, and related disturbances," and he repeatedly referred
to "the ACLU's position," the "ACLU professional brief," and "the *Wainwright*

forces." If the times were troubled, Seither wanted the Court to know that the ACLU was a troublemaker, and this case was part of the trouble.[22]

That said, unlike many government officials tasked with defending vagrancy laws, Seither was eager to discuss them. He did not try to avoid the issue, argue that the case should not have been granted, or recommend dismissal. On the merits, Seither was nonetheless deeply ambivalent. Speaking especially to Justice Douglas, Seither explained that, prior to 1958, it was the official policy of the New Orleans Police Department, blessed by the city attorney's office, to charge "everybody with no. 107 vagrancy pending investigation for everything from murder to rape to incest to petty larceny" and to hold such suspects for seventy-two hours or more without counsel or a phone call. As early as 1953, New Orleanians criticized the police for making vagrancy arrests just because some member of the city police force had a personal dislike for the person in question. The following year, the Criminal Courts Bar Association decided to study "the abuses" of the law as a "holding" statute, and the police superintendent sought a new law authorizing shorter detentions for investigation. According to the *Times-Picayune*, Deputy Police Superintendent Joseph I. Giarrusso defended the law as needed to combat vagrancy itself, issuing orders "that the vagrancy charge be used only as a vagrancy charge and [that] arrested persons were to be booked directly with the crime they were accused of committing."[23]

Policy and practice did not always match, and Giarrusso soon reestablished a "flying squad" to step up anti-vice and vagrancy enforcement. As the city arrested hundreds for vagrancy, the police no longer officially used the vagrancy law as an investigative holding charge. Instead, the department returned to an even older justification for the link between vagrancy and crime: because vagrants were likely to commit more serious crimes, vagrancy arrests constituted preventive policing. Into the late 1960s, as Giarrusso rose to superintendent, the New Orleans police remained committed to vagrancy authority.[24]

Perhaps galled by the distance between his own efforts to end pretextual vagrancy arrests and their persistence, Seither emphasized policy over practice at oral argument. "There is no community in the nation who agrees more [that it is] a wrong practice." But Seither's job in *Wainwright* was to defend his city's policing and prosecutorial judgments. Even as he confessed that he had been "part and parcel of this bad system," then, he tried to differentiate Wainwright's arrest and conviction.[25]

That is where Seither ran into some trouble, as the justices used oral argument to pepper him with questions about the validity of Wainwright's vagrancy charge. By 1968, the justices were already fairly well educated about both vagrancy laws generally and the pretextual use of vagrancy laws in crime control specifically. In addition to *Edelman v. California, Thompson v. Louisville, Arceneaux v. Louisiana,* and *Shuttlesworth v. Birmingham*, the Court had heard oral arguments in the ACLU's *Hicks* case before dismissing it as improvidently granted. The justices had also denied, often over Justice Douglas's persistent dissents, several other vagrancy petitions and appeals in recent years.[26]

Most relevant to *Wainwright* was another vagrancy case the Court did actually decide in the mid-1960s. *Preston v. United States* involved the vagrancy arrest of "three suspicious men acting suspiciously" who gave "unsatisfactory and evasive" answers to police questions. When the police later found two loaded revolvers, "caps, women's stockings (one with mouth and eye holes), rope, pillow slips," and an illegal license plate cover, the men were convicted of conspiring to rob a federally insured bank. The vagrancy charges never went to trial. When defendant Preston petitioned the Supreme Court pro se, the Court found his arguments of sufficient import that it asked prominent Washington lawyer Francis M. Shea to represent him. The Court held that Preston's conviction could not stand because the search and seizure were not valid under the Fourth Amendment. Searches incident to arrest were justified by the possibility of harm to an officer by a weapon on the accused or by the possibility that evidence would be destroyed prior to the procurement of an arrest. Here, however, the search took place long after the arrest, when the car was not accessible to the defendants. The Court adopted Shea's argument that it was odd even to contemplate "articles which can be the 'fruits' or 'implements' of the crime of vagrancy."[27]

The justices were equally skeptical of what seemed an equally pretextual vagrancy arrest in *Wainwright*. Seither's first move was to claim that the vagrancy arrest of a murder suspect was not a problem: "There is no conflict because vagrants have been known to commit murder and murderers have been known to be vagrants." One was no less a "vagrant, loiterer, drifter or idler" because he had also committed a felony. When asked what made Wainwright a vagrant, Seither appealed to conventional ideas of the crime. "He looked like a vagrant. His demeanor was that of a vagrant. He had no identification on him." When pressed about the clothing, Seither stated that they were "shabby clothes," which was followed up by the question, "Ever been around a university?" "This was not around a university, Mr. Justice," he responded. "This was down the French Quarter." When asked whether anyone could go to the French Quarter, he retreated, "We're not pegging this vagrancy charge strictly on shabby clothes. It's the overall picture. Shabby clothes, he had no identification on him." A justice asked how many people on Bourbon Street were dressed like Wainwright, and Seither replied, "This was before the hippies invaded New Orleans, or the malcontents, or whatever the mode of the moment is." Seither also contended that Wainwright's reluctance to give his name was an element of vagrancy, though he could not, when pressed, cite any cases that made noncooperation with the

police alone a form of vagrancy. He wanted to talk holistically: "He had no identification, no draft card though he was of draft age. All this put together would
make out a good case of vagrancy. . . . The whole picture together and the actions
of Mr. Wainwright were precisely the actions you would have expected of a man
who was wanted for something."[28]

It was that last bit that was the problem, because Wainwright's vagrancy
seemed to keep coming back to the murder investigation. The justices were
unconvinced that Wainwright really seemed like a vagrant, because the police
clearly thought he was not a vagrant but a murderer. At one point, Justice
Fortas asked whether a person suspected of murder would have been arrested
for vagrancy if he had been "extremely well-dressed and had $156 in his pocket
and an identification card that showed that instead of going to law school, which
was notorious behavior, lots of vagrants do that, instead of going to law school,
he was honestly employed in some way." When Seither said no, Justice Fortas
referred to the vagrancy charge as "phony," and Seither got agitated, insisting,
"We don't do that in New Orleans." Annoyed, Fortas replied, "I hear you, but
here they arrested him for vagrancy, and perhaps it is a phony charge." Seither
repeatedly protested that in the old days, the vagrancy charge would have been
dropped as soon as Wainwright had shown his arm at the police station. In light
of Wainwright's claim that the charges lingered for eight months as retribution,
it seems that New Orleans not only continued a practice it had allegedly stopped
but made it even more harassing than before.[29]

Seither's claim that Wainwright really had looked like a vagrant foundered
even more when he explained what happened to Wainwright's vagrancy
charge—disposed of while the defendant was in France. "Once the case came up,
and we realized that this man was a responsible citizen in the community, he got
a $25 suspended sentence. We weren't going to extradite him from Europe to try
him for a vagrancy charge." The irony was too rich to be overlooked. One justice
asked, "Do I understand you to say that this man who was dressed as a tramp has
since then been spending a year vacationing in Europe?" Indeed. Not only that,
but during the oral argument in October 1967, some three years after the arrest,
Wainwright sat at counsel's table along with ACLU legal director Mel Wulf, also
back from Europe in time to argue the case. A practicing Massachusetts lawyer,
Wainwright was dressed in a suit and looked little like the shabbily dressed law
student the police had targeted one late night in the French Quarter.[30]

The oral argument proved somewhat challenging for Wulf as well, though
for different reasons. As the justices learned more about the procedural posture
of the case, they became "confused" about what issues were actually before the
Court. One stated specifically that he had thought the Court could address the
street encounter, not the police station scuffle. But the police station convictions
were the only ones technically under review. Wulf tried to finesse the problem.

The police station arrests were the only thing at issue, but whether the convictions there could stand was contingent on whether the original French Quarter arrest was lawful or not. As one justice echoed Wulf, if Wainwright was arrested in violation of his rights, then he had a right to resist the search at the station.[31]

When the oral argument ended, it was unclear whether the justices would reach the questions with which they had been battering Seither. What was clear was that if they did, Wainwright would likely win. *Wainwright*'s potential for "landmark" status seemed to Wainwright himself on the verge of fulfillment. Wainwright wrote Wulf, "May I be the first to congratulate you on winning the case."[32]

Vagrancy Law, Stop and Frisk, and the Relationship between Them

It was October 1967 when the *Wainwright* oral argument vetted questions of pretextual vagrancy arrests. Only a few months later, the Court heard arguments in the stop and frisk case of *Terry v. Ohio*. Pretty much everyone who thought about either vagrancy or the constellation of practices that went under the names of field interrogation, street stop, stop and question, temporary field detention, aggressive patrol, and most prominently, stop and frisk in the 1960s concluded that they both provided routes—on their own or in tandem—to a similar end of granting police discretion to prevent and investigate crime in the absence of probable cause to search or arrest. Whether vagrancy laws' substantive law method of achieving that goal or stop and frisk's procedural approach was superior was an open question that prompted multiple and changing answers both outside the Court and within it.[33]

Laws granting authority to detain had been on the books for centuries. With citations going back to the thirteenth century, numerous courts had also upheld such power even in the absence of a statute. In 1942, the Interstate Commission on Crime promulgated a Uniform Arrest Act (UAA) that proposed granting a law enforcement officer authority to "stop any person abroad who he has reasonable ground to suspect is committing, has committed or is about to commit a crime." The UAA limited the stop to two hours, during which time the officer could question the person about his name, address, business, and destination. The officer would then be able to detain and investigate, but not formally arrest, the person. Several states passed laws based on the act in the 1940s and 1950s.[34]

Prior to the mid-1960s, a number of scholars concerned about vagrancy laws had favored such grants of police discretion to detain as the better option. Detention was shorter and thereby less liberty depriving or stigmatizing than arrest for vagrancy. Moreover, where police officers had an incentive to prosecute those arrested in order to immunize themselves from later suits for false arrest, the detention statutes created no such incentive. As for the rule-of-law problems that plagued the use of vagrancy law, the purported visibility of stop and frisk could be superior to the invisibility of pretextual vagrancy arrests. Explicitly licensing discretion and legalizing currently illegal practices would enable discretion to be controlled and mitigate disrespect for law by both police officers themselves and those witnessing police lawlessness.[35]

By the middle of the 1960s, however, liberal scholars and advocates began to oppose any such relaxation of procedural constraints on street policing. As early as 1957, Caleb Foote had articulated the key question as "whether the law should be made to conform to the practice or vice versa." He viewed with "extreme skepticism" the theory that "if the police are given more 'reasonable' limits, then it will be possible to enforce police compliance with the law." In other words, Foote and those who embraced his reasoning worried about the law enforcement officers as much as the laws themselves.[36]

To some extent, though, stop and frisk fell out of favor with liberals because of the favor it found at virtually the same moment with an entirely separate and politically antagonistic constituency: police advocates. The two groups conceptualized stop and frisk differently. They envisioned the ideal, constitutional street-level interaction between the police officer and the citizen in quite incompatible ways. In a prominent article in 1964 and book in 1968, legal scholar Herbert Packer crystallized the two viewpoints. What he called the "crime control" model of criminal justice was centrally concerned with procedural efficiency—with viewing the criminal process as an assembly line intended to turn suspects into defendants into convicts the way one might turn pieces of steel, plastic, and cloth into a car. Advocates of the crime control model wanted authorities to have the power they needed to effectuate their job of minimizing crime. By contrast, the "due process" model took a more skeptical view of the criminal process and worried about its potential for abuse more than its efficiency. Where the crime control model largely assumed the guilt of suspects and wanted to hasten their punishment in order to protect law-abiding citizens, the due process model took procedural fairness as the touchstone.[37]

To the extent that due process–oriented anti-vagrancy advocates might stomach stop and frisk, it was only as a concession to policing "real" crime upon the removal of vagrancy laws. To the extent that they opposed it, it was because the substantive and procedural enhancements of police power similarly contradicted the due process model.

For their part, police advocates proposed stop and frisk as a solution to a related but differently framed set of problems: a mismatch between what felt like exploding crime and disorder and newly stringent constitutional rules on searches and seizures. The real, if sometimes overstated, increase in the crime rate was not the only thing that put the police on high alert. The racial violence of the summer of 1967 had hardly been unexpected. Beginning in the summer of 1964, such "civil disturbances"—which many called "riots" but some deemed "rebellions" in service of a "liberation struggle"—had become regular summer events. They were marked annually along with Memorial Day, Independence Day, and Labor Day. Although riots, social movements, and street crime were often causally and culturally distinct from one another, conservative political rhetoric capitalized on their temporal coincidence and heightened their threat by linking them together. Almost two-thirds of police in one survey thought that "demonstrations [were] a main cause of violence these days," as civil rights activists, students calling themselves a "New Left," and hippies who refused to bathe proved equally, if differently, ungovernable. As the *Chicago Tribune* reported in the spring of 1967, FBI Director J. Edgar Hoover "said riots and anarchic demonstrations have joined rape, murder, and aggravated assault as major crime problems of many communities across the nation each summer."[38]

The police felt keenly the responsibility of containing all this disorder. They felt even more keenly the tightening constraints on their ability to do. Prior to the late 1950s, the Court's supervision of criminal justice had been limited to the federal government itself and to the occasional condemnation of a particularly egregious state or local practice—like a "legal lynching" in the 1930s South. As the Court's hesitation in *Thompson v. Louisville* had signaled, the justices were still reluctant to intervene in state criminal procedures as late as 1960. But that is precisely what liberal justices like Warren, Brennan, Douglas, and Black—joined by one or another additional colleague in any given case—began to do. They did so not only in *Thompson* and the southern civil rights cases that followed, but in garden variety criminal cases from across the country.

Warren's background made him an unlikely defendants' advocate. He had been a district attorney and then attorney general of California before serving three terms as the state's Republican governor. But Warren turned out to be far more of a liberal than President Eisenhower had anticipated when he appointed him in 1953. When it came to criminal procedure, the criminals Warren encountered as a justice in the 1960s—poor minorities who seemed forced into crime—were a far cry from the hardened professionals he had prosecuted in earlier decades. Though he retained his respect for law enforcement, Warren thought he could best support it by removing its more coercive aspects. Quite abruptly, in what came to be called the Warren Court "criminal procedure revolution," the Court began interfering with arrests, investigations, and criminal adjudications.[39]

That revolution seemed to the police like a frontal constitutional assault on their authority, expertise, and discretion. They were not pleased. Prominent conservative commentator William F. Buckley Jr. captured prevalent police sentiment when he noted, "The doctrine that a man is innocent until proven guilty seems to have been stretched to the point where the man who apprehends the criminal is guilty until proven innocent." According to a 1966 survey, 90 percent of police interviewed thought that the Supreme Court had "gone too far in making rules favoring and protecting criminal offenders." In Chicago, Superintendent of Police O. W. Wilson, a prominent advocate for police professionalization, pointedly complained that "the ever-increasing restrictions imposed on the police by legislation and court decisions in the field of arrest, [and] search and seizure" might be to blame for increases in crime and decreases in conviction rates. He specifically fingered the Court's 1961 decision in *Mapp v. Ohio*. After California's pioneering *People v. Cahan*, almost half the states adopted the exclusionary rule—prohibiting the use of evidence for prosecution purposes if the police had lacked probable cause to search or arrest. In extending the rule to the whole country, *Mapp* reinforced the felt need for either stops and frisks requiring less evidence or some lawful charge that could justify a search or arrest. According to Wilson, the exclusionary rule had "the effect of setting criminals free on the peculiar theory that this is a method of 'punishing' the police. It is not the police who are 'punished,' of course; it is society," and the "daily victims of 'four serious crimes a minute.' "[40]

To Wilson and other police advocates, enhancing police authority with stop and frisk was necessary to compensate the police for curtailing their power in cases like *Mapp*. Stop and frisk was harmless as well as necessary. It did not "threaten the lives or health of the innocent"; the inconvenience of a two-hour detention "is experienced only by the innocent person who inadvertently or by poor judgment" somehow arouses suspicion; and these harms were "a small price to pay for the privilege of living securely and peacefully." Wilson and others hoped that calling the police interactions "stops" and "frisks" meant that such interactions would be immune from Fourth Amendment regulation altogether. If the amendment spoke in the register of "searches" and "seizures," then anything else did not come under its purview.[41]

Before the Supreme Court took up vagrancy and stop and frisk in tandem as questions of constitutional litigation in the 1967 Term, the issue came to a head in academic and legislative arenas. Consider the "principled pragmatism" approach of the American Law Institute (ALI). The ALI's Model Penal Code (MPC) served as a marker of mainstream, generally utilitarian and consequentialist, ideas about criminal law and criminal liability. In principle, the drafters thought the Code should "substantially jettison the offense of 'vagrancy' as largely obsolete, duplicating other specifically defined offenses, unconstitutionally vague, and restrictive of liberty." In practice, the drafters worried that nobody would "pay the slightest bit of attention" to a Code that eliminated vagrancy law altogether. Governor Brown's veto of the first effort to repeal California's vagrancy law without a substitute suspicious loitering clause in 1959 underlined the point. Fears about police capacity to control serious crime seemed to require some residual reservoir of authority, even if traditional vagrancy was increasingly illegitimate. The ALI thus concluded that if any part of the vagrancy laws was to be retained it should be a "suspicious loitering" provision that best served crime control. The drafters were not entirely comfortable with that middle position, however. They wondered whether instead of criminalizing suspicious behavior, they should treat the issue "as a matter of procedure, outside the Penal Code, relating to definition of police power to question and detain."[42]

This was no idle question. The ALI began drafting a procedural companion to the MPC in 1963—the Model Code of Pre-Arraignment Procedure (MCPP). The drafters of the MCPP, many of whom were simultaneously involved in the MPC, explicitly authorized stop and frisk. In fact, they viewed that authorization as "one of the major innovative features" of the code. Drawing on the scholarly literature on discretion, the Code made "one of the central conceptions . . . that those powers which are indispensable in a rational scheme of police activity should be explicitly recognized, so that standards for their exercise may be created, and limitations may be imposed on them to prevent their abuse." The ALI concluded that if the authority to stop and frisk was necessary and effective, then it could also be reasonable under the Fourth Amendment.[43]

As the members of the ALI wrestled with the problem of police power and vagrancy laws, then, they hesitated to withdraw what seemed necessary authority from the police. So long as they eliminated most of the traditional, status-bound vagrancy concept, they thought they could save conduct-based suspicious loitering provisions as a matter of substantive law for crime control. But the ALI did not stop there. It offered states considering penal revisions both a substantive and a procedural fix to the police power problem. In fact, as police who defended stop and frisk and vagrancy laws well knew, the combination of the two was even more powerful than stop and frisk alone. In the absence of vagrancy laws, a stop that failed to uncover probable cause for arrest theoretically required the police officer to walk away. With both options available, however, the officer could instead arrest the suspect for vagrancy. A decade's worth of criticism had led to the proliferation and enhancement, rather than the elimination, of forms of police authority on the street.

The same thing happened—with far more publicity and vitriol—when the issue arose in the political arena. As advocates of Herbert Packer's two contending views increasingly clashed in the mid-1960s, New York passed a stop and frisk law in 1964 that "serve[d] to focus the attention of the legal world upon this particular police practice." *Mapp* and the withdrawal of vagrancy law leeway—in the prior two years, the New York Court of Appeals went from permitting the pretextual use of vagrancy laws to unanimously condemning the practice—served as the catalysts, and the Combined Council of Law Enforcement Officials of the State of New York was the catalyzer. As Richard Kuh, former assistant district attorney in Manhattan and the coordinator of the council, put it, police officers "would be able to work effectively under the exclusionary rule" if they could stop and frisk potential suspects without probable cause. As the law's supporters made the usual favorable comparisons of stop and frisk to pretextual arrests, they also defended its constitutionality under the Fourth Amendment. Setting to one side those circumstances that required warrants, the Constitution prohibited only "unreasonable" searches and seizures, and the bill allowed only those stops and frisks that were "reasonable."[44]

Mainstream groups like the Committee on Criminal Courts of the city's bar association opposed the bill as oppressive and likely illegal. The state bar association concluded: "Nowhere in the history of Anglo-Saxon jurisprudence have we so closely approached a police state." Unsurprisingly, the usual suspects who adhered to Packer's due process model also protested: liberal Democrats, especially those from New York City; the New York Civil Liberties Union; the NAACP; the Congress for Racial Equality; and new groups that formed specifically to oppose the bill. Police abuse of power in the South might have dominated media attention, but the discriminatory practices of the police had never been lost on either minority communities or civil rights advocates elsewhere. Indeed, in the year before the New York legislature proposed stop and frisk authority, several clashes between African Americans and police in both New York and other cities resulted in rioting and violence. Even though some liberal academics might have preferred stop and frisk to vagrancy in principle, in practice, such an expansion of police power at the behest of the police looked like an effort to undermine recent constitutional protections for criminal defendants. As the black newspaper the *Chicago Daily Defender* later put it, "The stop-and-frisk issue has been transformed from a question of police technique to an emotion-charged social issue because many civil rights leaders believe such laws would make legitimate one of the 'most pervasive causes' of friction between Negroes living in the ghettos and the legal structure of American society."[45]

After the law passed in a party-line vote, the council followed through on a promise to try to control the discretion the law granted by establishing guidelines for implementation. Police saw the administrative restrictions on what was supposed to be increased authority as "negat[ing] the benefits of the law." Officers' responses left considerable doubt about whether the new restrictions would be followed, reinforcing the impression that the police were at least part of the problem. "I won't do anything I didn't do before, only I'll do it less," remarked one officer. Another indicated that justifying stops would be difficult because "half the time you make a pinch it's because you think the bum is no good or because he's hanging around where he don't belong." Another said that when faced with a suspicious person, "I guess . . . I'll have to make sure he looks wrong before I stop him." Officers readily admitted to the *New York Times* that "under previous procedure a policeman merely used his judgment." Civil rights lawyers agreed. Quipped one, "A lot of us folks in Harlem thought that was the law already because they've been doing it that way for years."[46]

At the same legislative session that passed the stop and frisk law, New York also revised its vagrancy law. Like the California legislature, New York was trying to get ahead of constitutional vagrancy challenges like those brought by Emanuel Redfield. Viewing loitering as "generally unsalutary or unwholesome from a social viewpoint," the legislature eliminated the criminalization of idle poverty (the most clearly anachronistic feature of the law), replaced "vagrancy" with "loitering," and couched the law's prohibitions in terms of conduct rather than status. "A person [was] guilty of loitering when he" committed certain acts, like loitering for the purposes of begging, gambling, soliciting "deviate sexual intercourse," or when he loitered in particular places, like schools or transportation facilities. The new law also criminalized one who "loiters, remains or wanders in or about a place without apparent reason and under circumstances which justify suspicion that he may be engaged or about to engage in crime, and, upon inquiry by a peace officer, refuses to identify himself or fails to give a reasonably credible account of his conduct and purposes." As in California, the legislature cemented, rather than eliminated, the link between vagrancy law and crime control.[47]

The uproar of civil rights groups against the new stop and frisk law was nowhere to be found when it came to the new loitering law. Perhaps the elimination of status crimes and criminalized poverty were deemed enough of an improvement. Perhaps the abuse of police power, regardless of the law, seemed at a moment of highly publicized police brutality and police-provoked riots the more worrisome problem. Or perhaps, as suggested by the NYCLU's Paul Chevigny, who later challenged the new law, the difference was that stop and frisk represented the authorization of a new form of police power, whereas the loitering law was simply the continuation of long-legitimate prohibitions on criminality. Like the ALI, vagrancy critiques and police complaints culminated in the retention of loitering authority and the sanction of even greater police discretion in the form of stop and frisk.[48]

Officials elsewhere described problems similar to those in New York and tried similar solutions. Whether one perceived the threat as emanating from black teens, white college kids, or hardened felons, widespread fears of what conservative politicians purposefully lumped together as "lawlessness" heightened the perceived need for greater police authority. Two major federal reports, the President's Commission on Law Enforcement and Administration of Justice and the National Advisory Commission on Civil Disorders, recommended the authorization of brief stops. In July 1966, the *Washington Post* reported that Maryland's deputy attorney general called for stop and frisk legislation because he felt "recent decisions of the U.S. Supreme Court ha[d] created a situation in which 'the police can't even talk to a man in suspicious circumstances.'" In Wainwright's own New Orleans, Police Superintendent Joseph I. Giarrusso and an assistant district attorney asked the city council for a stop and frisk law in February 1967. Perhaps in light of *Wainwright,* Giarrusso claimed that the "criminal element is enjoying an immunity it has never before enjoyed because police officers hesitate to approach them on the street." The ACLU, CORE, and the NAACP in New Orleans protested accordingly, as did Loyola law professors Stephen Raphael and Kendall Vick. Vick noted that the Court would not look kindly on the proposed law as it "embodies all of the lawless law enforcement that the Supreme Court has been trying to root out."[49]

When Vick offered his prediction, the Court had already granted certiorari ("cert") in *Wainwright.* Over the next several months, as the Court decided to review not just *Terry* but two other affirmed convictions in stop and frisk cases in the spring of 1967, things did not look any better for the police. Indeed, the district attorney in one of *Terry's* companion cases was worried enough about an adverse outcome to tell the Court that the prosecution and affirmance had been "mistake[s]" and that his was not a good test case. Unsurprisingly, according to the *New York Times,* the defendant's lawyers saw the admission as "a tactic to avoid an adverse decision in a weak case."[50]

In part because it was perceived as a stronger case, *Terry v. Ohio* quickly took center stage among the Court's 1967 Term stop and frisk cases. The case began when Terry and Richard Chilton, both African American, appeared to be casing a jewelry store in Cleveland's Playhouse Square on Halloween afternoon, 1963. Detective Martin McFadden watched them walk back and forth several times. McFadden, white and a local police legend with thirty-nine years on the police force, was the kind of officer regularly dispatched to represent his department at presidential inaugurations and other events. According to Terry's lawyer, the prominent African American attorney Louis Stokes, McFadden was "a real character—a tall, stately guy, and basically a good policeman." Stokes recalled that with McFadden, "You did not have to worry about him misrepresenting what the facts were. He would come straight down the line, and as a defense lawyer I could appreciate that." This straight shooter was downtown that day as a "door shaker," assigned "for [the] benefit of the merchants" in Cleveland's business district. As Terry and Chilton peered into the jewelry store window each time they walked down the block, they "didn't look right to" McFadden. After the two met and conferred with a third man, a short white fellow named Carl Katz, McFadden approached the men and asked them questions. Dissatisfied with their answers, he patted them down, found a gun on Terry, and arrested all three.[51]

Because the facts were fraught for both sides—a white officer found a mixed-race group of men suspicious (a point of controversy for civil rights advocates) but the men turned out to have guns and the officer's life was potentially in danger (a point of vindication for law enforcement advocates)—the case became a lightning rod for intensifying debates about law and order. Arrayed on the government's side were organizations like Americans for Effective Law Enforcement (founded to "offset the influence of the ultra-liberal American Civil Liberties Union in the area of anti-crime legislation versus constitutional rights") and the National District Attorney's Association as well as the New York attorney general and United States Solicitor General Erwin Griswold. Their amicus briefs echoed arguments long made in the vagrancy law context. Citing the ALI, they claimed that temporary field detention was necessary and effective to police work. They amassed statistics that showed the effectiveness of on-the-street detention for crime prevention and investigation. The National District Attorneys Association recommended California's recently adopted rule: that detention was proper "when the circumstances are such that they would indicate to a reasonable man in a like position that such a course is necessary to proper discharge" of an officer's duties.[52]

On the other side were the usual civil rights and civil liberties suspects. At the same time that Mel Wulf was challenging the pretextual vagrancy arrest in *Wainwright*, he and his colleagues at the national and Ohio ACLUs also filed amicus briefs in the stop and frisk cases. Echoing the organization's *Wainwright* arguments, they argued that stops and frisks without probable cause were "inefficient as well as unconstitutional."[53]

An NAACP LDF amicus brief, written by Anthony Amsterdam with help from James Nabrit III and Jack Greenberg, also raised many of the problems commonly ascribed to vagrancy laws. These vagrancy law veterans resisted the law enforcement effort to flatten *Terry* into a case solely about public safety. Citing *Shuttlesworth* and *Thornhill*, they connected a possible jewelry store robbery to the unbridled police suppression of "First Amendment liberties." Though Terry was on a public street when he was arrested, Amsterdam also referenced the argument that would become prominent in vagrancy cases: like Charles Reich, he claimed a right to be let alone, and a right to privacy, even in public.[54]

The LDF also raised arguments that emerged more organically from *Terry* itself—arguments about the discretionary and discriminatory nature of on-the-street policing that had long permeated the dual critique of the vagrancy law problem. "The essence of stop and frisk doctrine is the sanctioning of judicially uncontrolled and uncontrollable discretion by law enforcement officers.

History . . . has taught that such discretion comes inevitably to be used as an instrument of oppression of the unpopular." The brief cited the 1947 report of President Truman's civil rights committee about who was likely to bear "the brunt" of such discretion: "suspected vagrants, . . . union organizers, . . . unpopular racial and religious minorities, such as Negroes, Mexicans, or Jehovah's Witnesses. . . . Unpopular, weak, or defenseless groups are most apt to suffer." Amsterdam thus found "hardly very reassuring" the New York Court of Appeals' statement in a *Terry* companion case that "where a person's activities are perfectly normal, he is fully protected from any detention or search."

Amsterdam tried to give the justices—cloistered in their marble palace—a sense of how police officers were instructed and expected to engage in such discrimination in the name of crime control. He quoted from an instructional article written by a police officer for other police officers: "Be suspicious. This is a healthy police attitude. . . . Look for the unusual," which included "persons who do not 'belong' where they are observed." The article described police-citizen interactions like this: "Meet . . . head on. Let the subject get up even with you or slightly beyond you. Then turn toward the subject facing his side. Your hand should either be holding onto the subject's arm at the elbow or in a ready position so that you will be able to spin him forward and away from you in a defensive move. . . . You should make a habit of interrogating from this position. Your greatest hazard is the unknown." Though those in favor of the stop portrayed it as relatively unintrusive, just a "Hey, there" by the police, this description suggested otherwise. Even without the aggressive physicality, Amsterdam pointed out, "Hey, there" (even when not followed by "boy," as it would have been "in the ghetto") was itself "a significant intrusion" when the speaker was a police officer. It was always a challenge, a threat of force, "an act of domination by the Fuzz." Especially given that as few as two out of ten of those stopped were found with weapons, stop and frisk "was perceived . . . as a tool for police control of the street corner in Harlem and . . . almost every other ghetto in the country." Moreover, such stops were rarely singular events, especially in the lives of young, minority men.[55]

The relationship between the police and such men was of more than passing interest to the LDF. As worried as Amsterdam and his colleagues were about police discretion and unpopular minorities generally, they were lawyers for an advocacy organization centrally concerned with race. The race of the *Terry* protagonists had disappeared from the official record quite early in the case, and it made no appearance in Ohio's brief to the Supreme Court. But Amsterdam would not let it be forgotten. The Court had shown itself sympathetic to the plight of African Americans for more than a decade. That sympathy seemed partly responsible for its pro-defendant criminal procedure doctrine. Perhaps it would prove significant here too. Amsterdam made clear that just as race had been central to *Shuttlesworth*, it was central to *Terry* and to stop and frisk more generally.[56]

Crime Control at the Supreme Court, Fall 1967–Spring 1968

When the Court granted *Wainwright* and *Terry*, the odds had looked good for defendants and the anti-vagrancy law forces. By the time the justices met in conference after the argument in *Wainwright* in October 1967, however, the New Orleans case had lost its momentum. Though the justices' skepticism of pretextual vagrancy arrests had been apparent during the *Wainwright* oral argument, their confusion about what was at the Court for review now overwhelmed those doubts. Chief Justice Warren said that he had thought the vagrancy charge at issue when the Court had granted cert. He did not think Wainwright could have been arrested for vagrancy, but he was now not sure that the Court could reach that question. Warren's uncertainty left him open to a variety of dispositions. Long-time vagrancy foe William O. Douglas was adamantly in favor of deciding the case on the vagrancy merits. The rest of the justices, however, were done with *Wainwright*. They voted to dismiss the case as improvidently granted (DIG).[57]

Perhaps those seven justices were frustrated by the state of the record, the two different sets of charges, and the lack of clarity on what was before them. Perhaps they worried about the implications of sanctioning Wainwright's physical, if passive, resistance to the police—crouching in a corner so that he "caused the officers to be butted around the room." Especially in light of the Long Hot Summer between granting and deciding *Wainwright*, police authority might have become a more pressing concern. Validating Wainwright's behavior might have seemed to validate physical resistance by those stopped or arrested by the police in other contexts, most critically riots, the civil rights movement, and protests against the Vietnam War. In Wainright's view, "a majority of the court backed off . . . because they knew you had the right to resist an illegal arrest but they weren't about to say." Just weeks into the Court's 1967 Term, the potential landmark case of *Wainwright v. New Orleans* seemed all played out.[58]

Wainwright and vagrancy laws nonetheless remained on the justices' minds as they decided what to do about stop and frisk. During the post-argument conference in *Terry* in December, the justices reaffirmed their decision to DIG *Wainwright* and decided to hold the case for final resolution after the Court had decided the stop and frisk cases. More important, *Wainwright*'s unanswered questions about whether and to what extent a citizen was required to answer the questions of a police officer on the street resurfaced in *Terry*. There was considerable disagreement, with Warren suggesting that the citizen did not have to answer and could walk away, Black disagreeing, Brennan wanting the Court not to get into it, and Stewart wanting the Court not to say that citizens "can refuse to answer a cop."[59]

Wainwright's problem of pretext also kept resurfacing as the justices thought about *Terry*. Brennan clearly had the continued validity of vagrancy laws in mind when he thought about the consequences of granting stop and frisk authority. In a memo to Warren in *Terry*, he noted that the police saw stop and frisk and vagrancy (and similar) laws as alternative ways of apprehending suspects who had not given them probable cause to arrest for other crimes. Because Brennan's view of the police was that they would attempt to find ways to stop suspicious people in some possibly plausible constitutional way, he worried about the potential consequences of withholding stop and frisk authority. "I recognize that police will frisk anyway and try to make a case that the frisk was incident to an arrest for public drunkenness, vagrancy, loitering, breach of the peace, etc. etc.— but at times I think these abuses would be more tolerable than those I apprehend may follow our legitimating of frisks on the basis of suspicious circumstances."[60]

Brennan did not expand on why he thought the "abuses" of the vagrancy route would be "more tolerable" than those of stop and frisk. He might have assumed that judges would automatically credit the police when it came to stop and frisk. Alternatively, he might have been convinced that there would be at least some review as vagrancy arrests became vagrancy convictions. As ineffective as suits for false arrest had been when vagrancy arrests proved baseless, they might have seemed more likely to succeed than efforts to discipline police officers for baseless stops. Moreover, the Court had already moved toward excluding evidence of other crimes found after a vagrancy arrest in *Preston*, whereas that question remained open in the stop and frisk context. In any event, presumably in part because *Wainwright* was at the Court at the same time as *Terry*, the continuing availability of vagrancy laws was a palpable presence in Brennan's thoughts about stop and frisk.

Whether these many nuances of the vagrancy/stop-and-frisk relationship were cause or effect, *Terry* proved even more unfavorable for defendants than *Wainwright* did. When the justices met in conference after *Terry's* oral argument in December 1967, it was essentially a foregone conclusion that even the Court's most liberal justices would affirm the conviction on some basis. The vote to do so was unanimous. Perhaps the justices were convinced that, as a matter of law, McFadden's stop and frisk of Terry were constitutional. Or perhaps they viewed McFadden as an experienced police officer whose efforts they wanted to support in a world in which crime was an ever more pressing problem. Certainly, the guns McFadden found on Terry and Chilton illustrated the need for the police to have authority to protect their own lives. Perhaps the issue was less McFadden specifically and the need for more police authority generally, or less about crime and disorder than the public's perception that the justices themselves were responsible for it.

Whatever the reason, the justices unanimously agreed that Detective McFadden had had probable cause to stop and frisk in *Terry*. That disposition was not entirely pro-police: it retained probable cause, and not something less stringent, as the standard for stop and frisk, just as it was for search and seizure. In fact, Warren—who kept the opinion for himself—was excited to "lay down hard rules for stop and frisk."[61]

That turned out to be trickier than Warren initially thought. Questions abounded about when McFadden had probable cause, when he arrested his subjects, and what he knew when. In his efforts to justify McFadden's actions, Warren's initial draft in February 1968 ended up pro-police in both disposition and rhetoric, if not Fourth Amendment doctrine. It satisfied few of his brethren.[62]

Brennan, often the mastermind of the Court's liberal opinions, suggested changes to the opinion that simultaneously expanded formal police authority beyond Warren's approach and tried to recognize the "individual liberty" interests at stake in the case. For the police, Brennan abandoned probable cause and latched onto the Amendment's language prohibition "unreasonable searches and seizures." He concluded, as the ALI had suggested, that if the authority to stop and frisk was necessary and effective, then it could also be reasonable under the Fourth Amendment.[63]

For potential suspects, Brennan tried to soften the tone. He told Warren that he had "become acutely concerned that the mere fact of our affirmance in *Terry* will be taken by the police all over the country as our license to them to carry on, indeed widely expand, present 'aggressive surveillance' techniques which the press tells us are being deliberately employed in Miami, Chicago, Detroit and other ghetto cities." Brennan thus explicitly acknowledged the larger context for the Court's ambivalence—"the 'crime in the streets' alarums being sounded in this election year in the Congress, the White House and every Governor's office." Brennan worried that parts of Warren's opinion were "susceptible to being read as sounding the same note," especially because "our affirmance surely does this: from here on out, it becomes entirely unnecessary for the police to establish 'probable cause to *arrest*' to support weapons charges; an officer can move against anyone he *suspects* has a weapon and get a conviction if he 'frisks' him and finds one." This created "the terrible risk that police will conjure up 'suspicious circumstances,' and courts will credit their versions." Brennan feared that it would "not take much of this to aggravate the already white heat resentment of ghetto Negroes against the police—and the Court will become the scapegoat."

If the Court was going to affirm the conviction, "the tone of our opinion may be even more important than what we say."[64]

As recirculated in May 1968 (and published a month later), Warren's opinion drew heavily on Brennan's revisions. Doctrinally, *Terry* held that "reasonableness," not "probable cause," governed, and that a particular Fourth Amendment "intrusion" would be reasonable if an officer could "point to specific and articulable facts" to justify it. Rhetorically, though the Court avoided mentioning the race of the officer (white) or of the suspects (black and white suspiciously together), it did acknowledge that granting stop and frisk authority would "exacerbate police-community tensions in the crowded centers of our Nation's cities." "The wholesale harassment by certain elements of the police community, of which minority groups, particularly Negroes, frequently complain," the Court went on, "will not be stopped by the exclusion of any evidence from any criminal trial" because innocent victims would not be tried for any criminal offense. The Court cited presidential commissions and American Bar Foundation studies about the "friction" caused by field interrogations motivated by a " 'perceived need to maintain the power image of the beat officer, an aim sometimes accomplished by humiliating anyone who attempts to undermine police control of the streets.' "[65]

Warren's efforts to recognize the harms to defendants notwithstanding, Douglas was apoplectic. He had originally joined the unanimous majority—when it had seemed the Court would adhere to probable cause even while affirming Terry's conviction. Perhaps Douglas was misguided to think that insisting on "probable cause" but finding it here would rein in the police more than using the less stringent "reasonableness" standard. Still, he saw the new opinion as fundamentally more pro-police than what he thought the Court had decided at conference. In the first week of June, Douglas circulated a dissent. In it, he argued that the Fourth Amendment required probable cause for searches and seizures, that McFadden's actions here were searches and seizures, and that probable cause did not exist. Douglas deemed the new power given police officers "a long step down the totalitarian path." Though it might be "desirable" as a way of "cop[ing] with modern forms of lawlessness," such a change was more appropriate for constitutional amendment than interpretation. "There have been powerful hydraulic pressures throughout our history that bear heavily on the Court to water down constitutional guarantees and give the police the upper hand. That hydraulic pressure has probably never been greater than it is today." Douglas worried that the individual was "no longer . . . sovereign" because "the police can pick him up whenever they do not like the cut of his jib."[66]

Douglas was the only justice to dissent in *Terry*, but a few others, as well as some clerks, expressed doubts and concerns in private. Though he joined the majority, Abe Fortas worried whether Warren's "detailed description of what the cops can get away with might not incite them to greater use of the latitude described!" His clerk wrote on Douglas's draft, "Darn it, this is a fine dissent." Warren's clerk Earl Dudley, who did much of the drafting and redrafting of the Chief's opinions, worried that allowing temporary detentions of people on the street would intrude on individual liberties involving political beliefs and conduct. Douglas's clerk also worried that *Terry* would "set a dangerous precedent for a watering down of Fourth Amendment guarantees." Raymond Fisher, the clerk who advised Brennan on the case, even went so far as to suggest that an "alternative approach to that set forth in the draft would call for a different result: reversing *Terry's* conviction."[67]

For his part, Warren transferred his outstanding misgivings about expanding police power from *Terry* to *Wainwright*, where he published a dissent from the Court's DIG. *Wainwright*, after all, raised questions not only about pretextual vagrancy arrests but more generally about police behavior after a street stop failed to yield incriminating evidence. As the *Washington Post* put it, *Wainwright* "had been considered a key test of police powers on urban streets, especially since, in contrast to the conventional search-and-seizure case, Wainwright was not trying to suppress evidence taken from him." At oral argument, Wulf had said that *Wainwright* "goes well beyond stop and frisk and seems to me to be a case of detention for investigation without probable cause." Warren clerk Earl Dudley agreed, finding Wainwright, despite his "belligerence," the more appealing defendant precisely because he was not the murderer the police had thought him to be. Dudley deemed *Wainwright* "the proper companion case for *Terry*" and suggested that Warren might use *Wainwright* to articulate *Terry's* limits. Though Wainwright's initial stop was justified, once no probable cause was found, the police "were required to let [Wainwright] go and were most emphatically not empowered to take him to the station."[68]

Indeed, Warren's dissenting *Wainwright* opinion bore little resemblance to his majority opinion in *Terry*. Warren described *Wainwright's* vagrancy and other street-encounter charges as "baseless" and "groundless," and he viewed their abandonment by the prosecution as an acknowledgment of that fact. He called out the City of New Orleans for continuing to engage in a practice they claimed to have ended, finding it "perfectly plain . . . that the police in this case were, to say the least, not confident that petitioner was the murder suspect, and that the vagrancy charge here was used as a pretext for holding petitioner for further questioning concerning the murder. This technique, using a minor and imaginary charge to hold an individual, in my judgment deserves unqualified condemnation." Taken together, Warren's opinions in *Terry* and *Wainwright* clearly favored stop and frisk over vagrancy authority: give police explicit, but purportedly bounded, authority to stop and frisk while simultaneously withdrawing the abuse of pretextual vagrancy arrests.[69]

Douglas did not see it that way. Until *Terry* was fully decided, Douglas had both joined Warren's *Wainwright* dissent and written his own. Douglas's anger about *Terry* now infected *Wainwright*. Warren might be satisfied splitting the difference between stop and frisk and vagrancy, but Douglas wanted the Court clearly on the side of the anti-vagrancy law forces along both substantive and procedural dimensions. Two days after the Court announced *Terry* in June 1968, Douglas withdrew from Warren's opinion and circulated a new dissent that made three separate digs at *Terry*. *Wainwright*, he argued, "point[ed] up vividly the dangers which emanate from the Court's decision in *Terry*." The police claims that Wainwright had stood still for five to ten seconds, did not have identification on him, and had "very little funds" "obviously could not be ingredients of a crime under our present system of government." (Douglas conveniently ignored the fact that they were often ingredients in the crime of vagrancy, and the Court had not yet invalidated vagrancy laws.) He condemned such arrests "on suspicion" as unconstitutional, "at least prior to . . . [the] ill-starred case" of *Terry v. Ohio*.[70]

In what was becoming characteristic, Douglas also linked *Wainwright* to themes that arose in other vagrancy cases but seemed distant from the crime control context. Just as he cited *Edwards v. California* and the right to travel in the civil rights case of *Shuttlesworth v. Birmingham*, here he linked a crime control vagrancy case to American freedom writ large with reference to "the philosophy of Walt Whitman, Vachel Lindsay, and Carl Sandburg." Douglas thought that "if this 'seizure' was constitutional, then the sleepless professor who walks in the night to find the relaxation for sleep is easy prey to the police, as are thousands of other innocent Americans."[71]

Douglas clearly had in mind his friend, former Hugo Black clerk and Yale law professor Charles Reich. Reich and Douglas were both walkers. They often walked together on Sunday mornings, their rapid pace leaving even the hardiest of interlopers in the dust. But Reich also often walked and drove at night, in places police officers did not think he should. Officers frequently stopped this Oberlin- and Yale-educated former Supreme Court clerk and law firm lawyer. As Douglas wrote *Wainwright* in 1966, Reich was publishing his article in the *Yale Law Journal* about his own frequent arrests during nighttime wanderings. Reich grounded his opposition to such police intrusions in the qualities of "independence, boldness, creativity, high spirits."[72]

Douglas thus linked a case about a potential murder suspect to his vision of how vagrancy laws thwarted American freedom and nonconformity. This was vintage Douglas-as-hobo, Douglas-as-protector-of-the-American-wanderer. "I fear," he concluded, "that with *Terry* and with *Wainwright* we have forsaken the

Western tradition and taken a long step toward the oppressive police practices not only of Communist regimes but of modern Iran, 'democratic' Formosa, and Franco Spain, with which we are now even more closely allied."[73]

Wainwright took heart from these dissents. For years after the case was decided, he carried in his briefcase the *Wainwright* opinions the Court had mailed to him. When he ran into Warren at a peace conference in Yugoslavia, he pulled out Warren's dissent and asked him to sign it. As Wainwright recalls, "Not only did he remember the case, but he remembered me and discussed with me why his opinion was the correct one."[74]

Few other defendants took much solace from the *Wainwright* dissents, given the far more important loss in *Terry*. Though some police advocates suggested that because stops and frisks had not previously been covered at all by the Fourth Amendment, *Terry* represented new oversight, theirs was a minority view. Whatever had been the prediction a year earlier when the Court had granted cert, whatever efforts Warren had made to avoid the "polar extremes" of the case, the decision was understood as emphatically expanding police discretion on the street. The Cleveland Police Department, for one, clearly viewed the case as a victory. When the Department nominated Detective McFadden for an award two years after the Court's decision, it cited the arrest as not only revealing McFadden's "highly professional manner and courage," but also leading to "a landmark decision which gives the Policeman the right to stop and frisk under certain conditions." Moreover, the overwhelming public view of the case was, in the words of the *New York Times*, to give "the police virtually the full range of powers that law enforcement representatives had asked of the Court." Other observers agreed that "the ruling could help soften widespread criticism that the court has 'handcuffed the police' and 'coddled criminals.'" That anti-vagrancy law advocates and police critics saw the case as a defeat was equally clear. As an editorial in the black newspaper the *Cleveland Post-Call* put it, "Sundry minions of the law . . . are now hailing it as though it were a renewal of their long-held license to stop any Negro, at any time, anywhere, and subject him to a search of his person."[75]

The coup de grace to the vagrancy law challengers came in May, when the Court refused one last opportunity to jettison vagrancy laws during the waning days of the 1967 Term. While the justices were still hashing out their opinions in *Terry* and *Wainwright*, they had to decide what to do with *Johnson v. Florida*. When Harvey Johnson was arrested at 4:30 AM on March 20, 1966, the white eighteen-year-old was sitting on a dark bus-stop bench with a friend. His answers to questioning from two officers of the Dade County (Florida) Sheriff's Department were not very good. He had been waiting for a bus for a while, even though the next bus was not due to arrive until morning. He had been to the movies with his girlfriend, but he couldn't remember her last name. He was thinking of taking a taxi home, but he had only eighty cents in his pocket. He should not have left home in the first place, as he was under a probationary curfew from a prior breaking and entering conviction. Suspecting that Johnson was really out in the middle of the night for some criminal purpose—and despite the fact that he had been sitting on the bench for hours—the officers arrested him for "vagrancy by wandering."[76]

The justices' handling of *Johnson* confirmed that it was not just the mess that was *Wainwright* that made them balk at invalidating vagrancy laws in the spring of 1968. *Johnson* was procedurally clean, and the case raised the same pretextual vagrancy issues that had clearly troubled the justices in *Wainwright*. Moreover, the Florida law seemed ideal for constitutional adjudication. In addition to making a vagrant of anyone "wandering or strolling around from place to place without any lawful purpose or object," its provisions also included "rogues and vagabonds," "persons who use juggling, or unlawful games or plays, common pipers and fiddlers," and "common railers and brawlers."[77]

Johnson's lawyer was the same Phillip Hubbart who sometimes collaborated with legal services lawyer Bruce Rogow. The assistant public defender in the Miami-Dade County office of Florida's brand-new, first-in-the-nation, statewide public defender system argued that the law was vague, that it "aimed at the oppression of the poor and at giving the police an overbroad tool for making 'preventive' arrests without probable cause when they either do not like someone's looks or wish in reality to investigate him for another crime." Hubbart did not argue, as one of the law clerks noted, that reversal under *Thompson v. Louisville* was possible, given the lack of evidence that Johnson had "wandered and strolled," nor that he had no lawful purpose in being on the bench. The clerk concluded that Hubbart's failure to argue this point was strategic: Johnson's "counsel is the public defender who apparently wants the statute struck down."[78]

Initially, it seemed that Hubbart might get his wish, and *Johnson* might do what *Wainwright* had not. At least six justices seemed ready to grant argument in the case. They did not seem deterred, as the state had hoped they would be, by the fact that a recent change in the Court's rules had rendered Johnson's appeal fifty-six days late. Nor were they apparently swayed by the state's argument—increasingly the preferred defense of vagrancy laws—that the law was not about "putting the idle to work, but . . . preventing crime." Though such arguments had been persuasive in shaping new laws in California and New York, in the spring of 1968, they raised more questions than they answered.[79]

At the end of the day, at the end of the term, at the end of months of struggle with related constitutional issues in other cases, however, a majority voted to avoid the constitutionality of the statute and instead reverse Johnson's conviction summarily. Douglas wrote a somewhat tortured per curiam opinion that followed the clerk's *Thompson* suggestion. Johnson "was not wandering, or strolling, only sitting. The bench where he sat was made for sitting and he was using it for that purpose in the precise place where the bench had been placed."[80]

The lineup was as puzzling as the reasoning. The four other most liberal justices on the Court—Warren, Brennan, Fortas, and Marshall—signed on to the per curiam. White and Harlan dissented, as they had in *Miranda, Escobedo*, and other pro-defendant Warren Court cases. The dissent was classic Justice White, a Kennedy appointee and former deputy attorney general with a law-and-order streak and a keen eye for incongruous facts. Given that "most inhabitants of park benches reach their bench by wandering or strolling," enough evidence existed on which to base the conviction. More important, the summary reversal skirted the real issue: the constitutionality of the Florida statute. White and Harlan called the constitutional claim "substantial," and they shamed the Court for not tackling it. Though they did not indicate what they thought the outcome of such attention would be, Harlan had previously commented that he could not "say vagrancy acts are unconstitutional."[81]

Why did Douglas, long the champion of vagrancy invalidation, lead the liberals to avoid decision in *Johnson* while more conservative justices clamored for constitutional resolution? Apparently, vagrancy invalidation no longer seemed like either a sure or a good thing in the spring of 1968. If much had changed in the public perception of policing and crime between the time the Court took *Wainwright* in early 1967 and the arguments in *Wainwright* and *Terry* the following fall, even more had changed by June of 1968. The April 4 assassination of Martin Luther King Jr. and the more than one hundred nationwide riots that followed might have convinced the justices of the dire need for more law and order. In particular, the justices lived through the riots in Washington, in which twelve people were killed, almost two thousand injured, and more than six thousand arrested. The damage to the 1,200 or so buildings that burned in the city was estimated at $27 million. Across the street from the Supreme Court, Marines mounted a machine gun on the Capitol steps and some of the 13,000 dispatched military troops ringed the building.[82]

Within this context of violence and disorder, the politics of crime control and the attacks on the Court grew more vitriolic. In early March, a Gallup poll found that 63 percent of Americans thought the Court was too lenient on crime. Just over a week later, Republican presidential candidate Richard M. Nixon began a frequent refrain of declaring that "some of the courts have gone too far in weakening the peace forces against the criminal forces." Just as *Johnson* came before the Court, Congress was debating the Omnibus Crime Control and Safe Streets Act. Though the act had begun as a Democratic initiative under President Lyndon B. Johnson, it had become a Republican attack on the Court's criminal procedure cases. North Carolina Democratic Senator Sam Ervin argued that only "those who are in favor of self-confessed murderers and rapists going free" should oppose the law.[83]

Within developing constitutional doctrine as well, the tea leaves were inauspicious. In addition to the resounding support for the police in *Terry* and the justices' reluctance to reverse in *Wainwright*, the Court's surprising response to another case in the midst of the spring tumult did not augur well for the vagrancy law challengers. *Powell v. Texas* had been expected to invalidate a public drunkenness law as the culmination of a long, and relatively successful, legal and medical reform effort against the criminalization of chronic alcoholism. Though many American vagrancy laws included prohibitions on being a "common" or "habitual" drunkard, other locales separately criminalized "public drunkenness," and those arrests made up one-third of all arrests in the United States. Like the lawyers in vagrancy cases, *Powell's* argued that *Robinson v. California's* Eighth Amendment prohibition on the status crime of being a narcotics addict applied equally to public drunkenness.[84]

The Court's 5-4 decision to uphold the law the same day it DIG'ed *Wainwright* was "a surprise action" and "a severe blow to libertarian and medical groups." (In fact, until May, a majority of the Court had planned to invalidate the law.) To some extent, *Powell* did not have to bode poorly for the vagrancy law challenge. The case distinguished, rather than overruled, *Robinson*. Rejecting a constitutional prohibition on criminalizing a "condition" or "illness," it maintained that "status" could not be criminalized. Moreover, the limitation of the *Powell* ordinance to "public" drunkenness only took it out of the pure status crime category. To the extent that vagrancy law challengers could convince the Court that those laws punished pure status, vagrancy lawyers might just be able to thread the *Robinson/Powell* needle.[85]

Whether bellwether or cause, the overwhelming effect of the constitutional reasoning in *Powell* was almost as bad for the vagrancy law challenge as it was for the arrested alcoholic Leroy Powell. Conceptually, the plurality rejected the H. L. A. Hart critique of the moral content of the criminal law. Its approval of the criminalization of the "moral defect" of alcoholism applied equally to many aspects of vagrancy regulation. Jurisprudentially, the affirming justices worried about what an invalidation would do to both criminal law and federalism. It had been just a decade since the justices had begun intruding seriously into state criminal justice practices, and they were still feeling their way. What was pretty clear, though, was that the Warren Court was engaged in a "criminal procedure revolution": an attempt to supervise the procedures, rather than the substance, of criminal justice. If the Court were to invalidate a public drunkenness law, a law like those on the books in states and cities across the nation, the plurality worried that the Court would become "the ultimate arbiter of the standards of criminal responsibility, in diverse areas of the criminal law," including the difficult issue of the insanity defense. The justices also worried that such a decision would "depart . . . from the ancient faith based on the premise that experience in making local laws by local people themselves is the safest guide for a nation like ours to follow." These concerns about intervening into state substantive criminal law had always been present in the vagrancy law challenge, but *Powell* heightened their visibility and indicated that they might be more sizable obstacles than previously believed.[86]

Adding the last-minute *Powell* decision to *Terry, Wainwright*, and the political tumult of the moment, it might have been disheartening, but not surprising, that Douglas lacked the votes to strike down the Florida vagrancy law on its face in *Johnson*. A majority of justices found Johnson's conviction troubling, but the best Douglas could get was his Shuffling Sam Thompson reversal. By pursuing the summary reversal approach, Douglas might have avoided an even worse alternative: upholding the law on its merits.

Given how long Douglas had been fighting to invalidate vagrancy laws, it was no wonder that he found a way to avoid the question altogether. An issue that had seemed likely to go one way when *Wainwright* was granted in early 1967 now looked like it might actually go the other. The justices were not at that moment ready or willing to overcome their reluctance to intervene in state substantive criminal law, identify ways around such intervention, or find answers to some tricky jurisprudential questions. The spring of 1968 turned out to be a moment for law and order, for security, for policing. It was not a moment, especially not for a beleaguered Warren Court trying to maintain its legitimacy, for undermining hundreds of years of vagrancy law, legal precedent, and police practices across the country. Doing so might have threatened to deplete any political capital *Terry* had just generated.

The *Congressional Quarterly* turned out to be very wrong in its fall 1967 prediction that *Wainwright* would be the "most significant criminal case of the year." By the time the term ended the following spring, the Court had indeed made "landmark" law. But it was not the landmark that the CQ had predicted. In both *Wainwright* and *Johnson*, the Court once again sidestepped the constitutionality of vagrancy laws, leaving the regime intact. In *Terry*, after much hand-wringing, the Court licensed greater police discretion by constitutionally blessing the stop and frisk. The *Los Angeles Times* captured prevalent sentiment when it overlooked *Wainwright* completely and dubbed *Terry* "the most important [case] in the field of criminal law" in June of 1968.[87]

Wainwright and *Johnson* became, if anything, barely footnotes to *Terry*. This was not surprising. The justices had ensured that *Wainwright* and *Johnson* were both doctrinally and politically unimportant. Their vagrancy-related substantive law questions had been eclipsed by the question of how to authorize appropriate police discretion in the constitutional criminal procedure context. *Terry* and its companion cases, rather than *Wainwright* or *Johnson*, provided both the vehicle and the context for that issue.[88]

Because of the erasure of *Wainwright* and *Johnson* from historical memory, scholars have sometimes concluded that *Terry* was the Court's way of compensating the police for the demise of vagrancy laws. The Court assumed that vagrancy laws were on the wane and offered up stop and frisk instead. But that story implies a foresight and will on the justices' part not in evidence during the 1967 Term. It also has the timing backward. No doubt, when the Court decided *Terry*, some state and lower federal courts, as well as some legislatures, were already withdrawing vagrancy authority. It was also common, however, for legal actors to retool vagrancy laws precisely to retain them for the kinds of crime control functions they served in *Wainwright* and *Johnson*. Some legal scholars may have seen vagrancy laws and stop and frisk laws as largely interchangeable, but advocates on both sides, as well as legislatures and courts, most certainly did not. Like the ALI and the New York legislature, the Court now enhanced police power by adding new stop and frisk to old vagrancy authority.[89]

Had the Court seen an easy stop and frisk for vagrancy trade, it likely would have struck down vagrancy laws as it granted stop and frisk authority in the spring of 1968. It had the opportunity to do so in *Johnson* or *Wainwright* or both. But the Court did not take those opportunities, and its validation of public drunkenness laws in *Powell* suggested that it might not want to for doctrinal and jurisprudential reasons. Indeed, it was not just the landmark case that had changed over the course of the 1967 Term, but the tenor of the Court's whole criminal procedure project. It had hardly seemed likely when the justices decided to hear *Wainwright* in early 1967 that they would lean so far toward law enforcement interests. By the time the dust cleared in June of 1968, the anti-vagrancy law forces had lost twice over. Though the Court had avoided affirming either vagrancy conviction, it both relaxed Fourth Amendment restrictions in *Terry* and left vagrancy laws intact in *Johnson* and *Wainwright*.[90]

The determination of the stop and frisk question in *Terry* was decisive for the future of the vagrancy challenge. Since the beginning of the concerted anti-vagrancy law effort, critics like Ernest Besig and Louis Lusky had articulated the problem as one of both laws and law enforcement, and they had pursued litigation as one among several strategies. The abuse of police discretion, and especially the violent abuse of that discretion, had already begun to provoke its own responses before *Terry*—task forces, civilian complaint review boards, internal affairs bureaus. Though concerns about law enforcement would continue to surface in vagrancy cases and criminal procedure cases of various kinds would become a constitutional staple, never again would they share equal billing in the constitutional challenge to the vagrancy law regime.

Perhaps in the long run, the Court would use the political and doctrinal capital the 1968 cases produced to invalidate vagrancy laws. But that was not at all
clear in light of the powerful message those cases sent to advocates, scholars,
politicians, and the American people. The message was of a Court with police
needs in mind. It was of a Court less amenable to the marginal characters, novel
arguments, and new constitutional paradigms than most had come to expect
from the Warren Court. It was of a Court chastened or threatened or scared. It
was of a Court that seemed to have moved further from, not closer to, invalidating vagrancy laws after some fifteen years of constitutional challenge.

Hippies, Hippie Lawyers,
and the Challenge of Nonconformity

Just days after the Supreme Court ended its term in June of 1968, the Boulder, Colorado, police raided a "hippie house" expecting to find drugs. When the officers came up empty-handed, they charged two of those arrested with vagrancy. A few months later, police in San Antonio, Texas, began arresting hippies in "crash pads" and local hangouts and charging them with vagrancy. All through that summer and fall of 1968, police arrested hippies for vagrancy in places as geographically and culturally distinct as Spokane, Washington; Tuscaloosa, Alabama; Charlotte, North Carolina; and Sarasota and Key West, Florida.

Hippies—with their hair long, clothing odd, and sexuality confusing—were literally proliferating. They made many people, older people, more conventional people, distinctly uncomfortable. The presence of hippies provoked intense conflict on streets and in parks. Their very existence unnerved many "straights." New social and cultural phenomenon that they were, hippies became a new problem for law enforcement.

As police were wont to do when confronted by aggressive nonconformity—of heterodox hoboes and tramps beginning in the late nineteenth century and Beats in the mid-twentieth—they turned to the vagrancy laws the Court had left very much intact in the 1968 cases of *Wainwright v. New Orleans* and *Johnson v. Florida*. Indeed, a few years earlier, just before hippies seemed suddenly to materialize in 1967's "Summer of Love," the Supreme Court had specifically tackled the problem of vagrancy arrests of cultural nonconformists. *Hicks v. District of Columbia*, the ACLU defense of a Washington, DC, guitar player, had failed to resolve the constitutional question. Even so, the case augured radical changes to come. As the counterculture exploded shortly after the Court dismissed *Hicks* in 1966, a loose network of ACLU lawyers across the country argued with increasing confidence that vagrancy arrests of nonconformists were unconstitutional.[1]

The results were dramatic. The aggressive use of vagrancy laws against often white, often middle-class young people sometimes arrested in their homes for a crime unsuited to either their station or their circumstances went far toward highlighting the anachronistic nature of the laws and the illegitimate authorization of police discretion. Despite the setbacks in both *Terry v. Ohio* and the crime control vagrancy cases of 1968, this new type of vagrancy target made the police and the vagrancy laws, rather than those arrested, look increasingly out of place in late 1968 and 1969. Moreover, even as hippie-specific facts drove these cases, the key to their doctrinal success was the use of those facts in combination with constitutional arguments from other contexts. The synthetic nature of the hippies' arguments made it possible to generalize from their vagrancy victories. And victories they were. As one lawyer crowed, "Vagrancy laws are falling like ninepins, and 1969 is clearly the banner year."[2]

Flashback, 1963: A "Spontaneous Hootenanny" in Dupont Circle

" 'Gaily the Troubadour Touch'd His Guitar.' And then the Interior Department's Park Police descended upon him, and the court of Judge Thomas C. Scalley convicted him of violating the vagrancy statute." These opening lines of a *Washington Post* editorial captured both the essence and the attraction of Eddie Hicks's 1963 Dupont Circle vagrancy case. Like Isidor Edelman, Hicks had been something of a fixture at his particular park. Like Edelman, the day of Hicks's arrest was not his first introduction to law enforcement. A few weeks earlier, the same park police officers had come upon Hicks and a few others making music for a sizable audience. The police had chased them away and warned Hicks not to play there again. When Hicks returned, the police arrested him for vagrancy.[3]

The press waxed poetic about the "spontaneous hootenanny" of Hicks the "balladeer," "aspiring poet," and "minstrel." Other descriptions stressed Hicks's itinerancy—he had only recently arrived in the city—calling him a "wandering guitarist," a "wandering troubadour," and "a grail-seeking young troubadour." All of these appellations were based on the assumption that Hicks's folk music placed him somewhere to the left of mainstream American culture. He was a bohemian, though not of the well-educated northern elite type. Hicks was no Columbia intellectual like Jack Kerouac or Allen Ginsberg. Poor, uneducated, and from a southern Virginia coal-mining town, Hicks would have listed jobs as diverse as cotton picking and acting on his resume—if he had had one.[4]

Hicks's cultural position helped make him an instant cause célèbre. For Hicks was not the only young bohemian in Dupont Circle in the spring of 1963. Lately bohemians had fled there from the rising rents of Georgetown and Foggy Bottom. One observer later called the Hicks arrest itself the "real tilt into the Boho Zone" for Dupont Circle.[5]

Figure 7.1 Eddie Hicks and his supporters playing music in Washington, DC's Dupont Circle in 1963. When Hicks was arrested for vagrancy, he was viewed as a "bohemian," though he preceded the more visible hippie counterculture that erupted a few years later. Hicks's Supreme Court case raised the question of whether vagrancy laws could be used to suppress cultural nonconformists. *Washington Post*/Getty Images.

Bohemians were not the only ones who flocked to Hicks's defense. Of the seven hundred-odd people who protested his arrest with a Dupont Circle "strum-in," some leaned more to the "campfire sing-along" than the Pete Seeger/ Woodie Guthrie (or even Bob Dylan) musical protest. Staking out their cultural space, Hicks and his "balladeers and bohemians" repeatedly broke away to form their own group far from the "bourgeois" intruders. Some of Hicks's "straight" defenders viewed playing music as a wholesome activity, especially in contrast to the less wholesome pastimes—souping up a hot rod and cruising down the main drag—of juvenile delinquents. Arthur E. Neuman, a Washington lawyer walking by the park with his camera when the police first rousted Hicks, found it "commendable and refreshing to see and hear young people engaged in good social behavior rather than roaming the streets committing crimes." The director of the National Park Service and the assistant to the secretary of the interior agreed. Said the former, "I like music myself. There's no rule I know against playing a guitar in a park. A lot depends on whether it is a public nuisance."[6]

Even the judge who tried Hicks could not hide his sympathy. Park police officer James E. Thomas testified that he had told Hicks that "he couldn't play and sing because he was disturbing others." According to Hicks's lawyer, Charles

Wolfram—a recent graduate of the University of Texas Law School, full-time associate at the prestigious firm of Covington & Burling, and volunteer ACLU lawyer—Thomas was one of a small minority of African American police officers in DC at the time. Though Hicks fashioned himself a "minstrel," the officer viewed him more as a "street person." When Thomas asked Hicks whether he had a job, Hicks replied in the negative. Hicks did, however, show Thomas a $20 bill to prove, as the *Post* reported it, that "he wasn't a bum." Thomas, Wolfram projected, thought, "Here was this white kid and he could be working, there are all sorts of jobs for white kids, and he's not." Thomas warned Hicks to stay out of the park and stop playing his guitar or face a vagrancy arrest. When Thomas arrested Hicks a few weeks later, Hicks's guitar had been in his case, and he had had money in his pocket. Despite these details, no one, not even Hicks, denied that Hicks was legally a vagrant—a "person leading an immoral or profligate life who has no lawful employment and who has no lawful means of support realized from a lawful occupation or source." Feeling simultaneously sympathetic and law-bound, Scalley suspended Hicks's sentence, released him, and found him a "job"—a guitar gig at the Colonial Inn.[7]

Scalley's lenience was not enough to assuage Hicks's defenders. One neighbor protested, "If they are going to stick that boy with a vagrancy conviction just for playing a guitar, they're going to have to arrest several hundred of us. We've been playing guitars there for years." Neuman asked, "If a man chooses to spend his life playing a guitar, who has the right to insist that he engage in some sort of servitude?" Because the answer was clearly the District of Columbia, the *Washington Post* opined that it was "not enough for the Interior Department to express regret at the harassment of the troubadour and his friends. So far as is possible, they are obliged to right the wrong he has been done by the police and to remove a blot from his record. . . . [T]he incredible vagrancy statute under which [Hicks] was apprehended and convicted must be amended." This inside-the-beltway paper pointed out that so long as the law "makes it an offense to lead a 'profligate life' . . . [n]o member of the 88th Congress is safe from the interpositions of the Park police. . . . In fact as long as this statute remains unaltered there is hardly a citizen who is immune to arbitrary arrest."[8]

The ACLU—which the *Post* described as "in the forefront of those believing that vagrancy statutes generally may be unconstitutional"—decided to pursue Hicks's appeal. Hicks's countercultural identity and the circumstances of his arrest were both a draw and a potential problem for the ACLU. Hicks and people like him had long been ACLU clients. Before Lawrence Speiser moved to DC to head the ACLU's new office there in 1959, he had spearheaded the ACLU's defense of Allen Ginsburg's *Howl* and the City Lights Bookstore as well as a diverse group of vagrancy litigants in San Francisco. Once in DC, he found himself explaining in yet another Beat-defending case that the ACLU's "central purpose [was] to plead for tolerance of the unorthodox." When Hicks's conviction came to Speiser's attention the following year, it combined people the ACLU was committed to defending—bohemians—and a type of law it had long found problematic—vagrancy.[9]

Hicks's attractiveness as a vagrancy challenger could, however, undermine the ACLU's goal of making sweeping new constitutional doctrine on vagrancy. According to David Carliner of the National Capital ACLU, Hicks's "lovely case" was "perhaps too good, because the offending act was the playing of a guitar by a folk-singing guitarist at a public park on a Sunday afternoon." If Hicks was too exceptional, his case might only apply to appealing nonconformists like himself.[10]

Wolfram's sense of this problem was heightened by the fact that he was simultaneously writing an amicus brief to the Supreme Court in *Arceneaux v. Louisiana*, the rural Louisiana farmworker vagrancy case. Despite the vast cultural differences between the cases, Wolfram thought both raised "the question whether a mere condition can constitutionally be punished as a crime." He wanted to get the Court a proper vehicle for answering that question quickly because he feared that Justice William O. Douglas, who had already been on the court for twenty-four years by 1963, might soon depart. "Mr. Justice Douglas has very outspoken views on vagrancy statutes and the abuses to which they are put and he might be expected to be a forceful advocate for striking down the vagrancy statutes involved." Wolfram worried that if he let the *Hicks* facts be known, the Court would not answer the bigger question and would instead "merely find the vagrancy statute unconstitutional as applied, . . . leaving it alive for misuse in arguably distinguishable factual settings."[11]

From the beginning, then, Wolfram and his colleagues hoped to move the case beyond Hicks and his particular facts. They agreed to a joint record on appeal that included almost nothing about the circumstances of the arrest, almost nothing that would either confirm or exonerate Hicks as a vagrant. The law would stand or fall on its own. "Vagrancy statutes in the main are designedly written in broad and all-inclusive terms so as to facilitate the conviction of vaguely undesirable persons who have committed no crime," Wolfram argued to the Court. Given that the opposite of "immoral and profligate" was "decent, upright, good and right," he contended that the law was void for vagueness because it was "patently unconstitutional" to "let a policeman loose on the streets with the word 'good' as his law and all that he need show in order to justify an arrest." Foreshadowing the tensions over public and private justifications for criminal vagrancy that were about to emerge in prostitution and sexuality cases, he asked, "Does 'leading an immoral or profligate life' refer to interference with other people, interference with other people's property or simply the interference with other people's sensibilities?"[12]

In their efforts to move the case beyond Hicks himself, the ACLU lawyers also tried to find additional vagrancy cases they could bring to the Court
at the same time. "It would be a tremendous accomplishment if the diverse
provisions and applications of the vagrancy statutes and ordinances could be
brought to the Supreme Court simultaneously. . . . I am sending a copy of this
letter to certain of the affiliates in the hope that there may be vagrancy cases
pending which might be accelerated to join ours," Carliner wrote national legal
director Mel Wulf in early 1965. Wulf told Carliner that he would canvass the
local affiliates to amass information on how widespread the vagrancy law problem was, "asking them to send us the vagrancy or vagrancy type statutes in
their states."[13]

As it turned out, Hicks was not the perfect vehicle. The opposing side was
quick to identify procedural problems with the case. Assistant District of
Columbia Corporation Counsel Hubert Pair argued that the Court should not
decide Hicks because it had been filed late—a nonjurisdictional problem the justices had recognized and chosen to overlook when they granted certiorari—and
because it was moot—the time during which the DC court could have imposed
sentence on Hicks had run.[14]

Other problems stemmed from the ACLU lawyers' own strategy, and especially the facts they had tried to omit. The case's anemic record hinted that
Officer Thomas had it right: in addition to playing the guitar in the park, Hicks
might also have been living in a public bathroom. There was a world of aesthetic
and cultural difference between a bathroom-living vagrant and a solvent if idle
bohemian. There was also little reason in constitutional doctrine for Wolfram to
think that a challenge to the fundamental anti-poverty basis of vagrancy laws was
likely to succeed in 1963. The Supreme Court had yet to decide many of its cases
protecting poor people; the welfare rights movement was still a few years from
prominence; and cases undermining the anti-poverty justifications for vagrancy
laws had not yet made much headway.[15]

The facts and their omission turned out to be quite important to several of
the justices. Cincinnati moderate Potter Stewart asked pointedly about the
public bathroom allegations at oral argument in October 1965. John Marshall
Harlan, one of the more conservative justices, thought the lack of a record dis-
positive. The only justice to defend vagrancy laws outright at the time, Harlan
described the DC law as "typical" of many that served "a fine public purpose."
Given that the Court had "traditionally approached such constitutional issues
warily by considering the statute as applied to the facts of the particular case
before it," Harlan asked how one could "strike . . . down a 73-year-old statute
of the District of Columbia" without a record. Aided by Hicks's brief, Harlan
listed all of the "similar statutes [endangered] in not a few of the states." The
ACLU lawyers who had worked so hard on their list might not have realized

that it could cut both ways. In highlighting the extent of the problem, it raised the stakes for a blanket invalidation.[16]

Justice William J. Brennan Jr. argued that the lack of a record was not Hicks's fault. Hicks had not been tried in a court that provided a court reporter, and he was unable to pay for one himself. Even if some of Hicks's procedural problems were strategic or contingent, others, Caleb Foote had long ago shown, were structural and systematic. If the Court insisted that vagrancy defendants provide trial transcripts before deciding whether vagrancy laws were constitutional, the justices might never determine the laws' constitutionality. As Justice Abe Fortas put it, "On the rare occasions when an underlying constitutional issue is presented for review after this type of police-court conviction it is likely that the case raising it will fall far short of compliance with our rules as to completeness of record, timeliness, preservation of points, and the like. It is infrequent that a thoroughly conventional process allows appellate courts to reach one of these issues."[17]

As an initial matter, the justices seemed amenable not only to that view but also to Wolfram's arguments on the merits. The Court voted to strike down the law in November 1965. Hugo Black, the New Dealer who had spearheaded both Isidor Edelman's and Sam Thompson's cases at the Court, drafted the opinion. He found the words "immoral and profligate" void for vagueness. Such language was subject to differing interpretations dependent on "country, locality, state, city, religion, home training, school training, college training, and a multitudinous host of other influences that go to make up the beliefs and convictions of a person's mind." Of constitutional import to Black was the opacity of the language of morality, not the moral content of Hicks's behavior.[18]

Black might not have had misgivings about the facts of Eddie Hicks's arrest, but he did harbor anxiety about the doctrinal basis of the case. That anxiety distanced him from Douglas, his anti-vagrancy law brother in arms in both *Edelman* and *Thompson*. Though in both of those cases Black and Douglas had openly embraced void for vagueness, Black now worried that the doctrine was inconsistent with his other jurisprudential commitments. As the decision in the contraception case of *Griswold v. Connecticut* indicated, the Court seemed on the verge of embracing a new, privacy-related substantive due process some thirty years after its New Deal-era rejection of economic substantive due process. Just as Louis Lusky had in *Thompson*, Black now saw an opportunity to distinguish the procedural and the substantive by tying void for vagueness to a narrow, procedural, and historically bounded due process clause that originated with the Magna Carta.[19]

Douglas was "greatly bothered" by Black's cramped vision of due process and told him that he had decided to "go on an alternate ground" in his own opinion. Although Douglas remained skeptical of substantive due process, both *Griswold* and *Hicks* revealed that he was more open than Black to new constitutional interpretations. Douglas described the law in *Hicks* "as an attempt by the Government to regulate the status of being a vagrant," in contravention of the 1962 narcotics addiction case of *Robinson v. California*. Rejecting the historical justification for vagrancy laws, Douglas's opinion both foreshadowed and provided fodder for the poverty cases that would develop over the next year. "Insofar as that status reflects pauperism, it suggests the need for welfare; and insofar as it reflects idleness, it suggests the need for the intervention of employment agencies. I do not see how, under our constitutional system, either of those elements can be made a crime."[20]

A few weeks after Douglas cleaved off, Black precipitously recommended that the Court DIG *Hicks*. Black was frustrated with how "divided [the Court was] on the question of our power to consider the constitutionality of the statute," but he might also have been trying to avoid either the vagueness issue or a reprise of *Griswold*'s dueling Black/Douglas opinions or both. Douglas alone opposed the DIG. "I don't see any objection to having a whole series of opinions. It has happened before, as you know. The questions presented are substantial ones, and I think they are here for decision."[21]

When Douglas lost that argument, he published a lone dissent to the DIG that revealed not only his openness to new constitutional interpretations but also his affinity for Hicks himself. *Edelman, Thompson, Arceneaux,* and *Shuttlesworth* had all raised issues Douglas found deeply problematic. But *Hicks* did more. *Hicks* raised issues that went to the core of Douglas's sense of his public identity, his sense of his own American-ness, his sense of the nation itself. The people Eddie Hicks seemed to represent, these were Douglas's people. In a lecture Douglas gave at Princeton in 1960, he had quoted Carl Sandburg as saying, "There always ought to be beatniks in a culture, hollering about the respectables." In the speech-cum-law review article he wrote as the Court was deciding *Thompson* that same year, Douglas had written, "Those exiled are not traitors or even thieves. They are wanderers, men of the 'open road'; persons whose only crime in many cases is in being jobless and homeless, the same people who have been the heroes of much of our great literature and whose way of life has been glorified and envied by others for generations." Douglas began in that article a litany of celebrating the wanderer and the hobo that he would reprise and reshape for more than a decade to come. He invoked songs like "The Happy Wanderer" and "Waltzing Matilda"; poets like Robert Louis Stevenson and his "old friend" and "Fellow Hobo" Carl Sandburg. The hobo, he wrote, "implies independence, a restless spirit, the quest for a better life, rebellion against submission to orthodoxy." This paean had come not out of the facts of *Thompson*—the furthest Thompson seemed to go in his lifetime was from the downtown to the outskirts of Louisville. It came instead out of Douglas's own imagination about the role of vagrancy laws in the American cultural and historical landscape.[22]

Hicks was the case Douglas could really place in the context of the American spirit of restlessness into which he tried in various ways to cram both earlier and later cases. "History tells the story from the point of view of the Establishment: that wandering bands of people, who had left their masters, committed all sorts of crimes, and hence must be punished for wandering," he wrote in his *Hicks* dissent in February 1966. Such a "philosophy" followed the laws to this country, but they engendered "incongruity" here, given the generally footloose approach of Americans. Quoting Foote, Douglas wrote, "America invited migration with the lure of free land. The same elements of the population who, on one side of the Atlantic, were rogues and vagabonds, on the other were frontiersmen."[23]

It was not every day that a Supreme Court justice wrote critically of "the Establishment," a term with roots going back to Henry David Thoreau's *Walden.* After all, it was hard to imagine a definition of the American Establishment that would exclude Douglas and his brethren. In his personal life too in the 1960s, Douglas reinforced his identification with the youthful, the eccentric, and the countercultural. Five days after his second divorce in August 1963 and at age sixty-four, Douglas married Joan Martin, a twenty-three-year-old law student. Three years later, two weeks after his third divorce and at age sixty-seven, Douglas married his fourth and final wife (they remained married until Douglas died) in July 1966. Cathleen Heffernan was twenty-two and in college.[24]

Perhaps as a result of these young wives—or perhaps part of their allure—Douglas was increasingly taken with a growing youth culture that, like its predecessors, shared much with Douglas's own vision. The America Douglas imagined was the America they imagined—without boundaries or rules, or at least celebrating those who crossed the boundaries and ignored the rules. (Douglas certainly did in his choices of marriage partners.) In a 1969 book entitled *Points of Rebellion,* Douglas went further than referencing some long ago English "Establishment." He also railed against "the Establishment" of contemporary America. He set himself decidedly on the side of young people trying to escape convention, encouraging "revolution" within the democratic system, and criticizing "goose-stepping and the installation of conformity as king." In an article he published in *Avant Garde* magazine the same year on "The Appeal of Folk Singing," Douglas renewed his autobiographical claims to have spent "a few months each year" as a young man as "part of the restless, unhappy, but stoutly independent group of migratory workers" in the Pacific Northwest. As he "sojourned with IWW's," Douglas recalled, he listened to folk songs with titles like "Hallelujah, I'm a Bum!" and Woody Guthrie songs about spending thirty days in jail because "we spoke at a union and we ain't got bail." Douglas noted that though "folk songs and law may seem far apart, . . . the compassion of folk songs sometimes finds its way into law." Perhaps that had been Douglas's hope in his *Hicks* opinion.[25]

The fact remained that Douglas's countercultural paean in *Hicks* in 1966 was offered alone and in dissent. Despite the justices' apparently warm reception at oral argument—"The argument in the Hicks case last Thursday seemed to go fairly well for 'our side' and the District of Columbia was handled rather roughly by the court," Wolfram had written Mel Wulf—an overwhelming vote in favor of invalidating a vagrancy law had split into yet another fractured DIG. *Hicks* thus echoed *Edelman* and *Arceneaux*, and it foreshadowed *Wainwright* two years later. Even though a majority of the justices had been convinced that either vagrancy laws in general or their uses against nonconformists like Eddie Hicks were unconstitutional, they had not yet found the way, or the case, to tell the public. [26]

The Threat of a New Counterculture

Hicks's bohemianism was no doubt what recommended him to Douglas—what made Douglas like him or at least the idea of him. Even as Douglas wrote, however, Hicks's brand of nonconformity was giving way to a new, more overwhelming and threatening, one. At worst, when arrested in 1963 Hicks had seemed a relatively harmless remnant of the Beats. His arrest took place when the Beatles were still cleanshaven; Indiana was still manufacturing Studebakers; and John F. Kennedy, with his boyish American optimism, was still president. Young people like Hicks could be a problem—at least Officer Thomas thought so—but they were a small and contained problem.

Not so the hippies, whose more widespread revolt—made possible by the postwar baby boom—became nationally visible shortly after the Supreme Court DIG'ed *Hicks* in 1966. Though the first Acid Test took place at the Fillmore before Hicks was arrested, it was not until 1967 that San Francisco columnist Herb Caen popularized the word "hippie," CBS aired a documentary called "The Hippies," and Billboard hit-song lyrics exhorted those heading to San Francisco's Summer of Love "to wear some flowers in [their] hair."[27]

Generationally and aesthetically distinct from the Beats, the hippies nonetheless inherited the Beats' bohemianism, combining it with the lawless rebellion of juvenile delinquents. Generalizations are dangerous, but hippies largely condemned materialism and shunned regular work. They idealized the avantgarde and all things natural and primitive. They wanted peace, not war; love, not hate. In Timothy Leary's famous phrase, they "turned on, tuned in, and dropped out." Where the Beats wallowed in alienation, the hippies joyously celebrated connection. As the burgeoning sexual revolution liberated many Americans to disentangle sexual pleasure from procreation, hippies pushed the boundaries further than most. They refused to be limited by heterosexuality, monogamy, or conventional ideas about how men and women should look, dress, groom themselves, or behave. In all these things, and unlike their counterparts in the ascendant New Left and the movement against the war in Vietnam, hippies were more cultural dissidents than political ones.[28]

The Haight-Ashbury in San Francisco and the East Village in New York City anchored the counterculture on the two coasts. But they were hardly the only places one could catch a glimpse of long hair on men or a whiff of pot or patchouli. Across the country, from Los Angeles to Philadelphia, Boulder to Tuscaloosa, hippies and their ilk were trumpeting their values and aesthetics in underground newspapers, music like that of the Grateful Dead, and movies like *Alice's Restaurant* and *Easy Rider*, not to mention frequent "love-ins," "be-ins," and "strum-ins."[29]

Like the hoboes riding the rails and the Beats "On the Road," hippies not only lived across the country; they moved across it. Ken Kesey, who described himself as "too young to be a beatnik, and too old to be a hippie," gained fame and notoriety from the trips he and his Merry Pranksters took in the bus they named "Furthur." That the bus became an emblem of the moment was no accident. It was a symbol of "People in motion" (as a hit song put it) and a literal vehicle for making that happen. Hippies played on their transiency. A mid-sixties band even called themselves "The Vagrants," and Bob Dylan captured both the poignancy and freedom of being untethered in 1965's "Like a Rolling Stone." Hippies lived in vans, group homes, communes. Their lack of attachment to a particular bourgeois place was purposeful and it was public. They moved with their homes, and where they were became the place to be.[30]

Even as this new breed of young American was alluring—the hippie aesthetic rapidly crossed over into mainstream consumer culture—it was also frightening. The gap, gulf, conflict—pick your preferred word of discord and distance—between the young and old grew wider and more intense every day. To some extent, the threat of this new counterculture was its challenge to public mores and public spaces. Hippies intended such a challenge. They went out in public to be seen in their natural state—barely clad and barefoot—and to be smelled in their natural odor. They wanted to shame the straights, who hid their humanity and individuality. Being seen in public was one way to defy and provoke the Establishment.[31]

Provoke they did. Many straights did not want hippies walking on their streets, lounging in their parks, living in their communities, or eating in their restaurants. Some complained, "Where ever these flute tooters, Buddhist love chanters, bongo whackers, and guitar strummers congregate THERE IS TROUBLE." After a 1967 clash in New York City's Tomkins Square Park between hippies and the local Ukrainian community led to hippie arrests, the presiding judge recognized that "the local police had a problem. The local, usual habitués of the park resented the invasion by this new group which is non-conforming, whose dress is bizarre, and whose conduct is unconventional. There is, however, no law against that nor is there any law granting exclusive use of a public park to any one group to the exclusion of others." In the wake of the confrontation, the parks department designated a "troubador [*sic*] area" at Tomkins. Even after the *Village Voice* declared that the hippies "had won the park," tensions continued between hippies and neighborhood Puerto Rican teens. Municipal attorney Jerry King summed up the problem, "The hippies have a right to go to the park, but the problem is that when they get there, they take over parts of it[;] in almost every city now there are one or two parks that are known as 'hippie parks.' The 'straights,' the rest of the people, will not go there, will not let their children go there, and as a result . . . a group of people are *de facto* barred from the parks."[32]

Much of the time, however, the harm of the hippie was a moral, not a public and spatial, one. Hippies led purposefully "immoral and profligate" lives of "free love, homosexuality, and drugs," as one North Carolina politician put it. To many straights, hippies represented the deterioration of the family, the workplace, and the church—the bedrocks of democracy and capitalism. Youngsters with all the hippie accoutrements were among the most visibly unpatriotic Vietnam War protestors. Congress accused hippies of trying to defraud the government by taking student loans with no intent of ever paying them back, and of claiming their communes as households in order to receive Food Stamps. In 1971, Congress amended the Food Stamp Act purposefully to exclude the unrelated members of hippie communes.[33]

The frequently in-your-face racial integration of hippies, like the frequent hippie dress of civil rights activists, was particularly galling. According to one Charlotte "hippie house" visitor, "The first thing you saw when you entered . . . was a bed. And in the bed was a white boy, a colored boy and a pretty little girl"— no doubt the "white" was implied and unnecessary—"of about 15." As municipal attorney King explained, older people witnessing such a counterculture "had a real feeling of *terror* because they realized that the rules with which they were comfortable, that had protected them all their lives, were not there anymore."[34]

By the late 1960s, hippies had come to be associated with far more gruesome transgressions. The murder of an audience member while the Rolling Stones played the Altamont Free Concert in Northern California in late 1969 seemed like the end of hippie innocence. Even before then, hippies and murders seemed increasingly related. The brutal murders that Charles Manson and his "Family" perpetrated the previous summer confirmed what many had already concluded about the counterculture: it was evil, in league with the devil, and lacking any moral compass. The Manson murders led communities and law enforcement authorities to turn to hippies as suspects in other crimes and generally to fear, isolate, and avoid them. According to the California Supreme Court, the townspeople of Santa Cruz had already "felt a deep-seated antagonism towards

hippies" long before murders there in 1970 prompted finger-pointing at the
"'hippie' element." Locals began to call for laws specifically targeting hippies.
The chairman of the local board of supervisors said, "I know some people will
scream about their rights getting stepped on but we are going to have to start
looking at the transient element, and those people who come here with no visible way of making a living."[35]

Responses to this counterculture were as diverse as the hippies themselves.
Parents, worried that their middle- or upper-class white hippie children were
mentally ill, at times had them committed to psychiatric institutions. In more
than one reported case, intermittent work, illegal drug use, interracial dating, and illegitimate children—right alongside suicidal tendencies—justified
involuntary commitment. Though many parents had their children's own best
interests at heart, courts occasionally implied that financial strain, social embar-
rassment, or outright revulsion at children who seemed like strangers also motivated parental action.[36]

Universities also responded with a mix of paternalistic concern and generational disgust. Their in loco parentis authority had long given them power over
where students lived (single-sex institutions or at least dorms), when they went
to bed (lights out at 11), with whom they consorted (other college students),
when, where, and under what conditions they spent time with the opposite sex
(three feet on the floor, door open, before curfew), and how they could express
their political opinions (not on campus, and not very stridently). By prohibiting
long hair and beards—the "badge of hippies"—university and college officials
hoped also to keep protests and riots at bay.[37]

Pretty much everywhere hippies went, at least some business owners,
bona fide community members, and local homeowners treated them as pari-
ahs. Fearing a loss of "straight" clientele and property values, business owners
posted signs that said, "No shirts, no shoes, no service." Everyone knew that
referred to hippies. Who else went around half-clad and shoeless on a regular
basis? Other signs were more straightforward: "Hippies not served here," read
a sign in Boulder. Large billboards in upstate New York exhorted rather than
excluded: "Keep America Clean: Take a Bath" or "Keep America Clean: Get a
Haircut." In Key West, according to a California newspaper, the local "conchs"
had tolerated all types over the years—"gamblers, ship wreckers, kooky artists,
derelict alcoholics." But they found hippies beyond the pale.[38]

As such signs and attitudes suggest, individuals, sometimes with the assistance of law enforcement, often took upon themselves the suppression of
the counterculture. In Meadville, Pennsylvania, the initial curiosity of locals
prompted the police to station officers on a road that passed by a hippie commune to keep gawking drivers moving. After some local teenagers left home to

join the commune, rumors of prostitution and drugs began to circulate. Some locals set the house on fire, shot the commune's dogs, and generally harassed its members. Storekeepers refused to serve hippies. The police in a nearby town arrested a few communards for vagrancy. After officers raided the farm and arrested its inhabitants, a jeering crowd of two hundred surrounded the bus that brought the hippies to the courthouse. Police nailed an injunction to the front of the farmhouse forbidding the use of the premises for fornication, assignation, and lewdness. The hippies tried to complain to the justice of the peace, but he wasn't home and his wife wouldn't let them in because of their filth. The district attorney agreed to drop the charges against them if they would leave the farm within two weeks and not return for a year. They scattered.[39]

In other circumstances, straights refrained from acting on their own behalf; instead, they went to the police to ask for help ejecting the "hippie-hoodlum element" from "their" parks and "their" neighborhoods. One court speculated that the Philadelphia police "undoubtedly received complaints from area residents appalled by the sinister appearance" of hippies, their drug use, "overt" homosexuality, and the fact that "some have so completely rejected the middle-class value of cleanliness that their very presence in the courtroom was an olfactory affront." An officer who arrested hippies camped on a mountain near Boulder explained that "the conditions of that camp, plus the complaints that we received from area residents, that live in the area, would indicate very definitely that we had to take some action of some kind." City attorney King lamented "the confusion in the public mind between criminal behavior and behavior which departs from the norm of orderly conduct. A lot of people have the feeling that if behavior is unusual enough, bizarre enough, disgusting enough, then it should be controlled through the use of criminal sanctions." Echoing H. L. A. Hart, King argued that the criminal law was not meant to protect "the sensibilities of the public."[40]

The police were not solely reacting to citizen concerns, though it was not always easy to decipher where the impetus to arrest hippies came from—the beat officer, the police chief, the community nearby. Law enforcement officers' own opinions and concerns also generated conflict with hippies. Prominent studies from the 1960s identified "the authoritarian police personality," which was characterized by conventionalism, cynicism, and suspicion. Others emphasized that the political inclinations of many officers—like the white working-class communities from which they hailed—tended toward "a Goldwater type of conservatism." It was the job as much as any predisposition, sociological and legal scholarship suggested, that required the police to suspect anyone out of place. One scholar noted: "Beginning with the fact that deviance may be a sign of danger, the police tend to see all deviance as dangerous. Policemen's work thus tends to make policemen socially conservative in the most fundamental sense." This view helped "to explain the strong negative responses that the police tend to display toward such events as picketing, wearing beards and sandals, and other socially disassociative activities." It also inclined the police "to classify as crime all behavior that they see as discrepant with 'ordinary' behavior, regardless of whether such behavior is technically a violation of law."[41]

Hippies in particular were, in the words of a *New York Times* opinion piece, "the living refutation of just about everything the average cop stands for. They are unstructured, flower-carrying, bearded, nonaggressive, turned-on, and as one admirer put it, 'always having interesting sex.'" The police deemed them "wastrels infiltrated by hard-core criminals and left-wing political extremists, and prone to panhandling, marijuana smoking and other objectional [*sic*] public behavior." The outright disrespect hippies and other young people displayed toward law enforcement officers had the effect of making this professional skepticism seem more like personal hostility. One police chief asked, "How often can a policeman be called a pig . . . and a fascist [expletive]? How long can he take it before the top of his head blows off?"[42]

Whether hippie arrests reflected community sentiment or law enforcement initiative or, most likely, both, such arrests were clearly intended to harass as much as convict. In many arrests, like those in Philadelphia's upscale Rittenhouse Square in the summer of 1967, the police never even got as far as identifying what law the hippies had supposedly broken, let alone charging them. Certainly the Rittenhouse Square officers could have found some charge to bring against the hippies had convictions been their goal. In part, as a California reporter noted, the police "always find a statute to fit the occasion."[43]

In part, however, the laws that could justify such arrests and prosecutions were many and diverse because hippies *were* often a law enforcement problem. Hippies routinely and ostentatiously violated laws regulating fornication, adultery, and sodomy. They publicly and on a mass scale ingested illegal drugs like LSD, marijuana, peyote, and psychedelic mushrooms at the Fillmore in San Francisco; at the Woodstock festival on Max Yasgur's New York farm; and at parks, concerts, communes, and street corners in between. Their (often self-imposed) poverty led them to violate laws like those prohibiting hitchhiking. Suffice it to say, hippies did not generally make a big show of abiding by the law.[44]

Even so, like white southerners responding to civil rights protests and farmers responding to farm labor organizing, straights were not always satisfied with the existing laws they could use against hippies. In response to hippie "invasions" that turned certain areas into "freak zone[s]," Beverly Hills began closing its parks at night and the police imposed a curfew on the Sunset Strip. As Gonzo journalist, countercultural hell-raiser, and Aspen, Colorado, immigrant Hunter S. Thompson put it in the late 1960s, "Rich merchants . . . didn't want dirty hippies moving into Aspen and frightening away the big spenders. They began busting people in the streets" on the basis of a vagrancy ordinance passed just for that purpose.[45]

Carmel-by-the-Sea, California, was the poster child for the urgently felt need for new legal tools to deal with hippies. In the summer of 1968, the city council passed an ordinance regulating the use of its parks and public property. Although the ordinance itself used neutral language to describe the new prohibitions, the "Declaration of Urgency" that triggered fast-track implementation made clear who the city was targeting when it prohibited lying on the lawn. The city "has observed an extraordinary influx of undesirable and unsanitary visitors to the City, sometimes known as 'hippies,' and finds that unless proper regulations are adopted immediately the use and enjoyment of public property will be jeopardized if not entirely eliminated."[46]

Prosecutors and trial judges at times joined the anti-hippie chorus of police and legislators. In one case, the prosecutor blatantly violated a trial court order that he not use the word "hippie" or suggest anything similar by referring to the defendant as a "guru," a "Messiah," or a leader of people with a similar "life style." In another case, an Illinois appeals court reversed the sentencing of a hippie for marijuana possession because the trial judge had lamented that "it is the hippies and it is a few other people who have a complete disregard for laws that are tearing down the very basis of this country." In addition to the drug use, the judge thought the defendant's cohabitation with his girlfriend and lack of masculinity were harming "the morals of this society." "Stand up like a man," he exhorted. "For once in your life be a man for your mother's sake.... This might be the making of a man out of you, I hope it is."[47]

The use of "haircut sentences" similarly responded to the androgeny of the hippies. One police chief explained that the "rule isn't applied to women because of the nature of their dress, because it's been a custom for years for women to wear long hair. When you cut a woman's hair, you detract from her feminine appearance, but when you cut a man's hair, if you detract from his feminine appearance, it's okay."[48]

As much as law enforcement officials sought new legal authority and relied on specific criminal prohibitions that hippies violated, they turned—no surprise here—to ever-elastic vagrancy laws as well. Vagrancy justified arrests for publishing "objectionable four-letter word[s]" in underground newspapers. It enabled judges to tell hippies that if they changed their attitudes, got jobs, and quit causing trouble, they would release them to their parents. In the late 1960s and early 1970s, police arrested hippies for vagrancy in places like Bronson, Florida; Cambridge Springs, Pennsylvania; South Padre Island, Texas; Vancouver, Canada; Timbrook, Louisiana; and Atlanta, Georgia. In some places, they eventually had to suspend such arrests because the jails were already full of hippie vagrants.[49]

Like many of the clashes between hippies and straights generally, these arrests were often deeply bound up with public space and its regulation—with restricting how people could look and behave when they had to share the same physical location with others. Past vagrancy cases often emphasized these public-regarding concerns. *Edelman, Thompson, Tinsley, Shuttlesworth, Ricks,* and *Talley* all involved individuals in public, where others would see them, encounter them, perhaps be discomfited by them. So did many hippie cases. At times, hippies in public were a vagrancy law problem because, like many of these predecessors, they were politically vocal and unruly—especially when it came to the Vietnam War. But the use of vagrancy laws against hippies in public had as much to do with their mere presence as their politics. Take the "thousands" of the "hippie herd" who followed the lead of *Easy Rider* and descended on New Orleans for Mardi Gras in 1970. Though Police Chief Joseph I. Giarruso knew that the ACLU would object, his officers nonetheless arrested more than two hundred hippies for vagrancy for "the crime of sleeping in the open-air on the banks of the Mississippi River and Lake Pontchartrain." The chief urged them not to be too sensitive about their rights. "This is not their city, it's our city," he said. "We'd be far better off without them."[50]

Still, the public space element of vagrancy laws had never been ironclad. When Bull Connor arrested the three Montgomery ministers in Birmingham, they had been invited guests in Fred Shuttlesworth's home. Hippie-seeking police shared the southern law enforcement instinct that vagrancy laws could apply in private homes and establishments. The youth of many hippies reinforced that instinct. By the time hippies proper came on the scene, parents, law enforcement, and legislators had been consumed with the problematic behavior of young adults for more than a decade. As juvenile delinquents became hippies, or at least the perception of the problem shifted from the former to the latter, the old juvenile delinquency apparatus turned its gaze to the new threats to, and of, the nation's youth. The same Senate Subcommittee that had held hearings on comic books in 1954 aired the "LSD problem" in 1968. Juvenile courts in California gained jurisdiction over minors who were "in danger of leading an idle, lewd, dissolute, or immoral life," language that echoed the state's repealed vagrancy law. Other states and cities instituted curfews resembling vagrancy laws. North Carolina passed a law in the spring of 1969 that authorized sheriffs to enter buildings to retrieve minors at the request of their parents. When police raided "hippie houses" or communes or stopped young people on the street because they carried backpacks or sleeping bags, then, they often were, or at least claimed to be, seeking runaways. These assertions of police authority bled over to hippies who were not actually juveniles, opening them up to charges of "contributing to the delinquency of a minor" as well as vagrancy.[51]

Police raids of private homes or quasi-private spaces like cafés, bars, and hippie "establishments" spurred the most vociferous legal responses. In the college town of Tuscaloosa, Alabama, in October 1968, police raided a student-owned "'mod' or 'hippy' curio shop" called the Haight Hut, the name an obvious nod to that bastion of hippiedom half a continent away. Looking for drugs with no warrant, the officers were only able to make one narcotics arrest. They charged everyone else with vagrancy. In San Antonio, the police used the vagrancy law with what the hippies' lawyers later called "remarkable gusto" in the fall of 1968. They raided private homes and "hippy crash pads" like Little Ned's Renaissance, which sold "periodicals of minority viewpoint, many of which were highly critical of police behavior and authority." Police told thirty-two adults that they were "being booked for vag." One of the arresting officers later testified that "most . . . were barefooted . . . unshaven. They had long hair, and were filthy." Asked to describe a dance he mentioned witnessing, a police officer on the stand said that he couldn't. "I'm not with it," he explained.[52]

In Charlotte, which the *Charlotte Observer* described as "North Carolina's answer to Greenwich Village," police harassment of hippies in private was more sustained and continuous. A federal judge later described the residents of the local "hippie house": "In dress, manner, length of hair, speech, slouch and activity most of the plaintiffs appear to fit the 'hippie' image. In court some wore beards and love beads. The gait and stance of the boys was anything but military. Some of the girls wore long pants. None fit the Horatio Alger picture of a young person setting out to 'strive and succeed.' None had much money. Most had no job. Some appeared truly to have 'tuned out of the rat race.' "[53]

Beginning in mid-December of 1968, vice squad officers visited the Charlotte hippie house fourteen times. On additional occasions, the officers explored the street outside, questioning guests and tenants and flashing searchlights into the house. Of these various police visits, only once did the officers bring a warrant, and then they failed to show it. In January of 1969, officers went to the house on a "routine patrol," allegedly heard profanity through a broken window, and entered. Though the police denied it, one resident claimed the police "kicked [him] into a corner" when he asked for a search warrant. Officers arrested eighteen people for vagrancy, took them to the police station, photographed some, and fingerprinted all. Joy Kelley, whose name was on the lease, was told that if she ever returned to the house, she would be arrested. The police continued this pattern of harassment in the days that followed. They also served an eviction notice, telling the hippies that if they did not vacate by midnight, everyone would be arrested. The situation prompted a series of firsts. One officer stated that he had never before arrested people for vagrancy while they were in their own occupied house. A division commander with thirty-five years' experience said he had never before served an eviction notice. A month later, the police dropped all the charges.[54]

Cases like these suggest that vagrancy arrests of hippies were about more than what was or was not appropriate behavior for public display. They were about eliminating the existence of a nonconforming subculture. According to an Aspen editorial in the late 1960s, "The hippie movement is as radical and undesirable to the essence of Aspen as can be produced by any group or individual. This conglomeration of disenchanted misfits who are unable and unwilling to meet the competition which prevails under the long-established concept of society in America would foster their level of existence upon others, dragging down everything with them."[55]

Given that vagrancy had been the go-to crime for communist soapbox orators and skid row alcoholics; Beat poets, "loose women," and sexual minorities; African Americans and civil rights activists, it should come as little surprise that they often seemed the right tool for containing hippies as well. That was the beauty of vagrancy laws: they could be deployed and redeployed on a moment's notice. The police were just doing what they always had when they arrested hippies at home and abroad. What the police had not anticipated was that their time-tested invocations of vagrancy laws would confront a changing social and legal context. They had certainly not counted on a growing if scattered group of lawyers ready to go to the vagrancy law mat.

The Constitutional Appeal of the Pie-Baking Hippie and the "Banner Year" of 1969

The pies were the last straw for Robert Bruce Miller. His latest vagrancy clients had been baking pies at 3:30 in the afternoon on an unseasonably hot June day in Boulder, Colorado. That is not what the police expected to find when they knocked on the door of a basement apartment after a tip about illegal activity from a neighbor. For the year was 1968, and the folks baking the pies were hippies.

The police who came to the door of the Boulder "hippie hangout" or "hippie haven" were in search of illegal drugs. They had no search warrant, but the young people let them in anyway. Even though the police found no evidence of illegal activity, they arrested several of those hanging around on suspicion of violating narcotics laws. When no drugs and or other evidence of illegality ever turned up—only pies—the police released everyone but Charles Goldman and John Kirkland. These two they charged under the Colorado state vagrancy law, which made a vagrant of "Any person able to work and support himself in some honest and respectable calling, who shall be found loitering or strolling about, frequenting public places, or where liquor is sold, begging or leading an idle, immoral or profligate course of life, or not having any visible means of support."[56]

Maybe the police singled out Goldman and Kirkland because they had no identification and no money. Maybe it was because the hippie hangout was not their home; they were only guests there. Perhaps it was that Kirkland was known as "STP John," after the powerful hallucinogen that had become popular during the summer of love in San Francisco in 1967. If the problem was drugs, he seemed a likely target. Or perhaps it was that Goldman and Kirkland were not from around Boulder—the two nineteen-year-olds were from the Northeast.[57]

In any event, what Bob Miller found at the local jail made him angry. "It was a frontier sort of jail, with the bars, and the deputy is over there drinking coffee. . . . And they said they were arrested on vagrancy. I said I'd just had it with vagrancy." Miller was just a few years out of the University of Colorado Law School, practicing as a criminal defense attorney, and isolated as an ACLU lawyer in northern Colorado. Miller would not have described himself as a hippie, but others saw him as "the hippie lawyer," in his Levis and T-shirts rather than the more conventional business suit when he was not in court. Even in court, "I had this big 'fro. They eventually were calling me the white panther" as well.[58]

Miller had "had it with vagrancy" because Goldman and Kirkland were not the first hippies the Boulder police had arrested and the local courts had convicted for the crime. The city had been a magnet for hippies and the counterculture; vagrancy arrests played a frequent role in the clash between newcomers and old-timers; and Miller had lost "trial after trial." He recalled, "They were arresting all these people for vagrancy . . . [a]nd the jails were full. . . . It just made no sense to me. And it was just accepted that this was how it was."[59]

Before Goldman and Kirkland's trial, police conducted another hippie raid, at a mountain camp outside of Boulder. By this time, Goldman and Kirkland had managed to scare up enough money to make bail. It had taken Goldman ten days and Kirkland forty-five—half of the maximum ninety-day sentence. But their jail time was not yet over. For this raid, the police were better prepared. They had a warrant for narcotics, and though they found drugs, they could not link them to anyone in particular. Undeterred, they arrested twenty-four people and held ten of them, including Goldman and Kirkland, on a new set of vagrancy charges. Miller saw these new arrests as retribution for challenging the prior charges. He brought petitions for habeas corpus to the federal district court, which granted them.[60]

Days after this second arrest, Goldman and Kirkland were tried and convicted on the original charges by a jury in the Boulder County Court. Miller later recalled that District Attorney John Purvis referred to the defendants as "'lolly-gagging around.' . . . I had never heard that word. I was like, 'What are you talking about? Is it a bad thing?'" The trial judge made it known that regardless of the constitutional arguments Miller raised against the law, he intended to find Miller's clients guilty. He also refused to count time served against the thirty-day sentences he imposed, even though Goldman had already been in jail a third and Kirkland one and a half times that period.[61]

With backing from the statewide ACLU and assistance from a few Colorado law students, Miller and his then-law partner Roger Stevens brought a civil suit in the federal district court. They wanted the court to declare the ordinance unconstitutional and enjoin the Boulder police from using it. Another Colorado public defender, Morgan Smith, also a graduate of the University of Colorado Law School's class of 1966, submitted an amicus brief on the hippies' behalf.[62]

Miller and his crew may have felt somewhat beleaguered in their corner of Colorado, but in this pro-hippie, anti-vagrancy law crusade, they were emphatically not alone. The rash of hippie arrests in the summer and fall of 1968 led to a rash of hippie lawsuits against vagrancy laws all around the country—in places as disparate as Boulder, Aspen, Charlotte, Sarasota, San Antonio, Los Angeles, and Tuscaloosa.

The key to this explosion of hippie vagrancy cases was the will and capacity of hippies and their lawyers. Though many hippies were aggressively apolitical, many, as one observer put it in the *New York Times*, knew "more about the Bill of Rights than Justice Black. They consider that these rights are theirs by virtue of being an American." At least in some places, hippies overcame their perceived aversion to politics when it came to protecting themselves from police harassment. In Haight-Ashbury, hippies established a local communication center called the Switchboard in 1967, with its own legal aid to help those arrested for vagrancy, possession of marijuana, and other charges. After the mass arrests in New York City's Tompkins Square Park that same year, the hippies put out the call for backup, announcing a "be-in at night court." As the *Village Voice* described the scene, "The entrance to the courtroom was blocked by a chain of [Tactical Police Forces] and the kids paraded before them, in provocative splendor, complete with bells and bare feet. They sat underfoot to sing Hare Krishna. They burned incense, and they carved what was perhaps the first watermelon to enter the hall of justice. Defiant, they slid down the banisters. Determined, they posed in lotus position on the floor of telephone booths."[63]

For some things, hippies needed lawyers. Though the lawyers who defended hippies were, like Miller, overwhelmingly affiliated with the ACLU, they were not coordinated in any major way. Their convergence on constitutional challenges to vagrancy laws reflected similarities in both the social reality that produced hippie vagrancy arrests and in the legal resources that were visibly available. That said, their ACLU affiliation was meaningful. At the heart of what a federal judge called the "loosely-knit coalition" that challenged the Alabama vagrancy law on behalf of the "student community" in Tuscaloosa in 1968 was Alabama's only ACLU chapter. It was started by a few law students and young professors from outside the state who had been recently hired by law school dean Dan Meador—Alabama native, Tuscaloosa law grad, former law clerk to Justice Black, and former professor at the University of Virginia—to raise the profile and intellectual currency of the law school. These included Stephen Raphael, who had opposed New Orleans' efforts to pass a stop and frisk law and had written a law review article about *Wainwright* and *Terry* in 1968. Steve Suitts, one of the plaintiffs, recalled asking Meador if he "knew what [he was] doing back then." Meador replied, "Yeah, I knew they were going to stir things up. That's why we have tenure." Suitts said, "But they didn't have tenure." That did not matter, Meador pointed out, because "folks thought they did."[64]

Even when ACLU vagrancy challenges had less local support than in Tuscaloosa, the national organization provided information and sometimes even funding. Mel Wulf made sure to grease the wheels of the various litigation efforts, to serve as the hub of the lawyers' loose network. Wulf's philosophy as legal director was clearly influenced by his own days as a volunteer ACLU attorney in upstate New York after graduating from Columbia and Columbia law school and serving in the Navy. "My tendency always when dealing with the affiliates was to say yes. . . . If they dreamed up a case, I said yes. And if an issue came to me that needed affiliate support, I helped find that support." After Wulf sent Dan Struve in San Antonio papers from a recent ACLU vagrancy victory in 1969, Struve copied their arguments almost verbatim in his own case. He then sent Wulf a full set of papers from his case, as he felt that he had "come up with some motions which might be helpful to other attorneys in similar situations." When Struve had to withdraw from the case because he was not licensed in federal court, David Richards, another volunteer ACLU lawyer, took it over.[65]

These lawyers had more in common than just the fact that they were often the only ACLU lawyers in their particular city. For a number of them, the affiliation with the ACLU was accompanied by an identification with their hippie clients. The ACLU was so intimately associated with hippies that that image filtered into popular culture. In the hit underground 1969 movie *Easy Rider*, Wyatt, played by Peter Fonda, and Billy, by Dennis Hopper, leave California on their motorcycle hoping to reach Mardi Gras in New Orleans. Along the way, they face the usual mix of wonderment and hostility from straights. At one point, in jail for crashing a small-town parade without a permit, they meet and befriend a fellow inmate named George Hanson, played by Jack Nicholson. In addition to being the local drunk, Hanson is also an ACLU lawyer who waxes eloquent about the movie's central theme: "It's real hard to be free when you are bought and sold in the marketplace," he tells Billy. "Of course, don't ever tell anybody that they're not free, 'cause then they're gonna get real busy killin' and maimin' to prove to you that they are. Oh, yeah, they're gonna talk to you, and talk to you, and talk to you about individual freedom. But they see a free individual, it's gonna scare 'em." The words are prescient. After joining Wyatt and Billy on their journey, Hanson comes to a violent and unfortunate end before the trio makes it to New Orleans.[66]

Putting these words in the mouth of an ACLU lawyer was no accident. Like Hanson, some real-life hippie lawyers engaged in not-always-legal countercul-ture behaviors. Though some ACLU lawyers involved in hippie vagrancy cases grew pot along with their clients, others did not necessarily, or at least as vis-ibly, break the law. They were not necessarily very straight either. Joe Edwards was the ACLU lawyer who challenged Aspen's anti-hippie vagrancy and loiter-ing enforcement. When Hunter S. Thompson decided to start the Freak Power Party in Aspen, he convinced Edwards to run for mayor on the ticket in 1969 because he was "weird enough." (Thompson himself ran for sheriff with a shaved head—so that he could call his conservative opponent a "long-hair.") By his own account, San Antonio ACLU-affiliated lawyer David Richards "wouldn't have qualified as a hippie," but he represented many in the counterculture, and he and his wife (future Texas governor Ann Richards) "ran with the fringe . . . with writ-ers and malcontents and what have you." Mel Wulf similarly rejected the label looking back, though in 1973 one interviewer described him as "casually attired in mod, ivy league clothes . . . , living the life of the Village, left-wing bachelor."[67]

Like Miller in Boulder, George Daly also found himself called "the hippie lawyer" in Charlotte, North Carolina. Born and bred in Mississippi, educated at Princeton and then Harvard, Daly spent some time in San Francisco before marrying, moving to North Carolina, and starting his law practice. When he was representing the city's "hippie house" residents, he told the *Charlotte Observer*, "I'm sort of an ex-beatnik. At least, I thought beat thoughts." Though he later said he had not looked like a hippie in San Francisco, news reports about the vagrancy case suggested that he had neither looked nor lived like a straight either. During his Beat years, he had grown "a mustache, wor[n] blue jeans all the time, slept in a sleeping bag and worked only when it was necessary." He described where he had lived as "kind of a commune similar to a bachelor flat except that we didn't hold steady jobs. I guess it would be called a Hippie house now."[68]

After moving to Charlotte, Daly worked to support his wife as expected: "Harvard had taught me to be a business lawyer, so I tried to do that." But it was not for him. Because of the proliferation of new lawyering opportunities in legal aid offices, public defender services, and in and with the support of advocacy organizations, he knew he had other options. Right around the time Daly got a call about police harassment of the hippie house, he helped estab-lish a local chapter of the ACLU. Having worked with the NAACP LDF before, Daly and his colleagues also received assistance from Anthony Amsterdam, Jack

Greenberg, and the usual LDF vagrancy crew in defending the hippies. When Daly went to the hippie house, he realized, "It was very familiar because I had lived in places like that in California. So I was right at home there, and I was also a lawyer, so it was perfect. For years people referred to me as 'the hippie lawyer.' And it was true in both senses. They thought it was an insult, but I thought it was an accurate description."[69]

Daly's bohemian instincts often found their way not only into his choice of clients—he represented a bevy of Charlotte's countercultural characters—but his practice of law. He delighted in, as he put it, allowing his "imagination take hold of the case." In one flag desecration prosecution, he recalled, "I printed my opinion on desecrated flags. . . . No rule says what kind of paper you have to use. So I just copied all the desecrated flags. Abby Hoffman's, and Raquel Welch and Maya Breckinridge's flag bikini. My [defendant] desecrated the flag by sewing it to his bottom. And I put in my brief, 'If Raquel Welch can wear a flag bikini, then my client can wear it on his bottom.'" According to Daly, the judge loved it. "He came in with a bunch of fliers from the biggest department store in Charlotte with all these flags on them, and he dumped them on the table. He asked the prosecutor why he wasn't going after the department store if he was worried about flag desecration."[70]

Such an approach surfaced in Daly's vagrancy law challenge as well. Thirty-seven pages of his brief came under the heading "Literary and Historical Vagrants." Daly's cultural romp was so unusual that it prompted the *Charlotte Observer* to write an article about it, entitled " 'Vagrants' Are Spice of Literature." According to Daly, under the vagrancy law, "Huck Finn would never have made it on the Mississippi; Gascoyne would have hanged himself; Steinbeck's sharecroppers-gone-West in "Grapes of Wrath" would never have gotten to California; [and] Whitman would have been scared to write "Song of the Open Road."[71]

There is little question that Daly's appendix would have struck a chord with Justice Douglas. The more immediate question was whether it would strike a chord with the judges who would hear the Charlotte hippie-house case before Daly got the chance to strut his literary stuff for the Supreme Court. It was going to take more than poetry to make that case. It would also require some serious constitutional arguments.

When Daly, Miller, and others decided to bring lawsuits challenging hippie vagrancy arrests in 1968 and 1969, it was not just that they identified with their clients. It was also that they were outraged by the facts of the cases. The incongruity between laws conventionally applicable to the "wretchedly poor" and arrests of white, middle-class college kids, and between laws generally understood as regulating public space and intrusions into private homes made for juicy and provocative fact sections in legal briefs. The lawyers contrasted the banality of the hippies' activities, or rather inactivity, at the moment of arrest and the aggressive stance of the police. Miller referenced a Boulder police "vendetta against certain groups," and Daly called the Charlotte arrests an "egregious example" of the "dictatorial power" the police exercised through vagrancy laws.[72]

The facts that provoked these lawyers might have come from the specifics of the hippie raids, but the legal strategies they employed and the legal arguments they made linked the cases closely to other types of vagrancy targets. On a procedural level, civil rights lawyers' successes removing southern cases from state to federal courts, bringing affirmative civil rights suits in federal courts, and convincing those courts to keep jurisdiction opened up new strategic possibilities for the hippie vagrancy cases. The new federal court receptiveness was key, as state court procedures often made it difficult to challenge vagrancy laws as part of a defense to hippie prosecutions. Unlike Miller's Boulder cases, prosecutors and judges quickly dismissed many of the more startling hippie vagrancy arrests. In Tuscaloosa, the charges against some hippies were dropped even before a committal hearing. The rest of the defendants came to court a week after the raid only to learn that their cases had not been docketed, or that the sheriff had failed to bring their warrants. The same thing happened a week later. Every time they asked about the status of the prosecution, they got nowhere. By the time they brought their own civil rights suit to federal court, they could not say where the state prosecution stood. Elsewhere, things were clearer. In San Antonio, the prosecutor dropped some vagrancy charges and then announced in open court "that he had new vagrancy charges drawn and 'ready to file' and that they might be filed at any time." The defendants understood this to be "an ultimatum to leave town." Louis Lusky, who had crusaded against the similar Louisville practice of "filing away," would have been appalled.[73]

Such episodes made it obvious that many of the hippie arrests were for harassment, rather than conviction, purposes. Without convictions, hippie vagrancy targets could not make constitutional arguments on appeal. By expanding federal jurisdiction to cases in which constitutional rights could not be vindicated in state courts, then, the recent civil rights developments enabled the hippie lawyers to move cases to friendlier judicial turf, to avoid the convictions that threatened to linger in state courts, and to get definitive rulings on the constitutionality of vagrancy laws. It also enabled them to bring their clients to court as civil rights plaintiffs rather than convicted vagrants.[74]

Once the lawyers had found a way into federal court and gotten the judges good and worked up about the facts, they had to offer them doctrinal reasons that the vagrancy laws were unconstitutional. The arguments they made were both rooted in their own particular context and drew on arguments made by other groups in the vagrancy law challenge. Running through, in, and around the facts, one could discern a central, abiding, and new(ish) theme: a constitutional challenge to the obvious singling out of hippies because of what was increasingly called their "lifestyle." In the San Antonio case, the hippies claimed that law enforcement was using the vagrancy laws "to enforce personal notions of acceptable behavior and appearance, and to stifle legitimate political and social dissent." At one point during the hippies' federal court hearing in Boulder, Miller's co-counsel Roger Stevens asked, "All over Boulder, there were people making pies that day, why these young men?" Miller and Stevens's answer: "The purpose and practical effect of the State Vagrancy Statute is to harass, intimidate, and jail those individuals whose ideas, dress, or manner of living infringes upon the sensitivities of those in authority."[75]

Underlying these arguments was the idea that people were free to choose a lifestyle different from the monogamous, heterosexual, market-oriented, Ozzy-and-Harriet mold. In part because of the anti-vagrancy law challenge itself, and in part benefiting it, that idea was gaining legal currency in the late 1960s. Just a few months after the Supreme Court dismissed *Hicks*, Justice Douglas's walking buddy Charles Reich published his autobiographical law review article. In it, he built on some of the themes Douglas had articulated in his *Hicks* dissent and would again echo in *Wainwright* in 1968. Reich argued that "in a society that presses toward sameness and safeness these all too perishable qualities [of independence, boldness, creativity, and high spirits] must be given some help—they must be fostered and nourished." When people sought Reich's "protected crannies for the soul" on a public street in the middle of the night, the police should be prevented from destroying them. Indeed, Reich would soon change his own life in dramatic ways. In the early 1970s, he rejected the cloistered world of the Yale law professor in favor of publishing a bestselling anthem of the counterculture, finding himself in Berkeley, and coming out as gay.[76]

Reich was not alone in championing such individuality. In the spring of 1968, the recently launched *Harvard Civil Rights-Civil Liberties Law Review* published an article on the invalidation of several vagrancy laws, and it devoted most of an issue to "The Legitimate Scope of Police Discretion to Restrict Ordinary Activity" the following year. To Beverly C. Moore Jr., "Vagrancy and Related Offenses" forced " 'bums,' 'hippies,' and 'drifters' to abandon [their] entire lifestyle," not because such people were "criminogenic but because they compete with and somehow threaten dominant values of the Establishment." In Moore's view, the "Establishment" feared that hippies would "win converts to their cause in a free marketplace of life styles—thus posing alternatives that make social change possible." He called on courts to "closely scrutinize vagrancy statutes which may in fact represent legislative attempts to 'abolish' minority life styles under the guise of a crime control measure." Moore's and other articles underscored a shared and growing awareness among young legal scholars and lawyers that adopting a lifestyle identifiably different from, and challenging to, main-stream norms could get one arrested for vagrancy. So too they bolstered the idea that "the existence of laws which can be used to enforce conformity is not a matter which, in the long run, can be or should be evaded by the US Supreme Court."[77]

What was less clear was how best to translate that argument into constitu-tional doctrine. It was hard to find a constitutional framework for protecting hip-pies as hippies, hard to find protection for a bohemian "lifestyle" that was lived both in private and very much in public. Neither an equal protection argument prohibiting anti-hippie legislation nor a fundamental rights argument to an alternative lifestyle seemed doctrinally available in 1968 and 1969. Instead, the lawyers tried to shoehorn their key concern with nonconformity into existing or potentially emerging doctrinal and constitutional categories. As for existing doctrine, the lawyers claimed that being a hippie was the sort of status prohib-ited by *Robinson v. California*'s 1962 interpretation of the Eighth Amendment, even in the face of the Court's limitations on that argument in the 1968 pub-lic drunkenness case of *Powell v. Texas*. To punish hippies "for maintaining an habitual lifestyle 'below' a predetermined level, for being social inferiors (if such they are), is to impose cruel and unusual punishment," wrote Daly.[78]

Even more commonly, the lawyers used void for vagueness, which had long lent itself to such overtones of discrimination. "If one may be arrested for vagrancy, as the plaintiffs in this case were . . . , while sitting in the [living] room of their home, surely the abuse of the law is epidemic in this State," argued Daly. In his San Antonio trial memorandum, Dan Struve recounted that when he had asked the prosecutors' investigator in San Antonio what vagrancy was, the dis-trict attorney had objected, "That is a pretty global question. I don't think it can be answered." Struve noted the irony that the lawyer was "prosecuting under a law which he does not find comprehensible."[79]

The lawyers also argued more explicitly for fundamental rights that would undergird constitutional lifestyle protection. Legal scholar Louis Henkin located the Court's "unwilling[ness] to accept broadside constitutional chal-lenges" to vagrancy, loitering, drunkenness, and other laws in its fear of "substan-tive due process" and "the ghost of *Lochner*." But that did not stop the lawyers from viewing *Griswold*, *Edwards v. California*, and other cases as creating new space for the protection of "the right to travel, to free movement, to peaceable assembly, to privacy, to be free from arbitrary and illegal arrests, to equal protec-tion of the laws, and to be free from forced labor." Some of these arguments, and especially those that relied on *Griswold*, emphasized the violations of privacy in home-intruding vagrancy arrests. Others, following Reich and Moore, insisted on rights that were not limited to the private sphere. Daly argued that "the Ninth and Fourteenth Amendment rights of 'liberty' include the right to be socially different, socially deviant, socially 'inferior,' so long as one is not thereby socially harmful." Struve criticized vagrancy laws for attempting "to codify attitudes toward morality which do not seem to be entirely consistent with the so-called more modern view."[80]

Perhaps because they recognized the fragility of such arguments, perhaps because of the increasingly obvious connections between the hippies' predicament and the anti-vagrancy law arguments of other groups, the lawyers also built on the claims of other types of vagrancy targets. Supreme Court doctrine did not provide much help. The Court had failed to resolve the specific problem of vagrancy regulation of nonconformists before the hippie explosion in *Hicks* in 1966, and it had hit the vagrancy law challenge hard in 1968's *Terry-Wainwright-Johnson* triple whammy. But the Court proved little hindrance either. By the fall of 1968, vagrancy-condemning judicial and scholarly authorities outside the hippie context were growing like weed in a hippie house. Vagrancy foes had seen victories in the poverty case of *Fenster v. Leary* and the prostitution case of *Ricks v. District of Columbia*, as well as a number of others. Indeed, there were not only positive precedents for vagrancy cases now but there were also conventions to follow. From the anachronism of laws rooted in feudal England to the long lists of violated constitutional provisions—including the First, Fourth, Fifth, Sixth, Eighth, Ninth, Thirteenth, and Fourteenth Amendments—the lawyers applied vagrancy lessons from other contexts to this one.[81]

In so doing, the lawyers equated, assimilated, and analogized. They compared hippies to other groups of people they presumed more likely to receive constitutional protection. The police were inclined to treat hippies—whose vices ran the gamut from sex crimes to narcotics—as "undesirables." The lawyers tried to link them more closely to constitutionally protected citizens. Like prostitutes, homosexuals, and others, hippies likened themlves to the worthy poor, First Amendment speakers, and racial minorities.

Take poverty and unemployment. Many hippies had no jobs, and they looked it. That made them ripe for vagrancy arrests. In *Gallant v. Barlow*, the 1969 San Antonio case, the defense lawyer tried to question the investigator about what he had asked the defendant, and the prosecutor interjected, "Your Honor, he has testified to all of that. He said that he didn't have a job. He told him he didn't have any money. He said that he looked like a bum." Elsewhere the investigator said, "As I understand the vagrancy law here, if a person doesn't have a home, he is a bum."[82]

If the hippies' poverty made them ripe for vagrancy prosecutions, it also made them ripe for newly circulating arguments about the constitutional protection of the poor in the late 1960s. Even as some lawyers claimed that the status of being a hippie should not be criminalized, others argued that hippies were a kind of poor person, and that *Robinson* prohibited the criminalization of the status of poverty. As for equal protection, the North Carolina *Wheeler* brief argued, "Whatever may be the respective incidents of affluence and poverty that would support other sorts of discriminations between rich and poor, it is wholly beyond conception that incidents can be found which would justify letting rich men lead idle, vagrant and suspicious lives while forbidding poor men the same sort of lives." In San Antonio's *Gallant*, Struve contended, "In this leisure time-early retirement era," the association between idleness, poverty, and criminality "is patently unfounded."[83]

Many of the arguments thus synthesized the poverty of the hippies with their nonconformity. "Does one have a visible means of support when one is wearing a coat and tie (as opposed to wearing levis and a sweatshirt)? Does one have a visible means of support when one carries a briefcase (as opposed to a duffel bag of indeterminate contents)?" They claimed equal protection violations from a law that facially "discriminates against the indigent and, under its practical effect, it discriminates against those whom the State authorities disagree with in dress, thought, and manner of living."[84]

One can readily see how such analogies were fraught with complications and imperfections. Even as the hippies built on the emerging rights of the poor, such rights were still relatively new and uncertain. Moreover, the poverty of the hippie—the suburban, middle-class white kid gone awry—was often voluntary and fleeting. Because hippies and the other poor people who were also challenging vagrancy laws were not the same in many respects, hippies offered up equivocal specimens for claims against both the Eighth Amendment status crime and poverty-based equal protection critiques of vagrancy laws.

More stable as successful models of the constitutionally protected were both free speakers and racial minorities. Some of the hippies' lawyers wondered if the First Amendment might be the central framework for the hippie vagrancy cases. One national ACLU staff lawyer scribbled at the top of some hippie vagrancy correspondence, "file" and then "free speech??" Might free speech be implicated because living as a hippie in a hippie house, dressing and acting as a hippie, was expressive and associational? So the lawyers tried to argue. *Wheeler*, for example, invoked the now staple New Deal-era labor organizing loitering case of *Thornhill v. Alabama*. Daly likened the modern-day hippie to "unpaid civil rights workers, labor organizers, persons attempting to promote boycotts or strikes, itinerant preachers" and others "indisputably engaged in the free (if sometimes unseemly) speech protected by the First Amendment." Given that hippies were not conventional First Amendment speakers, *Shuttlesworth v. Alabama* seemed even more on point. "There, no overt First Amendment activity in the traditional sense was involved or denied by the application of the challenged ordinance to the conduct of its constitutional challengers. . . . Yet the Court there had observed that '[i]nstinct with its ever-present *potential* for arbitrarily suppressing First

Amendment liberties, that kind of law bears the hallmark of a police state.'" The lawyers hoped that "[t]he analogy to the instant case [was] manifest."[85]

The problem for the hippie lawyers was that *Shuttlesworth* was as much a race case as a free speech case, and in crucial ways hippies were unlike African Americans. Though the hippies frequently cited civil rights cases, they had not wrested away the mantle of the free speaker; they could not claim the same moral high ground. One fair housing case espoused prohibitions against race discrimination while validating a building's policy against admitting "drunks, hippies, children and belligerent appearing applicants" as reasonably "necessary and practical . . . to keep undesirables of any race out of the building." Discriminating against hippies, on this view, was different from discriminating against African Americans. It was not legally problematic.[86]

In part, the two groups may have differed because the hippies chose their outsider status. They sealed their own fates as outcasts by rejecting mainstream culture. African Americans lacked such choice. To be sure, arrests often came when African Americans challenged the status quo, when they pressed on the boundaries of their place. If hippies were arrested for rejecting the Establishment, African Americans were often arrested for insisting on their inclusion in it. But African Americans frequently fell victim to vagrancy laws even when in place, even when not threatening any particular status quo. They were "undesirable" because of the color of their skin, the racial makeup of their ancestors. African Americans had been forcibly brought to this country on slave ships. They had been bought, sold, exploited, oppressed, and excluded for centuries. They could escape their racial legacy only by denying or escaping their racial heritage.

Lawyers nonetheless hoped that highlighting their hippie clients' shared experience of oppression, unpopularity, and police harassment would reap doctrinal rewards. In the Carmel-by-the-Sea case, the lawyers argued, "If we substitute 'Negroes' for the word 'hippies' in the declaration we have the paradigm for an ordinance designed to preserve the purity of the lawns of Biloxi." In North Carolina, George Daly identified the category of those police harassed as "the civil rights workers, the black, the hippie, the draft resister." More caustically, he echoed *The Village Voice*, which declared hippies "the new niggers" in 1967, in commenting, "There's just a lot more niggers in the world today. . . . Hippies are niggers. Some blacks are niggers. Long hairs are niggers. Draft resisters are niggers. And police beat on niggers. It's an attitude, not a color thing." Using different language, Justice Abe Fortas also grouped hippies with racial minorities, at least in their alienation. The impact of police interactions was "generally felt by the most sensitive, emotional, and overreactive members of our society: our young people, and members of minority groups emerging from a background of oppression."[87]

In different ways, the 1969 cases of *Broughton v. Brewer* in Alabama and *Gallant v. Barlow* in San Antonio highlighted the kinds of analogies, combinations, and recombinations that marked the maturation of the vagrancy law challenge. *Broughton*, a federal challenge to Alabama's vagrancy law, consolidated cases from Mobile and Tuscaloosa into a single class action. The Tuscaloosa case involved a college-town ACLU seeking protection for hippies and their Haight Hut as well as college students engaged in political speech. The Mobile case involved vagrancy arrests of school-age African Americans distributing handbills for a boycott of allegedly discriminatory downtown white businesses. Tuscaloosa plaintiff Steve Suitts discussed the consolidated cases years later with Vernon Z. Crawford, a cooperating lawyer with the NAACP LDF, founder of the first black law firm in Mobile, the "dean" of African American lawyers in that city, and the lawyer for the Mobile vagrancy plaintiffs. According to Suitts, Crawford thought putting the cases together was important because "it created a more biracial profile of what these issues were all about." That profile likely redounded to the benefit of both groups: the hippies might have engendered empathy, but the black students likely inspired greater sympathy.[88]

Dan Struve's choice of plaintiffs in San Antonio's *Gallant* also highlighted similarities and relationships across categories of vagrancy victims. His original complaint included biographical background about his diverse clients, including whether they looked like hippies or "undesirables," and how many times they had been arrested. Named-plaintiff Gallant had been arrested for vagrancy some twenty times, spending some two hundred days in jail on the charge. Another plaintiff was a migrant farm worker (arrested about ten times), another a prostitute (for whom vagrancy arrests were "almost a weekly occurrence"), and another African American. They were, Struve summarized, "the younger, disaffected, non-affluent members of society." When Struve handed the case over to David Richards, Richards's amended complaint left out much of the biographical information at the request of the district court judge. Instead of showing through individual lives how varied were the uses to which vagrancy laws were put, how varied its victims, Richards abstracted the argument: the police used the vagrancy law to "enforce personal notions of acceptable behavior and appearance, and to stifle legitimate political and social dissent."[89]

"Personal notions" or not, police officers, prosecutors, and state attorney generals responding to the hippies' anti-vagrancy law challenges had to decide what to do with these cases. In addition to dismissing charges on an ad hoc basis, some city attorneys made it a policy no longer to use the vagrancy laws at all. Before the federal court decided *Broughton*, for example, Tuscaloosa city attorney (later U.S. senator) Dick Shelby had already stopped making arrests under the state vagrancy law. According to plaintiff Steve Suitts, Shelby had been a "pragmatic Southern moderate" who had seen "the handwriting on the judicial wall and wanted to keep town-gown relations in Tuscaloosa from souring to a boiling point." Shelby told the city that it could not, as Suitts put it, "continue to arrest students because it did not like what they're doing and then call them vagrants."[90]

Other officials were less convinced that the laws would fall. They were, rather, convinced that the laws were necessary and constitutional, and they fought the hippie cases with all the legal ammunition at their disposal. A federal judge described Charlotte and North Carolina officials as deeply "stubborn" and betraying their fiduciary duty to the residents of their city with their defense to the hippie suit. In Texas, the state both conceded most and fought longest and hardest. As the federal court in *Gallant* put it, "In the face of numerous cases holding similar statutes unconstitutional for the grounds alleged in the plaintiff's petition," the state conceded that several sections of the state law were unconstitutional. Nonetheless, the state claimed that the plaintiffs could not constitute a class and that they lacked standing to challenge the law in its entirety, as they had not been arrested under every section of the Texas law.[91]

The government lawyers often fought hard not only in their briefs and arguments but also in interactions with the hippies and their lawyers. Officials in Charlotte claimed that the ACLU had coerced the hippies into filing suit. When the judge questioned the plaintiffs, however, they said that the only improper coercion they faced was from the police—the plaintiffs wanted to withdraw from the case because they feared police retaliation. Lawyer Daly recalled that "the police were very aggressive about attacking civil rights lawyers back then. . . . . [T]hey played hardball." In one case in the early 1970s, North Carolina Attorney General Robert Morgan discovered a possible way to thwart Daly. He wrote Daly about his thought process. " 'Well,' " I said to myself, 'let it ride. After all, George [Daly] did not move for summary judgment against you when you showed up for trial without an answer.' 'On the other hand,' myself replied, 'now that you've got a civil rights lawyer with his trousers about his ankles, why not be a real son of a bitch?' "[92]

Such official sentiment was sometimes reflected in the media. A radio editorial in San Antonio noted that though it usually found some "merit" in ACLU positions, it could find none in *Gallant*. "The vagrancy statutes are necessary tools if our police department is to keep this city from being overrun by undesirables. Intelligent application of the vagrancy laws cannot be considered 'harassment.' . . . We hope the judge who hands down the ultimate decision here will back the police officers and not do anything to 'tie their hands.' " Op-eds in the *San Antonio Express* and the *New York Times* likened hippies to animals who might be hunted (in Texas) or go extinct (in New York).[93]

Government recalcitrance and public vitriol or no, the ACLU lawyers, backed by growing lists of precedents and extensively footnoted law review articles, were confident about their cases. They were right to be. In every published federal civil rights hippie vagrancy case, the hippies and their lawyers won.

It was not that the judges who invalidated vagrancy laws on behalf of hip-pies were any kind of "hippie judges." Indeed, generationally distant as they usually were, they seemed somewhat perplexed by this new breed of young person. The judges worked hard to account for litigants one awkwardly described as "profess[ing] to be what is commonly referred to as a 'hippie.'" In the Rittenhouse Square case, the judge confessed to finding the "phenom-enon . . . difficult to define." He turned to quotations taken from the coun-terculture itself: "The first wave of an approaching ocean of technologically unemployable people; ' . . . escapists from the affluent society that produces and sustains them . . . opposed to the everyday middle-aged values of affluent America—its commercialism, mechanism and bureaucracy; its car culture, hygiene and unquestioned acceptance of the work ethic and the quick buck.'" It was not often that such language found its way into the *Federal Supplement*.[94]

However mystifying they found the hippies, judges—several of whom were recent appointments of Democratic president Lyndon B. Johnson—generously found in their favor. Police officers were using well-established laws as they long had, but the world had changed around them. By 1969, the judges were dis-turbed both by the laws' anachronism and by the laws' newly "outrageous" uses. As to the age of the laws, one judge noted that "vagrancy control dates back to the fourteenth century" and was used "to shore up the crumbling structure of feudal society." He marveled that a vagrant refusing hard labor could "be put in irons and kept on bread and water until he shall comply." As to current uses, the judges criticized police officers for harassing young people who displayed "a high degree of intelligence, clarity of speech, frankness and sense of relevance." The *Goldman* court condemned the vagrancy law because it could be used "against every member of the community who is not living in the style . . . which the particular authorities set as a standard" at "the whim of the authorities." The "egregious" facts of the cases and the antiquated language of the laws not only grabbed the attention of the judges but they also seemed to justify federal juris-diction as necessary to counteract the hostility of state court procedures.[95]

When it came to adjudicating the merits of the cases, these federal district judges found an abundance of doctrinal support for the invalidity of the laws both within the hippies' own cases and well beyond them. These judges took neither the absence of favorable Supreme Court precedence as of 1969, when they began deciding these cases, nor the crime control setbacks of June 1968 as constraints. Though the Court had not invalidated vagrancy laws, neither had it explicitly upheld them. In fact, the persistent trickle of cases at the Court—and especially the repeated dissents—suggested that the Court was not finished with the issue. Moreover, the crime control context was quite different from the hippie one. Even if, as law enforcement advocates were arguing, some residual vagrancy-like authority was necessary for crime control, that hardly justified this harassment of hippies. Though their conduct might be "unconventional, unproductive, and unattractive by everyday standards," it was not "unlawful."[96]

Void for vagueness dominated the judges' reasoning, as it did the lawyers', but the opinions also relied on the First, Fourth, Fifth, Eighth, and Fourteenth Amendments. Some courts embraced the lawyers' claims for constitutional protection of nonconformity. They also invoked the poverty of the hippies, finding both equal protection and *Robinson* Eighth Amendment status crime violations. "Hippies, like more conventional householders, are entitled to the protection of the constitution, and the court would be remiss if it allowed the length of a man's hair or the thinness of his purse to affect the measure of his cvil rights." Courts also accepted the racial and free speech analogies the lawyers offered. One court described itself as "consistently vigilant to protect racial groups from the effects of official prejudice, and we can be no less concerned because the human beings currently in disfavor are identifiable by dress and attitudes rather than by color." In *Wheeler*, the court concluded, "a man is free to be a hippie, a Methodist, a Jew, a Black Panther, a Kiwanian, or even a Communist, so long as his conduct does not imperil others, or infringe upon their rights. In short, it is no crime to be a hippie."[97]

As these federal judges synthesized and analogized, they adamantly and lavishly condemned vagrancy laws as unconstitutional. The archaic laws, the disturbing facts of the cases, and the apparent similarities between hippies and more obviously protected groups all made vagrancy laws look increasingly out of place. By the end of 1969, so many new precedents had accumulated that the *Wheeler* court described its holding as "bolstered by numerous holdings in 1969 alone that condemn vagrancy as unconstitutional." In Colorado, a cartoon showed Robert Bruce Miller as a knight slaying the dragon of the vagrancy laws. The newspaper called him a "diligent young attorney," for whom the court's decision "came like a winning ticket in the Irish Sweepstakes." Even the state attorney general, Duke Dunbar, was not surprised at the outcome in the case. "It was a tough one."[98]

The battle between the police and the hippies nonetheless raged on. Though the Denver district attorney recognized that Denver's ordinance was "in jeopardy" after the Boulder invalidation, the city attorney was convinced that an older state court precedent would save it. The practical response at least would not be long in coming: the Denver public defender announced that he would move to have vagrancy charges dismissed against five clients then in court and for the release of anyone then serving jail terms for the crime—around thirty people were released from the county jail.[99]

'Anything Else?'

Figure 7.2 Boulder ACLU lawyer Robert Bruce Miller slaying the dragon of the illegitimate vagrancy law. The cartoon reveals how, by 1969, the tide of public opinion had turned against the laws due to their aggressive and obviously discriminatory deployment against white, middle-class hippies. *Colorado Daily*, Rob Pudim.

In North Carolina, even before the federal court declared the vagrancy law invalid in Daly's Charlotte hippie case of *Wheeler*, a police department legal adviser acknowledged that arresting hippies for vagrancy was a mistake because even though hippies were different, they were not dangerous. "Neighbors had complained. These people were not conformists, but that's not against the law. We arrested them for vagrancy. We agree now, with some hindsight, that a vagrancy charge is unconstitutional." Even though government officials had fought the case tooth and nail, once the decision was in, the city appealed only that portion expunging the arrest records. The city was still convinced, with good cultural if not legal reason, that where hippies went, drugs went. As part of the city's ongoing investigation, it wanted to keep the arrest records for future use.[100]

The police/hippie clash continued with hippie arrests under other laws in a series of cases in which Daly represented "famous Charlotte hippie" Marvin Sparrow and his wife Katherine. When Richard Nixon visited for Billy Graham Day, for example, the Sparrows and other members of the counterculture and the political opposition were excluded from the Charlotte Coliseum. They sued the local police, the Secret Service, and others for their exclusion. Daly recalled, "When the presidential motorcade came into the coliseum, the hippies were singing 'The Star Spangled Banner' off key with the accompaniment of the kazoo. . . . [A]s part of the hearing, I told the court that I wanted the hippies to come to the front of the courtroom and recreate the whole scene and the song." U.S. Attorney David Sentelle (later a federal appellate judge) "quite correctly pointed out that we don't recreate things in court, we talk about things." Daly prevailed because the judge wanted to witness the song himself. According to Daly, they "devised a special oath that they would 'well and truly recreate the scene out there without fear or favor.' The hippies sang 'The Star Spangled Banner' off key in the courtroom. The courtroom was packed—and all the hippies on my side stood up. And the policemen on the other side were put to this terrible choice—do you stand up? It's 'The Star Spangled Banner' after all. About half of them stood up. So the hippies started singing along, it was so infectious. So Sentelle yelled, 'I object, I object, they're humming along!'" The judge said nothing. Sentelle just put his head on his desk. The hippies were singing and the judge was red in the face and Sentelle had his head on the table.[101]

After these victories, at least some legislators began to take possible legal challenges—usually ACLU challenges—more seriously as they considered new statutes or ordinances targeting hippies. In October 1968, Eason Monroe, the head of the ACLU of Southern California, which had spearheaded anti-vagrancy law efforts under A. L. Wirin and Leo Gallagher in the 1930s, challenged Los Angeles' new "anti-hippie loitering law." The city council passed the law unanimously, but the mayor worried that the city attorney would find it unconstitutional in light of *Shuttlesworth*. When Charlotte considered a new ordinance prohibiting loitering near places of prostitution and gambling and where drugs and alcohol were illegally sold, at least one councilman worried that Daly would "have a field day with this." Suddenly, it was to be expected that an ACLU hippie lawyer might object to a loitering or vagrancy law. Plaintiffs were finding lawyers, lawyers were quick with lawsuits and legal arguments, and judges seemed inclined to agree with them.[102]

Within a year of the 1968 defeats in *Terry* and *Wainwright*, the lower federal courts had managed to do what the Supreme Court had not: definitively strike down vagrancy laws. The kind of "lawless" activity vagrancy laws had long licensed was on full and open display in the hippie cases, with their constant surveillance and multiple raids of private homes. The police had overreached. The hippie arrests highlighted just how far the vagrancy laws could be pressed, and how out of place they increasingly seemed. No doubt, judicial shock was enhanced by who many of the hippies were: privileged white kids. The social position of these "vagrants" likely made hippies familiar to lawyers, reporters, and judges, who might have had children, siblings, or other relatives making similar, if disparaged, choices.[103]

The success of the hippie cases drew not only on the identity of the victims and the overreaching of law enforcement, but also on the arguments that other groups had been making about the defects of vagrancy laws for years. The cases showed that finding constitutional protection for hippies required synthesizing, analogizing, and building on arguments by poor people, free speakers, and racial minorities. Because the hippies turned to arguments others had made before them, the benefits of their cases extended far beyond the counterculture. What might have seemed disparate aspects of the decade had come together to bring down vagrancy laws, at least in the lower courts. The judicial decisions hippies and their lawyers secured became key victories and new resources in the ongoing vagrancy battle. The Supreme Court had seemed at the leading edge of the legal curve when it first took *Edelman v. Caliornia* in 1953. By 1971, it was decidedly behind it.

The Beginning of the End of Vagrancy Laws

On a sunny, snow-melting day in the spring of 1970, Cleveland lawyer Niki Schwartz was in a meeting for much of the morning. When it ended, he learned two things. One: at Kent State University, members of the Ohio National Guard had shot and killed four students protesting the Vietnam War and the invasion of Cambodia. Two: the Supreme Court had decided to hear *Palmer v. City of Euclid*. The case involved a black man convicted of violating a "suspicious persons" law in a mostly white city. "It was May 4, 1970," Schwartz recalled. "I won't forget that date."[1]

It would have been hard to forget, for these were not some distant events for Schwartz. As the incoming chair of the ACLU of Ohio, he played a key role in litigation arising out of the Kent State shootings. As a lawyer with the Cleveland ACLU, Schwartz had agreed to represent Palmer. He was headed to the Supreme Court in what the national organization predicted might finally be the "landmark" case that would "nullif[y]" "similar laws existing throughout the country."[2]

Two weeks later, attorney Robert Lavercombe learned that the Supreme Court had also taken his clients' vagrancy-related case, *Coates v. City of Cincinnati*. Dennis Coates was a long-haired, war-protesting, Antioch College student. Coates was luckier than his peers at Kent State and Jackson State, a black college where police had killed two more student war protestors shortly after Kent State. Instead of lethal force, Coates suffered arrest under a local loitering ordinance. The same ordinance had previously brought Lavercombe's law firm several other, very different, types of clients. Some, like labor union members arrested while picketing, were consolidated with *Coates* in the Ohio Supreme Court and were formally before the Court. Others, like Lathan Johnson, an African American community leader arrested during the 1967 Cincinnati riots, were not. All, however, were crucial to Lavercombe's understanding of the case.

Palmer and *Coates* brought the Supreme Court simultaneous opportunities to invalidate two of the classic vagrancy-related laws—suspicious persons and loitering—in two very different cases. Palmer, like Sam Thompson, Stephen Wainwright, and Harvey Johnson before him, was making neither a political nor a cultural statement by driving in Euclid at 2 AM. Whether he was, as he claimed, merely dropping off a friend or, as the police claimed, about to commit a serious crime, he was just out of place as a black man in a white city. The racial cast of Palmer's arrest raised warring frames of reference. One deemed Palmer out of place because of a racial hierarchy the Supreme Court had already condemned. The other found him out of place because of an apparent crime epidemic that made young black men particularly suspect and the justices particularly nervous. *Palmer* thus raised the specter of both racialized policing and racialized criminality in a world where civil rights protests seemed to have morphed into racialized violence.

Coates presented a very different problem. Dennis Coates was not out of place by happenstance or context; he was out of place very much on purpose. Like Isidor Edelman and Fred Shuttlesworth, Coates was the political opposition. Like Eddie Hicks, the Beats, and the hippies, he was culturally nonconforming. Coates was claiming a right to express his political views and his personal lifestyle, a right not only to be in public but to be witnessed and tolerated by the public. The justices had encountered many folks like Coates in recent years. They had been trying to find ways to respect the First Amendment rights of increasingly unruly free speakers while allowing government officials enough leeway to maintain order. They had been trying to distinguish between acceptable dissent and what sometimes felt like imminent anarchy. Coates's lawyers made drawing such a line in his case difficult by refusing to tell the justices exactly what Coates had done to get arrested.

The justices thus seemed poised to take sides in the battle that had been escalating for fifteen years. On one side, as a news report put it, were "the familiar claims that loitering laws are a symbol of oppression to blacks, labor pickets and war dissenters, subjecting them to arrest for activity that is constitutional, and permissible if carried on by other citizens." On the other side, government officials sought "wide latitude to protect city streets, businesses and homes in the face of rising crime rates."[3]

Choosing between those two sides—or finding a way to satisfy both—was particularly fraught in 1970 and 1971. Ohio seemed to be exploding, and it was not alone. Protests against racially discriminatory policing and the Vietnam War had grown increasingly strident in recent years, and both protestors and law enforcement officers had turned more frequently to violence. That violence and those protests had provided some of the context for the Supreme Court's 1968 policing cases, and it continued to bedevil liberal justices who both sympathized with some police targets and recognized the need for law enforcement authority. In May 1971, at the very moment the justices were considering the constitutionality of the vagrancy-related laws in *Palmer* and *Coates*, the chaos of the era literally, physically breached the justices' customary seclusion. As anti-war activists protested on the steps and then within the hallowed halls of the Supreme Court, debates about the validity of vagrancy laws generated urgent, insistent questions that demanded resolution.[4]

Race, Crime, and Vagrancy Redux

When Niki Schwartz agreed to take on *Palmer v. City of Euclid*, he had no idea that it would propel him to his first Supreme Court argument. Growing up in Bexley, Ohio, Schwartz first identified as a civil libertarian when his high school principal pulled his editorials from the school paper. As both an undergraduate and a law student at Ohio State University, Schwartz became embroiled in political battles. He later joined the local ACLU chapter while teaching law at the University of Toledo. Just after moving to Cleveland to practice law, Schwartz attended a meeting of volunteer ACLU lawyers. As he recalled, "they announced that someone had sent a letter requesting help with an appeal to the Supreme Court. Knowing nothing else and nothing about its odds at the Supreme Court, I said I would help. Las Vegas wouldn't book such a case at any odds."[5]

Once Schwartz began to look carefully at *Palmer*, he thought, "This case has real potential." As an initial matter, the ordinance itself "made it very sexy in terms of . . . being accepted by the Supreme Court." Palmer had been "sentenced to thirty days in jail for being a suspicious person. So he was being punished for his status." Though not labeled "vagrancy," the category could often be found in vagrancy laws, and the stand-alone suspicious persons law shared with vagrancy laws its historical roots in local suspicion of strangers, its target of potential criminals, and its criminalization of status. It was the third law in the frequent litany of exceptional—and exceptionally suspect—vagrancy, loitering, and suspicious persons laws. Schwartz knew from his ACLU connections and his own experience that status crimes, and vagrancy-related laws specifically, had recently been falling to constitutional challenges. Schwartz still viewed *Robinson v. California*'s prohibition on status crimes as an available and promising doctrinal resource even after *Powell v. Texas* upheld a public drunkenness law against a similar Eighth Amendment challenge. In his brief to the Supreme Court, he extended *Robinson*'s argument that a person could not be penalized for having a disease to ask "whether the status of being suspicious may be criminally punished."[6]

As a defense lawyer representing a suspected criminal against a "suspicious persons" charge, Schwartz also emphasized possible Fourth and Fifth Amendment violations—that Palmer was arrested without probable cause and that he had been forced to incriminate himself. Even if the criminal procedure problems likely seemed more apparent in this context than in others, Schwartz went beyond such crime prevention-related arguments to embrace other aspects of the vagrancy law challenge. He made the standard claims about the vagueness of the law's language and the law's "potential for suppressing noncriminal but unconventional persons and behavior." He reprised arguments about police manuals equating "suspicious" with "unusual" behavior. He quoted from 1959's *The Practical Patrolman*: "What makes a 'suspicious' person. . . ? In part it's a matter of not 'belonging,' of being unusual." He cited recent scholarship arguing that police officers had "a commitment to conventionalism"—perhaps due to an "authoritarian personality," perhaps not. Aided by his correspondence with Mel Wulf about recent victories in other ACLU vagrancy cases—including both the prostitution case of *Ricks v. District of Columbia* and the Charlotte, North Carolina, hippie case of *Wheeler v. Goodman*—Schwartz pointed out that nine state and lower federal courts had struck down laws with similar language in the previous five years.[7]

This general preoccupation with "not belonging" was intimately related to the second reason Schwartz thought the *Palmer* case had "sex appeal": what he called its "racial ingredients." These ingredients made the problem of Palmer's presence in Euclid systematic and profound rather than contingent and idiosyncratic. The first hint of the racial character of the case was just a notation on a police affidavit. It appeared right alongside the fact that at two o'clock in the morning on April 19, 1967, in Euclid, Ohio, the weather was clear. In the section describing the defendant, the officers had noted James Palmer's birthdate—he was on the cusp of his thirty-fifth birthday—and his height and weight—six foot one inche tall and 180 pounds. The key piece of information was the one that need not have been there. On the line requiring the sex of the defendant, the officers had entered "M-Colored." The form nowhere asked about race. It created no space for such a notation. But Palmer's race was important to the officers, and they squeezed it in.[8]

Granted, Palmer's race had not been the first thing about him that had made Joseph Zupanic suspicious. Zupanic, a policeman for the city of Euclid for more than twelve years, was moonlighting as a private security guard. He saw Palmer driving very slowly without his headlights through the 2,000-space parking lot of the Indian Hills Colony Apartments. Zupanic became more suspicious when Palmer pulled up in front of the large building and let out of his car "a colored female." Zupanic was candid at Palmer's trial that a black woman looked suspicious to him. He happened to know that not a single black woman lived in the massive apartment complex. In fact, *Palmer* was not the first time Euclid had been hauled before the Supreme Court. A half century earlier, the Court affirmed Euclid's power to pass a zoning ordinance in what became the canonical case of *Village of Euclid v. Amber Realty*. The lower court opinion forthrightly described "the result to be accomplished" as "classify[ing] the population and segregat[ing] them according to their income or situation in life." By the 1960 census, Euclid was home to only 105 people of color. They lived alongside 62,893 white people.[9]

When Zupanic saw a black woman get out of a car driven by a black man in an all-white apartment complex in a mostly white city, he thought something might be amiss. Moreover, after Palmer let his passenger off, he began talking into a two-way radio. When Zupanic questioned him, Palmer gave evasive answers. He claimed not to know his "friend's" name, and he offered up more than one home address. Zupanic called for backup and "marched" Palmer into the building at gunpoint to look for the woman. Palmer led them to an apartment, but the man who answered the door said that there was no woman inside. Without attempting to verify, Zupanic and on-duty Euclid police officer August Zach, a thirty-two-year department veteran, arrested Palmer under the ordinance making it "unlawful for any suspicious person to be within" the city limits. Among those deemed suspicious persons was anyone "who wanders about the streets or other public ways or who is found abroad at late or unusual hours in the night without any visible or lawful business and who does not give a satisfactory account of himself." To Zupanic and Zach, that was Palmer in a nutshell.[10]

Palmer represented himself in a jury trial in the Euclid municipal court. Though he had only a fifth-grade education, he shepherded his case adeptly through the Ohio courts. According to Schwartz, Palmer had "filed all the right papers in all the right places at all the right times. He never won, but I was dealt a good hand." Procedurally, Palmer had succeeded in cuing up for Schwartz and the ACLU that rare vagrancy case that had complied with all the rules. Substantively, Palmer raised many of the points any lawyer would have tried to get across at trial: neither he nor his friend had actually broken a single law (the suspicious persons law notwithstanding). Each of the apparently suspicious circumstances on its own was innocuous. Most significantly, Palmer identified the importance of race to his arrest. His companion's race played a significant—and, to him, problematic—role in the officers' suspicion.

The police prosecutor, Robert Steel, did not deny the importance of race to Zupanic's policing. Instead, he denied that it was problematic. After establishing that Zupanic had seen Palmer drop off a black woman at the apartment building, he asked, "Patrolman, do you know whether or not there was [sic] any colored females living at the Colony Hills Apartments on the 19th of April?" When Zupanic replied, "No, there are not, none whatsoever," Steel was content to rest. In Palmer's view, the race of his companion was an illegitimate justification. In Steel's, it was good reason to be suspicious.

In arguing Palmer's case to the Court, Schwartz brought to the fore these contending views about the legitimacy of race in policing. Anthony Amsterdam and the NAACP LDF had tried to bring out such themes in *Terry v. Ohio* a few years earlier, but Officer McFadden had denied that race had played any role in his suspicions of John Terry that day in Cleveland. The Court had managed to keep race, and the racial politics of policing, from playing much of a role in its opinion in *Terry*.

Now Schwartz tried again, aided by the fact that Officers Zupanic and Zach forthrightly acknowledged that race had been important to their arrest of James Palmer in nearby Euclid. Moreover, Schwartz cited national statistics showing that African Americans were not only more likely to be stopped and frisked but they were also "disproportionately burdened by suspicious person arrests." The President's Commission on Law Enforcement and Administration of Justice had found that African Americans accounted for 45.3 percent of arrests on "suspicion" but only 27.5 percent of total arrests.[11]

All of this race talk in the police records and at the trial offended Schwartz on two levels. The first was simply that "race was an element of suspicion." Schwartz agreed with Palmer that that was unacceptable. The second "was that you had this massive apartment complex where only white people lived." Schwartz knew that at least some of the justices worried about residential segregation, which had become salient in school desegregation cases. Schwartz emphasized how such segregation also facilitated racialized policing. He quoted from policing books like 1967's *Detection of Crime*, which stated, "A person of one race observed in an area which is largely inhabited by a different racial group may be stopped and questioned." More specifically, a black person in a white neighborhood "is more suspect than a white in the same area." Whites in black neighborhoods might also be detained, but "the purpose . . . is not usually to detect crime but to warn the person of the danger of being in the area particularly if he is alone." Even the presumption of racially identifiable neighborhoods was to Schwartz "a tragic reminder of the long history of housing discrimination and segregation, both governmental and private, that facilitates the use of race as a sign of being out of place." He acknowledged that race might be "viewed as a neutral and rational basis for determining who is 'out of place,'" but he argued that "it may not be so employed, because it is the product of, and contributes to, a long and tragic national history of housing discrimination and segregation." Because minorities were minorities, moreover, they were "out of place" more often than were members of the majority race, a fact that had "a differential impact on the freedom of movement of the minority race."[12]

Even as Schwartz linked *Palmer* to the larger questions about race in policing and the challenge to status crimes in the vagrancy law challenge, he assumed that *Terry*, far more than *Shuttlesworth*, *Thompson*, or *Wainwright*, was likely to be on the justices' minds. Schwartz knew he had to address the problem that anti-vagrancy advocates had faced for years: convincing the Court that the police could continue to do their jobs effectively without vagrancy-related laws, that they should be denied the power to "nip crime in the bud," to engage in "preventive policing," to get someone patently suspicious off of streets that seemed increasingly dangerous and insecure.[13]

In this task, Schwartz had it easier than Mel Wulf in *Wainwright* or Phillip Hubbart in *Johnson v. Florida* precisely because of the liberals' defeat in *Terry*. *Terry* did two things to and for the vagrancy law challenge. First, despite the Supreme Court's other pro-defendant cases, *Terry* made litigation efforts to rein in the police directly, as distinct from those challenging the validity of vagrancy laws, seem less likely to succeed. It was not that criminal defense and civil liberties lawyers had stopped challenging perceived procedural injustices. It was that within the vagrancy law challenge, constitutional litigation of vagrancy laws themselves now seemed the more promising approach.

Once the lawyers conceded that defeat, however, *Terry* could become a weapon in their fight against vagrancy laws. Unlike Besig and Lusky, Schwartz jettisoned the procedural attack, accepted a stop-and-frisk-for-vagrancy trade-off, and argued that now that the police had *Terry*, the Court could finally relinquish vagrancy law authority. "There is no necessity for the Euclid suspicious persons ordinance, and to the extent that it serves legitimate purposes, other means less destructive of personal liberty, are available," Schwartz argued. "If ever there was a necessity for suspicious persons ordinances . . . , that necessity has been dissipated by this Court's decision in *Terry v. Ohio*."[14]

Schwartz offered "a number of feasible alternatives," including the Uniform Arrest Act, the New York stop and frisk law, and the Model Code of Pre-Arraignment Procedure. Though Schwartz did not want to be understood as approving of these alternatives, he did find them "less destructive of important federal constitutional rights than the Euclid ordinance." Such alternatives "do not permit arrests or convictions on mere suspicion, they do not make it a crime to exercise the privilege against self-incrimination, and they do not shift the burden of proof to the defendant, while still affording ample police authority."[15]

In fact, the drafters of the American Law Institute (ALI) themselves were having second thoughts about the provision they had proposed in the Model Code of Pre-Arraignment Procedure. Although still "convinced" that stop and frisk was "essential to the control of crime in an urban, mobile and anonymous environment" and that police power could be executed with a minimum of abuse if explicitly granted, they also acknowledged that they could not "be sure . . . that the limitations we have chosen in this draft represent the optimum solution to the problem." Statistics like those out of San Diego gave them pause. The city reported 200,000 field interrogations annually in a city of 600,000 people. So too did a dawning realization of what a new section in the comments called "The dangers: resentment, harassment and abuse." The drafters identified two kinds of costs: one was the cost for innocent people "even when the police stay within the terms of the authority granted." The second was that the stop "may be used not for its authorized purpose, but to harass persons to whom the police may be hostile or about whom they feel a generalized suspicion or apprehension—e.g., youths, unconventionally attired persons, Negroes in white areas, whites in Negro areas." The 1969 Model Penal Code (MPC) draft accordingly narrowed the stop and frisk provision, an attempt to strike "a balance between filling the need [for crime control] and minimizing the costs and dangers."[16]

Niki Schwartz thus placed what could have seemed Palmer's quotidian crime prevention arrest into the larger context of both the racial politics of policing and ongoing debates about the best way to authorize and control police discretion. Conceding the Court's view in *Terry*, he did not suggest that the police need for legal authority was somehow illusory or overblown. Rather, he argued that "all sides of the crime control versus individual liberty debate" agreed that "the subterfuges of vague suspicious person and vagrancy laws be abandoned in favor of a direct resolution of the question of police power to deal with persons encountered in suspicious circumstances." He thought that it had "been abundantly demonstrated that suspicious person and vagrancy type laws are calculated to circumvent these constitutional standards and facilitate detention, arrest, search, interrogation and conviction of suspected criminals with respect to whom the authorities do not have the requisite quantum of evidence." He played to the justices' aspirations as well as their pragmatism by suggesting that they could "make a significant contribution to constitutional liberty at no cost to law enforcement by striking down the Euclid suspicious persons ordinance." In his view, whatever the crime rate, the use of race in street policing was questionable. The criminalization of suspicion was not only constitutionally questionable but, after *Terry*, not even necessary.[17]

Robert Lavercombe's framing of *Coates* offered the Court a distinct but related vision of the relationship between race, policing, and vagrancy-type laws. By the time *Coates* reached the Supreme Court, Lavercombe's clients were all white, and their arrests fit more obviously within the speech and protest, rather than the racial, strain of vagrancy enforcement. Race nonetheless infused the background to Lavercombe's challenge to Cincinnati's loitering law, and Lavercombe wanted the justices to know it.

The roots of Lavercombe's race, policing, and vagrancy story were not all that different from Schwartz's. Where Schwartz focused on how the police used suspicious persons laws in crime control against African Americans, however, Lavercombe emphasized the conflicts that grew out of such racialized policing. Tense relations between African Americans and (mostly white) law enforcement officials went back to slave patrols in the antebellum period. There were trumped-up charges that practically enslaved African Americans after the end of slavery, and police complicity in lynchings and "legal lynchings" in the late nineteenth and twentieth centuries. As early as the 1940s, discriminatory police practices had become a heated civil rights issue. By 1961, the U.S. Commission on Civil Rights was warning about the problem of police brutality and harassment, which its hearings revealed was as frequent a subject of African American complaint as unemployment, housing, and education.[18]

In fact, even as the southern freedom struggle dominated public perceptions of civil rights in the early 1960s, African Americans protested against the police across the country. "Looks as if we have Birmingham in Westchester County," wrote one New York reporter, referencing the notorious sheriff Bull Connor. The police task force report of the President's Commission on Law Enforcement and Administration of Justice concluded that whereas friction between police and African Americans in the South often occurred in the context of law enforcement suppression of protests, elsewhere the cause was street policing and field interrogations. Friction stemmed not only from what the police did, or were perceived to do, but also what they did not do, or were perceived not to do: actually protect inner-city residents. Complaints thus abounded not only about improper police behavior but also about the lack of police protection for law-abiding citizens.[19]

To some extent, African Americans turned to the usual forms of civil rights protest to challenge what they viewed as unacceptable discrimination by the police. Mainstream organizations like the NAACP and the ACLU took up the issue, holding hearings and complaining to local officials. The push for police task forces, civilian complaint review boards, and internal affairs bureaus was in large part an effort to find an institutional solution to this very problem.[20]

As the antagonism between many African Americans and the police reached a fever pitch by the mid-1960s, some young African Americans adopted more confrontational rhetoric and approaches. Themes of separatism, self-defense, and self-determination had long run through the black freedom struggle, but they now took on greater prominence. The process of arrest, jail, and prison time radicalized many civil rights participants. It left them cynical about the law, the efficacy of nonviolence and mainstream political participation, and the likelihood of eradicating American racism with the old methods. Some black leaders had been taking what were described as "militant" stances for years, but when SNCC and CORE, two previously interracial and nonviolent organizations, began to embrace greater racialism and exclusion of whites, these attitudes gained new visibility.[21]

A fair bit of the energy of the rising movements for black power and greater militancy was directed against the criminal justice system, the "power structure," and the police specifically. The Northern California Black Panthers embraced the slogan, "Off the pigs," which black students also chanted at San Francisco State University. In St. Louis, in 1967, a CORE leaflet referred to white police officers as "dogs" and called for African Americans to "Fight!! Fight!! Fight The Hunkie!!"[22]

The violence of this language took physical form as violence on the streets of hundreds of American cities in the 1960s. Harlem and Bedford-Stuyvesant erupted in the summer of 1964 (1 dead, 100 injured, almost 500 arrested, millions of dollars' worth of property destroyed). Rochester, Philadelphia, and other cities followed suit. The next summer, Los Angeles' Watts neighborhood took the spotlight (34 dead, more than 1,000 injured, nearly 4,000 arrested, tens of millions of dollars' worth of property destroyed). Chicago, Cleveland, San Francisco, Atlanta, Omaha, and Dayton rioted in 1966. The following summer, it was Boston, Nashville, Cincinnati, Newark, Milwaukee, and Detroit (the last resulting in 43 deaths, 467 injuries, 7,200 arrests, $50 million in property destroyed). According to a relatively conservative accounting of the wreckage, within four years, 329 incidents in 257 different places left 220 dead, 8,371 injured, and 52,629 arrested. Most in each category were African American.[23]

Such violence was scary to whites who felt threatened by black violence. It was scary to property owners who lost their livelihoods. It was scary to African Americans who lost life, limb, and liberty. And it was scary to the police officials charged with quelling it. The Kerner Commission appointed by President Lyndon B. Johnson to analyze the riots concluded that in almost every instance but the King assassination in 1968, the police themselves instigated the violence. In New York in 1964, after a police officer shot a black junior high school student, black teens carried signs that read "Save Us from Our Protectors," and "Stop Killer Cops." In Boston in 1967, the police confronted Mothers for Adequate Welfare protesting at the welfare office. A police official issued the order, "Beat 'em, kill 'em, just get 'em out of here." The officers followed it, corralling and beating the protesting mothers. For many African Americans, stated the report, the "police have come to symbolize white power, white racism, and white repression."[24]

The Kerner Commission singled out loitering and vagrancy laws as particular targets of black protest. Such laws were as commonly used in the North as in the South. Police sometimes allowed the underemployed black men who "loitered" on particular street corners in search of employment to remain, as their presence served the interests of employers in search of cheap and expendable day laborers. (One such corner in Detroit was called the "slave market.") Often, however, the police dispersed them. A group of black men on a street corner did not bring to the white or law enforcement mind an image of industrious laborers looking for work. Instead, especially as industrial jobs began to disappear from northern and midwestern cities, it broadcast poverty, idleness, alcohol, potential crime—all of the problems vagrancy and loitering laws were made to combat.[25]

Young black men in particular seemed a threat when they congregated in public places—which they often did, especially in summer, due to inadequate housing and small living spaces. These apparently idle black men in their own neighborhoods posed a very different threat from Palmer's lone black man in a white neighborhood, but they were equally amenable to vagrancy-type arrests. The police saw it as their job to break up groups of young black men and put them in their places, calling them "boy," "nigger," "monkey," and "punk." The police referred to these corners as "indicted corners," places where mere standing amounted to a crime.[26]

By the mid-1960s, such repeated street-corner scuffles made vagrancy and loitering laws a special point of contention and a provocation to violence. The President's Crime Commission found that arrests for crimes like vagrancy and loitering were "predominantly made in slum neighborhoods," and they created "great antagonism against police officers in slum communities." These laws were "of questionable legal validity and usually of considerable harm to community relations." The city of Hartford, Connecticut, for example, fielded complaints when the police arrested for loitering members of Puerto Rican, but not white, motorcycle gangs. In Atlanta, the loitering arrest of black power advocate and SNCC leader Stokely Carmichael was followed by two nights of violence in which one African American was killed and several people were injured. When told to leave a neighborhood the police called a "trouble area," Carmichael responded, "Man, don't tell me where to go. . . . I walk where I walk to and go where I want to go." A *Los Angeles Times* opinion piece recommended changing vagrancy and disorderly conduct laws because the "resentment against these laws in most cities, among the blacks, as among the young, is so intense that it seems unwise to keep them on the books for whatever value they might once have had."[27]

When violence broke out on city streets, as it did again and again and again, it was these very same police officers—in extreme circumstances backed up by the National Guard—who were charged with restoring order. Unsurprisingly, the police viewed this violence, the potential for violence, and the appropriate response to such violence quite differently from those who engaged in it. As African Americans stoned police cars and openly taunted officers, the police were often not only the rhetorical targets but also the actual targets of violence. (In 1967, one out of eight policemen across the country was assaulted.) Officers felt themselves hemmed in on all sides. They could not do enough to maintain order, but they were frequently criticized for doing too much against the disorderly. When Chicago police officers showed restraint during the violence that followed the assassination of Martin Luther King Jr., Mayor Richard Daley criticized them for not shooting to maim looters and kill arsonists. But when police officers then brutally removed anti-war demonstrators from downtown, a citizens' commission called for investigations of their behavior.[28]

These interactions took their toll on police perceptions of their jobs and their charges. Anger was high, morale low. As Los Angeles Police Chief William H. Parker put it after the Watts riot, the police were "the most downtrodden, oppressed, dislocated minority in America." After Detroit, Eljay Bowron, head of the Detroit Detectives Association, said, "Morale is lower than whale shit." According to one police commissioner, the police were "puzzled, bitter, and deeply resentful . . . that the public image of law enforcement . . . was unfairly distorted and smeared today as never before in our history." While protestors and minorities charged police brutality, local officials and police officers decried the "police brutality lobby" with some even calling for "breaking [the] heads [of troublemakers] both figuratively and literally." Some officers did not necessarily mind being criticized for police brutality, as they deemed that better than treating lawbreakers with "kid gloves."[29]

Against this backdrop of hostility, resentment, and fear, the police responded to outbreaks of violence with riot gear, tear gas, and their own violence. They also, of course, responded with arrests—hundreds and thousands of them. Some arrests were intended to lead to conviction and punishment—many states and cities announced that participation in racial disturbances would meet with certain charges and harsh sentences. Arrests in the midst of violence did not always, however, lead to prosecutions or convictions. Many of them, according to the Kerner Commission, were intended simply to get people off the streets and stop the violence. Such arrests often led to dropped or lesser charges or relatively lenient sentences.[30]

Vagrancy and loitering figured prominently among police charges against alleged rioters, though the Kerner Commission recommended the use of assault, arson, burglary, murder, and other felonies instead. The ACLU condemned "mass arrests of black people who were not looters and/or snipers, but rather by-standers, occupants of buildings in which looters lived." Some of these were "swept up, taken to jail, held on open charges (i.e., without bail) or vagrancy and loitering charges (with extremely high bail)." They were subject to "massive searches of whole blocks at a time, including the indiscriminate breaking down of doors and harassment and intimidation of the occupants."[31]

This explosive situation was key to Robert Lavercombe's understanding of *Coates v. Cincinnati*. Cincinnati was the poster child for both the loitering-inspired anti-police riot and the inappropriate police use of loitering during such riots. It all began in June of 1967, when African Americans in the city protested the discriminatory use of a loitering ordinance that made it "unlawful for three or more persons to assemble, except at a public meeting of citizens, on any of the side-walks, . . . and there conduct themselves in a manner annoying to persons pass-ing by." For the prior year and a half, 170 of the 240 (71 percent) loitering arrests had been of African Americans, even though they comprised only 27 percent of the city's population. Recent high-profile arrests led the black community to include repeal of the law among its demands. The Kerner Commission would later conclude that the selective enforcement of the loitering law had sparked the violence that lingered for two sweltering June days.[32]

Cincinnati was also a prime example of the dubious use of loitering laws to con-trol such violence. For Robert Lavercombe, the arrest of one African American in particular served as a prime example of that dubious use. At one point during the uprising, as young people threw bottles and rocks and taunted the police, community leader and social worker Lathan Johnson ventured out in an attempt to help calm things down. Johnson already had two master's degrees and was in the midst of a third. (He would go on to win a Macarthur Foundation "genius" award later in his career.) Just two weeks before the riots began, Johnson, a key player in Ohio's National Welfare Rights Organization, had warned the National Conference on Social Welfare that unless Cincinnati's "white power order" gave more control over social services spending to affected black communities, local goodwill would deteriorate and "open conflict" would ensue.[33]

Johnson was thus not surprised when the rioting began, but he was worried. He knew some of the teens out on the streets through his work with social ser-vice agencies, and he "didn't want to see them going to jail." After he had quieted one group of kids, "all of a sudden . . . came this phalanx of police." An officer ordered the crowd to disperse, and though the crowd moved back, Johnson did not. Like Fred Shuttlesworth a few years earlier, Johnson ignored repeated police requests to move, asking why he should. The officer said, "Well, you'll have to be placed under arrest because we can't allow anyone to stand here." Johnson thought the officer arrested him because the police "were severely outnumbered and a little scared. And they figured that if anyone was brave enough or fool enough to act like [the officers] weren't intimidating, they had to arrest them." The officer thought he "had not acted like a good colored boy" and "just wanted to prove a point that if I tell you to move, you move."[34]

Perhaps the police officers saw the irony of charging Johnson under the very same loitering ordinance that had prompted the violence he was attempting to stop. Perhaps not. After the arrest, the police transferred Johnson from place to place, making it difficult for his colleagues to find him. They were finally able to locate and bail him out early the next morning. His employers also contacted Lavercombe and Fox, who informed Johnson "all about the loitering law and how unconstitutional it was. . . . [T]hey told me when I got out of jail that I didn't need to worry. That I should pack my bags and get out of town." As previously planned, the day after his arrest, Johnson left to begin a doctoral program at Brandeis University in Boston. He returned to Cincinnati for the one-day trial in the police court. Although he was convicted and sentenced to thirty days in the workhouse plus a fine and costs, both his lawyers and his friends assured him "that they had the case won."[35]

So they did. On August 19, three "out-of-town judges" sitting as the Ohio Court of Appeals—presumably chosen for their greater potential neutrality—reversed Johnson's conviction. Though Lavercombe had argued that the ordinance was unconstitutional, and though the court expressed "grave doubts" about its constitutionality, the court avoided those issues and instead based its decision on "a failure of proof" under *Thompson v. City of Louisville.* The court found that Johnson was not part of the "unruly mob" that could have been described as illegally "annoying." To have included him within the ordinance would have meant basing his conviction on "guilt by association only," a doctrine with "no place in this case."[36]

Because Johnson's conviction was reversed in the Ohio courts, Johnson was no longer Lavercombe's client, and his case was not consolidated into *Coates.* Even so, in his *Coates* Supreme Court arguments, Lavercombe highlighted Johnson's arrest and the Kerner Commission's commentary on the role of the loitering law in both provoking and controlling the Cincinnati riot. "Negroes generally believe the Cincinnati Loitering Ordinance is a thing of substantial interest to them and their aspirations to be accorded equal treatment in the community," he wrote in the *Coates* jurisdictional statement. Like Schwartz, Lavercombe thought this racial backdrop to his case would attract the Supreme Court justices and make them sympathetic.[37]

Five years earlier, such a strategy would have seemed almost certain to succeed. In the early 1960s, arrested civil rights activists could rarely win in local and state courts, but they could not lose once—if—they got to the Supreme Court. In numerous civil rights cases, the high court reversed convictions, allowed federal civil rights actions, and scolded state courts and state and local officials. Into the late 1960s and early 1970s, the Court continued to find in favor of African American activists, including reversing the protest-related convictions of black-comedian-turned-civil-rights-activist Dick Gregory.[38]

As NAACP LDF lawyer Jack Greenberg put it in 1968, however, justices increasingly "expressed disquiet" about the violence that "lurked" behind civil rights protests. Starting in 1964, with the explosion of racial violence in a number of cities, the Court began refusing to hear challenges to civil rights-related convictions, thereby leaving them intact. In January of 1965, the Court rejected the idea that civil rights protest could take place "at any public place and at any time," given the governments' duty "to keep their streets open and available for movement." The proverbial writing was on the wall: peaceful, nonobstructing protests were one thing. But other types of protest were already in the making, and the Court was not going to take kindly to them.[39]

By the end of the decade, the justices' impatience with protestors undermining the rule of law was more pronounced. Earl Warren himself—followed by all the Warren Court liberals but Douglas—led the way in cases like Terry, which downplayed the problem of race in criminal justice. Even when the standard-bearers of the movement protested peacefully, the Court was less hospitable. When Martin Luther King Jr. and his colleagues proceeded with a planned march in Birmingham, Alabama, despite a judicial injunction, the Supreme Court upheld their contempt convictions in 1969. Though the Court explained that violating an injunction was worse than violating a law, participants and observers were unconvinced. They thought the case evidenced hostility to the movement. By 1968, Greenberg worried about the "easy tendency to lump together the growing civil dissonance" of anti-war and student protest, "summer riots," and civil rights "as a single phenomenon" less deserving of protection than the Court had previously deemed civil rights cases alone.[40]

In fact, racial protest was changing. The challenge to the status quo no longer seemed limited to the South, limited to black civil rights, limited to a claim to legal equality and the chance to sit at the proverbial table. No longer did protestors wear jackets and ties, presenting themselves as the picture of civility as they enacted symbolic civil disobedience against unjust laws. Not that the challenge ever was so limited. This circumscribed and stylized—but reassuring—image of the early 1960s black civil rights movement obscured so much. Civil rights activists had long challenged the status quo north and south, east and west. Mexican Americans, Puerto Ricans, Asian Americans, and Native Americans had all opposed discrimination. Activists had long contested economic orderings as well as legal rules, entrenched social hierarchies as well as governmental segregation. They had not always been orderly, and they had certainly not been perceived as such by Bull Connor and other law enforcers.[41]

The recent violence of the inner cities nonetheless contrasted sharply with the continuing sway of these myths. The rising crime rate and the equation of the imagined criminal with young black men—replacing white mobsters and juvenile delinquents—belied the myths. So did the rising prominence of Black Power. Seen as rejecting coalitions between whites and blacks and eschewing the nonviolence that had given the civil rights movement moral stature, black power undermined the legitimacy of protest in many white eyes and some black ones. Despite the social service and community-building efforts of many black power organizations, the image of black power in the media—which could not seem to cover enough of it—was of violence, hyper-masculinity, and virulently anti-white sentiment. Deliberate efforts by conservatives to link the civil rights struggle, black power, riots, and regular old crime undermined the legitimacy of even nonviolent racial protest. Even as race riots abated after 1968, the image of black America that was increasingly prevalent in media reports and legal cases dissipated rather than evoked the sympathies of whites, including several Supreme Court justices. The Court became ever more vigilant that African Americans, no less than southern whites, comply with the dictates of law and order.[42]

The Court's approach to race cases also changed because the Court itself was changing. After Republican Richard M. Nixon won the presidency in 1968, he had the good fortune to appoint four new justices to the Supreme Court, including Republican stalwart Warren Burger as chief. Over the next three years, the more conservative William H. Rehnquist, Lewis F. Powell, and Harry A. Blackmun replaced the more liberal Abe Fortas and Hugo L. Black, as well as moderate John Marshall Harlan.

Even with all of these changes, however, both lower courts and the justices of the Supreme Court continued to express concerns about vagrancy cases in racially inflected circumstances. It was 1969 by the time the Court considered the case of Sandra Adickes, the New York teacher who was arrested for vagrancy after trying to eat at a Kress department store lunch counter during the Hattiesburg Freedom Project in 1963. After removing Adickes's criminal case from the Mississippi courts and getting the charge dismissed, attorney Eleanor Jackson Piel had proceeded to bring a federal civil rights suit for $550,000 in damages in New York (where Adickes was a citizen and Kress was incorporated). After losing in the lower courts and with help from the national ACLU, Piel petitioned the Supreme Court for certiorari.[43]

By the time the Supreme Court considered the case, it no longer centrally concerned the vagrancy law. The main context was Kress' custom of not serving mixed-race groups in Hattiesburg. The main legal issue was whether Kress had properly been granted summary judgment despite an alleged conspiracy between the restaurant and the police. Vagrancy was nonetheless a prominent issue during oral argument, and it was apparent that the justices understood the Jim Crow use of vagrancy laws they encountered in *Shuttlesworth v. Birmingham*. One justice asked what to do "when the police uniformly enforce the custom [of segregation] by vagrancy statute?" Others repeatedly referred to Adickes's vagrancy arrest. They wanted to know whether "there [was] any allegation at all that this Petitioner was broke" and whether there was "any evidence that this teacher was anything like a vagrant." One noted that Adickes had been "arrested by the police for a charge that they themselves . . . didn't feel inclined to defend." Though *Adickes v. Kress* did not make any new constitutional doctrine concerning vagrancy laws, it revealed that even at the very end of the decade—even as the "sexy" racial angle of a case might lead to judicial impatience as much as sympathy—the justices still viewed the racialized use of vagrancy laws as deeply problematic.[44]

As one might have predicted, and Schwartz did, Thurgood Marshall in particular found the racial issues in *Palmer* troubling. A Johnson appointee, Marshall was the first African American justice on the Supreme Court. He was also the former head of the NAACP Legal Defense Fund. He pressed on the race question at oral argument, and during the justices' conference he commented that the ordinance was "used only against the Blacks."[45]

If race set the stage, the use of vagrancy-related laws for crime control purposes starred in the production. The question was not only whether the crime of being a suspicious person could pass constitutional muster but whether on a pragmatic level the Court could or should jettison that crime given its decision in *Terry*. Throughout the case, Schwartz insisted that it should. "While the nation debates preventive detention, the City of Euclid wants preventive conviction," he said. City prosecutor David J. Lombardo vacillated between contending that the law did not create a status crime and that the status crime was necessary. On the one hand, Lombardo argued that the city had punished Palmer for his "irregular behavior," a power the city viewed as "vital to . . . local governments to protect its [*sic*] citizens." On the other hand, the city identified the offense of being a suspicious person as "not consist[ing] of particular acts, but a mode of life, the habits and practices of the accused in respect to the character or traits which it is the object of the ordinance creating the offense to suppress." Palmer exhibited such a mode of life. Like Schwartz, Lombardo urged the Court to think practically: invalidating the Euclid ordinance "would do violence to the whole theory of preventive law enforcement." Exactly. The issues were joined.[46]

Lombardo did not shy away from the implications of his argument. In stating frankly that he was asking the Court "to extend *Terry*," Lombardo articulated what had been left largely unspoken when the New York and California legislatures, the Model Penal Code, and the Supreme Court had all left vagrancy authority intact while licensing stop and frisk authority: the police did not think that stop and frisk was enough. It was also necessary also to have some legal basis for arrest—often vagrancy, loitering, or suspicious persons—if officers remained suspicious but failed to find probable cause to arrest for another crime. Invoking the crime rate, Lombardo concluded, "In *Terry* . . . , this Court started to give the streets back to the people. . . . I would ask you in this case to take the next step and give them back."[47]

The lawyers were candid about the choice that had faced the Court in 1968 and continued to face it three years later. So were the justices. As the case progressed, Justice Harry Blackmun, for example, moved from skepticism to reluctant acceptance. A lifelong Republican, Blackmun held two degrees from

Harvard and had led a distinguished career in private practice and as resident counsel for the Mayo Clinic before President Nixon appointed him to the Court in 1970. Blackmun and Chief Justice Burger were referred to as the "Minnesota Twins," both because they were childhood friends and because of their similar, generally conservative voting records in Blackmun's early years on the Court. Blackmun viewed Euclid's "poorly drawn local ordinance" as "typical vagrancy" and agreed that there were a number of "on point" lower court invalidations. He was concerned, however, "that the individuals concerned here were clearly up to no good." It was difficult to deny police authority in the face of what seemed like real danger. Blackmun thus initially resisted the possibility that statutes like Euclid's were no longer necessary after *Terry*, writing next to the contention in a bench memo, "I wonder."[48]

By oral argument, Blackmun was more receptive to the *Terry* point. When he noted Schwartz's argument that any need for such a law had been dissipated by *Terry*, he wrote, "Good point." He thought it "fairly obvious that the ordinance gives entirely too much leeway to the authorities. . . . As a consequence, it is to be anticipated that this conviction will be reversed. The Court may well be unanimous in this holding." In the end, he found "some comfort . . . in that this kind of a fact situation may be covered by the approach to probable cause to stop and even to frisk. Thus, one can say that *Terry v. Ohio* and probable cause give a community sufficient protection."[49]

Blackmun had his finger on the pulse of the Court. Chief Justice Burger started off the conference discussion after oral argument by describing the Euclid ordinance as "typical of vagrancy statutes." He stated that he was leaning toward invalidating on void for vagueness grounds. The rest of the justices agreed.[50]

In January of 1971, almost twenty years after the Court first considered the constitutionality of a vagrancy law in *Edelman v. California*, the justices decided to strike down a vagrancy-related law. The problem for the anti-vagrancy law forces, however, was that Justice Byron R. White convinced his colleagues to strike it down only "as applied" to Palmer, rather than "facially" for all cases and all times. After conference, White, who was more pro-law enforcement than many of his colleagues, distributed a memo to the conference that eventually became a per curiam opinion for the Court. He argued that there were many situations in which the Euclid ordinance could constitutionally apply—as when one wandered the streets without explanation while "pandering for a prostitute . . . obstructing traffic or peering into windows of private residences." Because the ordinance "gave insufficient notice to the average person that discharging a friend at an apartment house and then talking on a car radio while parked on the street was enough to show him to be 'without any visible or lawful business,'" it was vague as far as Palmer was concerned. But only that far.[51]

White's opinion allowed the justices to avoid addressing issues on which conflict remained. A concurrence that Stewart authored and Douglas joined stated that they "would go further and hold that the ordinance is unconstitutionally vague on its face." They thought that the government lacked the power to make wandering "the streets late at night without apparent lawful business" a criminal offense on its own. On the other side were Harlan, Blackmun, and Black. The latter two justices considered writing their own opinions, but they eventually signed on to the per curiam when they found the case more difficult than it had originally seemed.[52]

The Court thus did both more and less than it might have in *Palmer*. It did more by deciding the constitutionality of the ordinance. It did not dismiss *Palmer* as improvidently granted, as it had *Edelman, Arceneaux, Hicks,* and *Wainwright*. It also did not take what had been a common avoidance technique: the *Thompson v. Louisville* no-evidence approach. A little more than a decade after *Thompson*, the Court seemed ready to move beyond it. It did decide the law's constitutionality. Still, the move was incremental, and the decision only invalidated the law as applied.[53]

As the justices well knew, however, *Palmer* was not the only vagrancy-related case at the Court during the 1970 Term. A facial invalidation was still a possibility, and Robert Lavercombe was determined to realize it.

Loitering, Protest, and the Importance of Facts

Consider the "facts" as Lavercombe did: six months after Lathan Johnson's June 1967 arrest during the Cincinnati riot, Dennis Coates was arrested, apparently while "loitering" with six other people in front of the local draft board office in Cincinnati's downtown business district. One of Lavercombe's law partners, Bernard Fox, represented Coates at trial in the Hamilton County Municipal Court. Despite Fox's many motions challenging the constitutionality of the ordinance, the trial went forward. Coates waived a jury, and the judge heard the case, convicted Coates, and sentenced him to a year of probation and a fine. The discrimination of the loitering law, it seemed, operated at sentencing as well as arrest. African American Lathan Johnson was sentenced to the workhouse, white Dennis Coates to probation.[54]

A few weeks after Coates's trial in March, James Hastings, Wendell Saylor, Arnold Adams, and Clifford Wyner were arrested under the same loitering ordinance for their involvement in labor picketing. Fox represented them too. After these men were also convicted, their case was consolidated with Coates's. The five came to the Supreme Court together as *Coates v. Cincinnati*.[55]

June. December. April. Black social worker in a riot. White college student in a war protest. White workers in a union picket line. Defending this assortment of characters against the same loitering ordinance convinced the lawyers that the issue was not what their particular clients had done but how city officials understood their authority under the local loitering law. Lavercombe viewed the law as having "nothing to do with loitering but rather . . . used to quell such activity as incurs the displeasure of . . . officials." It was "useful for a government of men rather than a government of laws." The ordinance was "used to excuse police transportation of nonconformists (to the jailhouse) from the immediate area where they have displeased or irritated or annoyed Cincinnati officialdom—it has come to symbolize repression, discrimination, intolerance and arrogance to the groups whose members have been charged with 'loitering.'" To Lavercombe, the crucial issue was not the specifics of any given arrest but the abuse of official discretion by "Police State functionaries" against anyone who "merits the displeasure of a Cincinnati official."[56]

Lavercombe not only thought the facts were irrelevant to his case. He also thought the Ohio courts had sometimes been too preoccupied with facts in previous loitering cases. Between 1940 and 1968, lower Ohio courts had repeatedly found Cincinnati's and similar ordinances void for vagueness. The courts had relieved from convictions for annoyance the owners of barking dogs, Halloween revelers, businessmen, and "possible Socialist sympathizers." One court went so far as to write a poem on the subject. "In other words, the laws so passed/Must plainly be effective/Inaptly framed, they lack the force/To meet their planned objective." But the courts had also avoided the constitutional question in several cases by deciding that particular facts did not come within the ordinance. Lavercombe pointed out the tremendous consequences of this avoidance. The "eventual acquittal of the more sophisticated or more affluent defendant" left the law intact for "use on the unsophisticated miscreants who, dragged off to the Police Station in the evening, plead guilty the next morning and thus have an established record for conviction of an ill-defined offense which may well have been, legally, no offense at all." This process gave "lazy officers or, worse, malevolent officials . . . less reason to adhere to the principles of law, order and justice which must necessarily prevail for the continuation of our form of government." With this injustice in mind, Lavercombe, like the ACLU lawyers in *Hicks* a few years earlier, set out intentionally to deprive the higher state courts of the facts of his cases in hopes of getting an invalidation once and for all.[57]

Ohio state law, which did not forward case records on appeal unless a lawyer filed a bill of exceptions, helped Lavercombe keep the facts hidden. He offered very little in the way of what had happened during either the war protest or the picketing cases, which by then had been consolidated. The Supreme Court of Ohio surprised Lavercombe by calling his bluff, affirming the convictions outright in a 4–3 vote, and upholding the law. In Lavercombe's view, this represented a change in judicial approach to the ordinance. He saw the decision as a "backlash" against the "racial disturbances" of the summer of 1967 and the fact that "the police and perhaps more significantly, other city officials frequently found themselves irritated or provoked, annoyed by the conduct of those who complained and those who disturbed."[58]

When Lavercombe brought the case to the United States Supreme Court, then, it was devoid of the facts of the war protestor or the labor pickets. Lavercombe did, however, provide a full record of the Lathan Johnson case in an appendix. Indeed, between *Hicks* and *Coates*, the Court had reinforced the lesson that sympathetic facts could serve as an escape hatch when the Court decided *Johnson v. Florida* on *Thompson v. Louisville* grounds in 1968. Whether Lavercombe did not want to give the Court that out or thought that the *Coates* facts would alienate the justices because they revealed not only that Lavercombe's clients were different and unpopular but also disorderly and potentially dangerous is hard to say. If his clients had been truly "annoying," then the anti-vagrancy lawyer's interest in challenging laws on their face and clients' interests in a reversal on any ground might point in the same direction.[59]

Some at the Court were unperturbed by the absence of the facts because the case seemed, as one clerk put it, "to be a classic void-for-vagueness law that tells the policeman to go arrest whomever his whim directs." Others wanted to know more. Blackmun's clerk, Michel A. Lafond, the same clerk working on *Palmer*, scared up all the facts he could find for his justice. A city brief from the appeals court proved illuminating. After a police officer asked Coates and his companions to leave a protest of the Vietnam War and the Selective Service System, the protestors instead gathered in front of the federal building "in such a way that normal pedestrian flow was disrupted." While the protestors were gathered, "loud and boisterous remarks were directed at the police officers." As to the pickets of the Whiteway Manufacturing Company, they apparently "blocked the path of a moving truck" and refused to disperse despite police orders.[60]

Blackmun himself considered the facts key. "This is the kind of case which would not be here at all if it were not for the nature of the protest. These people were arrested as a result of demonstrations against the Vietnam war [*sic*] and the Selective Service System," he wrote. "Certainly they would not have been arrested, or at least the case would not be here, had it been the result of a football celebration." These loaded sentences make three things apparent. First, Blackmun implicitly acknowledged potential discrimination by police officers—the nature of the protest had something to do with why the protestors were arrested. Second, the union picketing did not particularly register with Blackmun. The political salience of the case, for both the police who made the arrests and the justices who took the case, inhered in the war protest, not the union picketing. Where labor unrest had once, not so long ago, provoked heated First Amendment battles in workplaces, on streets, and at the Court, now it did not. Labor unions had already yielded the mantle of the imagined free speaker to civil rights protestors earlier in the decade, and as Lavercombe and Schwartz both revealed in their high court strategies, race still seemed salient. New free speakers were now fighting for that mantle. The union pickets were at most background noise, a secondary concern, a sideshow to the real free speech battles of 1971—battles waged in part by students, battles fought over a war.[61]

Third, and most important, Blackmun thought the nature of the protest was what made it important to the justices themselves. They took the case because it concerned an anti-war demonstration. The first organized anti-war protests dated back to the summer of 1963, when they were often overshadowed by the drama of the southern civil rights movement. By the time President Lyndon B. Johnson escalated United States military involvement in Vietnam in 1965, war protests were harder to ignore. Some twenty thousand to twenty-five thousand people marched on Washington in response to Johnson's actions. Beginning in 1965, Americans witnessed the horrors of the war on nightly television news in what became known as "the living-room war." Anti-war organizations, anti-war activists, and anti-war tactics proliferated. Within the military, service members organized Resist Inside the Army and deserted in unprecedented numbers. From Students for a Democratic Society (SDS) to Women Strike for Peace, from the National Mobilization Committee to End the War in Vietnam to the Catholic Worker Movement to the Vietnam Veterans Against the War (VVAW), religious pacifists joined with students, women, and political radicals. African Americans interested in Third World nationalism increasingly, though hardly uniformly, concluded that they should not fight "in Viet Nam for the White Man's freedom, until all the Negro People are free in Mississippi." Hundreds of thousands of people from all walks of life protested the war all across the country in the second half of the 1960s.[62]

Anti-war activists were often grown-ups, they were mainstream, they had short hair and bathed regularly. But that was rarely the media portrayal or, likely, the justices' perception. Diverse as the anti-war movement was, the popular image of the movement linked it to people like Dennis Coates—long-haired, countercultural college students who seemed everywhere to be in revolt. As early as 1960, when SDS was founded, young Americans had begun to make known their opposition to the status quo. The usual complacency of youth was shattered by the ongoing threat of nuclear holocaust and the novel and empowering challenge to Jim Crow. Self-described New Leftists celebrated, in the words of SDS's 1962 Port Huron Statement, their "unrealized potential for self-cultivation, self-direction, self-understanding, and creativity." Their statement encapsulated and espoused a vision of "participatory democracy," critiquing the everyday life of a self-satisfied, consumerist America. Warning each other not to "trust anybody over thirty," young radicals targeted universities as big bureaucracies, hierarchical bureaucracies, paternalistic bureaucracies, government— and defense—embroiled bureaucracies. Arguing in favor of lowering the voting age, one senator channeled the youth movement with the slogan "Old enough to fight, old enough to vote." Direct conflict between students and universities escalated when students in California organized the Berkeley Free Speech Movement against university regulations of political speech on or near campus.[63]

Even as some of those who looked like Coates took it as their mantra to "tune in, turn on, and drop out," then, many turned on to serious political and social protest. Within the ranks of the youth generation, the hippies' politics were lived through their rejection of mainstream culture, whereas the New Leftists' cultural style was an adjunct to their fundamentally political program. The more politically committed of the New Leftists sometimes resented the bad name, the nihilism, "the whole hippie contagion" which was not just "apolitical but antipolitical," as one New Left journalist put it. To the typical hippie, the New Left sometimes seemed too uptight, too dogmatic, too much like the mainstream work they were intent on rejecting. Such differences notwithstanding, the confluence of the political opposition with the countercultural compounded the threat each posed and accordingly the vulnerability of each to police repression.[64]

What was happening on college campuses turned out not to look that different from what was happening on inner-city streets. The images both produced in the mass media were similar: angry young people antagonizing law enforcement, police in riot gear, tear gas exploding, National Guardsmen patrolling streets and campuses. The students were often, though hardly always, whiter than those in the inner city. They were certainly more privileged. Though they might have felt themselves immune from the kind of violent state response that was quickly forthcoming in the ghetto, they were not. This was clear when officers killed black students during desegregation protests at South Carolina State University in the 1968 "Orangeburg Massacre," and then war-protesting students at Kent State and Jackson State two years later.[65]

Campus disruptions were so frequent and so ubiquitous that newspapers would compile long articles that chronicled all their vital statistics: where and for how long the protest had occurred; what the basis of student grievances was; what forms of law enforcement were used; and how many students were involved, suspended, expelled, arrested, and jailed. One article alone described the following: two hundred white students in Buffalo forced their way into an administration building and took over the president's office. Three hundred black students held an eighteen-story YMCA college in Chicago's Loop for seven hours. Fifty students at Holy Cross in Worcester, Massachusetts protested in the lobby of the campus center against Marine recruiters. Classes were suspended at Chicago State College when racial tensions mounted. Students at the University of Chicago occupied the university administration building for sixteen days. And on. And on.[66]

Conflict between law enforcement and both young people and anti-war protestors became more direct and oppositional over time. In a process that generally paralleled that of civil rights activists, what began as protests against the war ended as protests against the police. At Kent State, just before the shootings, for example, students chanted, "Pigs off campus." When the National Guard asked the students to disperse, many did not. As one later recalled, "A very adversarial atmosphere existed, and we felt that this was our campus, that we were doing nothing wrong, and that they had no right to order us to disperse. If anyone ought to leave, it's them, not us." With roots in the anti-war movement and Dada-influenced art, a semi-anarchist, non-student SDS chapter called "Up Against the Wall Motherfucker" used extreme and inflammatory rhetoric. One leaflet noted, "Sitting on the stoop to them is a revolutionary act. Your [*sic*] a Che Guevara if you stand on the corner." They lamented, "Its [*sic*] against the law to be young in this country. . . . Its [*sic*] within the law to be a fat old pig." "Stop busting or we will bust back," the leaflet said. "This is a new breed of flower child—venus pig-trap/We are violent flowers—cactus—thorns."[67]

More mainstream responses came from other quarters. The ACLU and many of its affiliates supported challenges to the selective service system and its decentralized approach to deferments; to narrow definitions of conscientious objector status; to laws prohibiting the burning of draft cards; and to school prohibitions on various types of speech. The NYCLU challenged the "longstanding Police Department practice" of harassing "peaceniks" and others distributing political pamphlets. Modeled after suits brought by the NAACP LDF and civil rights lawyers in Jackson, Mississippi, an NYCLU lawsuit asked a federal court to enjoin the NYPD from such interference. The organization also created a whole new staff position—filled by the same Burt Neuborne who defended New York's prostitutes against loitering charges—to represent the thousands of war protestors arrested in New York City. Neuborne came to take as his guide what he called "the redneck/mandarin distinction." He believed that the higher up the ladder of education and elite status a decision maker was positioned, the more sympathetic he would be toward civil liberties. As a result, Neuborne tried to push decision-making authority from police officer to local judge to federal judge—to bring "redneck situations" before "mandarin judges." [68]

Coates was thus hardly the Supreme Court's first encounter with the new anti-war free speakers. As the NYCLU contended and Justice Blackmun noted in passing, the police seemed to single out war protestors for arrest. That meant that protests against the war brought case after case about the scope and limits of the

First Amendment to the Supreme Court. Some thought that the bid of Vietnam War protestors to become the new free speakers was likely to fail. Indeed, the Court often found against this new breed. In many cases involving opposition to the war, however, the Court viewed First Amendment protections rather expansively. In 1969's *Tinker v. Des Moines*, it protected the right of students to wear black armbands to school in protest of the war. In *Cohen v. California* two years later, it reversed a disturbing the peace conviction for wearing a jacket imprinted with the words "Fuck the Draft" in a courthouse hallway. These cases pushed the Supreme Court and other courts to think about First Amendment protections for what came to be called "symbolic speech," combining "speech" (which was often protected) and "conduct" (which was usually not). The Court seemed willing to protect war protestors, but how much it would protect them, against what types of laws, and for what speech/conduct combinations remained in 1970 and 1971 as unsettled as the status of the war itself. [69]

Coates offered the Court one such opportunity to delineate the contours of constitutional protection for anti-war protestors. That was what made the facts—or their absence—so important. As the justices were attempting in other cases, they wanted to parse out what was protected free speech and what was threatening and unprotected conduct. While some justices read the Cincinnati ordinance as suspect no matter the conduct, others thought that the law's validity depended on exactly what people were doing that had made them seem annoying. Were they annoying simply because they opposed the war? If so, then that might be a constitutional problem of viewpoint discrimination. If they were annoying because they were blocking traffic or impeding access to the induction office or engaging in some type of violence, however, then that might not be a constitutional problem. It might be a legitimate law enforcement problem.[70]

The question of what the First Amendment protected thus coincided with the question of what vagrancy and loitering laws could prohibit. Both raised versions of more abstract questions of what constituted a threat and what kinds of "harms" could be proscribed. Where the Hart/Devlin debates in the criminal law context asked whether particular behavior was threatening, dangerous, and therefore criminal, the First Amendment question was whether speech should be protected even if it might be harmful. Free speech cases also reprised the status/conduct distinction, as general loitering was increasingly seen as lacking sufficient conduct to make its prohibition constitutional, but specific types of loitering were seen as legitimately prohibitable conduct.

By *Coates*, police use of loitering laws against speech-related conduct precisely in the context of campus and anti-war protests had already raised such questions for several years. Just as inner-city racial violence sometimes ended with loitering arrests, so too did war protests. During nationwide anti-war demonstrations in October of 1965, police arrested for loitering eleven demonstrators outside Truax Air Force Base near the college town of Madison, Wisconsin. The following March, several young men in Boston were convicted of loitering and sauntering during a protest in front of the gates of the Boston Army base. In October of 1967, a major demonstration in Washington, DC, included a march of some 50,000 from the Capitol to the Pentagon, where protestors did everything from storm the building to plant daisies in gun barrels. Soldiers and federal marshals did everything from beat protestors to arrest them for loitering. When members of the political performance group Bread and Puppet Theater planned an event with masked performers protesting the war, the police warned them that they would be arrested under the new loitering version of the same New York anti-masquerading vagrancy law that had snared cross-dressing men like Martin Hirshhorn. (They decided not to take the chance and performed maskless.) When students at Colorado State University vowed to prevent Dow Chemical, maker of the napalm used in the Vietnam War, from conducting job interviews by taking over a campus building, they were arrested and booked for "investigation of loitering," littering, and damaging property. In July of 1969, peaceful demonstrators who tried to read the names of the war dead on the Pentagon's concourse were arrested for "loitering and unseemly conduct" in government buildings. A month later, those trying to participate in a Catholic mass for peace and return their draft cards to the secretary of defense were also arrested for loitering.[71]

As in other contexts, police sought additional authority to contain violence and disorder by more vigorously enforcing existing loitering laws or convincing legislatures to pass new ones. The same National Guard troops who had been sent to the Watts area of Los Angeles after the riots there in 1965 later found themselves policing mostly white college students at the University of California at Santa Barbara after three days of violence. The guardsmen were armed with specialized plastic shields, the young people with makeshift garbage can lids. Officials instituted a curfew and prohibited loitering. Republican Governor Ronald Reagan—who had been elected partly on the basis of promises that he would "send the welfare bums back to work" and "clean up the mess at Berkeley"—called the demonstrators "cowardly little bums." Over the course of one night, seventy people were arrested, most on "suspicion of loitering." Adapting their procedures for the crisis, police booked the students "on the spot," using the hood of a patrol car as a desk.[72]

Similarly, when the Berkeley city manager declared a state of emergency after several nights of anti-war violence in 1968, he invoked a nighttime loitering prohibition. The following spring, the cycle was repeated—protest, tear gas, arrests, curfew. The Berkeley-Albany chapter of the ACLU served as a legal clearinghouse, providing information about bail and legal procedures to those arrested, helping coordinate legal counsel, and serving as a conduit for grievances. After studying 404 complaints, the chapter concluded that the "state of emergency" regulations had been selectively enforced against young men, especially those who were "hip," "defiant," or using cameras. Many of those arrested were taken to the Santa Rita Rehabilitation Center. In something of a reprise of the treatment of civil rights activists at the Jackson, Mississippi, fairgrounds, they complained that they were physically abused, beaten, and generally mistreated. Those arrested likened their treatment to that of victims of state violence in Vietnam, Birmingham, and elsewhere.[73]

Judicial responses to these loitering arrests varied. In the years before *Coates*, lower courts were busy sorting out unconstitutional loitering ordinances from constitutional ones, protected protest activities from unprotected ones. A number of courts faced with unruly student, anti-war, or civil rights demonstrators recognized the growing consensus against loitering laws generally. They nonetheless distinguished certain types of loitering laws that they could conclude were constitutional. Criminalizing loitering wholesale might be problematic, but specific types of loitering laws could still survive.

Take the "unwarranted loitering" provision that the General Services Administration (GSA) used to regulate the public on federal property. When the October 1967 anti-war protests at the Pentagon led to the arrest of such countercultural celebrities as Jerry Rubin and Norman Mailer, the court distinguished between loitering simpliciter, which many lower courts had invalidated, and the "unwarranted loitering" prohibited on public property. Citing *Shuttlesworth*, *Thornhill*, and other cases, one federal court noted that, in contrast to the more targeted GSA regulation, the laws that had been invalidated "were operating in an unlimited spectrum, unlimited in their scope and in their application, statutes which could be applied against virtually anyone in accordance with the whims of public officials." When the issue arose again after the arrest of sixty-two more Pentagon protestors in the summer of 1969, however, a magistrate judge found the regulation "obscure and devoid of meaning." That view eventually gained traction, and the following year the GSA replaced "unwarranted loitering" with a new regulation that prohibited "disorderly conduct on property," or conduct making loud noises, creating obstructions, or impeding or disturbing either employees or the general public.[74]

Loitering laws targeting school property were more resilient. Though some judges refused to apply loitering laws to student sit-ins, others upheld laws that specifically prohibited loitering on or near school grounds against civil rights and anti-war activists. Courts emphasized that laws making vagrants of anyone not a student, parent, guardian, or employee who "willfully loiters about" school buildings protected students from "degenerates, dope peddlers, pornographers, vandals, [and] troublemakers in general." Though the courts were concerned about protecting free speech, such rights were "relative" and could not completely override other interests. Like the GSA cases, these cases distinguished between "willful," and therefore proscribable, and "innocent" loitering. As one court concluded, "The enactment concerns itself with a form of conduct—willful loitering—by a designated class of persons carried on about a particular quasi public area—school premises."[75]

Yet another distinction courts drew was the one the Court had suggested in *Shuttlesworth v. Birmingham*: loitering that obstructed traffic deserved less constitutional protection than did loitering that did not obstruct traffic. When Michigan State University students demonstrating to support passage of a fair housing ordinance sat down in the street and blocked traffic, the Michigan Court of Appeals had little difficulty distinguishing *Shuttlesworth*. The East Lansing loitering ordinance clearly prohibited only loitering that "obstruct[ed] the free and uninterrupted passage of the public," and the students' behavior fit that description. In another case, the court struck down all the sections of a New Orleans vagrancy ordinance except those involving orders to move on, which it interpreted narrowly in light of *Shuttlesworth*.[76]

Where protestors did lie in the streets, obstruct traffic, or otherwise disrupt public order, they opened themselves up to disorderly conduct and breach of the peace charges as well as loitering and vagrancy. It is hard to draw a strict line between these various laws, but if loitering laws were formally more conduct-based than vagrancy, disorderly conduct was more conduct-based than loitering. Disorderly conduct laws typically read something like this: "Every person who shall be found . . . acting in a disorderly manner to the disturbance of the public peace, upon any street or highway" shall be guilty of disorderly conduct and punished accordingly. During the 1960s and 1970s, many of the same criticisms leveled against vagrancy laws applied to disorderly conduct laws as well, and a number of civil rights cases eventuated in the invalidation of disorderly conduct and breach of the peace laws. Still, many viewed vagrancy, loitering, and suspicious persons as distinct from disorderly conduct, and more constitutionally problematic. Disorderly conduct laws were better positioned to survive constitutional challenge precisely because they were more conduct oriented, and jurisdictions worried about the validity of their loitering or vagrancy laws increasingly turned to disorderly conduct laws instead.[77]

Anti-war protestors, black power activists, and student demonstrators who deliberately crossed the line from harmless to threatening made that shift easy. Where civil rights protestors early in the decade had often tried to comply with legal dictates about where, when, and how to demonstrate, that was no longer of as much concern to either black militants or anti-war protestors. (Anthony Amsterdam recounted giving African American comedian and activist Dick Gregory "sage and sober" advice on how to obey traffic rules so as not to get arrested during a 1965 march protesting de facto segregation in Chicago's public schools. "There was a long pause and then Dick Gregory turned to us and said, 'You know if the mafia had lawyers like you guys, there would be no horse sold in this country, absolutely no heroin.'") Especially in the wake of the violent police response to the protests at the 1968 Democratic Convention in Chicago, the student-led New Left took on a more oppositional stance. Some activists shifted from participating in sit-ins and civil disobedience to seizing campus buildings and engineering disruptive demonstrations. They proclaimed themselves the vanguard and identified with Third World revolutionaries. A few joined groups like the Weatherman and took their protests to new heights of violence by bombing government buildings and robbing armored cars.[78]

These protestors wanted not only to publicize their grievances but also to disrupt the orderly workings of the Establishment. They wanted to harass those trying to conduct the war and to shut down induction centers. They refused to play by the rules—to get permits, or abide by the terms if they did. They blocked streets when police tried to pursue law-breaking demonstrators. They burned draft cards in front of marshals, troops, and the Pentagon itself. They destroyed the records of draft boards. They bombed, stole, and destroyed, spawning criminal prosecutions colloquially referred to as the "Boston Five" and the "Boston Eight," the "Milwaukee Fourteen," the "Pasadena Three," the "Chicago Fifteen," or the "Akron Two."[79]

As courts dealt with the legal detritus of such conduct, they tried to flesh out a set of rules by which both protestors and law enforcement officers would have to abide. Justice Fortas described his understanding of these emerging rules in a book he published while a sitting justice in 1968. He drew a stark line between peaceful protest, even on a mass scale, and protest that harmed people or property. He defended civil disobedience, but only insofar as the law being violated was itself the target of the moral objection. In his view, protests that violated "secondary" laws like disorderly conduct moved from "dissent" to "rebellion." The trickiness of distinguishing between legitimate civil disobedience and lawlessness can be seen as well in the report on civil disobedience of the National Commission on the Causes and Prevention of Violence—the only non-unanimous report of this commission. A majority of commissioners determined that they could not give their blessing to civil disobedience because they worried that they would thereby encourage anarchy.[80]

Some version of that anxiety no doubt lurked behind the justices' concern for the missing facts in Coates. Coates reflected debates not only about vagrancy laws writ large but also about the constitutionality of loitering laws in the context of student and anti-war protests. Without the facts, Coates provided no opportunity to determine what was acceptable and unacceptable loitering. For those justices primarily concerned about the behavior of the protestors, the facts were key. Facts were what would enable them to establish concrete constitutional rules for what types of laws the police could use to arrest demonstrators, and under what conditions.

Toward that end, Burger and others pressed Lavercombe for more details about his clients' protests. Lavercombe largely stood his ground. He did describe Coates and his gang as "dirty, unkempt, unshaven, Antioch college demonstrators," but that was all he gave up. Lavercombe insisted that he was not trying to game the Court, that the lack of facts was merely an unintended consequence of his Ohio court strategy. Even so, he was candid that at this court too he was hoping for a decision on the face of the ordinance.[81]

When the justices intimated that prosecutor Nichols might provide some facts, Nichols also demurred. Perhaps Nichols and Lavercombe were trying to follow procedural norms that frowned on the introduction of facts outside the record. But Nichols made clear that he too preferred a decision about the law on its face, one that rejected the void for vagueness argument. "There are some men who will never understand that which meets their purpose not to understand. The Constitution does not require impossible standards of legal draftsmanship." It only required "that laws be drafted so men of common intelligence, who would be law-abiding, can determine with reasonable precision what acts it is their duty to avoid." Annoying, he said, was the antonym of "peaceably." As such, it was clear and constitutional. By 1971, not only protestors but also police and prosecutors were hoping that the Court would provide some constitutional clarity.[82]

Close Encounters with the Anti-War Movement, Spring 1971

The same day as the oral argument in both *Palmer* and *Coates*, and before the justices met in conference to discuss the cases, Burger took the unusual step of pre-circulating a per curiam opinion dismissing the appeal in *Coates*. Despite the arguments on both sides, he said, the case lacked a properly presented federal question.

Burger was angry. "I would not lift a finger to help Appellant have his way 'to force the Court to decide the Constitutional question,'" he wrote to the other justices. "We should not encourage this kind of business." Having circulated one per curiam dismissing the case, Burger then circulated another affirming the ordinance on its face. The two circulations created confusion. Some justices signed onto one. Other justices dissented from the other. It was unclear who thought what about which possible disposition. Burger did not seem to feel strongly about which of the two possibilities prevailed—he was just looking for a majority that would not strike down the ordinance. He did, however, like that the dismissal would seem punitive, that it would discourage "these 'eager beavers' who thrust constitutional issues on us prematurely." He also suggested, perhaps with *Palmer* in mind, that "the Court ought to be more cautious than it has been in striking down statutes and ordinances on vagueness just because they may be vague as applied in some circumstances."[83]

By early May, and with the end of the term approaching, the stakes in *Coates* had escalated. It was not only that the justices were aware of vagrancy and loitering cases elsewhere, or that the Court had previously dealt with war protest cases, or that the justices knew that war protests continued around the county. It was also that at the very moment the Court was deciding *Coates*—and deciding how important the facts of a war protest were to the determination of a loitering law's constitutionality—war protest came right to the halls of the Court itself. Between the time the Court held oral argument in *Coates* and *Palmer* in January of 1971 and the time it decided the cases that June, protests against the war took a turn for the dramatic, the large scale, and the very close at hand. The Court became an integral player in a tense drama over the bounds and boundaries of public protest against the war, and especially over limitations on the protestors' uses of public space.

Over the course of April and May of 1971, protestors accumulated in the capital. Sixteen days of April witnessed anti-war protests. The Vietnam Veterans Against the War (VVAW) began the festivities by renouncing their medals and throwing them over a protective fence at the Capitol. Soon thereafter, some 500,000 others from a variety of organizations joined them. By early May, the Mayday Tribe was calling for thousands of protestors to "literally," as the *Washington Post* described it, "halt the machinery of government by a massive exercise in civil disobedience." In response, more than 15,000 law enforcement and military personnel were placed on duty or alert. Officers arrested some 12,000 protestors and bystanders over the course of three days. With so many arrested, law enforcement had to turn, like Mississippi and Berkeley authorities, to makeshift holding pens. In this case, they used Robert F. Kennedy Stadium. Those arrested complained of a lack of food, water, shelter, toilets, or arraignment. Though the arrests would later lead to an ACLU lawsuit and a rare instance of federal compensation (of over $12 million) for the violation of the right to free assembly, at the time even sympathetic observers referred to the incident as the "Peace Freak Follies of 1971" and less a "protest" than a "rampage."[84]

It was the VVAW that brought these issues from the nearby Capitol and National Mall to the Court itself shortly before the May Day chaos. The organization called its protest Dewey Canyon III, after covert military operations in Laos. As part of their "limited incursion into the country of Congress," the veterans planned to set up an encampment on the Mall for the duration of the multi-day protest. They would sleep outdoors to evoke their "in country" experiences and symbolically represent their sacrifice for their nation and their poor treatment on return. The camp would also link the veterans with earlier attempts to use the Mall as a base for petitioning Congress. In 1932, World War I veterans calling themselves the Bonus Army camped there as they sought early payment of their pensions to get them through the Depression years. In 1968, civil rights and poverty rights activists calling for an "economic bill of rights" created their own "Resurrection City."[85]

As was the case with those earlier efforts, government officials were less than pleased. The Nixon Justice Department asked a federal district court in Washington for a prophylactic injunction to stop the veterans. The court granted the injunction—which allowed dancing, singing, and even a rock concert to take place overnight but prohibited camping or sleeping. The appellate court modified the injunction to allow use of the Mall as "a so-called campsite base." After the veterans gathered, the Justice Department continued to fight them. It presented an emergency application for a stay to Chief Justice Warren Burger, who was the justice with jurisdiction over the Court of Appeals for the DC Circuit. Burger, and later the full court, vacated the appellate court's order and reinstated the original injunction. The protestors had lost.[86]

That night, against the advice of their lawyer, the veterans remained on the Mall. They watched cast members of *Hair* perform for them, and, yes, they lay down in their bedrolls and slept. Despite the court order that made such actions illegal, and despite the Nixon administration's request for that court order, the police did not disturb them. Administration officials belatedly realized that there was much public sympathy for the veterans, and they changed their minds about what to do with, about, or to them. George L. Hart Jr., the district court judge who had originally granted the Department of Justice its injunction only to see it go unenforced, was not happy. If the Justice Department lawyers had not planned to enforce the injunction, they should have had it dissolved. He fumed that his branch of government had been "degraded by this whole affair," which had left the veterans "in the position of openly defying the laws of the courts of this country." The *New York Times* described the Justice Department's "pursuit of these technical violations by nonviolent protestors—some so nonviolent that they were protesting in wheelchairs"—as giving "a political tone to law enforcement." The administration "made the whole process ludicrous by marching all the way to the highest court for an injunction, seeing it flouted, and then asking that it be dissolved when a backlash of sympathy developed for the veterans."[87]

On April 21, 1971, the veterans brought both legal papers and protests to the Supreme Court. Eleven demonstrators had wanted to witness in person the Court's ruling on the encampment injunction. One veteran delivered a letter of protest to Chief Justice Burger's chambers. The visitors either refused or failed to leave the Court fast enough when ordered to do so by the police. The police arrested them in the main hall that led to the courtroom. The next day, police arrested 110 anti-war veterans on the outside steps of the Court as the veterans pressed the Court to rule "on the constitutionality of the Vietnam war." Though the active justices stayed out of sight, the press reported that they could see former Chief Justice Earl Warren watching the arrests through his window. The *New York Times* editorialized that these arrests were "a technical breach of the law forbidding obstruction of the administration of justice." It linked the protest on the steps directly to the Court's reinstatement of the injunction against camping on the Mall.[88]

Figure 8.1 Police arrest a member of the Vietnam Veterans Against the War during a protest on the steps of the Supreme Court in April 1971. The proximity of these protests likely affected the justices' deliberations in the Cincinnati loitering case of war protestor Dennis Coates, which the Court was considering at the same moment. Associated Press, Charles Harrity.

Lavercombe's efforts to force the Court to consider the facial constitutionality of the Cincinnati ordinance in *Coates* had already infuriated Chief Justice
Burger before these events occurred. Afterward, the justices were no longer
mere bystanders; they had become targets of the war protests. In fact, the day
after the arrests at the Court, Justice Douglas wrote a memo to his incoming
law clerks asking one of them to spend the summer writing a memo about the
"recurring questions" raised by "dissident groups" who protested at or near
the Court, the Capitol, and the Mall. Douglas wanted a handbook of all of
the relevant regulations and any decisions concerning them. The problem,
Douglas emphasized, "usually reaches the Court in a[n] emergency situation
where there is no time for any research or oral argument, but where action
must be taken immediately." He thus hoped to create a brochure to be "made
available for distribution as, if, and when a nasty situation develops as it did in
April 1971."[89]

Against this backdrop, *Coates* remained a contested mess. There had been a
flurry of memos between the justices early in the year. But by February, they had
come to a complete halt. As Burger reinitiated discussion on May 10 in anticipation of the end of the term, his count of the votes put Black, Harlan, White,
and Blackmun signing onto his first per curiam dismissing the appeal. Stewart,
Marshall, Brennan, and Douglas had stated no position there. Instead, Stewart
had written a dissent to Burger's second per curiam upholding the law on the
merits, and the three liberal justices had all signed on. It looked like the Court
would reject Coates's claims 5 to 4.[90]

Justice Stewart was as exercised about Burger's handling of the case as
Burger was about Lavercombe's. A moderate and frequent swing vote on the
Burger Court, his interest in *Coates* seemed both doctrinal and biographical.
Doctrinally, Stewart had written the majority opinion in the loitering case
of *Shuttlesworth v. Birmingham*, and he had taken a strong stance in *Palmer*
against the constitutionality of the suspicious persons ordinance. In a number of other cases, he had recently taken positions that suggested a willingness to involve the Court in questions the war prompted. On the personal
side, Stewart was from an elite Cincinnati family. His father had been mayor
of the city. Stewart himself had twice been elected to the Cincinnati City
Council and once to the vice mayoralty. Given these close ties to city's governance, one might have expected Stewart to defend the need for order and
the ordinance that might provide it. That was not the case. Instead, Stewart
seemed to take his hometown's unconstitutional ordinance—and Burger's
defense of it—as a personal affront.[91]

Stewart found the proposed dismissal of the appeal for want of a properly
presented federal question "almost unbelievable." He pointed out that the appeal

was at the Court not as a matter of a totally discretionary grant of certiorari but "as a matter of absolute right" under federal law. "The federal question it involves is presented not only 'properly,' but presented in the clearest and least 'cloudy' way imaginable," Stewart argued. "The federal question, quite simply, is whether a Cincinnati ordinance is or is not unconstitutional on its face. It is exactly the kind of question that this Court is here to decide, and exactly the kind of question that, Term after Term, we have routinely decided." Stewart cited a recent case that had clearly been set up without facts in order to force consideration of an ordinance on its face, and which the Court, with no protest, had decided.[92]

Stewart's ire was exacerbated by the fact that the Court had recently "drastically limited the power of federal district courts to pass upon the constitutionality of state laws." (Indeed, the new doctrine had led the Court to reject several of the hippie-related federal civil rights suits challenging vagrancy laws.) The Court's recent restrictions on federal court jurisdiction, Stewart concluded, "make it imperative that we here never abdicate our own responsibility to pass on the constitutionality of a state or local law" properly before the Court. "For where else is a litigant to turn for constitutional vindication?" Liberals Douglas, Brennan, and Marshall joined the opinion. So did the more conservative Harlan, surprisingly and with little explanation about why he had overcome his long skepticism of the vagrancy law challenge. Stewart now had five votes to vindicate Coates.[93]

As published, Stewart's majority opinion in *Coates* addressed the absence of facts explicitly. "We need not lament that we do not have before us the details of the conduct found to be annoying. It is the ordinance on its face that sets the standard of conduct and warns against transgression." Stewart found it troubling that the Ohio court "did not indicate upon whose sensitivity a violation does depend—the sensitivity of the judge or jury, the sensitivity of the arresting officer, or the sensitivity of a hypothetical reasonable man." People "must conduct themselves so as not to annoy any police officer or other person who should happen to pass by." Given such uncertainty, Stewart deemed the ordinance void for vagueness on its face.[94]

Taking what some viewed as the unusual step of relying on not one but two constitutional arguments, Stewart also deemed the ordinance unconstitutionally "overbroad." Overbreadth was useful for Stewart because it meant that even if the ordinance might legitimately prohibit harmful conduct that could be prohibited, it was nonetheless unconstitutional because it could also be used to squelch protected speech. Overbreadth also enabled Stewart to protect Coates regardless of whether Coates himself had been annoying because it meant that he could challenge the law on behalf of other, protected, defendants as well. This helped Stewart hedge on Coates's behavior. "The First and Fourteenth

Amendment do not permit a State to make criminal the exercise of the right of assembly simply because its exercise may be 'annoying' to some people." The Court could not allow "the right of the people to gather in public places for social or political purposes" to be subject to determinations about what police officers thought was annoying. Stewart quoted at length from a Toledo Municipal Court opinion involving a similar local Ohio ordinance, to the effect that the ordinance "would have been effective as against . . . Patrick Henry, Thomas Jefferson, George Washington and others for loitering and congregating in front of Raleigh Tavern . . . in Williamsburg, Virginia, at any time during the summer of 1774 to the great annoyance of Governor Dunsmore and his colonial constables." Stewart thus likened some labor pickets and "unkempt" students to the nation's Founding Fathers.[95]

Stewart's point was essentially Lavercombe's: that laws like Cincinnati's were used discriminatorily against those considered annoying due to "their ideas, their lifestyle or their physical appearance." These words, in the context of 1971, readily call to mind the students, Vietnam War protestors, and hippies who were involved in *Coates*. But the footnote following the statement turned immediately to race. "The alleged discriminatory enforcement of this ordinance figured prominently in the background of the serious civil disturbances that took place in Cincinnati in June 1967." Perhaps "physical appearance" in the text meant "race," but that was not the usual way of writing about race. Rather, it seems that just after noting the discrimination against certain ways of living, Stewart thought it important to mention discrimination on the basis of race as well. Lavercombe's strategy had borne some fruit. Once again, what might have seemed disparate aspects of the era—race riots and war protests—came together in the vagrancy law challenge.[96]

As vagrancy cases repeatedly revealed in various contexts, people and behaviors that had previously been invisible, marginal, or condemned prompted reevaluation of what types of difference were actually dangerous. During the *Coates* oral argument, in fact, the justices had spent considerable energy trying to figure out whether and how much agreement there could be about what was "annoying." Though they used hypotheticals involving cigarette smoke and loud talking instead of picketing or anti-war protests, they debated both among themselves and with the lawyers whether "annoying" was sufficiently objective and identifiable. At one point Lavercombe suggested that American legionnaires would not be arrested under the ordinance. Burger resisted, "But sometimes American legionnaires do get arrested on these circumstances too, don't they?" he asked. No, replied Lavercombe, "I don't think they get arrested for the Cincinnati loitering ordinance, Your Honor." When Nichols repeatedly invoked "common sense" as the basis for defining what was annoying, one got the impression that others wondered whose common sense and whether it was even comprehensible to speak in such terms any more. As Marshall put it, "There is no yard stick."[97]

This impression of a disintegrating yardstick, a dissipating center, was perhaps what made the four more conservative justices uneasy. Stewart's comparison to the Founding Fathers was not one they would have found persuasive. Justice White's opinion for Chief Justice Burger and Justice Blackmun took an even stronger stance. For them, the absence of facts required affirming the ordinance on its face. By prohibiting "annoying" "conduct," White concluded, the Cincinnati ordinance did "not purport to bar or regulate speech as such." The Court had not treated demonstrations and picketing as pure speech in the past, and in some prior cases it had allowed regulation of such conduct even though "there is incidental impact on speech." With the ordinance a regular criminal law with no First Amendment implications, only vagueness applied, and there, facts were necessary to determine constitutionality as applied. Those facts were missing here, and White would have affirmed the convictions and upheld the law. To White, Coates was not a hero. He was a criminal.[98]

Justice Black took a similar approach. By the spring of 1971, a few months from retirement and death, Black was no longer as liberal as he had once been. He had become skeptical of people like Coates—criminals with little regard for the rules trying to masquerade as protected free speakers. Coates brought to Black's mind not august political leaders as much as a "gathering of persons in the mouths of alleys to annoy passersby by throwing rocks." The ordinance, he thought, could clearly and constitutionally apply to such conduct. But Black was uncomfortable validating a type of law he had long opposed. He found it impossible to decide the case without information about the annoying behavior. In his own opinion suggesting that the parties supplement the record, he sided neither with the liberals ready to invalidate nor the conservatives ready to uphold the law. To Black, then, the ordinances in *Palmer* and *Coates* seemed similar—both could constitutionally apply to some but not all conduct—but the defendants were differently situated with regard to what was known about their conduct. Palmer's was innocent (even though it suggested possible criminality), while Coates's was unknown (even though it suggested both possible criminality and possible protected speech).[99]

In a way, the Cincinnati ordinance itself, though intended to take the side of the so-called Establishment, undermined White's and Black's views of the case. It framed the key question not as whether its targets were criminals or heroes but whether they were annoying or not. When Stewart wrote that the ordinance invited "discriminatory enforcement against those whose association [was] 'annoying,'" he domesticated exactly what those nonconforming people and ideas did to the public space and the fellow citizens. "Annoy" would not likely have been the word of choice for moderates and conservatives witnessing or interacting with people like Coates. Demonstrators, hippies, and students were not just "annoying." They were threatening, dangerous, and morally offensive. Because the ordinance used the language of "annoyance," though, that became a focal point of the case and the image it projected. Annoyance was far less fundamental a divide than other words the city of Cincinnati, the public, or the Supreme Court might have used. The word belittled the concerns on the side of those who were threatened or offended and implicitly took on the perspective of those who were doing the "annoying."[100]

The differences between the justices' handling of *Palmer* and *Coates*—*Palmer* was unanimous and *Coates* 5–4; *Palmer* only decided as applied but *Coates* decided on its face—had not been foreseeable when the Court first took up the cases in the spring of 1970. In fact, from the very beginning, observers and participants had viewed them together. Both involved local, low-level ordinances in Ohio—Euclid's suspicious loitering law in *Palmer*, Cincinnati's loitering law in *Coates*. (With *Coates* in mind, Blackmun described the law in *Palmer* as "another poorly drawn local ordinance.") Both were part of the escalating vagrancy law challenge. In some respects, *Coates*'s Cincinnati law more closely resembled an unlawful assembly or disorderly conduct law than a traditional loitering law. Because it was, as Lavercombe noted, "whimsically labeled" "loitering," it made lawyers, justices, and the media group it together with *Palmer* and with challenges to vagrancy, loitering, and related laws more generally. The connections went in the other direction too. During oral argument, Schwartz linked *Palmer*, his case about a black criminal suspect, to a "law review literature . . . replete with discriminatory enforcement of these kinds of ordinances against Hippies, Yippies, beatniks, bums, people of unconventional dress, behavior, length of hair and so on."[101]

Even so, *Coates* had divided the justices more starkly than *Palmer* from the beginning. It might seem odd in retrospect that the Court was more willing to offer protection to a potential criminal than to a potential free speaker, that as Justice Blackmun—who went along in *Palmer* but dissented in *Coates*—warned, the momentum to invalidate the ordinance in *Palmer* might "taint the result in the Cincinnati case as well." (Perhaps it did.) But Coates's status as a free speaker was not initially obvious, and it was always contested. Moreover, perhaps the Court found *Palmer* easier to resolve because the Euclid law was clearly status based and looked more like a traditional, and illegitimate, vagrancy law, whereas the Cincinnati law was more conduct based. Though the *Palmer* Court did not cite *Robinson v. California*, perhaps Schwartz's arguments on that score had made an impression. Or perhaps the difficult questions about the scope of First Amendment protection for conduct-embroiled speech that *Coates* raised seemed harder to parse. Perhaps it was the more central presence of race in

Palmer, or that the justices truly agreed with Schwartz's arguments that *Terry* obviated any further need for suspicious persons laws.[102]

The remaining paper trail suggests that at least in part the difference stemmed from the presence and absence of facts. However potentially unsavory, more facts were known in *Palmer* than *Coates*. True, exactly what Palmer and his friend were doing at the Indian Colony Apartments in the middle of the night was never discovered. Even so, the facts the police had at the moment of arrests were known, and they were not sufficient to label Palmer a criminal. Whether the justices would have struck down the Euclid ordinance on its face in the absence of such facts is impossible to say. *Palmer* could be, and ultimately was, decided as applied. Even though those facts implied threat and criminality, they had not outright revealed it. To those like White, Burger, and Blackmun, who had apparently not yet settled on a view of the constitutional legitimacy of vagrancy-related laws, that disposition made *Palmer* an easier sell than *Coates*. Lavercombe's strategy had been a risky one. He had almost lost the whole case, and he did lose four of the justices. But it ultimately paid off in a big win.

Coates was front-page news in the *New York Times*, the *Los Angeles Times*, and the *Washington Post*. Though media reports on *Palmer* were less spectacular, the press still announced that the Court had issued a "warning" about the potential invalidation of laws like Euclid's. Not only did news coverage announce that the Supreme Court had found both ordinances unconstitutional to one extent or another. It also identified as important much of what Schwartz and Lavercombe had emphasized and the published opinions had not. Whatever the justices might have thought or discussed, Schwartz and Lavercombe were right that race mattered to the broader cultural understanding of their cases. Almost every article mentioned Palmer's race, his companion's race, and the Cincinnati riots. [103]

In addition, though neither Supreme Court opinion said much about the larger anti-vagrancy law context for the cases, the press did. The *Washington Post* noted, "Although loitering laws differ from city to city, the high court's broad condemnation of a Cincinnati ordinance raised fresh questions in Washington and other urban areas where loosely phrased laws have been challenged as weapons used chiefly against minorities and the poor." *Coates* was important because the ordinance was "similar to laws that a number of cities have passed in recent years in efforts to control boisterous or disruptive sidewalk gatherings." *Palmer* was important because it was similar to laws "common in most jurisdictions." City papers would describe their own equivalent laws, noting where their differences might save them from constitutional attack. Cincinnati City Solicitor William McLain underscored *Coates*'s significance. He thought that the Court had "changed its opinion in reference to fundamental rights of the citizens." As a result, the city would "have to draft a new ordinance in accordance with this new philosophy."[104]

In predicting that *Coates* "probably spelled the doom of many umbrella-type statutes" in 1971, Fred Graham of the *New York Times* offered up something of a primer on the vagrancy law challenge. After describing the breadth of the laws, he explained, "The reason so many persons managed to stay out of jail is that these laws are enforced selectively—and therein lies a controversy that has been gathering momentum for the past decade." The controversy was one between "law enforcement officers [who] assert that policing the modern city requires broad, flexible powers to deal with the infinite variety of annoying or menacing conduct that can make life miserable for others in a congested city" and "Negroes, hippies and political dissenters [who] claim that such umbrella laws are little more than a police license to discriminate." Graham thus highlighted what the lawyers had been pointing out for some time: that vagrancy law enforcement crossed perceived boundaries between different types of people out of place. It affected racial minorities, cultural nonconformists, and political rabble-rousers alike.[105]

Graham also offered readers who may not have been paying close attention a partial history of the vagrancy law challenge. That challenge, he wrote, "had as its catalyst the civil rights movement and one of its foremost legal theoreticians a young professor named Anthony G. Amsterdam." Amsterdam's 1960 note, Graham explained, had provided a "constitutional measuring stick" for laws that had rarely been challenged until the 1950s, when they began to be used not only against "drunks, Negroes, and the poor" but also against civil rights activists. As the activists' lawyers challenged the laws, courts "almost invariably" invalidated them. The extent of the invalidations had remained unclear prior to *Coates*. Some courts had determined that vagrancy laws could not even be used in their traditional way, "to control the neighborhood rowdies or the town drunk." Others had validated only those with special prohibitions, like loitering near schools or men's bathrooms. Other courts, Graham acknowledged, "insisted that congested urban living would be unbearable unless the police could deal with truly 'annoying' conduct." To them, the laws were legitimate except when the goal was "to crush dissent."[106]

Such a synthesis of the vagrancy law challenge is hard to imagine before the Court's decisions in 1971 and 1972. Three years earlier, *Wainwright, Johnson,* and *Terry* had stalled the Supreme Court's previously halting movement toward vagrancy law invalidation over the prior fifteen years. Though lower courts became more aggressive just afterward, and their invalidations garnered increasing publicity and visibility, it was not until *Coates* and *Palmer* that a story of origins, progress, connections, and (at least partial) vindication could be told.

9

"Vagrancy Is No Crime"

The race was on to get to the Supreme Court. For years, the justices had been equivocating. They had been obfuscating. They had been denying. Between 1969 and 1971, events had begun to overtake them. State and lower federal courts had struck down vagrancy, loitering, and suspicious persons laws. States and cities across the nation had repealed, substantially revised, or simply stopped using their laws. The scales of scholarly authority had tipped precipitously to the side of invalidation. Finding themselves on the defensive, local officials began narrowing their justifications for the constitutionality of such laws.[1]

In *Coates v. City of Cincinnati* and *Palmer v. City of Euclid*, the Supreme Court had belatedly, if still equivocally, embraced the vagrancy law challenge. A traditional vagrancy law might have seemed like a more obvious constitutional problem than either a loitering law that entailed some amount of conduct or a suspicious persons law that had a better crime control rationale. But the Court had not yet taken the step of invalidating a traditional vagrancy law on its face. Perhaps it would not. Perhaps this would prove to be one of those instances where legal change would happen without conclusive Supreme Court intervention. If the Court refused to go further than it already had, that legal change would be patchwork indeed. For despite all the anti-vagrancy successes, many states and cities continued to defend and aggressively use vagrancy laws, especially for crime control purposes. If the justices did think that emerging but contested local anti-vagrancy law trends should be nationalized—and *Coates* and *Palmer* suggested that a majority of the justices thought so—then they might, eventually, conclude that they would have to do it.

That was certainly what lawyers across the country had determined by the late 1960s. Though they still deemed law enforcement part of the problem, these lawyers had largely coalesced around constitutional litigation over the substantive validity of vagrancy laws. Challenging police power directly seemed less promising after *Terry v. Ohio*, and challenging vagrancy laws themselves seemed more promising after the accumulation of lower court victories. The liberal lawyers at the hub of the vagrancy law challenge, like other liberal lawyers of the time, had determined that even if the discretion of law enforcement officers was in part to blame for the harms of the vagrancy law regime, the substance of the laws nonetheless mattered. It *had* to matter, or the project of liberal law reform—the project that had championed *Brown v. Board of Education* and other Supreme Court victories—was doomed from the start.

Even as vagrancy lawyers narrowed their strategy, however, the sheer diversity of vagrancy litigants and anti-vagrancy law arguments broadened the scope of the attack. Consider the wide array of cases lawyers hoped would be the Supreme Court headliner. In Boulder, after ACLU lawyer Robert Bruce Miller had slain the dragon of the Colorado vagrancy law in federal district court, he had begged the assistant attorney general on the case to appeal, to no avail. With its hippies arrested for vagrancy while innocently baking pies in the middle of the afternoon, he had thought it "just such a perfect case . . . to take up to the Supremes." Monroe Freedman of the National Capital ACLU also lamented when he convinced a federal appellate court to strike down the capital's vagrancy law on behalf of prostitute Hattie Mae Ricks. He had thought that the police testimony he had procured about enforcement abuses made his the perfect case to do what the Supreme Court had refrained from doing in *Edelman v. California* and *Hicks v. District of Columbia*. In Cleveland, Ohio, Niki Schwartz was also disappointed. Schwartz had wanted *Palmer* to be the case that finally and unambiguously dismantled the vagrancy law regime, but his client had been the only one to benefit directly. In each context, in each place, each lawyer thought his the quintessential vagrancy case, the perfect vehicle.[2]

The real race came out of Florida. At least three different lawyers across the state pursued three different cases they thought might be the big one. Miami legal aid lawyer Bruce Rogow had won his case against the Florida vagrancy law in 1969's *Lazarus v. Faircloth*, but the state's appeal kept his Supreme Court hopes alive. Rogow's friend and sometime collaborator Philip Hubbart was also his competitor when it came to the vagrancy law hunt. The Miami-Dade public defender whose *Johnson v. Florida* had eked out a limited reversal in 1968 was on the lookout for a new and better case. Then there was Samuel Jacobson, a law school classmate and friend of Hubbart's who regularly trolled the Jacksonville Municipal Court for the perfect test case.[3]

That these Florida lawyers in a legal aid agency, a public defender's office, and private practice all thought they had a shot at the high court stemmed partially from the wide diffusion of the anti-vagrancy law challenge by the late 1960s. Though Rogart and Hubbart both did some work for the ACLU, Jacobson did not. None of the three received assistance from either organization in his vagrancy litigation efforts. The challenge was no longer the provenance of those in the know. Or, rather, those in the know now extended far beyond the cadre of ACLU and NAACP LDF lawyers who had long propelled the movement forward.

The particulars of the Florida law and its local counterparts made these and other Sunshine State lawyers especially attuned to the constitutional defects in vagrancy laws. The state statute was originally passed in 1832, and it remained essentially the same in the early 1970s as a slightly amended 1907 version. The "Elizabethan" language of this "garbage pail" of the criminal law announced that "rogues and vagabonds, idle or dissolute persons who go about begging, common gamblers, persons who use juggling, or unlawful games or plays, common pipers and fiddlers, common drunkards, common night walkers, thieves, pilferers, traders in stolen property, lewd, wanton and lascivious persons, keepers of gambling places" were vagrants. "Common railers and brawlers, persons who neglect their calling or employment, or are without reasonable continuous employment or regular income and who have no sufficient property to sustain them, and misspend what they earn without providing for themselves or the support of their families" were also vagrants. So too were "persons wandering or strolling around from place to place without any lawful purpose or object, habitual loafers, idle and disorderly persons neglecting all lawful business and habitually spending their time by frequenting houses of ill fame, gaming houses or tippling shops, persons able to work but habitually living upon the earnings of their wives or minor children and all able bodied male persons over the age of eighteen years who are without means of support and remain in idleness."[4]

The law created somewhere in the range of twenty different types of vagrants, though the number was in flux. In 1971, the city of Jacksonville made two changes to the similar ordinance Jacobson hoped to challenge. First, it eliminated "juggling." Second, it reduced the maximum imprisonment from ninety to seventy-five days and the maximum fine from $500 to $450 in order to avoid federal court decisions that required state provision of counsel at the higher levels. That same year, the Florida legislature removed "tippling shops" in an effort to modernize its laws involving drunkenness. It left the rest of the law intact.[5]

"Archaic," "anachronistic," "antiquated," "vestigial," and downright "old," the law's genealogy and vocabulary made it particularly ripe for challenge. Four hundred years of vagrancy laws now seemed a distinct mark against them rather than conclusive evidence in favor. One thing lawyers had learned from watching the justices make procedural hay of vagrancy cases for more than a decade, though, was that they would have to take care to bring the right kind of case in the right kind of context. Each in his way, Jacobson, Hubbart, and Rogow tried to do exactly that.

Race to the Court

Classroom seating at Duke Law School was alphabetical, and in many of their classes, Phil Hubbart sat just to the left of Sam Jacobson. The two became good friends. When they took first-year constitutional law in the fall of 1958, Caleb Foote's pioneering vagrancy exposé was just two years old. Though few other scholars had yet picked up on Foote's themes, Hubbart and Jacobson's constitutional law professor did. Douglas Maggs had served as solicitor of labor during World War II. By 1958, he was already on record as in favor of prompt school desegregation in North Carolina (for which he was denounced as a communist). Maggswas also affiliated with the ACLU. Though Maggs might have read Foote's article, it was just as likely that he had pinpointed vagrancy laws as problematic because he circulated in the same small but growing group of civil libertarians who were coming to the same conclusion Foote had. Maggs told his students that vagrancy laws were likely unconstitutional.[6]

Jacobson would later identify Maggs's lecture as "the moment" when he first thought about challenging such laws. As a child in Orlando—then the celery-farming capital of the world—Jacobson "had heard about vagrancy law all growing up. The fact that bums were vagrants was just common knowledge. The idea that something so fundamental could be unconstitutional piqued my curiosity."[7]

Jacobson first experienced vagrancy law in action when he began working as an assistant United States attorney in Jacksonville shortly after law school. He heard "officers saying that we need these laws, when we don't have anything on [suspects], but we think they might be wanted somewhere else, so we can detain them for 8 or 10 days so we can check them out. If it turns out that they aren't wanted, then no harm no foul. You drop the charges, no one gets convicted. No problem." Jacobson later reported that he was shocked that "this was all said with a straight face." When he left the prosecutor's office for private practice in 1965, he started looking for vagrancy defendants to represent.

Unbeknownst to Jacobson, his law school friend Phil Hubbart was also seeking a vagrancy test case. Hubbart had grown up in Illinois but headed south for law school at Duke and eventually farther south to Miami. Hubbart and Jacobson would see each other periodically after graduation, when each ventured into the other's neck of the Florida woods. But they never discussed their passion against vagrancy laws. Neither knew that the other was looking for vagrancy cases to challenge. For years.

In the first go-round, Hubbart beat Jacobson to the Court. Though the two budding lawyers had sat right beside each other in that constitutional law course at Duke, Hubbart's germinal vagrancy moment had come later, when he was working appeals as an assistant public defender in Miami-Dade County. As he put it, "I got interested in the vagrancy statutes principally because it was our clients who were the victims of these laws. . . . [T]hey made unemployment in effect a crime—being out of work, no visible means of support, and all that nonsense. And I thought that was clearly unconstitutional. So I started looking around for a case to take up to the Supreme Court." Hubbart eventually found young Harvey Johnson, who had been arrested while hanging out at a bus stop in the middle of the night. By describing Johnson as not having violated the terms of the vagrancy law, the Supreme Court had skirted the underlying constitutional issue. Hubbart had been disappointed when the Court had decided *Johnson v. Florida* on *Thompson v. Louisville* no-evidence grounds in the spring of 1968.[8]

Hubbart learned his lesson: if you give the Court an innocent vagrancy defendant, the Court will use it as an excuse not to strike down the vagrancy law itself. So Hubbart said to himself, "Ok, I'll find a guy who was doing something wrong so they couldn't reverse on the ground that there was no evidence of wrongdoing. . . . I thought they would have to face the constitutionality of the law then." Hubbart found Raymond Smith. Smith had been convicted of vagrancy and attempting to break and enter a railroad car after a special agent had heard, but not seen, Smith tampering with a freight car door. With both of Smith's convictions affirmed on appeal, Hubbart felt confident that the Court would not be able to *Thompson* him again.[9]

Sam Jacobson was looking for a different kind of test case. Like Hubbart, he "was very cognizant of those cases where cert had been granted and dismissed as improvident"—*Edelman v. California, Arceneaux v. Louisiana, Hicks v. District of Columbia*, and *Wainwright v. New Orleans*—and where the Supreme Court "would take one case and deal with it on its facts"—*Thompson v. Louisville, Shuttlesworth v. Birmingham, Johnson v. Florida*. Jacobson's goal, pursued with what he called "malice aforethought," however, was to create a "package" of cases "that came from so many angles that [the justices] couldn't with intellectual honesty throw out the writ." Hubbart hoped to challenge the justices with a single defendant who raised the most controversial crime control issues. Jacobson wanted to overwhelm them with the sheer diversity of vagrancy law's targets.[10]

Jacobson's client-hunting grounds were the Jacksonville Municipal Court, which operated with the same informal procedures that Foote had described in Philadelphia in 1956. Sam Jacobson "started letting it be known that [he] would represent anyone on a charge of vagrancy." He would approach potential clients. "You are charged with vagrancy. I'm a lawyer, and I'll be happy to defend you. It won't cost you anything. I just don't like this type of charge." Given that few vagrancy defendants had counsel, they would usually agree. "Some would want to know what the rub was. But for most of them it was like manna from heaven for me to be their lawyer." Jacobson had never met most of these defendants before, and he would never see most of them again. The few minutes Jacobson spent with his client before trial was often his only chance to learn about the facts of the case.[11]

John Santora, the municipal court judge, did not help Jacobson any. Santora had a "rough and ready" sense of justice, Jacobson recalled. The judge viewed the young lawyer as "an annoyance and a bother. . . . I was helping these people who he thought didn't deserve any help. He thought I was a meddling do-gooder." In some of the most transparently illegal cases, Santora would acquit "either because he could see it was such a bad abuse or because he didn't want to give me a really good fact situation" for appeal. When the judge did not like what the defendant had done, or the police made it clear that they wanted to hold the suspect for further investigation, Santora would convict.[12]

The "package" Jacobson eventually put together included four individual cases and one case with four defendants. All eight defendants were between the ages of twenty-one and twenty-six. Four were black. Four were white. Jacobson's desire to hem in the justices meant that he, like Hubbart, did not shy away from unsympathetic defendants. Three of the arrests Jacobson chose were clearly motivated by crime control concerns. Two of the white defendants—Thomas Owen Campbell and Henry Edward Heath—were separately arrested for "vagrancy-common thief," with "loitering" thrown in for Heath. At the time of their arrests, Campbell had been driving in his neighborhood and Heath had been standing in his girlfriend's driveway. Jacobson was under no illusions about the men—he called Heath "a flat-out thief." But Jacobson's point was that even men known to be criminals should not be arrested for vagrancy at times when they "hadn't done anything at all."[13]

The third crime-control case Jacobson added to his package would turn out to be the trickiest. According to the stipulated facts, Hugh Brown, a twenty-one-year-old African American, was "reported to be a thief, narcotics pusher, and generally opprobrious character." According to Jacobson, he had "very few moral limitations." On the night that would bring Brown to the Supreme Court, an officer found heroin on him. Because the officer lacked probable cause, Brown was eventually convicted only of "vagrancy-disorderly loitering on street" and resisting arrest. Jacobson "thought it would be better to round out the package with somebody like that, rather than not acknowledge that [the ordinance] got put to use against any really bad guys."[14]

To three potential "bad guys" who had not "done anything," Jacobson added five others who represented wholly different vagrancy concerns, concerns that went more to the dangers of nonconformity than the dangers of serious crime. One was Jimmy Lee Smith (no relation to Hubbart's freight car-tampering Raymond Smith). The police arrested Smith and a co-defendant in downtown Jacksonville on a weekday morning—cold, and Smith without a jacket—while they waited for a ride to potential job openings. The men came up clean in a search, but the police arrested them for "vagrancy-vagabonds" because, according to one officer, "their story just didn't seem to work from what we could see." Smith's co-defendant had no prior record and he was acquitted. But Smith—with several arrests, one conviction, a common law wife, three "illegitimate" children, a part-time produce job, and a part-time job with "a Negro political organization"—was convicted. These characteristics led to what the stipulated facts called a judicial "tongue lashing about [Smith's] character." Judge Santora denounced Smith's "'open adultery,' his 'bastard children,' his arrests, and his general demeanor." He concluded: "You are not what we call a good citizen, a respectable citizen."[15]

It was the last four defendants, the four who had all been arrested together, that were at the heart of Jacobson's case. Two of the four were Margaret "Lorraine" Papachristou and Betty Jean Calloway. Both were white, tall, blonde, and in their early twenties. Papachristou was in a job-training program at the Florida Junior College, separated from her husband and living with her parents. Calloway, a typing and shorthand teacher at a state mental institution, had lived her whole life near Jacksonville. Had she and Papachristou been the only occupants of her car on the night of April 20, 1969, no doubt they would not have been arrested. But they were not alone. They were accompanied by Eugene F. Melton and Leonard Johnson, "Negro males," in the parlance of the stipulated facts. Each man was twenty-four, six foot four inches tall, and weighing nearly two hundred pounds. Melton was a Vietnam War veteran and a full-time college student with a part-time computer job in Jacksonville. Johnson worked in a warehouse and was a lifelong Jacksonville resident. In fact, some of his family members happened to pass by during the arrest, and they tried "unsuccessfully to vouch for him."[16]

What vouching would have looked like under the circumstances is an open question. The four were in Calloway's car on their way from a restaurant (owned by Johnson's uncle) to a nightclub. According to the stipulated facts, "The arresting officer denied that the racial mixture of the defendants played any part in the decision to arrest them." Though the officers claimed that the four had "stopped near a used car lot which had been broken into several times," they had not pursued the car-theft theory. The four were charged with "vagrancy–prowling by auto," a type of vagrancy nowhere to be found in the ordinance's long list of prohibitions. (Indeed, of the arrest notations for all of Jacobson's clients—"prowling by auto," "loitering," "common thief," "disorderly loitering on street," and "vagabond"—only the last was actually listed in the ordinance.) Of the four in the car that night, only Papachristou had a prior record—for a municipal offense. They were, Jacobson later reflected, "law-abiding citizens" who "just offended the sensibilities of the police officer who saw them."[17]

The officers' were not the only sensibilities offended. Municipal court judge Santora set bail at $500, the maximum allowable amount. According to Jacobson, Santora saw the situation as "the equivalent of miscegenation. It deeply offended him and it was something that just wasn't supposed to happen." The stipulated facts also noted that "an unidentified caller from the Police Department telephoned Papachristou's parents that she had been out with a Negro." Melton, who had given his unlisted phone number to the booking officer as required, "began receiving threatening telephone calls." If Jimmy Lee Smith's scolding suggested that Jacksonville officials used vagrancy laws to enforce social norms, *Papachristou* provided clear confirmation.[18]

Once he had his "package," Jacobson said to the city attorney, "These cases are a pain in the butt for you, but they're a cause for me. Why don't we consolidate them?" Jacobson told the circuit court judge hearing his first appeal, "We really just need to get through you to get to the higher state courts. I'll give you a brief but I don't really expect you to rule for me." According to Jacobson, "It was fine with [the judge], because he wasn't involved in any cause or anything." From there, Jacobson went to the Florida appeals court, where he "was afraid that this so affronts fundamental justice that they would say they couldn't find it constitutional." Though his clients no doubt would have liked a reversal of their convictions at any level of the justice system, Jacobson faced the same ethical issues Monroe Freedman had faced in the prostitution case of *Ricks v. District of Columbia*. Focused on what he called his "cause," Jacobson's goal was less to reverse the convictions anywhere than to overturn the vagrancy laws at the Supreme Court. As he later recounted, "I didn't write a very strong brief [in the appellate court]. Plus, there were earlier cases upholding the Florida law, which I knew. So I really kind of invited the affirmance."[19]

After the affirmance that predictably followed, Jacobson could have taken his case to the Florida Supreme Court. Florida law allowed him to skip that court, however, and so he did. He was afraid it would invalidate the law or reverse the convictions, and, as he put it, "My eye was on Washington."[20]

When Jacksonville police decided that a vagrancy arrest was the proper response to Papachristou, Calloway, Melton, and Johnson, they brought together two venerable and intertwined targets of vagrancy law regulation: racial mores and women's sexuality. As African American men as different as the Reverend Fred Shuttlesworth and Euclid's James Palmer well knew, vagrancy regulation of race had taken many forms and censured many different types of racial insubordination. Alleged prostitutes like Hattie Mae Ricks and Dorothy Kirkwood knew just as well that the police had long used vagrancy laws to regulate women's sexuality generally, and especially the sexuality of poor and minority women. But the police had also turned to vagrancy laws to constrain white women—especially those who became sexually involved with men of other races—and the men with whom they became involved.

Seeing people of different races in the same physical or social space often put law enforcement in mind of criminality. When John Terry and Richard Chilton met up with their white colleague Carl Katz in downtown Cleveland, veteran officer Martin McFadden concluded that the trio could be up to nothing but trouble. As the President's Crime Commission task force report on the police noted, "Members of minority groups were often stopped, particularly if found in groups, in the company of white people, or at night in white neighborhoods." Though whites in African American company or neighborhoods were also suspect, police often chose to return them to their proper places rather than arrest them.[21]

Mixed race, mixed sex associations were particularly disreputable, as the vagrancy arrests of interracial Beat groupings in 1950s San Francisco had made clear. A jazzy 1967 *Playboy* piece on "The Fuzz" noted that some of the threat of the mixed-race couple began in vice. "If you see a nigger and a white woman together, chances are it's a pimp and a whore." Wayne R. LaFave had reported in a more scholarly fashion in his seminal work on arrest that in Detroit, "Association of a woman with men of another race usually results in the immediate conclusion that she is a prostitute. If a Negro woman is found in the company of a white man, she is usually confronted by the police and taken to the station unless it is clear that the association is legitimate." The president's task force on the police echoed these findings: "Negro women with white men were almost always charged," though the men often went free.[22]

Vice and criminality were not the only threats of the interracial couple. Interracial sex was itself often a "racial taboo," and it had been so with considerable, though not complete, consistency for much of American history. The suppression of forbidden interracial sex had taken many forms—violence, lynchings, "legal lynchings," legal prohibitions—especially when it involved white women and black men. Sometimes officials pressed into service race-neutral laws that they enforced aggressively against interracial couples; at other times, they enacted and enforced explicitly discriminatory laws. In particular, anti-miscegenation laws that dated back to the colonial era restricted marriage and sometimes cohabitation between whites and various minorities. These laws waxed and waned across the nineteenth and twentieth centuries in part due to whether legislatures imagined the illicit coupling of a rights-less black man and "his" rights-less white woman (waxed) or marriage between a rights-bearing white man and "his" black wife (waned). In other words, the law functioned to enable white men control over black female sexuality while suppressing the sexuality of both white women and black men.[23]

The United States Supreme Court placed its imprimatur on anti-miscegenation laws in 1883 and kept it there for eighty years. When the Court invalidated a Florida law that prohibited cohabitation of unmarried, mixed-race couples in 1964, Justice Stewart's concurrence questioned the constitutional validity of any law that made "the criminality of an act depend upon the race of the actor." Even so, every southern state prohibited interracial marriage until 1967, when the Court invalidated Virginia's prohibition in the aptly named *Loving v. Virginia*.

When the police stopped the Jacksonville foursome for "vagrancy-prowling by auto," then, only two years had passed since the Supreme Court had declared anti-miscegenation laws anathema to the Constitution. During that time, *Guess Who's Coming to Dinner*, a movie made just before *Loving* that depicted interracial marriage in a positive light, had won several awards and become a box office hit, even in the South.[24]

The invalidation of anti-miscegenation laws was not the same, however, as the eradication of governmental harassment of interracial couples. An outpouring of commentary made clear that such specialized laws were not the only way government officials thwarted interracial couplings. In his path-breaking book on the police, *The Big Blue Line: Police Power vs. Human Rights*, Ed Cray concluded, "Interracial couples are constantly stopped, not only in the nation's capital, but in every other city." Anthony Amsterdam highlighted the same in his NAACP LDF brief in *Terry v. Ohio*. In part because of the selective enforcement of adultery and fornication against interracial couples, the American Law Institute decided to omit such prohibitions from its Model Penal Code.[25]

Vagrancy laws frequently played their part in this regulation. Sometimes, officers perceived vagrancy laws as an easier way to suppress interracial sexuality than anti-miscegenation laws themselves. In one 1942 Denver case, a black man and a white woman were living together "as though married" when the police arrested them for vagrancy. Because interracial marriage was illegal in Colorado, the couple's common law marriage was no marriage at all. They were leading "an immoral course of life" under the Denver ordinance. Even at that time, however, two dissenters found such arrests problematic. They objected to the "vindictive" execution of the vagrancy law. The officers had purposefully "waited until the hour of 11 o'clock p.m. . . . to invade [the couple's] home . . . without a warrant" and put them in jail for two days for investigation before procuring one. In Norfolk, Virginia, fifteen years later, a white GI and an African American woman wanted to marry. The man had asked permission to transfer to a state where such a marriage would be legal. Instead, the couple was arrested, convicted of vagrancy, and sentenced to thirty days "on the roads."[26]

Even when anti-miscegenation laws were less directly implicated, it was clear to at least some observers that vagrancy arrests were a way of enforcing Jim Crow's sexual segregation. One article in the *Baltimore Afro-American* described a New Orleans arrest of a black barroom operator and two white women as an indication that the police were "determined to enforce the South's outmoded segregation laws on intermingling of the races, particularly when white women are involved." According to the article, "The two white women who dared to cross the color line were held on vagrancy by loitering charges."[27]

Sometimes vagrancy arrests of interracial couples were wholly unconnected to anti-miscegenation laws and occurred in states without them. In 1951 Detroit, a "beautiful white girl" was arrested for vagrancy shortly before she married a forty-something black hotel porter. When interviewed after the wedding, she said, "When we go out together, people look at us like [we] are crazy, but we keep our heads raised and pay no attention. One of the best ways to spread democracy is to put it into reality through interracial marriage." The *New Amsterdam News*, a black newspaper in New York City, described how another black male-white female interracial couple had had to move, been arrested, and received hundreds of letters and phone calls in New York City in 1955. Though the couple had never been south of New Jersey, their experiences since their marriage had left them with "plenty of doubts about whether Georgia moved North on the map of the U.S." When a judge dismissed a prostitution charge against the woman, she was arrested for vagrancy and held incommunicado until the following day. While she was being held, the assistant district attorney asked her, as she later put it, "what I was doing married to a nigger."[28]

Such incidents continued well into the 1960s. An advice column in the *Chicago Defender* in 1966 printed a letter from a white woman and her black beau. Whenever they went out, she said, "We get into trouble with the law." Once a police officer accused the couple of loitering and ordered the man off the street. When he refused to move, he was jailed overnight. The paper reported later that same year, "The old bugaboo about the black man and the white woman is still getting Negro men into trouble with the law" in both the North and the South. In the South, the interracial interaction was criminalized "by calling it 'association with a Negro male or just plain vagrancy.'" A survey had found that in Chicago and Houston, charges lodged against African American men in such circumstances ranged from vagrancy to aggravated battery. As these incidents suggest, arresting interracial couples was not only part of vice and crime control; it was also, deeply, part of social control. It targeted both women's sexuality in a racial context and racial mores in a sexual one. The police were using vagrancy laws to enforce official policy in the South and social norms virtually everywhere else.[29]

What Papachristou, Calloway, Melton, and Johnson were engaged in was far less serious than the marriage or cohabitation that states had prohibited explicitly before the late 1960s. The four were simply out on the town. But it seems undeniable that "the criminality of [their acts depended] upon the race of the actor[s]." It was simply socially unacceptable for two white women and two black men to go out together in Jacksonville in 1969. Even if the evening had been wholly innocent, their shared ride in a car implied sexuality. For some time, cars had been deemed "brothels on wheels" as "courting" had moved from the proverbial "front porch" to the "back seat." The officer who arrested them, the officer who called Papachristou's parents with what seemed to him important information about their daughter, the person who threatened Melton with prank calls, and the appalled judge were all trying to use vagrancy law to enforce an anti-miscegenation policy the Court had declared unconstitutional when pursued by legislatures. The question now was whether the Court would allow state executive and judicial officials to do under cover of vagrancy laws what it had already prohibited the state legislatures from doing outright.[30]

Before the Court could answer that question, it had to decide whether to hear any of the Florida cases—Jacobson's *Papachristou v. Jacksonville*, Hubbart's *Smith v. Florida*, or Rogow's *Lazarus v. Faircloth*. *Lazarus* ran into trouble from the start. Like many of the lawyers who pursued vagrancy cases in the late 1960s, Rogow had been on the cutting edge when he decided to challenge the repeated arrests of Matthew Lazarus with a civil rights lawsuit in federal court. By the time *Lazarus* got to the Court in 1969, however, the justices were already reconsidering the circumstances under which federal courts could decide cases, like *Lazarus*, that might interfere with state criminal charges. For more than two years, *Lazarus* languished at the Court. When the Court finally decided to substantially narrow such federal court jurisdiction out of respect for state autonomy (in the seminal case of *Younger v. Harris*), it dashed not only Rogow's hope but also the hopes of a number of other vagrancy lawyers for Supreme Court glory.[31]

Unlike *Lazarus, Papachristou* and *Smith* were straight-ahead appeals from state criminal convictions. Though that meant that Jacobson's and Hubbart's clients came to the Court as convicts rather than civil rights supplicants, it also meant that their cases were procedurally unencumbered. The Court could focus on the constitutional question without any distractions. When Jacobson and Hubbart brought their separate vagrancy petitions to the Supreme Court in late 1970, however, the Court was already preparing to hear oral argument in *Palmer* and *Coates*. The justices decided to hold the new cases to see whether it would be necessary to decide them once the Court had disposed of the old ones.[32]

Shortly after the Court announced its decisions in *Palmer* and *Coates*, the justices unanimously voted to hear both *Smith* and *Papachristou*. It was clear that vagrancy law work remained, and Florida was exhibit "A." In fact, though Rogow failed to get *Lazarus* its own Supreme Court hearing, his efforts likely bolstered *Papachristou's* and *Smith's* chances by revealing the mess of Florida vagrancy laws. When the Supreme Court had reversed Harvey Johnson's conviction in Hubbart's 1968 case, the Florida Supreme Court had only grudgingly complied. Since then, state and federal courts in Florida had been engaged in open warfare over the validity of the state's vagrancy laws. A federal district court had declared the Florida vagrancy law unconstitutional in *Lazarus* in 1969. The police had stopped enforcing the law. Then the Florida Supreme Court had upheld the same law. Police officers took that decision as permission to resume enforcement. State courts had continued to uphold vagrancy arrests and federal courts had continued to cast doubt on them. In one case, the federal appeals court stated, "We think it bordering on the fantastic to contend that everything listed in this relic of the English statute of laborers can come within the power of the state to forbid, with criminal sanctions in this day."[33]

Given this context, the Court's invalidations in *Coates* and *Palmer*, and the fact that the lower courts in *Smith* and *Papachristou* had affirmed the various convictions, the Court's decisions to hear *Smith* and *Papachristou* were telling. The *Sarasota Herald-Tribune* reflected common sentiments when it reported that "those on both sides of the issue are predicting the ancient law will soon be ruled unconstitutional. . . . [E]ven supporters of the concept don't seem too optimistic that the law will be upheld. Similar statutes have been ruled invalid by federal courts throughout the country, or are presently under attack."[34]

The question for the Court was now clear: were the Jacksonville ordinance and the Florida law constitutional? Though Jacobson was mainly challenging the former and Hubbart the latter, and though they had developed their cases separately, the two lawyers converged on many of their answers to that question: the laws were vague, and they violated the right to travel, the *Robinson v. California* prohibition on status crimes, the "zone of privacy" that *Griswold v. Connecticut* protected, equal protection, and rights under the Fifth and Thirteenth Amendments. Jacobson highlighted the diverse functions of vagrancy laws that threatened "oppression and harassment" against "the unpopular, unconventional, and unestablished."[35]

The authorities for such arguments had been accreting for decades—slowly at first, and then far more quickly. When Al Wirin and Fred Okrand had represented Isidore Edelman and Ernest Besig his Beats, African Americans, and gay men and lesbians in the 1950s, they had been largely out on their own, with few citations to support their central claims. The sheer volume of the citations in Jacobson's and Hubbart's briefs showed the Court that it was perhaps a bit late to the vagrancy law invalidation party. Citations to *Palmer, Coates, Hicks, Shuttlesworth,* and *Adickes* nonetheless reminded the justices that the Court had been making preparations to join in for some time.[36]

The government lawyers defending the laws also followed many of the usual conventions in pressing both procedural and substantive objections. Edward Austin, Jacksonville's city attorney, took the by-then somewhat unusual position of defending the laws not only as used but as conceived. Following Devlin in the Hart/Devlin debates, he identified vagrancy law's "socially valid purpose" as guiding "each member of society toward socially desirable conduct by distinguishing between socially acceptable and socially destructive behavior." Though Austin contended that the long history of vagrancy laws buttressed, rather than undermined, their legitimacy, his reasons for not worrying about discrimination and abuse were entirely modern. The police would behave because they were "watched by the media, television, newspaper, they are watched by the prosecutor, they are watched by the Human Relations Committees, they are watched by the Civil Liberties Union, they are watched by the sheriff himself because he is the elected official."[37]

Assistant Attorney General Nelson E. Bailey, who defended Florida's law against Hubbart's challenge in *Smith*, preferred to rely on the narrower crime control defense that seemed more publicly acceptable by 1971. A "properly administered vagrancy statute appears to be a more appropriate tool of good law enforcement practices today than ever before in history." Stop and frisk simply did not give the police enough authority to protect society. The Court should not make law enforcement officers "stand idle, immobilized by non-essential constitutional restraints, while night time prowlers and apparently resolute thieves or designing rapists stalk without restraint."[38]

Bailey was not the only Florida official to make such arguments. A state attorney speaking on television had described the Florida law as "a very broad law that is really a law enforcement tool primarily for temporary detention of suspects. I think [that] is its primary objective." He suggested that "perhaps it should have another name," like "temporary detention of suspicious persons." In his view, the name of the law, not its substance, was the problem. Indeed, Jacksonville city attorney Austin informed the justices during the *Papachristou* oral argument that "amazingly" the Florida legislature was just then in the process of revising the state vagrancy law at the request of the State Association of Prosecuting Attorneys.[39]

If crime control was the context in which government officials held most tenaciously to vagrancy laws, it was also the context that most worried some of the justices contemplating the withdrawal of vagrancy authority. During oral argument, the justices peppered Jacobson with questions about the need for police authority over Hugh Brown, the heroin-holding *Papachristou* defendant who most directly raised the crime control issue. Jacobson explained that he had added the "Brown situation to round out the package of cases because we assume that the City would contend that there were circumstances in which something like [the] vagrancy statute and ordinance would be required [for] offenders or hardcore criminal[s] and we did want to bring [an] instance of at least that sort of alleged situation before the Court." When a justice suggested that if Brown had been the only petitioner, the case would have been "much more difficult," Jacobson conceded only that it would have been less appealing. In Jacobson's view, the fact that those like Papachristou and her friends and political organizer Jimmy Lee Smith "suffered really blatant oppression" made their cases more sympathetic, but it did not make them constitutionally more deserving.[40]

As a general matter, the justices seemed open to Jacobson's arguments in *Papachristou*. They were disturbed by what he told them about the actual operation of the law. Justice Stewart expressed some disbelief that once one was convicted of theft one was always vulnerable to arrest under the vagrancy law. Jacobson explained, "The vagrancy is a continuing offense . . . however long ago it had been or however minor it has been . . . he is subject to continuing incarceration." When Stewart pressed, "Everyday, could he be arrested?" Jacobson replied, "He cannot walk the streets of Jacksonville without being subject to arrest." Unwittingly channeling Louis Lusky, Chief Justice Burger reflected, "I suppose then the more he gets arrested the easier it is to sustain the charge because they can identify him."[41]

Having watched *Papachristou* go pretty well for the anti-vagrancy forces, Jacobson's Duke law classmate and friend Phil Hubbart thought, "Ok, I'm going to have the same reception" in *Smith*. Jacobson's trouble with the crime control vagrancy arrest of Hugh Brown augured otherwise. Hubbart's efforts to deny the Court a repeat of the *Thompson v. Louisville* safe harbor in 1968's *Johnson* by providing a guilty suspect—freight car-tampering Raymond Smith—pushed him into other, equally dangerous, currents. By avoiding the Scylla of "no evidence," Hubbart came close to hitting the *Palmer/Coates* Charybdis of "conduct the legislature could clearly prohibit."

As a result, the justices questioned Hubbart more aggressively than they had Jacobson. "It was a 30 minute argument. And Justice White was all over me. I got 3 or 5 minutes into my argument and he started in." White, who had served as deputy attorney general of the United States and was generally conservative on criminal law and procedure, pressed on Smith's criminal conduct. As Hubbart recalled, White "asked if it was a lawful object to break into a railroad car. . . . I kept bringing it back to the statute but he wanted to talk about the facts. Only the facts." White's were the same concerns that had given the justices pause two years earlier when they authorized the stop and frisk in *Terry* and simultaneously left vagrancy laws intact in *Wainwright* and Hubbart's own *Johnson*. Though the justices had seemed to acknowledge in *Palmer* that *Terry* had obviated the need for crime control vagrancy laws, they still seemed somewhat hesitant on that score in both *Papachristou* and *Smith*. Just as the problems of vagrancy laws and their enforcers seemed of a piece to vagrancy law challengers, the problems of inadequate police power and necessary laws seemed of a piece to the justices.[42]

At least some of the justices found the looming choice between freeing obvious criminals and upholding a vagrancy law so unappealing that they began exploring the possibility of getting rid of Hubbart's case on some procedural ground. Both Hubbart and Assistant Attorney General Bailey opposed that outcome. Bailey told the Court, "I am inclined to urge this Court to go ahead and decide the case. . . . because the State of Florida is in the process and has been for a while of redrafting its vagrancy statute. We know other states are also in the process. There is some confusion among state legislatures because of recent opinions by this Court and they need some guidelines and this is the time when they're redrafting the vagrancy statutes."[43]

In *Papachristou*, Jacobson practically begged the Court to act. He argued that "only a declaration that the entire legislation is unconstitutional can prevent the daily flagrant abuse being wrought under it." The more piecemeal approach the Court had taken in the past seemed to Jacobson unlikely to work. "It has taken nearly three years for the cases at hand to reach their present posture. There is no reason to believe that new attacks could be moved more quickly. Nor is this Court in a position to entertain eighteen separate vagrancy cases" for each section of the law. "Most important, having regard for the people upon whom the brunt of vagrancy enforcement falls, there is no way to estimate how much abuse will be acquiesced in while a point-by-point attack is carried out." He concluded, "Vagrancy has troubled this Court for years, but the Court has always restrained itself. Petitioners hope that the Court's patience is now at an end and that it will here issue a declaration putting vagrancy to rest."[44]

Constitutionalizing the Vagrancy Law Challenge, Winter 1972

Some twenty years after Isidore Edelman first brought his vagrancy case to the Supreme Court, the Court did just that. The justices voted unanimously to strike down Jacksonville's vagrancy law as void for vagueness in *Papachristou*. In conference, Chief Justice Warren E. Burger announced that most vagrancy ordinances were "on their way out" and that the Jacksonville one "wins a prize."[45]

As the oral arguments had indicated, however, the justices' crime control concerns shaped their views of vagrancy laws and their enforcement. Take Harry Blackmun. He had not always been on board in vagrancy cases. He had gone along hesitantly in *Palmer* and dissented in *Coates*. But he found *Papachristou* easy. He wrote to himself, "I do not have very much difficulty with this case, and can easily vote to reverse it." The ordinance was "a wonderful composite of ancient words. It is almost limitless in its sweep, and affords police the authority to detain and arrest one for almost any conceivable and imagined offense. . . . Certainly this ordinance and the corresponding state statute are vague if any language ever is in this day and age. I am content to strike it as unconstitutional on its face. Actually, we should do so." Blackmun did not view his dissent in *Coates* "a barrier to [his] feeling this ordinance is overbroad," given that some of the law's "provisions really reached non-criminal conduct or, if you will, pro-tected conduct." Even so, some of the defendants clearly seemed easier calls to him than others. Papachristou "and her companions" were most sympathetic, as it seemed they "were really convicted for racial intermingling." That all of

Blackmun's questions for oral argument had concerned Hugh Brown, his nar-cotics charge, and his coverage under the ordinance reflected the justice's main hesitation.[46]

Accordingly, Blackmun found *Smith* harder than *Papachristou*. He wrote to himself, "I initially thought that [*Smith*] automatically would follow [*Papachristou*], but now I am not so sure." Wandering about a railroad yard with-out valid business "is the type of thing a vagrancy statute might lawfully aim at," so the law might facially apply to *Smith*. Ultimately, Blackmun predicted "that on the whole the Court will make *Papachristou* the pivotal case and will throw out the Jacksonville statute, and this one will disappear in the afterfall."[47]

Blackmun's prediction was almost exactly right. *Papachristou* (and the Jacksonville ordinance) became the headline case and *Smith* (and the Florida statute) the little-known companion. Where *Papachristou* generated consensus at conference, *Smith* generated confusion. By Burger's count, six of the seven jus-tices then on the Court—Lewis F. Powell Jr. and William H. Rehnquist had not yet replaced the recently retired and deceased Hugo Black and John Marshall Harlan II—voted to dismiss *Smith* as improvidently granted (DIG). In Douglas's view, a number of justices wanted to reverse, some were fine with either revers-ing or dismissing, and some preferred dismissal. Hubbart's strategy seemed on the verge of failure. His guilty client made the justices just as uncomfortable as his earlier innocent client had.[48]

When it came to deciding the cases, *Papachristou* was thus easier than *Smith*. But when it came time to draft the opinions, the opposite was true. Douglas wrote both. *Smith* went through a few drafts, largely as Douglas stripped away much of its content and played with dispositions that might avoid a DIG. At the end of the day, Douglas settled on vacating and remanding the case in light of *Papachristou*. All six other justices signed on.[49]

For *Papachristou*, the consensus of the conference vote threatened to dis-integrate when it came to the content of the opinion itself. The justices' crime control concerns completely disappeared as Douglas condemned the police and valorized alleged vagrants. Douglas, of the Hoboes of America and the riding-the-rails autobiography, of *Points of Rebellion* and a *Washington Post* story about his C&O Canal tramping, finally had an opportunity to constitutionalize not only his problems with vagrancy laws but also his vision of America, his vision of the sixties, his vision of what the sixties had brought to America. He planned to make the most of it.

Douglas was never one for taking direction. That trait was in full flower when he sat down to write *Papachristou* in December of 1971. As the conference vote had recommended, Douglas's early drafts discussed vagueness. But that was only the beginning.

Douglas had a larger goal for this opinion. He wanted to identify a new set of constitutionally protected, fundamental, individual rights. Before 1972, the Court's hint in *Griswold v. Connecticut* of a new generation of rights had remained just that: a hint. Though Sam Jacobson had occasionally suggested that vagrancy laws violated such rights in *Papachristou*, and other lawyers and scholars had occasionally offered up similar arguments over the course of the vagrancy law challenge, these arguments had remained largely undeveloped and unlikely to succeed. In fact, Louis Lusky had probably resisted challenging the constitutionality of Louisville's loitering ordinance in 1960's *Thompson v. Louisville* in part to avoid the possibility of just such an argument.[50]

Now, as Douglas wrote *Papachristou*, he made clear that the problem with the Jacksonville ordinance was not just that it was hard for potential targets to understand and police officers to enforce. It was also, and perhaps even predominantly, that the law criminalized certain conduct that could not be criminalized because it was constitutionally protected. In articulating the content of such fundamental rights, Douglas seemed to be trying both to identify what freedom was lost to vagrancy regulation and to distill some essence of the "sixties" into a constitutional right. This was no small task—articulating an essential right from the chaotic events of a chaotic decade. Even as vagrancy laws had served as something of a unifying target for many of the social movements of the era, each movement had simultaneously pointed in multiple and disparate directions.

What Douglas settled on was a constellation of rights around the idea of being out of place, both physically and metaphorically. He described activities like "walking, strolling, wandering, [and] loafing" as "historically part of the amenities of life contained in those rights 'retained by the peopl[e]' within the meaning of the Ninth Amendment." People were entitled, Douglas intimated, to be out of place in public space. Linking that physical liberty to a right to be out of place culturally, socially, or politically, he continued, "These unwritten amenities have been in part responsible for giving our people the feeling of independence and self-confidence, the feeling of creativity. These amenities have dignified the right of dissent and have honored the right to be nonconformists and the right to defy submissiveness. They have encouraged lives of high spirits rather than hushed, suffocating silence."[51]

This was a capacious understanding of individual rights that sounded in both mobility and nonconformity. The concern with mobility came directly out of the vagrancy law challenge itself and Douglas's own self-conception as a wanderer and champion of wanderers. The Jacksonville ordinance was typical in prohibiting wandering about with no apparent purpose, and mobility had been a common theme in the vagrancy law challenge. Over the course of more than thirty years on the bench, Douglas had been the spokesman for the widely held idea that the right to travel was constitutionally protected and crucially important to some deep American spirit. As early as 1941 in *Edwards v. California*, Douglas rhapsodized about the "right to move freely from State to State." In the 1965 civil rights case of *Shuttlesworth v. Birmingham*—in which the only mobility consisted of Shuttlesworth pausing on a street corner in his home city—Douglas nonetheless described the United States as "a country where freedom of locomotion is honored." The following year in the counter-culture case of *Hicks v. District of Columbia*, Douglas came closest to articulating the American mythology of the expansive frontier that he would embrace in *Papachristou* when he described the "incongruity in superimposing the English anti-migratory policy upon the law of America." Douglas must have been delighted when Justice Byron White's join memo for *Papachristou* was addressed to "Bill*," with the handwritten footnote specifying Bill Douglas and not Bill Brennan as "*the walking and strolling one."[52]

This constellation of rights went far beyond literal mobility, however. Such freedom, both for Douglas himself and for the vagrancy law challenge writ large, had as much to do with lofty ideals of individualized self-fulfillment as with physical movement for its own sake. Recall that in Douglas's construction of his identity, he was not only a perpetual wanderer but a perpetual rebel as well. He saw a straight line from Henry David Thoreau and Walt Whitman—whose "Excursions" and "Song of the Open Road" he cited in *Papachristou*—through himself to the Beats and the hippies. Douglas's advocacy of nonconformity, tolerance, and pluralism and his rejection of the idea that difference was dangerous were deeply embedded in long-standing and common themes of American individualism. They were central to the vagrancy law challenge. And they were nearly pervasive, if hotly debated, during the long 1960s. Law professors wrote books called "The Right to Be Different." Anthropologists created matrices in which hierarchy and coercive community were pitted against egalitarianism and individuation.[53]

Douglas's decades-long friendship with Charles Reich reinforced this relationship between physical mobility and cultural transgression—even as Douglas took his inspiration more from the rugged individualism of the frontier and Reich took his more from newly emerging lifestyles. From Douglas's *Hicks* dissent to Reich's anti-police-questioning *Yale* article to Douglas's *Points of Rebellion* to Reich's *Greening of America* to Douglas's opinion in *Papachristou*, Reich and Douglas seemed to share a conversation about the youth culture, the state of the nation, the importance of the wanderer, and constitutional protections for the whole shebang. They shared an outlook, a vocabulary, and an attitude toward the protagonists on both sides of the vagrancy battle.[54]

As Douglas used *Papachristou* to identify this radical new set of rights as fundamentally antagonistic to the vagrancy law regime, he tried to integrate the rights into the existing structure of constitutional doctrine. First Amendment ß

Supreme Court of the United States
Washington, D. C. 20543

CHAMBERS OF
JUSTICE BYRON R. WHITE

February 8, 1972

Re: No. 70-5030 - Papachristou v.
     City of Jacksonville

Dear Bill:

     Please join me in your

January 28, 1972, circulation in

this case.

                         Sincerely,

                         B.R.W.

Mr. Justice Douglas

cc: Conference

* the walking and strolling one

Figure 9.1 Memo from Justice Byron White to Justice William O. Douglas joining Douglas's majority opinion invalidating a vagrancy law in *Papachristou v. Jacksonville*. Douglas, who fashioned himself something of a vagrant, must have been tickled at the way White distinguished him from the Court's other "Bill," Justice William J. Brennan Jr., by calling Douglas "the walking and strolling one." William O. Douglas Papers, Library of Congress.

rights to speech and assembly had achieved "preferred" status by the 1940s, but over the course of the 1960s, the justices had added other rights they had deemed worthy of special constitutional protection. Douglas suggested that the same kind of heightened scrutiny that the Court had applied to already established rights should apply to these new ones as well. "As we have often stated, laws in more sensitive areas, such as walking, strolling, wandering, loafing, must be narrowly drawn to meet a precise evil."[55]

Even as Douglas identified these new rights and assimilated them into an existing constitutional framework, he remained uncertain about the specific doctrinal basis for their protection. A Franklin D. Roosevelt appointee who had arrived on the Court just after it had ceased using substantive due process to thwart economic regulation, Douglas, like Lusky, had long resisted the siren call of a potentially expansive due process clause. Indeed, between the late 1930s and 1971, the Court in general had continued to disparage the economic substantive due process rights the Court had earlier protected in cases like *Lochner v. New York*. The rights the Court had safeguarded instead—those of racial minorities and free speakers—had generally echoed Louis Lusky's suggestions in *Carolene Products*'s footnote four.[56]

With substantive due process still a bugaboo, Douglas's initial instinct in *Papachristou* was to avoid it. Still, he was not sure where to turn. After some vacillation, he did invoke it, but he also relied on the Ninth Amendment—which suggested that the Constitution might protect rights not explicitly mentioned. Whatever the remaining doctrinal uncertainties, Douglas's first stab at *Papachristou* made clear that he deemed vagrancy laws inimical to an emerging conception of individual rights.[57]

As Douglas was constructing his new rights and wrestling with their constitutional basis, the fate of his efforts became entwined with other cases at the Court in the winter of 1971. Two weeks before the Court heard arguments in *Papachristou* and *Smith*, it heard arguments challenging a state law restricting the distribution of contraception in *Eisenstadt v. Baird*. Even more significant was another argument the Court heard the week after *Papachristou*: the Texas case of *Roe v. Wade*, which raised the question of whether abortion prohibitions violated women's fundamental rights.[58]

On the surface, *Papachristou*'s concerns with loafing, wandering, and living a life of high spirits might seem to have little in common with the regulation of sexuality and reproduction. On the most concrete level, however, as the Jacksonville foursome and the earlier prostitution vagrancy cases revealed, vagrancy laws were often used to regulate sexuality. Such laws criminalized the sexual choices of Papachristou and her companions, just as the contraceptive and abortion laws criminalized the choices of the petitioners in the other cases.[59]

In fact, to both Douglas and Justice William J. Brennan Jr., who was writing the opinion in *Eisenstadt*, the *Roe/Eisenstadt/Papachristou* connection was far more fundamental than a quirk of the facts. It went to central questions in both sets of cases: what were fundamental rights, and what in the Constitution, if anything, justified their protection? In both contexts, the laws at issue criminalized people or conduct that commentators at the time described as at least "victimless" in the H. L. A. Hart sense and perhaps even constitutionally protected.[60]

In both vagrancy and abortion cases, moreover, the justices were ambivalent about whether even to broach the fundamental rights issue. While Douglas intended to do so in *Papachristou*, the conference vote there had been limited to vagueness. The opposite was true for abortion: despite an apparent focus on fundamental rights at conference, Justice Harry A. Blackmun's initial efforts for the majority in *Roe* originally relied on vagueness precisely to avoid "the more complex" issue of fundamental rights.[61]

A remarkable eleven-page memo from Brennan to Douglas shows how the Court's simultaneous consideration of *Roe, Eisenstadt,* and *Papachristou* led Brennan to agree with Douglas that the time was right to articulate new fundamental rights. Where most Supreme Court memos hewed closely to a single case, this memo did not. Writing after Douglas sent him a preview of his *Papachristou* draft, Brennan took the *Papachristou/Roe* convergence as an opportunity to propose a holistic theory of constitutional rights. Like Douglas, Brennan was still doctrinally ambivalent, wavering between the Ninth and Fourteenth Amendments. On the substance, where Douglas began with the vagrancy defendant's rights to mobility and moved outward from there, Brennan began with the idea of privacy that *Roe* had inherited from *Griswold* and other prior cases. Brennan described privacy as "a species of liberty" and identified "three groups of fundamental freedoms that 'liberty' encompasses." The first group included "freedom from bodily restraint or inspection, freedom to do with one's body as one likes, and freedom to care for one's health and person." The second group included "freedom of choice in the basic decisions of life, such as marriage, divorce, procreation, contraception, and the education and upbringing of children." The third group included "autonomous control over the development and expression of one's intellect and personality." Brennan thought that the decision to have an abortion "obviously fits directly within each of the categories of fundamental freedoms," and therefore "should be held to involve a basic individual right."[62]

Other than a reference to a 1928 opinion of Justice Louis Brandeis about a "right to be let alone," most of the cases Brennan invoked, like most of those Douglas cited in his *Papachristou* draft, were of recent vintage. More than a decade of piecemeal but dramatic Supreme Court elaboration of new constitutional interpretations in areas ranging from race discrimination to free speech to criminal procedure to sexuality called out for greater systematic consideration and articulation. To Douglas and Brennan, the presence of *Roe* and *Papachristou* at the Court together seemed to enhance the chances that the Court would actually attempt such a task in one case, the other, or both.[63]

As it turned out, the *Roe/Papachristou* convergence marked a narrowing of the broadest notions of individual freedom that the vagrancy epic helped to inspire.

Even as Brennan shared Douglas's enthusiasm for new constitutional protections for individual rights, he speculated that other justices might not. With the addition to the Court of the four more conservative Nixon appointees—Chief Justice Burger and his "Minnesota Twin" Blackmun, as well as Rehnquist and Powell—the center of gravity was clearly shifting to the right. Thinking strategically about how that shift might affect these cases, Brennan sent Douglas another memo after reading Douglas's *Papachristou* draft. "I think *Papachristou* is just fine. As I recall[,] vagueness was the consensus ground at conference. Will the 'fundamental rights' approach scare away votes? It keys in so perfectly with my views in the abortion cases that I fervently hope not. Does the possible risk argue for holding up circulation until Harry's Texas case comes around[?]" "Harry's Texas case" was Blackmun's *Roe*. Brennan was clearly worried that agreement on fundamental rights might be more fragile than Douglas realized. To the extent that Blackmun circulating *Roe* and Douglas circulating *Papachristou* simultaneously might just shatter that agreement, Brennan seemed to think *Roe* either less controversial or more important than *Papachristou*.[64]

Douglas, who tended to be less politic and more iconoclastic than Brennan, ignored Brennan's warning and sent his draft to the full Court anyway. As circulated, the opinion dealt with protected rights in two steps. First, after discussing walking, strolling, loafing, and wandering, as well as the importance of dissent and nonconformity, it stated, "The difficulty is that these activities are historically part of the amenities of life as we have known it. They are not mentioned in the Constitution or in the Bill of Rights." That seemed to acknowledge that Douglas intended to protect unwritten rights. The second step was to conclude that "these amenities are so basic and elemental in our scheme of values that . . . they are part of the 'liberty' of the individual that is protected by the Due Process Clause of the Fourteenth Amendment against infringement by the States." Whether he envisioned the change as a concession to Brennan's fears about *Roe*, a resistance to them, or neither, the result was a much-clarified doctrinal basis for the opinion. The Ninth Amendment was gone. Douglas had finally succumbed to substantive due process.[65]

Douglas's changes notwithstanding, Brennan had been right to worry. It was Eisenhower-appointee and longtime Warren Court moderate Potter Stewart, rather than the new conservatives, who objected to Douglas's approach in *Papachristou*. In recent years, Stewart had become a relatively aggressive participant in the anti-vagrancy law challenge. He had written the majority opinion in *Shuttlesworth*, joined the majority in *Palmer*, and angrily defied the chief justice to lead the majority in *Coates*. Now he signed on to *Papachristou*, however, only to the extent that it held "the ordinance before us to be unconstitutionally vague." In other words, he rejected that part of Douglas's holding that relied on fundamental rights.[66]

Stewart did not explain his opposition. Perhaps he was committed to continuing the vagueness approach he had used in *Coates* because it would apply to a broader swath of vagrancy challenges than any particular individual right. Perhaps he thought vagueness the more effective way to control police discretion. Though both vagueness and substantive due process regulated the police by regulating legislatures, vagueness analyzed a law's effects not only on the conduct of those it regulated but also on the power of those who enforced it. Alternatively, Stewart might have hesitated to embrace the entire project of reviving fundamental rights. Stewart had been galled by the justices' apparent fishing expedition to find some rationale for the *Griswold* decision, and in criminal procedure cases, he had objected to finding a *"general* right to privacy" in the Constitution. He had seemed open to certain types of public rights in *Coates*, where he suggested that the public sphere had to allow those with alternative "lifestyle[s]" to "annoy" the more conventional. That case turned on vagueness and overbreadth, however, and *Papachristou* might have prompted him to draw the line at explicit constitutional rights protection. Or perhaps Stewart agreed with Douglas that something substantive was at stake, but he disagreed about— or had trouble identifying—precisely what the substantive problem was. Anthony Amsterdam had suggested in his 1960 note that vagueness often hid substantive concerns. Perhaps Stewart preferred to leave those concerns hidden. If so, there would have been some irony to the possibility that vagueness doctrine criticized legislatures for failing to define precisely what they were prohibiting even while the Court refused to define precisely what it was protecting.[67]

By the time *Roe* was finally decided in early 1973—after reargument before a full Court of nine justices—the fundamental rights implicated by abortion laws had garnered the votes that Douglas failed to secure in the vagrancy context. Justice Stewart now joined the majority in finding a "right to privacy . . . in the Fourteenth Amendment's concept of personal liberty." Perhaps between his opposition to finding such rights in *Papachristou* and his (still somewhat reluctant) embrace in *Roe*, Stewart had been worn down by time and necessity. Or perhaps he viewed the liberty protected in *Roe*—which in his view encompassed a relatively narrow category of "personal choice in matters of marriage and family life"—as preferable to, more limited than, or more important than "the right to be nonconformists and the right to defy submissiveness" that Douglas had proposed in *Papachristou*.[68]

Whatever had made Stewart balk in *Papachristou* but not *Roe*, Douglas changed his *Papachristou* opinion to keep Stewart, as well as others who might have silently agreed, on board. For some twenty years, Douglas had been dissenting from denials of certiorari and dismissals of cases as improvidently granted. He had gone along with narrow reversals and pushed for broader grounds. He had kept a subject file entitled "Vagrancy," had made speeches on the topic and published them in law reviews. So close to resolution, Douglas was not going to let this one get away. *Papachristou's* sole constitutional basis in the final opinion was that the "ordinance [was] void for vagueness" because of both its lack of notice to ordinary people and its licensing of "arbitrary and erratic arrests and convictions."[69]

The end result of the *Papachristou/Roe* convergence, then, was not the whole-sale elevation of all the fundamental rights Douglas and Brennan had in mind. Doctrinally, the two cases switched places. *Roe* admitted its embrace of funda-mental rights, while *Papachristou's* reliance on vagueness masked the connec-tions between *Papachristou* and the new fundamental rights in *Roe*. On the basis of an unwritten right to privacy that Louis Lusky would decry for the rest of his life, the *Roe* Court instructed legislatures that they could no longer prohibit all abortions. They could regulate abortions only so long as they did not violate fundamental rights. In *Papachristou*, by contrast, the Court told legislatures not that certain conduct was protected, but that they had to prohibit it with greater specificity. *Roe*, not *Papachristou*, became the canonical case that articulated new constitutional rights.

As for the content of those rights, *Roe* represented a narrow and limited ver-sion of what Douglas had suggested in his *Papachristou* draft and Brennan in his memo to Douglas. In *Papachristou*, Douglas had not shied away from the wide-ranging and publicly expressed rights that had run through the vagrancy law challenge. Douglas's Constitution would protect people who engaged in unconventional behavior—or simply were unconventional, even "undesir-able"—precisely where others could, and likely would, have to encounter them. *Roe* embraced only a segment of those rights. It became a protector of "privacy" of a certain kind—that closely linked to marital and family life.[70]

Even as *Roe* narrowed the rights implicit in *Papachristou*, it nonetheless revealed how instrumental the vagrancy law challenge had been to the revival of substantive freedom. *Roe's* elaboration of new fundamental rights was forged at a moment when vagrancy litigation had put such rights squarely in the justices' line of vision. In a concurrence in *Roe*, Douglas closely tracked the taxonomy of constitutionally protected "liberty" Brennan had proposed in his lengthy memo. Douglas departed from Brennan's vision most sharply where *Papachristou* was concerned. Douglas added to the "freedom to care for one's health and person" and "freedom from bodily restraint or compulsion" the public rights he had envi-sioned in *Papachristou*. Quoting *Papachristou*, he called "walking, strolling, and wandering" "historically part of the amenities of life as we have known them." Although the final draft of *Papachristou* had not constitutionalized these "rights," Douglas's earlier drafts remained alive in his reimagining and reworking of the opinion. Douglas's opinion in *Roe* reads as if his draft of *Papachristou* had actu-ally been published.[71]

Papachristou and the Long 1960s

To describe *Papachristou* in terms of its relationship to *Roe* risks obscuring what *Papachristou* did on its own terms: after twenty years of false starts and hesitations, the Supreme Court unanimously struck down a vagrancy law on its face. Sam Jacobson was jubilant—the Court had overcome its "piece-meal" approach and "knocked out" the law in its entirety. To most observers, *Papachristou*'s import was as described in a front-page headline in the *New York Times*: "Broad Ruling Expected to Void Many Similar Statutes across the Nation." *Papachristou* was "a sweeping new application of the Constitution in the field of criminal law."[72]

Those who had even casually followed the vagrant winds of change, however, recognized that *Papachristou* manifested no abrupt departure. Despite the fanfare, the end of vagrancy laws already seemed inevitable to many. The Nixon appointees to the Burger Court were clearly more conservative than the liberals who had dominated the Warren Court, and observers were already noting the Court's move to the right. But by the time the Burger Court got to the vagrancy question, and in contrast to the Warren Court's repeated hesitations, the answer already seemed overdetermined. One observer concluded that even if Nixon's newest conservative appointees, Rehnquist and Powell, had participated in *Papachristou*, the case "doubtless" would have remained unanimous.[73]

Those who had been paying particularly close attention—the legal scholars, lawyers, judges, and commentators with stakes in the cases or especially astute sensibilities—would also have seen something else in *Papachristou*. They would have seen the imprint of the cumulative and overlapping movements, campaigns, and litigation efforts that had made the vagrancy law challenge and *Papachristou* itself what it was. Twenty years earlier, when Douglas and Black had first dissented from the dismissal of Isidore Edelman's case in 1953, they had thought about the problem largely in terms of Edelman's own free speech context. Moreover, they could muster few citations for their position. In 1972, the Supreme Court opinion that finally and somewhat belatedly answered the call of that dissent looked dramatically different. It was shot through with quotes from seminal anti-vagrancy law articles by Foote, Amsterdam, Reich, and California's Arthur Sherry, and from key Supreme Court dissents in *Edelman* and *Hicks*. The Supreme Court citation of an article (by Amsterdam) entitled "Crimes of Obnoxiousness, Crimes of Displeasing Police Officers, and the Like," would have been unthinkable twenty years earlier. One can imagine Douglas's glee when he included it.[74]

In part, the differences between *Edelman* and *Papachristou* were due to Jacobson's success in putting together such a wide-ranging package of defendants. They were also due to what had transpired both within and outside the

Court during the intervening years. In the past, vagrancy arrests had flown under the radar of public consciousness. Now such arrests served to make visible growing contradictions between vagrancy laws and changing concepts of constitutional rights and criminal law and procedure. The magnitude of the problem was now apparent, a fact Douglas emphasized by citing statistics that showed around 100,000 people arrested for vagrancy in each of the previous three years.[75]

The complexity of the vagrancy law problem—and the many functions the vagrancy law regime served—was equally apparent if one knew where to look. Take free speech. *Papachristou* was nobody's idea of a free speech case. Nonetheless, those who had been following anti-vagrancy law litigation for the previous two decades would have seen the role free speakers had played. In the form of Jimmy Lee Smith, the organizer for a "Negro political group" who had suffered a vitriolic harangue from the trial judge, they would have seen all of the political dissidents felled or stymied by vagrancy suppression: civil rights activists Ruth Tinsley and Fred Shuttlesworth, soapboxing Wobblies, organizing farmworkers, communists like Isidore Edelman, and anti-war protestors like Dennis Coates. Such suppression was deeply suspicious to a Court that had expanded First Amendment protections in the decades after World War II. When Douglas condemned vagrancy and loitering laws as "a convenient tool for 'harsh and discriminatory enforcement by local prosecuting officials, against particular groups deemed to merit their displeasure,'" he alluded in *Papachristou* to these generations of "vagrant" free speakers. Insiders would have recognized that quote from the labor organizing case of *Thornhill v. Alabama* and the mention of "a regime in which the poor and the unpopular are permitted to 'stand on a public sidewalk . . . only at the whim of any police officer'" from the civil rights case of *Shuttlesworth*.[76]

Shuttlesworth's presence in *Papachristou* signaled to the cognoscenti not only the historically free speech-suppressing function of vagrancy laws, but also the laws' role in regulating race more broadly. The persistence of vagrancy arrests of African Americans into the civil rights era had exposed the fundamental role of vagrancy laws in keeping African Americans physically, geographically, economically, socially, sexually, and culturally in place. Though Douglas did not articulate this challenge to vagrancy regulation of race in explicit analytical terms—perhaps he worried that readers might unduly limit the case to its racial implications—the facts spoke for themselves to anyone who had come across the outrageous and much-publicized arrests of civil rights leaders in private homes. Indeed, virtually every law clerk, justice, newspaper reporter, and legal scholar who commented on the case highlighted the facts of Papachristou and her friends. They described the foursome as having been, in Blackmun's words, "really convicted for racial intermingling." Douglas's prominent recitation of the circumstances of the interracial arrests thus confirmed what the vagrancy law challenge and *Shuttlesworth* itself had already foreshadowed: that in the wake of the civil rights struggle, north and south, east and west, the Constitution constrained the police as much as the legislature, the vagrancy law as much as the anti-miscegenation law, from translating racial mores into racial law.[77]

It was less Jacobson's facts than Douglas's reflections on them that hinted at the fundamental objection within the vagrancy law challenge to ideas about poverty and the poor. Despite the centrality of idle poverty to the vagrancy concept, and the Court's own protection of the poor in other contexts, the Court had not decided a poverty-focused vagrancy case since 1960's *Thompson v. Louisville*. It had DIG'ed *Arceneaux v. Louisiana*, remanded *Lazarus*, and denied certiorari in a number of cases. During that time, one of the things that had become clear was that full-throated defenses of the criminalization of poverty had diminished in both frequency and ferocity. The welfare rights movement, poverty lawyers, social workers and advocates, and government agencies and officials in the War on Poverty had made almost incomprehensible the fundamental basis of the criminalization of idle poverty. The decriminalization of vagrancy was equally important at the other end of the economic spectrum—where it potentially legitimated the unemployment essential to a rising free market ideology. "The conditions which spawned these laws may be gone," Douglas wrote in *Papachristou*, "but the archaic classifications remain." Quoting *Edwards v. California*, he announced that "the theory of the Elizabethan poor laws no longer fits the facts." He echoed the vagrancy critique of those forced into idleness through unemployment—"unemployed people out of the labor market, by reason of a recession or disemployed by reason of technological or so-called structural displacements"—as well as those, like handyman Sam Thompson, who in some sense had chosen what might seem to others a life of undue material deprivation. Those in the know would have recognized Anthony Amsterdam's words when Douglas condemned the presumption that " 'if some carefree type of fellow is satisfied to work just so much, and no more, as will pay for one square meal, some wine, and a flophouse daily, but a court thinks this kind of living subhuman, the fellow can be forced to raise his sights or go to jail as a vagrant.' "[78]

The tolerance for nonconformity, for the idiosyncratic or culturally overdetermined choice, was apparent to the vagrancy challenge insider far beyond choices an individual might make about his or relationship to the market. Though there were no Beats or hippies in *Papachristou*, Papachristou and her companions' flouting of racial and sexual mores made them nonconformists nonetheless. And though Douglas omitted the doctrine of fundamental rights at Stewart's request, his published *Papchristou* opinion still read as a fervent defense of both physical freedom and cultural nonconformity. It continued to describe wandering, strolling, and loafing as "historically part of the amenities of life as we have known them." To the surprise of some commentators, a unanimous

Burger Court glorified the "independence," "self-confidence," "creativity," and "nonconformi[ty]" that such mobility both depended upon and enhanced. Douglas condemned the Jacksonville authorities for using the vagrancy law to require people "to comport themselves according to the lifestyle deemed appropriate by the Jacksonville police and the courts."[79]

What might also have surprised avid watchers of vagrancy law challenges, though not observers of Douglas himself, was Douglas's complete rejection of the compromise position—frequently staked out by law enforcement advocates—that gave up social control vagrancy policing but retained vagrancy laws for crime control purposes. Despite the justices' considerable anxiety about defendants like Hugh Brown in *Papachristou*, one could scour Douglas's opinion and find no sign of concern about withdrawing vagrancy authority for major crime control. Douglas found that a "presumption that people who might walk or loaf or loiter or stroll or frequent houses where liquor is sold, or who are supported by their wives or who look suspicious to the police are to become future criminals is too precarious for a rule of law." He also argued that "arresting a person on suspicion" was "foreign to our system. . . . A direction by a legislature to the police to arrest all 'suspicious' persons would not pass constitutional muster. A vagrancy prosecution may be merely the cloak for a conviction which could not be obtained on the real but undisclosed grounds for the arrest." After *Papachristou*, vagrancy laws no longer authorized the police to arrest and convict for either "past" or "future" criminality. *Papachristou* thus finally consummated the stop-and-frisk-for-vagrancy swap the Court had resisted since at least 1968. After *Terry*, the police could stop and frisk suspects without probable cause. But after *Papachristou*, vagrancy laws no longer provided either an alternative or a backstop.[80]

Indeed, even as the vagrancy law challenge had come to attack vagrancy laws rather than police power, it was possible to see in Douglas's opinion—if one had been educated about where to look by Louis Lusky, Ernest Besig, Caleb Foote, and others—the point that the vagrancy law problem was really two related problems: the laws and the people who enforced them. The problem, Douglas noted, inhered partly in the lower courts, in "the procedural laxity which permits 'conviction' for almost any kind of conduct." The vagrancy law challenge had made clear that even such trivial charges as vagrancy, as Douglas put it in a case extending the right to counsel, "often bristle[d] with thorny constitutional questions." Even more pointedly, *Papachristou* highlighted the deep skepticism of the police that was a hallmark of both the vagrancy law challenge and many of the social movements of the era. Douglas, the lone dissenter in *Terry*, had never accepted the licensing of increased police power. In *Papachristou*, he took the opportunity to speak for the whole Court—and the whole Court allowed him—in condemning "the unfettered discretion [the vagrancy law] places in the hands of the Jacksonville police." Though Douglas's colleagues did not all fully share Douglas's distrust of the police—just four months after *Papachristou*, the Court reaffirmed *Terry* for the first time—such distrust was visible in other invalidations of petty criminal laws. Speaking for the Court, the Nixon-appointed Justice Powell commented that another low-level offense the Court invalidated "tend[ed] to be invoked only where there is no other valid basis for arresting an objectionable or suspicious person." As the vagrancy law challenge had taught in so many cases and so many places over the prior twenty years, "The opportunity for abuse, especially where a statute has received a virtually open-ended interpretation, is self-evident."[81]

The truly sophisticated *Papachristou* reader would have seen that the real culmination of the vagrancy law challenge lay not in the opinion's allusions to any one of the social transformations that had produced it but in their simultaneous appearance in a single opinion. Quoting Foote's flagship 1956 article, Douglas reflected that vagrancy laws acted upon "a motley assortment of human troubles" and offered imprisonment "for problems that appear to have no other immediate solution." When Douglas described the types of people "generally implicated by the imprecise terms of the ordinance," then, people who would otherwise occupy distinct legal, social, and cultural space came together: "the poor among us, the minorities, the average house-holder"; the "vaguely undesirable" and the "so-called undesirables"; "particular groups deemed to merit [official] displeasure"; "the poor and the unpopular"; and "poor people, nonconformists, dissenters, [and] idlers." All those who could not "comport themselves according to the lifestyle deemed appropriate by the Jacksonville police and the courts" were understood together as targets of vagrancy laws and dangers to the status quo. They were the people with whom Douglas identified, the people whose "independence," "self-confidence," "creativity," and "nonconformity" were threatened by vagrancy's reservoir of coercive police power.[82]

This is not to say, of course, that astute observers would have found references to every aspect of the vagrancy law challenge in *Papachristou*. They might have been disappointed that, for some reason—out of an effort to make *Papachristou* seem more innovative than it was, annoyance at how long it took the Court to get at the problem, or sheer laziness—Douglas failed to cite many of the state and federal cases that had paved the way. Moreover, the opinion omitted reference to many of the types of constitutional claims that lawyers and judges had proposed over the years. Notably absent was any comment on one of the most prominent constitutional arguments: that vagrancy laws constituted status crimes, and that status crimes were unconstitutional. Perhaps Douglas thought the public drunkenness case of *Powell v. Texas* had cast too much doubt on the fledgling doctrine. Perhaps the mix of status and conduct in the *Papachristou* defendants' arrests made it unevenly applicable. In any event, though one might—and some did—read Douglas's thorough condemnation of Jacksonville's ordinance as a condemnation of status crimes, the opinion avoided any explicit invocation of the argument.[83]

Most consequentially, observers would have missed some of the movements that had raised significant vagrancy law challenges. Poverty was present but not drunkenness or prostitution; drug possession but not addiction; interracial sex but not women's rights. Even as the Court had begun inching toward special constitutional scrutiny of sex discrimination, for example, this movement was still tentative and could barely be detected in *Papachristou*. Papachristou and Calloway's story was not a lesson about women's empowerment. It was a lesson about the South's continued resistance to racial integration. In addition, even as the Court's decision vindicated the sexual autonomy of *Papachristou* and her companions, Douglas offered no larger context within which to think about such autonomy and nowhere suggested how narrow or expansive it might be. In part, this was because *Papachristou* relied on vagueness, not fundamental rights. But in part, it was because of the limitations of the emerging fundamental rights doctrine itself. The Court had loosened strictures on sexuality in *Griswold*, *Eisenstadt*, and *Roe*. But this deregulation had remained bounded by notions of family, privacy, gender, and heterosexuality. Despite the efforts of gay rights advocates both before and after *Papachristou* to fit sexual orientation within that doctrinal framework and to challenge the use of vagrancy laws against gay men, lesbians, and "genuine transvestites," the Burger Court seemed as loath as its predecessor to accept arguments that any deregulation of sexuality should benefit sexual minorities. Even as observers could see in *Papachristou* many of the aspirations of the vagrancy law challenge, then, the limitations were equally present.[84]

Still, the overwhelming impression *Papachristou* offered vagrancy-law-challenge insiders was that the constitutional rules for how the frontline representatives of the state treated all people, and especially people out of place, had changed. *Papachristou* reflected crucial questions the challenge had raised about how to interpret the Constitution for a self-consciously new era, an era in which many, though emphatically not all, thought that the Constitution should provide protection for difference and a greater toleration for the danger that might accompany that difference.

This impulse toward greater toleration was apparent elsewhere in constitutional law in the years around *Papachristou*, once *Papachristou* taught one how to see it. Even as the Burger Court was already pulling back in some areas of Warren Court jurisprudence, it nonetheless continued to wrestle with a variety of constitutional questions the vagrancy law challenge had prominently raised. Whether the criminal law should be used for social control purposes was a question, for example, that extended far beyond vagrancy in the early 1970s. Support for some decriminalization was so widespread at the time that even Republican president Richard M. Nixon supported it. Before the Supreme Court had decided *Palmer v. Euclid, Coates v. Cincinnati,* or *Papachristou,* Nixon had told the National Conference on the Judiciary, "We have to find ways to clear the courts of the endless streams of what are termed 'victimless crimes' that get in the way of serious consideration of serious crimes. There are more important matters for highly skilled judges and prosecutors than minor traffic offenses, loitering and drunkenness."[85]

Within the Supreme Court, one could discern a clear decriminalization trend. In addition to the vagrancy cases, the status crime and notice cases of *Lanzetta v. New Jersey, Lambert v. California,* and *Robinson v. California*; the abortion and sexuality cases of *Griswold v. Connecticut, Eisenstadt v. Baird,* and *Roe v. Wade*; the anti-miscegenation cases of *McLaughlin v. Florida,* and *Loving v. Virginia*; and even *Yoder v. Wisconsin,* which shielded from criminal prosecution Amish parents who removed their teenagers from high school, all placed new limits on the states' power to criminalize. Taken separately those cases might have looked like vagueness or substantive due process or race equal protection or free exercise cases. They were. But they were also something else. They were part of a process of dismantling the criminal law as a method of social control. That process was incomplete even on its own terms—carving out mostly conventional sexual relations for protection, for example—and it never came to full fruition. It was nonetheless both significant in its own right and emblematic of the shift in orientation toward difference and danger. If vagrancy law, "the traditional wastebasket of the criminal law," could be constitutionalized, then anything could be.[86]

Protection for the alternative "lifestyle" Douglas invoked in *Papachristou*—so new a term that it was sometimes a single word, sometimes two, sometimes hyphenated, sometimes not—also popped up elsewhere in the Supreme Court reports during the 1970s. Suddenly people as different as women seeking abortions and *Yoder's* Amish parents seemed as entitled to their "preferred lifestyle" as the hippies and hoboes Justices Douglas and Stewart protected in vagrancy cases. In 1977, even such moderate legal scholars as J. Harvie Wilkinson III (appointed to the federal bench by Ronald Reagan in 1984) and University of Virginia law professor G. Edward White argued for greater "Constitutional Protection for Personal Lifestyles." With *Papachristou* prominently in their minds and their citations, they identified the ongoing trend toward such constitutional protection as among the most significant of the moment. Their understanding of the scope of the right to a lifestyle also echoed the vagrancy law challenge in assimilating the often distinctive concerns of the long 1960s. Protecting people on the basis of race, they wrote, "has the stated purpose of freeing persons from the bondage of racial and other stereotyping and of encouraging them to seek their destinies as individual human beings." Indeed, the scholars' main lament about *Papachristou* was that Justice Douglas—who had been the Court's most "ardent and explicit champion of lifestyle freedom"—had "left much in the way of stirring words and phrases, precious little in the way of analytic definition."[87]

Closely related to the question of protecting individuals' choices about how to live their lives was the question of whether particular types of people deserved, or needed, an extra measure of constitutional protection. Beginning in the mid-1960s, the Court had made clear that it would scrutinize governmental acts affecting racial minorities particularly carefully. By the early 1970s, many groups—women, the poor, hippies, children born to unmarried parents—were hoping for similar treatment. Though the Court had trouble rationalizing its decisions in these cases, it nonetheless found in favor of many of the unpopular groups seeking constitutional protection. That many of these contenders were the same ones involved in the vagrancy law challenge is no accident. While the end of vagrancy laws gave them a minimum baseline of toleration, they still hoped, and fought, for outright constitutional protection.[88]

The justices were thus struggling across a number of contexts to determine how, and to what extent, to constitutionalize the new pluralism it had helped cultivate during the long 1960s. As it turns out, *Papachristou* was less outlier or exception than epitome.

That is certainly what Justice Douglas thought. To the very end of his life, Douglas believed that of all of his opinions in thirty-six years on the Court, *Papachristou* best captured his view of the essence the long 1960s, the American spirit, and his own constitutional vision. Douglas had made efforts in a few other opinions in the early 1970s to identify and integrate what he saw as key aspects of the 1960s. None was as ambitious, as rhetorically stirring, or as close to his heart as *Papachristou*. When he died in 1980, Douglas left specific instructions for his funeral. They included the singing of Woody Guthrie's "This Land Is Your Land," often considered the national anthem of the left, with its "roam[ing]," "rambl[ing]" narrator "walking that ribbon of skyway." The Senate chaplain who eulogized Douglas quoted the justice's explanation for that choice: it represented "many of the freedoms that are explicit or implicit in the Constitution, such as the right to move from place to place to look for a job or to establish a new home, and the right to move interstate without payment of a fee, as some states within the last thirty years have tried to impose. In other words, it expressed the vagrancy issue as I have expressed it and as it has become ingrained in the law. See my opinion expressed in *Papachristou v. City of Jacksonville*." *Papachristou* was the opinion Douglas chose to represent his constitutional vision even at his death. He still treated the case as if it had managed to make that vision a reality.[89]

When Phil Hubbart returned to his work at the public defender's office after the Court's decisions in *Smith* and *Papachristou*, it quickly became clear that neither his own nor the larger vagrancy crusade was over. "Cities and states facing urban problems not touched by Lindsay or Whitman or Thoreau will be faced with a difficult task if they hope to create a valid anti-vagrancy law directed toward restraining muggings and street-gang crime by preventing them rather than punishing the perpetrators," commented one legal scholar. "Whether they can do it at all is certainly a question that the Court will be called upon to answer after the newly tailored statutes are offered for judicial evaluation."[90]

Indeed, almost as soon as the Florida Supreme Court reversed Raymond Smith's conviction on remand—and as Jacksvonville state attorney Edward Austin had predicted—the Florida legislature moved to replace at least the crime control function of its now invalid vagrancy law. As instructed by the Court, the legislature tried to come up with more specific—less vague—language that would authorize law enforcement to arrest in the presence of suspicion but the absence of probable cause. The state's new "loitering and prowling" law followed the Model Penal Code—making it "unlawful for any person to loiter or prowl in a place, at a time or in a manner not usual for law-abiding individuals, under circumstances that warrant a justifiable and reasonable alarm or immediate concern for the safety of persons or property in the vicinity."[91]

Hubbart challenged the new law just as he had the old. The Florida courts upheld it, distinguishing it from *Smith* and *Papachristou.* "We are not here dealing with the historical loitering and vagrancy statute that makes status a crime and gives uncontrolled discretion to the individual law enforcement officer to make the determination of what is a crime."[92]

A few years later, Hubbart won a seat on the court that had stymied him in so many vagrancy cases. As a judge, he again encountered the loitering and prowling law. In this new role, he found it hard to invalidate altogether—the law seemed to comply (just) with the Court's new rules. But he did narrow it. He warned that the law should not be used as "a catchall crime whereby a person may be charged and convicted by prosecutors when there is an insufficient basis to sustain a conviction on some other charge." He described the law as "plainly reach[ing] the outer limits of constitutionality."[93]

Sam Jacobson had brought *Papachristou* the case, and Bill Douglas had crafted *Papachristou* the opinion. But it was Phil Hubbart, first as lawyer and then as judge, who would join other state and local officials, legal professionals, laypeople, and law enforcement officers across the country in remaking the law in *Papachristou*'s image. Whatever that meant.

What it meant for Lorraine Papachristou became clear to her lawyer one day in the fall of 1971 when Sam Jacobson happened to walk into the restaurant near the Jacksonville courthouse where Papachristou was waiting tables. It was two years after her vagrancy arrest, and Papachristou recognized Jacobson immediately. She smiled at him. She was highly solicitous of him. As he was not the kind of man who usually captured the attention of attractive women like Papachristou, his lunch companions teased him that she had "taken a shine" to him. Finally, Papachristou realized that although she knew Jacobson, he had not recognized her. She said, "You don't remember me, do you? . . . Well, you're my lawyer." Jacobson, who had met Papachristou only once briefly in the Jacksonville municipal court while assessing her potential as a vagrancy law challenger, responded, "I'm sorry. I don't remember." She said, "I'm Lorraine Papachristou." Jacobson replied, "Well this is a coincidence, because your case is still going, and I just sent the briefs to the Supreme Court in Washington, and you're going to be famous."

Papachristou was not particularly pleased to hear that she might be famous for this particular incident. But after a moment, she started asking Jacobson questions. "What does it mean?" she wanted to know. "Do I have to go to Washington?" She left the table but returned a few minutes later. She said, "Tell me something. You go to Washington, and you win, and then it's over." Jacobson said that it would be. And she said, "If you lose, do I still have to do those ten days?" The question came as something of a surprise to Jacobson, who later recalled, "It's terrible to say it, but I had forgotten about those ten days. She had been a real live person, but to me she had been a battleground. . . . To me, it was a cause."[94]

To Papachristou, it had been a trial. The case had been hanging over her head for years. The city of Jacksonville had arrested, convicted, and demeaned her. Unless the Supreme Court intervened on her behalf, she would lose ten days of her life to the city jail. When the Court did intervene a few months later, it was Papachristou who called Jacobson. With Jacksonville's ordinance invalidated and her conviction reversed, she could put the case behind her.

In 1953, when Isidore Edelman had faced his own vagrancy charge, he had not been so lucky. Nor had most of the millions of others arrested for vagrancy in the intervening twenty years. Where earlier efforts to resist the vagrancy label had come to naught, now Papachristou's struggle not to be deemed a vagrant and a criminal had finally succeeded. Between *Edelman* and *Papachristou*, the country, the Constitution, and criminal law and procedure had changed in fundamental ways. Whatever the future would bring, one thing was clear: vagrancy laws, rather than the people they had long regulated, now seemed very much out of place.

Conclusion

The afterlife of the vagrancy law regime has in some sense mirrored the life, and death, of the regime itself. One of vagrancy law's most impressive feats during its reign was its relative obscurity—it systematically rendered itself invisible. The litigants, lawyers, and legislators who objected to vagrancy laws changed all that. They made the laws visible and, in doing so, made them illegitimate. It seems surprising, then, that the history of the regime and its demise has itself been relegated to relative obscurity in the intervening decades. It is not that vagrancy cases are completely unknown. *Papachristou v. Jacksonville* especially makes frequent if brief appearances in casebooks, treatises, and law review articles. But the cases, and the history that made them, are understood separately, mostly by legal specialists, only in their barest outlines, and often only for their most obvious consequences.[1]

This invisibility is partly a function of the campaign's own success. Once the Constitution no longer allowed the police to keep people in place with vagrancy laws, the various groups that had converged on these laws no longer shared that common target. They shifted energies that had gone toward vagrancy challenges to resisting less universal legal strictures in a host of judicial and administrative forums. That fragmentation has made it hard to see vagrancy law as a coherent category with its own history. Scholars who have examined discrete parts of the story have divvied up the cases by litigant (civil rights protestor, skid row drunk, soapbox orator), constitutional claim (free speech, due process, criminal procedure), or historical framework (race, labor, poverty, crime, sexuality, geography). The various uses of vagrancy laws have accordingly been subsumed within, and viewed as adjuncts to, the specific contexts in which they arose.

What have we lost as a result of this disappearance, and what do we gain now that we have recovered the whole story? At the most general level, the history of vagrancy law and its downfall revises our sense of how legal change happens. Like most legal campaigns, this one did not appear fully formed with Isidore Edelman in 1949 and remain static until vindicated with Lorraine Papachristou in 1972. In fact, the campaign's relatively spontaneous and loosely networked

form made especially pronounced the contingencies always present when people try to change the law. As with most social problems that become constitutional ones, both the scope of the problem and the identity of the legal target
were initially unclear. When Al Wirin and Leo Gallagher first brought *Edelman
v. California* to the Supreme Court, vagrancy enforcement seemed limited to
a few types of undesirables: poor people, gangsters and other criminals, and
unpopular free speakers like Edelman. As vagrancy challengers emerged from
more and more social worlds, the scope of the challenge exploded. In mature
form in the early 1970s, the campaign implicated many of the era's key cultural
figures—Beats, hippies, New Left students, and war protestors; civil rights activists, Black Power adherents, and young, urban, minority men; poor people, prostitutes, single women, and sexual minorities.

At the same time, the vagrancy law challenge narrowed along other dimensions. When Ernest Besig first encountered vagrancy law in San Francisco in
the 1950s, he perceived a two-dimensional problem—an overly permissive law
and abusive law enforcers. He brainstormed numerous methods of solving that
problem—legislation, police reform, public education, and citizen complaint
boards, as well as constitutional litigation. Though the duality of law and law
enforcer remained a theme, the problem of vagrancy laws and the problem of
police discretion eventually diverged. Though litigation over procedural protections in the criminal justice system continued elsewhere, within the vagrancy
law challenge, the target narrowed. As the reform and control of police power
took on its own shape, as *Terry v. Ohio*'s "stop and frisk" put the Court on the side
of police authority on the street, and as vagrancy lawyers steeped in the constitutional possibilities of the 1960s looked optimistically toward a Warren Court
that seemed sympathetic to their critique, attacks on the constitutionality of the
laws crowded out other possible solutions to the problem.[2]

The recovery of these fluid and improvisational aspects of constitutional
change brings into relief two more specific, and very different, sets of insights and
questions. On the one hand, that so many diverse groups joined the campaign
changes our historical understanding of the 1960s. It highlights forgotten commonalities, reveals the law's centrality to the pre-1960s world, and suggests how
the vagrancy law challenge helped transform that world. On the other hand, the
campaign's eventual focus on invalidating vagrancy laws raises a distinct complex of issues: how much policing would change from what went before, as well
as what it might mean for litigation campaigns like this one that new forms of
power immediately tried to fill the void that vagrancy law's downfall left behind.

Much has been written about the 1960s, but like histories of vagrancy law itself,
sixties histories have largely been disjointed and partial. The sixties was the time
of the African American freedom struggle, or the time of the counterculture, the

student movement, and the Vietnam War. It was the time when gay men and lesbians openly embraced their liberation, or when women demanded equality. There is the early sixties and the late; the Warren Court and the Burger Court; the New Left and the emerging right; legitimate protest and violence and disorder.

In an effort to find unity, historians have recently described the era as a "movement of movements." Synthesis has nonetheless remained somewhat elusive. Certain aspects of "the sixties" still often stand in for the whole, other aspects get left out, and differences across movements resist attempts to find some plausible but abstract common ground. To some extent, that is because scholars remain somewhat preoccupied with close-to-the-ground sectarian concerns—about "liberal" versus "left" versus "conservative" contributions to the era. To some extent, it is because efforts to integrate often float above real people and events, articulated in global and abstract terms.[3]

Fragmentation is especially noticeable in legal histories of the era, which have mostly followed specific types of people seeking specific types of legal change. Each group or movement had discrete goals—of racial equality, sexual freedom, or a better standard of living—that made them target discrete laws—segregation laws, sodomy laws, or welfare regulations—enforced by different agencies and institutions—boards of education, "morals squads," or welfare agencies. Beginning with particular people, social movements, or reform efforts invites narrative and analytical isolation (if not chauvinism) and produces an image of the law as an agglomeration of disconnected and episodic mechanisms of oppression.[4]

The history—and especially the incredible breadth—of the vagrancy law challenge organically grounds and synthesizes these distinct histories. It allows us to understand how things actually worked into the 1960s, and how they then fell apart. Vagrancy law made an enormous legal bulls-eye in the center of the sixties dartboard. It provided a unifying target, forum, language, and set of institutional arrangements and personnel against which the movement of movements fought. It was not only that so many people of the era came up against these laws and tried to challenge them. It was also that in doing so, they did not treat themselves as insular movements with insular legal claims. The arguments they and their lawyers made crossed social boundaries and doctrinal categories, copied and compared, piggy-backed and built on. The usual process of analogical, common law, constitutional reasoning facilitated such integration. So did the fact that vagueness—the failure of the laws to adequately instruct either potential suspects or law enforcers about what was prohibited—became the dominant constitutional argument. Where other claims—of discrimination, privacy, or free speech—applied more to some litigants than to others, vagueness highlighted commonalities in both the experience of unwitting arrests and the exercise of unfettered discretion.

On a conceptual level as well, vagrancy law linked the various movements. Even as the many vagrancy law contenders had their own problems, goals, and constitutional claims—which sometimes conflicted with those of other contenders—vagrancy laws prompted convergence on the shared constitutional problem of being out of place. They forced alleged vagrants to ask how their difference made them dangerous, and how they might follow in the footsteps of those who seemed able to trade in that danger for constitutional protection. Vagrancy cases functioned as a common route through which marginal people created places for themselves, a manifestation of their claims to those places, and even a limit to the recognition of those places in the law. Though stories abound about the winners and losers in the new, more pluralist order—and especially about the consequences of the rise of "identity politics" for class politics—this history suggests that people who were out of place for very different reasons stood to gain together when vagrancy laws fell. The image of the 1960s that emerges from the vagrancy law challenge, then, is one of far more synthesis than previously recognized.[5]

Because it is the vagrancy law regime that does that work of integration, our image of the 1960s must also make room for a new understanding of the relationship between law and the great controversies of the era. It is not that law is absent from most sixties histories. Rather, its presence is often segmented and unacknowledged, its force intermittent. What the vagrancy law challenge shows is that the law's role in the hierarchies and inequalities of pre-1960s America was neither episodic nor limited to particular arenas of repression. Law—not just any law, but the coercive and always implicitly violent power of the criminal law—was ubiquitous. People were fighting not just specific types of law for specific groups, but a regime whose function had been to keep in check so many groups all at once.

The campaign against vagrancy laws was thus part of a generational battle about the circumstances under which people could be allowed to escape from such criminal law supervision, and how to tell when their escape was dangerous to, or merely uncomfortable for, mainstream Americans. Where did the need for security against danger end and the need for tolerance of pluralism begin? The line between the two had always been contested and shifting. It was particularly so during the long 1960s. And it was particularly so in the battles over vagrancy laws both because there the state's frontline defenders clashed directly with so many people out of place and because the vagrancy law challenge threatened to shift the line not with regard to one particular group of newly unruly people but virtually all of them.

The successful challenge to that extensive legal regime helped make both what we call "the sixties" and the world we know as our own. The end of the vagrancy law regime, the same regime that had been a fundamental component of the basic governing structures of English and then American society since the Elizabethan "rogues and vagabonds," amounted to a radical and fundamental historical break. That break was neither complete nor singular. Not everyone out of place now found constitutional embrace. Nor did the downfall of vagrancy laws transform the sixties on its own. The campaign's success was as much the result as the cause of the salient controversies of the time. It would have been inconceivable without the free speech revolution at mid-century, the civil rights movement a decade later, the welfare rights movement, the New Left, Second Wave feminism, gay liberation, and more.

Indeed, the claims of the vagrancy law challenge were as deeply limited as they were revolutionary. They were revolutionary in resisting the daily harassment and vulnerability that many people had long endured and that law enforcement had long taken for granted. Challengers argued that this hidden, ubiquitous, protean, criminal, four-hundred-year-old means of keeping people in place was no longer acceptable in a society in which place was, at the least, contested. The campaign's claims were nonetheless limited in that they did not demand complete equality, inclusion, or freedom. They sought only the barest immunity from limitless arrest under a single category of criminal law. In other words, neither the vagrancy law challenge nor "the sixties" it helped to make led to a society devoid of coercion, hierarchy, inequality, or exclusion.

Even so, ours is not the same world as the one in which Edelman was arrested in 1949 or Papachristou in 1969. It is sometimes hard to recall what the past looked like once it has receded. It is hard to recall that a beard, or a date, or a guitar made a person a criminal. It is hard to recall that millions of people were made vagrants simply for being who they were. Continuing disagreements about what else changed during the 1960s notwithstanding, the success of the vagrancy law challenge—limited as it was—meant that the United States Constitution no longer sanctioned this particular, systematic criminalization of nonconformity, dissent, and disorder. Even as today's debates over new issues of pluralism, toleration, and freedom bear the imprint of the vagrancy law challenge, they are different precisely because of its success. Vagrancy law's downfall was a critical part, perhaps even the epitome, of a new cultural baseline that has since been both frequently contested and utterly taken for granted.

If the expanding social reach of the vagrancy law campaign revises our understanding of the 1960s, the campaign's narrowing legal target—its ultimate convergence on the goal of invalidating vagrancy laws—raises questions about the decades that followed. The vagrancy law story prompts us to customize a perennial question for legal scholars and historians alike: how did the constitutional invalidation of vagrancy laws affect the world outside the law books?

That question has neither pat nor easy answers. On an individual level, the stories told here had as many endings as there were lives and litigants. Lorraine Papachristou is the poster child for the way we often imagine constitutional law to work. Recall that after the Supreme Court invalidated the Jacksonville ordinance under which she had been convicted, Papachristou no longer had to serve her ten-day sentence. That is not always how things turned out, though. The Court also vindicated Louisville's Sam Thompson. Yet, as we know, he found himself—or made himself, depending on one's perspective—repeatedly subject to further arrests. On the flip side is Tulane law student and suspected murderer Stephen Wainwright. A Massachusetts attorney by the time the Court dismissed his case, Wainwright stayed out of Louisiana, and he stayed out of jail. He only returned to New Orleans once, for a law school reunion. He and his wife stayed at the Royal Orleans Hotel and made sure to steer clear of the police. The different vagrancy fates of an anxious Papachristou, a resigned Thompson, and an indignant Wainwright no doubt had as much to do with who they were before their vagrancy arrests as with the outcomes of their cases. But that was the way of the vagrancy law regime: its wide-ranging operations made its relationship to the lives of its subjects, and to social life more generally, always varied and dynamic.

The diversity of these individual stories thus serves as a microcosm of the larger one. This book promised a messy history, and the end is no neater than the rest. Few of the lawyers who had targeted vagrancy laws had ever thought that a litigation victory would solve every aspect of the issue they were trying to address. Rather, as they analyzed the dualism of discretion-enhancing laws and discretion-exercising enforcers, many lawyers came to see constitutional litigation against the laws as particularly promising. It was. The lawyers also knew that it was not, could not be, was never thought to be, a comprehensive solution to the constellation of problems that had prompted and sustained the vagrancy law challenge. It wasn't.

The Supreme Court's embrace of new constitutional rules in *Coates, Palmer,* and *Papachristou* was only one moment in a contingent process of change that had begun long before and continued long after those decisions. The Court's pronouncements did not initiate the destruction of the vagrancy law regime. Lawyers, scholars, judges, legislators, and executive officials had already substantially undermined the regime before the Court offered its belated intervention. Nor did the Court's decisions either immediately or completely change every vagrancy law everywhere—on the books or in action. Some officials tenaciously enforced invalidated laws. They evaded the kind of constitutional litigation that would void vestigial laws. Even when they found themselves defending such laws in court, they occasionally managed to convince judges to let them stand.[6]

What the Court's decisions did do was constitutionalize a previously overlooked legal issue. They withdrew sanction for vagrancy laws, questioned the legitimacy of unfettered police discretion, reinterpreted the Constitution, and reframed debates going forward. In other words, people out of place gained a constitutional resource in future conflicts over state authority, and police departments and legislators lost one. As Anthony Amsterdam noted in 1973, vagrancy and related laws had "undergone a marked revolution, and unless the legislatures [got] busy with new statutes, specifically addressed . . . to legitimate state concerns, the courts [had] no option but to knock out the present statutes, even though they may not word-for-word track those that the Supreme Court [had] already invalidated."[7]

As state and local officials attempted to reconstitute some of the authority that had previously resided in vagrancy laws, many tried to follow Amsterdam's knowing advice. They took seriously the doctrines the vagrancy law challenge had produced and tried to fit new forms of vagrancy or loitering authority within the rules courts had established. Because the Court had determined that the critical problem with vagrancy laws was their vagueness, specificity was the principle of the moment. Specificity of language required a greater specificity of purpose than the now disgraced vagrancy laws had evinced. In an effort to construct legal authority that would serve some of the crime and social control purposes of vagrancy laws and still satisfy the Constitution, legislators passed more specific loitering laws—not only suspicious loitering, but also loitering for the purposes of prostitution, narcotics, and "deviant sexual behavior." As judges assessed these laws, they came to differing conclusions about their validity and about what precisely *Coates, Palmer,* and *Papachristou* prohibited.[8]

When the Supreme Court faced the constitutionality of vagrancy law's crime control replacements in the decades that followed, advocates on all sides conceded that *Papachristou* meant that old-style, status-based, broad and ambiguous vagrancy laws were dead. Other things were different too. New threats to public safety—like the spread of crack cocaine and the related rise in gang-related violence—prompted new types of vagrancy law replacements like "gang loitering" and "stop and identify" laws. Moreover, though much of the cultural pluralism sought by vagrancy law's challengers was entrenched by the mid-1970s, the Court decided *Papachristou* as national politics shifted decisively to the right. Less than a year after the decision, President Nixon was reelected in a landslide. Over the next two decades, existing fissures within liberalism would grow, and Republican appointees would make the Supreme Court less hospitable to liberal claims. Reigning ideas about criminal justice also changed—from the Warren Court's embrace of the due process model to what has been dubbed a "retributive" model of broad laws, harsh sentences, and mass incarceration. The momentum for decriminalization of victimless crimes dissipated, while that for increased criminalization and law enforcement power increased.[9]

Some things nonetheless remained uncannily similar. For one, when it came to crime control, African American men continued to be frequent victims, too frequent in the eyes of critics. The lawyers, for another. Many of the individuals and organizations that had challenged vagrancy laws during their heyday now challenged the new contenders. Two vagrancy veterans participated in a key vagrancy follow-up that made it to the Supreme Court in 1983. In *Kolender v. Lawson,* an African American man repeatedly arrested in white neighborhoods sought to invalidate one of the first victories of the vagrancy law challenge: the 1962 disorderly conduct law that Ernest Besig had helped to pass in California. Dreadlocked and rights-conscious Edward Lawson challenged the compromise suspicious loitering provision that had been necessary to ensure passage of the vagrancy law repeal. Among his lawyers were Fred Okrand, who had first challenged California's law in *Edelman* in the early 1950s, and whose partner Al Wirin had first challenged the law in the farm labor fights of the 1930s. There as well was Anthony Amsterdam, back at the Court more than two decades after beginning his work as advocate and scholar in the vagrancy law trenches.[10]

Justice Douglas's presence in these cases remained a kind of constant as well, at least into the 1980s. Though he retired in 1975 and died five years later, Douglas and his personal connection to vagrancy laws were still very much in evidence when the Court heard *Kolender.* In a slight variation on Stephen Wainwright's own New Orleans arrest, Douglas's son, William O. Douglas Jr. had once been arrested while on his way to a deli in Hollywood under the very California law at issue in *Kolender.* The police held Douglas for nine hours while he refused to give his name. They finally released him when they determined that he was not their suspect. In one of his memoirs, the justice identified the incident, and especially Douglas Jr.'s refusal to trade on his famous name, as the reason for his high regard for his son. Justices Blackmun and Brennan were familiar with the story. As Brennan prepared for the justices' conference that would determine the constitutionality of the California law in *Kolender,* he noted to himself, "Tell story about William O. Douglas, Jr. if it seems appropriate."[11]

Whether it seemed appropriate or not, the Court did invalidate the California replacement. It also invalidated the gang loitering law that came its way fifteen years later. The stop-and-identify law the Court faced several years after that survived scrutiny. The dynamic of legislative creativity, statutory specificity, and judicial review continues to this day, with *Papachristou* still largely the touchstone.[12]

It would be wrong to conclude, however, that no such dynamic would exist had *Papachristou* only relied on fundamental rights instead of vagueness, that if Douglas had resisted Justice Stewart's changes, nothing would have filled the vacuum left by vagrancy law's invalidations. Given the Court's relatively robust history of supervising the police through vagueness doctrine, vagueness might actually have enhanced, rather than weakened, the judiciary's ability to intervene in the discretion granted by low-level policing. More fundamentally, the functions of vagrancy laws were simply too widespread and important to too many people simply to fade away. Some of the contours of the laws and regulations that followed might have been different if the doctrine had been different, but the efforts to find new forms of regulation would no doubt have been equally vigorous.

Indeed, even as attempts to reconstruct laws as close to vagrancy as possible were the most doctrinally obvious legacy of vagrancy law's downfall, they were by no means its only legacy. As predicted and contemplated, police across the country turned to "*Terry* stops," as the stop and frisk sanctioned in *Terry v. Ohio* came to be known. Local and state officials also continued to use vague but more conduct-oriented disorderly conduct and breach of the peace laws to fill the vacuum. Though *Papachristou* nowhere mentioned Eighth Amendment status-crime prohibitions, both courts and officials took from the larger vagrancy law challenge the belief that such formally conduct-based laws were constitutionally safer than status-based ones. Officials also increasingly deployed stringent drug laws and trespass and housing violation infractions—sometimes called "lingering" to distinguish them from the now-discredited but eerily similar "loitering"—to name only the most obvious extant laws that filled some of vagrancy law's crime control space. Moreover, with new forms of "broken windows" and "order maintenance" policing, officials adapted the centuries-old idea that vagrancy law's challengers had largely rejected: because petty crime would lead to more serious crime, law enforcement should take aim at the former in order to prevent the latter. These neo-vagrancy-type justifications for the regulation of incipient crime mimicked, though fell short of replicating, the old.[13]

Whether all these efforts were a good thing or a bad has been the subject of politicized debates that have often taken place explicitly in the shadow of, and with reference to, the end of vagrancy laws. Even with vagrancy laws' whole story submerged, the gaping hole left in crime control by the end of the regime has been readily apparent. Conservative scholars calling for "order maintenance" or "quality of life" policing have lamented that vagrancy laws were no longer doing such work. By contrast, liberal scholars have criticized such practices. When they have promoted "community policing," they have taken pains to distance it from both vagrancy laws and their conservative replacements. Moreover, when liberal scholars condemn drug possession arrests or trespass enforcement, they either explicitly or implicitly compare them to the "catch-alls" and "pretexts" of vagrancy laws. When they condemn the discriminatory cast of *Terry* stops, racial profiling, "Driving While Black," "the new Jim Crow," "the carceral state," or "mass incarceration," the historical discrimination of vagrancy enforcement is never far.[14]

Conservatives and liberals, advocates and government officials have disagreed as much about the consequences of vagrancy laws' absence for social control as for crime control. Officials have no longer been able to turn, on a dime and with no public input or knowledge, an infinitely elastic law to new social problems or new forms of old ones. Almost simultaneous with the withdrawal of vagrancy law's legitimacy, for example, and in part out of the same 1960s impulse toward liberty, autonomy, and nonconformity, state mental institutions began to discharge their patients on a massive scale. Officials faced with an increase in what they called "the derelict population" complained loudly about being hamstrung by the absence of vagrancy laws, and they blamed the Supreme Court. They turned instead to a variety of legal and nonlegal strategies for responding to the subsequent—and enduring—rise in homelessness. These ranged from laws prohibiting panhandling and sleeping on park benches and in cars, to technological changes (like armrests dividing park benches) that made such sleep impossible, to sheer avoidance through zoning regulations and gated communities.[15]

The response to the homeless might come to mind most readily as evidence that coercive governmental power survived the end of vagrancy laws, albeit in new forms. After all, the homeless always had best fit the popular label of "vagrants." They still do, even in the absence of constitutional vagrancy laws and the subsequent (and partial) linguistic shift from "vagrants" and "bums" to "homeless" and "unhoused."

Even so, vagrancy itself is only one of many examples in which vagrancy laws had made policing easier and cheaper in circumstances where policing tended to be difficult and expensive. For better or worse, the loss of vagrancy authority has made it harder to regulate all kinds of people: men whose children receive welfare because they do not provide for them; women and transwomen suspected of but not obviously engaged in prostitution; migrant farmworkers seeking legal or medical services; free speakers occupying public parks; day laborers gathering in public spaces in the hope of finding work; minority teens whose sartorial choices are found offensive and symbolically dangerous, just as the hippies' choices once were. The absence of a freewheeling, always available, infinitely flexible law enforcement tool serves as a reference point for these developments and then some. The vagrancy law regime also serves as a reference point for the status regulation of everyone from sex offenders to juveniles to undocumented workers. Regulating such people, tackling such threats, was work that would have been undertaken at least in part under the auspices of vagrancy enforcement before 1972. It was work that has produced new forms of legal authority ever since. The question of how much these countless regulatory efforts have reproduced the discredited vagrancy law regime haunted many who were involved in its destruction, and especially those, like Louis Lusky, who worried from the start that attacking the laws alone would accomplish little.[16]

Even as one can identify innumerable ways in which coercive government authority survived the downfall of vagrancy law, it is hard to resist three, more optimistic, conclusions about the forms that authority has taken. First, the necessity of passing new legislation in at least some contexts has meant greater regulatory transparency—with attendant distributional effects—than had characterized the vagrancy law era. Police may no longer turn ever-ready vagrancy laws to any new threat that arises. That constraint has required legislatures to articulate their goals and identify their targets. Because of both the changing constitutional baseline and the increased supervision of law enforcement procedures, even much of the vagrancy enforcement that has shifted to other "low-visibility" laws or practices has gained increased visibility in the post-vagrancy law world.

Consider stop and frisk. When a lawsuit in the 2010s challenged a New York City stop and frisk policy that had entailed hundreds of thousands of (mostly fruitless) stops of young African American and Latino men, the continuities with the past were far more immediately apparent than the discontinuities. Some forty years after *Papachristou*, police were still using enormous discretion in racially discriminatory ways, and misdemeanor arrests were still often serving as punishment in their own right. But the discontinuities were in evidence as well. *Terry* licensed stop and frisk, but it also brought it under (some) constitutional supervision. The New York lawsuit exploited that fact. Moreover, the suit was based on the substantive and procedural innovations of the 1960s civil rights movement. It was made possible by an assiduous record-keeping of stops and frisks unheard of during the vagrancy law era and only in existence because of the changes that the era had produced. The widespread public outcry, the agreement among so many different types of people that this was simply wrong, was not to be taken for granted. It was not something that existed before the vagrancy law challenge and the long 1960s.[17]

Second, none of the new laws, retooled laws, and novel methods of control has literally replaced vagrancy laws because, by their very nature, none can. The vagrancy law was written and used as an infinitely flexible license to arrest. It was understood to be the law that could do anything. Vagrancy laws were ubiquitous, protean, hidden, and almost never, before the era of their downfall, subject to much supervision, judicial or otherwise. There are so many contenders for vagrancy law's replacement today: traffic stops, drug possession laws, immigration status arrests, public housing violations. The list goes on. They vary in their vagueness, the discretion they license, the procedural informality through which they are enforced. But none of them, by definition, is as broad and flexible as vagrancy law. Each targets some people, some conduct, and some places more than others. That makes them all only contenders. No matter how they try, and no matter how many of them there are, they cannot legally do what vagrancy laws legally did precisely because they have to be specific and obvious while vagrancy laws were broad and hidden. Nothing can replace a vagrancy law but another vagrancy law. Unless and until the Court jettisons *Papachristou*, or the case otherwise loses its legitimacy, that is the one thing legislatures are denied.

Third, the invalidation of vagrancy laws was far more unsettling to state and local law than is typically understood. Given that vagrancy laws played more varied and substantial roles in both social and crime control than previously realized, the end of vagrancy laws has more fundamentally changed institutional and administrative arrangements for maintaining social order and public safety than we could have known. The vast and varied list of inheritances of vagrancy's downfall reveals how much work states and localities have done since 1972 to try to put back together what the vagrancy law challenge took apart. The monumental efforts that have gone into replacing a regime that for hundreds of years had enabled—and minimized the cost of—widespread surveillance and control represent massive outlays of governmental, intellectual, political, and policing capital.

These new techniques have taken very different forms and operated in very different contexts, but each in its way offers an ending to the vagrancy law story. Given the expanse of both the vagrancy law regime and the campaign that led to its downfall, myriad implications are to be expected. Following two decades of controversy, the Court did its best to construct new constitutional boundaries between danger and difference, acceptable and unacceptable police power, crime control and social control, freedom and order. Even as those new boundaries fundamentally changed the meaning of the Constitution and helped make the "sixties" as we know it, they were never understood as the last word on any of these subjects. So they weren't. The Court's boundaries were inherently unstable, and they proved difficult to maintain over time. Battles over what, if anything, should replace vagrancy laws, like battles over the legacy of the sixties transformations themselves, are far from over.

ACKNOWLEDGMENTS

I could not have completed this project without help from many people and institutions. I received generous financial support from University of Virginia School of Law deans John Jeffries and Paul Mahoney, and from the John Allan Love Professorship, the Justice Thurgood Marshall Distinguished Professorship, and the Caddell and Chapman Research Professorship. Fellowships from the Guggenheim Foundation and the American Council of Learned Societies enabled me to devote myself to the project for substantial chunks of time. My year at the Kluge Center of the Library of Congress as an ACLS Jacob Burkhardt Recently Tenured Faculty Fellow gave me exceptional access to the library's archives. It is also led me to the wonderful Roberta Schaffer, Elizabeth Pugh, David Mao, and the many others I was privileged to meet at the library. I am especially grateful to the staff in the Manuscript Division and to Hugo Black Jr. for access to the papers of Justice Hugo Black.

Archivists and librarians across the country were instrumental in providing access to archival materials. Thanks to Dan Linke and the staff of Princeton's Seeley G. Mudd Library; Gretchen Feltes and the NYU Law Library; and the California Historical Society; the Bancroft Library at UC Berkeley; the Columbia Law Library; the Dolph Briscoe Center for American History at the University of Texas at Austin; the Louisiana Law Library; the Martin Luther King, Jr., Center; the National Archives and Records Administration; the UCLA Special Collections Library; the Washington and Lee Law Library; and Alderman Library at the University of Virginia (with special thanks to Molly Schwartzburg for sharing the tramp and hobo collection). I am especially and deeply grateful to Michael D'Amelio for providing unmatched access to Anthony Amsterdam's unarchived papers and to Carmen Santiago and Art Eisenberg for access to the unarchived papers of the New York Civil Liberties Union.

When it comes to libraries, there is none finer than the Arthur J. Morris Law Library at the University of Virginia. Its librarians are smart, responsive, tenacious, and very patient. Special thanks go to Michelle Morris Beecy and Alison White who continued to help me even after they departed for greener pastures; Ben Doherty, Kristin Glover, and Amy Wharton for answering every question I ever thought of; Kent Olson for answering even the ones I didn't know enough to think of; and Loren Moulds for the hard and time-consuming work of tracking down illustrations and permissions. Leslie Ashbrook went above and beyond in supervising research assistants and cite-checking the entire manuscript. Knowing that that monstrous project was in her extremely capable hands gave me confidence and relief during the final months of editing.

An army of research assistants deserves credit for doing so much to make this project possible. For archival assistance, I am grateful to Gina Finke, Alison Gocke, Marnie Kaplan, Allison Lauterbach, Jennifer Wells, and Victor Yu. For assistance when I visited NYU and Columbia law schools, thanks go to Brian Bolin, Gideon Hart, Patryk Labuda, Nicole Peles, Aaron Slater, and Allison Westfahl Kong. I feel so lucky to have had dedicated and outstanding student assistants at Virginia every step of the way. My sincerest thanks to Virginia Blanton, Rebecca Caruso, Lauren Cassady, Benjamin Cohen, Nick Crown, Erik Erlandson, Sara Feldenkris, Jon Gryskiewicz, Evan Guimond, Sidney Helfer, Stew Inman, Matt Jobe, Elizabeth Katz, Sarah McCracken, Nate Nichols, Chris Pavlacka, Kelly Phipps, Sandy Piracci, Emily Riff, Gillet Rosenblith, Cassie Ross, Jennifer Roy, Priya Roy, Greg Rustico, Julie Schiff, Caroline Schmidt, Garrick Smith, Jesse Stewart, Sam Strongin, John Sullivan, Rachel Wade, Joseph Wilkinson, and Justin Zelikovitz.

I imagine that my colleagues at UVA will celebrate the publication of this book, just so they won't have to read any more draft installments. I feel so fortunate to have colleagues who always leave my work far better than they find it during (and often after) faculty retreats, faculty workshops, incubator lunches, and legal history workshops and writing groups. I am especially appreciative of my UVA legal history posse: Paul Halliday, Jessica Lowe, Chuck McCurdy, Cynthia Nicoletti, and Ted White. In the wider university, I have been fortunate to have help from colleagues who read or responded to my work at the History Department faculty lunch, the Working Group on Racial Inequality, the Woodson Institute for African-American and African Studies, the Center for the Study of Race and the Law, the Society of Fellows, and the Miller Center Scholars Workshop. Thanks also to my astute students in Constitutional History II, Regulating Public Space in Theoretical and Historical Perspective, and UVA's student scholarly lunches. Thank you also to the students at the J. Willard Hurst Institute; the Harvard Legal History Workshop (twice); and the University of Michigan Law School Public Law Workshop. Special thanks to Brian Balogh and his students in American Political Development for providing insightful feedback on the entire manuscript at a critical moment.

I was fortunate to present parts of this manuscript at a number of other institutions. I received helpful reactions, new leads, and important revisions from colleagues at the American Society for Legal History and the University of Alabama Symposium on Law's History, and participants in workshops at Cardozo Law School, Columbia Law School, the George Washington University History Department, Harvard Law School, the NYC Area Scholarship Group, NYU Law School, the Modern America Workshop at Princeton University's History Department, Princeton's Program in Law and Public Affairs, the University of Chicago Law School, the University of Hawai'i Law School, the University of Michigan Law School, the Constitutional Theory Conference at the University of Southern California, Yale Law School, the Yale Research Initiative on the History of Sexualities Lecture Series, and the American History Seminar of the Woodrow Wilson International Center for Scholars and the American Historical Association. I am also thankful for comments I received at public lectures at the Kluge Center, Constitution Day, and Law Day at the Library of Congress; the Virginia Bar Association; and the Charlottesville-Albemarle Bar Association.

For ideas, inspiration, information, sources, and new directions, I am grateful to Paul Baier, Gary Bass, Derrick Bell, Joel Black, Richard Bonnie, Mark Brilliant, Marvin Campbell, Margot Canaday, Mitch Dunier, Alex Elkins, Dan Ernst, David Garland, Sally Gordon, Tom Green, Helen Hershkoff, Laura Kalman, Randy Kennedy, Linda Kerber, Liz Magill, Keith Mayes, Sarah Milov, Elisa Alvarez Minoff, Robert Post, Scot Powe, Gil Seinfeld, Jon Rose, Austin Sarat, Mike Seidman, Reva Siegel, Sarah Seo, Carol Stack, Chris Stansell, Bill Stuntz, David Thacher, Mark Tushnet, and Ahmed White. Thank you to Susie Blumenthal for the title, and to Hal Goluboff and Elisha Cooper for their artistic expertise and sensibilities. My agent, Geri Thoma, and my editor, Dave McBride, both gave me excellent advice about things large and small all the way through this process. Thank you also to Katie Weaver, Stacey Victor, and the fine folks at Oxford for seeing the book through to publication.

Readers are any writer's most important resource and biggest fear. I am grateful for critical feedback on chapters from Tomiko Brown-Nagin, Peter Low, Bryan Goluboff, Erik Goluboff, Hal Goluboff, Nicole Goluboff, Paul Halliday, Jessica Lowe, Chuck McCurdy, Nell Mermin, Jim Ryan, John Setear, and Steven Wilf. Thanks to Barry Friedman and John Jeffries for reading substantial portions of the manuscript. I am delighted to add John's elegant voice to those in my head as I write and edit in the future.

What can one say about the people who are willing to slog through a 600-plus-page manuscript for no reward but my eternal gratitude? My thanks go to Tony Amsterdam for his inspiration, his mind-boggling recall, and his affirmation that I had something here; Myriam Gilles for reading the book as if it were readable and helping make it so; Debbie Hellman for her analytical clarity at the end;

George Rutherglen for help deciphering judicial handwriting and for a keen editorial eye; Cynthia Nicoletti for reminding me of vagrancy fundamentals; Ted White for helping me keep the Court in mind; John Witt for highlighting the big picture; Mike Klarman for pushing me to refine my arguments; Dirk Hartog for keeping humanity and imagination alive; and my mother, Linda Goluboff, for her insights, her careful attention to detail, and (most of all) her love.

Without the amazing recollections of people who were involved in this story in some way, this book would be far less rich and certainly less meaningful. For answering my questions through correspondence, I thank Jean Ares, Jerome Falk Jr., Ronald Krelstein, John Lusky, Arthur E. Neuman, George Shadoan, and Jonathan Shapiro. I am honored to have had the chance to speak with Anthony Amsterdam, Paul Chevigny, George Daly, Norman Dorsen, Earl Dudley, Monroe Freedman, Jack Greenberg, Sam Jacobson, Ed Hopson, Dick Merrill, Robert Bruce Miller, Burt Neuborne, Eleanor Jackson Piel, David Richards, Bruce Rogow, Niki Schwartz, Steve Suitts, Stephen Wainwright, Charles Wolfram, and Mel Wulf.

I think every day about how fortunate I am to have family and friends who have maintained their enthusiasm for this project for so many years. I thank them for their feedback, advice, and, most simply, love and support.

Finally, I thank my children, Solly and Ellie, and my husband, Rich Schragger. My children were too young to notice when I started this book. Now they can (and will) tell anyone what it is about, and they know, happily, that it is coming to an end. I hope that when they are older, they will pick it up, read some, and conclude that it was at least a little bit worth the attention I gave it. As for Rich, he has lived with this book from the very beginning. He jokes that he has read every sentence a hundred times, but I would not dispute it. He always knew when to go easy, when to be tough, and when to celebrate. He was my ideal reader, as he is my ideal partner in all things.

NOTES

Introduction

1. She had once previously been arrested for a municipal violation.
2. Edelman v. California, 344 U.S. 357 (1953); United States v. Kilgen, 431 F.2d 627, 628 (5th Cir. 1970) (quoting appellant's brief); Papachristou v. City of Jacksonville, 405 U.S. 156, 158 (1972).
3. William Blackstone, *Commentaries on the Laws of England*, vol. 4 (Oxford: Clarendon Press, 1769), 169–70; Statute of Labourers, 1349, 23 Edw. 3, c. 1; Statute of Labourers, 1350, 25 Edw. 3, stat. 2; 1350, 25 Edw. 3, stat. 7; Vagrancy Act of 1597 (An Act for Punishment of Rogues, Vagabonds, and Sturdy Beggars), 39 Elizabeth I, c. 4; Ruthann Robson, "Beyond Sumptuary: Constitutionalism, Clothes, and Bodies in Anglo-American Law, 1215–1789," *British Journal of American Legal Studies* 2, no. 2 (2013): 477. See Markus Dubber, *The Police Power: Patriarchy and the Foundations of American Government* (New York: Columbia University Press, 2005); Ruth Wallis Herndon, *Unwelcome Americans: Living on the Margin in Early New England* (Philadelphia: University of Pennsylvania Press, 2001); Joan Crouse, *The Homeless Transient in the Great Depression* (Albany: State University of New York Press, 1986), 15; Jeffrey S. Adler, "A Historical Analysis of the Law of Vagrancy," *Criminology* 27, no. 2 (1989): 214–15. On American migration as controlled by government rather than an expression of individual freedom, see Paul Frymer, "'A Rush and a Push and the Land Is Ours: Territorial Expansion, Land Policy, and State Formation," *Perspectives on Politics* 12, no. 1 (2014): 119–44.
4. In West Virginia it was a common law crime, and in all other states, plus Washington, DC, it was prohibited by statute. US Department of Justice, Federal Bureau of Investigation, *Uniform Crime Reports* (Washington, DC: Government Printing Office) (showing, though underreporting, between 99,000 and 157,000 vagrancy arrests per year between 1950 and 1970). See, e.g., William L. Burdick, *The Law of Crime*, vol. 3 (New York: Fallon Law Book Co., 1946), 431; "Vagrancy," *American Jurisprudence*, vol. 55 (Rochester, NY: Lawyers Co-operative Publishing Company, 1946), 446.
5. Such discretion was long a hallmark of vagrancy enforcement. See infra Chapter One notes 7–8; see, e.g., Tim Hitchcock, Adam Crymble, and Louise Falcini, "Loose, Idle and Disorderly: Vagrant Removal in Late Eighteenth-Century Middlesex," *Social History* 39, no. 4 (2014): 509–27; Caleb Foote, "Vagrancy-Type Law and Its Administration," *University of Pennsylvania Law Review* 104, no. 5 (1956): 603, 649; Shuttlesworth v. Birmingham, 382 U.S. 87, 89 (1965). See generally Sanford F. Kadish, "The Crisis of Overcriminalization," *American Criminal Law Quarterly* 7, no. 1 (1968): 157, 168–69.
6. "Vagrancy," *Corpus Juris Secundum*, vol. 91 (Brooklyn: American Law Book Co., 1955), 778.
7. See, e.g., George T. Payton, *Patrol Procedure* (Los Angeles: Legal Book Store, 1964), 139 (describing how to select subjects for field interrogation as "A Subject That Is Out of Place"); Brief for Appellant at 7, 20, Palmer v. City of Euclid, 402 U.S. 544 (1971) (No. 143). See also "ACLU Challenges Vagrancy Statutes," *Baltimore Afro-American*, August 10, 1968, 17 (lawyer describing vagrancy laws as "keep[ing] black people and other minorities in their place").

8. Thomas F. Adams, "Field Interrogations," *Police* 7 (March–April 1963): 26, 29 (describing people as "legitimate").

9. U.S. Department of Justice, Federal Bureau of Investigation, *Uniform Crime Reports* (Washington, DC: Government Printing Office).

10. Del Martin, quoted in Nan Alamilla Boyd, *Wide Open Town: A History of Queer San Francisco to 1965* (Berkeley: University of California Press, 2003), 156; Stetson Kennedy and Elizabeth Gardner, "Jim Crow Guide to U.S.A.: Loafing—For Rich Whites Only: All Others Can Be Charged as Vagrants," *Afro-American*, February 25, 1950, 13. Draft Petition for Writ of Habeas Corpus with Motion for Stay of State Court Proceedings at 5, Hillegas v. Sams, No. EC-65-1 (N.D. Miss. Jan. 5, 1965), Hillegas v. Sams, DC File Papers, Papers of Anthony Amsterdam (on file with author).

11. Palmer v. City of Euclid, 402 U.S. 544 (1971); Coates v. City of Cincinnati, 402 U.S. 611 (1971); Papachristou v. City of Jacksonville, 405 U.S. 156, 158 (1972).

12. See generally Thomas Miguel Hilbink, "Constructing Cause Lawyering: Professionalism, Politics, and Social Change in 1960s America" (Ph.D. diss., New York University, 2006).

13. On deliberate litigation campaigns, see, e.g., Richard Kluger, *Simple Justice: The History of Brown v. Board of Education and Black America's Struggle for Equality* (London: Vintage, 2004); Mark V. Tushnet, *The NAACP's Legal Strategy against Segregated Education, 1925–1950* (Chapel Hill: University of North Carolina Press, 2005); but see Risa Goluboff, *The Lost Promise of Civil Rights* (Cambridge, MA: Harvard University Press, 2010).

14. "Ugly laws" that targeted people with disabilities were also used in tandem with vagrancy laws. See Susan M. Schweik, *The Ugly Laws: Disability in Public* (New York: New York University Press, 2010).

15. Paul Chevigny, *Police Power: Police Abuses in New York City* (New York: Pantheon Books, 1969), 220 (internal quotation marks omitted); Winters v. New York, 333 U.S. 507, 540 (1948) (Frankfurter, J., concurring). See also Anthony G. Amsterdam, "Federal Constitutional Restrictions on the Punishment of Crimes of Status, Crimes of General Obnoxiousness," *Criminal Law Bulletin* 3, no. 4 (1967): 207–8; Model Penal Code § 250.12, cmt. 1 (Tentative Draft No. 13, 1961); President's Commission on Law Enforcement and Administration of Justice, *Task Force Report: The Courts* (Washington, DC: Government Printing Office, 1976), 102–4.

16. Edwards v. California, 314 U.S. 160, 176 (1941); Lanzetta v. New Jersey, 306 U.S. 451, 458 (1939); Thornhill v. Alabama, 310 U.S. 88, 101-106 (1940). Cf. New York v. Miln, 36 U.S. 102, 142–43 (1837).

17. For conventional histories, see, e.g., Terry Anderson, *The Movement and The Sixties: Protest in America from Greensboro to Wounded Knee* (New York: Oxford University Press, 1996); Terry H. Anderson, *The Sixties*, 148–49 (1999 publication of *The Movement and The Sixties* with shortened title); Alice Echols, *Shaky Ground: The '60s and Its Aftershocks* (New York: Columbia University Press, 2002); Todd Gitlin, *The Sixties: Years of Hope, Days of Rage* (New York: Bantam Books, 1987); Mark H. Lytle, *America's Uncivil Wars: The Sixties Era: From Elvis to the Fall of Richard Nixon* (New York: Oxford University Press, 2006); Gerald J. DeGroot, *The Sixties Unplugged: A Kaleidoscopic History of a Disorderly Decade* (Cambridge, MA: Harvard University Press, 2008); Bernard Von Bothmer, *Framing the Sixties: The Use and Abuse of a Decade from Ronald Reagan to George W. Bush* (Amherst: University of Massachusetts Press, 2010). For brief discussions of the use of vagrancy laws against other minority groups, see infra, at Chapter Four, text accompanying notes 5–6. On the need for historians to look beyond black and white, see, e.g., Mark Brilliant, *The Color of America Has Changed: How Racial Diversity Shaped Civil Rights Reform in California, 1941–1978* (New York: Oxford University Press, 2010). On the gendered aspects of vagrancy laws, see Linda K. Kerber, *No Constitutional Right to Be Ladies: Women and the Obligations of Citizenship* (New York: Hill and Wang, 1998), 47–80. On the rise of conservatism in the 1960s, see, e.g., Mary Brennan, *Turning Right in the Sixties* (Chapel Hill: University of North Carolina Press, 2007); Donald T. Critchlow and Nancy Maclean, *Debating the American Conservative Movement: 1945 to the Present* (Lanham, MD: Rowman and Littlefield, 2009); David R. Farber, *The Conservative Sixties* (New York: Peter Lang, 2003); Eric Foner, *American History Now* (Philadelphia: Temple University Press, 2011); David Frum, *How We Got Here: The 70's, the Decade That Brought You Modern Life (for

Better or Worse) (New York: Basic Books, 2000); Laura Jane Gifford and Daniel K. Williams, eds., *The Right Side of the Sixties: Reexamining Conservatism's Decade of Transformation* (New York: Palgrave Macmillan, 2012); Godfrey Hodgson, *The World Turned Right Side Up: A History of the Conservative Ascendancy in America* (New York: Houghton Mifflin, 1996); Edward D. Berkowitz, *Something Happened: A Political and Cultural Overview of the Seventies* (New York: Columbia University Press, 2006); Lisa McGirr, *Suburban Warriors: The Origins of the New American Right* (Princeton, NJ: Princeton University Press, 2001); Sarah Barringer Gordon, *The Spirit of the Law: Religious Voices and the Constitution in Modern America* (Cambridge, MA: Harvard University Press, 2010); Matthew D. Lassiter, *The Silent Majority: Suburban Politics in the Sunbelt South* (Princeton, NJ: Princeton University Press, 2007); Kevin M. Kruse, *White Flight: Atlanta and the Making of Modern Conservatism* (Princeton, NJ: Princeton University Press, 2005); Kevin Kruse and Thomas Sugrue, eds., *The New Suburban History* (Chicago: University of Chicago Press, 2006).

Chapter 1

1. Seymour Korman, " 'Next Friend' of Rosenbergs Tells Spy Aid," *Chicago Daily Tribune*, June 18, 1953, 7. He sometimes went by the name "Irwin Edelman" as well.
2. "Spy Case Limelight Shines on Pershing Square Orator," *Los Angeles Times*, June 18, 1953, 2. See Melvyn P. Leffler, *For the Soul of Mankind: The United States, the Soviet Union, and the Cold War* (New York: Macmillan, 2007); Melvyn P. Leffler, *A Preponderance of Power: National Security, the Truman Administration, and the Cold War* (Palo Alto, CA: Stanford University Press, 1992); Elaine Tyler May, *Homeward Bound: American Families in the Cold War Era* (New York: Basic Books, 2008).
3. Transcript of Record at 18, Edelman v. California, 344 U.S. 357 (1953) (No. 86).
4. In re McCue, 96 P. 110, 111 (Cal. Ct. App. 1908). Cal. Penal Code § 647(5) (Deering 1949).
5. Transcript of Record, Edelman.
6. Ibid. at 45–47.
7. For Statute of Labourers, see Statute of Labourers, 1349, 23 Edw. 3, c. 1; Statute of Labourers, 1350, 25 Edw. 3, st. 2; Sir James Fitzjames Stephen, *A History of the Criminal Law of England*, Vol. 3 (London: Macmillan, 1883), 203. See also Elaine Clark, "Institutional and Legal Responses to Begging in Medieval England," *Social Science History* 26, no. 3 (2002): 461; Statute of Artificers, 1562, 5 Eliz. I c. 4; Stephen, *History of the Criminal Law of England*, 205. See William P. Quigley, "Five Hundred Years of English Poor Laws, 1349–1834: Regulating the Working and Nonworking Poor," *Akron Law Review* 30, no. 1 (1996): 89. For sixteenth- and seventeenth-century laws, see Vagrancy Act of 1597 (An Act for Punishment of Rogues, Vagabonds, and Sturdy Beggars), 39 Eliz. I, c. 4; see also 1388, 12 Rich. 2, cc. 3–10; 1405, 7 Hen. 4, c. 17; 1414, 2 Hen. 5, c. 4; 1427, 6 Hen. 6, c. 3; 1494, 11 Hen. 7, c. 2; 1503, 19 Hen. 7, c. 12; 1514, 6 Hen. 8, c. 3. See generally Stephen, *History of the Criminal Law of England*, 204–5; A. L. Beier, *Masterless Men, The Vagrancy Problem in England, 1560–1640* (New York: Methuen, 1985); Paul A. Slack, "Vagrants and Vagrancy in England, 1598–1664," *Economic History Review* 27, no. 3 (1974): 360–79; Tim Hitchcock, Adam Crymble, and Louise Falcini, "Loose, Idle and Disorderly: Vagrant Removal in Late Eighteenth-Century Middlesex," *Social History* 39, no. 4 (2014): 509–27; Patricia Fumerton, *Unsettled: The Culture of Mobility and the Working Poor in Early Modern England* (Chicago: University of Chicago Press, 2006); Paul Slack, *Poverty and Policy in Tudor England* (New York: Longman, 1988), 91–107. For political purposes of English vagrancy laws, see C. J. Ribton-Turner, *A History of Vagrants and Vagrancy and Beggars and Begging* (London: Chapman and Hall, 1887); Robert C. Palmer, *English Law in the Age of the Black Death, 1348–1381* (Chapel Hill: University of North Carolina Press, 1993), 17; Steve Hindle, *The State and Social Change in Early Modern England, 1550–1640* (New York: St. Martin's Press, 2002). See generally Tim Cook, ed., *Vagrancy: Some New Perspectives* (London: Academic Press, 1979); Paul Slack, *From Reformation to Improvement: Public Welfare in Early Modern England* (New York: Clarendon Press, 1999); Robert Humphreys, *No Fixed Abode: A History of Responses to the Roofless and the Rootless in Britain* (New York: St. Martin's Press, 1999); David Green, *Pauper Capital: London and the Poor Law, 1790–1870* (Farnham, Surrey: Ashgate Books, 2010).

8. David J. Rothman, *The Discovery of the Asylum: Social Order and Disorder in the New Republic*, rev. ed. (New York: Transaction, 2002); Stefan A. Riesenfeld, "The Formative Era of American Public Assistance Law," *California Law Review* 43, no. 2 (1955): 189–247; David M. Schneider, *The History of Public Welfare in New York State, 1609–1866* (Chicago: University of Chicago Press, 1938); Douglas Lamar Jones, "The Strolling Poor: Transiency in Eighteenth-Century Massachusetts," *Journal of Social History* 8, no. 3 (1975): 28–54; Margaret Creech, *Three Centuries of Poor Law Administration: A Study of Legislation in Rhode Island* (Chicago: University of Chicago Press, 1936; College Park: McGrath, 1969); William P. Quigley, "Work or Starve: Regulation of the Poor in Colonial America," *University of San Francisco Law Review* 31, no. 1 (1996): 40 n. 23; James W. Ely Jr., "American Independence and the Law: A Study of Post-Revolutionary South Carolina Legislation," *Vanderbilt Law Review* 26, no. 5 (1973): 939–72; Benjamin J. Klebaner, *Public Poor Relief in America, 1790–1869* (New York: Arno Press, 1976); John K. Alexander, *Render Them Submissive: Responses to Poverty in Philadelphia, 1760–1800* (Amherst: University of Massachusetts, 1980); William P. Quigley, "Reluctant Charity: Poor Laws in the Original Thirteen States," *University of Richmond Law Review* 31, no. 1 (1997): 111–78; William P. Quigley, "The Quicksands of the Poor Law: Poor Relief Legislation in a Growing Nation, 1790–1820," *Northern Illinois University Law Review* 18, no. 1 (1997): 1–98; Stephen, History of the Criminal Law of England, 267.

9. Amy Dru Stanley, "Beggars Can't Be Choosers: Compulsion and Contract in Postbellum America," *Journal of American History* 78, no. 4 (1992): 1265–93. Only Tennessee and Arkansas did not pass new vagrancy laws in the two years after the war ended. Tennessee passed a new law in 1875 and Arkansas in 1905, but both in the meantime maintained their antebellum laws. William Cohen, *At Freedom's Edge: Black Mobility and the Southern White Quest for Racial Control, 1861–1915* (Baton Rouge: Louisiana State University Press, 1991), 31, 240–41, table 12; William Cohen, "Negro Involuntary Servitude in the South, 1865–1940: A Preliminary Analysis," *Journal of Southern History* 42, no. 1 (1976): 31–46; Eric Foner, *Reconstruction: America's Unfinished Revolution, 1863–1877* (New York: Harper and Row, 1988).

10. John J. McCook, "A Tramp Census and Its Revelations," *The Forum* 15 (1893): 753; Michael B. Katz, *In the Shadow of the Poorhouse: A Social History of Welfare in America*, 10th ed. (New York: Basic Books, 1996), 95; Kenneth L. Kusmer, *Down and Out, On the Road: The Homeless in American History* (New York: Oxford University Press, 2002); Todd DePastino, *Citizen Hobo: How a Century of Homelessness Shaped America* (Chicago: University of Chicago Press, 2003); Frank Tobias Higbie, *Indispensable Outcasts: Hobo Workers and Community in the American Midwest, 1880–1930* (Urbana: University of Illinois Press, 2003); Alexander Keyssar, *Out of Work: The First Century of Unemployment in Massachusetts* (New York: Cambridge University Press, 1986); Paul T. Ringenbach, *Tramps and Reformers, 1873–1916: The Discovery of Unemployment in New York* (Westport, CT: Greenwood Press, 1973), 20–26.

11. John C. Schneider, *Detroit and the Problem of Order, 1830–1880: A Geography of Crime, Riot, and Policing* (Lincoln: University of Nebraska Press, 1980), 109–10; Sidney Harring, "Class Conflict and the Suppression of Tramps in Buffalo, 1892–1894," *Law and Society Review* 11, no. 5 (1977): 873–911; Joel E. Black, "Idlers, Outliers and Dependents: The Free Labor Order in Industrial Chicago, 1870–1930" (Ph.D. diss., University of Florida, 2010); David Montgomery, "Wage Labor, Bondage, and Citizenship in Nineteenth-Century America, International Labor and Working-Class," *International Labor and Working-Class History* 48 (Fall 1995): 19–20. See, e.g., "Miners' Trouble: Result of Arrest of Strikers in Colorado, Mining Town," *Evening News*, December 3, 1903, 5; "Strikes Still On at Carhartt," *Evening Herald*, June 17, 1920, 6.

12. Dennis E. Hoffman and Vincent J. Webb, "Police Response to Labor Radicalism in Portland and Seattle, 1913–19," *Oregon Historical Quarterly* 87, no. 4 (1986): 348–49; Kevin Starr, *Endangered Dreams: The Great Depression and California* (New York: Oxford University Press, 1996), 29; Melvin Dubofsky, *We Shall Be All: A History of the Industrial Workers of the World* (Chicago: Quadrangle Books, 1969), 349; Patrick Renshaw, *The Wobblies: The Story of Syndicalism in the United States* (New York: Doubleday, 1967); *Industrial Worker*, September 30, 1909, quoted in Dubofsky, *We Shall Be All*, 173; "Hordes of I.W.W. Summoned Here," *Oregonian* (Portland, OR), December 29, 1916, 16.

13. "I.W.W.'s Have Reached Minot," *Ward County Independent* (Minot, ND), August 3, 1916, 1, cited in Ahmed A. White, "A Different Kind of Labor Law: Vagrancy Law and the Regulation of Harvest Labor, 1913–1924," *University of Colorado Law Review* 75, no. 3 (2004): 711; "I.W.W.'s Finding It Tough: Armed Bands of Malcontents Roving over the Northwest States," *Fargo* (ND) *Forum and Daily Republican*, August 5, 1916, 6, cited in White, "Different Kind of Labor Law," 711. See generally White, "Different Kind of Labor Law," 711; Hoffman and Webb, "Police Response to Labor Radicalism," 346; "250 Alleged Reds Caught in Portland," *Daily Olympian* (Olympia, WA), October 20, 1922, 1; "Arrest Forty-One I.W.Ws.," *Chicago Tribune*, March 26, 1918, 9; "41 I.W.W. Arrested," *Duluth News-Tribune*, March 26, 1918, 4; "I.W.W. Marched Out; Strike Over," *Oregonian* (Portland, OR), July 11, 1917, 4.

14. White, "Different Kind of Labor Law," 712–26 (citing primary sources); "250 Alleged Reds Caught in Portland," 1; "Portland Police Thwart Invasion of I.W.W. Hordes," *San Jose* (CA) *Mercury Herald*, October 22, 1922, 1; Hoffman and Webb, "Police Response to Labor Radicalism," 344; Roberts v. Missouri, 14 Mo. 138, 138 (1851); Roberts v. Missouri, 15 Mo. 28 (1851); "I.W.W. So Quiet Coup Is Feared," *Oregonian* (Portland, OR), October 25, 1922, 4.

15. "I.W.W. So Quiet Coup Is Feared," 4; "Miss Flynn Arrested on Arrival in Duluth," *Aberdeen Daily American*, June 24, 1917, 1; "I.W.W. Marched Out; Strike Over," 4. See also American Civil Liberties Union, *Record of the Fight for Free Speech in 1923* (New York: ACLU, 1931), p. 14, box 82, American Civil Liberties Union of Southern California Records (collection 900), Charles E. Young Research Library, UCLA Special Collections (hereafter UCLA ACLU Records) (describing raids of Marine Transport Workers Union and vagrancy arrests); White, "Different Kind of Labor Law," 726–31 (quoting primary sources); "Hordes of I.W.W. Summoned Here," 16; "Miss Flynn Arrested on Arrival in Duluth," 1; "I.W.W. Marched Out; Strike Over," 4. See also "I.W.W. Ordered to Invade City," *Oregonian* (Portland, OR), October 25, 1922, 1; "I.W.W. Trial Set," *Oregonian* (Portland, OR), August 7, 1917, 12; Ex parte Clancy, 210 P. 487 (Kan. 1922). On additional use of vagrancy laws in Kansas, see James Gray Pope, "Labor's Constitution of Freedom," *Yale Law Journal* 106, no. 4 (1997): 1009–10; see also Ex parte Taft, 225 S.W. 457, 458 (Mo. 1920); Zechariah Chafee Jr., *Free Speech in the United States* (Cambridge, MA: Harvard University Press, 1941), 100 n. 107.

16. John Wertheimer, "Free-Speech Fights: The Roots of Modern Free-Expression Litigation in the United States" (Ph.D. diss., Princeton University, 1992), 194–95; David M. Rabban, *Free Speech in Its Forgotten Years, 1870–1920* (New York: Cambridge University Press, 1999); Dubofsky, *We Shall Be All*, 185–89; Starr, *Endangered Dreams*, 33; Hoffman and Webb, "Police Response to Labor Radicalism," 344.

17. 1919 Cal. Stat. 281 (c. 188); Woodrow C. Whitten, "Criminal Syndicalism and the Law in California: 1919–1927," *Transactions of the American Philosophical Society* 59, no. 2 (1969): 3–5, 15–26; Starr, *Endangered Dreams*, 48; Ahmed A. White, "The Crime of Economic Radicalism: Criminal Syndicalism Laws and the Industrial Workers of the World, 1917–1927," *Oregon Law Review* 85 (2007): 649.

18. Whitten, "Criminal Syndicalism," 27–28. Again, in November of 1919, more arrests for vagrancy and criminal syndicalism followed. Starr, *Endangered Dreams*, 55; "41 I.W.W. Arrested," 4; "I.W.W. Trial Set," 12. See also "Arrest Forty-one I.W.Ws," 9; "Miners Mistreated Union Man Charges," *Dallas Morning News*, September 21, 1922, 1.

19. The "usual summer prosecutions" of IWW "harvest hands" for vagrancy continued into the 1930s, however. ACLU, *The Fight for Civil Liberties 1930–1931* (New York: ACLU, 1931), p. 16, box 82, UCLA ACLU Records (collection 900). For examples of such arrests, see, e.g., Eason Monroe, interview by Joel Gardner, July–August, 1972, Safeguarding Civil Liberties, Oral History of Eason Monroe at 102–3, Oral History Program University of California Los Angeles, http://www.oac.cdlib.org/view?docId=ft4g5005d0&brand=oac4&doc.view= entire_text. For police breaking strikes, see *The Western Worker*, quoted in *Violations of Free Speech and Labor Right, Hearings before a Subcommittee of the Senate Committee on Education and Labor* (hereafter Free Speech and Labor Right Hearings, pt. 54, 74th Cong. 19,992 (1940)); Frank P. Barajas, "Resistance, Radicalism, and Repression on the Oxnard Plain," *Western Historical Quarterly* 35, no. 1 (2004): 45; Starr, *Endangered Dreams*, 158, 167; James Gray, "The American Civil Liberties Union of Southern California and Imperial Valley Agricultural Labor Disturbances: 1930, 1934" (Ph.D. diss., UCLA, 1966), 65, 101; "Peace Called Sure as Dock

Men Vote," *New York Times*, July 24, 1934, 1; Free Speech and Labor Right Hearings, *pts. 1–10, 51, 54*, 74th Cong. 19,992 (1936–1940), *pt. 70*, supplemental exhibits, 74th Cong. (1940), *pt. 72*, 74th Cong. 26,472 (1941) (as well as many other places in the hearings). For arrests of communists and workers, "Authorities Believe Men Were Imported for Strike Breaking," *Reading* (PA) *Eagle*, March 16, 1937, 1; "84 Arrested In Raid on CIO Headquarters," *Reading* (PA) *Eagle*, June 26, 1938, 5; "Danville Arrests Three Communists," *Washington Post*, July 31, 1934, 6; "State Prepares for Trouble in Danville Strike," *Washington Post*, September 6, 1934, 10; Free Speech and Labor Right Hearings, *pt. 11*, 74th Cong. 3,918 (1937); "100 Jailed in New Orleans," *New York Times*, November 5, 1936, 30. See also "16 Ships Here Sail Despite Walkout," *New York Times*, November 14, 1936, 4; "Police Order Texas Pickets to Quit," *Los Angeles Times*, November 11, 1936, 6; "Socialists Aid Fight to Release Imprisoned No. Carolina Strikers," *Baltimore Afro-American*, August 12, 1933, 8; "Norman Thomas Will Speak in Terre Haute," *Reading* (PA) *Eagle*, October 8, 1936, 3; "Mills May Stay Closed Even if Strike Is Ended," *Lewiston* (ME) *Evening Journal*, November 6, 1931, 1; Free Speech and Labor Right Hearings, *pt. 72*, 74th Cong. 26,472 (1941); "Use of Vagrancy-Type Laws for Arrest and Detention of Suspicious Persons," *Yale Law Journal* 59, no. 7 (1950): 1363 n. 35.

20. See, e.g., "Pea-Pickers' Strike Over in One Day," *Los Angeles Times*, November 22, 1933, 1; "Fruit Pickets Given Conditional Sentence," *Los Angeles Times*, July 23, 1939, 4; Free Speech and Labor Right Hearings, *pt. 74*, 74th Cong. 27,366 (1940), *pt. 54*, 74th Cong. 19,992 (1940), *pt. 61*, 74th Cong. 25,237 (1940). The organizer arrested repeatedly was Clarence E. Shauman: Starr, *Endangered Dreams*, 73. Free Speech and Labor Right Hearings, *pt. 54*, 74th Cong. 19,992, 20,013 (1940); "Summary Justice Dealt Coast Reds," *New York Times*, July 23, 1934, 2; "300 Put under Arrest," *New York Times*, July 18, 1934, 1; "Communists 'Mopped Up' by Vigilantes," *Washington Post*, July 18, 1934, 1; Free Speech and Labor Right Hearings, *pt. 60*, 74th Cong. 22,058 (1940).

21. Free Speech and Labor Rights Hearings, *pt. 11*, 74th Cong. 3,918–26 (1937) (describing incident in Harlan County, Kentucky); Jerold S. Auerbach, *Labor and Liberty: The La Follette Committee and the New Deal* (New York: Bobbs-Merrill, 1966); Free Speech and Labor Right Hearings, *pt. 48* 74th Cong. 17,613(1940); "Reds Rush City Hall," *New York Times*, October 17, 1930, 1.

22. Rabban, *Free Speech in Its Forgotten Years*, 81 n. 12, 88, 302.

23. See Laura M. Weinrib, "The Liberal Compromise: Civil Liberties, Labor, and the Limits of State Power, 1917–1940" (Ph.D. diss., Princeton University, 2011); Whitten, "Criminal Syndicalism," 57; Martin Zanger, "Politics of Confrontation: Upton Sinclair and the Launching of the ACLU in Southern California," *Pacific Historical Review* 38, no. 4 (1969): 383–406; Starr, *Endangered Dreams*, 52; Eason Monroe, interview by Joel Gardner, 100; Judy Kutulas, *The American Civil Liberties Union and the Making of Modern Liberalism* (Chapel Hill: University of North Carolina Press, 2006), 42; Laura M. Weinrib, "The Sex Side of Civil Liberties: *United States v. Dennett* and the Changing Face of Free Speech," *Law and History Review* 30, no. 2 (2012); Samuel Walker, *In Defense of American Liberties: A History of the ACLU* (Carbondale: Southern Illinois University Press, 1999).

24. John Kykyri, "Many Mourn Passing of Leo Gallagher," *People's World*, October 5, 1963, folder 1, box 1, Leo Gallagher Papers, MSS 012, Southern California Library of Social Studies and Research, Los Angeles (hereafter Leo Gallagher Papers); Larry S. Ceplair, "Leo Gallagher: A Man of Faith and Principle," n.d., folder 1, box 1, Leo Gallagher Papers;Carey McWilliams, "Leo Gallagher," *The Nation*, October 16, 1935, 437; Carey McWilliams, interview by Joel Gardner, July 19, 1978, Honorable in All Things: Oral History of Carey McWilliams at 469, Oral History Program University of California Los Angeles; Kutulas, *American Civil Liberties Union*, 50; McWilliams, "Leo Gallagher," 437. Ceplair, "Leo Gallagher," n.d., folder 1, box 1, Leo Gallagher Papers.

25. Free Speech and Labor Right Hearings, *pt. 51*, 74th Cong. 18,976 (1940) (quoting a news release of the Associated Farmers of California, Inc., Exhibit 8546-A); "Lynch Talk Enters Case," *Los Angeles Times*, February 22, 1935, 8; Ben Margolis, interview by Michael S. Balter, July 2, 1984, Law and Social Conscience: Oral History of Ben Margolis at 86, 278–79, 336, Oral History Program University of California Los Angeles. See also Communist Activity among Professional Groups in the Los Angeles Area, Hearing before the House Committee on Un-American Activities, *Part 3*, 82d Cong., 2d sess., 4024–29 (1952) (Testimony of J. Allan

Frankel); Communist Legal Subversion: The Role of the Communist Lawyer, Report by the Committee on Un-American Activities, H.R. Rep. No. 86–41, at 38–39 (1959); Gray, "American Civil Liberties Union of Southern California," 330; McWilliams, "Leo Gallagher," 437. Carey McWilliams, interview by Joel Gardner, 468–69; Starr, *Endangered Dreams*, 168. On Wirin, see Mark Brilliant, *The Color of America Has Changed: How Racial Diversity Shaped Civil Rights Reform in California, 1941–1978* (New York: Oxford University Press, 2010), 31; "Friends May Pay Respects Today to Attorney A. L. Wirin," *Los Angeles Times*, February 7, 1978, C3; Auerbach, *Labor and Liberty*, 178. Wirin's brother spent most of his career at the Department of Agriculture in Washington, DC. "Harry B. Wirin," *Washington Post*, November 26, 1998, D15; Ben Margolis, interview by Michael S. Balter, 98. See Walker, *In Defense of American Liberties*, 233. On the Popular Front and Communism, see Michael Denning, *The Cultural Front: The Laboring of American Culture in the Twentieth Century* (New York: Verso, 1998); Leffler, *For the Soul of Mankind*; Leffler, *A Preponderance of Power*. See Peter H. Irons, *Justice at War: The Story of the Japanese-American Internment Cases* (Berkeley: University of California Press, 1993).

26. Gray, "American Civil Liberties Union of Southern California," 344 n. 70 (quoting letter); Carey McWilliams, interview by Joel Gardner, 467; Eason Monroe, interview by Joel Gardner, 338–39.

27. Kolender v. Lawson, 461 U.S. 352 (1983); Starr, *Endangered Dreams*, 165, 176–73. See, e.g., Gray, "American Civil Liberties Union of Southern California," 318; "Summary Justice Dealt Coast Reds," 2.See, e.g., Ex parte Gutierrez, 36 P.2d 712 (Cal. Ct. App. 1934); People v. Chambers, 72 P.2d 746 (Cal. Ct. App. 1937). On an injunction Wirin obtained in Imperial Valley, see Gray, "American Civil Liberties Union of Southern California," 83, 89.

28. Free Speech and Labor Right Hearings, *pt. 54*, 74th Cong. 20,049 (1940); "Wirin Posts Reward for 'Kidnappers,'" *Los Angeles Times*, May 25, 1934, 18; "Man Seized in Strike," *Los Angeles Times*, January 24, 1934, 1; Gray, "American Civil Liberties Union of Southern California," 69–73, 237, 247, 250, 273–74, 278–79; "Wife of Attorney Fails in Probation Plea," *Los Angeles Times*, April 28, 1934, A7; Free Speech and Labor Right Hearings, *pt. 55*, 74th Cong. 20,308–20,309 (1940) (affidavit of Grover Johnson); Starr, *Endangered Dreams*, 159–60; Gray, "The American Civil Liberties Union of Southern California," 250, 273–74, 278–79.

29. "Reds at Plaza Battle Police," *Los Angeles Times*, August 2, 1930, A1; "Young Strikers Released," *Los Angeles Times*, November 2, 1933, 9; Barajas, "Resistance, Radicalism, and Repression on the Oxnard Plain," 28–51; "Strike Pair Held Guilty," *Los Angeles Times*, February 22, 1934, 6; Gray, "American Civil Liberties Union of Southern California," 300; "Budget Holds Up Action on Glassford's Report," *Los Angeles Times*, June 28, 1934, 6.

30. One argument they made was that the total lack of evidence to support Cutler's conviction constituted a due process violation. This is the same argument Louis Lusky would later make successfully in *Thompson v. Louisville*, 362 U.S. 199 (1960); Ex parte Cutler, 36 P.2d 441, 442–43 (Cal. Dist. Ct. App. 1934).

31. G. Edward White, "The First Amendment Comes of Age: The Emergence of Free Speech in Twentieth-Century America," *Michigan Law Review* 95, no. 2 (1996): 310–12. One exception to this general rule was "prior restraints," ibid; Rabban, *Free Speech in Its Forgotten Years*, 130 (discussing the Alien Immigration Act and other federal restrictions on free speech between 1801, when the Sedition Act expired, and World War I). In *Barron v. Baltimore*, the Supreme Court announced that the Bill of Rights governed only the federal government, not the states 32 U.S. (7 Pet.) 243 (1833). On early free speech claims, see Wertheimer, "Free-Speech Fights," 129–237; Rabban, *Free Speech in Its Forgotten Years*; Mark A. Graber, *Transforming Free Speech: The Ambiguous Legacy of Civil Libertarianism* (Berkeley: University of California Press, 1991).

32. Schenck v. United States, 249 U.S. 47, 52 (1919); Abrams, 250 U.S. 616 (1919). Gitlow v. New York, 268 U.S. 652 (1925); Fiske v. Kansas, 274 U.S. 380 (1927); Stromberg v. California, 283 U.S. 359 (1931). See also Near v. Minnesota, 283 U.S. 697 (1931). See generally Walker, *In Defense of American Liberties*; Christopher Cappazola, *Uncle Sam Wants You: World War I and the Making of the Modern American Citizen* (New York: Oxford University Press, 2010); John Fabian Witt, *Patriots and Cosmopolitans* (Cambridge, MA: Harvard University Press, 2009), 157–208; White, "The First Amendment Comes of Age," 312–26; Harry Kalven Jr., *A Worthy Tradition: Freedom of Speech in America* (New York: Harper and Row, 1988); Elaine Elinson and Stan Yogi, *Wherever There's a Fight: How Runaway Slaves, Suffragists, Immigrants, Strikers, and Poets Shaped Civil Liberties in California* (Berkeley: Heyday, 2009), 214.

33. Hague v. CIO, 307 U.S. 496 (1939); Carlson v. California, 310 U.S. 106, 112-13 (1940); Thornhill v. Alabama, 310 U.S. 88, 97–98, 100, 104-06 (1940). See also Ex parte Bell, 122 P.2d 22 (Cal. 1942) (striking down part of anti-picketing and anti-loitering law); Violations of Free Speech and Rights of Labor, S. Rep. No. 77–1150, *pt. 1*, at 53 (1942); Michael J. Klarman, "Rethinking the Civil Rights and Civil Liberties Revolutions," *Virginia Law Review* 82, no. 1 (1996): 1–68; Risa L. Goluboff, *The Lost Promise of Civil Rights* (Cambridge: Harvard University Press, 2007); Weinrib, "The Liberal Compromise."

34. See, e.g., DeJonge v. Oregon, 299 U.S. 353 (1937); Herndon v. Lowry, 301 U.S. 242 (1937); Lovell v. City of Griffin, 303 U.S. 444 (1938); Hague, 307 U.S. at 496; Jones v. City of Opelika, 316 U.S. 584 (1942); Murdock v. Pennsylvania, 319 U.S. 105 (1943); see generally Walker, *In Defense of American Liberties*, 110–11; Klarman, "Rethinking the Civil Rights and Civil Liberties Revolutions," 1–68; William McAninch, "A Catalyst for the Evolution of Constitutional Law: Jehovah's Witnesses in the Supreme Court," *University of Cincinnati Law Review* 55, no. 4 (1987): 997–1078; White, "The First Amendment Comes of Age," 330–36; Schneider v. New Jersey, 308 U.S. 147 (1939).

35. "Candidate for the Presidency," *Sunday Morning Star*, September 19, 1920, 12; "27 Alleged Communists Released," *Independent* (St. Petersburg, FL), January 9, 1932, 4-A; "Miami's Own Whirligig, the News behind the News—'Snooty Labor,'" *Miami News*, August 23, 1942, 1; "10 Radicals Jailed," *Pittsburgh Press*, August 23, 1928, 21; "Richly Gowned Woman Fined—Shoplifting Charge Is Cause of Arrest," *Milwaukee Journal*, August 10, 1914, 3; "Arrest 7 Active in Riot at Utica," *Schenectady* (NY) *Gazette*, July 8, 1932, 8; "Miss Thompson Arrested, Tried, Arrested Again," *Baltimore Afro-American*, May 26, 1934, 20; Owen L. Scott, "What's Going On in Washington," *Sunday Morning Star* (Wilmington, DE), September 26, 1937, 58; "Socialists Aid Fight to Release Imprisoned No. Carolina Strikers," 8; Free Speech and Labor Right Hearings, *pt. 48*, 74th Cong. 17,628–29 (1940), *pt. 61*, 74th Cong. 22,266 (1940), *pt. 68*, 74th Cong. 24,913 (1941).

36. "Lawyers Protest Raids on Radicals," *New York Times*, August 12, 1934, N1.

37. "Government by Police Chiefs," *New York Times*, October 2, 1936, 24; "Browder Is Jailed in Terre Haute; Held All Day to Prevent Speech," *New York Times*, October 1, 1936, 1; "Browder Jailed at Terre Haute in Move to Bar Campaign Talk," *Washington Post*, October 1, 1936, X1; "Government by Police Chiefs," *New York Times*, October 2, 1936, 24.

38. Charles H. Martin, "Communists and Blacks: The ILD and the Angelo Herndon Case," *Journal of Negro History* 64, no. 2 (1979): 131–41. Herndon was later the defendant in a case in which the Supreme Court invalidated Georgia's insurrection law; Herndon v. Georgia, 295 U.S. 441 (1935). See also Free Speech and Labor Right Hearings, *pt. 3*, 74th Cong. 760–61 (1937); Free Speech in Labor Right Hearings, *pt. 15C*, 74th Cong. 6315–16 (1938); Davis v. State, 34 N.E.2d 23 (Ind. 1941).

39. "Anything but Gentlemanly," *Time*, May 10, 1948 (quoting Bull Conner), cited in Diane McWhorter, *Carry Me Home: Birmingham, Alabama: The Climactic Battle of the Civil Rights Revolution* (New York: Simon and Schuster, 2001), 65; "Two Arrested in Drive on Reds in Birmingham," *Washington Post*, July 9, 1950, M1; Hallmark v. State, 185 So. 908 (Ala. Ct. App. 1939); Snitzer v. State, 199 So. 745 (Ala. Ct. App. 1940); Flandell v. State, 4 So.2d 264 (Ala. Ct. App. 1941); Ex parte Hall, 50 So.2d 264 (Ala. 1951); Hall v. City of Birmingham, 61 So.2d 773 (Ala. Ct. App. 1952).

40. Transcript of Record at 42–49, Edelman; Jack Liebau, "Judge Who Foiled Pickpockets Quits," *Los Angeles Times*, July 23 1981, SG6; "Richard Hayden Named Pasadena City Judge," *Los Angeles Times*, February 10, 1961, B3.

41. See, e.g., Paul Griffiths, *Lost Londons: Change, Crime, and Control in the Capital City, 1550–1660* (New York: Cambridge University Press, 2008); Forrest W. Lacey, "Vagrancy and Other Crimes of Personal Conduct," *Harvard Law Review* 66, no. 7 (1953): 1203; People v. Babb, 103 Cal. App. 2d 326, 229 P.2d 843 (1951).

42. See Marcus Dubber, *The Police Power* (New York: Columbia University Press, 2005), 130–38; Ernst Freund, *The Police Power: Public Policy and Constitutional Rights* (1904; repr., New York: Arno Press, 1976), 99; Bryan Wagner, *Disturbing the Peace: Black Culture and the Police Power after Slavery* (Cambridge, MA: Harvard University Press, 2009), 38–42; William J. Novak, *The People's Welfare: Law and Regulation in Nineteenth-Century America*

(Chapel Hill: University of North Carolina Press, 1996); Christopher Tomlins, *Freedom Bound: Law, Labor, and Civic Identity in Colonizing English America* (New York: Cambridge University Press, 2010); Christopher Tomlins, "Necessities of State: Police, Sovereignty, and the Constitution," *Journal of Policy History* 20, no. 1 (2008): 47. But see Christopher G. Tiedeman, *A Treatise on the Limitations of the Police Power in the United States Considered from both a Civil and Criminal Standpoint* (St. Louis: F. H. Thomas Law Book Co., 1886). See State v. Maxcy, 26 S.C.L. 501, 505 (S.C. Err. 1837); People v. Forbes, 19 How. Pr. 457 (N.Y. Sup. 1860); Morgan v. Nolte, 37 Ohio St. 23, 25–26 (Oh. 1881).

43. For critiques, see Freund, *Police Power*, 97, 99; Aubrey W. Grossman, "Who Is a Vagrant in California?" *California Law Review* 23, no. 5 (1935): 515. See also Black, "Idlers, Outliers and Dependents," 117. Even prominent critiques of the laws did not emphasize the problem of the status crime. See, e.g., Territory v. Anduha, 31 Haw. 459 (1930); Grossman, "Who Is a Vagrant in California?" 506–18; *Report of the New York Law Revision Commission* (1935), 591, quoted in Wayne R. LaFave, *Arrest: The Decision to Take a Suspect into Custody* (Boston: Little, Brown, 1965), 355 n. 50. The report stated, "The underlying purpose [of the vagrancy laws] is to relieve the police of the necessity of proving that criminals have committed or are planning to commit specific crimes." For continued defenses, see William A. Martin, "Vagrancy," in *Corpus Juris*, ed. William Mack and Donald J. Kiser, vol. 66 (New York: American Law Book Co., 1934), 399; Morgan v. Commonwealth, 191 S.E. 791, 794 (Va. 1937); see also State v. Harlowe, 24 P.2d 601 (Wash. 1933); "Vagrancy," in *Corpus Juris Secundum*, ed. Francis J. Ludes and Harold J. Gilbert, vol. 91 (Brooklyn: American Law Book Co., 1955), 778; Carl L. Shipley, "Guilt by Association," *Journal of the Bar Association of the District of Columbia* 21, no. 1 (1954): 16–20, discussed in 100 Cong. Rec. A280 (daily ed. January 18, 1954) (statement of Rep. Auchincloss) (praising vagrancy and other laws for criminalizing guilt by association).

44. Transcript of Record at 2–11, 19, Edelman.

45. E. P. Ryland, Chairman, SCACLU, to Leo Gallagher, January 5, 1943, folder 14, box 1, Leo Gallagher Papers; Clinton J. Taft, director, SCACLU, to Leo Gallagher, January 22, 1943, folder 14, box 1, Leo Gallagher Papers; Leo Gallagher to Clinton J. Taft, director, SCACLU, October 29, 1943, folder 14, box 1, Leo Gallagher Papers. See, e.g., Bridges v. Superior Court, 94 P.2d 983 (Cal. 1939); Bridges v. California, 314 U.S. 252 (1941) (Wirin and Gallagher both worked on the case in the lower courts, and Wirin in the Supreme Court); Ben Margolis, interview by Michael S. Balter, 124, 128, 131, 486; Leo Gallagher Biography, folder 1, box 1, Leo Gallagher Papers; Ceplair, "Leo Gallagher," n.d., folder 1, box 1, Leo Gallagher Papers.

46. Transcript of Record at 7, 11–14, Edelman.

47. Ibid. at 4, 15, 52, Edelman.

48. Ibid. at 10, 13, Edelman.

49. Fred Okrand, interview by Michael S. Balter, 1982, Forty Years Defending the Constitution: Oral History of Fred Okrand at 294, Center for Oral History Research, University of California, Los Angeles, http://oralhistory.library.ucla.edu/Browse.do?descCvPk=27430 (comparing Pershing Square to Hyde Park); Korman, " 'Next Friend' of Rosenbergs Tells Spy Aid," 7 (comparing it to Bughouse Square); "Rag of the 'Reds' Must Come Down," *Los Angeles Times*, March 3, 1908, I11. For Pershing Square arrests, "Arrest Three; Disperse Fabian Society Crowd," *Los Angeles Times*, November 17, 1919, II1; "To Drive Reds from the City," *Los Angeles Times*, November 16, 1919, IV14. Arrests continued in the 1920s and 1930s. "Complaints Delayed in Red Rioting," *Los Angeles Times*, November 1, 1931, A6; "Jury to Try Asserted Reds Being Picked," *Los Angeles Times*, November 6, 1931, A5; "Ten Suspects in Riot Held," *Los Angeles Times*, November 3, 1931, A8. And into the 1940s: see, e.g., "Lecturer without Permit Gets 10 Days, but It's Suspended," *Los Angeles Times*, March 2, 1946, 8; "The City in Brief," *Los Angeles Times*, May 2, 1907, I16; "The Police Court," *Los Angeles Times*, September 7, 1895, 7 (anarchist); "The Police Court," *Los Angeles Times*, September 8, 1895, 20; "The City in Brief," *Los Angeles Times*, September 30, 1902, 12 (religious orator); "Precautions by the Local Police," *Los Angeles Times*, September 8, 1901, B1; "Disturbed the Peace," *Los Angeles Times*, September 28, 1896, 10; "The Public Service—In the Courts and Offices," *Los Angeles Times*, September 30, 1909, I12; "Army Officers Aid Prisoner," *Los Angeles Times*, September 17, 1909, I12; "Park Spouters Not Tolerated," *Los Angeles Times*, June 4, 1904, A2; "Park Windjammers Must Keep Silent," *Los Angeles Times*, September 27, 1901, A6; "Plant Friend of Socialists," *Los Angeles*

Times, September 30, 1909, I12; "'Spouters' Nipped," *Los Angeles Times*, January 24, 1906, I14; "Squelching Spouters in Central Park," *Los Angeles Times*, August 26, 1902, 10; "Eminent Economists Fight," *Los Angeles Times*, July 3, 1907, I12; "Woman Orator in the Patrol," *Los Angeles Times*, July 3, 1905, I10; "Prominent Citizens May Be Arrested," *Los Angeles Times*, October 5, 1901, A2. See, e.g., "Wilshire on Patrol Wagon," *Los Angeles Times*, October 9, 1900, I10; Jack Smith, "The Boulevard of Token Dreams," *Los Angeles Times*, March 26, 1981, G1; Terry Lee Jones, "Downtown Tour Opens Some Eyes," *Los Angeles Times*, April 12, 1981, I25; "The Public Service—In the Offices and Courts," I10; "Spellbinders Arraigned," *Los Angeles Times*, October 5, 1900, I10; "Lawyer Shaw Guilty of Wife-Beating," *Los Angeles Times*, October 25, 1901, 10; Jack Smith, "All but the Kitchen Succinct," *Los Angeles Times*, March 5, 1978, H1; "Handbill Violation Costs Painter $10," *Los Angeles Times*, August 6, 1950, B3. At various times, the park also had its share of actual vagrants, who were also periodically purged. "Arrests in City Parks Continued," *Los Angeles Times*, January 16, 1923, I19. Judges sometimes balked at such arrests. "Another Judge Turns against Park Arrests," *Los Angeles Times*, June 29, 1928, A7; "Judge Upholds Pershing Park Perching Again," *Los Angeles Times*, June 1, 1928, A2; "Officer Curbed at Reds' Trial," *Los Angeles Times*, November 28, 1931, 14. See generally Mark Wild, *Street Meeting: Multiethnic Neighborhoods in Early Twentieth-Century Los Angeles* (Berkeley: University of California Press, 2005), 172.

50. Transcript of Record at 18–21, Edelman.
51. Ibid. at 18–21, Edelman.
52. Ibid. at 45, Edelman.
53. Ibid. at 2, 34–35, Edelman. Edelman received a concurrent ninety-day sentence for begging, based on his attempts to sell pamphlets. Ibid. at 37, 39, 58, Edelman; Brief of Petitioner at 1, Edelman v. California, 344 U.S. 357 (1953) (No. 86); Brief of Respondent in Opposition at 2, Edelman v. California, 344 U.S. 357 (1953) (No. 86).
54. Edelman v. California, 337 U.S. 949 (1949), rehearing denied 338 U.S. 842 (1949). Justice Stanley Reed, memorandum to conference, May 21, 1952, Edelman v. California (No. 86), box 311, Hugo LaFayette Black Papers, Library of Congress (hereafter Black Papers); Brief of Respondent in Opposition at 4, 6–7, Edelman; see also HJT (Howard J. Trienens), memorandum to conference, May 24, 1952, Edelman v. California (No. 86), box 179, Robert Houghwout Jackson Papers, Library of Congress (hereafter Jackson Papers).
55. Howard Ball, *Hugo L. Black: Cold Steel Warrior* (New York: Oxford University Press, 1996); Howard Ball, *The Vision and the Dream of Justice Hugo L. Black: An Examination of a Judicial Philosophy* (Tuscaloosa: University of Alabama Press); Steve Suitts, *Hugo Black of Alabama: How His Roots and Early Career Shaped the Great Champion of the Constitution* (Montgomery: NewSouth Books, 2005).
56. Daniel M. Berman, "The Racial Issue and Mr. Justice Black," *American University Law Review* 16, no. 3 (1967): 387–88; Howard Ball and Phillip Cooper, *Of Power and Right: Hugo Black, William O. Douglas, and America's Constitutional Revolution* (New York: Oxford University Press, 1992), 196.
57. "Howard Langer interviews Associate Justice, U.S. Supreme Court, William O. Douglas," produced by Howard Langer (New York City: Smithsonian Folkways Records, 1957); William O. Douglas, *Go East, Young Man: The Early Years, the Autobiography of William O. Douglas* (New York: Random House, 1974), 75–86; William O. Douglas, *Of Men and Mountains* (New York: Harper, 1950), 9–16; Hoboes of America documents and correspondence, Hoboes of America, Washington, DC, 1939–1966 folder, box 1762, William O. Douglas Papers, Library of Congress (hereafter Douglas Papers). See Bruce Allen Murphy, *Wild Bill: The Legend and Life of William O. Douglas* (New York: Random House, 2003), 118–23; G. Edward White, "The Anti-Judge: William O. Douglas and the Ambiguities of Individuality," *Virginia Law Review* 74 (1988): 17.
58. On the Cold War, see, e.g., Stanley I. Kutler, *The American Inquisition: Justice and Injustice in the Cold War* (New York: Hill and Wang, 1982); Hannah Arendt, *The Origins of Totalitarianism* (New York: Harcourt, Brace, 1951). For cases, see, e.g., Breard v. City of Alexandria, 341 U.S. 622 (1951); Dennis v. United States, 341 U.S. 494 (1951); Feiner v. New York, 340 U.S. 315 (1951). But see, e.g., Joint Anti-Fascist Refugee Committee v. McGrath, 341 U.S. 123 (1951); Rumely, 345 U.S. 41; Beauharnais v. Illinois, 343 U.S. 250

(1952); Adler v. Board of Education, 342 U.S. 485 (1952). On Black and Douglas dissents, see, e.g., Breard v. City of Alexandria, 341 U.S. 622 (Vinson, J., Black, J., and Douglas, J. dissenting); Dennis v. United States, 341 U.S. 494 (Black, J. and Douglas, J., dissenting); Feiner v. New York, 340 U.S. 315 (Black, J., Douglas, J., and Minton, J., dissenting). But see, e.g., McGrath, 341 U.S. 123; Rumely, 345 U.S. 41. Beauharnais, 343 U.S. 250 (Black, J., Reed, J., Douglas, J., and Jackson, J., dissenting); Adler, 342 U.S. 485 (Black, J., Douglas, J., and Frankfurter, J., dissenting). Of course, Black and Douglas did not always agree on every First Amendment case. See, e.g., American Communications Ass'n v. Douds, 339 U.S. 382 (1950); Osman v. Douds, 339 U.S. 846 (1950); Ball and Cooper, *Of Power and Right*. On the Warren Court generally, see, e.g., Leonard W. Levy, *The Supreme Court under Earl Warren* (New York: Quadrangle Books, 1972); Archibald Cox, *The Warren Court: Constitutional Decision as an Instrument of Reform* (Cambridge, MA: Harvard University Press,1968); Alexander, M. Bickel, *Politics and the Warren Court* (New York: Harper and Row, 1965); Michal R. Belknap, *The Supreme Court under Earl Warren, 1953–1969* (Columbia: University of South Carolina Press, 2005); Mark Tushnet, ed., *The Warren Court in Historical and Political Perspective* (Charlottesville: University of Virginia Press, 1993); Justin Driver, "The Constitutional Conservatism of the Warren Court," *California Law Review* 100 (2012): 1101.

59. Docket sheet (with voting tally), Edelman v. California, box 85, Douglas Papers.

60. Brief of Petitioner at 13–17, Edelman; see Justice Hugo Black, memorandum (draft dissent to the denial of cert.), Edelman v. California, May 19, 1952, box 311, Black Papers. For loitering and vagrancy considered together, see, e.g., In re Stegenga, 94 N.W. 385 (Mich. 1903); Burns v. District of Columbia, 34 A.2d. 714 (D.C. 1943). For examples of courts striking down such laws, see Anduha, 31 Haw. 459 (which Edelman's brief also neglected to cite). It is possible that the lawyers chose not to cite *Thornhill* and *Carlson* because, in the wake of 1947's Taft-Hartley amendments to the National Labor Relations Act, those cases had come in for no small abuse from commentators and courts. See, e.g., Charles O. Gregory, "Constitutional Limitations on the Regulation of Union and Employer Conduct," *Michigan Law Review* 49, no. 2 (1950): 191–212; Sylvester Petro, "Participation by the States in the Enforcement and Development of National Labor Policy," *Notre Dame Lawyer* 28, no. 1 (1952): 26 n. 71; AFL v. Vogt, 354 US 284, 290–91 (1957). Black and Douglas, for the most part, continued to stand by *Thornhill's* basic protection for peaceful picketing. AFL v. Vogt, 354 U.S. 295 (Douglas, J., dissenting).

61. Brief of Petitioner at 10–11, Edelman. See also Affidavit and Application for Leave to Prosecute Petition for Writ of Certiorari in Forma Pauperis, Edelman v. California, RG 267, box 42, US Supreme Court, 85 OT 1952, 17E3/11/31/05, National Archives and Records Administration; Winters v. New York, 333 U.S. 507, 515 (1948). On void for vagueness, see Anthony G. Amsterdam, "The Void-for-Vagueness Doctrine in the Supreme Court," *University of Pennsylvania Law Review* 109, no. 1 (1960): 67–116; John C. Jeffries Jr., "Legality, Vagueness, and the Construction of Penal Statutes," *Virginia Law Review* 71, no. 2 (1985): 189–245; Robert C. Post, "Reconceptualizing Vagueness: Legal Rules and Social Orders," *California Law Review* 82, no. 3 (1994): 491–508. Brief of Petitioner at 11, 13, Edelman.

62. Lanzetta v. New Jersey, 306 U.S. 451, 458 (1939). See Jerome Hall, "The Law of Arrest in Relation to Social Problems," *University of Chicago Law Review* 3, no. 3 (1936): 369; Carl V. Eimbeck, "Some Recent Methods of Harassing the Habitual Criminal," *St. Louis Law Review* 16, no. 2 (1930–1931): 155.

63. Liva Baker, *Felix Frankfurter* (New York: Coward-McCann, 1969); Helen Shirley Thomas, *Felix Frankfurter: Scholar on the Bench* (Baltimore: Johns Hopkins University Press, 1960); Winters v. New York, 333 U.S. at 540 (Frankfurter, J., dissenting).

64. Brief of Petitioner at 7, Edelman; Herbert Monte Levy to Irving Ferman, memorandum, November 14, 1952, Edelman v. California (No. 86), folder 22, box 750, American Civil Liberties Union Records, The Roger Baldwin Years, Department of Rare Books and Special Collections, Princeton University Library (hereafter Princeton ACLU Papers); Herbert Monte Levy to Paul S. Tenen, October 18, 1950, Edelman v. California (No. 86), folder 22, box 750, Series 3, Subseries 3A.4, Princeton ACLU Papers; "Constitutionality of Calif. Vag. Law Before Supreme Court," *American Civil Liberties Union-News* 17, no. 9 (September 1952), box 47, UCLA ACLU Records (collection 900).

65. Herbert Monte Levy to Emanuel Redfield, December 12, 1952, Edelman v. California, folder 22, box 750, Series 3, Subseries 3A.4, Princeton ACLU Papers; "Emanuel Redfield, 78, Civil Liberties Counsel," *New York Times*, January 24, 1983; "State Vagrancy Law Challenged in Suit," *New York Times*, March 7, 1952, 5; ACLU News Release, January 12, 1951, folder 18, box 1038, Series 3, Subseries 3B.5, Princeton ACLU Papers; John Paul Jones to Hon. Arthur H. Wickes, January 12, 1951, folder 18, box 1038, Series 3, Subseries 3B.5, Princeton ACLU Papers; handwritten note ("Round-up of 'Hoodlums'"), March 13, 1951, folder 18, box 1038, Series 3, Subseries 3B.5, Princeton ACLU Papers.

66. "Test Case Is Filed on Vagrancy Law," *New York Times*, July 26, 1951, 46; "Anti-Vagrant Law Attacked in Court," *New York Times*, August 16, 1951, 26; "City on Defensive on Vagrancy Act," *New York Times*, October 21, 1951, 26; "Vagrancy Law 'Problems' Will Get Court Scrutiny," *New York Times*, August 18, 1951, 8; Arnold v. Twomey, 105 N.E.2d 628 (N.Y. 1952).

67. Fred Okrand to Emanuel Redfield, November 12, 1952, folder 18, box 1038, Series 3, Subseries 3B.5, Princeton ACLU Papers; Herbert Monte Levy to Irving Ferman, memorandum, November 14, 1952, folder 18, box 1038, Series 3, Subseries 3B.5, Princeton ACLU Papers; Emanuel Redfield to Fred Okrand, November 20, 1952, folder 18, box 1038, Series 3, Subseries 3B.5, Princeton ACLU Papers.

68. Emanuel Redfield to Fred Okrand, November 20, 1952, folder 18, box 1038, Series 3, Subseries 3B.5, Princeton ACLU Papers.

69. Notes, Edelman v. California, box 179, Jackson Papers. Douglas initially passed and Black voted against. See WHR (William H. Rehnquist) to Justice Robert H. Jackson, memorandum, n.d., Edelman v. California (No. 86), box 179, Jackson Papers. For DIGs, see Arceneaux v. Louisiana, 376 U.S. 336 (1964); Hicks v. District of Columbia, 383 U.S. 252 (1966); Wainwright v. City of New Orleans, 392 U.S. 598 (1968).

70. Edelman v. California, 344 U.S. 357, 358–59 (1953).

71. Edelman, 344 U.S. at 362, 365 n. 2, 366.

72. Justice Hugo Black, memorandum (draft dissent to the denial of cert.), May 19, 1952, Edelman v. California (No. 86), box 311, Black Papers (emphasis added); Edelman, 344 U.S. at 366 (emphasis added). Moreover, where he cited *Lanzetta* in a draft of the DIG, he cited a free speech case that used vagueness in the final version.

73. "Spy Case Limelight Shines on Pershing Square Orator," 2; Ronald Radosh and Joyce Milton, *The Rosenberg File*, 2nd ed. (New Haven, CT: Yale University Press, 1997), 383.

74. Brad Snyder, "Taking Great Cases: Lessons from the *Rosenberg* Case," *Vanderbilt Law Review* 63, no. 4 (2010): 898, 902; Michael E. Parrish, "Cold War Justice: The Supreme Court and the Rosenbergs," *American Historical Review* 82, no. 4 (1977): 805–42; John F. Neville, *The Press, the Rosenbergs, and the Cold War* (Santa Barbara: Praeger, 1995), 121–30; Radosh and Milton, *Rosenberg File*, 397–412.

75. Snyder, "Taking Great Cases," 885–956, 919. Radosh and Milton, *Rosenberg File*, 405–6; Joseph H. Sharlitt, *Fatal Error: The Miscarriage of Justice that Sealed the Rosenbergs' Fate* (New York: Charles Scribner's Sons, 1989), 118, 130; Neville, *The Press, the Rosenbergs, and the Cold War*, 130; "The Last Appeal," *Time*, June 29, 1953; Rosenberg v. U.S., 346 U.S. 273, 291 (1953) (Jackson, J.).

76. Fred Okrand, interview by Michael S. Balter, 292–95; Transcript of Record at 17, Edelman.

77. "Spy Case Limelight Shines on Pershing Square Orator," 2; Korman, "'Next Friend' of Rosenbergs Tells Spy Aid." See also Walter Winchell, "Of New York: Peddoing His Papers," *Washington Post*, June 25, 1953, 35.

78. Dragna v. California, 344 U.S. 921 (1953), rehearing denied 344 U.S. 921 (1953). See also Notes, n.d., Dragna v. California, box 222, Douglas Papers; CEA (Charles E. Ares) to Justice William O. Douglas, memorandum, March 5, 1953, Dragna v. California, folder 8, box 224, Douglas Papers.

79. "Supreme Court Upholds Deportation of Ex-Red," *Los Angeles Times*, January 13, 1953, 7; "Edelman, Figure in Rosenberg Case, Convicted," *Los Angeles Times*, July 1, 1953, 29; "Edelman to Go Free if He Registers as Vagrant," *Los Angeles Times*, July 7, 1953, 25; "Speech Right Upheld after 5-Year Court Battle in L.A.," *American Civil Liberties Union-News* 19, no. 5 (May 1952), box 47, UCLA ACLU Records (collection 900); "Man Who Got Rosenberg Stay Haled to Court," *Los Angeles Times*, June 24, 1953, A6; "Edelman, Figure in Rosenberg

Case, Convicted," *Los Angeles Times,* July 1, 1953, 29; "Edelman to Go Free if He Registers as Vagrant," *Los Angeles Times,* July 7, 1953, 25.

80. "Court Upsets Conviction of Pamphleteer," *Los Angeles Times,* January 23, 1954, 3; "Speech Right Upheld after 5-Year Court Battle in L.A.," *American Civil Liberties Union-News* 19, no. 9 (September 1952), box 47, UCLA ACLU Records (collection 900).

81. Lacey, "Vagrancy and Other Crimes of Personal Condition," 1203, 1222; Henry Silver, "Vag Lewd: A Criticism of the California Statute," *Los Angeles Daily Journal* 7, reprinted in *Mattachine Review* 1, no. 1 (January–February 1955): 3; John M. Coe, "Practices of Police and Prosecution Prior to Trial," *Lawyers Guild Review* 17, no. 2 (1957): 62, 64.

Chapter 2

1. Ernest Besig to Governor Edmund G. Brown ("Pat"), typewritten letter, July 10, 1959, MS 3580, carton 36, folder 781, American Civil Liberties Union of Northern California records, California Historical Society, San Francisco (hereafter Cal. Hist. Soc'y Cal. ACLU Papers); Stephen Schwartz, "Ernest Besig," SFGate, November 21, 1998, http://www.sfgate.com/news/article/Ernest-Besig-2977857.php.

2. Ernest Besig to Governor Edmund G. Brown ("Pat"), typewritten letter, July 10, 1959, MS 3580, carton 36, folder 781, Cal. Hist. Soc'y ACLU Papers.

3. Leeanna McDuffy to Fowler, handwritten note, n.d., MS 3580, carton 36, folder 778, Series 2, Subseries 2.30, Cal. Hist. Soc'y ACLU Papers.

4. On earlier critiques of police abuse of African Americans, see, e.g., Martha Biondi, *To Stand and Fight: The Struggle for Civil Rights in Postwar New York City* (Cambridge, MA: Harvard University Press, 2006). On the raids and the ACLU response to them, see "Mass Arrests of Negroes in Lawless Raid; Union Secures Freedom for Seven Victims," *American Civil Liberties Union News,* April 1954, 1, MS 3580, carton 36, folder 788, Series 2, Subseries 2.30, Cal. Hist. Soc'y ACLU Papers; Ernest Besig to State Board of Equalization, typewritten letter, April 24, 1954, MS 3580, carton 36, folder 788, Series 2, Subseries 2.30, Cal. Hist. Soc'y ACLU Papers. See also "E. Bay Raids Put CLU into Action," *San Francisco News,* March 13, 1954, box 36, folder 778, Series 2, Subseries 2.30, Cal. Hist. Soc'y ACLU Papers; "23 Plead Innocent to Charges of Vagrancy," *Oakland Tribune,* March 9, 1954, 20, 23, box 36, folder 778, Series 2, Subseries 2.30, Cal. Hist. Soc'y ACLU Papers. On Besig's background and position within the ACLU, see "Safeguarding Civil Liberties: Oral History of Eason Monroe," by Joel Gardner (Los Angeles: Oral History Program of UCLA, 1974), 282; Judy Kutulas, *The American Civil Liberties Union and the Making of Modern Liberalism* (Chapel Hill: University of North Carolina Press, 2006), 51. On Speiser's background and work with the vagrancy cases, see Executive Committee meeting minutes, October 2, 1952, box 47, American Civil Liberties Union of Southern California records (collection 900), Charles E. Young Research Library, UCLA Library Special Collections (hereafter UCLA ACLU Papers); Noam S. Cohen, "Lawrence Speiser, 68, a Civil Liberties Lawyer," *New York Times,* September 1, 1991. Though the ACLU had contemplated bringing a federal civil rights suit in addition to the false arrest claims, it does not appear that the group ever filed such a suit. Other lawyers also filed claims, with some success. See, e.g., Onick v. Long, 316 P.2d 427 (Cal. Ct. App. 1957).

5. Ernest Besig, handwritten notes, n.d., MS 3580, carton 36, folder 778, Cal. Hist. Soc'y ACLU Papers.

6. Ibid. For states' attempts to equate a person's having only illegitimate means of support with lacking visible means altogether, see, e.g., People ex. rel. Sammons v. Snow, 173 N.E. 8 (Ill. 1930); Hallmark v. State, 198 So. 149, 150 (Ala. Ct. App. 1940); Snitzer v. State, 199 So. 745 (Ala. Ct. App., 1940); Flandell v. State, 19 So. 2d 401 (Ala. Ct. App., 1944); Reynolds v. State, 4 So. 2d 201 (Ala. Ct. App. 1941); People v. Belcastro, 190 N.E. 301 (Ill. 1934); Morgan v. Commonwealth, 191 S.E. 791 (Va. 1937); Joel E. Black, "Idlers, Outliers and Dependents: The Free Labor Order in Industrial Chicago, 1870–1930" (Ph.D. diss., University of Florida, 2010), 251. For Besig's complaints, see Ernest Besig to Stockton Chief of Police (Jack O'Keefe), September 22, 1955, MS 3580, carton 36, folder 779, Cal. Hist. Soc'y ACLU Papers; "Arrests for Vagrancy Hit," *Stockton Record,* September 27, 1955, MS 3580, carton 36,

folder 779, Cal. Hist. Soc'y ACLU Papers. See also Albert White, letter to the editor, *Stockton Record*, September 19, 1955 MS 3580, carton 36, folder 779, Cal. Hist. Soc'y ACLU Papers; Jack O'Keefe (Stockton Chief of Police) to Ernest Besig, September 30, 1955, MS 3580, carton 36, folder 779, Cal. Hist. Soc'y ACLU Papers; "Crackdown on Vagrants Lauded," *Stockton Record*, October 13, 1955, MS 3580, carton 36, folder 779, Cal. Hist. Soc'y ACLU Papers; Jack O'Keefe (Stockton Chief of Police), letter to the editor, Stockton Record, October 3, 1955, MS 3580, carton 36, folder 779, Cal. Hist. Soc'y ACLU Papers.

7. See, e.g., Police Complaints against Thornton Jones Junior and Thomas Richard Tryon in the Justice Court of the San Pablo Judicial District in Contra Costa County, MS 3580, carton 36, folder 778, Cal. Hist. Soc'y ACLU Papers.

8. "Civil Liberties Union Looks into Mass Arrests," *Mattachine Review*, vol. 2, Special Issue (March 1956): 4; Cal. Penal Code § 415 (1955). On the revocation of gay bars' liquor licenses, see Elaine Elinson and Stan Yogi, *Wherever There's a Fight: How Runaway Slaves, Suffragists, Immigrants, Strikers, and Poets Shaped Civil Liberties in California* (Berkeley: Heyday, 2009), 314–16; Patricia A. Cain, "Litigating for Lesbian and Gay Rights: A Legal History," *Virginia Law Review* 79 (1993): 1567–72; John D'Emilio, *Sexual Politics, Sexual Communities: The Making of a Homosexual Minority in the United States, 1940–1970* (Chicago: University of Chicago Press, 1983), 182–83; William N. Eskridge Jr., "Some Effects of Identity-Based Social Movements on Constitutional Law in the Twentieth Century," *Michigan Law Review* 100, no. 8 (2002): 2160, 2165; Christopher Agee, "Gayola: Police Professionalization and the Politics of San Francisco's Gay Bars, 1950–1968," *Journal of the History of Sexuality* 15, no. 3 (September 2006), 462–89, 466. See, e.g., Stoumen v. Reilly, 234 P.2d 969 (Cal. 1951); Vallegra v. Dep't of Alcoholic Beverage Control, 347 P.2d 909 (Cal. 1959). Hazel Nickola's license was revoked in 1957. "Pervert Charge Too Vague, Says Bar Owner," *San Francisco Chronicle*, June 18, 1957, MS 3580, carton 36, folder 782, Cal. Hist. Soc'y ACLU Papers.

9. D'Emilio, *Sexual Politics, Sexual Communities*, 41–53; Margot Canaday, *The Straight State: Sexuality and Citizenship in Twentieth-Century America* (Princeton, NJ: Princeton University Press, 2009), 168, 246; David K. Johnson, *The Lavender Scare: The Cold War Persecution of Gays and Lesbians in the Federal Government* (Chicago: University of Chicago Press, 2004), 149; Allan Bérubé, *Coming Out under Fire: The History of Gay Men and Women in World War II* (New York: Plume, 1991), 28; Robert J. Corber, *Homosexuality in Cold War America: Resistance and the Crisis of Masculinity* (Durham, NC: Duke University Press, 1997); Neil Miller, *Sex-Crime Panic: A Journey to the Paranoid Heart of the 1950s* (Los Angeles: Alyson Books, 2002); William N. Eskridge Jr., "Privacy Jurisprudence and the Apartheid of the Closet, 1946–61," *Florida State University Law Review* 24, no. 4 (1997): 726–27. For cases, see, e.g., United States v. Flores-Rodriguez, 237 F.2d 405 (1956); Lavoie v. Immigration and Naturalization Services, 360 F.2d 27 (9th Cir. 1966); Ganduxe y Marino v. Murff 183 F. Supp. 565 (S.D.N.Y. 1959); Babouris v. Esperdy, 269 F.2d 621 (2d Cir. 1959); see also Deborah W. Denno, "Life before the Modern Sex Offender Statutes," *Northwestern University Law Review* 92 (1998): 1318; Estelle B. Freedman, " 'Uncontrolled Desires': The Response to the Sexual Psychopath, 1920–1960," *Journal of American History* 74 (1987): 83–84, 94; John Howard, "The Library, the Park, and the Pervert: Public Space and Homosexual Encounter in Post-World War II Atlanta," *Radical History Review* 62 (1995): 170, 175.

10. The San Francisco gay and lesbian population grew by over 125,000 between 1940 and 1950. John D'Emilio, "Gay Politics, Gay Community: San Francisco's Experience," *Socialist Review* 11, no. 1 (January–February 1981): 81; D'Emilio, *Sexual Politics, Sexual Communities*, 40–53; Eskridge, "Privacy Jurisprudence and the Apartheid of the Closet," 722–723, 768. In Los Angeles, arrests for so-called sex perversion increased by 85 percent after 1950. Elinson and Yogi, *Wherever There's a Fight*, 317. For reactions to the increasing size and visibility of gay and lesbian populations in Marin County (California), Los Angeles, and Philadelphia, see "Drive on Homosexuals Announced by Police," *Mattachine Review* 5, no. 4 (April 1959): 14; "17 Cops Catch 1 Homosexual in Well-Planned Trap," *Mattachine Review* 5, no 5 (May 1959): 17; "Western-Adams Residents Seek Public Vice Action," *Los Angeles Times*, January 30, 1961, 2; Mark Stein, *City of Sisterly and Brotherly Loves: Lesbian and Gay Philadelphia 1945–72* (Chicago: University of Chicago Press, 2000), 170; Hal Schulz, "Homosexual Activities on Rise, City Informed," *Los Angeles Times*, March 9, 1966.

11. On early attempts to enforce sodomy proscriptions, see Elinson and Yogi, *Wherever There's a Fight*, 311; David Sklansky, "'One Train May Hide Another': *Katz*, Stonewall, and the Secret Subtext of Criminal Procedure," *University of California, Davis Law Review* 41, no. 3 (2008): 875. On enforcement attempts that implicated vagrancy, disorderly conduct, public lewdness, or solicitation laws, see D'Emilio, *Sexual Politics, Sexual Communities*, 146; Eskridge, "Privacy Jurisprudence and the Apartheid of the Closet," 725 n. 107. Two additional laws were used to police gays and lesbians in California: Penal Code § 650.5, "outraging public decency," and Penal Code § 185, prohibiting "wearing masks or personal disguise." Cal. Penal Code § 650.5 (1955); Cal. Penal Code § 185 (1955). Agee, "Gayola," 462–89. On the New York law, see Charles W. McCurdy, *The Anti-Rent Era in New York Law and Politics, 1839–1865* (Chapel Hill: University of North Carolina Press, 2001), 175, 274. Amendments to the UK's vagrancy law made it a misdemeanor for men to commit indecent assault, solicit other men for immoral purposes, or dress in "female attire." William N. Eskridge Jr., *Gaylaw: Challenging the Apartheid of the Closet* (Cambridge, MA: Harvard University Press, 1999), 389 n. 40. For arrests of "social vagrants," see, e.g., "Vice Squad Officers Round Up 19 Men," *Los Angeles Times*, April 13, 1948, 17; "19 Arrested by Vice Squad in Café Raid," *Los Angeles Times*, February 8, 1953, 3; "El Monte High Teacher Named in Morals Case," *Los Angeles Times*, September 15, 1955, A6; Eskridge, *Gaylaw*, 31. See generally Angus McLaren, *The Trials of Masculinity: Policing Sexual Boundaries, 1870–1930* (Chicago: University of Chicago Press, 1999); George Chauncey, *Gay New York: Gender, Urban Culture, and the Makings of the Gay Male World, 1890–1940* (New York: Basic Books, 1994), 294; Nan Alamilla Boyd, *Wide Open Town: A History of Queer San Francisco to 1965* (Berkeley: University of California Press, 2003), 103.

12. D'Emilio, *Sexual Politics, Sexual Communities*, 49; "19 Arrested by Vice Squad in Café Raid," 3; Elinson and Yogi, *Wherever There's a Fight*, 317; Boyd, *Wide Open Town*, 156. Both women and men (often called "female impersonators") were arrested under such laws. Eskridge, "Privacy Jurisprudence and the Apartheid of the Closet," 723 n. 98; Cain, "Litigating for Lesbian and Gay Rights," 1565–66 n. 85.

13. "Lecturer Jailed on Morals Charge," *Los Angeles Times*, January 23, 1953, 23. For consequences of these charges, see, e.g., Fountain v. Bd. of Educ., 320 P.2d 899 (Cal. Dist. Ct. App. 1958); DiGenova v. State Bd. Of Educ., 367 P.2d 865 (Cal. 1961); "El Monte High Teacher Named in Morals Case"; "Professor Admits Disturbing Peace," *Los Angeles Times*, March 17, 1949, A6; "Councilman Bennett Gets $100 Fine as Disturber," *Los Angeles Times*, November 28, 1950, A3; "Actor Pleads to Misconduct," *Los Angeles Times*, July 15, 1950, A5; "Lewd Vagrancy Sentence Given," *Los Angeles Times*, April 19, 1951, A26; "Salesman Denies Morals Charge," *Los Angeles Times*, June 6, 1951, 5. See also In re Boyd, 307 P.2d 625 (Cal. 1957). See generally Eskridge, *Gaylaw*, 98; C. Todd White, *Pre-Gay L.A.: A Social History of the Movement for Homosexual Rights* (Urbana: University of Illinois Press, 2009), 26; D'Emilio, *Sexual Politics, Sexual Communities*, 49. On involuntary commitment of "sexual psychopaths," see Elinson and Yogi, *Wherever There's a Fight*, 323–24; Robert L. Jacobson, "'Megan's Laws' Reinforcing Old Patterns of Anti-Gay Police Harassment," *Georgetown Law Journal* 87 (1999): 2431, 2440–45. On the 1947 California registration requirement, see Boyd, *Wide Open Town*, 175; Elinson and Yogi, *Wherever There's a Fight*, 323. Some registration requirements predated 1947, with one passed in 1945. Eskridge, "Privacy Jurisprudence and the Apartheid of the Closet," 716 n. 57. In addition, states and localities continued to pass stricter and more encompassing laws over the next several years. See, e.g., "Degenerate Ban Voted," *Los Angeles Times*, March 12, 1949, A1. For vag lewd arrestees' guilty pleas, see, e.g. "Professor Admits Disturbing Peace"; "Councilman Bennett Gets $100 Fine as Disturber"; Eskridge, "Privacy Jurisprudence and the Apartheid of the Closet," 720.

14. Bérubé, *Coming Out under Fire*; Elinson and Yogi, *Wherever There's a Fight*, 310, 313; D'Emilio, *Sexual Politics, Sexual Communities*, 58–70; Martin Meeker, *Contacts Desired: Gay and Lesbian Communications and Community, 1940s–1970s* (Chicago: University of Chicago Press, 2006).

15. Stuart Timmons, "The Trouble with Harry," *Los Angeles Times Magazine*, November 25, 1990, 21; D'Emilio, *Sexual Politics, Sexual Communities*, 70–71; Patricia Cain, *Rainbow Rights: The Role of Lawyers and Courts in the Lesbian and Gay Civil Rights Movement* (Boulder, CO: Westview Press, 2000), 54; Elinson and Yogi, *Wherever There's a Fight*, 324. Others had pleaded not guilty to vag lewd charges before Dale Jennings. See, e.g., "Lewd Vagrancy Sentence Given"; "Salesman Denies Morals Charge".

16. Alfred C. Kinsey, Wardell B. Pomery, and Clyde E. Martin, *Sexual Behavior in the Human Male* (Philadelphia: Saunders, 1948); Alfred C. Kinsey et al., *Sexual Behavior in the Human Female* (Philadelphia: Saunders, 1953); Leigh Ann Wheeler, *How Sex Became a Civil Liberty* (Oxford: Oxford University Press, 2013), 105.

17. John Stuart Mill, "Introductory," and "Of the Limits to the Authority of Society over the Individual," in *On Liberty*, 2nd ed. (London: John W. Parker and Son, 1859); Louis Lusky, "Invasion of Privacy: A Clarification of Concepts," *Columbia Law Review* 72, no. 4 (1972): 704 n. 34. For a contrary view, see James Stephen, *Liberty, Equality, Fraternity* (New York: Holt & Williams, 1873). See generally the famous exchange between H. L. A. Hart and Patrick Devlin: Patrick Devlin, *The Enforcement of Morals* (Oxford: Oxford University Press, 1965); H. L. A. Hart, *Law, Liberty and Morality* (Palo Alto, CA: Stanford University Press, 1963); H. L. A. Hart, *The Morality of the Criminal Law* (Jerusalem: Magnes Press, Hebrew University, 1964). See also Edwin M. Schur, *Crimes without Victims* (Englewood Cliffs, NJ: Prentice-Hall, 1965); . For the ALI position, see Model Penal Code, §§ 207.1 cmt. at 207, 207.5 cmt. at 277–78 (Tentative Draft No. 4 1955); Model Penal Code § 251.3 cmt. at 474–79 (Official Draft and Revised Comments 1980) (on solicitation); see also Louis B. Schwartz, "Morals Offenses and the Model Penal Code," *Columbia Law Review* 63, no. 4 (1963): 669–86. For the Wolfenden position, see Committee on Homosexual Offenses and Prostitution, *The Wolfenden Report*, Authorized American ed. (New York: Stein and Day, 1963), paras. 14, 61. The Supreme Court's decision in *One, Inc. v. Olesen*, 355 U.S. 371 (1958), which summarily reversed the U.S. Post Office's refusal to mail the Mattachine Society's magazine because it was obscene, also seemed to mark a possible softening of attitudes about homosexuality.

18. The California courts had repeatedly held that even though vagrancy was a status crime, a single act of lewdness "of such a nature that it reasonably justifies an inference that no one not of lewd or dissolute character would do such an act even once" was sufficient to support a vagrancy conviction under subdivision five. See, e.g., People v. Babb, 229 P.2d 843 (Cal. Ct. App. 1951); People v. Brandt, 306 P.2d 1069 (Cal. App. Dep't Super. Ct. 1957). Lanzetta v. New Jersey, 306 U.S. 451 (1939); Winters v. New York, 333 U.S. 507 (1948); Edelman v. California, 344 U.S. 357 (1953).

19. See Wheeler, *How Sex Became a Civil Liberty*, 156–57.

20. Boyd, *Wide Open Town*, 106; Elinson and Yogi, *Wherever There's a Fight*, 324.

21. Lawrence Speiser to Rowland Watts, letter, July 1, 1957, folder 30, box 968, American Civil Liberties Union Records, Series 3, Subseries 3B.1, Department of Rare Books and Special Collections, Princeton University Library (hereafter Princeton ACLU Papers). (Though it seems most likely these arrests were from Hazel's Inn, it is possible that they stemmed from some other police raid of a "bar in which men were dancing with men."); Rowland Watts to Northern California Civil Liberties Union, memorandum, August 29, 1957, folder 28, box 968, Series 3, Subseries 3B.1, Princeton ACLU Papers (copied to Lawrence Speiser). For Watts's efforts to encourage vagrancy challenges, see, e.g., Emil Oxfeld to Saturna Figueroa, letter, November 5, 1957, folder 30, box 968, Series 3, Subseries 3B.1, Princeton ACLU Papers (copied to Rowland Watts and the ACLU); Rowland Watts to Emil Oxfeld, letter, November 5, 1957, folder 30, box 968, Series 3, Subseries 3B.1, Princeton ACLU Papers. On friction between the national ACLU and its northern California branch, see Samuel Walker, *In Defense of American Liberties: A History of the ACLU*, 2nd ed. (Carbondale: Southern Illinois University Press, 1990), 142; Kutulas, *American Civil Liberties Union*, 47–48.

22. Wheeler, *How Sex Became a Civil Liberty*, 114; D'Emilio, *Sexual Politics, Sexual Communities*, 112, 117, 155–56; Walker, *In Defense of American Liberties*, 312 (quoting ACLU, Board of Directors, "Minutes" (January 7, 1957)); *NYCLU Penal Code Committee Report* (January 31, 1966), 12 (recommending deletion of New York's sodomy law); Board meeting minutes (February 5, 1959), UCLA ACLU Papers; Vern L. Bullough, "Lesbianism, Homosexuality, and the American Civil Liberties Union," *Journal of Homosexuality* 13, no. 1 (Fall 1986): 23–26.

23. "Civil Liberties Union Looks into Mass Arrests," 4.

24. Bill Morgan, *The Typewriter Is Holy: The Complete, Uncensored History of the Beat Generation* (New York: Free Press, 2010); Steven Watson, *The Birth of the Beat Generation* (New York: Pantheon Books, 1995); John Tytell, *Naked Angels: The Lives & Literature of the Beat Generation* (New York: McGraw-Hill, 1976); Michael Davidson, *The San Francisco*

Renaissance: Poetics and Community at Mid-Century (New York: Cambridge University Press, 1989); James Campbell, *This Is the Beat Generation: New York, San Francisco, Paris* (Berkeley: University of California Press, 1999); Brenda Knight, *Women of the Beat Generation: The Writers, Artists, and Muses at the Heart of Revolution* (Berkeley, CA: Conari Press, 2000); D'Emilio, *Sexual Politics, Sexual Communities*, 177–81; Francis B. O'Gara, "'Rousting' on Race Basis Here Denied," *San Francisco Examiner*, July 29, 1958, MS 3580, carton 36, folder 782, Cal. Hist. Soc'y ACLU Papers. For North Beach's nicknames in the press, see, e.g., "Cops Score in Beatland—Three Jugged," *San Francisco Examiner*, September 3, 1959, MS 3580, carton 36, folder 782, Cal. Hist. Soc'y ACLU Papers; "Brawl Opens Beatnik Trial," *San Francisco Chronicle*, August 1, 1959, MS 3580, carton 36, folder 782, Cal. Hist. Soc'y ACLU Papers; "Wendy Gets $50 Fine, Lecture and Probation," *San Francisco Examiner*, December 19, 1958, 1. See also "Fragile Girl vs. Burly Cop; Cause Celebre in Court," *San Francisco Examiner*, December 2, 5 (describing North Beach as the "Land of the Beats").

25. On Beats as the spiritual heirs of earlier wanderers, see Tom Lutz, *Doing Nothing: A History of Loafers, Loungers, Slackers, and Bums in America* (New York: Farrar, Straus and Giroux, 2006), 215–46. On the "vanishing American hobo" and the Beats' rehabilitation thereof, see Jack Kerouac, "The Vanishing American Hobo," in *Lonesome Traveler* (New York: McGraw-Hill, 1960); John D. Seelye, "The American Tramp: A Version of Picaresque," *American Quarterly* 15, no. 4 (Winter 1963): 535–53; Todd Depastino, *Citizen Hobo* (Chicago: University of Chicago Press, 2003), 235–37. See generally Ann Douglas, "Holy Fools: The Beat Generation and the Cold War," *Reviews in American History* 41, no. 3 (2013): 525–32. On realities, stereotypes, and authorities' perceptions of Beat culture, see Christopher Lowen Agee, *The Streets of San Francisco* (Chicago: University of Chicago Press, 2014), 56; Christopher Lowen-Engel Agee, "The Streets of San Francisco: Blacks, Beats, Homosexuals, and the San Francisco Police Department, 1950–1968" (Ph.D. diss., University of California, Berkeley, 2005), 44; "Judge Wins Debate on Beatnik—$50 Fine," *San Francisco Examiner*, September 30, 1959; Tom Christopher, "Beatnik!" originally printed in *Beat Scene Magazine* (2005), http://www.tomchristopher.com/?op=home/Beat%20Generation/Beatnik!; Allen Brown, "Police Keep Close Watch on Beatniks," *San Francisco Chronicle*, June 20, 1958, MS 3580, carton 36, folder 782, Cal. Hist. Soc'y ACLU Papers; Dennis McNally, *Desolate Angel: Jack Kerouac, the Beat Generation, and America* (Cambridge, MA: Da Capo Press, 2003).

26. See David Riesman, *The Lonely Crowd: A Study of Changing American Character* (New Haven, CT: Yale University Press, 1950); Norman Vincent Peale, *The Power of Positive Thinking* (New York: Prentice-Hall, 1952); David Morris Potter, *People of Plenty: Economic Abundance and the American Character* (Chicago: University of Chicago Press, 1954); Matthew S. Hedstrom, *The Rise of Liberal Religion* (New York: Oxford University Press, 2013); Kevin M. Schultz, *Tri-Faith America: How Catholics and Jews Held Postwar America to Its Protestant Promise* (New York: Oxford University Press, 2011); David A. Hollinger, *After Cloven Tongues of Fire: Protestant Liberalism in Modern American History* (Princeton, NJ: Princeton University Press, 2013); Joseph Kip Kosek, *Acts of Conscience: Christian Nonviolence and Modern American Democracy* (New York: Columbia University Press, 2011); Martin Halliwell, *Therapeutic Revolutions: Medicine, Psychiatry, and American Culture, 1945–1970* (New Brunswick, NJ: Rutgers University Press, 2013); Alan Cecil Petigny, *The Permissive Society, 1941–1965* (New York: Cambridge University Press, 2009).

27. Arthur Schlesinger Jr., *The Vital Center: The Politics of Freedom* (Boston: Houghton Mifflin, 1949); Elaine Tyler May, *Homeward Bound* (New York: Basic Books, 1988); John A. Andrew III, *The Other Side of the Sixties* (New Brunswick, NJ: Rutgers University Press, 1997), 12; Cain, "Litigating for Lesbian and Gay Rights," 1567–68; D'Emilio, *Sexual Politics, Sexual Communities*, 179–82.

28. D'Emilio, *Sexual Politics, Sexual Communities*, 179–82; Agee, "Streets of San Francisco," 53, 43–44.

29. Jack Kerouac, "Letter to Gary Snyder of 19 June 1958," in *Selected Letters, 1957–1969*, ed. Ann Charters (New York: Viking, 1999), 134, quoted in Tom Christopher, "Beatnik!"; D'Emilio, *Sexual Politics, Sexual Communities*, 177–81; George Dorsey, *Christopher of San Francisco* (New York: Macmillan, 1962); Ernest Lenn, "ACLU Clashes with Police on Vagrancy Arrests, 'Waterholes,'" *San Francisco Examiner*, May 21, 1957, MS 3580, carton 36, folder 782, Cal.

Hist. Soc'y ACLU Papers; "Ahern Drops Rookie Tests," *San Francisco Chronicle,* June 5, 1957, MS 3580, carton 36, folder 782, Cal. Hist. Soc'y ACLU Papers; "Ahern Orders Probe into That Case," *San Francisco Examiner,* May 19 May, MS 3580, carton 36, folder 782, Cal. Hist. Soc'y ACLU Papers; "Ahern Backs His Cops in Check on 'Beatnik' Bar," *San Francisco News,* July 8, 1958, MS 3580, carton 36, folder 782, Cal. Hist. Soc'y ACLU Papers; "Beatnik Hoppe Held as Drunk," *San Francisco Chronicle,* June 14, 1958, MS 3580, carton 36, folder 782, Cal. Hist. Soc'y ACLU Papers; Allen Brown,"Police Keep Close Watch on Beatniks," MS 3580, carton 36, folder 782, Cal. Hist. Soc'y ACLU Papers; "Beachnik Plan Stymied," *San Francisco Examiner,* July 16, 1958, MS 3580, carton 36, folder 782, Cal. Hist. Soc'y ACLU Papers; "Beatniks' Lawyer Demands Jury Trial," *San Francisco Examiner,* September 19, 1958, MS 3580, carton 36, folder 782, Cal. Hist. Soc'y ACLU Papers; "Cops Looking behind Beards," *San Francisco Chronicle,* March 25, 1960, MS 3580, carton 36, folder 782, Cal. Hist. Soc'y ACLU Papers; Richard G. Gould, letter to the editor, *San Francisco Chronicle,* March 25, 1960, MS 3580, carton 36, folder 781, Cal. Hist. Soc'y ACLU Papers.

30. Ernest Besig to Thomas Cahill (San Francisco Chief of Police), letter, October 3, 1958, MS 3580, carton 36, folder 779, Cal. Hist. Soc'y ACLU Papers; Agee, "Streets of San Francisco," 36–40, 45, 54, 57; "William C. Bigarini Obituary," Tributes.com, accessed May 18, 2015, http://www.tributes.com/show/William-Bigarani-87200756; Don McClure, "Barefoot Girl Booted Law Around, Husky Cop Testifies," *San Francisco Chronicle,* December 2, 1958, 3; David Henderson, "Introduction," in Bob Kaufman, *Cranial Guitar: Selected Poems* (Minneapolis, MN: Coffee House Press, 1996), 13; Thomas Cahill to Ernest Besig, March 20, 1959, MS 3580, carton 36, folder 781, Cal. Hist. Soc'y ACLU Papers; Ernest Besig to Thomas Cahill, March 13, 1959, MS 3580, carton 36, folder 781, Cal. Hist. Soc'y ACLU Papers; Agee, *Streets of San Francisco,* 64; Thomas Cahill to Ernest Besig, April 13, 1959, MS 3580, carton 36, folder 781, Cal. Hist. Soc'y ACLU Papers; Ernest Besig to Thomas Cahill, April 7, 1959, MS 3580, carton 36, folder 781, Cal. Hist. Soc'y ACLU Papers; handwritten notes, March 19, 1959, MS 3580, carton 36, folder 781, Cal. Hist. Soc'y ACLU Papers (by Ernest Besig).

31. Agee, *Streets of San Francisco,* 60 (quoting store owner); Elinson and Yogi, *Wherever There's a Fight,* 320, 323; affidavit of Roberta Hogan, Complaint for Violation of Civil Rights before the Police Commission for the City and County of San San [*sic*] Francisco, State of California, MS 3580, folder 781, carton 36, Series 2, Subseries 2.30, Cal. Hist. Soc'y ACLU Papers; Agee, "Streets of San Francisco," 59; Josh Sides, *Erotic City: Sexual Revolutions and the Making of Modern San Francisco* (New York: Oxford University Press, 2009), 27–28; Ernest Besig to Thomas Cahill (San Francisco Chief of Police), July 15, 1959, MS 3580, carton 36, folder 781, Cal. Hist. Soc'y ACLU Papers; Thomas Cahill to Ernest Besig, July 1, 1951, MS 3580, carton 36, folder 781, Cal. Hist. Soc'y ACLU Papers; Ernest Besig to Thomas Cahill, June 19, 1959, MS 3580, carton 36, folder 781, Cal. Hist. Soc'y ACLU Papers; Elizabeth Lenhart to Ernest Besig, June 2, 1959, MS 3580, carton 36, folder 781, Cal. Hist. Soc'y ACLU Papers. Two years later, John McFeeley, a NAACP lawyer, would note that interracial couples in North Beach attracted particular attention, as the police tried to deter what they saw as the beginnings of racial integration. Agee, "Streets of San Francisco," 60; American Civil Liberties Union of Northern California, *Freedom and Justice for All: Biennial Report, June 1956–June 1958* (San Francisco: 1958), 21, carton 47, folder 1, Cal. Hist. Soc'y Papers.

32. Ernest Besig to Thomas Cahill (San Francisco Chief of Police), October 3, 1958, MS 3580, carton 36, folder 780, Cal. Hist. Soc'y ACLU Papers; Agee, *Streets of San Francisco,* 57; "Are Beatniks Being Pushed Around Because They Are Nonconformists? *San Francisco Chronicle,* July 29, 1958, MS 3580, carton 36, folder 782, Cal. Hist. Soc'y ACLU Papers.

33. "Police 'Blitz' in Fillmore—12 Arrested," *San Francisco Chronicle,* August 30, 1957, MS 3580, carton 36, folder 782, Cal. Hist. Soc'y ACLU Papers; "Give Police Force More Manpower," *San Francisco Chronicle,* 22 January 1960, MS 3580, carton 36, folder 782, Cal. Hist. Soc'y ACLU Papers; Arthur Hoppe, "Let's Get Him!," *San Francisco Chronicle,* December 5,1958, MS 3580, carton 36, folder 782, Cal. Hist. Soc'y ACLU Papers. For statistics on the rising crime rate in 1950s San Francisco, see Federal Bureau of Investigation, *Uniform Crime Reports* 26, no. 1 (Washington, DC, 1955): 104, table 35 ("Number of Offenses Known to the Police, 1955, Cities Over 25,000 in Population"); Federal Bureau of Investigation, *Uniform Crime*

Reports 27, no. 1 (Washington, DC, 1956): 100, table 35 ("Number of Offenses Known to the Police, 1956, Cities Over 25,000 in Population"); Federal Bureau of Investigation, *Uniform Crime Reports* 28, no. 1 (Washington, DC, 1957): 105, table 35 ("Number of Offenses Known to the Police, 1957, Cities Over 25,000 in Population"); Federal Bureau of Investigation, *Uniform Crime Reports* (Washington, DC, 1959): 89, table 15 ("Number of Offenses Known to the Police, 1958, Cities Over 25,000 in Population"); Federal Bureau of Investigation, *Uniform Crime Reports* (Washington, DC, 1960): 95, table 15 ("Number of Offenses Known to the Police, 1959, Cities Over 25,000 in Population").

34. See People v. Allington, 229 P.2d 495 (Cal. App. Dep't Super. Ct. 1951).
35. Christopher G. Tiedeman, *A Treatise on the Limitations of Police Power in the United States* (St. Louis: F. H. Thomas Law Book Co., 1886), 116–17, 121, 124.
36. Caleb Foote, "Vagrancy-Type Law and Its Administration," *University of Pennsylvania Law Review* 104, no. 5 (1956): 649.
37. Ibid.; People v. Craig, 152 Cal. 42, 47 (1907); Wayne R. LaFave, *Arrest: The Decision to Take a Suspect into Custody—The Report of the American Bar Foundation's Survey of the Administration of Criminal Justice in the United States*, ed. Frank J. Remington (Boston: Little, Brown, 1965), 355 n. 50 (quoting N.Y. Law Revision Comm. Rep. No. 591 (1935)). The earliest reported pretext case I have found is People v. Bealoba, 17 Cal. 389 (1861). For additional examples of lawmakers endorsing pretextual vagrancy arrests, see H.R. Rep. 70–1869 (1928); H.R. Rep. 77–1138 (1941); H.R. Rep. 77–659 (1941). See also Carl V. Eimbeck, "Some Recent Methods of Harassing the Habitual Criminal," *St. Louis Law Review* 16, no. 2 (1931): 148 (describing vagrancy as the most discussed method of "harassing the habitual criminal").
38. For the use of vagrancy laws against gangsters, see, e.g., Ex parte Lonardo, 89 N.E.2d 502, 503–04 (Ohio Ct. App. 1949); Hallmark v. State, 185 So. 908 (Ala. Ct. App. 1939); Snitzer v. State, 199 So. 745 (Ala. Ct. App. 1940); Flandell v. State, 4 So. 2d 264 (Ala. Ct. App. 1941); Lanzetta, 306 U.S. 451. For vagrancy-like laws tailored for use against gangsters, see Act of July 6, 1933, Laws 489 (amending Illinois's Vagabond Act to include criminal reputation as evidence of vagrancy); Lanzetta, 306 U.S. 451. For the application of vagrancy laws' "means of support" provisions to gangsters, see Chicago City Council, *Report of the City Council Committee on Crime* (Chicago, 1915), 172, quoted in Black, "Idlers, Outliers and Dependents," 81. See also Eimbeck, "Some Recent Methods of Harassing the Habitual Criminal," 156. For ACLU concern about these vagrancy arrests, see, e.g., Osmond K. Fraenkel to Marjorie Goldstein, letter, May 7, 1940, roll 184, volume 2198, American Civil Liberties Union Records, 1917–1950, Series 1, Subseries 17, microfilm (hereafter ACLU microfilm). For accounts of the arrests themselves, see Laurence Greene, "Owney Madden Seized at Garden, Held as Vagrant," *New York Post*, roll 184, volume 2198, page 244, Series 1, Subseries 17, ACLU microfilm; "Waxey Gordon, Picked Up as Vagrant, Is Told by Police to Stay Out of New York," roll 195, volume 2288, page 85, Series 1, Subseries 17, ACLU microfilm; "Johnny Torrio Arrested Here as Undesirable," *New York Herald-Tribune*, November 30, 1941, roll 198, volume 2314, page 242, Series 1, Subseries 17, ACLU microfilm.
39. For the use of vagrancy laws against "moneyed hoodlums," see "Hoodlums and the Law," *Chicago Tribune*, October 20, 1930, quoted in Eimbeck, "Some Recent Methods of Harassing the Habitual Criminal," 156; Berry v. State, 27 S.E.2d 563 (Ga. Ct. App. 1943) (defense attorney objecting to prosecutor's mention of defendant's nice clothing). For gangsters' resources used to fight vagrancy charges, see *Chicago Tribune*, September 7, 1930, quoted in Eimbeck, "Some Recent Methods of Harassing the Habitual Criminal," 155. See also "2 'Enemies' Give Up; Quickly Freed," *Chicago Daily Tribune*, September 30, 1930, 1. On Clarence Darrow, see Kevin Boyle, *Arc of Justice: A Saga of Race, Civil Rights and Murder in the Jazz Age* (New York: Henry Holt, 2004); John Aloysius Farrell, *Clarence Darrow: Attorney for the Damned* (New York: Doubleday, 2011); Phyllis Vine, *One Man's Castle: Clarence Darrow in Defense of the American Dream* (New York: Armistad, 2005). For vagrancy laws used to get criminals off the street, see, e.g., "Drop Vagrancy Cases against Two Public Foes," *Chicago Tribune*, April 11, 1931, 18; Black, "Idlers, Outliers and Dependents," 250. In Chicago, for example, the conviction rate for these public enemies for the meager crime of vagrancy was about one in three. Black, "Idlers, Outliers and Dependents," 250. "2 'Enemies' Give Up; Quickly Freed," 1. For high bail set or discussed in gangsters' vagrancy cases, see, e.g., Ex parte

Lonardo, 89 N.E.2d 502, 503–04 (Ohio Ct. App. 1949) (The appeals court lowered the sum to a mere $15,000.); "2 'Enemies' Give Up; Quickly Freed," 1; People ex parte Sammons, 173 N.E. 8, 469 (Ill. 1930). For bail lowered or charges dismissed in gangsters' vagrancy cases, see, e.g., American Civil Liberties Union to Leonard McGee, letter, December 3, 1931, roll 195, volume 2288, page 84, Series 1, Subseries 17, ACLU microfilm; People ex. rel. Sammons v. Snow, 173 N.E. 8 (Ill. 1930); Morgan v. Commonwealth, 191 S.E. 791 (Va. 1937). But see Flandell v. State, 19 So. 2d 401 (Ala. Ct. App., 1944) (affirming gambling/vagrancy conviction). See also Reynolds v. State, 4 So.2d 201 (Ala. App. 1941); Hallmark v. State, 198 So. 149, 150 (Ala. Ct. App. 1940); Snitzer v. State, 199 So. 745 (Ala. Ct. App., 1940); People v. Belcastro, 190 N.E. 301 (Ill. 1934).

40. Petition for a Writ of Certiorari at 2, Dragna v. California, 344 U.S. 921 (1953) (No. 365); Brief of Respondent in Opposition to the Granting of Petition for Writ of Certiorari at 2, Dragna v. California, 344 U.S. 921 (1953) (No. 365). For press accounts of the arrest, the case, and Dragna's death, see, e.g., "Jack Dragna's 180-Day Jail Term Cut to 30," Los Angeles Times, June 6, 1952, 5; "Dragna Rule Seen in Bookie Racket," Los Angeles Times, May 11, 1953, 2; "U.S. Nabs Jack Dragna on Illegal Entry Charge," Los Angeles Times, December 9, 1952, 2; "Jack Dragna Sentenced to 180 Days in Jail," Los Angeles Times, July 27, 1951, 2; "Dragna Seized on Vagrancy Charge," Los Angeles Times, April 11, 1951, 16; "Jack Dragna Found Dead in Sunset Bld. Hotel," Los Angeles Times, February 24, 1956, 1.

41. People v. Cahan, 282 P.2d 905 (Cal. 1955); "L.A. Crime Survey Urged by Parker," Los Angeles Times, April 20, 1956, 7.

42. "Hoodlums Hide as Cops Step Up Raids," San Francisco Chronicle, September 6, 1957, MS 3580, carton 36, folder 782, Cal. Hist. Soc'y ACLU Papers; "Police Continue . . . [unreadable]," San Francisco Chronicle, September 8, 1957, MS 3580, carton 36, folder 782, Cal. Hist. Soc'y ACLU Papers; "Hoodlum Roundup Still On," San Francisco Examiner, September 6, 1957, MS 3580, carton 36, folder 782, Cal. Hist. Soc'y ACLU Papers; "The 'Roust,'" San Francisco Examiner, September 13, 1957, MS 3580, carton 36, folder 782, Cal. Hist. Soc'y ACLU Papers. For additional press accounts of these raids, see, e.g., "Police 'Blitz' in Fillmore—12 Arrested," MS 3580, carton 36, folder 782, Cal. Hist. Soc'y ACLU Papers; "40 Police Men [sic] Join in the New Hoodlum Roundup," San Francisco Chronicle, September 5, 1957, MS 3580, carton 36, folder 782, Cal. Hist. Soc'y ACLU Papers.

43. Ernest Besig to Governor Edmund G. Brown ("Pat"), typewritten letter, July 10, 1959, MS 3580, carton 36, folder 781, Cal. Hist. Soc'y ACLU Papers.

44. Aubrey W. Grossman, Comment, "Who Is a Vagrant in California?," California Law Review, 23, no. 5 (1935): 506. There were a few others that Besig did not cite. See, e.g., "Use of Vagrancy-Type Laws for Arrest and Detention of Suspicious Persons," Yale Law Journal 59, no. 7 (1950): 1358.

45. Stan Windhorn, "Anyone Can Be a Vagrant," Sarasota Herald-Tribune, November 19, 1954, 4; "Vagrancy Law Study Is Slated," New Orleans Times-Picayune, February 26, 1957, 4.

46. Rollin M. Perkins, "The Vagrancy Concept," Hastings Law Journal 9, no. 3 (1958): 252–53; George McClure, "Vagrants, Criminals and the Constitution," Denver Law Center Journal 40, no. 6 (1963): 335.

47. Forrest W. Lacey, "Vagrancy and Other Crimes of Personal Condition," Harvard Law Review 66, no. 7 (1953): 1224–25; Foote, "Vagrancy-Type Law and Its Administration," 648, 649. See also Caleb Foote, "Law and Police Practice: Safeguards in the Law of Arrest," Northwestern University Law Review 52, no.1 (1957): 28, 34 (suggesting the need for research into "the extent to which such easy and necessarily haphazard techniques tend to be substituted for more thoroughgoing investigation or degenerate into harassment of reputed criminals as an alternative to solution of crimes"). See also "Use of Vagrancy-Type Laws for Arrest and Detention of Suspicious Persons," 1358; Jerome Hall, "Police and Law in a Democratic Society," Indiana Law Journal 28, no. 2 (1953): 157, 159; James Blair, "Act 378 Vagrancy," Arkansas Law Review 9 (1954–1955): 400–401; Foote, "Vagrancy-Type Law and Its Administration," 614; Arthur H. Sherry, "Vagrants, Rogues and Vagabonds—Old Concepts in Need of Revision," California Law Review 48, no. 4 (1960): 567–568; "Over-Expanded Application of Vagrancy Statutes," Washington University Law Quarterly 6 (1961): 425; Donald H. Whaley, "The Constitutionality of Loitering Ordinances," St. Louis University Law

Journal 6 (1960–61): 247; Gary V. Dubin and Richard H. Robinson, "The Vagrancy Concept Reconsidered: Problems and Abuses of Status Criminality," *New York University Law Review* 37, no. 1 (1962): 129; William O. Douglas, "Vagrancy and Arrest on Suspicion," *Yale Law Journal* 70, no. 1 (1960): 9.

48. Beail v. District of Columbia, 82 A.2d 765, 767 (D.C. 1951) (The case was later reversed on appeal. Beail v. District of Columbia, 201 F.2d 176 (D.C. Cir. 1952)); Jenkins v. United States, 146 A.2d 444, 447 (D.C. 1958). For cases allowing vagrancy arrests prior to other charges, see, e.g., Adamson v. Hoblitzell, 279 S.W.2d 759, 760 (Ky. 1955); State v. Solomon, 62 So. 2d 481 (La. 1952); Ringo v. State, 275 S.W.2d 121 (Tex. Crim. App. 1955); People v. Simpson, 339 P.2d 156 (Cal. Dist. Ct. App.1959); Rinehart v. State, 114 So. 2d 487 (Fla. Dist. Ct. App. 1959). See also *Ex rel* Jackson, 168 N.Y.S.2d 1018 (App. Div. 1957); People v. Allington, 229 P.2d 495, 501 (Cal. App. Dep't Super. Ct. 1951).

49. People v. Wilson, 301 P.2d 974, 977 (Cal. Dist. Ct. App. 1956); State v. Salerno, 142 A.2d 636, 639 (N.J. 1958); "False Arrest Gets $11,000," *Milwaukee Journal*, February 8, 1958, 1; People v. Molarius, 303 P.2d 350, 352 (Cal. Dist. Ct. App. 1956); Brown v. State, 99 N.E.2d 103 (Ind. 1951); Soles v. City of Vidalia, 90 S.E.2d 249 (Ga. Ct. App. 1955);People v. Harris, 304 P.2d 178 (Cal. Dist. Ct. App. 1956). For vagrancy convictions reversed on lack of evidence, see, e.g., Hainsworth v. District of Columbia, 72 A.2d 776 (D.C. 1950); People v. Reilly, 105 N.Y.S.2d 845 (N.Y. App. Part 1951); People ex. rel. Harrington v. Marcial, 110 N.Y.S.2d 361 (N.Y. City Magis. Ct. 1952); Prince v. State, 59 So. 2d 878 (Ala. Ct. App. 1952); Green v. District of Columbia, 91 A.2d 712 (D.C. 1952); State v. Scavo, 55 N.W.2d 509 (Minn. 1952); Able v. State, 62 So. 2d 239 (Ala. Ct. App. 1952); City of Xenia v. Burton, 128 N.E.2d 134 (Ohio Ct. App. 1953); Houston v. State, 65 So. 2d 830 (Ala. Ct. App. 1953); Rainbolt v. State, 260 P.2d 426 (Okla. Crim. App 1953); Johnson v. State, 67 So. 2d 902 (Ala Ct. App. 1953); People v. Gould, 118 N.E.2d 553 (N.Y. 1954); People v. Brandt, 306 P.2d 1069 (Cal. App. Dep't Super. Ct. 1956); People v. McCormack, 169 N.Y.S.2d 139 (N.Y. App. Part 1957); Commonwealth v. Clinton, 137 A.2d 463 (Pa. 1958); People v. Burgwin, 172 N.Y.S.2d 726 (N.Y. App. Part 1958); State v. Salerno, 142 A.2d 636 (N.J. 1958); Reed v. City and County of Denver, 342 P.2d 642 (Colo. 1959).

50. M.L.M., "Constitutional Law: Criminal Registration Ordinance Held Unconstitutional," *Howard Law Journal* 4, no. 2 (1958): 253. Also echoing criticisms of vagrancy laws, several commentators noted the possibly unconstitutional restraint on movement that such laws created. M.L.M., "Constitutional Law: Criminal Registration Ordinance Held Unconstitutional," 250–55; "Constitutional Law: Due Process Requirement of Notice in Felon Registration," *Iowa Law Review* 44, no. 1 (1958): 205–10. See also Thomas Milton Jones, "Constitutional Law: Knowledge of a Criminal Registration Act as a Requirement of Its Violation," *Georgia Bar Journal* 22, no. 2 (1959): 239; Frank C. Bozeman, "Mens Rea and Strict Liability Criminal Statutes," *Washington & Lee Law Review* 16, no. 2 (1959): 238; R.S.F., "'Ignorance of the Law' a Defense to Conviction under Criminal Registration Ordinance," *Utah Law Review* 6, no. 1 (1958): 124; Alexander M. Bickel, "The Supreme Court 1960 Term: Foreword, The Passive Virtues," *Harvard Law Review* 75, no. 1 (1961): 40; David C. Berg, "Constitutional Law: Due Process, Knowledge of the Law Required for Conviction under Criminal Registration Ordinance," *Michigan Law Review* 56, no. 6 (1958): 1008. See generally John C. Jeffries Jr., "Legality, Vagueness, and the Construction of Penal Statutes," *Virginia Law Review* 71, no. 2 (1985): 189; Robert C. Post, "Reconceptualizing Vagueness: Legal Rules and Social Orders," *California Law Review* 82, no. 3 (1994): 491; Peter W. Low and Benjamin Charles Wood, "Lambert Revisited," *Virginia Law Review* 100, no. 8 (2014): 1603–82.

51. Walker, *In Defense of American Liberties*, 246–49. For the work of police practices committees, see, e.g., "Strange Interruption in Testing of Police," *San Francisco Chronicle*, June 7, 1957, MS 3580, carton 36, folder 782, Cal. Hist. Soc'y ACLU Papers; "Mental Testing of Rookies Ended Poor Scores," *San Francisco Chronicle*, June 5, 1957, MS 3580, carton 36, folder 782, Cal. Hist. Soc'y ACLU Papers; Emilie Tavel, "Police Trial Door Opened in Boston," *Christian Science Monitor*, June 6, 1959, MS 3580, carton 36, folder 782, Cal. Hist. Soc'y ACLU Papers; "Civilian Board to Check Complaints against Police Urged by Illinois CLU," press release, April 6, 1959, MS 3580, carton 36, folder 780, Cal. Hist. Soc'y ACLU Papers; "Police Have Rights, Too," *San Francisco News*, December 7, 1959, MS 3580, carton 36, folder 782, Cal. Hist.

Soc'y ACLU Papers; Emilie Tavel, "If You Should be Arrested . . . an Intimate Message from New England," *Christian Science Monitor,* February 15, 1960, MS 3580, carton 36, folder 780, Cal. Hist. Soc'y ACLU Papers; State v. Alfred F. Tinston, 163 N.Y.S.2d 554 (1957); Thomas A. Nielsen (Chief Inspector of New York City Police Department) to All Commands, memorandum, July 11, 1957, MS 3580, carton 36, folder 781, Cal. Hist. Soc'y ACLU Papers; Ernest Besig to John R. May (Executive Secretary of the San Francisco Foundation), draft of letter sent June 3, 1959, MS 3580, carton 36, folder 781, Cal. Hist. Soc'y ACLU Papers; "Cincinnati CLU Sees 'Dragnet-Like Campaign' by Police as Civil Liberties Invasion," *American Civil Liberties Union Weekly Bulletin* #1984, February 16, 1959, MS 3580, carton 36, folder 781, Cal. Hist. Soc'y ACLU Papers.

52. Albert Rocklin to Ernest Besig, December 6, 1958, MS 3580, carton 36, folder 780, Cal. Hist. Soc'y ACLU Papers; "Police Raid Fillmore," flyer, n.d., MS 3580, carton 36, folder 782, Cal. Hist. Soc'y ACLU Papers; "Police Continue . . . [unreadable]," MS 3580, carton 36, folder 782, Cal. Hist. Soc'y ACLU Papers.

53. "ACLU Clashes with San Francisco Police on Vagrancy Arrests," reprinted in *The Ladder* 1, no. 9 (June 1957): 19; Elinson and Yogi, *Wherever There's a Fight,* 310; D'Emilio, *Sexual Politics, Sexual Communities,* 70, 182–84; Eskridge, "Privacy Jurisprudence and the Apartheid of the Closet," 786; Timmons, "The Trouble with Harry," 21; James Leonard, "But He Still Has Faith in Chief Cahill," *San Francisco News-Call Bulletin,* n.d., MS 3580, carton 36, folder 782, Cal. Hist. Soc'y ACLU Papers.

54. Charles Raudebaugh, "33 Cases of Wiretapping in California," *San Francisco Chronicle,* July 29, 1958, MS 3580, carton 36, folder 782, Cal. Hist. Soc'y ACLU Papers; "Negroes Open Fight on Crime," *San Francisco Examiner,* April 6, 1959, MS 3580, carton 36, folder 782, Cal. Hist. Soc'y ACLU Papers, San; "Negro Minister Says Police Are Brutal in Fillmore," *San Francisco News-Call,* October 28, 1959, MS 3580, carton 36, folder 782, Cal. Hist. Soc'y ACLU Papers; Donovan McClure, "Negro Crime Statistics Argued Here," *San Francisco Chronicle,* January 29, 1960, MS 3580, carton 36, folder 782, Cal. Hist. Soc'y ACLU Papers; William Mackey, "Cahill Cites S.F. Negro Crime Rise," *San Francisco Examiner,* January 29, 1960, MS 3580, carton 36, folder 782, Cal. Hist. Soc'y ACLU Papers; "New Police Job—Easing Race Tension," *San Francisco Chronicle,* August 7, 1959, MS 3580, carton 36, folder 782, Cal. Hist. Soc'y ACLU Papers; "Charge on Dr. Dropped," *San Francisco Chronicle,* August 6, 1959, MS 3580, carton 36, folder 782, Cal. Hist. Soc'y ACLU Papers. See also Donovan Bess, "Police Urged to 'Organize' Their Critics, Talk to Them," *San Francisco Chronicle,* January 25, 1961, MS 3580, carton 36, folder 782, Cal. Hist. Soc'y ACLU Papers.

55. Pierre Delattre, *Episodes* (St. Paul, MN: Graywolf Press, 1993), 31, 59; "Religion's Voice in North Beach," *San Francisco Chronicle,* June 16, 1959, MS 3580, carton 36, folder 782, Cal. Hist. Soc'y ACLU Papers; Wes Willoughby, "Beatniks Find Champion in 28-year-old Pastor," *San Francisco News,* April 14, 1959, MS 3580, carton 36, folder 782, Cal. Hist. Soc'y ACLU Papers. For an example of harassment, see Bruce Higgins, statement submitted to San Francisco Police Department, n.d., MS 3580, carton 36, folder 781, Cal. Hist. Soc'y ACLU Papers.

56. For the committee's resolution to "fight," see Willoughby, "Beatniks Find Champion," MS 3580, carton 36, folder 782, Cal. Hist. Soc'y ACLU Papers. See also Ernest Besig to John R. May (Executive Secretary of the San Francisco Foundation), draft of letter sent June 3, 1959, MS 3580, carton 36, folder 781, Cal. Hist. Soc'y ACLU Papers. For the suggestion that the loitering law be applied to police, see Sanford Weinberg, "North Beach Citizens Committee," handwritten note, MS 3580, carton 36, folder 780, Cal. Hist. Soc'y ACLU Papers. The loitering they referred to was likely section 3 or 6 of the vagrancy law. For the poems, the officers' response, and the ACLU's position, see Arthur Hoppe, "Beatniks Go after Cops—In Verse," *San Francisco Chronicle,* August 14, 1959, MS 3580, carton 36, folder 782, Cal. Hist. Soc'y ACLU Papers; "San Francisco: 'Fuzz' with Feelings," *San Francisco Chronicle,* August 23, 1959, MS 3580, carton 36, folder 782, Cal. Hist. Soc'y ACLU Papers; Board meeting minutes, "Lawless enforcement referred to NoCal police practices committee" (February 5, 1959), UCLA ACLU Papers.

57. Board Meeting minutes, "Lawless enforcement referred to NoCal police practices committee," UCLA ACLU Papers; Ernest Besig to Governor Edmund G. Brown ("Pat"), typewritten letter, July 10, 1959, MS 3580, carton 36, folder 781, Cal. Hist. Soc'y ACLU Papers;

Leeanna McDuffy to Fowler, handwritten note, n.d., MS 3580, carton 36, folder 778, Series 2, Subseries 2.30, Cal. Hist. Soc'y ACLU Papers.

58. "Wendy Gets $50 Fine, Lecture and Probation." See also "Fragile Girl vs. Burly Cop; Cause Celebre in Court"; McClure, "Barefoot Girl Booted Law Around, Husky Cop Testifies"; Agee, *Streets of San Francisco*, 58.

59. American Civil Liberties Union of Northern California, "False Arrest Suits," in *Freedom and Justice for All*, carton 47, folder 1, UCLA ACLU Papers; ACLU of Northern California Board of Directors, "Minutes," (January 3 1957), box 46, UCLA ACLU Papers; "Damage Suits Filed in 2 'Vag' Arrest Cases," *ACLU News*, September 1957, box 47, UCLA ACLU Papers; "'Abuse' of Law: ACLU Challenges Vagrancy Arrests," *San Francisco Chronicle*, July 4, 1957, in MS 3580, carton 36, folder 782, Cal. Hist. Soc'y ACLU Papers; Ernest Besig, Draft Complaint, Besig v. San Francisco, Superior Court of California, n.d., MS 3580, carton 39, folder 876, Cal. Hist. Soc'y ACLU Papers; Wirin v. Parker, 313 P.2d 844 (Cal. 1957).

60. Francis W. H. Adams (with Richard De Lancie and Stephen Thiermann), "Report of Police Practices Committee," n.d., MS 3580, carton 36, folder 781, Cal. Hist. Soc'y ACLU Papers. See also Ernest Besig to John R. May (Executive Secretary of the San Francisco Foundation), June 3, 1959, MS 3580, carton 36, folder 781, Cal. Hist. Soc'y ACLU Papers.

61. American Civil Liberties Union of Northern California, *Freedom and Justice for All*, 4, carton 47, folder 1, UCLA ACLU Papers; Ernest Besig to George Christopher, December 23, 1958, MS 3580, carton 36, folder 780, Cal. Hist. Soc'y ACLU Papers. For Besig's correspondence with police officials, see also, e.g., letter from Ernest Besig to Thomas Cahill, October 3, 1958, MS 3580, carton 36, folder 780, Cal. Hist. Soc'y ACLU Papers; letter from Thomas Cahill to Ernest Besig, October 6, 1958, MS 3580, carton 36, folder 780, Cal. Hist. Soc'y ACLU Papers; letter from Ernest Besig to Thomas Cahill, December 16, 1958, MS 3580, carton 36, folder 780, Cal. Hist. Soc'y ACLU Papers; letter from Thomas Cahill to Ernest Besig, December 30, 1958, MS 3580, carton 36, folder 780, Cal. Hist. Soc'y ACLU Papers.

62. Gladwin Hill, *Dancing Bear: An Inside Look at California Politics* (New York: World Publishing, 1968), 151–53; Lisa McGirr, *Suburban Warriors* (Princeton, NJ: Princeton University Press, 2001), 67; Agee, *Streets of San Francisco*, 56–58; "Hearing on Cop's Tactics Opens Today," *San Francisco Examiner*, July 28, 1958, MS 3580, carton 36, folder 782, Cal. Hist. Soc'y ACLU Papers; O'Gara, "'Rousting' on Race Basis Here Denied," MS 3580, carton 36, folder 782, Cal. Hist. Soc'y ACLU Papers; "Revise Vagrancy Law, Say Experts," reprinted in *The Ladder* 2, no. 12 (September 1958): 18–19. See also "Report on ACLU Discussion Group Meetings" (Spring 1958), 1, ACLU Papers.

63. Sherry, "Vagrants, Rogues and Vagabonds," 567–68; "Revise Vagrancy Law, Say Experts," 17–20; "Beatniks' Lawyer Demands Jury Trial," MS 3580, carton 36, folder 782, Cal. Hist. Soc'y ACLU Papers; O'Gara, "'Rousting' on Race Basis Here Denied," MS 3580, carton 36, folder 782, Cal. Hist. Soc'y ACLU Papers; Raudebaugh, "33 Cases of Wiretapping in California," MS 3580, carton 36, folder 782, Cal. Hist. Soc'y ACLU Papers; United Press International, "DA Lynch States Vagrancy Law Needs Revision," *Modesto Bee*, July 30, 1958, A14; Boyd, *Wide Open Town*, 217–18; American Civil Liberties Union of Northern California, *Freedom and Justice for All*, 20, carton 47, folder 1, UCLA ACLU Papers.

64. "Pair Protest Police Drive on Hoodlums," *San Francisco Examiner*, September 8, 1957, MS 3580, carton 36, folder 782, Cal. Hist. Soc'y ACLU Papers; "Revise Vagrancy Law, Say Experts," 4; American Civil Liberties Union of Northern California, *Freedom and Justice for All*, 20, carton 47, folder 1, Cal. Hist. Soc'y ACLU Papers; "Democratic Platform Highlights Set Forth," *Los Angeles Times*, August 10, 1958, 24. Members of the state bar association also criticized the law. "Revise Vagrancy Law, Say Experts," 4.

65. O'Gara, "'Rousting' on Race Basis Here Denied," MS 3580, carton 36, folder 782, Cal. Hist. Soc'y ACLU Papers; "Police Chiefs Hit at Supreme Court," *New York Times*, October 6, 1957, 62; "'Abuse' of Law: ACLU Challenges Vagrancy Arrests," MS 3580, carton 36, folder 782, Cal. Hist. Soc'y ACLU Papers; Lenn, "ACLU Clashes with Police," MS 3580, carton 36, folder 782, Cal. Hist. Soc'y ACLU Papers.

66. O'Gara, "'Rousting' on Race Basis Here Denied," MS 3580, carton 36, folder 782, Cal. Hist. Soc'y ACLU Papers; Raudebaugh, "33 Cases of Wiretapping in California," MS 3580, carton 36, folder 782, Cal. Hist. Soc'y ACLU Papers.

67. Charles Raudebaugh, "Cahill Ends '$1000 Vag' Bookings," *San Francisco Chronicle*, October 4, 1958, MS 3580, carton 36, folder 782, Cal. Hist. Soc'y ACLU Papers; Cahill Ends '$1,000 Vag' Arrest Policy," *San Francisco Examiner*, October 3, 1958, MS 3580, carton 36, folder 782, Cal. Hist. Soc'y ACLU Papers; Gloria S. Napier to Ernest Besig, December 22, 1958, MS 3580, carton 36, folder 780, Cal. Hist. Soc'y ACLU Papers; Thomas Cahill to Mayor George Christopher, December 30,1958, MS 3580, carton 36, folder 780, Cal. Hist. Soc'y ACLU Papers; "The American Way of Life," *Militant*, February 9, 1959, MS 3580, carton 36, folder 782, Cal. Hist. Soc'y ACLU Papers. On the differences between Cahill's and Ahern's crime prevention strategies, see, e.g., "Cahill's Operation S.," *San Francisco Chronicle*, October 1, 1959, MS 3580, carton 36, folder 782, Cal. Hist. Soc'y ACLU Papers; "How Operation 'S' Hunts Down Toughs," *San Francisco Chronicle*, December 8,1958, MS 3580, carton 36, folder 782, Cal. Hist. Soc'y ACLU Papers; "29 Arrested by Special Crime Team," *San Francisco Chronicle*, October 27, 1958, MS 3580, carton 36, folder 782, Cal. Hist. Soc'y ACLU Papers; "Crime Squad Gets Results First Night," *San Francisco Chronicle*, October 26, 1958, MS 3580, carton 36, folder 782, Cal. Hist. Soc'y ACLU Papers.
68. William Keller, "Police Abuses Denied by Cahill," *San Francisco Chronicle*, November 16, 1958, MS 3580, carton 36, folder 782, Cal. Hist. Soc'y ACLU Papers; "How Operation 'S.' Hunts Down Toughs," MS 3580, carton 36, folder 782, Cal. Hist. Soc'y ACLU Papers; Baron Muller, "Major S. F. Crime Is Slashed 15.9%," *San Francisco News*, February 17, 1959, MS 3580, carton 36, folder 782, Cal. Hist. Soc'y ACLU Papers.
69. Ernest Besig to John R. May (Executive Secretary to the San Francisco Foundation), June 3, 1959, MS 3580, carton 36, folder 781, Cal. Hist. Soc'y ACLU Papers; Sherry, "Vagrants, Rogues and Vagabonds," 566–67. For Sherry's background, see Adrian A. Kragen, "Arthur H. Sherry—In Memoriam," *California Law Review* 75, no. 2 (1987): 547; Adrian A. Kragen, "Arthur H. Sherry—A Tribute," *California Law Review* 64, no. 2 (1976): 232. Sherry had also been the project director of the American Bar Foundation's Survey of the Administration of Criminal Justice, commenced in 1953. LaFave, *Arrest: The Decision to Take a Suspect into Custody*, ix.
70. Sherry, "Vagrants, Rogues and Vagabonds," 562 n. 38, 569–72.
71. "Modern 'Vag' Bill Wins Senate Test," *San Francisco News*, June 19, 1959, MS 3580, carton 36, folder 782, Cal. Hist. Soc'y ACLU Papers.
72. William Steif, "Model Vagrancy Law Nearing Enactment," *San Francisco News*, June 16, 1959, MS 3580, carton 36, folder 782, Cal. Hist. Soc'y ACLU Papers.
73. John O'Connell to Ernest Besig, July 8, 1959, MS 3580, carton 36, folder 781, Cal. Hist. Soc'y ACLU Papers; Ernest Besig to Governor Edmund G. Brown ("Pat"), typewritten letter, July 10, 1959, MS 3580, carton 36, folder 781, Cal. Hist. Soc'y ACLU Papers.
74. United Press International, "Governor Signs Last of Bills; Vetoes 168," *Lodi News Sentinel*, July 25, 1959; Clint Mosher, "Pat Brown Plans Drive on Crime," *San Francisco Examiner*, November 10, 1958, MS 3580, carton 36, folder 782, Cal. Hist. Soc'y ACLU Papers; Ernest Besig to Edmund G. Brown ("Pat"), July 31, 1959, MS 3580, carton 36, folder 782, Cal. Hist. Soc'y ACLU Papers.
75. Ernest Besig to Julian Beck, July 25, 1959, MS 3580, carton 36, folder 781, Cal. Hist. Soc'y ACLU Papers.
76. Edmund G. Brown to Ernest Besig, August 26, 1959, MS 3580, carton 36, folder 781, Cal. Hist. Soc'y ACLU Papers.
77. John A. O'Connell, Proposed Agenda for Meeting of the Assembly Interim Committee on Criminal Procedure, February 18–19, 1960, MS 3580, carton 36, folder 781, Cal. Hist. Soc'y ACLU Papers; Ernest Besig to John O'Connell, February 17, 1960, MS 3580, carton 36, folder 781, Cal. Hist. Soc'y ACLU Papers; *In re* Newbern, 350 P.2d 116 (Cal. 1960); "Prisoners Freed by Court Ruling on Vagrancy Law," *Lodi News-Sentinel*, March 19, 1960; "Drunk Freed after Getting Others Out," *San Francisco Chronicle*, March 26, 1960, MS 3580, carton 36, folder 782, Cal. Hist. Soc'y ACLU Papers; "34 Drunks Free—Some Not Long," *San Francisco Chronicle*, March 26, 1960, MS 3580, carton 36, folder 782, Cal. Hist. Soc'y ACLU Papers; " 'Common Drunk' Law Invalidated," *San Francisco Examiner*, March 9, 1960, MS 3580, carton 36, folder 782, Cal. Hist. Soc'y ACLU Papers.
78. Sherry, "Vagrants, Rogues and Vagabonds," 564–66. For the California case, see "Modesto Judge Rules Drunk Law Illegal," *Modesto Bee*, September 9, 1958; see also "Law Governing Vagrancy Will Be Tested in Court," *Modesto Bee*, May 24, 1958; "Appeal Is Filed over Ruling

on Drunk Law," *Modesto Bee*, October 13, 1958; "'Common Drunkard' Term Is Held Constitutional," *Modesto Bee*, February 18, 1959.

79. "'Common Drunk' Law Invalidated," MS 3580, carton 36, folder 782, Cal. Hist. Soc'y ACLU Papers; "'Common? I'm No Such Thing,'" *San Francisco Examiner*, April 1, 1960, MS 3580, carton 36, folder 782, Cal. Hist. Soc'y ACLU Papers.

80. Sherry, "Vagrants, Rogues and Vagabonds," 570–72.

81. California Penal Code § 647 (Supp. 1961), quoted in LaFave, *Arrest: The Decision to Take a Suspect into Custody*, 355 n. 50. For the bill's passage, see Associated Press, "Vagrancy Law Repealer Gets Final Approval," *Modesto Bee*, May 12, 1961 (the dissenter was Lee Backstrand, Republican of Riverside County); "Brown Gives Outline of 1961 Program," *Los Angeles Times*, May 16, 1960, B1; "Governor Signs Legislation Changing Vagrancy Statutes," *Sacramento Bee*, June 1, 1961, MS 3580, carton 36, folder 782, Cal. Hist. Soc'y ACLU Papers; "New Vagrancy Law," *San Francisco News-Call*, June 6. 1961, MS 3580, carton 36, folder 782, Cal. Hist. Soc'y ACLU Papers.

82. "New Vagrancy Law May Curb Abuse of Rights," *Sacramento Bee*, June 6, 1961, MS 3580, carton 36, folder 782, Cal. Hist. Soc'y ACLU Papers. On "suspicious loitering," see Lawson v. Kolender, 658 F.2d 1362, 1369 (9th Cir. 1981), *aff'd and remanded*, 461 U.S. 352 (1983). On the new law, see, e.g., "Selected 1960–1961 California Legislation," *Journal of the State Bar of California* 36, no. 5 (1961): 801–2; Associated Press, "Vagrancy Law Bill Gets Okeh of Assembly," *Modesto Bee*, March 15, 1961; "The Day in Sacramento," *Los Angeles Times*, March 16, 1961, 27; "The Day in Sacramento," *Los Angeles Times*, May 13, 1961, 8; Associated Press, "Vagrancy Law Repealer Gets Final Approval."

83. "Project: The Consenting Adult Homosexual and the Law: An Empirical Study of Enforcement and Administration in Los Angeles County," *UCLA Law Review* 13, no. 3 (1966): 643. See also D'Emilio, *Sexual Politics, Sexual Communities*, 194; Boyd, *Wide Open Town*.

84. "Governor Signs Legislation Changing Vagrancy Statutes," MS 3580, carton 36, folder 782, Cal. Hist. Soc'y ACLU Papers.

85. American Civil Liberties Union of Northern California, *Report of the American Civil Liberties Union of Northern California: July 1, 1960–June 30, 1963* (San Francisco: 1963), 28, box 47, folder 1, Cal. Hist. Soc'y Papers; Kolendar v. Lawson, 461 U.S. 352 (1983).

Chapter 3

1. Transcript of Record at 53, 63, Thompson v. Louisville, 362 U.S. 199 (1960) (No. 59) ("Transcript of Record"); Marvin Morse, telephone interview with author, June 23, 2014.

2. The record of the case and Morse's recollections indicate that this was an African American bar, though toward the end of his life, Lusky said that it was a white bar. Louis Lusky, interview by Cate Fosl, April 20, 1999, interview 2006OH216 AB 022, transcript and recording, Anne Braden Oral History Project, Louie B. Nunn Center for Oral History, University of Kentucky Libraries, https://nyx.uky.edu/oh/render. php?cachefile=2006OH213_AB22_Lusky_access.xml; Marvin Morse, telephone interview with author, June 23, 2014. On Walnut Street, see Catherine Fosl and Tracey E. K'Meyer, *Freedom on the Border: An Oral History of the Civil Rights Movement in Kentucky* (Lexington: University Press of Kentucky, 2009), 24–26; James Sydnor, quoted in Luther Adams, *Way Up North in Louisville: African American Migration in the Urban South, 1930–1970* (Chapel Hill: University of North Carolina Press, 2010), 149–52; J. Harvey Kerns, *A Survey of the Economic and Cultural Conditions of the Negro Population of Louisville, Kentucky, and a Review of the Program and Activities of the Louisville Urban League* (Louisville: Louisville Urban League, 1948), quoted in Mervin Aubespin, Kenneth Clay, and J. Blaine Hudson, *Two Centuries of Black Louisville: A Photographic History* (Louisville: Butler Books, 2011), 162–63; Bruce M. Tyler, *African-American Life in Louisville* (Charleston, SC: Arcadia, 1998), 13; Bruce M. Tyler, *Louisville in World War II* (Charleston, SC: Arcadia, 2005), 7.

3. U.S. Census Bureau, Jefferson County, Kentucky, Population Schedule, Louisville; ED 56–106, Sheet 10B, Dwelling #129, Family #147, Thompson household; digital image, Ancestry.com, accessed 26 April 2011, http://www.ancestry.com; Transcript of Record at 48, Thompson.

4. Joseph P. Blank, "The High Court and 'Shufflin' Sam,'" *Reader's Digest*, November 1961, 95; Transcript of Record at 38, Thompson; Charlotte G. Moulton, "Supreme Court Takes Up Appeal over Two $10 Fines in Tavern Dance," *Washington Post*, January 13, 1960, C6; Anthony Lewis, "High Court Hears a $10 Police Case," *New York Times*, January 13, 1960, 14; "Fines of 'Shufflin' Sam' Upset by Supreme Court," *Washington Post*, March 22, 1960, A8. On life expectancy, see, e.g.,Tenants' Relocation Bureau, *The Homeless Man on Skid Row* (Chicago: Tenants' Relocation Bureau, 1961), 39, http://www.archive.org/details/homelessmanonskiOOchic.

5. Transcript of Record at 1–3, 21, 25, Thompson; Jeffrey W. Davis, "A Kentucky Response: The Founding of the Kentucky Civil Liberties Union, 1955–1960" (master's thesis, University of Washington, 1981), 115; Petition for a Writ of Certiorari to the Police Court of the City of Louisville at 9, Thompson, 326 U.S. 199 (1960) ("Cert Petition"); Brief for the City of Louisville and the Commonwealth of Kentucky at 13, 25–26, Thompson, 326 U.S. 199 (1960) ("Brief for Louisville"); Morton O. Childress, *Louisville Division of Police: History & Personnel: 1806–2002* (Paducah, KY: Turner Publishing, 2005), 110, 121, 154. Some called the café the Liberty End Saloon. See testimony of Officer William Lacefield, Transcript of Record at 6, Thompson.

6. Transcript of Record at 57–58, 63, Thompson; Childress, Louisville Division of Police, 116; David E. Schancupp, "The Saga of Shufflin' Sam," *Connecticut Bar Journal* 39, no. 3 (1965): 405–6. Thompson's public drunkenness arrests came under Ky. Rev. Stat. Ann. § 244.020 (West 1955) ("Drinking or being under influence of alcoholic beverages in public place prohibited"). It is unclear under what law he was arrested for "perversion." It might have been Ky. Rev. Stat. Ann. § 436.075 (1955), Prostitution, Lewdness and Assignation ("The term 'lewdness' shall be construed to include any indecent or obscene act") or, less likely, Ky. Rev. Stat. Ann. § 244.150 (1955), Profane Swearing or Cursing ("Any person who profanely curses or swears shall be fined one dollar, and every oath shall be deemed a separate offense").

7. Transcript of Record at 4, Thompson; Stewart Dean, "My Father, Dr. William Wynant Dean," accessed February 4, 2015, http://www.sdean.net/moredad.

8. Davis, "A Kentucky Response," 113–14; Childress, Louisville Division of Police, 61; Dean, "My Father, Dr. William Wynant Dean"; Marvin H. Morse, "Profiles in Public Practice: Retired Administrative Law Judge," Federal Lawyer 50, no. 7 (2003): 21; Marvin Morse, telephone interview with author, June 23, 2014.

9. Blank, "The High Court and 'Shufflin' Sam,'" 94–98.

10. Transcript of Record at 36–37, 49, Thompson. On the segregated waiting room, see Aubespin, Clay, and Hudson, *Two Centuries of Black Louisville*, 163–65; Adams, *Way Up North in Louisville*, 3; Fosl and K'Meyer, *Freedom on the Border*, 78.

11. Transcript of Record at 69, Thompson; Davis, "A Kentucky Response," 114.

12. Albert J. Rosenthal, "Louis Lusky—An Outstanding Scholar and a Dedicated Crusader for Justice," *Columbia Law Review* 101, no. 5 (2001): 986; Davis, "A Kentucky Response," 33; Louis Lusky, "Minority Rights and the Public Interest," *Yale Law Journal* 52, no. 1 (1942): 1–41. For Lusky's cases with Clark, see, e.g., Minersville Sch. Dist. v. Gobitis, 310 U.S. 586 (1940); Hague v. Comm. for Indus. Org., 307 U.S. 496 (1939).

13. Davis, "A Kentucky Response," 13, 38; Rosenthal, "Louis Lusky," 988; Louis Lusky, *Harold Leventhal 1915–1979: An Appreciation* (Chicago: University of Chicago Press, 1980), 10; John Kleber, ed., *The Encyclopedia of Louisville* (Lexington: University Press of Kentucky, 2001), 28–29; *American Civil Liberties of Kentucky: 1955 to 1995, A Celebration* (Madison, IN: American Civil Liberties Union of Kentucky, 1995), 3; Louis Lusky, interview by Cate Fosl, April 20, 1999. On the KCLU, see Davis, "A Kentucky Response."

14. Jack Greenberg, "In Memoriam, Louis Lusky," *Columbia Law Review* 101, no. 5 (2001): 981; Rosenthal, "Louis Lusky," 986–89; *American Civil Liberties of Kentucky*, 10; Davis, "A Kentucky Response," 37. Lusky's cases with the KCLU included Colbert v. Commonwealth of Kentucky, 306 S.W.2d 825 (1957).

15. For exposés, studies, and policy prescriptions, see, e.g., Francis E. Feeney et al., "The Challenge of the Skid Row Alcoholic: A Social, Psychological and Psychiatric Comparison of Chronically Jailed Alcoholics and Cooperative Alcoholic Clinic Patients," *Quarterly Journal of Studies on Alcohol* 16, no. 4 (1955): 645–67; George J. Dudycha, *Psychology for Law Enforcement Officers* (Springfield, IL: Charles C. Thomas, 1959); Norman L. Clowers, *Patrolman Patterns, Problems, and Procedures* (Springfield, IL: Charles C. Thomas, 1962);

Los Angeles Police Department, *Daily Training Bulletin* (1954), accessed February 4, 2015, http://archive.org/stream/dailytrainingbul00losarich/dailytrainingbul00losarich_djvu.txt; Charles Hoch and Robert A. Slayton, *New Homeless and Old: Community and the Skid Row Hotel* (Philadelphia: Temple University Press, 1989), 107–14. On the *Chicago Daily News* series, see Kenneth L. Kusmer, *Down and Out, on the Road: The Homeless in American History* (New York: Oxford University Press, 2002), 229. See also " 'Operation Cleanup' in Full Swing Here," *Atlanta Daily World*, July 29, 1957, 5.

16. U.S. Census Bureau, *County and City Data Book: A Statistical Abstract Supplement*, (1962), 578 tbl.A-1; Irwin Deutscher, "The Petty Offender: Society's Orphan," *Federal Probation* 19, no. 2 (1955): 12–13.

17. Kleber, *Encyclopedia of Louisville*, 69; Morton O. Childress, *Louisville Division of Police: History & Personnel*, 42.

18. On the main stem and its inhabitants, see Hoch and Slayton, *New Homeless and Old*, 29–33; John C. Schneider, "Skid Row as Urban Neighborhood, 1880–1960," in *Housing the Homeless*, eds. Jon Erickson and Charles Wilhelm (New Brunswick, NJ: Center for Urban Policy Research, 1986), 169–73; Eric H. Monkkonen, "Walking to Work," in *Walking to Work: Tramps in America, 1790–1935*, ed. Eric H. Monkkonen (Lincoln: University of Nebraska Press, 1984), 11; Eric H. Monkkonen, *The Dangerous Class: Crime and Poverty in Columbus, Ohio, 1860–1885* (Cambridge, MA: Harvard University Press, 1975); John C. Schneider, "The Police on Skid Row: A Historical Perspective," *Criminal Justice Review* 13, no. 2 (1988): 17. See also Chapter 1, this volume. On perceptions and portrayals of hoboes, see Nels Anderson, *The American Hobo: An Autobiography* (Leiden: Brill, 1975), 2, quoted in John C. Schneider, "Tramping Workers 1890–1920: A Subcultural View," in Monkkonen, *Walking to Work*, 215, 219; Tom Lutz, *Doing Nothing: A History of Loafers, Loungers, Slackers, and Bums in America* (New York: Farrar, Straus and Giroux, 2006), 161–71; Jack London, *The Road* (New York: Macmillan, 1907); Schneider, "Police on Skid Row," 15–20. On the diversity of main stem populations, see Towne Nylander, "The Migratory Population of the United States," *American Journal of Sociology* 30, no. 2 (1924): 130–36; Eric H. Monkkonen, "A Disorderly People? Urban Order in the Nineteenth and Twentieth Centuries," *Journal of American History* 68, no. 3 (1981): 539–40, 545; Todd DePastino, *Citizen Hobo: How a Century of Homelessness Shaped America* (Chicago: University of Chicago Press, 2003), 228–31.

19. Schneider, "Skid Row as Urban Neighborhood," 174; Nels Anderson, *The Hobo: The Sociology of the Homeless Man* (Chicago: University of Chicago Press, 1923); DePastino, *Citizen Hobo*, 175–81; 184–85, 201, 206, 209; Margot Canaday, *The Straight State: Sexuality and Citizenship in Twentieth-Century America* (Princeton, NJ: Princeton University Press, 2009), 91–92 and generally 91–134. See John Steinbeck, *The Grapes of Wrath* (New York: Viking Press, 1939); John Dos Passos, *The Big Money* (New York: Harcourt, Brace, 1936), 446–48.

20. Walt Whitman, "Song of the Open Road," in *Leaves of Grass* (New York: Modern Library, 1921), 125–34. On the federal transient program and the changing face of the main stem, see, e.g., Kusmer, *Down and Out, on the Road*, 193, 209, 226; Schneider, "Skid Row as Urban Neighborhood," 184; Joan M. Crouse, *The Homeless Transient in the Great Depression: New York State, 1929–1941* (Albany: State University of New York Press, 1986); Errol Lincoln Uys, *Riding the Rails: Teenagers on the Move during the Great Depression* (New York: TV Books, 1999).

21. For positive studies and accounts, see, e.g., Keith Arthur Lovald, "From Hobohemia to Skid Row: The Changing Community of the Homeless Man" (Ph.D. diss., University of Minnesota, 1960), cited in Kusmer, *Down and Out, on the Road*, 230–33; Hoch and Slayton, *New Homeless and Old*; Leonard Blumberg et al., *The Men on Skid Row: A Study of Philadelphia's Homeless Man Population* (Philadelphia: 1960) (typescript); George Nash, *The Habitats of Homeless Men in Manhattan* (New York: Columbia University, Bureau of Applied Social Research, 1964) (typescript); W. Jack Peterson and Milton A. Maxwell, "The Skid Row 'Wino,' " *Social Problems* 5, no. 4 (1958): 309, 313; DePastino, *Citizen Hobo*, 231–32. For more negative views from the 1950s though the 1970s, see, e.g., Howard M. Bahr, *Disaffiliated Man: Essays and Bibliography on Skid Row, Vagrancy, and Outsiders* (Toronto: University of Toronto Press, 1970); Howard M. Bahr and Theodore Caplow, *Old Men Drunk and Sober* (New York: New York University Press, 1974); Donald J. Bogue, *Skid Row in American Cities* (Chicago: University of Chicago Community and Family Study Center, 1963), 2; William J. Plunkert, "Skid Row Can Be

Eliminated," *Federal Probation* 25, no. 2 (1961): 41–42. For popular writing from that period, see, e.g., Sara Harris, *Skid Row U.S.A.* (Garden City, NY: Doubleday, 1956); Elmer Bendiner, "'Immovable Obstacle' in the Way of a New Bowery," *New York Times Magazine*, January 21, 1962, 22. On community and social attachments on skid row, see Kusmer, *Down and Out, on the Road*, 225, 227; James F. Rooney, "Group Processes among Skid Row Winos," *Quarterly Journal of Studies on Alcohol* 22, no. 3 (1961): 450–51; Peterson and Maxwell, "The Skid Row 'Wino,'" 308; Joan K. Jackson and Ralph Conner, "The Skid Road Alcoholic," *Quarterly Journal of Studies on Alcohol* 14, no. 3 (1953): 470.

22. On continuities between skid row and the main stem, see Schneider, "Skid Row as Urban Neighborhood," 184. On the home guard, see Schneider, "Tramping Workers," 228–29; Schneider, "Skid Row as Urban Neighborhood," 178. On urban renewal and declining skid row populations, see, e.g., Bendiner, "'Immovable Obstacle' in the Way of a New Bowery," 22; Peter H. Rossi, *Down and Out in America: The Origins of Homelessness* (Chicago: University of Chicago Press, 1989), 32; Howard M. Bahr, "The Gradual Disappearance of Skid Row," *Social Problems* 15, no. 1 (1967): 41–45; DePastino, *Citizen Hobo*, 232–35. The population of New York's Bowery skid row went from 14,000 in 1949 to fewer than 8,000 in 1964. Chicago's West Madison Street skid row went from 30,000 to 21,000 in 1951 and 13,000 in 1958. Kusmer, *Down and Out, on the Road*, 225, 236–37. In Louisville, urban renewal began in 1959. Kleber, *Encyclopedia of Louisville*, 389, 904–5.

23. Canaday, *The Straight State*, 98–99; Kusmer, *Down and Out, on the Road*, 141–42; Nels Anderson, *On Hobos and Homelessness* (Chicago: University of Chicago Press, 1998), 203, quoted in Canaday, *The Straight State*, 101; Axel Kleiboemer and Frank L. Schneider, "The Law on Skid Row," *Chicago-Kent Law Review* 38, no. 1 (1961): 29, 39; Stanley Rosenman, "The Skid-Row Alcoholic and the Negative Ego Image," *Quarterly Journal of Studies on Alcohol* 16, no. 3 (1955): 450. See also Edwin H. Sutherland and Harvey J. Locke, *Twenty Thousand Homeless Men: A Study of Unemployed Men in the Chicago Shelters* (New York: Arno Press, 1936), 23–24; Josiah Flynt, "Homosexuality among Tramps," appendix A to Havelock Ellis, ed., *Studies in the Psychology of Sex*, vol.1, by Havelock Ellis (New York: Random House, 1940), cited in Canaday, *The Straight State*, 100; Carlton H. Parker, *The Casual Laborer and Other Essays* (New York: Harcourt, Brace and Howe, 1920), 73–74, quoted in Canaday, *The Straight State*, 101.

24. Kusmer, *Down and Out, on the Road*, 229; Jackson and Conner, "The Skid Road Alcoholic," 469; Leonard Blumberg et al., "The Development, Major Goals and Strategies of a Skid Row Program: Philadelphia," *Quarterly Journal of Studies on Alcohol* 27, no. 2 (1966): 249; Deutscher, "The Petty Offender," 13. See also Kleiboemer and Schneider, "The Law on Skid Row," 26 (describing the "overwhelming ugliness" of both the men and the places they lived).

25. On the original and continued use of vagrancy laws against idle and out-of-place people, see Chapter 1, this volume. On the presumed immorality of idle poverty, see F. B. Sanborn, "The Year's Work in Administration and Legislation," in *Proceedings of the Sixth Annual Conference of Charities*, ed. F. B. Sanborn (Boston: A. Williams, 1879), 25, http://name. umdl.umich.edu/ACH8650.1879.001; Dr. Luther, "Causes and Prevention of Pauperism," in Sanborn, *Proceedings of the Seventh Annual Conference of Charities and Correction*, 248; Francis Wayland and F. B. Sanborn, "Tramp Laws and Indeterminate Sentences" in Sanborn, *Proceedings of the Seventh Annual Conference of Charities and Correction*, 277–81, cited in Kusmer, *Down and Out, on the Road*, 53; Paul T. Ringenbach, *Tramps and Reformers 1873–1916: The Discovery of Unemployment in New York* (Westport, CT: Greenwood Press, 1973), 23–24. For the Supreme Court's acceptance of this view, see Mayor of N.Y. v. Miln, 36 U.S. (11 Pet.) 102, 142–43 (1849). On the "social crime" approach, see Michael Willrich, *City of Courts: Socializing Justice in Progressive Era Chicago* (New York: Cambridge University Press, 2003); Roscoe Pound, "Introduction," in Francis Bowes Sayre, *A Selection of Cases on Criminal Law* (Rochester: Lawyers Co-Operative Publishing, 1927), xxxvi. See also Markus Dirk Dubber, *The Police Power: Patriarchy and the Foundations of American Government* (New York: Columbia University Press, 2005), 167; Joel Elan Black, "Idlers, Outliers, and Dependents: The Free Labor Order in Industrial Chicago, 1870–1930" (Ph.D. diss., University of Florida, 2010), 77; Michael Willrich, "The Two Percent Solution: Eugenic Jurisprudence and the Socialization of American Law, 1900–1930," *Law and History Review* 16, no. 1 (1998): 80 n. 47.

26. Edwards v. California, 314 U.S. 160, 174, 177 (1941). See also Chapter 1.
27. On the applicability of jurisprudential assumptions about regulating the poor to the vagrancy law context, cf. City of New Orleans v. Postek, 158 So. 553 (La. 1934). For the view that vagrancy laws were incompatible with aspects of midcentury society, see, e.g., Aubrey W. Grossman, "Who Is a Vagrant in California?" *California Law Review* 23, no. 5 (1935): 518; Arthur H. Sherry, "Vagrants, Rogues and Vagabonds—Old Concepts in Need of Revision," *California Law Review* 48, no. 4 (1960): 557–59. See also People v. Sohn, 199 N.E. 501, 502 (N.Y. 1936); State v. Grenz, 175 P.2d 633, 639–40 (Wash. 1946) (Millard, C. J., dissenting); Olof Kinberg, "On So-Called Vagrancy (Concluded)—A Medico-Sociological Study," *Journal of the American Institute of Criminal Law and Criminology* 24 (1933–1934): 552. On the failure of full employment, see Alan Brinkley, *The End of Reform: New Deal Liberalism in Recession and War* (New York: Alfred A. Knopf, 1995); Mordecai Ezekiel, *Jobs for All through Industrial Expansion* (New York: Alfred A. Knopf, 1939).
28. Egon Bittner, "The Police on Skid-Row: A Study of Peace Keeping," *American Sociological Review* 32, no. 5 (1967): 703–4. On Bittner's influence, see, e.g., J. M. Moynahan, "Perceptions of Police Legal Powers," *Police Law Quarterly* 2, no. 4 (1972): 6; John F. Galliher, "Explanations of Police Behavior: A Critical Review and Analysis," *Sociological Quarterly* 12, no. 3 (1971): 309; Charles B. Saunders, *Upgrading the American Police: Education and Training for Better Law Enforcement* (Washington, DC: Brookings Institution, 1970), 23.
29. Bittner, "The Police on Skid-Row," 700–01. See also Voices of the Oral History Project of the Gay and Lesbian History Society of Northern California, Thomas Cahill, July 28, 1997, 43–45 (describing such policing).
30. On the police as peacekeepers, see Dubber, *The Police Power*, 53–55; Richard Danzig, "Toward the Creation of a Complementary, Decentralized System of Criminal Justice," *Stanford Law Review* 26, no. 1 (1973): 27; Paula R. Markowitz and Walter I. Summerfield, Jr., "Philadelphia Police Practice and the Law of Arrest," *University of Pennsylvania Law Review* 100, no. 8 (1952): 1201 (describing that, in Philadelphia, "three-quarters of the arrests for disorderly conduct appear to be illegal, in that the charge is used to cover lawful conduct of which the police disapprove"); David R. Johnson, *American Law Enforcement: A History* (St. Louis: Forum Press, 1981), 3–4, 38–39, 62–64; John J. Flinn with assistance of John E. Wilkie, *History of the Chicago Police* (Chicago: Police Book Fund, 1887; repr., New York: Arno Press, 1971), 55–56. On the police as professional crime fighters, see Hoch and Slayton, *New Homeless and Old*, 105; Johnson, *American Law Enforcement*, 69–71; Robert M. Fogelson, *Big-City Police* (Cambridge, MA: Harvard University Press, 1977), 84–90; David Alan Sklansky, *Democracy and the Police* (Stanford, CA: Stanford University Press, 2007); Samuel Walker, *A Critical History of Police Reform: The Emergence of Professionalism* (Lexington, MA: Lexington Books, 1977); Elizabeth Dale, *Criminal Justice in the United States, 1789–1939* (New York: Cambridge University Press, 2011).
31. Emmet Daly, "Reports on Government-Sponsored Programs," *Quarterly Journal of Studies on Alcohol* 13 (June 1952): 346; Schneider, "Police on Skid Row," 19; Lovald, "From Hobohemia to Skid Row," quoted in Kusmer, *Down and Out, on the Road*, 234; Kleiboemer and Schneider, "The Law on Skid Row," 25, 25 n. 14. See also Hoch and Slayton, *New Homeless and Old*, 105.
32. On discretionary police management and containment of skid row, see Bittner, "The Police on Skid-Row," 703–7, 715; Raymond Nimmer, "Court Directed Reform of Vagrancy-Type Laws," *Judicature* 54, no. 2 (1970): 50; Raymond T. Nimmer, "Public Drunkenness: Criminal Law Reform," *Valparaiso University Law Review* 4, no. 1 (1969): 87, 91, 93; John M. Murtagh, "The Derelicts of Skid Row," *Atlantic*, March 1962, 78; Schneider, "Police on Skid Row," 18; Kusmer, *Down and Out, on the Road*, 233–35; Hoch and Slayton, *New Homeless and Old*, 88. On politically motivated roundups, see Kusmer, *Down and Out, on the Road*, 233–35; Samuel E. Wallace, *Skid Row as a Way of Life* (Totowa, NJ: Bedminster Press, 1965), 94–95; Bittner, "The Police on Skid-Row," 701–2. For officials' opinions of these practices, see, e.g., Murtagh, "The Derelicts of Skid Row," 80–81. See also Alan H. Levine, "Disorderly Conduct: Catch-all Device for New York City's 'Undesirables,'" *Civil Liberties in New York*, June 1966, 2 (quoting Justice Bernard Botein about sweeping vagrants under the carpet).
33. Bittner, "The Police on Skid-Row," 702–03.

34. Bittner, "The Police on Skid-Row," 707–08, 710–11, 713. On arrestees who did not conform precisely to the requirements of the law invoked, see Kleiboemer and Schneider, "The Law on Skid Row," 42–43. Brandeis once described himself as a "lawyer for the situation." The skid row police officer could be considered an officer for the situation. See Clyde Spillenger, "Elusive Advocate: Reconsidering Brandeis as People's Lawyer," *Yale Law Journal* 105, No. 6 (1996): 1502–12.

35. For vagrant status persisting until "reformation," see, e.g., People v. Craig, 91 P. 997 (Cal. 1907); Cf. Robinson v. California, 370 U.S. 660, 666 (1962).

36. William Ker Muir, *Police: Streetcorner Politicians* (Chicago: University of Chicago Press, 1977), 78, cited in Schneider, "Police on Skid Row," 18; Bittner, "The Police on Skid-Row," 707–08, 715.

37. Bittner, "The Police on Skid-Row," 713–14; Kleiboemer and Schneider, "The Law on Skid Row," 37.

38. Schneider, "Police on Skid Row," 19–20; Wallace, *Skid Row as a Way of Life*, 92; Bittner, "The Police on Skid-Row," 708; Kleiboemer and Schneider, "The Law on Skid Row," 39; on shakedowns and quotas, see Kleiboemer and Schneider, "The Law on Skid Row," 40; Leonard U. Blumberg, Thomas E. Shipley, and Irving W. Shandler, *Skid Row and Its Alternatives: Research and Recommendations from Philadelphia* (Philadelphia: Temple University Press, 1973), 60–75; Lovald, "From Hobohemia to Skid Row"; Jacqueline P. Wiseman, *Stations of the Lost: The Treatment of Skid Row Alcoholics* (Englewood Cliffs, NJ: Prentice-Hall, 1970); Bittner, "The Police on Skid-Row," 711; Schneider, "Police on Skid Row," 19.

39. Dubber, *The Police Power*, 131–32; Kleiboemer and Schneider, "The Law on Skid Row," 33 n. 52, 38; Bittner, "The Police on Skid-Row," 711–12. For the historically paternalistic use of police power, see, e.g., In re Nott, 11 Me. 208, 208 (1834); Schneider, "Police on Skid Row," 17; Kleiboemer and Schneider, "The Law on Skid Row," 37–41.

40. Marty Mann, "The Challenge of Alcoholism," *Federal Probation* 24, no. 1 (1960): 18–22; Kleiboemer and Schneider, "The Law on Skid Row," 36, 43–44, 47–52.

41. Murtagh, "The Derelicts of Skid Row," 77–81. On penal welfarism, see David Garland, *The Culture of Control: Crime and Social Order in Contemporary Society* (Chicago: University of Chicago Press, 2001), 34; Kleiboemer and Schneider, "The Law on Skid Row," 39. See also President's Commission on Law Enforcement and the Administration of Justice, *Task Force Report: Drunkenness* (1967), 4.

42. On the elimination of skid rows through urban renewal, see Kusmer, *Down and Out, on the Road*, 235–37; Hoch and Slayton, *New Homeless and Old*, 119; Chester Hartman, *Yerba Buena: Land Grab and Community Resistance in San Francisco* (San Francisco, CA: Glide, 1974), cited in Kusmer, *Down and Out, on the Road*; Stephen Metraux, "Waiting for the Wrecking Ball: Skid Row in Postindustrial Philadelphia," *Journal of Urban History* 25, no. 5 (1999): 690–715, cited in Kusmer, *Down and Out, on the Road*, 317. For the Model Penal Code dispute, see Kleiboemer and Schneider, "The Law on Skid Row," 47; Model Penal Code § 250.11, cmt. at 56 (Tent. Draft No. 13, 1961). For cities' arrest patterns, see Kleiboemer and Schneider, "The Law on Skid Row," 47–48 n. 116; Murtagh, "The Derelicts of Skid Row," 80. New York and Chicago had similar skid row populations.

43. Childress, *Louisville Division of Police*, 13–15; Fosl and K'Meyer, *Freedom on the Border*, 225; Aubespin, Clay, and Hudson, *Two Centuries of Black Louisville*, 168–70; Adams, *Way Up North in Louisville*, 119–20; Ed Hopson, telephone interview with author, May 13, 2011.

44. Leonard Blumberg, Thomas E. Shipley Jr., and Joseph O. Moor Jr., "The Skid Row Man and the Skid Row Status Community," *Quarterly Journal of Studies on Alcohol* 32, no. 4 (1971): 917 (describing similarities between men who lived on skid row and those who were similar and "skid-row-like"); Transcript of Record at 54, Thompson.

45. *American Civil Liberties of Kentucky*, 5.

46. See Chapter 2.

47. On the legal targets common to civil libertarian and welfarist reformers, see Edwin M. Schur, review of *The Road to H: Narcotics, Delinquency, and Social Policy*, by Isidor Chein et al. and *The Addict and the Law* by Alfred R. Lindesmith, *Stanford Law Review* 17, no. 6 (1965): 1189–99; *New York City Magistrates' Courts Annual Report* (1955), 2, cited in "Metropolitan Criminal Courts of First Instance," *Harvard Law Review* 70, no. 2 (1956): 320, 349.

48. On police courts and their counterparts, see Barbara Bintliff, "A Jurisdictional History of the Colorado Courts," *University of Colorado Law Review* 65, no. 3 (1994): 609, 630 ("Local courts, whether referred to as Municipal Courts, Police Magistrate's Courts, or Police Courts, have been in existence since the state was created"); Albert Wickersham, *The Judicial System of Metropolitan Chicago* (Chicago: University of Chicago Press, 1932), 23 (stating that the term "justice court," referred both to justice of the peace courts and police magistrate courts in Illinois); see also President's Commission on Law Enforcement and Administration of Justice, *The Challenge of Crime in a Free Society* (Washington, DC: Government Printing Office,1967), 128-30; National Commission on Law Observance and Enforcement (Wickersham Commission), *Report on Criminal Procedure*, vol. 8 (Washington, DC: Government Printing Office, (1931), 6, 11. On Jack London's ordeal, see London, *The Road*, 70.
49. Childress, *Louisville Division of Police*, 60.
50. "In Memoriam: Caleb Foote, Professor of Law, Emeritus, UC Berkeley 1917–2006," Jonathan Simon, Sanford Kadish, and Robert Cole, University of California, accessed February 5, 2015, http://senate.universityofcalifornia.edu/inmemoriam/calebfoote.html; Douglas Martin, "Caleb Foote, Law Professor and Pacifist Organizer, 88," *New York Times*, April 3, 2006, B6; Jerry Skolnick, "Reflection on Foote on Vagrancy-Type Laws" (lecture, Berkeley Center for Criminal Justice Symposium: The Caleb Foote Symposium: Connecting Criminal Justice Scholarship with Criminal Justice Reform, March 23, 2007), 2–3, https://www.law.berkeley.edu/files/Skolnick.pdf.
51. London, *The Road*, 72; Caleb Foote, "Vagrancy-Type Law and Its Administration," *University of Pennsylvania Law Review* 104, no. 5 (1956): 605, 620; William O. Douglas, "Vagrancy and Arrest on Suspicion," *Yale Law Journal* 70, no. 1 (1960): 9–10; "Use of Vagrancy-Type Laws for Arrest and Detention of Suspicious Persons," *Yale Law Journal* 59, no. 7 (1950): 1357–58. On legal realism, see generally John Henry Schlegel, *American Legal Realism and Empirical Social Science* (Durham, NC: University of North Carolina Press, 1995).
52. Kleiboemer and Schneider, "The Law on Skid Row," 39; Murtagh, "The Derelicts of Skid Row," 78.
53. Gertrud Neuwirth, "Participant Observation Journal" (unpublished research report, University of Minnesota, 1958), quoted in Wallace, *Skid Row as a Way of Life*, 104. See also Kleiboemer and Schneider, "The Law on Skid Row," 36, 43–44.
54. Neuwirth, "Participant Observation Journal," quoted in Wallace, *Skid Row as a Way of Life*, 98, 100.
55. On the historical view of vagrancy laws as not requiring the same protections as criminal offenses, see Markus Dirk Dubber, "'The Power to Govern Men and Things': Patriarchal Origins of the Police Power in American Law," *Buffalo Law Review* 52, no. 4 (2004): 1286–92. On magistrates' workload, qualifications, and sympathy for police viewpoints, see Foote, "Vagrancy-Type Law and Its Administration," 607; "Use of Vagrancy-Type Laws for Arrest and Detention of Suspicious Persons," 1357 n. 20; Kleiboemer and Schneider, "The Law on Skid Row," 39. For crtiticism of magistrates' practices in vagrancy cases, see Foote, "Vagrancy-Type Law and Its Administration," 611–12, 630. LaFave similarly found little effort on the part of many police officers in the ABF study to justify arrests for investigation at all. Wayne R. LaFave, *Arrest: The Decision to Take a Suspect into Custody* (Boston: Little, Brown, 1965), 342.
56. On appointed counsel in misdemeanor cases, see Richard H. Rahl, "The Right to Counsel in Misdemeanor Cases," *California Law Review* 48, no. 3 (1960): 501–15; John M. Junker, "The Right to Counsel in Misdemeanor Cases," *Washington Law Review* 43, no. 4 (1968): 685–734. See generally Sara Mayeux, "Ineffective Assistance of Counsel before Powell v. Alabama: Lessons from History for the Future of the Right to Counsel," *Iowa Law Review* 99, no. 5 (2014): 2161–84. On the cost of appeals and other factors protecting vagrancy and related laws from oversight, see "Use of Vagrancy-Type Laws for Arrest and Detention of Suspicious Persons," 1357–58 n. 21; Gary V. Dubin and Richard H. Robinson, "The Vagrancy Concept Reconsidered: Problems and Abuses of Status Criminality," *New York University Law Review* 37, no. 1 (1962): 132. On police officers' routine failure to offer vagrancy defendants a phone call or the possibility of bail, see Kleiboemer and Schneider, "The Law on Skid Row," 34 n. 56, 43.

57. Davis, "A Kentucky Response," 82–89, 91–99, 110–12. For KCLU attacks on procedural defects, see, e.g., Brown v. Hoblitzell, 307 S.W.2d 739 (Ky 1957); Brief for Kentucky Civil Liberties Union, Amicus Curiae, Brown, 307 S.W.2d 739 (Ky. 1956) (No. V-59-55).

58. Davis, "A Kentucky Response," 112; *38th Annual Meeting, American Law Institute Proceedings, May 17–20, 1961* (American Law Institute, 1962). See also Louis B. Schwartz, "Morals Offenses and the Model Penal Code," *Columbia Law Review* 63 (1963): 669–86.

59. Davis, "A Kentucky Response," 83, 86–87, 93; Tom Karsell, "Are 'Vagrancy' and 'Filed Away' Acceptable Police Tools as Used Here?" *Courier-Journal* (Louisville, KY), February 3, 1957; Tom Karsell, " 'Vagrancy' and 'Filed Away' Can Hurt a Man's Job Chances," *Courier-Journal* (Louisville, KY), February 3, 1957. For the successful KCLU challenge, see Van Arsdale v. Caswell, 311 S.W.2d 404 (Ky. 1958).

60. Marvin Morse, telephone interview with author, June 23, 2014; Kentucky, Louisville City, 1930 U.S. Census, population schedule.

61. Transcript of Record at 36, Thompson.

62. Brief for Louisville at 25–26, Thompson; Ky. Rev. Stat. Ann. § 436.520 (West 1955).

63. Transcript of Record at 43–44, 50–51, 58–62, Thompson.

64. Ibid. at 31, 40, 53–54.

65. Ibid. at 63.

66. William F. Maher and William E. Williams, "Vagrancy—A Study in Constitutional Absolescence," *University of Florida Law Review* 22, no. 3 (1970): 393 (quoting a California judge's jury instruction, as cited in Edelman v. California, 344 U.S. 357, 365 (1952) (Black, J., dissenting).

67. Transcript of Record at 63, Thompson.

68. Ibid.

69. Ibid. at 62–64.

70. Ibid. at 33; Joseph P. Blank, "The High Court and Shufflin' Sam," *Reader's Digest*, November 1961, 95–96.

71. Cert Petition at 9, Thompson, 362 U.S. 199 (1960); Nickell v. Commonwealth, 285 S.W.2d 495 (Ky. 1956); Schancupp, "The Saga of Shufflin' Sam," 408; Richard A. Buckner, Joshua F. Bullitt, and Alvin Duvall, eds., Civil and Criminal Codes of Practice of Kentucky § 39 (1876).

72. Transcript of Record at 18, Thompson.

73. Ibid. at 31.

74. Blank, "The High Court and 'Shufflin' Sam,' " 95–96.

75. 28 U.S.C. § 1257 (1958); Ky. Rev. Stat. Ann. § 26.080 (1955). Lusky did have alternatives in the state courts. He could have brought a malicious prosecution suit on the bus station arrests, as the jury acquitted Thompson on both vagrancy and loitering on appeal. Cert Petition at 8, Thompson, 362 U.S. 199 (1960). He also could have attacked the loitering law itself with an extraordinary writ in the Kentucky state courts. For reasons discussed below, he declined to do so. See Schancupp, "The Saga of Shufflin' Sam," 411.

76. Lynch to Levy, December 12, 1955, quoted in Davis, "A Kentucky Response," 29; Brief for Petitioner at 47, Thompson, 362 U.S. 199 (1960).

77. In 1968, the Supreme Court changed mootness doctrine in such a way that Thompson's case would no longer have faced these obstacles. See "The Supreme Court, 1967 Term—IV. Business of the Court—A. Mootness in Criminal Cases," *Harvard Law Review* 82 (1968): 296–97.

78. Cert Petition at 30, Thompson, 362 U.S. 199 (1960); Lusky, *Harold Leventhal*, 10–12; "Jewish Politicians in Kentucky," Political Graveyard, accessed February 5, 2015, http://political-graveyard.com/geo/KY/jewish.html; Marvin Morse, telephone interview with author, June 23, 2014; Karsell, "Are 'Vagrancy' and 'Filed Away' Acceptable Police Tools as Used Here?"; Thompson, 362 U.S. at 202–203; Thompson v. Taustine, No. 40715, Jefferson (Ky.) Cir. Ct., Feb. 4, 1959 (Judge Grauman's opinion), quoted in Schancupp, "The Saga of Shufflin' Sam," 413.

79. Taustine v. Thompson, 322 S.W.2d 100, 102 (Ky. 1959). See also Cert Petition at 11–14, Thompson, 362 U.S. 199 (1960); Lowell H. Harrison and James C. Klotter, *A New History of Kentucky* (Lexington: University Press of Kentucky, 1997), 385–86; Fosl and K'Meyer, *Freedom on the Border*, xii–xiii.

80. Greenberg, "In Memoriam, Louis Lusky," 978; Henry P. Sailer to Justice John Marshall Harlan, bench memorandum on case No. 59 (Thompson v. Louisville), box 86, John Marshall Harlan II Papers, Seeley G. Mudd Manuscript Library, Princeton University (hereafter Princeton Harlan Papers). Lusky and Morse had help strategizing about the case and drafting their cert petition from Harold Leventhal and Eugene Gressman, another Washington lawyer who had served as a law clerk to Justice Frank Murphy for a record-breaking five years. John Charles Boger, "Eugene Gressman: In Memoriam," *North Carolina Law Review* 89, no. 1 (2010): 1–8.

81. Brief for Petitioner at 13, 23–24, Thompson.

82. Cert Petition at 17, 22–24, Thompson, 362 U.S. 199 (1960).

83. Brief for Petitioner at 13, Thompson.

84. Ibid. at 25–26; Petitioner's Reply Brief at 2, Thompson, 326 U.S. 199 (1960).

85. Cert Petition at 15, Thompson, 362 U.S. 199 (1960); Brief for Petitioner at 15, Thompson; see Chapter 2.

86. Winters v. New York, 333 U.S. 507 (1948); "Justices Sharply Ask about Action of Police in Shuffle-Dance Case," *Courier-Journal* (Louisville, KY), January 13, 1960, 1; Henry P. Sailer to Justice John Marshall Harlan, bench memorandum on case No. 59 (Thompson v. Louisville), box 86, Princeton Harlan Papers. For cases making vagrancy laws vulnerable, see, e.g., Thornhill v. Alabama, 310 U.S. 88, 100 (1940); Territory v. Anduha, 31 Haw. 459 (1930); City of St. Louis v. Gloner, 109 S.W. 30 (Mo. 1908); Commonwealth v. Carpenter, 91 N.E.2d 666 (Mass. 1959). See generally "Use of Vagrancy-Type Laws for Arrest and Detention of Suspicious Persons," 1351–64, 1353–54 nn. 9–10.

87. Brief for Petitioner at 64, Thompson; Oral Argument, Thompson, 326 U.S. 199 (1960), January 11–12, 1960, transcript and audio, The Oyez Project, IIT Chicago-Kent College of Law, http://audio.oyez.org/cases/1950–1959/1959/1959_59 (hereafter Oyez Project).

88. The doctrine was only called "substantive due process" after the Lochner era ended. G. Edward White, *The Constitution and the New Deal* (Cambridge, MA: Harvard University Press, 2002). For different views on the Lochner era, compare John Hart Ely, *Democracy and Distrust: A Theory of Judicial Review* (Cambridge, MA: Harvard University Press, 1980); Arnold M. Paul, *Conservative Crisis and the Rule of Law: Attitudes of Bar and Bench, 1887–1895* (Ithaca, NY: Cornell University Press, 1960); with David E. Bernstein, *Rehabilitating Lochner: Defending Individual Rights against Progressive Reform* (Chicago: University of Chicago Press, 2011); Owen Fiss, *Troubled Beginnings of the Modern State, 1888–1910* (New York: Macmillan, 1993); Howard Gillman, *The Constitution Besieged: The Rise and Demise of Lochner Era Police Powers Jurisprudence* (Durham, NC: Duke University Press, 1993); Morton J. Horwitz, *The Transformation of American Law, 1870–1960: The Crisis of Legal Orthodoxy* (New York: Oxford University Press, 1992), 3–230; Michael Les Benedict, "Laissez-Faire and Liberty: A Re-Evaluation of the Meaning and Origins of Laissez-Faire Constitutionalism," *Law and History Review* 3 (1985): 293–331; Charles W. McCurdy, "The 'Liberty of Contract' Regime in American Law," in *The State and Freedom of Contract*, ed. Harry N. Scheiber (Stanford, CA: Stanford University Press, 1998), 161–97. See generally Gary D. Rowe, "Lochner Revisionism Revisited," *Law and Social Inquiry* 24 (1999): 221–52.

89. United States v. Carolene Products, 304 U.S. 144, 152 n. 4 (1938). On the delayed influence of the footnote, see Felix Gilman, "The Famous Footnote Four: A History of the Carolene Products Footnote," *South Texas Law Review* 46 (Fall 2004): 163; Risa L. Goluboff, *The Lost Promise of Civil Rights* (Cambridge, MA: Harvard University Press, 2007). On Lusky, see Louis Lusky, *By What Right? A Commentary on the Supreme Court's Power to Revise the Constitution* (Charlottesville, VA: Michie, 1989), 364. Roe v. Wade, 410 U.S. 113 (1973).

90. For pre-1959 judicial criticisms of vagrancy laws, see, e.g., Edelman, 344 U.S. 357, 362–66 (1953) (Black, J., dissenting). Anduha, 31 Haw. 459 (1930); Thornhill, 310 U.S. 88, 100–101 (1940); Lanzetta, 306 U.S. 451 (1939). For Amsterdam's criticism, see Anthony G. Amsterdam, "The Void-for-Vagueness Doctrine in the Supreme Court," *University of Pennsylvania Law Review* 109, no. 1 (1960): 74 n. 38. See also "Void for Vagueness: An Escape from Statutory Interpretation," *Indiana Law Journal* 23, no. 3 (1948): 278 ("But it seems a coincidence of some moment that the device of invalidating a statute for vagueness should develop on the federal level concurrently with the growth of the tool of substantive due process"). See generally Robert C. Post, "Reconceptualizing Vagueness: Legal Rules and

Social Orders," *California Law Review* 82, no. 3 (1994): 498. For judicial confusion regarding the distinction between procedural and substantive due process, and the interaction of the status/conduct distinction and the void-for-vagrancy doctrine therewith, see Lambert v. California, box 1192, William O. Douglas Papers, Library of Congress (hereafter Douglas Papers); Lanzetta, 306 U.S. 451 (1939).

91. Robinson, 370 U.S. 660, 689 (1962) (White, J., dissenting); Herbert L. Packer, "Making the Punishment Fit the Crime," *Harvard Law Review* 77, no. 6 (1964): 1071; Gary V. Dubin, "Mens Rea Reconsidered: A Plea for a Due Process Concept of Criminal Responsibility," *Stanford Law Review* 18, no. 2 (1966): 392–93. See generally Erik Luna, *Robinson v. California: From Revolutionary Constitutional Doctrine to Model Ban on Status Crimes, in Criminal Law Stories,* eds. Robert Weisberg and Donna Coker (New York: Foundation Press, 2012).

92. Brief for Petitioner at 45–48, 61, Thompson. See generally A. E. Dick Howard, *Magna Carta: Text and Commentary,* rev. ed. (Charlottesville, VA: University Press of Virginia, 1998), 15.

93. Brief for Petitioner at 26–28, 62, Thompson; Petitioner's Reply Brief at 11, Thompson.

94. Brief for Louisville at 6–16, Thompson. For ease, I will refer to the legal documents created by this team of city and state lawyers as the city's brief, as it was ultimately the city that defended the law at oral argument. Oral Argument, Thompson, 326 U.S. 199 (1960), Oyez Project.

95. Brief for Louisville at 16–18, Thompson.

96. Ibid. at 21.

97. Ibid. at 7–8, 21.

98. Petitioner's Reply Brief at 5n*, Thompson; Louis Lusky to James R. Browning (Supreme Court Clerk), January 14, 1960, box 343, Hugo LaFayette Black Papers, Library of Congress (hereafter Black Papers).

99. "Justices Sharply Ask About Action of Police in Shuffle-Dance Case," 1; "Supreme Court Upsets $10 Fines of Man Here," *Courier-Journal* (Louisville, KY), March 22, 1960, 1. As Morse recalls it, Thompson was in jail on a concealed weapons charge when the decision was handed down. Marvin H. Morse, "Terror in the Pocket: Carrying Concealed," President's Message, Federal Lawyer 43, no. 4 (1996): 2. He points out that this was Thompson's first felony charge and his first possibility of real time in the penitentiary. Thompson was ultimately sentenced to a year but served less for good behavior. See also Moulton, "Supreme Court Takes Up Appeal over Two $10 Fines in Tavern Dance," C6.

100. Schancupp, "The Saga of Shufflin' Sam," 424–25; "High Court Hears a $10 Police Case," 14; Oral Argument, Thompson, 326 U.S. 199 (1960), Oyez Project.

101. Thompson v. Louisville, 362 U.S. 199, 206 n. 13 (1960); Justice John M. Harlan to Justice Hugo Black, memorandum, March 17, 1960, box 343, Black Papers; Justice John M. Harlan to Justice Hugo Black, memorandum, March 18, 1960, box 86, Princeton Harlan Papers. On the unanimity of the decision, see Blank, "The High Court and 'Shufflin' Sam,'" 97–98; Justice William J. Brennan to Justice Hugo Black, memorandum, March 16, 1960, box 343, Black Papers; Justice William O. Douglas to Justice Hugo Black (handwritten note on draft opinion), n.d., Box 343, Black Papers; Justice Tom C. Clark to Justice Hugo Black, memorandum, March 18, 1960, box 343, Black Papers; Chief Justice Earl Warren to Justice Hugo Black, memorandum, March 17, 1960, box 343, Black Papers; Justice Potter Stewart to Justice Hugo Black, memorandum, March 17, 1960, box 343, Black Papers; Justice Charles E. Whittaker to Justice Hugo Black, memorandum, box 343, Black Papers. For Justice Harlan's misgivings regarding *Thompson,* see Justice John Marshall Harlan II to Justice Hugo Black, memorandum, March 18, 1960, Princeton Harlan Papers. On Justice Harlan's background and jurisprudence, see David Shapiro, *The Evolution of a Judicial Philosophy: Selected Opinions and Papers of Justice John M. Harlan* (Cambridge, MA: Harvard University Press, 1969); Tinsley E. Yarbrough, *John Marshall Harlan: Great Dissenter of the Warren Court* (New York: Oxford University Press, 1992); Norman Dorsen, "The Second Mr. Justice Harlan: A Constitutional Conservative," *New York University Law Review* 44 (1969): 249; Henry Friendly, "Mr. Justice Harlan as Seen by a Friend and Judge of an Inferior Court," *Harvard Law Review* 85 (1971): 382; Gerald Gunther, "In Search of Judicial Quality on a Changing Court: The Case of Justice Powell," *Stanford Law Review* 24 (1972): 1000; J. Harvie Wilkinson, III, "Justice John M. Harlan and the Values of Federalism," *Virginia Law Review* 57 (1971), 1185; G. Edward White, *The American Judicial Tradition* (New York: Oxford University Press),

291–94. See generally Gerald L. Neuman, "The Constitutional Requirement of 'Some Evidence,'" *San Diego Law Review* 25, no. 4 (1988): 651–56.

102. Thompson, 362 U.S. 199 (1960).

103. Howard Ball and Phillip Cooper, *Of Power and Right: Hugo Black, William O. Douglas, and America's Constitutional Revolution* (New York: Oxford University Press, 1992), 196; Daniel M. Berman, "The Racial Issue and Mr. Justice Black," *American University Law Review* 16, no. 3 (1967): 387–88; Thompson v. Louisville, 362 U.S. 199 (1960).

104. Douglas, "Vagrancy and Arrest on Suspicion," 7.

105. "Inn Snubs 'Tramps': Udall and 2 Douglases," *New York Times*, May 8, 1961, 1.

106. Douglas, "Vagrancy and Arrest on Suspicion," 7–13.

107. "Shufflin' Sam's Long Step," *Time*, April 4, 1960, 17; Blank, "The High Court and 'Shufflin' Sam,'" 96.

108. "Court Works Overtime to Hear an Old Man's Case," *Register-Pajaronian* (Watsonville, CA), January 15, 1960, 4, box 343, Black Papers; Blank, "The High Court and 'Shufflin' Sam,'" 98. See also Silvia S. Bennet to Justice Hugo Black, March 22, 1960, box 343, Black Papers; "Sam Thompson, the Handyman of Legal Fame," *Courier-Journal* (Louisville, KY), March 23, 1960; Nat Hentoff, "The Supreme Court," *Playboy*, November 1966; Anthony Lewis, "High Court Voids 2 Kentucky Fines," *New York Times*, March 22, 1960, 1.

109. Michael Pulitzer, "Louis Lusky: Defender of Civil Liberties," *Courier-Journal* (Louisville, KY), March 27, 1960, 4; "Sam Thompson, the Handyman of Legal Fame"; *American Civil Liberties of Kentucky*, 12; Bill Woolsey, "War on Slipshod Justice Goes On: For Saint or Sinner . . . The Civil Liberties' Union Fights," *Louisville Times*, March 31, 1960, 6. See also Blank, "The High Court and 'Shufflin' Sam,'" 98.

110. "Sam Thompson, the Handyman of Legal Fame"; Davis, "A Kentucky Response," 122.

111. Davis, "A Kentucky Response," 122; "Thompson Case Cited; Man Freed of Charge," *Courier-Journal* (Louisville, KY), September 13, 1960; "Taustine Frees Accused in Case like Thompson's," *Courier-Journal* (Louisville, KY), April 2, 1960.

112. See Certiorari Memorandum, Robinson v. California, n.d., box 149, Princeton Harlan Papers; John Marshall Harlan to Potter Stewart, memorandum, June 13, 1962, box 149, Princeton Harlan Papers; NL [Nathan Lewin], Supplementary Memo, n.d., Box 149, Princeton Harlan Papers; Conference Notes, Robinson v. California, April 20, 1962, Box 1277, Dougles Papers.

113. Blank, "The High Court and 'Shufflin' Sam,'" 98; "Shufflin' Sam's Long Step," *Time*, April 4, 1960, 17; "Fines of 'Shufflin' Sam' Upset by Supreme Court," A8; "Supreme Court Upsets $10 Fines of Man Here," 1.

114. Childress, *Louisville Division of Police*, 61. For Lusky's accounts of his role in *Thompson*, see, e.g., Louis Lusky, *By What Right? A Commentary on the Supreme Court's Power to Revise the Constitution* (Charlottesville, VA: Michie, 1975), 1; Louis Lusky, "Justice with a Southern Accent," *Harper's Magazine*, March 1964, 70. For Lusky's friends' memorials, see, e.g., Jack Greenberg, "In Memoriam: Louis Lusky," *Columbia Law Review* 101, no. 5 (2001): 977–81; Alfred Hill, "In Memory of Louis Lusky," *Columbia Law Review* 101, no. 5 (2001): 983; Arthur W. Murphy, "In Memory of Louis Lusky," *Columbia Law Review* 101, no. 5 (2001): 984–85; Rosenthal, "Louis Lusky," 986–89.

115. For criminal cases implicating the *Thompson* no-evidence rule, see, e.g., *In re* Winship, 397 U.S. 358 (1970); Jackson v. Virginia, 443 U.S. 307 (1979); Ex parte Reed, 402 S.W.3d 39, 46 (Tex. App. 2013).

116. Schancupp, "The Saga of Shufflin' Sam," 414 n. 27. See also Marvin Morse, telephone interview with author, June 23, 2014.

117. On the civil rights cases that culminated in *Brown v. Board of Education*, see Risa L. Goluboff, *The Lost Promise of Civil Rights* (Cambridge, MA: Harvard University Press, 2007); Michael J. Klarman, *From Jim Crow to Civil Rights* (New York: Oxford University Press, 2004); Mark V. Tushnet, *Making Civil Rights Law: Thurgood Marshall and the Suprme Court, 1936–1961* (New York: Oxford University Press, 1994); Tomiko Brown-Nagin, *Courage to Dissent: Atlanta and the Long History of the Civil Rights Movement* (New York: Oxford University Press, 2011). On pressure to desegregate public accommodations in Louisville, see Adams, *Way Up North in Louisville*, 128–34; Aubespin, Clay, and Hudson, *Two Centuries of Black Louisville*, 185–87.

118. Petitioner's Reply Brief at 2–3, Thompson.
119. "Precedent for Sitdowns?" *Richmond Times-Dispatch*, March 24, 1960, 12, box 343, Black Papers.
120. Jack Greenberg, *Crusaders in the Courts: Legal Battles of the Civil Rights Movement*, ann. ed. (New York: Twelve Tables Press, 2004), 392; Greenberg, "In Memoriam, Louis Lusky," 979.
121. Childress, *Louisville Division of Police*, 61.
122. Jack Greenberg, interview with author, June 9, 2009; Greenberg, "In Memoriam, Louis Lusky," 979.

Chapter 4

1. Ala. Code §§ 14.80.437–439 (1940).
2. "Birmingham: Smoldering Hotbed of Terror and Hatred," *Philadelphia Tribune*, April 19, 1960, 1.
3. Patrick Murphy Malin, ACLU Executive Director, to Martin Luther King Jr., October 30, 1958, folder 42, box 1074, American Civil Liberties Union Records, series 3, subseries 3B: 9, Department of Rare Books and Special Collections, Princeton University Library (hereafter Princeton ACLU Papers). See also United Press International, "U.S. Probes Alabama Arrests," *Chicago Daily Defender*, October 30, 1958, A1, 2. United Press International, "3 Negro Pastors Seized in Birmingham Home," *Washington Post and Times Herald*, October 28, 1958, A11; see also Frank L. Stanley, "Being Frank ... About People, Places and Problems," Chicago Defender, September 27, 1958, 10; "Plantation Days Are Over," Our Opinions, *Chicago Daily Defender*, September 20, 1958, 10; NNPA News Service, "Continuation of NNPA Roundup of News Highlights—July to Dec.," *Baltimore Afro-American*, January 10, 1959, 2; United Press International, "Arrest of Ministers under Government Investigation: If Civil Rights Violated Action Will Be Taken," *Atlanta Daily World*, October 31, 1958, 1; "Reign of Terror in Birmingham: 3 Negro Ministers Jailed," *Cleveland Call and Post*, November 1, 1958, 1A; "FBI Probes Birmingham Terror after Five Pastors Are Jailed," *Norfolk New Journal and Guide*, November 1, 1958, B1; "FBI Probes Arrest of Three Ministers: Action Follows NAACP Protest," *Chicago Daily Defender*, November 15, 1958, 21; United Press International, "Federal Grand Jury to Probe Birmingham Arrests," *Norfolk New Journal and Guide*, November 15, 1958, B2; Louis Lautier, "To Probe Arrest of Clergymen," *Baltimore Afro-American*, November 22, 1958, 1; Helen Thomas, "U.S. Maps War on Terrorism: Drafts Plan for Complete Rights," *Chicago Daily Defender*, November 22, 1958, 1; "Record in Birmingham: 22 Bombings, 4 Fires," Norfolk New Journal and Guide, December 20, 1958, 2; Helen Thomas, "Try to Register Again, Hampered Citizens Urged: Attempts Would Pile Up More Rights Evidence," *Atlanta Daily World*, January 16, 1959, 1; Louis Lautier, "Ala. Judge Defies U.S. Atty. Gen'l," *Cleveland Call and Post*, January 24, 1959, 1A; United Press International, "U.S. Wants Case on Voting Bars," *Chicago Daily Defender*, January 24, 1959, 1; Enoc P. Waters Jr., "Dilemma in the South: Birmingham Headed for Showdown on Rights," *Chicago Daily Defender*, March 3, 1959, 7.
4. Cliff Mackey, "Wanta Hike (Back) with Ike?" The Week's News in Tabloid, *Baltimore Afro-American*, April 12, 1952, 4; Diane McWhorter, *Carry Me Home: Birmingham, Alabama: The Climactic Battle of the Civil Rights Revolution* (New York: Simon & Schuster, 2001), 65; "Two Arrested in Drive on Reds in Birmingham," *Washington Post*, July 9, 1950, M1; Ex parte Hall, 50 So.2d 264 (Ala. 1951); Hall v. City of Birmingham, 61 So.2d 773 (Ala. Ct. App. October 8, 1952); clipping, Baltimore Afro-American, nd, box 4, folder 8, Fred Shuttlesworth Papers, King Library and Archive, Martin Luther King Jr. Center for Nonviolent Social Change (hereafter King Papers).
5. Paul A. Slack, "Vagrants and Vagrancy in England, 1598–1664," *Economic History Review* 27, no. 3 (August 1974): 365; Mark Netzloff, " 'Counterfeit Egyptians' and Imagined Borders: Johnson's *The Gypsies Metamorphosed*," *ELH* 68, no. 4 (2001): 763–93; Paul Slack, *Poverty and Policy in Tudor and Stuart England* (New York: Longman, 1988), 98; A. L. Beier, *Masterless Men, the Vagrancy Problem in England, 1560–1640* (New York: Methuen, 1985), 58–62, 64–65.

6. Stefan A. Riesenfeld, "The Formative Era of American Public Assistance Law," *California Law Review* 43, no. 2 (1955): 207; Nathaniel B. Shurtleff, ed., *Records of the Governor and Company of the Massachusetts Bay in New England Printed by Order of the Legislature*, vol. 4, bk. 2, 1661–1674 (Boston: William White, 1854), 2–4. The colony repealed it at the request of the king. Douglas Lamar Jones, "The Strolling Poor: Transiency in Eighteenth-Century Massachusetts," *Journal of Social History* 8, no. 3 (Spring 1975): 43. See also Douglas Lamar Jones, "The Transformation of the Law of Poverty in 18th Century Massachusetts," in *Law in Colonial Massachusetts, 1630–1800: A Conference Held 6 and 7 November 1981, by the Colonial Society of Massachusetts*, Daniel R. Coquilette ed. (Boston: The Society, 1984), 153 (describing removal law used against non-Puritans); James W. Loewen, *Sundown Towns: A Hidden Dimension of American Racism* (New York: New Press, 2005); An Act for the Government and Protection of Indians, ch. 133, 1850 Cal. Stat. 408; An Act to Punish Vagrants, Vagabonds, and Dangerous and Suspicious Persons, ch. 175, 1855 Cal. Stat. 217; Jesse Alemán, "Citizenship Rights and Colonial Whites," in *Complicating Constructions: Race, Ethnicity, and Hybridity in American Texts*, ed. David S. Goldstein and Audrey B. Thacker (Seattle: University of Washington Press, 2007), 7; Tomás Almaguer, *Racial Fault Lines* (Berkeley: University of California Press, 1994), 133–34; Robert F. Heizer and Alan J. Almquist, *The Other Californians: Prejudice and Discrimination under Spain, Mexico, and the United States to 1920* (Berkeley: University of California Press, 1971), 48–49; Kimberly Johnston-Dodds, *Early California Laws and Policies Related to California Indians*, in *California Water Plan Update 2009*, 13–15, http://www.waterplan.water.ca.gov/docs/cwpu2009/0310final/v4c19a02_cwp2009.pdf, originally published by California Research Bureau, 2002; F. Arturo Rosales, *¡Pobre Raza!: Violence, Justice, and Mobilization among Mexico Lindo Immigrants, 1900–1936* (Austin: University of Texas Press, 1999), 4, 78–79, 157; 1896 Haw. Sess. Laws 87 (Act 36); see also Haw. Rev. Stat. §§ 315–1 to 7 (1955); 1850 Penal Code of the Hawaiian Islands 91–92 (ch. 38); Edward J. Escobar, *Race, Police, and the Making of a Political Identity: Mexican Americans and the Los Angeles Police Department, 1900–1945* (Berkeley: University of California Press, 1999), 49–50, 129–30; see Matt S. Meier and Margo Gutierrez, *Encyclopedia of the Mexican American Civil Rights Movement* (Westport, CT: Greenwood Press, 2000), 232; see, e.g., Hawaii v. Moritaro, 16 Haw. 267, 268 (1904); Gary Okihiro, *Cane Fires: The Anti-Japanese Movement in Hawaii, 1865–1945* (Philadelphia: Temple University Press, 1991), 239; Ronald Takaki, *Pau Hana: Plantation Life and Labor in Hawaii 1835–1920* (Honolulu: University of Hawaii Press, 1983), 72; see also George Chaplin, *Presstime in Paradise: The Life and Times of the Honolulu Advertiser* (Honolulu: University of Hawai'i Press, 1998), 139; Walter G. Beach, *Oriental Crime in California* (New York: AMS Press, 1971), 71; see D. David Dreis, "The Cat of Kung-Fu," *Black Belt*, December 1968, 46; "Zoot-Suit War," *Time*, June 21, 1943, 20; Lisa Magana, *Mexican Americans and the Politics of Diversity* (Tucson: University of Arizona Press, 2005), 20; Rick Baldoz, *The Third Asiatic Invasion: Empire and Migration in Filipino America, 1898–1946* (New York: New York University Press, 2011), 58–59, 182–83; "Recent Antinarcotic Activities," *National Association of Retail Druggists Journal* 21 (1915–16): 1184; Josh Sides, *Erotic City: Sexual Revolutions and the Making of Modern San Francisco* (New York: Oxford University Press, 2009), 27–28; Sonia Emily Wallovits, *The Filipinos in California* (thesis, University of Southern California, 1972, reprinted San Francisco: R and E Research Associates, 1972), 59; Carey McWilliams, *Factories in the Field: The Story of Migratory Farm Labor in California* (Boston: Little, Brown, 1939), 38–39, 180–81, 225, 251, 311; "Anti-loiter Law Rapped," *Toronto Leader-Post*, June 9, 1972, G2.

7. On the plight of free African Americans in the antebellum era South, see Ariela J. Gross, *Double Character: Slavery and Mastery in the Antebellum Courtroom* (Athens: University of Georgia Press, 2006); Ariela Gross, *What Blood Won't Tell: A History of Race on Trial in America* (Cambridge. MA: Harvard University Press, 2009); Rebecca Scott, *Degrees of Freedom* (Cambridge, MA: Harvard University Press, 2009); William P. Quigley, "The Quicksands of the Poor Law: Poor Relief Legislation in a Growing Nation, 1790–1820," *Northern Illinois University Law Review* 18, no. 1 (1997): 79–81. June Axinn and Herman Levin, *Social Welfare: A History of the American Response to Need* (New York: Harper and Row, 1975), 83; Mimi Abramowitz, *Regulating the Lives of Women*, rev. ed. (Boston: South End Press, 1996), 154; William P. Quigley, "Rumblings of Reform: Northern Poor Relief Legislation in Antebellum

America, 1820–1860," *Capital University Law Review* 26, no. 4 (1997): 743–44; An Act to define and punish Vagrancy in free persons of color, and for other purposes, 1859 Ga. Laws 69 (no. 93); see also Act of February 19, 1820, ch. 26, 1819 Va. Acts 22; James W. Ely Jr., "'There Are Few Subjects in Political Economy of Greater Difficulty': The Poor Laws of the Antebellum South," *American Bar Foundation Research Journal* 10, no. 4 (Autumn 1985): 868; William Waller Hening, *The New Virginia Justice* (Richmond: Johnson and Warner, 1810), 566, 589; Benjamin Swaim, *The North Carolina Justice* (Raleigh: Henry D. Turner, 1839), 148–49, 457–58; Ruth Herndon, "'Who Died an Expence to This Town': Poor Relief in Eighteenth-Century Rhode Island," in *Down and Out in Early America*, ed. Billy G. Smith (University Park: Pennsylvania State University Press, 2004), 146–47; Douglas Lamar Jones, "Poverty and Vagabondage: The Process of Survival in Eighteenth-Century Massachusetts," *New England Historical and Genealogical Register*,133 (October 1979): 248–50; Benjamin Joseph Klebaner, *Public Poor Relief in America, 1790–1869* (New York: Arno Press, 1976), 519, 565–82. Similar lists, likening African Americans—both fugitive slave and free—to vagrants and other undesirables could also be found in nineteenth-century Supreme Court opinions. See, e.g., Prigg v. Com. of Pennsylvania, 41 U.S. (16 Pet.) 539, 625 (1842); Moore v. Illinois, 55 U.S. (14 How.) 13, 18 (1853). On vagrants as runaway servants, see David Montgomery, *Citizen Worker: The Experience of Workers in the United States with Democracy and the Free Market during the Nineteenth Century* (Cambridge: Cambridge University Press, 1996), 27– 29; Gerald L. Neuman, "The Lost Century of American Immigration Law (1776–1875)," *Columbia Law Review* 93 (1993): 1865–66. On discrimination against and restrictions on free blacks generally, see Ira Berlin, *Slaves without Masters: The Free Negro in the Antebellum South* (New York: New Press, 1974); Barbara J. Fields, *Slavery and Freedom on the Middle Ground: Maryland during the Nineteenth Century* (New Haven, CT: Yale University Press, 1985); John H. Franklin, *The Free Negro in North Carolina 1790–1860* (New York: Russell and Russell, 1969); A. Leon Higginbotham Jr., *In the Matter of Color: Race and the American Legal Process*, vol. 1, *The Colonial Period* (New York: Oxford University Press, 1978); Leon F. Litwack, *North of Slavery: The Negro in the Free States 1790–1860* (Chicago: University of Chicago Press, 1961); Paul Finkelman, "Prelude to the Fourteenth Amendment: Black Legal Rights in the Antebellum North," *Rutgers Law Journal* 17 (1986): 430–43; A. Leon Higginbotham Jr. and Greer C. Bosworth, "'Rather Than the Free': Free Blacks in Colonial and Antebellum Virginia," *Harvard Civil Rights–Civil Liberties Law Review* 26 (1991): 17–66.

8. On Union treatment of escaped slaves, see John W. Blassingame, *Black New Orleans, 1860–1880* (Chicago: University of Chicago Press, 1973), 30–31, 51–53 (quoting primary sources). Of the former Confederate states, only Tennessee and Arkansas did not pass new vagrancy laws in the two years after the war ended. William Cohen, *At Freedom's Edge: Black Mobility and the Southern White Quest for Racial Control 1861–1915* (Baton Rouge: Louisiana State University Press, 1991), 28, 30–31, 242–46; Theodore B. Wilson, *The Black Codes of the South* (Tuscaloosa: University of Alabama Press, 1965), 68. See also Eric Foner, *Reconstruction: America's Unfinished Revolution, 1863–1877*, updated ed. (New York: Harper Perennial, 2014), 199–201, 205. This portion of the vagrancy law was omitted from the reconstructed Mississippi Code of 1871.

9. Wilson, *The Black Codes of the South*, 117 (citing *New York Times* articles from January 25, 1866, and March 11, 1866); Foner, *Reconstruction*, 200. On hiring out vagrancy convicts, see Cohen, *At Freedom's Edge*, 29–30, 33 (quoting 1865 General Laws of Mississippi, 83–85, 90–92). Act of November 29, 1865, ch. 23, 1865 Miss. Laws 165, 167 quoted in Ahmed A. White, "A Different Kind of Labor Law: Vagrancy Law and the Regulation of Harvest Labor, 1913–1924," *University of Colorado Law Review* 75, no. 3 (2004): 680.

10. Cohen, *At Freedom's Edge*, 34–35. Eric Foner, *Reconstruction*, 200–201, 363, 372, 593; see also Gary V. Dubin and Richard H. Robinson, "The Vagrancy Concept Reconsidered: Problems and Abuses of Status Criminality," *New York University Law Review* 37, 132 (quoting Hicks v. State, 76 Ga. 326, 328 (1886)); Joseph H. Cartwright, *The Triumph of Jim Crow: Tennessee Race Relations in the 1880's* (Knoxville: University of Tennessee Press, 1975), 18, quoted in Cohen, *At Freedom's Edge*, 228–29; Report and Testimony of the Select Committee of the United States Senate to Investigate the Causes of the Removal of the Negroes from the Southern States to the Northern States, 46th Congress, 2d Session, Rpt. 693, Pt. 3 (1880),

500–501. Cf. Dan M. Kahan and Tracey L. Meares, "Foreword: The Coming Crisis of Criminal Procedure," *Georgetown Law Journal* 86 (1998): 1153, 1156.

11. Cohen, *At Freedom's Edge*, 239–41, table 12; Alabama, Laws, 1903, 244–45, quoted in ibid. at 242; William Cohen, "Negro Involuntary Servitude in the South, 1865–1940: A Preliminary Analysis," *Journal of Southern History* 42, no. 1 (February 1976): 47–48; *Atlanta Constitution*, September 2, 1904, quoted in Cohen, "Negro Involuntary Servitude," 50; Andrew W. Manis, *A Fire You Can't Put Out: The Civil Rights Life of Birmingham's Reverend Fred Shuttlesworth* (Tuscaloosa: University of Alabama Press, 1999), 33. See also Linda K. Kerber, *No Constitutional Right to Be Ladies: Women and the Obligations of Citizenship* (New York: Hill and Wang, 1998), 78. On vagrancy arrests during World War II, see John T. Elliff, *United States Department of Justice and Individual Rights, 1937–1962* (New York: Garland, 1987), 72; Cohen, "Negro Involuntary Servitude," 51–52 (quoting primary sources); Risa L. Goluboff, *The Lost Promise of Civil Rights* (Cambridge, MA: Harvard University Press, 2007), 51–80.

12. Jackson v. City & Cnty. of Denver, 124 P.2d 240 (Colo. 1942); see also State v. Bonnie, 206 S.W.2d 989 (Mo. App. 1947); State v. Hall, 52 A.2d 845 (N.J. Ct. Spec. Sess. 1947); People v. Simpson, 339 P.2d 156 (Cal. Dist. Ct. App. 1959); "Civic Groups Laud Maloney's 850 Arrests, 256 This Week," *Courier* (Pittsburgh), June 23, 1951, 1; "266 'Guests' Register at No. 2 Station," *Courier* (Pittsburgh), July 28, 1951, 6; "267 Arrests on Maloney's Scoreboard," *Courier* (Pittsburgh), October 13, 1951; " 'Maloney's Scoreboard' Shows 187 Arrests," *Courier* (Pittsburgh), December 22, 1951, 6; "Summary of Arrests of All Kinds at Center Avenue Station during 1951," *Courier* (Pittsburgh), February 9, 1952, 6; "Hill Crime Rate Still Normal at Awful Pace of 1,000 Arrests Each Month," *Courier* (Pittsburgh), May 9, 1953, 15; People v. Bell, 125 N.Y.S.2d 117 (Co. Ct. 1953), aff'd, 306 N.Y. 110, 115 N.E.2d 821 (1953). See also Chapter Nine, this volume.

13. Cohen, "Negro Involuntary Servitude," 31–60, 48–49; Va. Code Ann. §2808 (1942); Tenn. Code Ann. §5248 (Michie 1938); Ark. Stat. 41–4301 (1947); Tex. Penal Code Ann. 607 (Vernon 1938); Tex. Penal Code Ann. 607 (Vernon Supp. 1952); Ga. Code Ann. §26–7001 (1936); Fla. Stat. §856.02 (1944); Ala. Code §437 (1940). For a discussion of the history of vagrancy laws in the post-Civil War era, see Amy Dru Stanley, *From Bondage to Contract: Wage Labor, Marriage, and the Market in the Age of Slave Emancipation* (Cambridge: Cambridge University Press, 1998), 98–137; Jane Dailey, "Introduction," and "The Limits of Liberalism in the New South: The Politics of Race, Sex, and Patronage in Virginia," in *Jumpin' Jim Crow: Southern Politics from Civil War to Civil Rights*, ed. Jane Dailey, Glenda Gilmore, and Bryant Simon (Princeton, NJ: Princeton University Press, 2000), 3–6, 88–114.

14. Report of the Southern Regional Council, "The Student Protest Movement: A Recapitulation" (1961), cited in Joel B. Grossman, "A Model for Judicial Policy Analysis: The Supreme Court and the Sit-in Cases," in *Frontiers of Judicial Research*, eds. Joel B. Grossman and Joseph Tanenhaus (New York: John Wiley, 1969), 427; Martin Oppenheimer, "The Movement—a 25-Year Retrospective," *Monthly Review* 36, no. 9 (February 1985): 50.

15. Numan V. Bartley, *The Rise of Massive Resistance: Race and Politics in the South during the 1950s* (Baton Rouge: University of Louisiana Press, 1969); Neil R. McMillen, *Dark Journey, Black Mississippians in the Age of Jim Crow* (Champaign: University of Illinois Press, 1984); see also Kevin Kruse, *White Flight: Atlanta and the Making of Modern Conservatism* (Princeton, NJ: Princeton University Press, 2005); Matthew D. Lassiter, *The Silent Majority: Suburban Politics in the Sunbelt South* (Princeton, NJ: Princeton University Press, 2006); Dennis Robert's Journal, accessed March 10, 2015, http://www.crmvet.org/lets/dr_63_journal. pdf; Seth Cagin, and Philip Dray, *We Are Not Afraid: The Story of Goodman, Schwerner, and Chaney and the Civil Rights Campaign for Mississippi* (New York: Macmillan, 1988); John R. Rachal, " 'The Long, Hot Summer': The Mississippi Response to Freedom Summer, 1964," *Journal of Negro History* 84, no. 4 (Autumn 1999): 323–24; Samuel Walker, *In Defense of American Liberties: A History of the ACLU* (Carbondale: Southern Illinois University Press, 1999), 265–66; Townsend Davis, *Weary Feet, Rested Souls: A Guided History of the Civil Rights Movement* (New York: W.W. Norton, 1998), 197.

16. Anthony Lester, *Justice in the American South* (London: Amnesty International, n.d.), folder 7, box 1872, American Civil Liberties Union Records, Series 4, Subseries 4B, Princeton ACLU Papers; John H. McCray, "Pending High Court Sit-In Rulings Pose New Legal

Problems," *Pittsburgh Courier*, December 16, 1961, A6 (mentioning loitering and loafing convictions of demonstrators); "Ga. Judge Gives Coed 18 Months," in *The Student Voice, 1960–1965: Periodical of the Student Nonviolent Coordinating Committee*, ed. Clayborne Carson (Westport, CT: Meckler, 1990) (hereafter *The Student Voice*), 125, 128; Jack Greenberg, *Crusaders in the Courts: How a Dedicated Band of Lawyers Fought for the Civil Rights Revolution* (New York: Basic Books, 1994), 344–45; Allard K. Lowenstein (Chairman, Advisory Committee, Henry for Governor), statement, n.d., folder 1, box 1873, American Civil Liberties Union Records, Series 4, Subseries 4B, Department of Rare Books and Special Collections, Princeton University Library; Summary of Events (Mississippi), October 22 through October 28, n.d., folder 1, box 1873, American Civil Liberties Union Records, Series 4, Subseries 4B, Princeton ACLU Papers; Events in Mississippi, November 1 and 2, folder 1, box 1873, American Civil Liberties Union Records, Series 4, Subseries 4B, Princeton ACLU Papers; letter to Birch Bayh., folder 1, box 1873, American Civil Liberties Union Records, Series 4, Subseries 4B, Princeton ACLU Papers ; Part 23, Series A, Reel 15, Papers of the NAACP, Library of Congress (microfilm) (hereafter NAACP Papers); "Jails Fill as Protests Rise," January 27, 1964, 1, in *The Student Voice*, 109; Herbert Timothy Lovelace Jr., "International Legal History from Below: The Civil Rights Movement and the U.S. Origins of the International Convention on the Elimination of All Forms of Racial Discrimination, 1960–1965" (unpublished Ph.D. dissertation, University of Virginia, May 2012), 51–53 (discussing aspirin arrests).

17. "Court Ruling Due on Trespass Law," May 5, 1964, 1, in *The Student Voice*, 143; Lester, *Justice in the American South*, 14–15, folder 7, box 1872, Series 4, Subseries 4B, Princeton ACLU Papers; "Here's How Americus' [sic] Officials React to Rights Demonstrations," *New Journal and Guide*, November 9, 1963, 11; "Pass 3 New Laws in La. to Halt Rights Actions," *Chicago Defender*, August 24, 1963, 6. On newly passed laws, see Rachal, "'The Long, Hot Summer,'" 316, 320–21; John Dittmer, *Local People: The Struggle for Civil Rights in Mississippi* (Urbana: University of Illinois Press, 1994), 229 (transfer to state prison farm); "Lawyers Plot Strategy to Aid Demonstrators," *Michigan Chronicle*, June 13, 1964, A3.

18. Tomiko Brown-Nagin, *Courage to Dissent: Atlanta and the Long History of the Civil Rights Movement* (New York: Oxford University Press, 2011), 165, 177–79, 221–23, 237, 279–80.

19. Joes Elvin Atkins, Direct Examination Exhibit "F", *Florida v. Atkins* (Polk Co., Fla., Crim. Ct. Record), part 23, series A, reel 14, NAACP Papers.

20. See, e.g., *Tinsley v. City of Richmond*, 119 S.E.2d 488 (Va. 1961).

21. For examples of vagrancy and loitering leading to additional charges, see Frank Hunt, "FBI Investigates Police Freedom Riders' Beating: 3 Arrested, Let Go after Lecture," *Baltimore Afro-America*, August 26, 1961, 3; "'Criminal Anarchy': Went to Visit Student Prisoner; 2 Land in Jail," *New Journal and Guide*, March 3, 1962, 1. For examples of the charges on their own, see United Press International, "Jail Youth for Brushing against White Man: Threats, Firings in N.O. Aid Boycott," *Chicago Daily Defender*, December 12, 1960, 1; "Helped Sit-Ins: White Minister Tells of Police Attacks," *New York Amsterdam News*, May 6, 1961, 18 (no additional charges after vagrancy and disturbing the peace); "73 on 'Partial' Hunger Strike in Baton Rouge," *Chicago Daily Defender*, December 19, 1961, 3; "Faculty Lashes Southern Head: Clark Told He Handled Affair Badly," *Baltimore Afro-American*, February 10, 1962, 1; John G. Warner, "Nab 17 of Jeering Mob at Integrated School: Whites Boycott Classes," *Chicago Daily Defender*, November 16, 1960, 1; "Here Is the Score on 'Mississippi Project,'" *Baltimore Afro-American*, August 1, 1964, 12. For vagrancy and (or by) loitering, see, e.g., "Street Fight in Tenn. over 'Sitdown' Protests," *Chicago Daily Defender*, March 5, 1960, 12; "Discuss Florida Problem," *Baltimore Afro-American*, September 10, 1960, 3; "Cause Police Sit-In," *Pittsburgh Courier*, September 2, 1961, 8; "Arrest CORE Members 2 Days after Meeting," *New York Amsterdam News*, November 4, 1961, 6; "6 CORE Members Charged with Vagrancy, Loitering," *Chicago Daily Defender*, November 8, 1961,19; "Albany Rights Fighters near 'Breaking Point,'" *Chicago Daily Defender*, July 1, 1963, 4; Julius Higgenbotham, "Marchers Camp in Montgomery: Overcome Bombs, Weather, Counter-March," *Courier* (Pittsburgh), March 27, 1965, 1; "SNCC Secretaries Detained in Sumter," *Atlanta Daily World*, March 22, 1963, 2; Homer Bigart, "10 in Pool Episode Guilty in Georgia: Judge at Trial of Negroes Assails Outside 'Agitators,'" *New York Times*, July 10, 1964, 11. For vagrancy, see, e.g., "Dixie and the Law," *Chicago Daily Defender*, January 15, 1964, 11; "Jail SNCC Leader in

Albany, Ga.," *Chicago Daily Defender*, August 7, 1962, 9; "Four Arrested in Miss. Library; One Illinoisan," *Chicago Daily Defender*, August 20, 1964, 8; "73 on 'Partial' Hunger Strike in Baton Rouge," 3; Tananarive Due and Patricia Stephens Due, *Freedom in the Family: A Mother-Daughter Memoir of the Fight for Civil Rights* (New York: One World, 2009), 177–78. For loitering, see, e.g., "Summer Project: Mississippi, 1964," *National Lawyers Guild Review* 24, no. 2 (1965): 37 (describing vagueness challenge to one such ordinance in Meridian, Mississippi); Daniel H. Pollitt, "Dime Store Demonstrations: Events and Legal Problems of First Sixty Days," *Duke Law Journal* 1960, no. 3 (1960): 334; Dennis Roberts's Journal, accessed March 10, 2015, http://www.crmvet.org/lets/dr_63_journal.pdf; Brief of Plaintiff-in-Error, Part 1, Harris v. City of Albany, n.d., folder 57.10, container 111, Meiklejohn Civil Liberties Institute Collections, BANC MS 991281 c, The Bancroft Library, University of California, Berkeley (hereafter Civil Liberties Institute Collections); Adam Fairclough, *Race and Democracy: The Civil Rights Struggle in Louisiana, 1915–1972* (Athens: University of Georgia Press, 2008), 330; Daniel J. Lanahan, *Justice for All: Legendary Trials of the 20th Century* (Bloomington, IN: Authorhouse, 2006), 67.

22. Bryce Miller, "Ark. Leader Acts to Curb NAACP," *Chicago Daily Defender*, October 14, 1958, 4; "SNCC Secretaries Detained in Sumter," 2; David L. Chappell, *Inside Agitators: White Southerners in the Civil Rights Movement* (Baltimore: Johns Hopkins University Press, 1994), 135.

23. See, e.g., "FBI Enters Case: Probes Attack on Minister," *Chicago Daily Defender*, April 28, 1960, A1; "FBI Pr[o]bes Arrest of Ala. Pastor," The Week's Newsmakers, *Baltimore Afro-American*, May 7, 1960, 6; Fairclough, *Race and Democracy*, 278; James Smallwood, *Reform, Red Scare, and Ruin: Virginia Durr, Prophet of the New South* (Philadelphia: Xlibris, 2008), 185; Blaine T. Browne and Robert C. Cottrell, *Modern American Lives: Individuals and Issues in American History since 1945* (Armonk, NY: M. E. Sharpe, 2008), 169; Doug Rossinow, *The Politics of Authenticity: Liberalism, Christianity, and the New Left in America* (New York: Columbia University Press 1998), 137; Judith N. McArthur and Harold L. Smith, "Not Whistling Dixie: Women's Movements and Feminist Politics," in *The Texas Left: The Radical Roots of Lone Star Liberalism*, ed. David O'Donald Cullen and Kyle G. Wilkison (College Station: Texas A&M University Press, 2010), 144–45; Hunt, "FBI Investigates Police Freedom Riders' Beating," 3; Due and Due, *Freedom in the Family*, 177–78; Bob Zellner, *Wrong Side of Murder Creek* (Montgomery, AL: New South Books, 2008), 190–93; copy of telegram to James Farmer et al., February 1962, part 21, no series, reel 18, fr. 141, NAACP Papers; Denise Nicholas, "A Grand Romantic Notion," in *Hands on the Freedom Plow: Personal Accounts by Women in SNCC*, ed. Faith S. Holsaert, Martha Prescod Norman Noonan, Judy Richardson, Betty Garman Robinson, Jean Smith Young, and Dorothy M. Zellner (Urbana: University of Illinois Press, 2010), 262.

24. Miss. Code Ann.§ 2666(c) (1956); Edward Ranzal, "Civil Rights Worker Sues Kress for Arrest at Mississippi Store," *New York Times*, November 14, 1964, 16; Complaint and Jury Demand at 3, Adickes v. S.H. Kress & Co., 252 F.Supp. 140 (S.D.N.Y. 1966), file 552.NY.2, container 111, Civil Liberties Institute Collections; Eleanor Jackson Piel, interview with author, February 14, 2012; Draft Brief for the Petitioner at 18, Adicks v. S.H. Kress & Co., 398 U.S. 144 (1970) (No. 79), box 1197, American Civil Liberties Union Records, Series 4, Subseries 4A, Princeton ACLU Papers; Achtenberg v. State of Miss., 393 F.2d 468, 472–74 (5th Cir. 1968).

25. Complaint and Jury Demand at 5, Adickes v. S.H. Kress & Co., 252 F.Supp. 140 (S.D.N.Y. 1966), file 552.NY.2, container 111, BANC MS 991281 c, Civil Liberties Institute Collections.

26. Marlise James, *The People's Lawyers* (New York: Holt, Rinehart, and Winston, 1973), 293–94; Dennis Roberts, "Georgia Justice," *The Progressive*, March 1964, at 17; Ellen Lake, "C. B. King," *Harvard Crimson*, May 13, 1964, http://www.thecrimson.com/article/1964/5/13/cb-king-pcb-king-is-a/.

27. Ann Fagan Ginger and Eugene M. Tobin, *The National Lawyers Guild: From Roosevelt through Reagan* (Philadelphia: Temple University Press, 1988), 196–97.

28. Charles F. Wilson to Herbert Wright, July 14, 1961, part 21, no series, reel 18, fr. 490, NAACP Papers; S.W. Georgia Voter Program Continues Despite Legal Losses," at 2, in *The Student Voice*; On the use of inordinately high bail, see, e.g., "Will He Get Away with It?" *Baltimore*

Afro-American, August 11, 1962, 4; "'Criminal Anarchy': Went to Visit Student Prisoner; 2 Land in Jail," 1; "73 on 'Partial' Hunger Strike in Baton Rouge," 3; "Faculty Lashes Southern Head,"1; "'Criminal Anarchy' Charges Filed in La. Jail Visit," *Atlanta Daily World*, February 20, 1962, 1; "Jailing of Leader Is Costly Mistake," Sit-In Roundup, *Baltimore Afro-American*, July 20, 1963, 1.

29. Rachal, "'The Long, Hot Summer,'" 316; Richard Hammer, "Yankee Lawyers in Mississippi Courts," *Harper's*, November 1, 1966, 79–88; Dennis Robert's Journal, accessed March 10, 2015, http://www.crmvet.org/lets/dr_63_journal.pdf; Summary of Events (Mississippi), October 22 through October 28, n.d., folder 1, box 1873, Series 4, Subseries 4B, Princeton ACLU Papers; Ginger and Tobin, *The National Lawyers Guild: From Roosevelt through Reagan*, 196 (case of white SNCC workers); Cathy Cade, *My Family, the Movement and Me: How My Being in the Civil Rights Movement Affected My White Family* (2002), last modified 2005, http://www.crmvet.org/nars/cadec.htm; Charles Oldfather, letter to the editor, *Harvard Law Record*, March 12, 1964, 16; Ginger and Tobin, *The National Lawyers Guild: From Roosevelt through Reagan*, 196. Sometimes law enforcement deliberately avoided vagrancy arrests for locals when arresting outsiders; see, e.g., "FBI Probes Birmingham Terror," B1; "Four Arrested in Miss. Library; One Illinoisan," 8.

30. See also Zellner, *Wrong Side of Murder Creek*, 223–29 ; Zellner later brought a civil rights suit against many state and local officials for damages arising out of this incident. Zellner v. Wallace, 233 F. Supp. 874 (M.D. Ala. 1964); see also "Reign of Terror in Birmingham," 1A; Bryce Miller, "Ark. Leader Acts to Curb NAACP," *Chicago Daily Defender*, October 14, 1958, p. 4; Chester M. Hampton, "Northern Schools Join in Protest," *Baltimore Afro-American*, April 2, 1960, p. 1; "Sitdowners Irk White Atlantans," *Baltimore Afro-American*, April 9, 1960, p. 6; "Helped Sit-Ins: White Minister Tells of Police Attacks," *New York Amsterdam News*, May 6, 1961, p. 18; "3 Integrationists Placed on Parole," *Chicago Daily Defender*, June 6, 1961, p. 19; "SNCC Teams in College after Summer in South," *Baltimore Afro-American*, September 22, 1962, p. 18; "SNCC Teams in College after Summer in South," *Baltimore Afro-American*, September 22, 1962, 18. See also Bruce Payne, "Race and Poverty in American Politics: The Quiet War," in *The New Student Left: An Anthology*, ed. Mitchell Cohen and Dennis Hale (Boston: Beacon Press, 1966), 50–58; Rossinow, *The Politics of Authenticity*, 137; McArthur and Smith, "Not Whistling Dixie," 144–45; Council of Federated Organizations, *Mississippi Black Paper* (New York: Random House, 1965), 67, see also p. 86 (activist couple arrested for vagrancy after being told to leave town); "3 Integration Fighters Arrested in Pine Bluff," *Chicago Daily Defender*, January 17, 1963, 8; "2 Registration Drive Workers Arrested in Georgia: Both Were Warned at Vote Rally," *New Journal and Guide*, August 11, 1962, 15; see, e.g., "Jail Youth for Brushing against White Man," 1; Glenn T. Eskew, *But for Birmingham: The Local and National Movements in the Civil Rights Struggle* (Chapel Hill: University of North Carolina Press, 1997), 157–58.

31. For lunch counter and soda fountain arrests, see, e.g., United Press International, "Albany Desegregates 'Chairless' Library," *Atlanta Daily World*, March 12, 1963, 1; United Press International, "Tear Gas, Gestapo Tactics: Georgia State Troopers Sent against Students," *New Journal and Guide*, March 19, 1960, B1; "Woolworth, Kresge to Continue 'Fence-Riding' Policy in Dixie States," Sit-Down Roundup, *Philadelphia Tribune*, May 24, 1960, 1; "Woolworth Mgr. Sloshes Ammonia on Three Sit-Ins," Sitdown Roundup, *Philadelphia Tribune*, July 26, 1960, 1; "Discuss Florida Problem," 3; "73 on 'Partial' Hunger Strike in Baton Rouge," 3; "Dixie and the Law," 11; United Press International, "Arrest Two Whites in 'Mississippi Project,'" *Chicago Daily Defender*, June 25, 1964. For voter registration arrests, see, e.g., "Jail SNCC Leader in Albany, Ga.," 9; "Vote Advocates Jailed as Vagrants," *Baltimore Afro-Americans*, August 11, 1962, 18; "Will He Get Away with It?" 4; "Vote Work Jails La. NAACP Aide," *Baltimore Afro-American*, September 22, 1962, 17. For arrests on college campuses, see, e.g., "High Court Hears Boycott Case," in *The Student Voice*, 128; "Charge Dixie Officials with Using Power for Bias," *Chicago Daily Defender*, March 7, 1962, 8. For arrests involving underground newspapers, see, e.g., David Doggett, "The Kudzu: *Birth and Death in Underground Mississippi*," in *Voices from the Underground*, ed. Ken Wachsberger (Tempe, AZ: Mica's Press, 1993), 213, 219–20. For arrests trying to integrate pools, see, e.g., United Press International, "Plan to Appeal in Convictions," *Chicago Daily Defender*, July 13, 1964, 17; United Press International, "U.S. Protection Plea Is

Renewed," *Baltimore Afro-American*, August 1, 1964, 1; "Four Arrested in Miss. Library," 8; Higgenbotham, "Marchers Camp in Montgomery," 1.

32. Rachal, "'The Long, Hot Summer,'" 316. See also Dennis Robert's Journal, accessed March 10, 2015, http://www.crmvet.org/lets/dr_63_journal.pdf; Doggett, "The Kudzu," 219–20; Cade, *My Family, the Movement and Me*; George Todd, "How It Is: In Jail, in Dixie!" *New York Amsterdam News*, July 13, 1963, 1; United Press International, "Arrest Two Whites in 'Mississippi Project,'" A3; Gertrude Wilson, "White-on-White: Mississippi Justice," *New York Amsterdam News*, May 2, 1964, 1; Fairclough, *Race and Democracy*, 313–14.

33. See generally Benjamin Muse, *The American Negro Revolution: From Nonviolence to Black Power* (Bloomington: Indiana University Press, 1968), 131–47; Karl Fleming, *Son of the Rough South: An Uncivil Memoir* (New York: Public Affairs Books, 2005), 239–343; "Vote Advocates Jailed as Vagrants," 18; "Ask U.S. Probe of Trumped-Up Ala. Vagrancy Arrest," *Chicago Daily Defender*, January 14, 1963, 7; Wilson, "White-on-White: Mississippi Justice," 11; "Albany Rights Fighters near 'Breaking Point,'" 4; Cliff MacKay, "U.S. Moves to Force Shutdown in Albany: 5 Lawyers of Justice Dept. There," *Baltimore Afro-American*, August 11, 1962, 1; "For Integration? You're a Vagrant," The Week's Newsmakers, *Baltimore Afro-American*, January 19, 1963, 12.

34. On the training of nonsouthern civil rights workers, see Cade, *My Family, the Movement and Me*; see also Rachal, "'The Long, Hot Summer,'" 322–24; George Barner, "Ride Towards Freedom! Mississippi! Get on Board! Amsterdam Newsman Arrested with Freedom Bus Riders," *New York Amsterdam News*, May 27, 1961, 1; Brown-Nagin, *Courage to Dissent*, 175–76.

35. Draft Petition for Writ of Habeas Corpus with Motion for Stay of State Court Proceedings at 3, 5–6, Hillegas v. Sams, No. EC-65-1 (N.D. Miss. Jan. 5, 1965), Hillegas v. Sams, DC File Papers, Papers of Anthony Amsterdam (on file with author) (hereafter Amsterdam Papers); Albert Gleaves Cohen, Affidavit, Hillegas v. Sams, No. EC-65-1 (N.D. Miss.), December 30, 1964), Hillegaas v. Sams, Work Papers, Amsterdam Papers; Dennis Gaston, Affidavit, Hillegas v. Sams, No. EC-65-1 (N.D. Miss.), December 30, 1964, Hillegas v. Sams, Work Papers, Amsterdam Papers.

36. "A Strange Land," *Chicago Daily Defender*, November 28, 1964, 8; "Reign of Terror in Birmingham,"1A; Manis, *A Fire You Can't Put Out*, 184; Achtenberg, 393 F.2d 468, 474 (5th Cir. 1968); Complaint and Jury Demand at 5, Adickes v. S.H. Kress & Co., 252 F.Supp. 140 (S.D.N.Y. 1966), file 552.NY.2, container 111, BANC MS 991281 c, Civil Liberties Institute Collections; Cade, *My Family, the Movement and Me*; Rosenberg v. U.S., 346 U.S. 273, 291 (1953) (Jackson, J.); see generally, Brad Snyder, "Taking Great Cases: Lessons from the *Rosenberg* Case," *Vanderbilt Law Review* 63, no. 4 (May 2010): 885. See Chapter One, this volume.

37. Council of Federated Organizations, *Mississippi Black Paper*, 30; "Charge Dixie Officials with Using Power for Bias," 8; "Albany Rights Fighters near 'Breaking Point,'" 4; MacKay, "U.S. Moves to Force Shutdown in Albany," 1; "College Kicks Out Ten after 'Sit-Ins,'" *Baltimore Afro-American*, February 23, 1963, 18. Ray Abrams, "'This Is the Greatest Thing since 1865': Alabama Student Leader Tells His Story to Afro," *Baltimore Afro-American*, April 9, 1960, 7; Chester M. Hampton, "Northern Schools Join in Protest," *Baltimore Afro-American*, April 2, 1960, 1; "Sitdowners Irk White Atlantans," *Baltimore Afro-American*, April 9, 1960.

38. Oldfather, letter to the editor, 15–16; see also Clarice T. Campbell, *Civil Rights Chronicle: Letters from the South* (Jackson: University Press of Mississippi, 1997), 178; Dennis Robert's Journal, accessed March 10, 2015, http://www.crmvet.org/lets/dr_63_journal.pdf.

39. For reporting on what were perceived as outrageous arrests, see, e.g., "Judge Gives Nashville Sit-In Demonstrator $100 Fine," The Sit-In Scene, *Philadelphia Tribune*, December 24, 1960, 11; Anthony Lewis, "Racial Protestor Loses Court Fight," *New York Times*, February 25, 1964, 20; Charles Tyler, "Dion Diamond Vows Lasting War on Bias," *Afro-American*, May 12, 1962, 9; "High Court Hears Boycott Case," 128; see also "Charge Dixie Officials with Using Power for Bias," 8; Zellner, *Wrong Side of Murder Creek*, 190–92; "'Criminal Anarchy': Went to Visit Student Prisoner; 2 Land in Jail," 1; "'Criminal Anarchy' Charges Filed in La. Jail Visit," 1.

40. "'Criminal Anarchy' Cases Reset for June 13 Hearing," *Cleveland Call and Post*; "Lunch-Counter Victory Won, Augustans Press Job Drive," *Baltimore Afro-American*, April 14, 1962, 7; copy of

telegram to James Farmer et al., February 1962, part 21, no series, reel 18, fr. 141,NAACP Papers; "Attendance of 'Anarchy' Hearing for Youths Asked," *Atlanta Daily World*, March 11, 1962, 1; Steve Gerstel, "Man Who Aided Evicted Farmers Reveals Torture: Teacher Tells of Electric Shock Probe by Policemen," *Atlanta Daily World*, May 26, 1962, 1.

41. "Stars Move to Aid Students and Dr. King," *Chicago Daily Defender*, April 12, 1960, 17; Todd, "How It Is: In Jail, In Dixie!" 1.

42. "FBI Probes Birmingham Terror," B1; "FBI Probes Arrest of Three Ministers," 21; United Press International, "Federal Grand Jury to Probe Birmingham Arrests," B2; Lautier, "To Probe Arrest of Clergymen," 1; "FBI Pr[o]bes Arrest of Ala. Pastor," 6; "6 CORE Members Charged with Vagrancy, Loitering,"19; " 'Criminal Anarchy': Went to Visit Student Prisoner; 2 Land in Jail," 1; Council of Federated Organizations, *Mississippi Black Paper*, 30; "Vote Advocates Jailed as Vagrants," 18; "Ask U.S. Probe of Trumped-Up Ala. Vagrancy Arrest," 7. On the FBI investigations, see Hunt, "FBI Investigates Police Freedom Riders' Beating," 3; "Investigation of Unusual Arrests of Ministers Urged," *Atlanta Daily World*, April 10, 1960, 1; "FBI Enters Case: Probe Attack on Minister," A1; "Attendance of 'Anarchy' Hearing for Youths Asked," 1; MacKay, "U.S. Moves to Force Shutdown in Albany,"1; Council of Federated Organizations, *Mississippi Black Paper*, 30; "High Court Hears Boycott Case," 128; see also United Press International, "Judge Elliot Refuses U.S. Request to Restrain Terrell County Law Officer Threats," *Atlanta Daily World*, August 15, 1962, 1. On the Federal Civil Rights Commission investigation, see Steven Gerstel, "Rights Inquiry on Justice May Be Nationwide," *Atlanta Daily World*, November 15, 1959, 1; "Perverted Justice," *Baltimore Afro-American*, May 21, 1960, 4.

43. For black press condemnation, see, e.g., " 'Criminal Anarchy': Went to Visit Student Prisoner; 2 Land in Jail," 1; "In La. a Student Is a Vagrant," *Baltimore Afro-American*, November 4, 1960, 1; see also Louis Lautier, "Randolph Gets Top Elk Award, Sees Rights Emerging," *Atlanta Daily World*, August 29, 1957, 1; MacKay, "U.S. Moves to Force Shutdown in Albany," 1; "Not against Sitdowns—Dr. Atwood," *Baltimore Afro-American*, May 7, 1960, 1; "Woolworth Mgr. Sloshes Ammonia on Three Sit-Ins," 1; Todd, "How It Is: In Jail, In Dixie!"1; Hampton, "Northern Schools Join in Protest," 1; Adolph J. Slaughter, "Student Finds Fight for Rights 'Anarchy,' " *Chicago Daily Defender*, April 21, 1962, 1; "Reign of Terror in Birmingham," 1A; "Investigation of Unusual Arrests of Ministers Urged,"1; "Perverted Justice," 4; "6 CORE Members Charged with Vagrancy, Loitering,"19; "Vote Advocates Jailed as Vagrants," 18; "Will He Get Away with It?," 4; "Arrest CORE Members 2 Days after Meeting," 6.

44. Bigart, "10 in Pool Episode Guilty in Georgia," 11; "Journal Recounts Mississippi Summer," *Harvard Law Record*, November 5, 1964, 13–14; "3 Negro Pastors Seized in Birmingham Home," A11; Elsie Carper, "Texas Contriving to 'Accommodate' Race Issue," *Washington Post and Times Herald*, May 8, 1958, E1; see also United Press International, "Plan to Combat NAACP Urged," *Washington Post*, October 3, 1958, B4.

45. Ginger and Tobin, *The National Lawyers Guild: From Roosevelt to Reagan*, 203; Greenberg, *Crusaders in the Courts*, 273–74, 348; Ernest Gellhorn, "The Law Schools and the Negro," *Duke Law Journal* 1968 (1968): 1073–74, 1098 (indicating that in 1968 there were 20 black lawyers in Alabama, 10 in Arkansas, 44 in Florida, 34 in Georgia, 55 in Louisiana, 9 in Mississippi, 90 in North Carolina, 30 in South Carolina, 62 in Tennessee, 85 in Texas, and 67 in Virginia); Greenberg, *Crusaders in the Courts*, 273 ("It was a very rare Southern white lawyer who handled a demonstration case at that early phase of the movement [during the 1960 Greensboro sit-ins], although more did later"); M. F. III, "The Negro Lawyer in Virginia: A Survey," *Virginia Law Review* 51 (1965): 521 (indicating that there were "51 Negro lawyers in active practice" in Virginia in 1965); Vernon E. Jordan Jr., *Vernon Can Read! A Memoir*, with Annette Gordon Reed (New York: Public Affairs, 2008), 127 ("There [were] fewer than fifteen practicing black lawyers in the whole state [of Georgia in 1952].").

46. On the mobilization of the civil rights bar, see Greenberg, *Crusaders in the Courts*, 272–75, 348–49; Arthur Kinoy, *Rights on Trial: Odyssey of a People's Lawyer* (Cambridge, MA: Harvard University Press, 1983), 160; Michael Meltsner, *The Making of a Civil Rights Lawyer* (Charlottesville: University of Virginia Press, 2006), 86–87; Christopher W. Schmidt, "Divided by Law: The Sit-Ins and the Role of the Courts in the Civil Rights Movement," *Law and History Review* 33 (2015): 93. On generational interactions in the civil rights movement, see, e.g., Brown-Nagin, *Courage to Dissent*; Rebecca De Schweinitz,

If We Could Change the World: Young People and America's Long Struggle for Racial Equality
(Chapel Hill: University of North Carolina Press, 2011); William G. Weart, "100 Lawyers
Join New Rights Group: Will Seek Legal Solutions to Racial Problems," *New York Times,* July
11, 1963, 17; Thomas M. Hilbink, "Filling the Void: The Lawyers Constitutional Defense
Committee and the 1964 Freedom Summer" (senior honors thesis, Columbia University,
1993), http://ssrn.com/abstract=2416592; Walker, *In Defense of American Liberties,* 264–67;
Richard Hammer, "Taking Law to Mississippi," confidential paper for the Twentieth Century
Fund, February 1966, folder 21, box 651, American Civil Liberties Union Records, Series
2, Subseries 2B, Princeton ACLU Papers; Dittmer, *Local People,* 335–36; Ginger and
Tobin, *The National Lawyers Guild: From Roosevelt to Reagan,* 188, 191–92. On the threats
civil rights lawyers faced, see Walker, *In Defense of American Liberties,* 264; Report of Southern
Conference of the American Civil Liberties Union, Atlanta, May 16, 1964, 4box 18, folder 2,
Subseries 1B, National Mailings, Princeton ACLU Papers; Anthony Amsterdam, interview
with the author, April 14, 2009; civil rights lawyering faced similar, if less violent, obstacles
elsewhere as well—see Nat'l Ass'n for Advancement of Colored People v. Button, 371 U.S.
415 (1963); Nat'l Ass'n for Advancement of Colored People v. State of Ala. ex rel. Patterson,
357 U.S. 449 (1958); see also Juan Williams, *Thurgood Marshall: American Revolutionary*
(New York: Times Books, 1998), 258–59; Samuel Hoskins, "NAACP Defies Ala.: We'll
Never Expose Our Members to Violence," *Baltimore Afro-American,* August 4, 1954, 1; Harry
Kalven Jr., *The Negro and the First Amendment* 75–90, 91–95 (1965); Miller, "Ark. Leader Acts
to Curb NAACP," 4; "Summer Project: Mississippi, 1964," 39.

47. Com. v. Franklin, 92 A.2d 272 (Sup. Ct. Pa. 1952); Bell, 125 N.Y.S.2d 117, *aff'd,* 115 N.E.2d
821; Martin v. State, 98 A.2d 8 (Ct. App. Md, 1953); Com. v. Williams, 137 A.2d 903 (Sup.
Ct. Pa. 1958); Reed v. City & Cnty. of Denver, 342 P.2d 642 (Colo. 1959).

48. Cf. Sarah Hart Brown, *Standing against Dragons: Three Southern Lawyers in an Era of Fear*
(Baton Rouge: Louisiana State University, 1998), 166.

49. Bush v. Orleans Parish Sch. Bd., 194 F. Supp. 182, 185–86 (E.D. La.) *aff'd sub nom.* Gremillion
v. United States, 368 U.S. 11 (1961); see also Kinoy, *Rights on Trial,* 240; see generally Martha
Biondi, *To Stand and Fight: The Struggle for Civil Rights in Postwar New York City* (Cambridge,
MA: Harvard University Press, 2003); Leonard M. Moore, *Black Rage in New Orleans: Police
Brutality and African American Activism from World War II to Hurricane Katrina* (Baton
Rouge: Louisiana State University Press, 2010); Anders Walker, *The Ghost of Jim Crow: How
Southern Moderates Used* Brown v. Board of Education *to Stall Civil Rights,* 30–32, 34 (2009);
Brown v. State of Mississippi, 297 U.S. 278 (1936); Powell v. State of Ala., 287 U.S. 45 (1932);
Moore v. Dempsey, 261 U.S. 86 (1923); see generally Michael J. Klarman, "The Racial Origins
of Modern Criminal Procedure," *Michigan Law Review* 99 (2000): 48.

50. On the change in protests, see, e.g., Fairclough, *Race and Democracy,* 278; Cox v. State of La.,
379 U.S. 536 (1965); Adderley v. State of Fla., 385 U.S. 39 (1966); Lanahan, *Justice for All,* 74;
Forman v. City of Montgomery, 245 F. Supp. 17 (M.D. Ala. 1965) *aff'd without opinion,* 355
F.2d 930 (5th Cir. 1966). For the vagrancy and loitering arrests, see, e.g., "Cause Police Sit-In,"
8; "73 on 'Partial' Hunger Strike in Baton Rouge," 3; "A Follow-Up Report on the Student
Protest Movement after Two Months," n.d., part 21, no series, reel 21, fr. 571, NAACP Papers;
United States v. City of Jackson, Miss., 318 F.2d 1 (5th Cir. 1963).

51. Henry Schwarzschild, "Lawyers Constitutional Defense Committee of The American Civil
Liberties Union," remarks to Twentieth Century Fund, Conference on the Administration of
Justice in the South, October 6, 1966, folder 21, box 651, American Civil Liberties Union Records,
Series 2, Subseries 2B, Princeton ACLU Papers. For other similar examples, see, e.g., Dittmer,
Local People 163, 345; Davis, *Weary Feet, Rested Souls,* 209–11; "Albany, Ga., Called 'Police State,' "
Harvard Law Record, October 3, 1963, 7; "Summer Project: Mississippi, 1964," 40; Hammer,
"Taking Law to Mississippi," confidential paper for the Twentieth Century Fund, February 1966,
folder 21, box 651, Series 2, Subseries 2B, Princeton ACLU Papers; Brown-Nagin, *Courage to
Dissent,* 193; Anthony Amsterdam, interview with the author, April 14, 2009.

52. Len Holt, *An Act of Conscience* (Boston: Beacon Press, 1965), 26; Anthony G. Amsterdam,
"Criminal Prosecutions Affecting Federally Guaranteed Civil Rights: Federal Removal and
Habeas Corpus Jurisdiction to Abort State Court Trial," *University of Pennsylvania Law
Review* 113 (1965): 794–99; Michael Meltsner, "Southern Appellate Courts: A Dead End," in

Southern Justice, ed. Leon Friedman (New York: Pantheon Books, 1965), 139, 154; see also Schwarzschild, "Lawyers Constitutional Defense Committee of the American Civil Liberties Union," Princeton ACLU Papers; Meltsner, *The Making of a Civil Rights Lawyer*, 87.

53. Sometimes the mayor himself tried cases of disorderly conduct or loitering, as was the case in C. B. King's Fitzgerald, Georgia, part 23, series A, reel 15, NAACP Papers; "Judge Finds 11 Guilty," *Courier Journal* (Louisville, KY), April 12, 1960, 1; Dennis Robert's Journal, accessed March 10, 2015, http://www.crmvet.org/lets/dr_63_journal.pdf., 4; Oldfather, letter to the editor, 15.

54. Hammer, "Yankee Lawyers in Mississippi Courts," 81; see also Hammer, "Taking Law to Mississippi," confidential paper for the Twentieth Century Fund, February 1966, folder 21, box 651, Series 2, Subseries 2B, Princeton ACLU Papers; Robert H. Reynolds, "The Fee System Courts—Denial of Due Process," *Oklahoma Law Review* 17, no. 4 (1964): 373–74; Daniel M. Berman, "The Racial Issue and Mr. Justice Black," *American University Law Review* 16, no. 3 (1967): 387–88; Robert S. Keebler, "Our Justice of the Peace Courts—a Problem in Justice," *Tennessee Law Review* 9, no. 1 (1930): 14; Zellner, *Wrong Side of Murder Creek*, 193. See generally Nicholas R. Parrillo, *Against the Profit Motive: The Salary Revolution in American Government, 1780–1940* (New Haven, CT: Yale University Press, 2013), 255–94; John A. Pietrykowski, Note, "The Constitutionality of the Fee System in Justice of the Peace Courts," *Notre Dame Law Review* 29 (1954): 438; Hugh C. Simpson, "Constitutionality of the Fee System of Justices of the Peace," *Tennessee Law Review* 14 (1937): 565.

55. Marvin Braiterman, "Harold and the Highwaymen," in *Southern Justice*, ed. Leon Friedman (New York: Pantheon Books, 1965), 95; Hulett v. Julian, 250 F. Supp. 208 (M.D. Ala. 1966). The case was based on *Tumey v. Ohio*, 273 U.S. 510 (1927). See also Bennett v. Cottingham, 290 F. Supp. 759 (N.D. Ala. 1968) *aff'd*, 393 U.S. 317 (1969). Amsterdam also recalled challenging local fee practices among JPs in Florida. Anthony Amsterdam, interview with the author, April 14, 2009.

56. On the role of federal courts, see Gil Seinfeld, "The Federal Courts as a Franchise: Rethinking the Justifications for Federal Question Jurisdiction," *California Law Review* 97 (2009): 104–6; Wythe Holt, " 'To Establish Justice': Politics, the Judiciary Act of 1789, and the Invention of the Federal Courts," *Duke Law Journal* 1989 (1989): 1441–42, 1458. See generally Amsterdam, "Criminal Prosecutions Affecting Federally Guaranteed Civil Rights"; but see Louis Lusky, "Justice with a Southern Accent," *Harper's Magazine*, March 1964, 77; Louis Lusky, "Racial Discrimination and the Federal Law: A Problem in Nullification," *Columbia Law Review* 63, no. 7 (1963): 1179–91; Anthony Amsterdam, interview with the author, April 14, 2009; correspondence from Anthony Amsterdam, April 17, 2015.

57. For efforts to enjoin law enforcement from interfering with civil rights activities, see, e.g., Cottonreader v. Johnson, 252 F. Supp. 492 (M.D. Ala. 1966); Wells v. Hand, 238 F. Supp. 779 (M.D. Ga.) *aff'd sub nom*; Wells v. Reynolds, 382 U.S. 39 (1965); *Zellner v. Lingo* held that the court would not enjoin state criminal prosecutions; Zellner v. Lingo, 218 F. Supp. 513 (M.D. Ala. 1963) *aff'd*, 334 F.2d 620 (5th Cir. 1964). On removal, see Brown-Nagin, *Courage to Dissent*, 239–40; Ginger and Tobin, *The National Lawyers Guild: From Roosevelt to Reagan*, 204; David J. Langum, *William M. Kunstler: The Most Hated Lawyer in America* (New York: New York University Press, 1999), 60, 66; Dittmer, *Local People*, 230; Braiterman, "Harold and the Highwaymen," 91–92; Holt, *An Act of Conscience*, 37–38, 48–49, 51; Kinoy, *Rights on Trial*, 163–64, 190–201; Meltsner, *The Making of a Civil Rights Lawyer*, 48–49; Robert Jerome Glennon, "The Jurisdictional Legacy of the Civil Rights Movement," *Tennessee Law Review* 61 (Spring 1994): 905–13; Amsterdam, "Criminal Prosecutions Affecting Federally Guaranteed Civil Rights," 793, 841 n. 192, 895–896 n. 446; *In re Shuttlesworth*, 369 U.S. 35 (1962). Civil rights lawyers did not always win. See, e.g., McLaurin v. Burnley, 279 F. Supp. 220 (N.D. Miss. 1967) *aff'd*, 401 F.2d 773 (5th Cir. 1968); see, e.g., Anthony Amsterdam, interview with the author, April 14, 2009; Robert L. Carter, *A Matter of Law: A Memoir of Struggle in the Cause of Equal Rights* (New York: New Press, 2007), 105–7; Jack Oppenheim, "The Abdication of the Southern Bar," in *Southern Justice*, ed. Leon Friedman (New York: Pantheon Books, 1965), 130–32. For arguments against federal court abstention, see Lusky, "Justice with a Southern Accent," 75; Dombrowski v. Pfister, 380 U.S. 479 (1965); see also Brief for NAACP Legal Defense and Educational Fund, Inc. as Amicus Curiae Supporting Appellees, Zwickler v. Koota, 389 U.S. 241. Lawyers also filed suit for a writ of mandamus to force

the U.S. Justice Department (specifically Robert Kennedy and J. Edgar Hoover) to arrest and prosecute law enforcement officers in Mississippi who interfered with voter registration through violence, intimidation, and arrest in 1963. Memo from Mel Wulf to Board of Directors, ACLU, January 3, 1963 (discussing whether to file amicus brief in the case, Moses v. Kennedy), box 17, folder 7, Subseries 1B, National Mailings, Princeton ACLU Papers. See generally Note, "Theories of Federalism and Civil Rights," *Yale Law Journal* 75, no. 6 (1966): 1007. For cases based on these resurrected civil rights laws, see, e.g., Complaint, Crawford v. City of Jackson, n.d., folder 1, box 1873, American Civil Liberties Union Records, Series 4, Subseries 4B, Department of Rare Books and Special Collections, Princeton University Library; Hamer v. Musselwhite, 376 F.2d 479 (5th Cir. 1967); Monroe v. Pape, 365 U.S. 167 (1961); Adickes v. S. H. Kress & Co., 398 U.S. 144 (1970); Dombrowski, 380 U.S. 479.

58. Anthony Amsterdam, interview with the author, April 14, 2009; Anthony G. Amsterdam to Thomas M. Hilbink, March 1, 1993, 575.4 Civil Rights—Georgia v. Rachel—Atlanta Removal folder, Amsterdam Papers; Amsterdam, "Criminal Prosecutions Affecting Federally Guaranteed Civil Rights," 793, n A1; Lusky, "Racial Discrimination and the Federal Law,"1179; "Theories of Federalism and Civil Rights," *Yale Law Journal* 75 (1965): 1007; Kinoy, *Rights on Trial*, 237.

59. Brief in Support of Motion to Dismiss, Hillegas v. Sams (5th Cir.) (No. 22241), Hillegas v. Sams, CA File Papers, Amsterdam Papers; Petition for Rehearing En Banc, Hillegas v. Sams, Work Papers; Rehearing petition, Hillegas v. Sams, Amsterdam Papers; Denial, loose papers, Hillegas v. Sams, Amsterdam Papers; Petitioner's Memorandum of Law in Support of Application for a Writ of Habeas Corpus, n.d., Hillegas v. Sams, CA File Papers, Amsterdam Papers; also in Brief for Appellants, Hillegas v. Sams (5th Cir.) (No. 22241), n.d., Hillegas v. Sams, CA File Papers, Amsterdam Papers; Opposition to Motion to Dismiss Petition for Writ of Certiorari, Hillegas v. Sams (Supreme Court) (No. 704), n.d., Hillegas v. Sams, loose papers, Amsterdam Papers; Hillegas v. Sams, 383 U.S. 928 (1966); Anthony G. Amsterdam to Henry M. Aronson, March 15, 1966, Hillegas v. Sams, loose papers, Amsterdam Papers; Henry M. Aronson to Anthony G. Amsterdam, n.d., Hillegas v. Sams, loose papers, Amsterdam Papers.

60. Achtenberg 393 F.2d at 474; also 475 (Godbold, J., concurring in part, dissenting in part); Eleanor Jackson Piel, interviews with author, February 14 and 15, 2012; Adickes, 398 U.S. 144; Ranzal, "Civil Rights Worker Sues Kress for Arrest at Mississippi Store," 16.

61. James, *The People's Lawyers*, 32; Mary Ann Meyers, "Tony Amsterdam: Professor and Civil Rights Lawyer," *Pennsylvania Gazette*, March 1966; Fred R. Shapiro and Michelle Pearse, "The Most-Cited Law Review Articles of All Time," *Michigan Law Review* 110 (2012): 1489, table I. (no. 58, and the only student note on the list).

62. Anthony G. Amsterdam, "The Void-for-Vagueness Doctrine in the Supreme Court," *University of Pennsylvania Law Review* 109 (1960): 67–106, 91, n 116.

63. Anthony G. Amsterdam, "Federal Constitutional Restrictions on the Punishment of Crimes of Status, Crimes of General Obnoxiousness, Crimes of Displeasing Police Officers, and the Like," *Criminal Law Bulletin* 3, no. 4 (1967): 207, 233; Anthony Amsterdam, interview with the author, April 14, 2009; Anthony Amsterdam, phone interview with author, June 9, 2008.

64. Greenberg, *Crusaders in the Courts*, 274–75; Amsterdam, "Federal Constitutional Restrictions on the Punishment of Crimes of Status," 206, 224–25, 234.

65. James, *The People's Lawyers*, 33.

66. See, e.g., Alexander M. Bickel, "The Supreme Court 1960 Term Foreword: The Passive Virtues," *Harvard Law Review* 75 (1961): 62, 62, n 105; Button, 371 U.S. at 466; Harry H. Wellington and Lee A. Albert, "Statutory Interpretation and the Political Process: A Comment on *Sinclair v. Atkinson*," *Yale Law Journal* 72 (1963): 1560, n 42, 1564, n 51; Thomas P. Lewis, "The Sit-In Cases: Great Expectations," *Supreme Court Review* 1963 (1963): 109, n 24.

67. "Lawyers: Prodigious Professor," *Time Magazine*, December 10, 1965, 74; Greenberg, *Crusaders in the Courts*, 343; Mel Wulf, telephone interview with author, October 2, 2012; Meyers, "Tony Amsterdam."

68. Jack Greenberg, interview with author, June 9, 2009; letter from Anthony Amsterdam to author, April 17, 2015. See also Anthony Amsterdam to Henry Schwarzschild (Executive Secretary LCDC), August 8, 1966, folder 6, box 652, American Civil Liberties Union Records, Series 2, Subseries 2B, Princeton ACLU Papers; "Lawyers: Prodigious Professor," 74.

69. Cade, *My Family, the Movement and Me*; Goluboff, *The Lost Promise of Civil Rights*, 130–31; "Arrest CORE Members 2 Days after Meeting," 6; Anthony Amsterdam, interview with the author, April 14, 2009; Anthony Amsterdam, phone interview with author, June 9, 2008.

70. Letter from Anthony Amsterdam to author, April 17, 2015.

71. Lewis A. Randolph and Gayle T. Tate, *Rights for a Season: The Politics of Race, Class, and Gender in Richmond, Virginia* (Knoxville: University of Tennessee Press, 2003), 182–83. The photo became iconic and was reprinted frequently. See, e.g., Ronald L. Heineman, et al., *Old Dominion, New Commonwealth* (Charlottesville: University of Virginia Press, 2007): 356; Suzanne Lebsock, *Virginia Women, 1600–1945* (Richmond: Virginia State Library, 1987),133; Tinsley v. City of Richmond, 368 U.S. 18 (1961); Tinsley, 119 S.E.2d 488, http:// www.vahistorical.org/civilrights/introduction.htm#images; Peter Wallenstein, *Cradle of America: Four Centuries of Virginia History* (Lawrence: University Press of Kansas, 2007) 363; Marvin Caplan, Farther Along: A Civil Rights Memoir (Baton Rouge, LA: Louisiana State University Press, 1999), 56; Ruth Nelson Tinsley, *Crisis*, June–July 1970, 218; Larry Hall, "Ruth Nelson Tinsley," *Richmond Times-Dispatch*, February 1, 2006, http://www.richmond. com/special-section/black-history/article_81d322ba-6af7-11e2-a9c1-001a4bcf6878.html; "Street Fight in Tenn. over 'Sitdown' Protests,"12. The next time Virginia's vagrancy law was challenged, lawyers highlighted the race and class dimensions of the problem. A judge declared the law unconstitutional in 1969, though the legislature had already quietly repealed it. Oliver v. Button, Series 4, box 1603, Princeton ACLU Papers.

72. Jon Nordheimer, "Rev. Fred L. Shuttlesworth, 89, Dies; Fought on Front Lines for Civil Rights," *New York Times*, October 6, 2011, A6; "Investigation of Unusual Arrests of Ministers Urged," 1. See generally Manis, *A Fire You Can't Put Out*, 34, 280.

73. Shuttlesworth v. City of Birmingham, 382 U.S. 87, 89 (1965); Justice Abe Fortas, handwritten notes, Shuttlesworth v. City of Birmingham, n.d., MS 858, box 10, folder 250, Abe Fortas Papers, Yale University Library, hereafter Fortas Papers; Manis, *A Fire You Can't Put Out*, 308; Nesson (Charles R. Nesson) to Justice John Marshall Harlan, Memorandum, November 2, 1964, , John Marshall Harlan Papers, Seeley G. Mudd Manuscript Library, Princeton University (hereafter Harlan Papers); handwritten notes on the 1965 Shuttlesworth case, loose papers , Amsterdam Papers.

74. Section 1142 of Birmingham City Code (in effect 1965); Section 1231 of Birmingham City Code (in effect 1965); Shuttlesworth v. City of Birmingham, 161 So. 2d 796 (Ala. Ct. App. 1963) *rev'd*, 382 U.S. 87 (1965); Orzell Billingsley Jr. was also on the brief in the Alaabama appeals court. Manis, *A Fire You Can't Put Out*, 308.

75. Memorandum, n.d. Box 1362, William O. Douglas Papers, Library of Congress; Nesson (Charles R. Nesson) to Justice John Marshall Harlan, memorandum, January 28, 1965, Harlan Papers; Nesson (Charles R. Nesson), Memorandum, January 28, 1965, Harlan Papers; Boudin (Michael Boudin), Bench Memorandum, October 4, 1965, Harlan Papers; O.M.F. (Owen Fiss) to Justice J. Brennan, memorandum, n.d., box I-133, William J. Brennan Papers, Library of Congress..

76. Glennon, "The Jurisdictional Legacy of the Civil Rights Movement," 870; Stephen L. Wasby, Anthony A. D'Amato, and Rosemary Metrailer, *Desegregation from Brown to Alexander* (Carbondale: Southern Illinois University Press, 1977), 343–59.

77. "High Court Gets First Sit-in Test," *New York Times*, January 3, 1961, 17. For an example of the Court applying this canon, see, e.g., Warren, Garner v. Louisiana, 368 U.S. 157 (1961); Bell v. Maryland, 378 U.S. 226 (1964).

78. Thornhill v. Alabama, 310 U.S. 88 (1940). For examples of the Court's unsympathetic approach to communists in the 1950s, see Watkins v. United States, 354 U.S. 178 (1957); Sweezy v. New Hampshire, 354 U.S. 234 (1957). For the Court's expanded conception of First Amendment Protection, see NAACP v. Alabama, 357 U.S. 449 (1958). See generally Michael J. Klarman, "Rethinking the Civil Rights and Civil Liberties Revolutions," *Virginia Law Review* 82, no. 1 (1996): 34–46; Bevier, 1992 Sup. Ct. Rev. at 85; Harry Kalven Jr., "The Concept of the Public Forum: Cox v. Louisiana," *Supreme Court Review* (1965): 12; Garner v. Louisiana, 368 U.S. 157 (1961); Kalven, *The Negro and the First Amendment*, 3–6; Mark V. Tushnet, *Making Civil Rights Law: Thurgood Marshall and the Supreme Court, 1936–1961* (New York: Oxford University Press, 1994), 277, 300; Kalven, *The Negro and the First*

Amendment, 6; Thomas Emerson, "Freedom of Association and Freedom of Expression," *Yale Law Journal* 74, no. 1 (1964): 1–34.

79. Anthony Lewis, "High Court Hears First Three Pleas in Southern Sit-ins," *New York Times*, October 20, 1961, 1; Anthony Lewis, "High Court Voids Sit-in Conviction of 16 in Louisiana," *New York Times*, December 12, 1961, 1.

80. McKenzie Webster, "The Warren Court's Struggle with the Sit-in Cases and the Constitutionality of Segregation in Places of Public Accommodations," *Journal of Law and Politics* 17, no. 2 (2001): 377–78; Schmidt, "Divided by Law," 93; Christopher W. Schmidt, "The Sit-ins and the State Action Doctrine," *William & Mary Bill of Rights Journal* 18 (March 2010): 767.

81. Justice John M. Harlan to Justice Hugo Black, memorandum, March 17, 1960, box 343, Hugo LaFayette Black Papers, Library of Congress; Justice Hugo Black to Justice John M. Harlan, memorandum, March 18, 1960, box 86, Harlan Papers. See also "La. Sit-Ins Convictions Overturned," *Chicago Daily Defender*, December 12, 1961, 2; 368 U.S. 157, 190 (Harlan, J., concurring). Justice John M. Harlan to Justice Felix Frankfurter, " 'Sit-in' Cases," December 4, 1961, box 138, Harlan Papers; NL (Nathan Lewin) to Justice John M. Harlan, memorandum re: Taylor v. Louisiana (No. 773), n.d., box 150, Harlan Papers; Jack Greenberg, "The Supreme Court, Civil Rights and Civil Dissonance," *Yale Law Journal* 77, no. 8 (1968): 1528.

82. See also Fields v. Fairfield, 375 U.S. 248 (1963); Barr v. City of Columbia, 378 U.S. 146, 151 (1964); Shuttlesworth, 382 U.S. at 95; Gregory v. City of Chicago, 394 U.S. 111, 112 (1969). In other cases, the Court discussed *Thompson* grounds but did not necessarily rely on them. The plethora of such cases is an indication of how frequently the civil rights defendants included the claim among their arguments. See, e.g., Edwards v. South Carolina, 372 U.S. 229 (1963); Peterson v. City of Greenville, 373 U.S. 244, 259 (Harlan, J., concurring in part and dissenting in part); Wright v. State of Georgia, 373 U.S. 284, 285 (1963); Bell v. Maryland, 378 U.S. 226, 324 (1964) (Black, J., dissenting); Bouie v. City of Columbia, 378 U.S. 347, 350 (1964); Cox v. Louisiana, 379 U.S. 536, 544–45 (1965); Brown v. Louisiana, 383 U.S. 131, 139 (1966). Cf. Garner v. Louisiana, 368 U.S. 157 (1961); Taylor v. Louisiana, 370 U.S. 154 (1962); Fields v. City of Fairfield, 375 U.S. 248 (1963).

83. Norman Amaker to Anthony Amsterdam, May 14, 1965, Shuttlesworth v. Birmingham Loitering 577.7[1] file, Shuttlesworth v. Birmingham—Loitering and Parade Permit folder, Amsterdam Papers; Anthony Amsterdam to Norm (Norman Amaker) and Jim (James M. Nabritt III), July 23, 1965, Shuttlesworth v. Birmingham Loitering 577.7[1] file, Shuttlesworth v. Birmingham—Loitering and Parade Permit folder, Amsterdam Papers; Civil Rights and Civil Liberties Draft (1962), Series 3A.1, Princeton ACLU Papers; Draft Brief, Shuttlesworth v. Birmingham (O.T. 1964 No. 423), Shuttlesworth v. Birmingham Loitering 577.7[1] file, Shuttlesworth v. Birmingham—Loitering and Parade Permit folder, Amsterdam Papers; Oral Argument, Shuttlesworth v. City of Bimingham, 382 U.S. 87 (1965), Oyez Project at IIT Chicago-Kent College of Law, http://www.oyez.org/cases/1960-1969/1965/1965_5.

84. Brief for Petitioner at 15, Shuttlesworth v. City of Birmingham, 382 U.S. 87 (1965) (No. 5); Brief for Petitioner at 15, Shuttlesworth v. City of Birmingham, 382 U.S. 87 (1965) (No. 5); Draft Brief, Shuttlesworth v. Birmingham (O.T. 1964 No. 423), Shuttlesworth v. Birmingham Loitering 577.7[1] file, Shuttlesworth v. Birmingham—Loitering and Parade Permit folder, Amsterdam Papers.

85. Brief for Petitioner at 25–28, Shuttlesworth v. City of Birmingham, 382 U.S. 87 (1965) (No. 5); Territory of Hawaii v. Anduha, 48 F.2d 171 (9th Cir. 1931); Soles v. City of Vidalia, 90 S.E.2d 249 (Ga. Ct. App. 1955); Com. v. Carpenter, 91 N.E.2d 666 (Mass. 1950); City of St. Louis v. Gloner, 109 S.W. 30 (Mo. 1908); State v. Caez, 195 A.2d 496 (N.J. Super. Ct. App. Div. 1963); People v. Diaz, 151 N.E.2d 871 (N.Y. 1958); City of Akron v. Effland, 174 N.E.2d 285 (Ohio Ct. App. 1960); Ex parte Mittelstaedt, 297 S.W.2d 153 (Tex. Crim. App. 1956); Brief for Petitioner at 28 n.18, Shuttlesworth v. City of Birmingham, 382 U.S. 87 (1965) (No. 5); Brief for Petitioner at 25–26 & 26 n. 18, Shuttlesworth v. City of Birmingham, 382 U.S. 87 (1965) (No. 5); Draft Brief, Shuttlesworth v. Birmingham (O.T. 1964 No. 423), Shuttlesworth v. Birmingham Loitering 577.7[1] file, Shuttlesworth v. Birmingham—Loitering and Parade Permit folder, Amsterdam Papers; Brief for Petitioner at 28, Shuttlesworth v. City of Birmingham, 382 U.S. 87 (1965) (No. 5).

86. But cf. Justice William O. Douglas, Conference Notes, October 15, 1965, box 1362, William O. Douglas Papers, Library of Congress. Misc Folder, 2576; Shuttlesworth, 382 U.S. at 92, 94–96, 99–101; See, e.g., Middlebrooks v. City of Birmingham, 170 So.2d 424, 426 (Ala. Ct. App. 1964), Thomas v. City of Birmingham, 171 So. 2d. 84 (Ala. Ct. App. 1964); Smith v. City of Birmingham, 168 So. 2d 35 (Ala. Ct. App. 1964); Shelton v. City of Birmingham, 165 So. 2d 912 (Ala. Ct. App. 1964); Phifer v. City of Birmingham, 160 So. 2d 898 (Ala. Ct. App. 1963); Justice Douglas, draft concurrence and dissent, Shuttlesworth v. City of Birmingham, recirculated 9 November 1965, MS 858, box 10, folder 250, Fortas Papers; Justice Fortas, draft concurrence, Shuttlesworth v. City of Birmingham, n.d., MS 858, box 10, folder 250, Fortas Papers; Shuttlesworth, 382 US at 100–101. Harlan disagreed, but did not publish his view. Justice Harlan, draft concurrence, Shuttleworth v. City of Birmingham, n.d., Harlan Papers.
87. Because the Court had held that there was no evidence under the Shuffling Sam rule for the other charge, the state did not attempt to retry Shuttlesworth on that ground; Georgia v. Rachel, Memo to Amanker, Douglas, Hall, Zarr, June 24, 1966, Amsterdam Papers; Georgia v. Rachel, letter from Thurgood Marshall to Cullinan, April 13, 1966, Amsterdam Papers; Melvyn Zarr to Anthony Amsterdam, March 11, 1966, Georgia v. Rachel, Amsterdam Papers; Memo from Anthony Amsterdam to Norman Amanker, Nils Douglas, Peter Hall, Melvyn Zarr, June 24, 1966, Shuttlesworth, [2] Removal folder, Amsterdam Papers. Hillegas info, http://www.crmvet.org/vet/hillegas.htm.
88. Justice Abe Fortas memorandum, October 11, 1965, MS 858, box 10, folder 250, Fortas Papers; Justice Abe Fortas, handwritten note, Shuttleworth v. City of Birmingham, n.d., MS 858, box 10, folder 250, Fortas Papers; Shuttlesworth, 382 U.S. at 101–2,
89. J.B.F. (Jerome B. Falk) to Justice William O. Douglas, memorandum, n.d., box 1362, William O. Douglas Papers, Library of Congress;. Shuttlesworth, 382 U.S. at 86, 96.
90. See Laurence H. Tribe, "A Tale of Two Portraits," *Yale Law Journal* 95, no. 1328 (1986); Joel Jacobsen, *Remembered Justice: The Background, Early Career and Judicial Appointments of Justice Potter Stewart, Akron Law Review* 35, no. 227 (2002); Gayle Binion, "Justice Potter Stewart: The Unpredictable Vote," *Journal of Supreme Court History* 1992 (1992): 99.
91. Shuttlesworth, 382 U.S. at 87, 90–91, 91, nn. 5, 6.
92. "High Court Frees Rights Aide Again," *New York Times*, November 16, 1965, 38.

Chapter 5

1. Anthony G. Amsterdam, "A Selective Survey of Supreme Court Decisions in Criminal Law and Procedure," *Criminal Law Bulletin* 9, no. 5 (1973): 389, 390, 395; "Anthony G. Amsterdam, "Federal Constitutional Restrictions on the Punishment of Crimes of Status, Crimes of General Obnoxiousness, Crimes of Displeasing Police Officers, and the Like," *Criminal Law Bulletin* 3, no. 4 (1967): 207.
2. Mary Ann Meyers, "Tony Amsterdam: Professor and Civil Rights Lawyer," *Pennsylvania Gazette* (University of Pennsylvania's alumni magazine), March 1966; Anthony Amsterdam to author, April 17, 2015; Amsterdam, "Federal Constitutional Restrictions," 207.
3. Edelman v. California, 344 U.S. 357 (1953); Thompson v. Louisville, 362 U.S. 199 (1960); Shuttlesworth v. Birmingham, 382 U.S. 87 (1965); Hicks v. District of Columbia, 383 U.S. 252 (1966); Ricks v. District of Columbia, 414 F.2d 1097 (D.C. Cir. 1968).
4. Amsterdam, "Federal Constitutional Restrictions," 207; Brief of Appellant at 7, Ricks v. District of Columbia, 414 F.2d 1097 (D.C. Cir. 1968) (No. 20,919); see Stuart Auerbach, "City Vagrancy Statute Unlawful, Says Judge," *Washington Post*, June 17, 1966, A3.
5. For scholarly commentary, see, e.g., Donald H. Whaley, "The Constitutionality of Loitering Ordinances," *St. Louis University Law Journal* 6 (1960–61): 247; Gary Dubin and Richard Robinson, "The Vagrancy Concept Reconsidered: Problems and Abuses of Status Criminality," *New York University Law Review* 37 (1962): 102; William J. Chambliss, "Sociological Analysis of the Law of Vagrancy," *Social Problems* 12 (1964–65): 69; J. Knox Argo, "Constitutional Law—Criminal Law—Vagrancy Laws and the Fourteenth Amendment," *Alabama Law Review* 20 (1967–68): 141; Harvey David Brooks, "Vagrancy: A Constitutional Battle," *Syracuse Law Review* 16 (1964–65): 646; Anthony A. Cuomo, "Mens Rea and Status Criminality," *Southern California Law Review* 40 (1966–67): 463;

Paul G. Flynn, "Vagrancy Laws and the Right to Privacy," *University of San Francisco Law Review* 2 (1967–68): 337; Gerald E. Magaro, "Criminal Penalties for Vagrancy—Cruel and Unusual Punishment under the Eighth Amendment," *Western Reserve Law Review* 18 (1966–67): 1309; George M. McClure, "Vagrants, Criminals and the Constitution," *Denver Law Center Journal* 40 (1963): 314; John M. Murtagh, "Status Offenses and Due Process of Law," *Fordham Law Review* 36 (1967–68): 51; R. M. Robinson, "Constitutional Law: Vagrancy Ordinance Held Unconstitutional for Vagueness," *University of Florida Law Review* 18 (1965–66): 169; Margaret K. Rosenheim, "Vagrancy Concepts in Welfare Law," *California Law Review* 54 (1966): 511; "Over-Expanded Application of Vagrancy Statutes," *Washington University Law Quarterly* 1961 (1961): 425. For cases, see, e.g., In re Newbern, 350 P.2d 116 (Cal. 1960); Headley v. Selkowitz, 171 So.2d 368 (Fla. 1965); Soles v. City of Vidalia, 90 S.E.2d 249 (Ga. Ct. App. 1955); Territory v. Camelio Anduha, 31 Haw. 459 (1930), aff'd 48 F.2d 171 (9th Cir. 1931); People v. Belcastro, 190 N.E. 301 (Ill. 1934); People v. Alterie, 190 N.E. 305 (Ill. 1934); People v. Eisen, 191 N.E. 219 (Ill. 1934); Commonwealth v. Carpenter, 91 N.E.2d 666 (Mass. 1950); State v. Caez, 195 A.2d 496 (N.J. Super. Ct. App. Div. 1963); People v. Diaz, 151 N.E.2d 871 (N.Y. 1958); State v. Ashe, 161 S.E. 709 (N.C. 1932); City of Akron v. Effland, 174 N.E.2d 285 (Ohio Ct. App. 1960); United States v. Margeson, 259 F. Supp. 256 (E.D. Pa. 1966); Ex Parte Mittelstaedt, 297 S.W.2d 153 (Tex. Crim. App. 1957).

6. City of Reno v. Second Judicial Dist. Court, 427 P.2d 4 (Nev. 1967); Parker v. Municipal Judge of Las Vegas, 427 P.2d 642 (Nev. 1967); see also In re Hoffman, 434 P.2d 353 (Cal. 1967); City of Cleveland v. Forrest, 223 N.E.2d 661 (Cleveland Mun. Ct. 1967); City of Seattle v. Drew, 423 P.2d 522 (Wash. 1967). Fenster v. Leary, 229 N.E.2d 426 (N.Y. 1967). See also People v. Williams, 286 N.Y.S.2d 575 (N.Y. Crim. Ct. 1967); Alegata v. Commonwealth, 231 N.E.2d 201 (Mass. 1967); Baker v. Bindner, 274 F.Supp. 658 (D. Ky. 1967).

7. McCandlish Phillips, "Bus Terminal at Night: A Derelict's Haven," *New York Times,* January 8, 1967, 1; "Police Begin Times Sq. Cleanup After Night Workers Complain," *New York Times,* February 6, 1969, 78; "Unsavory Types Are Plaguing Bus and Rail Terminals Here," *New York Times,* February 8, 1969, 20; see also Robert D. McFadden, "Hustlers Harass Bus Terminal," *New York Times,* October 20, 1969, 49. For discussion of the harm principle versus the offense principle, see Bernard E. Harcourt, "The Collapse of the Harm Principle," *Journal of Criminal Law and Criminology* 90, no. 1 (1999): 109–94; "Unsavory Types Are Plaguing Bus and Rail Terminals Here," 20.

8. Edwin M. Schur, *Crimes without Victims: Deviant Behavior and Public Policy, Abortion, Homosexuality, Drug Addiction* (Englewood Cliffs, NJ: Prentice-Hall, 1965); H. L. A. Hart, *Law, Liberty and Morality* (Palo Alto, CA: Stanford University Press, 1963); Patrick Devlin, *The Enforcement of Morals* (London: Oxford University Press, 1965); Henry Hart, "The Aims of the Criminal Law," *Law & Contemporary Problems* 23, no. 3 (1958): 401, 411; Ronald Dworkin, "Lord Devlin and the Enforcement of Morals," *Yale Law Journal* 75, no. 6 (1966): 986; Graham Hughes, "Morals and the Criminal Law," *Yale Law Journal* 71, no. 4 (1962): 662. See also Joel Feinberg, "Moral Enforcement and the Harm Principle," in *Ethics and Public Policy,* ed. Tom L. Beauchamp (Englewood Cliffs, N.J.: Prentice-Hall, 1975), 283–99; Harcourt, "Collapse of the Harm Principle," 109; Joseph F. Winterscheid, "Victimless Crimes: The Threshold Question and Beyond," *Notre Dame Law Review* 52, no. 5 (1977): 995; Joel Westbrook, "Crimes without Plaintiffs" *Baylor Law Review* 25, no. 1 (1973): 37; H. L. A. Hart, *The Morality of the Criminal Law: Two Lectures* (Jerusalem: Magnes Press Hebrew University, 1964); Charles E. Moylan Jr., "Temple Bar to Megalopolis: The Criminal Law in Transition," *American Criminal Law Quarterly* 7, no. 1 (1968): 35; Sanford F. Kadish, "The Crisis of Overcriminalization," *American Criminal Law Quarterly* 7, no. 1 (1968): 17; Jerome H. Skolnick, "Coercion to Virtue: The Enforcement of Morals," *Southern California Law Review* 41, no. 3 (1968): 588; Ernest B. Furgurson, "The Harm of Some 'Victimless' Crimes," *Los Angeles Times,* June 11, 1972, G7; Norval Morris, "The Law Is a Busybody: Crimes without Victims," *New York Times Magazine,* April 1, 1973, 10; Sol Wachtler, "The High Cost of Victimless Crimes," *Record of the Association of the Bar of the City of New York* 28, no. 5 (May 1973): 357.

9. Nicholas N. Kittrie, *A Right to Be Different* (Baltimore: Johns Hopkins University Press, 1971).

10. Barbara Meil Hobson, *Uneasy Virtue: The Politics of Prostitution and the American Reform Tradition* (New York: Basic Books, 1987), 32–33; A. L. Beier, *Masterless Men: The Vagrancy Problem in England, 1560–1640* (New York: Methuen, 1985), 7, citing A. V. Judges, ed., *The Elizabethan Underworld* (London: G. Routledge & Sons, 1930); Paul A. Slack, "Vagrants and Vagrancy in England, 1598–1664," *Economic History Review* 27, no. 3 (1974): 367; Tim Hitchcock, Adam Crymble, and Louise Falcini, "Loose, Idle and Disorderly: Vagrant Removal in Late Eighteenth-century Middlesex," *Social History* 39, no. 4 (2014): 509–10.

11. On prostitution and women in public, see Mark Thomas Connelly, *The Response to Prostitution in the Progressive Era* (Chapel Hill: University of North Carolina Press, 1980), 8–9; Jeffrey S. Adler, "Streetwalkers, Degraded Outcasts, and Good-for-Nothing Huzzies: Women and the Dangerous Class in Antebellum St. Louis," *Journal of Social History* 25, no. 4 (1992): 737. On separate spheres, see Nancy F. Cott, *The Bonds of Womanhood: "Woman's Sphere" in New England, 1780–1835* (New Haven, CT: Yale University Press, 1997); Linda K. Kerber, "Separate Spheres, Female Worlds, Woman's Place: The Rhetoric of Women's History," *Journal of American History* 75, no. 1 (1988): 9; Barbara Welter, "The Cult of True Womanhood: 1820–1860," *American Quarterly* 8, no. 2 (1966): 151; Hobson, *Uneasy Virtue*, 26; Michael Willrich, " 'To Protect Her from the Greed as Well as the Passions of Man': The Morals Court," in *City of Courts: Socializing Justice in Progressive Era Chicago* (Cambridge: Cambridge University Press, 2003), 172–207.

12. See B. Anthony Morosco, *The Prosecution and Defense of Sex Crimes* § 6.01, rev. ed. (New York: Matthew Bender, 2014) (Lexis Advance); Jessica Drexler, "Governments' Role in Turning Tricks: The World's Oldest Profession in the Netherlands and the United States," *Dickinson Journal of International Law* 15, no. 1 (1996): 204–5; Coty R. Miller and Nuria Haltiwanger, "Prostitution and the Legalization/Decriminalization Debate," *Georgetown Journal of Gender and Law* 5, no. 1 (2004): 207. For the cases, see, e.g., People v. Santiago, 79 N.Y.S.2d 139 (N.Y. Magis. Ct. 1948); State v. McCorvey, 114 N.W.2d 703 (Minn. 1962); Harper v. State, 126 So.2d 232, 234 (Ala Ct. App. 1961); People v. Scott, 296 P. 601 (Cal. App. Dep't Super. Ct.1931); State v. Harlowe, 24 P.2d 601 (Wash. 1933); Kelly v. State, 14 So.2d 599 (Ala. Ct.App. 1943); Davis v. State 18 So.2d 695 (Ala. App. 1944). See also Jeff O'Neill, "Jail Terms for 2 Girls Explained," *Washington Post*, August 8, 1960, B1.

13. Model Penal Code § 207.12 cmt. at 171 (Tentative Draft No. 9 1959); John F. Decker, *Prostitution: Regulation and Control* (Littleton, CO: F. B. Rothman, 1979), 273; U.S. Department of Justice, President's Commission on Law Enforcement and Administration of Justice, *Task Force Report: The Police* (1967), 188; Thomas F. Adams, "Field Interrogation," *Police* (March–April 1963), quoted in Brief of the N.A.A.C.P. Legal Defense and Educational Fund, Inc. as Amicus Curiae at 45–46, Terry v. Ohio, 392 U.S. 1 (1968) (No. 67); State v. Armstrong, 162 N.W.2d 357, 362 (Minn. 1968). See also Maurine McLaighlin, "Judge Throws Out Prostitution Case: Stream of Males to Her Home Not Enough Evidence," *Washington Post*, May 23, 1970, B1.

14. Brief of Appellant at 11, Ricks (quoting officer). See also "Police Continue Crime Round-Up," *New York Times*, June 16, 1957, 67; "Unsavory Types Are Plaguing Bus and Rail Terminals Here," 20; Maurine Beasley, "Bordellos, White Slavers Are Gone—But Prostitutes Remain," *Washington Post*, May 24, 1971, C1.

15. Wayne R. LaFave, "Penal Code Revision: Considering the Problems and Practices of the Police," *Texas Law Review* 45, no. 3 (1967): 442–45; Hobson, *Uneasy Virtue*, 32–34; Sidney E. Zion, "Prostitution: The Midtown Roundup," *New York Times*, October 1, 1967, E6 (quoting Deputy Commissioner Jacques Nevard); Bernard Weintraub, "City Vice Squads in Midtown Drive," *New York Times*, September 17, 1966, 19; Williams, 286 N.Y.S.2d at 577–78; Kirkwood v. Ellington, 298 F. Supp. 461 (W.D. Tenn. 1969).

16. Nelson v. State, 133 So. 747 (Ala. Ct. App. 1931); Hallmark v. State, 30 S.E.2d 116 (Ga. Ct. App. 1944); Williams v. State, 394 S.W.2d 510 (Tex. Crim. App. 1965); Ashe, 161 S.E. at 709. See also "Woman Gets 2d Reversal under Statute," *Washington Post*, February 1, 1961, A3.

17. See, e.g., People v. Brandt, 306 P.2d 1069 (Cal. App. Dep't Super. Ct. 1956); Hunt v. District of Columbia, 47 A.2d 783 (D.C. 1946), *aff'd*, District of Columbia v. Hunt, 163 F.2d 833 (D.C. Cir. 1947); McCorvey, 114 N.W.2d 703; State v. Gustin, 419 P.2d 429 (Or. 1966); Curtis v. U.S., 222 A.2d 840 (D.C. 1966); Kansas City v. Mathis 409 S.W.2d

280 (Mo. Ct. App. 1966); Gene Hunter, "Parker Halts Prostitute Arrests under City Law," *Los Angeles Times*, December 28, 1961, 1; Johnson v. District of Columbia, 230 A.2d 483, 484 (D.C. 1967); People v. Choremi, 94 N.E.2d 81 (N.Y. 1950); People v. Hansuld, 114 N.Y.S.2d 243 (NY. Magis. Ct. 1952); People v. Cirile, 205 N.Y.S.2d 618 (N.Y. Magis. Ct. 1960).

18. Zion, "Prostitution: The Midtown Roundup," E5 (quoting Deputy Commissioner Jacques Nevard); Weintraub, "City Vice Squads in Midtown Drive," 19; Williams, 286 N.Y.S.2d at 577–78; Sidney E. Zion, "2,300 Seized in Prostitution Drive Here," *New York Times*, September 26, 1967, 62.

19. Zion, "Prostitution: The Midtown Roundup," E5.

20. Burt Neuborne, interview with author, November 8, 2008.

21. Williams, 286 N.Y.S.2d at 577–80; Zion, "Prostitution: The Midtown Roundup," E5 (quoting Judge Amos S. Basel); Burt Neuborne, interview with author, November 8, 2008.

22. Bernard Weintraub, "Grimness of Crime Unfolds at 100 Centre Street," *New York Times*, September 3, 1969, 49; Barry Newman, "Losing Battle? New York's Campaign to Stop Prostitution is Beset by Obstacles," *Wall Street Journal*, September 17, 1971, 1.

23. See, e.g., Clark v. District of Columbia, 34 A.2d 711, 712 n. 1 (D.C. 1943); "Judge Barse Indorses Law Council Plan," *Washington Post*, March 2, 1950, 1; John B. Layton (Metropolitan Police Chief) to David C. Carliner (Chair of the National Capital Area Civil Liberties Union), March 26, 1965, in Petition for a Writ of Certiorari, Hicks v. District of Columbia at App'x C, box 1433, American Civil Liberties Union Records, Series 4, Subseries 4A, Department of Rare Books and Special Collections, Princeton University Library (hereafter Princeton ACLU Papers); see generally "Law Studied to Get Convictions in Raid," *Washington Post*, February 5, 1952, B9.

24. Alfred E. Lewis, "Plainclothes Group Active Six Months in Downtown Area to Trap Culprits," *Washington Post*, November 13, 1956, B1; Alfred E. Lewis and Harry Gabbett, "Second Precinct Smallest But No Longer Wickedest," *Washington Post*, January 2, 1959, B1; S. L. Fishbein, "Police Use New Tool to Fight Vice," *Washington Post*, April 9, 1954, 21 (quoting Precinct Captain Jolin E. Winters). See Harris v. District of Columbia 132 A.2d 152, 153 (D.C. 1957) as an example of a case in which an officer arrested a suspect for disorderly conduct and upon discovering that "we had enough observations on her" for a vagrancy charge, changed the charge.

25. George W. Shadoan to Rowland Watts (Legal Director, ACLU) December 9, 1960, folder 25, box 971, American Civil Liberties Union Records, Series 3, Subseries 3B.1, Princeton ACLU Papers; Memorandum of Points and Authorities in Support of Motion to Dismiss, U.S. v. Vicks (D.C. Mun. Ct. Crim. Div.), n.d., folder 25, box 971, American Civil Liberties Union Records, Series 3, Subseries 3B.1, Princeton ACLU Papers; Rowland Watts (Legal Director, ACLU) to George W. Shadoan, December 14, 1960, folder 25, box 971, American Civil Liberties Union Records, Series 3, Subseries 3B.1, Princeton ACLU Papers.

26. Auerbach, "City Vagrancy Statute Unlawful, Says Judge," A3; Brief of Appellant at 3, 6, Ricks; "Trial Opens in Test of DC Vagrant Law," *Washington Post*, March 25, 1966, B1; Ricks v. District of Columbia, 414 F.2d 1097, 1098–99 (D.C. Cir. 1968).

27. "Trial Opens in Test of DC Vagrant Law," B1.

28. Monroe Freedman, phone interview with author, August 13, 2012.

29. Brief of Appellant at 15–37, Ricks (citing Alegata, Baker, Edelman, Edwards, Fenster, Anduha, Hicks); Brief of Appellant at 14, Ricks.

30. Brief of Appellant at 3–4 (internal citations and quotation marks omitted); Ricks, 414 F.2d at 1109.

31. Brief of Appellant at 7, Ricks; see Auerbach, "City Vagrancy Statute Unlawful, Says Judge," A3; Ricks v. United States, 228 A.2d 316 (1967), *rev'd* 414 F.2d 1097 (D.C. Cir. 1968), *rev'd* 404 F.2d 111 (D.C. Cir. 1968); Ricks, 414 F.2d at 1100 (striking down sections, 1, 3, 8); see also Ricks v. United States, 414 F.2d 1111 (D.C. Cir. 1968) (striking down Narcotic Vagrancy Statute).

32. Ronald Krelstein, email correspondence with author, May 20, 2013; Kirkwood, 298 F.Supp. 461. For other examples of running from the police, see, e.g., Seattle v. Jones, 488 P. 2d 750 (Wash. 1971); Mathis, 409 S.W.2d 280; Beail v. District of Columbia 82 A.2d 765 (D.C. 1951), *rev'd*, Beail v. District of Columbia, 201 F.2d 176 (D.C. Cir. 1952).

33. Ronald Krelstein, email correspondence with author, May 20, 2013; Kirkwood v. Loeb, 323 F.Supp. 611 (W.D. Tenn. 1971).

34. Kirkwood, 298 F.Supp. at 465; Kirkwood cited Smith v. Hill, 285 F.Supp 556 (E.D.N.C. 1968); Ricks, 414 F.2d 1097; Alegata, 231 N.E.2d 201; Baker, 274 F.Supp. 658 (D. Ky. 1967).

35. See Carolyn Lewis, *Prescription for Heterosexuality: Sexual Citizenship in the Cold War Era* (Chapel Hill: University of North Carolina Press, 2010); William H. Masters and Virginia E. Johnson, *Human Sexual Response* (New York: Bantam, 1966); William H. Masters and Virginia E. Johnson, *Human Sexual Inadequacy* (New York: Bantam, 1970); Alan Petigny, *The Permissive Society, America, 1941–1965* (New York: Cambridge University Press, 2009), 100–33.

36. Harry Ferguson, "500,000 U.S. Women Arrested Yearly," *Washington Post-Times Herald*, March 19, 1963, B6; Samuel Walker, *In Defense of American Liberties: A History of the ACLU* (Carbondale: Southern Illinois University Press, 1999), 301–04.

37. Alice Kessler-Harris, *Out to Work: A History of Wage-Earning Women in the United States* (New York: Oxford University Press, 1982). On women's experiences in other movements, see, e.g., Davis W. Houck and David E. Dixon, *Women and the Civil Rights Movement, 1954–1965* (Jackson: University Press of Mississippi, 2009), xi; Jean Stefancic, "On the Road without a Map: The Women of the Beat Writers," in "Symposium—Mania: The Lives, Literature, and Law of the Beats, Session I, Weaving Lives into Literature," *Seattle University Law Review* 37, no. 1 (2013): xv–xxxi; Gretchen Lemke-Santangelo, *Daughters of Aquarius: Women of the Sixties Counterculture* (Lawrence: University Press of Kansas, 2009); Philip S. Foner, *Women and the American Labor Movement: From Colonial Times to the Eve of World War I* (New York: Free Press, 1979); Philip S. Foner, *Women and the American Labor Movement: From World War I to the Present* (New York: Free Press, 1980); Betty Friedan, *The Feminine Mystique* (New York: W. W. Norton, 1963); Civil Rights Act of 1964, Pub. L. 88–352, 78 Stat. 241 (1964); Walker, *In Defense of American Liberties*, 304.

38. People v. Archibald, 296 N.Y.S.2d 834, 838 (N.Y. App. Div. 1968) (Markowitz, J. dissenting); Carol Hanisch, "The Personal Is Political," *Notes from the Second Year: Women's Liberation* (1970): 76.

39. Helen Gurley Brown, *Sex and the Single Girl* (New York: Pocket Books, 1963); *Women and Their Bodies* (Boston: New England Free Press, 1970). See John D'Emilio and Estelle B Freedman, *Intimate Matters: A History of Sexuality in America*, 3rd ed. (Chicago: University of Chicago Press, 2012), 350–52; Susan Brownmiller, "The Pornography Wars," in *In Our Time: Memoir of a Revolution* (New York: Dial Press, 1999), 295–325; Ronald J. Berger, Patricia Searles, and Charles E Cottle, *Feminism and Pornography* (New York: Praeger, 1991), 31–49; Lynn S. Chancer, "From Pornography to Sadomasochism: Reconciling Feminist Differences," *Annals of the American Academy of Political Science and Social Science* 571(September 2000): 79.

40. Roth v. United States, 354 U.S. 476 (1957); see also Butler v. Michigan, 352 U.S. 380 (1957); Jacobellis v. Ohio, 378 U.S. 184, 194 (1964) (Stewart, J., concurring); Memoirs v. Massachusetts, 383 U.S. 413 (1966); Miller v. California, 413 U.S. 15 (1973).

41. Minor v. Happersett, 88 U.S. 162 (1874); Bradwell v. Illinois, 83 U.S. 130 (1872); Hoyt v. State of Florida, 368 U.S. 57, 61–62 (1961).

42. Griswold v. Connecticut, 381 U.S. 479, 486 (1965). For an example of the Court's avoidance of substantive due process, see, e.g., Skinner v. Oklahoma, 316 U.S. 535 (1942). Justice William O. Douglas to Justice William Brennan, April 24, 1965, Griswold v. Connecticut, box I-126, William J. Brennan, Jr. Papers, Library of Congress. On Justice Brennan, see Hunter R. Clark, *Justice Brennan: The Great Conciliator* (New York: Carol, 1995); Kim I. Eisler, *A Justice for All: William J. Brennan, Jr., and the Decisions that Transformed America* (New York: Simon and Schuster, 1993); Roger Goldman with David Gallen, *Justice William J. Brennan, Jr.: Freedom First* (New York: Carroll and Graf, 1994); Seth Stern and Stephen Wermial, *Justice Brennan: Liberal Champion* (Boston: Houghton Mifflin Harcourt, 2010); Griswold, 381 U.S. at 515 (Black. J., dissenting).

43. Griswold, 381 U.S. at 498–99 (Goldberg, J. concurring); ibid at 499 (quoting Harlan in Poe, 367 U.S. at 553). See Marc Stein, *Sexual Injustice: Supreme Court Decisions from Griswold to Roe* (Chapel Hill: University of North Carolina Press, 2010).

44. Webster Schott, "Civil Rights and the Homosexual," *New York Times Magazine*, November 12, 1967, 44; *In re* Davis, 51 Cal. Rptr. 702, 706–07 (Cal. Dist. Ct. App. 1966).

45. For cases, see, e.g., Hamm v. Jones, 353 S.W.2d 544 (Ky. Ct. App. 1962); Brandt, 306 P.2d 1069. Johnson v. State, 197 So.2d 466 (Ala. Ct. App. 1967). Lesley Oelsner, "Customers of Prostitutes Are Difficult to Prosecute," *New York Times*, July 15, 1971, 35; Lacey Foseburgh, "Criminal Laws Called Discriminatory to Women," *New York Times*, September 25, 1970, 1, 2; George Barner, "ASHA Aims at 'Pay for Play Boys,'" *New York Amsterdam News*, November 28, 1964, 1.

. 46. Phyllis Schlafly, "The Feminist Assault on Reasonableness," *The Phyllis Schlafly Report* (1996); Phyllis Schlafly, "A Short History of the E.R.A.," *The Phyllis Schlafly Report* (1986) (emphasis in original), http://www.eagleforum.org/psr/1986/sept86/psrsep86.html.

47. Beasley, "Bordellos, White Slavers Are Gone—But Prostitutes Remain," C1.

48. Jean M. White, "49 States and the District Punish Overt Homosexual Acts as Crimes," *Washington Post*, February 3, 1965, A1; see generally Jonathan Ned Katz, *The Invention of Heterosexuality* (New York: Dutton, 1995); Rob Cole interview with Dr. John B. Williams, 1971, "The View from the Vice," in *Long Road to Freedom: The Advocate History of the Gay and Lesbian Movement*, ed. Mark Thompson (New York: St. Martin's Press, 1994), 61; Schott, "Civil Rights and the Homosexual," 44; Robert C. Doty, "Growth of Overt Homosexuality in the City Provokes Wide Concern," *New York Times*, December 17, 1963, 1; Ronald Maiorana, "Hempstead Plans Patrol to Combat Influx of Deviates," *New York Times*, January 30, 1965, 29. On the continued use of vagrancy arrests of gay men and lesbians, see, e.g., Corbet Grenshire, "A Night at the Hollywood Jail," in *Long Road to Freedom*, 12; Harold Jacobs, "Decoy Enforcement of Homosexual Laws," *University of Pennsylvania Law Review* 112, no. 2 (1963): 259; "Police Continue Crime Round-Up," 67; Milton Bracker, "Police Arrest 145 Youths in Growing Crime Drive," *New York Times*, September 6, 1959; Eve Edstrom, "'Hopeless' Youths Sent Back to Slum by Punitive Rules Which Don't Cure," *Washington Post*, July 21, 1960, A1; "Six Accused of Perversion in Park Quiz," *Chicago Daily Tribune*, September 8, 1960, C2; Gene Blake, "Easing of Law against Homosexual Act Urged," *Los Angeles Times*, April 28, 1966, 21. See generally John D'Emilio, *Sexual Politics, Sexual Communities: The Making of a Homosexual Minority in the United States, 1940–1970* (Chicago: University of Chicago Press, 1983), 146; William N. Eskridge Jr., "Privacy Jurisprudence and the Apartheid of the Closet, 1946–1961," *Florida State University Law Review* 24, no. 4 (1997): 721; "The Consenting Adult Homosexual and the Law: An Empirical Study of Enforcement and Administration in Los Angeles County," *UCLA Law Review* 13, no. 3 (1966): 673, 719; The History Project, comp., *Improper Bostonians: Lesbian and Gay History from the Puritans to Playland* (Boston: Beacon Press, 1998), 171.

49. On the obstacles, see "The Consenting Adult Homosexual and the Law," 760. The typical charge was $1,000 to $1,500, which was, according to the UCLA study, a lot given how mechanical and simple the defenses and the process usually were; ibid., 763–92; C. Todd White, *Pre-Gay L.A.: A Social History of the Movement for Homosexual Rights* (Urbana: University of Illinois Press, 2009), 26. See also Eskridge, "Privacy Jurisprudence," 722; Schott, "Civil Rights and the Homosexual," 44. On avoidance of stigma, see, e.g., People v. Anonymous, 111 N.Y.S.2d 679 (NY Magis. Ct. 1952). On increasing assertiveness and organization, see Franklin E. Kameny to *The Advocate*, 1967, in *Long Road to Freedom*, 9; D'Emilio, *Sexual Politics, Sexual Communities*, 14–15; David Carter, *Stonewall: The Riots That Sparked the Gay Revolution* (New York: St. Martin's Press 2004): 104–5; Christopher Agee, "Gayola: Police Professionalization and the Politics of San Francisco's Gay Bars, 1950–1968," *Journal of the History of Sexuality* 15, no. 3 (2006) 462. See Nancy L. Ross, "Homosexual Revolution," *Washington Post*, October 25, 1969, C1; Simon Hall, *American Patriotism, American Protest: Social Movements since the Sixties* (Philadelphia: University of Pennsylvania Press, 2011), 28–33.

50. Joyce Murdoch and Deb Price, *Courting Justice: Gay Men and Lesbians v. The Supreme Court* (New York: Basic Books, 2001), 143–46.

51. See Simon Hall, "The American Gay Rights Movement and Patriotic Protest," *Journal of the History of Sexuality* 19, no. 3 (2010): 536; Simon Hall, "Protest Movements in the 1970s: The Long 1960s," Journal of Contemporary History 43 no. 4 (2008): 655, 657; Enid Neemy, "Young Homosexual Women Are Rebelling," *Cleveland Plain Dealer*, November 23, 1969, 20-E; Martin Duberman, *Stonewall* (New York: Penguin, 1993), 278–79.

52. Ross, "Homosexual Revolution," C1; Thompson, *Long Road to Freedom*, 52–53.

53. "Jurist Parley Asks Easing of Penalties on Sexual Behavior," *New York Times*, August 30, 1964, 36; see also "The Consenting Adult Homosexual and the Law," 647–56 (introduction by Judge Stanley Mosk); Schott, "Civil Rights and the Homosexual," 44; Elaine Elinson and Stan Yogi, *Wherever There's a Fight: How Runaway Slaves, Suffragists, Immigrants, Strikers, and Poets Shaped Civil Liberties in California* (Berkeley, CA: Heyday, 2009), 325; see also Stein, *Sexual Injustice*, 149.

54. State v. Sharpe, 205 N.E.2d 113, 114 (Ohio Ct. App. 1965); Harris v. State, 457 P.2d 638, 644–45 (Alaska 1969).

55. D'Emilio, *Sexual Politics, Sexual Communities*, 49; Claudia Levy, "District Homosexuals Note Decrease in Arrest Totals," *Washington Post*, July 2, 1971, B1; "Morals in the Parks," *Washington Post*, January, 1 1966, A6; Ross, "Homosexual Revolution," C1.

56. See, e.g., People v. Gillespi, 204 N.E.2d 211 (N.Y. 1964). A few lawyers brought constitutional claims against sodomy laws in the 1950s, but they did not really pick up until the mid-1960s. Harris, 457 P.2d 638; People v. Hurd, 85 Cal. Rptr. 718 (Cal. Ct. App. 1970); Gilmore v. People, 467 P.2d 828 (Colo. 1970); Estes v. State, 195 N.E.2d 471 (Ind. 1964); State v. White, 217 A.2d 212 (Me. 1966); Neville v. State, 430 A.2d 570 (Md. 1981); Joquith v. Commonwealth, 120 N.E.2d 189 (Mass. 1954); People v. Dexter, 148 N.W.2d 915 (Mich. Ct. App. 1967); Hogan v. State, 441 P.2d 620 (Nev. 1968); Jones v. State, 456 P.2d 429 (Nev. 1969).

57. N.Y. Crim. Proc. § 887(7) (McKinney 1945); Archibald, 296 N.Y.S.2d at 837 (Markowitz, J., dissenting). See Gillespi, 204 N.E.2d 211; see also People v. Miller (App. Term, 1st Dept., Nov. 1964, No. 394), cited in Archibald, 296 N.Y.S.2d at 837. See generally Charles W. McCurdy, *The Anti-rent Era in New York Law and Politics, 1839–1865* (Chapel Hill: University of North Carolina Press, 2006).

58. Craig J. Konnoth, "Created in Its Image: The Race Analogy, Gay Identity and Gay Litigation in the 1950s–1960s," *Yale Law Journal* 19, no. 2 (2009): 331; Margaret Canady, *The Straight State* (Princeton, NJ: Princeton University Press, 2009); Michael Foucault, *The History of Sexuality* (New York: Pantheon Books, 1978); Murdoch and Price, *Courting Justice*, 111.

59. Robinson v. State, 370 U.S. 660 (1962); Petition for a Writ of Certiorari at 13–14, Hirshhorn v. New York, 386 U.S. 984 (1967) (No. 1058) (cert. denied); Gerald Margaro, "Cruel and Unusual Punishment under the 8th Amendment," *Western Reserve Law Review* 18, no. 4 (1967): 1319–24. See also Perkins v. North Carolina, 234 F. Supp. 333, 336–37 (W.D. N.C. 1964).

60. Petition for a Writ of Certiorari at 11, Hirshhorn v. New York, 386 U.S. 984 (1967) (No. 1058) (cert. denied).

61. Ibid. at 12.

62. Respondent's Brief in Opposition to Petition for Writ of Certiorari at 7, Hirshhorn v. New York, 386 U.S. 984 (1967) (No. 1058).

63. Archibald, 296 N.Y.S.2d at 838–39.

64. Hughes v. Rizzo, 282 F. Supp 884 (E.D. Pa. 1968); Gomez v. Wilson, 323 F. Supp. 87 (D.D.C. 1971); Phillips, "Bus Terminal at Night," 1.

65. See, e.g., "Police Continue Crime Round-Up," 67; Bracker, "Police Arrest 145 Youths in Growing Crime Drive," 1; Mary Ellen Leary, "The Trouble with Troubleshooting," *Atlantic*, March 1969, 95; Franklin E. Kameny to Robert F. Kennedy, quoted in William N. Eskridge Jr., "Challenging the Apartheid of the Closet: Establishing Conditions for Lesbian and Gay Intimacy, Nomos, and Citizenship, 1961–1981," *Hofstra Law Review* 25, no. 3 (1997): 909–910; Konnoth, "Created in Its Image," 331.

66. Murdoch and Price, *Courting Justice*, 143–46.

67. Murdoch and Price, *Courting Justice*, 145–46 (quoting Selwyn).

68. See One Eleven Wines & Liquors, Inc. v. Div. of Alcoholic Beverage Control, 235 A.2d 12, 18 (N.J. 1967); "The Consenting Adult Homosexual and the Law," 666–67, 793; State v. Finrow, 405 P.2d 600, 601 (Wash. 1965); Boutilier v. INS, 387 U.S. 118 (1967); Stein, *Sexual Injustice*, 57–92.

69. Schott, "Civil Rights and the Homosexual," 44; Cole, "The View from the Vice," in *Long Road to Freedom*, 61; Respondent's Brief in Opposition to Petition for Writ of Certiorari at 9, Hirshhorn v. New York, 386 U.S. 984 (1967) (No. 1058). See generally Martha C. Nussbaum, *From Disgust to Humanity: Sexual Orientation and Constitutional Law* (New York: Oxford University Press, 2010).

70. See, e.g., White, "49 States and the District Punish Overt Homosexual Acts as Crimes," A1; "The Consenting Adult Homosexual and the Law," 740; Levy, "District Homosexuals Note Decrease in Arrest Totals," B1 (quoting Inspector Walter Bishop); Bruce McCabe, "On the Vice Beat," *Atlantic*, March 1969, 122; Nan Alamilla Boyd, *Wide Open Town: A History of Queer San Francisco to 1965* (Berkeley: University of California Press, 2003), 156; Elinson and Yogi, *Wherever There's a Fight*, 314.

71. Schott, "Civil Rights and the Homosexual," 44; "The Consenting Adult Homosexual and the Law," 685, 791 (emphasis in original).

72. Model Penal Code § 251.3 cmt (Official Draft and Revised Comment 1980); Louis B. Schwartz, "Morals Offenses and the Model Penal Code," *Columbia Law Review* 63, no. 4 (1963): 674–75; *In re* Davis, 51 Cal. Rptr. at 706–07. For another take on the public/private question, see Patricia A. Cain, *Rainbow Rights: The Role of Lawyers and Courts in the Lesbian and Gay Civil Rights Movement* (Boulder, CO: Westview Press, 2000).

73. On police surveillance cases, see Bielicki v. Superior Court, 371 P.2d 288 (Cal. 1962); William N. Eskridge, Jr, *Gaylaw: Challenging the Apartheid of the Closet* (Cambridge, MA: Harvard University Press, 1999), 102–3; David Alan Sklansky, "'One Train May Hide Another': Katz, Stonewall, and the Secret Subtext of Criminal Procedure," *U.C. Davis Law Review* 41, no. 3 (2008): 875–934. For commentators on privacy, see Charles Reich, "Police Questioning of Abiding Citizens," *Yale Law Journal* 75, no. 7 (1966): 1172; William O. Douglas, "The Attack on the Right to Privacy," *Playboy*, December 1967, 244; Carl C. Rachlin, "The Police Order: The Right to Disobey," *Santa Clara Lawyer* 6 (1965): 158. See also Flynn, "Vagrancy Laws and the Right to Privacy," 337–54.

74. D'Emilio, *Sexual Politics, Sexual Communities*, 14, 49; John Howard ed., *"Carryin' On in the Lesbian and Gay South"* (New York: New York University Press, 1997), 216; Craig M. Loftin, *Masked Voices: Gay Men and Lesbians in Cold War America* (Albany: State University of New York Press, 2012), 97; Schott, "Civil Rights and the Homosexual," 44.

75. Charles Grutzner, "Mafia Buys Clubs for Homosexuals," *New York Times*, November 30, 1967; Doty, "Growth of Overt Homosexuality in the City Provokes Wide Concern"; Levy, "District Homosexuals Note Decrease in Arrest Totals," B1; Charles Grutzner, "Bar in 'Village' Yields on License: Police Call Café Flagrant Center of Homosexuals Incidents Cited," *New York Times*, October 23, 1963, 30.

76. Gomez, 323 F. Supp. 87.

77. More than thirty years later, the Supreme Court struck down a sodomy law. See Lawrence v. Texas, 539 U.S. 558 (2003); see also Romer v. Evans, 517 U.S. 620 (1996). See generally Felicia Kornbluh, "Queer Legal History: A Field Grows Up and Comes Out," *Law and Social Inquiry* 36, no. 2 (2011): 537–59.

78. Dunn, N.C., Vagrancy Ordinance, ch. H, art. I, sec. 2, as referenced in Smith v. Hill, 285 F.Supp. 556, 558 n. 2 (E.D.N.C. 1968); Smith, 285 F. Supp. at 558–59 and n. 4 (referencing *The Daily Record* (Dunn, NC), a local newspaper).

79. Smith, 285 F. Supp. at 558, 558 n. 4, 562–63, 563 n. 15.

80. Ibid. at 562.

81. For scholarly commentary, see Chapter 2. For earlier cases, see Lanzetta v. New Jersey, 306 U.S. 451 (1939); Thornhill v. Alabama, 310 U.S. 88 (1940); Edwards v. California, 314 U.S. 160 (1941); Belcastro, 190 N.E. 301; Alterie, 190 N.E. 305; Eisen, 191 N.E. 219; Ashe, 161 S.E. 709. For 1950s and 1960s cases, see, e.g., Griffin v. Illinois, 351 U.S. 12, 17 (1956); Gideon v. Wainwright, 372 U.S. 335 (1963); Douglas v. California, 372 U.S. 353 (1963); Harper v. Virginia Bd. of Elections, 383 U.S. 663 (1966). U.S. Const. amend. XXIV.

82. H.R. Doc. No. 392, 77th Cong., 1st Sess. (1941); Arceneaux v. Louisiana, 376 U.S. 336 (1964); Oral Argument, Arceneaux v. Louisiana, as quoted in Paul R. Baier, "Review of Louisiana Legal Memoirs: *Law in the Cajun Nation,* by J. Minos Simon with David Leon Chandler," *Louisiana Law Review* 54, no. 5 (1994): 1451; Brief for Petitioner at 4–8, Arceneaux v. Louisiana, 376 U.S. 336 (1964) (No. 76); Reply and Supplemental Brief on Behalf of Sidney Arceneaux at 8–11 (App'x B, Sidney Arceneaux's deposition), Arceneaux v. Louisiana, 376 U.S. 336 (1964) (No. 76); Arthur J. Goldberg, "Equality and Governmental Action," *New York University Law Review* 39, no. 2 (1964): 221 (reprinting Madison Lecture, February 11, 1964.)

83. William O. Douglas, "The Bill of Rights Is Not Enough," *New York University Law Review* 38, no. 2 (1963): 207, 234; Complaint for Declaratory Judgment at 6, Gallant v. Barlow (W.D. Tex.), n.d., roll 180, American Civil Liberties Union Archives, 1950–1999, series 4, microfilm. See Michael Harrington, *The Other America* (New York: Macmillan, 1962). The sense that some types of poor people were more morally deserving of government assistance than others was written into New Deal legislation itself. See, e.g., Linda Gordon, *Pitied but Not Entitled: Single Mothers and the Origins of Welfare* (Cambridge, MA: Harvard University Press, 1995); Theda Skocpol, *Protecting Soldiers and Mothers: The Political Origins of Social Policy in the United States* (Cambridge, MA: Harvard University Press, 1995).

84. Thomas Jackson, *From Civil Rights to Human Rights: Martin Luther King, Jr., and the Struggle for Economic Justice* (Philadelphia: University of Pennsylvania Press, 2007).

85. Felicia Kornbluh, *The Battle for Welfare Rights* (Philadelphia: University of Pennsylvania Press, 2007); Felicia Kornbluh, "The Goals of the National Welfare Rights Movement: Why We Need Them Thirty Years Later," *Feminist Studies* 24, no. 1 (1998): 68–74. For judicial victories, see, e.g., Levy v. Louisiana, 391 U.S. 68 (1968); Shapiro v. Thompson, 394 U.S. 618 (1969); King v. Smith, 392 U.S. 309, 324–25 (1968); Goldberg v. Kelly, 397 U.S. 254 (1970). See generally Elisa M. Alvarez Minoff, "Free to Move? The Law and Politics of Internal Migration in Twentieth-Century America" (Ph.D. diss., Harvard University, 2013).

86. *Report of the National Advisory Commission on Civil Disorders* (1968) (The Kerner Report) Economic Opportunity Act of 1964, Pub. L. No. 88–452, 78 Stat. 508.

87. See John A. Andrew, *The Other Side of the Sixties: Young Americans for Freedom and the Rise of Conservative Politics* (New Brunswick, NJ: Rutgers University Press, 1997), 18–19; Jill Quadagno, *The Color of Welfare: How Racism Undermined the War on Poverty* (New York: Oxford University Press, 1994); Michael B. Katz, *The Undeserving Poor: From the War on Poverty to the War on Welfare* (New York: Pantheon Books, 1989); Martin Gilens, *Why Americans Hate Welfare: Race, Media, and the Politics of Antipoverty Policy* (Chicago: University of Chicago Press, 1999). See also, e.g., Donald T. Critchlow and Nancy MacLean, *Debating the American Conservative Movement: 1945 to the Present* (Lanham, MD: Rowman and Littlefield, 2009); Eric Foner and Lisa McGirr, eds., *American History Now* (Philadelphia: Temple University Press, 2011); David Frum, *How We Got Here: The 70's, the Decade That Brought You Modern Life (For Better or Worse)* (New York: Basic Books, 2000); Edward D. Berkowitz, *Something Happened: A Political and Cultural Overview of the Seventies* (New York: Columbia University Press, 2006); Lisa McGirr, *Suburban Warriors: The Origins of the New American Right* (Princeton, NJ: Princeton University Press, 2001); Sarah Barringer Gordon, *The Spirit of the Law: Religious Voices and the Constitution in Modern America* (Cambridge, MA: Belknap Press of Harvard University Press, 2010); Matthew D. Lassiter, *The Silent Majority: Suburban Politics in the Sunbelt South* (Princeton, NJ: Princeton University Press, 2006); Kevin M. Kruse, *White Flight: Atlanta and the Making of Modern Conservatism* (Princeton, NJ: Princeton University Press, 2005); Kevin M. Kruse and Thomas J. Sugrue, eds., *The New Suburban History* (Chicago: University of Chicago Press, 2006).

88. J. Skelley Wright, "The Courts Have Failed the Poor," *New York Times*, March 9, 1969; see also "Unsavory Types Are Plaguing Bus and Rail Terminals Here," 20; Alan H. Levine, "Disorderly Conduct: Catch-all Device for New York City's 'Undesirables,'" *Civil Liberties in New York*, June 1966, 2 (quoting Justice Bernard Botein discussing the use of vagrancy to sweep undesirables under the carpet).

89. Martha F. Davis, *Brutal Need: Lawyers & the Welfare Rights Movement, 1960–1973* (New Haven, CT: Yale University Press, 1993); Thomas Miguel Hilbink, "Constructing Cause Lawyering: Professionalism, Politics, and Social Change in 1960s America" (Ph.D. diss. New York University, 2006); Earl Johnson, *Justice and Reform: The Formative Years of the OEO Legal Services Program* (New York: Russell Sage Foundation, 1974).

90. "Police Begin Times Square Cleanup after Night Workers Complain," 78; "Unsavory Types Are Plaguing Bus and Rail Terminals Here," 20; Wright, "The Courts Have Failed the Poor."

91. Anthony Amsterdam, interview with author, April 14, 2009; Jack Greenberg, *Crusaders in the Courts: Legal Battles of the Civil Rights Movement*, ann. ed. (New York: Twelve Tables Press, 2004), 371–72, 435–41.

92. Recommendation for the 1966 Biennial Conference: Agenda and Schedule, January 6, 1966, folder 4, box 1872, American Civil Liberties Union Records, Series 4, Subseries 4B, Princeton ACLU Papers; Tom Litwack, memorandum, n.d., Paul Chevigny Papers (folder L-Z), New York Civil Liberties Union Headquarters (made available to author); Walker, In Defense of American Liberties, 313–16. See, e.g., King, 392 U.S. 309; Powell v. State, 392 U.S. 514 (1968).

93. R. W. Apple Jr., "Costello Sought as U.S. Witness," *New York Times*, June 5, 1964; Fenster, 229 N.E.2d 426. N.Y. Crim. Pro. Law §. 887(1) (McKinney 1945); Fenster v. Criminal Court of City of New York, 259 N.Y.S. 2d 67 (Sup. Ct. 1965), aff'd 216 N.E.2d 342 (N.Y. 1966); Fenster v. Leary, 264 F. Supp. 153 (S.D.N.Y. 1966), cert denied 386 U.S. 10 (1967); LBM (Lewis B. Merrifield), memorandum, February 6, 1967, Fenster v. Leary, box 1381, William O. Douglas Papers, Library of Congress (hereafter Douglas Papers); Docket sheet, n.d., Fenster v. Leary, box 1374, Douglas Papers.

94. Richard L. Madden, "Law on Vagrancy Voided in Albany as a Usurping Act," *New York Times*, July 8, 1967. Philip J. Hirshkop similarly attacked Virginia's vagrancy law in 1968 on behalf of the ACLU. See Documents and correspondence, Oliver v. Button (E.D. Vir. No. 5904-R), box 1603, American Civil Liberties Union Records, Series 4, Subseries 4A, Princeton ACLU Papers; Fenster v. Leary, 20 N.Y.2d 309, 315–16 (N.Y. 1967).

95. Bruce Rogow, phone interview with author, May 17, 2013.

96. Ibid.; Ackies v. Purdy, 322 F. Supp. 38 (S.D. Fla. 1970); Fuentes v. Shevin, 407 U.S. 67 (1972).

97. LAP (Lucas A. Powe), memorandum, April 27, 1971; Shevin v. Lazarus, box 1493, Douglas Papers.

98. Bruce Rogow, phone interview with author, May 16, 2013; Lazarus v. Faircloth, 301 F. Supp. 266, 268, 271 (quoting Landry v. Daley, 280 F. Supp. 968, 972 (N.D. Ill. 1968)), 272 (S.D. Fla, 1969).

99. See also, e.g., Documents and correspondence, Oliver v. Button (E.D. Vir. No. 5904-R), box 1603, American Civil Liberties Union Records, Series 4, Subseries 4A, Princeton ACLU Papers; Jones v. Jefferson City Court (Colorado), 2 Crim. L. Rep. 2498–99 (February 21, 1968); Phillip Hubbart, phone interview with author, May 23, 2013; Lazarus, 301 F. Supp. 266. Wallace v. State, 161 S.E.2d 288 (Ga. 1968) cert denied 393 U.S. 1123 (1969).

100. Wallace, 161 S.E.2d at 291.

Chapter 6

1. Wainwright v. City of New Orleans, 392 U.S. 598, 600 (1968) (Warren, C.J., dissenting). Wainwright sometimes recalled that he had gone out to a nightclub where he played the banjo rather than to get something to eat. John Q. Barrett, "Deciding the Stop and Frisk Cases: A Look Inside the Supreme Court's Conference," *St. John's Law Review* 72, no. 3 (1998): 761.

2. Hirshhorn v. New York, 386 U.S. 984 (1967); Talley v. California, 390 U.S. 1031 (1968); Fenster v. Leary, 386 U.S. 10 (1967); Georgia v. Wallace, 393 U.S. 1123 (1960). The Court also passed on cases that presented loitering laws with additional elements, like loitering around schools or loitering under circumstances that seemed to threaten public safety. See, e.g., Sprowal v. New York, 385 U.S. 649 (1967); Weger v. California, 389 U.S. 1047 (1968).

3. On rising crime, see, e.g., Michael W. Flamm, *Law and Order: Street Crime, Civil Unrest, and the Crisis of Liberalism in the 1960s* (New York: Columbia University Press, 2005), 125; "The Fear Campaign," *Time*, October 4, 1968, 21–27. (Beckett and Alexander both arguing that increase in crime rate was overblown). See also David R. Johnson, *American Law Enforcement: A History* (St. Louis: Forum Press, 1981), 135. There is some dispute about whether the increase in crime was extraordinary, overblown, or continuous from previous decades. Compare Katherine Beckett, *Making Crime Pay: Law and Order in Contemporary American Politics* (New York: Oxford University Press, 1997); Michelle Alexander, *The New Jim Crow: Mass Incarceration in the Age of Colorblindness*, rev. ed. (New York: New Press, 2010), 41, with Vesla M. Weaver, "Frontlash: Race and the Development of Punitive Crime Policy," *Studies in American Political Development* 21, no. 2 (2007): 233; Malcolm M. Feeley,

"Crime, Social Order and the Rise of Neo-Conservative Politics," review of *The Culture of Control: Crime and Social Order in Contemporary Society*, by David Garland, Theoretical Criminology 7, no. 1 (2003): 124 n. 9; see also David Garland, *The Culture of Control: Crime and Social Order in Contemporary Society* (Chicago: University of Chicago Press, 2001). On responses to crime rate, see Flamm, *Law and Order*; Samuel Walker, *Popular Justice: A History of American Criminal Justice*, 2nd ed. (New York: Oxford University Press, 1998), 201–02; David R. Colburn and Jeffrey S. Adler, eds., *African-American Mayors: Race, Politics, and the American City* (Urbana: University of Illinois Press, 2001), 9; Michael Stern, "Fear Soars with Rate of Crime: Fear of City Residents Soaring with Crime Rates," *New York Times*, December 11, 1968, 49; "Even Baltimore Police Lock Doors," *Washington Post*, November 15, 1967, C6; see also Richard Phalon, "Rising Prices and Crime Create Burglary Insurance Chaos," *New York Times*, June 1, 1970, 38; "Merchants Attack High Crime Rate," *Washington Post*, January 27, 1968, A14; D. J. R. Bruckner, "Midwest Cities React to Year of Crime, Riots: Detroit, Tense with Continuing Violence, Finds Fault with Its Law Enforcement," *Los Angeles Times*, September 28, 1967, 16. For cases, see Miranda v. Arizona, 384 U.S. 436 (1966); Escobedo v. Illinois, 378 U.S. 478 (1964); Massiah v. United States, 377 U.S. 201 (1964);. On linking street crime with activism, riots, and assassinations, see, e.g., Flamm, *Law and Order*.

4.	For precedent skeptical of pretextual vagrancy arrests, see, e.g., Preston v. United States, 376 U.S. 364, 368 (1964). On views that the Supreme Court was pro-defendant, see Bernard A. Berkman to Melvin L. Wulf, June 9, 1967, quoted in Barrett, "Deciding the Stop and Frisk Cases," 769 n. 122; "Another Defeat for Criminals," *Chicago Tribune*, June 1, 1967, 22; James J. Kilpatrick, "Decision Time Starts to Run," *Plain Dealer* (Cleveland), October 1, 1967, 32; Ronald J. Ostrow, "Marshall Takes Formal Oath as Justice Today: High Court's First Negro Member Could Hold Key Vote in Curbing Police Powers," *Los Angeles Times*, October 2, 1967, 5. For the quote, see "Supreme Court Begins New Term," Congressional *Quarterly Weekly Report* 25 (September 29, 1967): 1963.

5.	Stephen Wainwright, interview with author, January 2013; Wesleyan Class of 1961 Reunion Book, 116 (copy of article on file with author).

6.	Brief for Petitioner at 4, 4 n. 3, 5–6, Wainwright v. City of New Orleans, 392 U.S. 598 (1968) (No. 13); Petition for Certiorari at 4–5, Wainwright v. City of New Orleans, 392 U.S. 598 (1968) (No. 13). There was some disagreement about whether the resisting arrest charge was simultaneous with the vagrancy charge or came after the initial arrest. See Oral Argument, Wainwright v. City of New Orleans, 392 U.S. 598 (1968), Oyez Project at IIT Chicago-Kent College of Law, http://www.oyez.org/cases/1960-1969/1967/1967_13 (hereafter Oyez Project).

7.	Wainwright, 392 U.S. at 601–2 (1968) (Warren, C. J., dissenting).

8.	Petition for Certiorari at 8–9, 39, Wainwright v. City of New Orleans, 392 U.S. 598 (1968) (No. 13); Brief for Petitioner at 7, Wainwright. Spencer's conviction was reversed on appeal.

9.	Transcript of Record, 2–3, Wainwright v. City of New Orleans, box 1814, American Civil Liberties Union Records, Series 4, Subseries 4A, Department of Rare Books and Special Collections, Princeton University Library (hereafter Princeton ACLU Papers); Petition for Certiorari at 20, 27, Wainwright v. City of New Orleans, 392 U.S. 598 (1968) (No. 13).

10.	Though at oral argument, the state said that Wainwright had been given a suspended sentence on the original charges, Wainwright said the state described them as "long abandoned" in his petition; Brief for Petitioner at 8, Wainwright; Petition for Certiorari at 11, 42, Wainwright v. City of New Orleans, 392 U.S. 598 (1968) (No. 13); Oral Argument, Wainwright v. City of New Orleans, 392 U.S. 598 (1968), Oyez Project.

11.	Stephen Wainwright, interview with author, January 2013; Petition for Certiorari at 15, 33, Wainwright v. City of New Orleans, 392 U.S. 598 (1968) (No. 13); Stephen R. Wainwright to Marvin M. Karpatkin, February 20, 1967, Wainwright v. City of New Orleans, box 1814, Series 4, Subseries 4A, Princeton ACLU Papers.

12.	"Expect High Court Testing of Frisk Law," *Chicago Tribune*, March 12, 1967, 21; "Court to Review Frisking Power," *New York Times*, January 10, 1967, 28; Kilpatrick, "Decision Time Starts to Run," 32; John P. MacKenzie; "Court Studies Police Powers vs. Individual," *Washington Post*, October 12, 1967, G5.

13. "Court to Review Frisking Power," 28; Stephen R. Wainwright to ACLU Office of Counsel, April 5, 1966, Wainwright v. City of New Orleans, box 1814, Series 4, Subseries 4A, Princeton ACLU Papers. For input to the ACLU, see Eleanor H. Norton to Alan Helseth (Louisiana CLU), June 29, 1966, Wainwright v. City of New Orleans, box 1814, Series 4, Subseries 4A, Princeton ACLU Papers; Alan E. Helseth to Melvin L. Wulf, August 18, 1967, Wainwright v. City of New Orleans, box 1814, Series 4, Subseries 4A, Princeton ACLU Papers; Eleanor Holmes Norton to Melvin L. Wulf, handwritten note, n.d., Wainwright v. City of New Orleans, box 1814, Series 4, Subseries 4A, Princeton ACLU Papers; Jeremiah S. Gutman to Marvin Karpatkin, March 3, 1967, Wainwright v. City of New Orelans, box 1814, Series 4, Subseries 4A, Princeton ACLU Papers; Wayne S. Woody to Stephen R. Wainwright, September 8, 1967, Wainwright v. City of New Orelans, box 1814, Series 4, Subseries 4A, Princeton ACLU Papers; Marvin M. Karpatkin to Stephen R. Wainwright, February 1, 1967, Wainwright v. City of New Orleans, box 1814, Series 4, Subseries 4A, Princeton ACLU Papers; Mel Wulf, interview with author, October 2012.

14. Paul Chevigny, interview with author, April 2009; Paul Chevigny, *Police Power: Police Abuses in New York City* (New York: Pantheon Books, 1969); see also Ed Cray, *The Big Blue Line: Police Power vs. Human Rights* (New York: Coward-McCann, 1967); Paul Chevigny, *Cops and Rebels: A Story of Provocation* (New York: Pantheon, 1972); see generally Marilynn Johnson, *Street Justice: A History of Police Violence in New York City* (Boston: Beacon Press, 2003).

15. See Paula R. Markowitz and Walter I. Summerfield, "Philadelphia Police Practice and the Law of Arrest," *University of Pennsylvania Law Review* 100, no. 8 (1952): 1182–1236; American Bar Foundation, *Survey of the Administration of Criminal Justice in the United States, July 1959: History and Status Report* (Chicago: American Bar Foundation, 1959); American Bar Association Project on Standards for Criminal Justice, *Standards Relating to the Administration of Criminal Justice* (Chicago: ABA, 1974); President's Commission on Crime in the District of Columbia, *Report on the Metropolitan Police Department* (Washington, DC: Government Printing Office, 1966); Walter P. Armstrong, "Administration of Criminal Justice: The American Bar Foundation Project," *American Bar Association Journal* 54, no. 3 (1968): 261–63; Kenneth Culp Davis, *Discretionary Justice: A Preliminary Inquiry* (Baton Rouge: Louisiana State University Press, 1969); Kenneth Culp Davis, *Police Discretion* (St. Paul, MN: West Publishing Co., 1975); Wayne R. LaFave, *Arrest: The Decision to Take a Suspect into Custody* (Boston: Little, Brown, 1965), 61–62, 63–82; Walker, *Popular Justice*, 202–04; Samuel Walker, "Origins of the Contemporary Criminal Justice Paradigm," *Justice Quarterly* 9, no. 1 (1992): 66.

16. LaFave, *Arrest*, 87–89, 151–52, 354–57. Bail for vagrancy could be set at an amount between $100 and $1,000, and it was usually set high when the goal was to keep the suspect for investigatory purposes. Ibid., 302, 338–39. In Wisconsin, officers used what they called a "ten-day vag check" to investigate suspicious persons. Ibid., 354. On pretextual arrests, see Kelley v. U.S., 298 F.2d 310 (D.C. Cir. 1961); People v. Harris, 304 P.2d 178 (Cal. Dist. Ct. App. 1956); People v. Fischetti, 273 Ill. App. 215 (Ill. App. Ct. 1933); Brown v. State, 99 N.E.2d 103 (Ind. 1951). On validating searches incident to vagrancy arrest and prosecution of crimes after the vagrancy arrest, see Hanks v. State, 195 So.2d 49 (Fla. Dist. Ct. App. 1967); Sutherland v. State, 167 So.2d 236 (Fla. Dist. Ct. App. 1964); Rinehart v. State, 114 So.2d 487 (Fla. Dist. Ct. App. 1959); Evans v. State, 400 S.W.2d 536 (Tenn. 1966); State v. Grenz, 175 P.2d 633 (Wash. 1946); Gray v. State, 9 N.W.2d 68 (Wis. 1943). See generally Forrest W. Lacey, "Vagrancy and Other Crimes of Personal Condition," *Harvard Law Review* 66, no. 7 (1953): 1218. LaFave noted that courts had begun to question the validity of these arrests by the time he wrote in 1965. LaFave, *Arrest*, 151–52; see U.S. v. Thomas, 49 F. Supp. 547 (W.D. Ky. 1943); State v. Utley, 91 N.E.2d 355 (Ind. 1950). Vagrancy laws were not the only laws used as pretexts. Disorderly conduct was common, too. Markowitz and Summerfield, "Philadelphia Police Practice," 1201–2. In Kansas, those held for investigation were often booked for "vagrancy and investigation." LaFave, *Arrest*.

17. Chevigny, *Police Power*, 226; Caleb Foote, "The Coming Constitutional Crisis in Bail: II," *University of Pennsylvania Law Review* 113, no. 8 (1965): 1147; Jerome H. Skolnick, *Justice without Trial: Law Enforcement in Democratic Society* (New York: John Wiley, 1966); Joseph Goldstein, "Police Discretion Not to Invoke the Criminal Process: Low-Visibility Decisions in

the Administration of Justice," *Yale Law Journal* 69, no. 4 (1960): 580; Caleb Foote, "Law and Police Practice: Safeguards in the Law of Arrest," *Northwestern University Law Review* 52, no. 1 (1957): 34–36; Jerome Hall, "Police and Law in a Democratic Society," *Indiana Law Journal* 28, no. 2 (1953): 133; Malcolm M. Feeley, *The Process Is the Punishment* (New York: Russell Sage Foundation, 1979).

18. On police discretion, see LaFave, *Arrest*, 64; B. Hargrove, "Police Discretion," *Solicitor* 25, no. 12 (1958): 337–38; Foote, "Law and Police Practice," 22–27; Caleb Foote, "Vagrancy-Type Law and Its Administration," *University of Pennsylvania Law Review* 104, no. 5 (1956): 612, 629–30. According to a student note in the *New York University Law Review*, within the forty-eight American states with vagrancy laws in 1962, there were thirty different definitions of a vagrant, including the "common law vagrant," "the healthy beggar," "the loiterer," and "the night walker." Gary V. Dubin and Richard H. Robinson, "The Vagrancy Concept Reconsidered: Problems and Abuses of Status Criminality," *New York University Law Review* 37, no. 1 (1962): 108–13. See D.C. Code § 22–3302 (Supp. VIII 1960); see also, e.g., Cal. Penal Code § 647 (West 1970). Vagrancy laws were often sponsored by the police force of a given city. Donald Whaley, "The Constitutionality of Loitering Ordinances," *St. Louis University Law Journal* 6, no. 2 (1960): 248; see Alegata v. Commonwealth, 231 N.E.2d 201 (Mass. 1967). On arrests, see, e.g., Commissioner's Committee on Police Arrests for Investigation, *Report and Recommendations* (Washington, DC, 1962), 8, quoted in Herbert L. Packer, *The Limits of the Criminal Sanction* (Stanford, CA: Stanford University Press, 1968),184; Frank J. Remington, "The Law Relating to 'On the Street' Detention, Questioning and Frisking of Suspected Persons and Police Arrest Privileges in General," *Journal of Criminal Law and Criminology*, 51, no. 4 (1960): 386–87.

19. On sharing vagrancy information, see Hicks v. District of Columbia, 382 U.S. 252 (1966); Melvin L. Wulf to J. Dan Struve, April 23, 1969, Gallant v. Barlow, roll 180, American Civil Liberties Union Archives, 1950–1999, Series 4, microfilm (hereafter ACLU microfilm); and Dan Struve to Melvin L. Wulf, August 4, 1969, Gallant v. Barlow, 1950–1999, Series 4, ACLU microfilm; Mel Wulf, interview with author, October 2012. See also Robert J. Krengel, memorandum, n.d., Wainwright v. City of New Orleans, box 1814, Series 4, Subseries 4A, Princeton ACLU Papers; Melvin L. Wulf to David Carliner, February 16, 1965, Hicks v. District of Columbia, box 1433, Series 4, Subseries 4A, Princeton ACLU Papers; David Carliner to Melvin L. Wulf, February 8, 1965, box 1433, Series 4, Subseries 4A, Princeton ACLU Papers. On Chevigny's experience, see Chevigny, *Police Power*, 220, 223; see also Paul Chevigny, interview with author, April 2009; Burmeister v. New York City Police Department, 275 F. Supp. 690, 697 (S.D.N.Y. 1967).

20. Brief for Petitioner at 11–12, Wainwright. American Civil Liberties Union, News Release, July 26, 1967, Wainwright v. City of New Orleans, box 1814, Series 4, Subseries 4A, Princeton ACLU Papers.

21. Stephen Wainwright, interview with author, January 2013; Brief for Petitioner at 20–21, Wainwright; see also Max Hochanadel and Harry W. Stege, "Criminal Law: The Right to Resist an Unlawful Arrest: An Out-Dated Concept," *Tulsa Law Journal* 3, no. 1 (1966): 44.

22. Brief for Respondent at 3, 5, 7, Wainwright v. City of New Orleans, 392 U.S. 598 (1968) (No. 13); Oral Argument, Wainwright v. City of New Orleans, 392 U.S. 598 (1968), Oyez Project.

23. Oral Argument, Wainwright v. City of New Orleans, 392 U.S. 598 (1968), Oyez Project; "Dayries to Seek New Law for Detention of Suspects: Will Ask Change at 1958 Legislature Session," *Times-Picayune* (New Orleans), April 9, 1957, 9; see also "Lawyer-Police Links Charged: Soliciting at Stations Will Be Topic of Bar Group," *Times-Picayune* (New Orleans), May 1, 1957, 20; R. R. Hunt, "Letter to the Editor," *Times-Picayune* (New Orleans), October 15, 1953, 16; "Vagrancy Law Study Is Slated," *Times-Picayune* (New Orleans), February 26, 1957, 4; "Rights of All Arrested to Be Shown at Stations," *Times-Picayune* (New Orleans), September 28, 1957, 7; " 'Job to Suppress Vice' Police Told," *Times-Picayune* (New Orleans), October 15, 1957, 17.

24. "Fiat Justitia," letter to the editor, *Times-Picayune* (New Orleans), March 20, 1958; "Squad Arrests 258 Undesirables," *Times-Picayune* (New Orleans), March 13, 1958, 50; see also "Carrying Weapons, Vagrancy Charged," *Times-Picayune*, March 13, 1958, 50; "Bucaro Offers to Aid Probers," *Times Picayune* (New Orleans), February 25, 1966; "Jury to Consider Probe

of Bucaro," clipping, n.d., Wainwright v. City of New Orleans, box 1814, Series 4, Subseries 4A, Princeton ACLU Papers.

25. Oral Argument, Wainwright v. City of New Orleans, 392 U.S. 598 (1968), Oyez Project.
26. Edelman v. California, 344 U.S. 357 (1953); Thompson v. Louisville, 362 U.S. 199 (1960); Arceneaux v. Louisiana, 376 U.S. 336 (1964); Shuttlesworth v. Birmingham, 382 U.S. 87 (1965); Hicks v. District of Columbia, 383 U.S. 252 (1966). For cert denials, see People v. Weinstein, 184 N.E.2d 312 (N.Y. 1962), cert. denied, 373 U.S. 904 (1963); People v. Weger, 59 Cal. Rptr. 661 (Cal. Ct. App. 1967), cert. denied, 389 U.S. 1047 (1968) (with Douglas dissenting); Talley, 390 U.S. 1031; Dragna v. California, petition for cert. filed, September 28, 1952; cert. denied, 344 U.S. 921 (1953) (with Black and Douglas dissenting); rehearing denied, 345 U.S. 914 (1953).
27. Preston, 376 U.S. at 365–66, 368 (1964); Brief for Petitioner at 6, 7–10, 13, 19–22, 28, 34–35, 37–40, 43–47, Preston v. United States, 376 U.S. 364 (1964) (No. 163).
28. Brief for Respondent at 6, Wainwright; Oral Argument, Wainwright v. City of New Orleans, 392 U.S. 598 (1968), Oyez Project.
29. Oral Argument, Wainwright v. City of New Orleans, 392 U.S. 598 (1968), Oyez Project.
30. Oral Argument, Wainwright v. City of New Orleans, 392 U.S. 598 (1968), Oyez Project; MacKenzie, "Court Studies Police Powers," G5.
31. Oral Argument, Wainwright v. City of New Orleans, 392 U.S. 598 (1968), Oyez Project; Paul G. Chevigny to Richard R. Sobol, June 19, 1967, Police File, Wainwright folder, Paul Chevigny Papers, New York Civil Liberties Union Headquarters (made available to author) (hereafter Chevigny Papers); Brief for Petitioner at 20, Wainright; see Draft Brief by Paul Chevigny, Wainright v. City of New Orleans, Police File, Wainwright folder, Chevigny Papers.
32. Stephen Wainwright to Mel Wulf, October 13, 1967, Wainwright v. City of New Orleans, box 1814, Series 4, Subseries 4A, Princeton ACLU Papers.
33. See Brief for National District Attorneys' Association as Amicus Curiae Supporting Respondents at 6, Terry v. Ohio, 392 U.S. 1 (1968) (No. 67); Brief for Americans for Effective Law Enforcement as Amicus Curiae at 6, Terry v. Ohio, 392 U.S. 1 (1968) (No. 67); LaFave, *Arrest*, 358–59. See generally Tracey Maclin, "*Terry v. Ohio's* Fourth Amendment Legacy: Black Men and Police Discrimination," *St. John's Law Review* 72, no. 3–4 (1998): 1282.
34. See, e.g., *The Colonial Laws of Massachusetts: Reprinted from the Edition of 1672, with Supplements through 1686* (Boston: Rockwell and Churchill, 1887), 198; Statute of Winchester, 1285, 13 Edw. 1, stat. 2, c. 4 (discussed in Model Code of Pre-Arraignment Procedure at 82 (Preliminary Draft No. 1, 1965). See also "Use of Vagrancy-Type Laws for Arrest and Detention of Suspicious Persons," *Yale Law Journal* 59, no. 7 (1950): 1359. Remington noted that a number of jurisdictions had rejected such police authority as well. Remington, "Law Relating to 'On the Street' Detention," 391 nn. 30–32 (collecting cases); Uniform Arrest Act § 2, in Interstate Commission on Crime, *The Handbook on Interstate Crime Control* (n.p., 1942), 87; John B. Warner, "The Uniform Arrest Act," *Virginia Law Review* 28, no. 3 (1942): 315. For examples of state laws passed in response to the Uniform Arrest act, see Del. Code. Ann. Tit. 11, § 1902 (1953); 1941 N.H. Laws 242 (c. 163); 1941 R.I. Acts & Resolves 22 (c. 982). See also Packer, *Limits of the Criminal Sanction*, 182; Brief for the American Civil Liberties Union, American Civil Liberties Union of Ohio, and New York Civil Liberties Union as Amici Curiae at 8, Terry v. Ohio, 392 U.S. 1 (1968) (No. 67) (hereafter Brief for ACLU as Amici Curiae).
35. "Use of Vagrancy-Type Laws," 1359–62. On the superiority of stop and frisk, see Herman Goldstein, "Police Discretion: The Ideal versus the Real," *Public Administration Review* 23, no. 3 (1963): 144; M. Glenn Abernathy, "Police Discretion and Equal Protection," *South Carolina Law Quarterly* 14, no. 4 (1962): 472; Sanford H. Kadish, "Legal Norm and Discretion in the Police and Sentencing Processes," *Harvard Law Review* 75, no. 5 (1962): 915; Remington, "Law Relating to 'On the Street' Detention," 386–87. Cf. George McClure, "Vagrants, Criminals and the Constitution," *Denver Law Center Journal* 40, no. 6 (1963): 340; Hall, "Police and Law," 159.
36. Foote, "Law and Police Practice," 43.
37. Packer, *Limits of the Criminal Sanction*; Herbert L. Packer, "Two Models of the Criminal Process," *University of Pennsylvania Law Review* 113, no. 1 (1964): 1. For an example of a

real-life debate between the two views on stop and frisk see "Police Detention and Arrest Privileges: An International Symposium," *Journal of Criminal Law, Criminology, and Police Science* 51, no. 4 (1960): 385.

38. On civil disturbances see Michael W. Flamm and David Steigerwald, *Debating the 1960s: Liberal, Conservative, and Radical Perspectives* (Lanham, MD: Rowman and Littlefield, 2008), 27–28; Harvard Sitkoff, *The Struggle for Black Equality: 1954–1992* (New York: Hill and Wang, 1993), 195. On the language of "revolt, rebellion, uprising, riot," see Thomas Sugrue, *Sweet Land of Liberty: The Forgotten Struggle for Civil Rights in the North* (New York: Random House, 2008), 334; see also Richard Newman, "Black Power, Black Nationalism, Black Rebellion," in *Black Power and Black Religion: Essays and Reviews* (West Cornwall, CT: Locust Hill Press, 1987), 25–32; Flamm, *Law and Order*, 4, 78; Seymour Martin Lipset, "Why Cops Hate Liberals—and Vice Versa," *Atlantic*, March 1969, 80; "Hoover Speaks Out against Summer Riots," *Chicago Tribune*, June 1, 1967, E2; Jerry E. Bishop, "Police vs. Riots: How Forceful Should They Be in Putting Down Disorders?" *Wall Street Journal*, July 28, 1964, 12.

39. G. Edward White, *Earl Warren: A Public Life* (New York: Oxford University Press, 1982), 252–78. See also Bernard Schwartz, *Super Chief: Earl Warren and His Supreme Court, a Judicial Biography* (New York: New York University Press, 1984). For key cases, see Miranda, 384 U.S. 436 (1966); Gideon v. Wainwright, 372 U.S. 335 (1963); Mapp v. Ohio, 367 U.S. 643 (1961). See Corinna Barrett Lain, "Countermajoritarian Hero or Zero? Rethinking the Warren Court's Role in the Criminal Procedure Revolution," *University of Pennsylvania Law Review* 152, no. 4 (2004): 1361–452.

40. People v. Cahan, 282 P.2d 905 (Cal. 1955); Mapp, 367 U.S. 643 (1961); Wong Sun v. United States, 371 U.S. 471 (1963); "The 'No-Knock' and 'Stop and Frisk' Provisions of the New York Code of Criminal Procedure," *St John's Law Review* 38, no. 2 (1964): 400; "Buckley Praises Police of Selma," *New York Times*, April 5, 1965, 35; Lipset, "Why Cops Hate Liberals," 80; O. W. Wilson, "Police Authority in a Free Society," *Journal of Criminal Law and Criminology* 54, no. 2 (1963): 176–77; see generally Bradley C. Canon, "Testing the Effectiveness of Civil Liberties Policies at the State and Federal Levels: The Case for the Exclusionary Rule," *American Politics Quarterly* 5, no. 1 (1977): 57; Dallin H. Oaks, "Studying the Exclusionary Rule in Search and Seizure," *University of Chicago Law Review* 37, no. 4 (1970): 665. See LaFave, *Arrest*, 342–43; Loren G. Stern, "Stop and Frisk: An Historical Answer to a Modern Problem," *Journal of Criminal Law, Criminology, and Political Science* 58, no. 4 (1967): 533; Brief for American Civil Liberties Union of Ohio as Amicus Curiae Supporting Petition for Writ of Certiorari at 2, Terry v. Ohio, 392 U.S. 1 (1968) (No. 67) (hereafter Brief for ACLU Supporting Certiorari); Anders Walker, " 'To Corral and Control the Ghetto': Stop, Frisk, and the Geography of Freedom," *University of Richmond Law Review* 48, no. 4 (2014): 1223.

41. O. W. Wilson, "Police Arrest Privileges in a Free Society: A Plea for Modernization," *Journal of Criminal Law and Criminology* 51, no. 4 (1960): 400; Wilson, "Police Authority in a Free Society," 175; Brief for ACLU Supporting Certiorari at 10–11, Terry; see also Johnson, *American Law Enforcement*, 118–19.

42. Herbert L. Packer, "The Model Penal Code and Beyond," *Columbia Law Review* 63, no. 4 (1963): 594; Herbert Wechsler, "Symposium on the Model Penal Code: Foreword," *Columbia Law Review* 63, no. 4 (1963): 590; Model Penal Code at 3 (Council Draft No. 29, 1961) (memorandum to the council); see also Model Penal Code at xii (Tentative Draft No. 13, 1961), American Law Institute, *38th Annual Meeting: Proceedings, 1961* (Philadelphia: American Law Institute, 1961), 252–53; American Law Institute, *98th Annual Meeting: Proceedings, 1962* (Philadelphia: American Law Institute, 1962), 211–12. See generally Paul H. Robinson and Markus D. Dubber, "The American Model Penal Code: A Brief Overview," *New Criminal Law Review* 10, no. 3 (2007): 324–25. In worrying about the practical and political ramifications of eliminating the suspicious loitering provision altogether, the ALI treated it as it did a few other select provisions, like the penalties for attempt of serious crimes and the death penalty. In each case, when the Institute decided to retain the provision, it did so because it worried that if it omitted it altogether knowing that states wanted such provisions, it would be leaving them without any guidance at all on these key, and controversial, issues. See Model Penal Code at 114, 122–23 (Council Draft No. 29, 1961); see also Model Penal Code at 60 (Tentative Draft No. 13, 1961).

43. Model Code of Pre-Arraignment Procedure at 4 (Reporters' Memorandum on the November Meeting of the Advisory Committee, 1965); Model Code of Pre-Arraignment Procedure at 86–87 (Preliminary Draft No. 1, 1965). See also Model Code of Pre-Arraignment Procedure at vii–viii (Council Draft No. 1, 1965).

44. A. Fairfield Dana, ed., *New York State Legislative Annual, 1964* (New York: New York Legislative Services, 1964), 64, 67. On the New York law as pioneering, see Wayne R. LaFave, "'Street Encounters' and the Constitution: *Terry, Sibron, Peters*, and Beyond," *Michigan Law Review* 67, no. 1 (1968): 44. Although a Rhode Island law based on the Uniform Arrest Act had been passed in 1956, New York saw itself, and was seen by others, as an innovator. "Criminal Law— New York Authorizes Police to 'Stop-and-Frisk' on Reasonable Suspicion—N.Y. Sess. Laws 1964, ch. 86, § 2, N.Y. code crim. proc. § 180(a)," *Harvard Law Review* 78, no. 2 (1964): 473. On the New York doctrine, compare People v. Weinstein, 184 N.E.2d 312 (N.Y. 1962), *cert. denied*, 373 U.S. 904, with People v. Davis, 191 N.E.2d 674 (N.Y. 1963); People v. Robinson, 196 N.E.2d 261 (N.Y. 1963). On politics, see Combined Council of Law Enforcement Officials, *Let Your Police Police!* (1963), 4, cited in "'No-Knock' and 'Stop and Frisk'," 400; see also Anthony Lewis, "Bench v. Stop-and-Frisk: High Court Decisions Cast Doubt on Constitutionality of State Crime Laws," *New York Times*, March 9, 1964, 24 (discussing the connection between *Mapp* and the law); Richard H. Kuh, "Reflections on New York's 'Stop and Frisk' Law and Its Claimed Unconstitutionality," *Journal of Criminal Law and Criminology* 56, no. 1 (1965): 37–38. On comparing stop and frisk to pretextual arrests, see, e.g., Emanuel Perlmutter, "New 'Frisk' Law Goes into Effect: Police Are Dubious about Curbs That Go with It," *New York Times*, July 2, 1964, 52 (Statement of New York City Police Commissioner, Michael J. Murphy).

45. Douglas Dales, "Rockefeller Signs Bills Increasing Powers of Police: Bar and Civil Rights Groups Call 'Stop-and-Frisk' and 'No-Knock' Laws Illegal: Harassment is Feared: But Governor Says Judicial Safeguards Are Provided—Calls Bill Imperative," *New York Times*, March 4, 1964, 1, 41. Groups formed to oppose the bill included the Emergency Committee for Public Safety, lawyers and businessmen who offered free legal services to victims of the new law; the Ad Hoc Committee for Fair Police Practice, affiliated with the NAACP and CORE; and the Committee on Police Community Relations, made up of clergymen and civic leaders in East Harlem. See also "NAACP Opposes Stop-and-Frisk Law: Contends Minority Groups Suffer," *Chicago Daily Defender*, November 22, 1967, 30. See generally Walker, "'To Corral and Control," 1248–49; Sugrue, *Sweet Land of Liberty*, 406.

46. "Limitations Noted in New 'Frisk' Law," *New York Times*, April 25, 1964, 14; Perlmutter, "New 'Frisk' Law Goes into Effect," 52; "New Police Laws Scored at Rally: 'No-Knock' and Frisk Bills Called Unconstitutional," *New York Times*, March 8, 1964, 63 (quoting Paul Zuber).

47. Pamela A. Roby, "Politics and Criminal Law: Revision of the New York State Penal Law on Prostitution," *Social Problems* 17, no. 1 (1969): 83. Compare N.Y. Crim. Proc. § 887(1) (McKinney 1958) to N.Y. Penal § 240.35 (McKinney 1967). See generally Ruthan Robson, *Dressing Constitutionally: Hierarchy, Sexuality, and Democracy from Our Hairstyles to Our Shoes* (New York: Cambridge University Press, 2013); N.Y. Penal § 240.35 (McKinney 1967); N.Y. Penal § 240.35(6) (McKinney 1967).

48. Paul Chevigny, interview with author, December 2008.

49. Flamm, *Law and Order*. See generally LaFave, "'Street Encounters,'" 43–46. See "Stop-and-Frisk Statute Is Urged for Maryland," *Washington Post*, July 26, 1966, C5; John Elmer, "Stop-Frisk Passed and Sent to Governor," *Chicago Tribune*, June 14, 1967, 1 (quoting Republican Representative Henry Hyde of Chicago); "Police Ask City for 'Frisk' Law," *New Orleans States-Item*, February 14, 1967, clipping, Wainright v. City of New Orleans, box 1814, Series 4, Subseries 4A, Princeton ACLU Papers; James H. Gillis, "Action on Stop and Search Postponed by City Council," *Times-Picayune* (New Orleans), February 24, 1967, 1, 7; "No More "Sun 'n Fun" as Miami Makes War on "Negro" Crime Wave," *Philadelphia Tribune*, December 30, 1967, 2.

50. Fred P. Graham, "Court to Review State 'Frisk' Law: Heroin Peddler Searched on Street Is Given Hearing," *New York Times*, March 14, 1967, 1; Sidney E. Zion, "Koota Concedes "Frisking" Error: Asks High Court to Reverse Conviction but Uphold Law," *New York Times*, December 2, 1967, 45 (quoting Aaron E. Koota). See Peters v. New York, 392 U.S. 40, 48–49 (1968).

51. Lewis Wm. Coffey, Chief of Police, to Mr. Quinn Tamm, Executive Director, July 9, 1970, Martin McFadden Papers, Western Reserve Historical Society, Cleveland, OH (hereafter Martin McFadden Papers); Louis Stokes, "Representing John W. Terry," *St. John's Law Review* 72, no. 3–4 (1998): 729; Reuben M. Payne, "The Prosecutor's Perspective on *Terry*: Detective McFadden Had a Right to Protect Himself," *St. John's Law Review* 72, no. 3–4 (1998): 733; Terry v. Ohio, 392 U.S. 1, 5–6 (1968).

52. "Model Crime Laws Are Sent Thruout U.S.: Ask Eavesdropping, Frisk Powers," *Chicago Tribune*, February 3, 1969, A3; see also Thomas Buck, "Bids to Upset Kerner's Veto on Police Bill," *Chicago Tribune*, August 5, 1967, 4; "NAACP Opposes Stop-and-Frisk Law," 30; Brief for Nat'l District Attorneys' Assn. at 16, Terry; RCF (Raymond C. Fisher, clerk) to Justice William Brennan, memorandum, n.d., Terry v. Ohio (No. 67), box I-168, William J. Brennan Papers, Library of Congress (hereafter Brennan Papers).

53. Brief for ACLU as Amici Curiae at 3, Terry.

54. Brief for the N.A.A.C.P. Legal Defense and Educational Fund, Inc., as Amicus Curiae at 24 n. 45, Sibron v. New York, 392 U.S. 40 (1968) (No. 63) ("Brief for LDF as Amicus Curiae") (quoting Cox v. Louisiana, 379 U.S. 536, 579 (1965) (Black, J., concurring in part and dissenting in part)); ibid. at 14, 14 n. 21 (citing Olmstead v. United States, 277 U.S. 438, 478–79 (1928) (Brandeis, J., dissenting) and Griswold v. Connecticut, 381 U.S. 479 (1965).

55. Brief for LDF as Amicus Curiae at 6 n. 7, Sibron; Thomas F. Adams, "Field Interrogation," *Police* 7 (1963): 28, quoted in ibid. 45–47; see also Geoffrey C. Hazard Jr., "Book Review," *University of Chicago Law Review* 34, no. 1 (1966): 228–29, quoted in ibid. at 43 n.74; Anthony Amsterdam, telephone interview with author, April 2009.

56. Brief for Petitioner at 31, Terry v. Ohio, 392 U.S. 1 (1968) (No. 67); Brief for Respondent on Writ of Certiorari to the Supreme Court of Ohio at 3, Terry v. Ohio, 392 U.S. 1 (1968) (No. 67); President's Commission on Law Enforcement and Administration of Justice, *Task Force Report: The Police* (Washington, DC: Government Printing Office, 1967), quoted in Brief for LDF as Amicus Curiae at 2 n. 2, Sibron; Brief for ACLU as Amici Curiae, Terry. The ACLU brief also highlighted that Terry and Chilton were African American. Brief for ACLU as Amici Curiae at 4, Terry.

57. Barrett, "Deciding the Stop and Frisk Cases," 776–77 (quoting Fortas conference notes); Justice William O. Douglas, handwritten conference notes, October 13, 1967, Wainwright v. City of New Orleans (no. 13), box 1413, William O. Douglas Papers, Library of Congress (hereafter Douglas Papers).

58. Wainwright, 392 U.S. at 610 (1968) (Douglas, J. dissenting); Barrett, "Deciding the Stop and Frisk Cases," 778, 780–81; Stephen Wainwright, telephone interview with author, January 2013. See Justice William O. Douglas, draft dissent, Wainwright v. City of New Orleans, recirculated December 13, 1967, Wainwright v. City of New Orleans, box 298, John Marshall Harlan Papers, Series 3, Department of Rare Books and Special Collections, Princeton University Library (hereafter Harlan Papers Princeton); Justice William O. Douglas to John Davis (clerk), memorandum, October 20, 1967, Wainwright v. City of New Orleans (no. 13), box 1413, Douglas Papers; Justice Harlan, draft concurrence, circulated October 24, 1967, Wainwright v. City of New Orleans, box 298, Harlan Papers Princeton; see also Per Curiam order, circulated October 24, 1967, Wainwright v. City of New Orleans (no. 13), folder 1161, box 55, Abe Fortas Papers (MS 858), Manuscripts and Archives, Yale University Library (hereafter Abe Fortas Papers).

59. Barrett, "Deciding the Stop and Frisk Cases," 780–81, 792.

60. Justice William Brennan to Chief Justice Earl Warren, memorandum, January 30, 1968, Terry v. Ohio (No. 67), box 624, Earl Warren Papers, 1864–1974, Library of Congress (hereafter Earl Warren Papers); see also Barrett, "Deciding the Stop and Frisk Cases," 796 n. 280 (quoting Justice William J. Brennan Jr. to Chief Justice Earl Warren, January 30, 1968) (available in Warren Papers, Manuscript Division, Library of Congress). Justice William Brennan to Chief Justice Earl Warren, memorandum ("Stop and Frisk" Cases), March 14, 1968, Terry v. Ohio, box 624, Earl Warren Papers.

61. Justice William O. Douglas, handwritten notes of the Conference, December 13, 1967, Terry v. Ohio, box 1416, Douglas Papers.

62. Chief Justice Earl Warren, Majority draft opinion, circulated February 9, 1968, Terry v. Ohio, box 624, Earl Warren Papers; Barrett, "Deciding the Stop and Frisk Cases," 800–21.

63. Justice William Brennan to Chief Justice Earl Warren, memorandum ("Stop and Frisk" Cases), March 14, 1968, Terry v. Ohio, box 624, Earl Warren Papers; see also Model Code of Pre-Arraignment Procedure at 86–87 (Preliminary Draft No. 1 1965).

64. Justice William Brennan to Chief Justice Earl Warren, memorandum ("Stop and Frisk" Cases), March 14, 1968, Terry v. Ohio, box 624, Earl Warren Papers.

65. Terry v. Ohio, 392 U.S. 1, 8–9, 12, 14–15, 15 (1968); Lawrence P. Tiffany, Donald M. McIntyre, and Daniel L. Rotenberg, *Detection of Crime: Stopping and Questioning, Search and Seizure, Encouragement and Entrapment* (Boston: Little, Brown, 1967), 47–48, quoted in ibid. at 14–15 n. 11.

66. Douglas was so committed to finding probable cause somewhere in *Terry*, that he suggested that McFadden might have had probable cause to arrest Terry for loitering. Terry v. Ohio, 392 U.S. 1, 35–39 (1968) (Douglas, J. dissenting).

67. Justice Abe Fortas to Chief Justice Earl Warren, handwritten letter, n.d., Earl Warren Papers, quoted in Barrett, "Deciding the Stop and Frisk Cases," 828 n. 467; H. David Rosenbloom, note, n.d., Abe Fortas Papers, quoted in ibid. at 832 n. 486; Earl C. Dudley (clerk) to Chief Justice Earl Warren, memorandum, March 12, 1968, Stop and Frisk cases and Wainwright v. New Orleans, referenced in ibid. at 819 n. 431; Carl J. Kim Seneker II (clerk) to Justice William O. Douglas, June 1, 1968, Douglas Papers, quoted in ibid. at 831 n. 480; RCF (Raymond C. Fisher, clerk) to Justice William Brennan, memorandum, n.d., Terry v. Ohio (No. 67), box I-168, Brennan Papers.

68. MacKenzie, "Court Studies Police Powers," G5; Oral Argument, Wainwright v. City of New Orleans, 392 U.S. 598 (1968), Oyez Project; see also Brief for Petitioner at 11 n. 8, Wainwright; Earl C. Dudley (clerk) to Chief Justice Earl Warren, memorandum, March 12, 1968, Stop and Frisk cases, and Wainwright v. New Orleans, referenced in Barrett, "Deciding the Stop and Frisk Cases," 819 n. 431.

69. Wainwright, 392 U.S. at 604 n. 2, 606–7, 607 n. 8 (1968) (Warren, C. J., dissenting).

70. Justice William O. Douglas, draft dissent, Wainwright v. City of New Orleans, recirculated December 13, 1967, Wainwright v. City of New Orleans, box 298, Series 3, Harlan Papers Princeton; Fay Aull (secretary) to Chief Justice Earl Warren, June 12, 1968, Wainwright v. City of New Orleans, box 650, Earl Warren Papers; Justice William O. Douglas, draft dissent, Wainwright v. City of New Orleans, recirculated June 12, 1968, Wainwright v. City of New Orleans, box 298, Series 3, Harlan Papers Princeton; Wainwright, 392 U.S. at 613 (1968) (Douglas, J., dissenting).

71. Wainwright, 392 U.S. at 614 (1968) (Douglas, J., dissenting).

72. Charles A. Reich, "Police Questioning of Law Abiding Citizens," *Yale Law Journal* 75, no. 7 (1966): 1161. See also Brief for ACLU as Amici Curiae at 15 n. 13, Terry. The ACLU *Terry* brief also cited Brandeis's "right to be let alone" in *Olmstead*. Ibid. at 19.

73. Johnson v. Florida, 391 U.S. 596, 615 (1968) (Douglas, J., dissenting).

74. *Wesleyan Class of 1961 Reunion Book*, 116 (copy of article on file with author).

75. Fay Aull (secretary) to Justice William Brennan, memorandum, June 7, 1968, Wainwright v. City of New Orleans, box 1413, Douglas Papers. For police views of *Terry*, see John P. MacKenzie, "Court Upholds Stop and Frisk, Education Suits: Police May Act if They See Risks of Harm," *Washington Post*, June 11, 1968, A1, A11; Frank Corrigan, police lieutenant, to Robert Gallagher, police captain, memorandum, June 22, 1970, Martin McFadden Papers. For public views of *Terry*, see John H. Averill, "High Court Approves Parts of Police 'Stop-and-Frisk' Tactic," *Los Angeles Times*, June 11, 1968, 1; Graham, "High Court Backs Rights," 1. See also "Stop Frisk Ruling," *Chicago Daily Defender*, June 22, 1968, 9; "A Victory for Law Enforcement," *Chicago Tribune*, June 11, 1968, 16; "Guest Editorial (from Cleveland *Call-Post*)," *Chicago Daily Defender*, June 26, 1968, 13; see also "Supreme Court Will Examine Stop-Frisk Law," *Chicago Daily Defender*, March 14, 1967, 8; but see Eric Miller, "The Warren Court's Regulatory Revolution in Criminal Procedure," *Connecticut Law Review* 43, no. 1 (2010): 1–82.

76. Johnson, 391 U.S. 596, 596–97 (1968).

77. Fla. Stat. Ann. § 856.02 (West 1965).

78. ECD (Earl Clark Dudley, clerk), memorandum, n.d., Johnson v. Florida, box 1427, Douglas Papers; WAR (William A. Reppy Jr.), memorandum, May 14, 1968, Johnson v. Florida, box 1427, Douglas Papers; WAR (William A. Reppy Jr.), memorandum, May 14, 1968, Johnson v. Florida, box 1427, Douglas Papers; see also CEL (Charles E. Lister), notations (n.d.) on ECD (Earl Clark Dudley), memorandum, n.d., Johnson v. Florida (No. 1393 Misc.), box 320, Harlan Papers Princeton.

79. ECD (Earl Clark Dudley, clerk), memorandum, n.d., Johnson v. Florida, box 1427, Douglas Papers.

80. Miscellaneous Docket Sheet, n.d., Johnson v. Florida (no. 1393), box 1393, Douglas Papers; Johnson, 391 U.S. at 598.

81. Conference Notes, January 17, 1964, Arceneaux v. Louisiana, box 1319, Douglas Papers; see also John Marshall Harlan II, Draft of Dissent, circulated November 10, 1965, Hicks v. District of Columbia, box 530, Earl Warren Papers. On Justice White, see Dennis J. Hutchinson, *The Man Who Once Was Whizzer White* (New York: Free Press, 1998); Bernard W. Bell, "Byron R. White, Kennedy Justice," review of *The Man Who Once Was Whizzer White*, by Dennis J. Hutchinson, *Stanford Law Review* 51, no. 5 (1999): 1410, 1417; William E. Nelson, "Justice Byron R. White: A Modern Federalist and a New Deal Liberal," *Brigham Young University Law Review*, no. 2 (1994): 333; Johnson 391 U.S. at 599 (1968) (White, J., dissenting).

82. Nan Robertson, "Johnson Leads U.S. in Mourning: 4000 Attend Service at Cathedral in Washington," *New York Times*, April 6, 1968, 25; Ben A. Franklin, "Army Troops in Capital as Negroes Riot; Guard Sent into Chicago, Detroit, Boston; Johnson Asks a Joint Session of Congress," *New York Times*, April 6, 1968, 1; Barrye L. Price, "The Role of Federal Troops in Quelling Civil Disturbances in Washington, D.C., April 1968" (master's thesis, Texas A&M, 1994), http://www.dtic.mil/dtic/tr/fulltext/u2/a270505.pdf; see generally Walter C. Rucker and James N. Upton, eds., *The Encyclopedia of American Race Riots* (Westport, CT: Greenwood Press, 2007), 2: 683.

83. Federal Bureau of Investigation, *Uniform Crime Reporting Statistics*, accessed October 22, 2014, http://www.bjs.gov/ucrdata/Search/Crime/State/RunCrimeTrendsInOneVar.cfm. Lucas A. Powe, Jr., *The Warren Court and American Politics* (Cambridge, MA: Belknap Press of Harvard University Press, 2000), 410. See also Flamm, *Law and Order*, 133–35,164; Richard Harris, *The Fear of Crime* (New York: Frederick A. Praeger, 1969), 72, 98.

84. President's Commission on Law Enforcement and the Administration of Justice, *Task Force Report: Drunkenness* (Washington, DC: Government Printing Office, 1967), 1; William Blackstone, *Commentaries on the Laws of England* (Oxford: Clarendon Press, 1769), 4: 41–42, 65; Motion for Leave to File Brief and Brief for American Civil Liberties Union et al. as Amici Curiae at 2, 32–35, Powell v. Texas, 392 U.S. 514 (1968) (No. 405). For successful public drunkenness cases, see Driver v. Hinnant, 356 F.2d 761 (4th Cir. 1966); Easter v. District of Columbia, 209 A.2d 625 (D.C. 1965), rev'd, 361 F.2d 50 (D.C. Cir. 1966). But see Seattle v. Hill, 435 P.2d 692 (Wash. 1967) (en banc) and People v. Hoy, 158 N.W.2d 436 (Mich. 1968). See generally Richard A. Merrill, "Drunkenness and the Reform of the Criminal Law," *Virginia Law Review* 54, no. 6 (1968): 1135; Charles E. Moylan, "Temple Bar to Megalopolis: The Criminal Law in Transition," *American Criminal Law Quarterly* 7, no. 1 (1968): 38. David E. Aaronson, C. Thomas Dienes, and Michael C. Musheno, *Public Policy and Police Discretion: Processes of Decriminalization* (New York: Clark Boardman, 1984), 182–83.

85. Powell v. Texas. 392 U.S. 514, 532 (1968) (White, J., concurring in the result). Powell also did not end the reform movement. See Aaronson, Dienes, and Musheno, *Public Policy and Police Discretion*, 187. By 1976, twenty-four states had enacted the Uniform Alcoholism Intoxication Treatment Act and even more had decriminalized public drunkenness. Ibid. at 187–88.

86. Powell v. Texas. 392 U.S. 514, 530–31 (1968). The main exceptions to the procedural nature of the cases were Robinson v. California, 370 U.S. 660 (1962); Lambert v. California, 355 U.S. 255 (1957); and Lanzetta v. New Jersey, 306 U.S. 451 (1939). See generally William J. Stuntz, *The Collapse of American Criminal Justice* (Cambridge, MA: Harvard University Press, 2011), 216–43; Powell, 392 U.S. 514. See also infra at Chapter 9, text accompanying n. 86.

87. "Supreme Court Begins New Term," 1963; Averill, "High Court Approves Parts of Police," 1.

88. But see Stephen M. Raphael, "Stop and Frisk" in a Nutshell: Some Last Editorial Thrusts and Parries before It All Becomes History," *Alabama Law Review* 20, no. 2 (1968): 297 (discussing Wainwright along with stop and frisk cases).

89. For the conventional wisdom, see William J. Stuntz, "Local Policing after the Terror," *Yale Law Journal* 111, no. 8 (2002): 2152 n. 42; "Orders to Move On and the Prevention of Crime," *Yale Law Journal* 87, no. 3 (1978): 603–4. For recognition of the role of *Mapp* and other cases, see, e.g., David A. Harris, "Particularized Suspicion, Categorical Judgments: Supreme Court Rhetoric versus Lower Court Reality under *Terry v. Ohio,*" *St. John's Law Review* 72, no. 3 (1998): 977–81.

90. The Court also left the New York stop and frisk law intact by avoiding the issue in two *Terry* companion cases. See Peters v. New York, 392 U.S. 40 (1968).

Chapter 7

1. Wainwright v. City of New Orleans, 392 U.S. 598 (1968); Johnson v. Florida, 391 U.S. 596 (1968); Hicks v. District of Columbia, 383 U.S. 252 (1966).

2. Plaintiff's Brief on Unconstitutionality of North Carolina Vagrancy Statute and on Expunction of Arrest and Other Records Pertaining to Plaintiffs (hereafter Plaintiff's Brief on Unconstitutionality) at 51–54, 78; Wheeler v. Goodman, 306 F.Supp. 58 (W.D. N.C. 1969) (No. Civ. 2431), box 1831, American Civil Liberties Union Records, Series 4, Subseries 4A, Department of Rare Books and Special Collections, Princeton University Library (hereafter Princeton ACLU Papers). See also Memorandum in Support of Motion for Permanent Injunction and Declaratory Judgment (hereafter Memorandum on Permanent Injunction) at 7, Goldman v. Knecht, 295 F.Supp. 897 (D. Colo. 1969) (No. C-974), box 1404, American Civil Liberties Union Records, Series 4, Subseries 4A, Princeton ACLU Papers.

3. "Vagrancy," *Washington Post,* June 17, 1963, A14.

4. "ACLU Wins Review for Eddie Hicks, Dupont Circle's Wandering Guitarist," *Washington Post,* February 2, 1965, A4; "Court Hears Troubadours 'Ballad,'" *Washington Post,* October 22, 1965, B3; Sterling Seagrave, "Guitarist Conviction Stirs Protest," *Washington Post,* June 14, 1963, B1; John D. Pomfret, "Vagrancy Issue," *New York Times,* February 7, 1965, E7.

5. Michael Dolan, "A Short History of a Very Round Place," *Washington Post Magazine,* September 2, 1990, W19.

6. Sterling Seagrave, "Bohemian Protest Ends in Bourgeois Sing-Along," *Washington Post,* June 17, 1963, B1; Arthur E. Neuman, e-mail message to author, May 23, 2008. Police also said they had had few complaints. Seagrave, "Guitarist Conviction Stirs Protest," B1.

7. Charles Wolfram, telephone interview with author, August 29, 2012; D.C. Code § 22–3302(3) (1961); "DuPont Guitarist Gets a Job," *Washington Post,* June 15, 1963, D3; "ACLU Wins Review for Eddie Hicks," A4; see James Forman, *Locking Up Our Own* (New York: Farrar, Straus, and Giroux: forthcoming).

8. "Vagrancy," A14.

9. "ACLU Wins Review for Eddie Hicks," A4; Samuel Walker, *In Defense of American Liberties: A History of the ACLU* (Carbondale: Southern Illinois University Press, 1990), 233. See Chapter 5, this volume, on DC vagrancy law.

10. David Carliner, "Lawyer and Immigration Advocate Is Dead at 89," *New York Times,* September 22, 2007; David Carliner to Melvin L. Wulf, February 8, 1965, box 1433, American Civil Liberties Union Records, Series 4, Subseries 4A, Princeton ACLU Papers; Charles Wolfram, telephone interview with author, August 29, 2012.

11. Charles W. Wolfram to Lawrence Speiser, October 22, 1963, box 1216, American Civil Liberties Union Records, Series 4, Subseries 4A, Princeton ACLU Papers; Charles Wolfram, e-mail message to author, October 8, 2012.

12. Brief for Petitioner at 21, Hicks v. D.C., 383 U.S. 252 (1966) (No. 51–496); Oral Argument, Hicks v. D.C., 383 U.S. 252 (1966) (No. 51), The Oyez Project, at IIT Chicago-Kent College of Law, http://www.oyez.org/cases/1960-1969/1965/1965_51 (hereafter Oyez Project). See also "Arguments before the Court: Vagrancy Statutes," *U.S. Law Week* 34, no. 15 (October 26, 1965): 3137.

13. David Carliner to Melvin L. Wulf, February 8, 1965, box 1433, American Civil Liberties Union Records, Series 4, Subseries 4A, Princeton ACLU Papers; Melvin Wulf to David Carliner, February 16, 1965, box 1433, American Civil Liberties Union Records, Series 4, Subseries 4A, Princeton ACLU Papers; see also Brief for Petitioner, Hicks v. D.C., 383 U.S. 252 (1966) (No. 51–496); Draft Brief for Petitioner, Hicks v. D.C., n.d., box 1433, American Civil Liberties Union Records, Series 4, Subseries 4A, Princeton ACLU Papers; Charles Wolfram to Larry, August 2, 1965, box 1433, American Civil Liberties Union Records, Series 4, Subseries 4A, Princeton ACLU Papers.

14. "Arguments before the Court," 3137–39. On nonjurisdictional tardiness, see *Supreme Court Practice* 6.1(a), (d), & (e); Bowles v. Russell, 551 U.S, 205, 211–12 (2007).

15. "Arguments before the Court," 3139.

16. Oral Argument, Hicks v. D.C., 383 U.S. 252 (1966) (No. 51), Oyez Project ; Hicks v. D.C., 383 US 252, 252 (1966) (Harlan, J., concurring); William O. Douglas, conference notes, Hicks v. D.C., 383 U.S. 242 (1966), October 22, 1965, box 1365, William O. Douglas Papers, Library of Congress (hereafter Douglas Papers). See also John Marshall Harlan, memorandum to the Court, November 5, 1965, box 1365, Douglas Papers; William O. Douglas, conference notes, January 17, 1964, Arceneaux v. Louisiana (No. 76), box 1319, Douglas Papers; John Marshall Harlan, draft dissent at 1, November 10, 1965, Hicks v. District of Columbia (No. 51), box 530, Earl Warren Papers, 1864–1974, Library of Congress.

17. Caleb Foote, "Vagrancy-Type Law and Its Administration," *University of Pennsylvania Law Review* 104, no. 5 (1956): 603; see also "Supreme Court Dismisses Minstrels Vagrancy Case," *Washington Post*, March 1, 1966, B1; William O. Douglas, conference notes, October 22, 1965, Hicks v. D.C., (No. 51), box 1365, Douglas Papers; Abraham Fortas, draft concurrence at 3, December 6, 1965, Hicks v. D.C. (No. 51), box 1365, Douglas Papers.

18. William O. Douglas, conference notes, Hicks v. D.C., (No. 51), October 22, 1965, box 1365, Douglas Papers (with deciphering help from George Rutherglen); Hugo Black, draft opinion at 8, November 4, 1965, Hicks v. D.C. (No. 51), box 389, Hugo LaFayette Black Papers, Library of Congress (hereafter Black Papers). Several of the clerks also favored invalidation. See Cert. Pool Memorandum, January 27, 1965, Hicks v. D.C. (No. 51), box 1365, Douglas Papers; Michael M. Maney, cert. memorandum, January 27, 1965, Hicks v. D.C. (No. 51), box 250, John Marshall Harlan Papers, Public Policy Papers, Princeton ACLU Papers.

19. Griswold v. Connecticut, 381 U.S. 479 (1965); West Coast Hotel v. Parrish, 300 U.S. 379 (1937); Hugo Black, draft opinion at 8, November 4, 1965, Hicks v. D.C. (No. 51), box 389, Black Papers.

20. William O. Douglas to Hugo Black, memorandum, November 16, 1965, Hicks v. D.C. (No. 51), box 1365, Douglas Papers; Hicks v. D.C., 383 U.S. 252, 257–58 (1966) (Douglas, J., dissenting) (footnotes and internal citations omitted).

21. Hugo LaFayette Black, memorandum for the conference, December 8, 1965, Hicks v. D.C. (no. 51), box 389, Black Papers; William O. Douglas to Hugo Black, memorandum, December 8, 1965, Hicks v. D.C. (No. 51), box 389, Black Papers.

22. William O. Douglas, *America Challenged* (Princeton, NJ: Princeton University Press, 1960), 5; William O. Douglas, "Vagrancy and Arrest on Suspicion," *Yale Law Journal* 70, no. 1 (1960): 2–3; see also William O. Douglas, "The Bill of Rights Is Not Enough," *New York University Law Review* 38, no. 2 (1963): 216.

23. Foote, "Vagrancy-Type Law and Its Administraiton," 617, quoted in William O. Douglas, draft concurring opinion at 2, November 18, 1965, Hicks v. D.C. (No. 51), box 1365, Douglas Papers; Hicks, 383 U.S. at 256 (Douglas, J., dissenting) (quoting Foote, "Vagrancy-Type Law and Its Administration," 603, 617).

24. Indeed, Douglas was one of only two Supreme Court justices to use the phrase that way, and the only one to imply, in more than one case, that he identified with those critical of it. Powell v. McCormack, 395 U.S. 486, 553 (1969) (Douglas, J., concurring) ("Today we proclaim the constitutional principle of 'one man, one vote.' When that principle is followed and the electors choose a person who is repulsive to the Establishment in Congress, by what constitutional authority can that group of electors be disenfranchised?"); Southeastern Promotions, Ltd. v. Conrad, 420 U.S. 546, 564 (1975) (Douglas, J., dissenting) ("There was much testimony in the District Court concerning the pungent social and political commentary which the musical 'Hair' levels against various sacred cows of our society: the Vietnam war, the

draft, and the puritanical conventions of the Establishment"). Burger was the other justice, but his use does not have quite the same anti-establishment ring to it as Douglas's uses do. See First Nat. Bank of Boston v. Bellotti, 435 U.S. 765, 800–01 (1978) (Burger, C.J., concurring) ("Soon after the invention of the printing press, English and continental monarchs, fearful of the power implicit in its use and the threat to Establishment thought and order—political and religious—devised restraints, such as licensing, censors, indices of prohibited books, and prosecutions for seditious libel, which generally were unknown in the pre-printing press era."). See generally Bruce Allen Murphy, *Wild Bill: The Legend and Life of William O. Douglas* (New York: Random House, 2003), 374, 392–98; James Simon, *Independent Journey: The Life of William O. Douglas* (New York: Harper and Row, 1980), 372–75, 380–83.

25. ; William O. Douglas, *Points of Rebellion* (New York: Random House, 1970), 16; William O. Douglas, "The Appeal of Folk Singing: A Landmark Opinion," *Avant Garde*, March 1969; see generally David McBride, "On the Fault Line of Mass Culture and Counterculture: A Social History of the Hippie Counterculture in 1960s Los Angeles" (Ph.D. diss., University of California, Los Angeles, 1998), 35.

26. Charles W. Wolfram to Melvin L. Wulf, October 25, 1965, box 1433, American Civil Liberties Union Records, Series 4, Subseries 4A, Princeton ACLU Papers.

27. See, e.g., Richard Fairfield, *Communes USA: A Personal Tour* (New York: Penguin, 1972); McBride, "On the Fault Line of Mass Culture and Counterculture," 121.

28. McBride, "On the Fault Line of Mass Culture and Counterculture," 133, 159; Martin A. Lee and Bruce Shlain, *Acid Dreams: The Complete Social History of LSD, The CIA, the Sixties, and Beyond* (New York: Grove Press, 1985), 141–42.

29. See, e.g., Carl Bernstin, "Commune 'Works' Because We Have Love, Trust," *Charlotte Observer*, August 7, 1969, Charlotte Observer clipping files, hippies, North Carolina Room, Charlotte Mecklenberg Library (hereafter Black Papers); Naomi Myles, "Communal Life Gains Appeal," *Charlotte Observer*, August 12, 1969, Charlotte Observer Clipping Files; Nick Taylor, "Hip Attorney Helps Hippies," *Charlotte Observer*, April 1969, Charlotte Observer Clipping Files; "ACLU Attorney Is Ex-Beatnik," *Charlotte Observer*, n.d., Charlotte Observer Clipping Files.

30. Rob Elder, "Down on the Peacock Farm," *Salon Magazine*, November 16, 2001, http://www.salon.com/2001/11/16/kesey99/.

31. McBride, "On the Fault Line of Mass Culture and Counterculture." See, e.g., Steven W. Roberts, "Tate Case Focuses New Attention on Hippie World," *Charlotte Observer*, c. 1969, Charlotte Observer Clipping Files.

32. *The Los Angeles Newsletter*, November 26, 1966, 4, quoted in McBride, "On the Fault Line of Mass Culture and Counterculture," 223; ibid., 256; Dan Katz, "National Coincidence," *The (East Village) Other*, June 5, 1967, 4, Police File, Tomkins Square Folder, Paul Chevigny Papers, New York Civil Liberties Union Headquarters (hereafter Chevigny Papers) (made available to author); Herman Weinkrantz, "The Court's Opinion" (People v. Wise et al.), June 30, 1967, Chevigny Papers; Don McNeill, "The Youthquake and the Shook-Up Park," *Village Voice* (New York), June 8, 1967, 1, Chevigny Papers; Hughes v. Rizzo, 282 F. Supp 881, 884 (E.D. Pa. 1968); Jerry F. King, "The Hippie Problem: Limitations of Police Powers," *Municipal Attorney* 12, no. 1 (1971): 3–7.

33. Jerry Adams, "Hippie-House Bill Clears House Unit," *Charlotte Observer*, June 26, 1969, Charlotte Observer Clipping Files; Maureen Tkacik, "The Student Loan Crisis That Can't Be Gotten Rid Of," *Reuters*, August 15, 2012, http://www.reuters.com/article/2012/08/15/us-student-loan-crisis-idUSBRE87E13L20120815; U.S. Dept. of Agriculture v. Moreno, 413 U.S. 528, 534 (1973). H.R. Rep. No. 91–1793, at 8 (1970); 116 Cong. Rec. 44439 (1970) (statement of Sen. Holland); see also Belle Terre v. Boraas, 416 U.S. 1 (1974).

34. Cathy Cade, *My Family, the Movement and Me: How My Being in the Civil Rights Movement Affected My White Family* (2002), http://www.crmvet.org/nars/cadec.htm; "Arrest Two Whites in 'Mississippi Project,'" *Chicago Daily Defender*, June 25, 1964, A3; George Todd, "How It Is: In Jail, In Dixie!" *New York Amsterdam News*, July 13, 1963, 1; Gertrude Wilson, "White-on-White: Mississippi Justice," *New York Amsterdam News*, May 2, 1964, 1; see also "48 Jailed in Pine Bluff Sits-In," *The Student Voice*, April 1963, 3, in *The Student Voice 1960–1965: Periodical of the Student Nonviolent Coordinating Committee*, ed. Clayborne Carson (Westport, CT: Meckler, 1990), 67; Adams, "Hippie-House Bill Clears House Unit"; King,

"Hippie Problem," 3–7. See also Adam Fairclough, *Race and Democracy: The Civil Rights Struggle in Louisiana, 1915–1972* (Athens: University of Georgia Press, 2008), 313–14; Forrest A. Deseran and Chang-Soo Chung, "Appearance, Role-Taking, and Reactions to Deviance," *Social Psychology Quarterly* 42, no. 4 (1979): 426.

35. See, e.g., Roberts, "Tate Case Focuses New Attention on Hippie World"; "Hippies Find They Are Prime Suspects," *Charlotte Observer*, February 21, 1970, Charlotte Observer Clipping Files; Frazier v. Superior Court, 486 P.2d 694, 696 (Cal. 1971).

36. In re Sealy, 218 So.2d 765, 766, 768 (Fla. Dist. Ct. App. 1969); People v. McAndrew, 239 N.E.2d 314, 318 (Ill. App. Ct. 1968).

37. See John Kifner, "Colleges Step Up Changes in Bid to Avert Disruption," *New York Times*, May 11, 1969, 1. For cases, see Calbillo v. San Jacinto Junior College, 305 F. Supp. 858, 858 (S.D. Tex. 1969); Zachry v. Brown, 299 F. Supp. 1360, 1362 (N.D. Ala. 1967); Westley v. Rossi, 305 F. Supp. 706 (D. Minn. 1969); Breen v. Kahl, 296 F.Supp. 702 (W.D. Wisc. 1969); Griffin v. Tatum, 300 F. Supp. 60, 63 (M.D. Ala. 1969); Roberts v. Thurston, 424 F.2d 1281 (1st Cir. 1970); Meyers v. Arcata Union High School Dist., 269 Cal. App. 2d 549 (Ct. App., 1969). Boyce v. Safeway Stores, 351 F. Supp. 402 (D.D.C. 1972). See generally J. Harvie Wilkinson III and G. Edward White, "Constitutional Protection for Personal Lifestyles," *Cornell Law Review* 62, no. 3 (1976): 563–626.

38. "Food for Thought," *Georgia Straight*, June 28, 1967, 4; Michael E. Brown, "The Condemnation and Persecution of Hippies," *Trans-Action* 6 (1969): 33; "'Conchs' Uneasy with Long-Haired Clan in Key West," *Times Standard* (Eureka, CA), February 12, 1973, 3; see William McKeen, *Mile Marker Zero: The Moveable Feast of Key West* (New York: Crown, 2011), 131–35.

39. Robert Houriet, "Life and Death of a Commune Called Oz," *New York Times Magazine*, February 16, 1969, 30; Bradley Martin, "Hippie House Abandoned: 'Too Much of an Attraction,'" *Charlotte Observer*, May 22, 1969, Charlotte Observer Clipping Files.

40. McKeen, *Mile Marker Zero*, 131–35; Hughes, 282 F. Supp at 884. Goldman v. Knecht, 295 F. Supp. 897, 900 (D. Colo. 1969); King, "Hippie Problem," 3–7; see also McBride, "On the Fault Line of Mass Culture and Counterculture," 331.

41. Arthur Niederhoffer, *Behind the Shield: The Police in Urban Society* (New York: Doubleday, 1967), 106–10; Seymour M. Lipset, "Why Cops Hate Liberals," *Atlantic Monthly*, March 1969, 76–78; Jerome H. Skolnick, *Justice without Trial: Law Enforcement in Democratic Society* (New Orleans: Quid Pro, 1994), 45; Geoffrey C. Hazard, review of *Justice without Trial: Law Enforcement in Democratic Society* by Jerome H. Skolnick, *University of Chicago Law Review* 34, no. 1 (1966): 228–29; Herman Schwartz, "Stop and Frisk (A Case Study in Judicial Control of the Police," *Journal of Criminal Law, Criminology, and Police Science* 58, no. 4 (1967): 447; Ramsay Clark, *Crime in America: Observations on Its Nature, Causes, Prevention and Control* (New York: Simon and Schuster, 1970); Jonathan Rubinstein, *City Police* (New York: Farrar, Straus and Giroux, 1973); William W. Turner, *The Police Establishment* (New York: G.P. Putnam's Sons, 1968).

42. Sidney E. Zion, "Policeman's Lot Is Not a Hippy One," *New York Times*, June 4, 1967, E3; Lipset, "Why Cops Hate Liberals," 82; Herman Goldstein, "Police Discretion: The Ideal versus the Real," *Public Administration Review* 23, no. 3 (1963): 143–44; see also McBride, "On the Fault Line of Mass Culture and Counterculture," 304, 312.

43. Hughes, 282 F.Supp at 883; Art Vinsel, "'True' Hippies Tune into Great Ills of Society," *Long Beach California Press-Telegram*, October 5, 1967, A-1.

44. See, e.g., Doug Smith, "Was Hippie Teen Profane? Yes, District Court Says," *Charlotte Observer*, May 26, 1969, Charlotte Observer Clipping Files; U.S. v. Pederson, 300 F. Supp. 669 (D.Vt. 1969); People v. Feltch, 483 P.2d 1335, 1336 (Colo. 1971); "Hitchhiking Hippies Get Nowhere Fast," *Long Beach California Press-Telegram*, October 28, 1970, P-3; McBride, "On the Fault Line of Mass Culture and Counterculture."

45. "Fear of Hippie Invasion May Bring Night Closing of Parks: B. H. Parks," *Los Angeles Times*, September 17, 1967, 1; see also "Anti-Hippie Bill Killed," *Chicago Tribune*, March 31, 1971, 5; Hunter S. Thompson, introduction to *To Aspen and Back* by Peggy Clifford (New York: St. Martin's Press, 1980), xiv; Lisa Sun-Hee Park and David Naguib Pellow, *The Slums of Aspen: Immigrants vs. the Environment in America's Eden* (New York: New York University Press, 2011), 87; McBride, "On the Fault Line of Mass Culture and Counterculture," 195.

46. Parr v. Mun. Court, 479 P.2d 353 (Cal. 1971).

47. Stein v. State, 492 S.W.2d 548, 551 (Tex. Crim. App. 1973); see also Renn v. State, 495 S.W.2d 922, 924 (Tex. Crim. App. 1973); Donald Janson, "'Bohemian' Father Pushes Suit in Iowa Court to Regain Custody of His Son," *New York Times*, April 3, 1966, 64; McAndrew, 239 N.E.2d at 318–19.

48. "'Haircut Sentences' Protested by ACLU," *Los Angeles Times*, July 28, 1968, G4; see also "2 Pacifist Are Jailed and Shaved in Wyoming," *New York Times*, June 29, 1968, 3; "'Hippies' Arrest Brings Protest," *Herald-Tribune* (Sarasota, FL), August 13, 1968, 1; "ACLU Challenges Arrest of Hippies," *Sarasota Journal*, August 13, 1968, 5; "Youth Nabbed in Police Drive on Hippies Draws Acquittal," *Herald-Tribune* (Sarasota, FL), August 22, 1968, 18.

49. "Hippie 'Editors' Denied Request," *Spokane Daily Chronicle*, November 23, 1968, 10; "Hippies' Arrest Brings Protest," 1; "ACLU Challenges Arrest of Hippies," 5; "Youth Nabbed in Police Drive on Hippies Draws Acquittal," 18; "12 Students Fined $100 Each for Nude Fling," *Chicago Tribune*, April 5, 1969, B20; "Hippies Let 'Sister' Take Rap," *Long Beach California Press-Telegram*, October 27, 1967, C-14; "State Candidates Continue Blasts," *Rome* (CA) *News-Tribune*, August 30, 1970, 1-B; "Hitchhiking Hippies Get Nowhere Fast," P-3; "'Conchs' Uneasy with Long-Haired Clan in Key West," 3.

50. Lee and Shlain, *Acid Dreams*, 145; Roy Reed, "New Orleans Ends the Most Violent Mardi Gras Season in Years with 600 in Its Jails," *New York Times*, February 11, 1970, 24; see generally J. Mark Souther, *New Orleans on Parade: Tourism and the Transformation of the Crescent City* (Baton Rouge: Lousiana State Univesity Press, 2006). For more on vagrancy and loitering arrests of Vietnam War protestors, see Chapter 8, this volume.

51. "Senators to Hold Teen Age Hearings," *New York Times*, September 19, 1963, 16; "No Harm in Horror, Comics Issuer Says," *New York Times*, April 22, 1954, 1; Lee and Shlain, *Acid Dreams*, 150; Adams, "Hippie-House Bill Clears House Unit"; "Hippie House Bill Swings," *Charlotte Observer*, June 27, 1969, Charlotte Observer Clipping Files. See generally H. L. and R. R. O, "Curfew Ordinances and the Control of Nocturnal Juvenile Crime," *University of Pennsylvania Law Review* 107 (1958): 66; Robert L. Harris, "California's Predelinquency Statute and Suggested Alternatives," *California Law Review* 60, no. 4 (1972): 1167–68, 1171. The federal government even got into the act, funding a series of houses for runaways in places like Haight-Ashbury, Berkeley, and Greenwich Village in response to the large numbers of runaways in the 1960s and stories about their vulnerability to violence. Anne B. Moses, "The Runaway Youth Act," *Social Services Review* 52, no. 2 (1978): 227. In Canada as well, vagrancy laws were used to control young people in conflict with authority figures, including, and perhaps most especially, their parents. Cliff Nelson and Ray Steele, "Vagrancy Dilemma: An Empirical Study," *Osgoode Hall Law Journal* 7, no. 2 (1969–1970): 177–98. For charges of contributing to the delinquency of a minor, see, e.g., State v. Sparrow, 173 S.E.2d 897 (N.C. 1970). See generally Anthony G. Amsterdam, "Federal Constitutional Restrictions on the Punishment of Crimes of Status, Crimes of General Obnoxiousness, Crimes of Displeasing Police Officers, and the Like," *Criminal Law Bulletin* 3, no. 4 (1967): 205, 240–42.

52. "Haight Hut Raid Plays Major Role in Vagrancy Ruling," *Tuscaloosa* (AL) *News*, March 14, 1969, 1; David Richards, *Once upon a Time in Texas: A Liberal in the Lone Star State* (Austin: University of Texas Press, 2002), 142; Transcript of Proceedings at 19, Texas v. Gallant, Justice of the Peace, Bexar County, TX, No. 75322, November 20, 1968, box K18, David Richards Papers, Briscoe Center for American History, University of Texas at Austin (hereafter David Richards Papers).

53. "Hippie House Bill Swings"; Wheeler v. Goodman, 298 F. Supp. 935, 937 (W.D.N.C. 1969).

54. Nick Taylor, "Police Brutality Claimed," *Charlotte Observer*, February 13, 1969, Charlotte Observer Clipping Files; Nancy Brachey, "Youths Seek End to Police Visits at 'Hippie House,'" February 14, 1969, Charlotte Observer Clipping Files; Wheeler, 298 F. Supp. at 939; "Hippie House Charges Dropped," *Charlotte Observer*, January 21, 1969, Charlotte Observer Clipping Files.

55. Park and Pellow, *The Slums of Aspen*, 87 (quoting editorial).

56. Goldman, 295 F. Supp. at 899.

57. Lawrence Young, "STP," *Drug Text*, January 15, 2010, http://www.drugtext.org/Recreational-Drugs/stp.html.

58. Robert Bruce Miller, e-mail message to author, August 17, 2012; Robert Bruce Miller, telephone interview with author, October 9, 2012; see also Anthony Ripley, "Spread of Marijuana Creates New Specialist: The Drug Lawyer," *New York Times*, September 2, 1971, 26.

59. Robert Bruce Miller, telephone interview with author, October 9, 2012.

60. Morgan Lawhorn, "Diligent Young Attorney Knocks Down Vagrancy Law," *Denver Post*, February 9, 1968, 61; Goldman, 295 F. Supp. at 899, 900 n. 3.

61. Robert Bruce Miller, telephone interview with author, October 9, 2012; Goldman, 295 F. Supp. at 900 n. 3.

62. The law students were William Redak and John Studholme. Smith's public defender office in Adams County was the first in the state, and served as a model for the later statewide system. Morgan Smith Biographical Note, Morgan Smith Papers, Denver Public Library, http://ead-srv.denverlibrary.org/sdx/pl/doc-tdm.xsp?id=WH2055_d0e33&fmt=text&base=fa.

63. Zion, "Policeman's Lot Is Not a Hippy One," E3; Vinsel, "'True' Hippies Tune into Great Ills of Society," A-1; Steve Abbot, "Karl and Groucho's Marxist Dance: *Columbus* (Ohio) *Free Press* and Its Predecessors in the Columbus Underground," in *Voices from the Underground*, ed. Ken Wachsberger et al. (Tempe, AZ: Mica Press, 1993), 325, 326–27; see also *Georgia Straight*, June 28,1967, 10; "Judge Says Laws Protect Hippies, Too," *Charlotte Observer*, July 1, 1967, Charlotte Observer Clipping Files; Herman Weinkrantz, "The Court's Opinion" (People v. Wise et al.), June 30, 1967, Chevigny Papers.

64. Steve Suitts, telephone interview with author, September 14, 2012.

65. David R. Richards to Wayne Oakes, November 19, 1969, Roll 180, Series 4, American Civil Liberties Union Archives, 1950–1999, microfilm (hereafter ACLU Archives, microfilm); Melvin Wulf, telephone interview with author, October 2, 2012; Melvin L. Wulf to J. Dan Struve, April 23, 1969, roll 180, Series 4, ACLU Archives, microfilm; Trial Memorandum at 2, n.d., Gallant v. Barlow (E.D. Tex.), roll 180, Series 4, ACLU Archives, microfilm; J. Dan Struve to Melvin L. Wulf (copying Boulder's Robert Miller), August 4, 1969, roll 180, Series 4 ACLU Archives, microfilm.

66. Dennis Hopper, *Easy Rider* (Columbia Pictures, 1969).

67. *In re* Cox, 474 P.2d 992 (Cal. 1970). See "A Tale of Pot and Politics: When the Cops Came They Found the Judge Had Planted Evidence," *Time Magazine*, October 8, 1979, 80; Paul Perry, *Fear and Loathing: The Strange and Terrible Saga of Hunter S. Thompson* (New York: Perseus Books Group, 1992), 131; William McKeen, *Outlaw Journalist: The Life and Times of Hunter S. Thompson* (New York: W. W. Norton, 2008), 139; "The Battle of Aspen," *Rolling Stone*, October 1, 1970, 30; Hunter S. Thompson, *Fear and Loathing in America: The Brutal Odyssey of an Outlaw Journalist, 1968–1976*, ed. Douglas Brinkley (New York: Simon and Schuster, 2000); David Richards, telephone interview with author, January 30, 2013; see, e.g., Bd. of Regents of Univ. of Texas Sys. v. New Left Ed. Project, 404 U.S. 541 (1972); see also Nora Varty, "A Q&A with David Richards," *Texas Monthly.com*, November 2002; Marlise James, *The People's Lawyers* (New York: Holt, Rinehart, and Winston, 1973), 24, 27.

68. "ACLU Attorney Is Ex-Beatnik," *Charlotte Observer*, n.d., Charlotte Observer Clipping Files; Taylor, "Hip Attorney Helps Hippies."

69. Wheeler, 298 F. Supp. at 943; "Hippie House Arrest Erasures Upheld," *Charlotte Observer*, July 3, 1971, 14C Charlotte Observer Clipping File; Norman Smith, telephone interview with author, September 5, 2012; "Youth Flying Back Here for 'Hippie House' Case," *Charlotte Observer*, February 12, 1969, Charlotte Observer Clipping Files; George Daly, telephone interview with author, September 18, 2012; see also Bob Fitzpatrick, "Federal Court Holds NC Vagrancy Laws Invalid," *Charlotte Observer*, November 15, 1969, Charlotte Observer Clipping Files.

70. George Daly, telephone interview with author, September 18, 2012; see also Parker v. Morgan, 322 F. Supp. 585 (W.D.N.C. 1971).

71. George Daly, telephone interview with author, September 18, 2012; Plaintiff's Brief on Unconstitutionality at 8–44, Wheeler v. Goodman, box 1831, American Civil Liberties Union Records, Series 4, Subseries 4A, Princeton ACLU Papers; Vivian Monts, "'Vagrants' Are Spicke of Literature," *Charlotte Observer*, n.d., Charlotte Observer Clipping Files.

72. J. Skelly Wright, "The Courts Have Failed the Poor," *New York Times Magazine*, March 9, 1969, 26; Memorandum on Permanent Injunction at 7, Goldman v. Knecht, 295 F.Supp. 897

(D. Colo. 1969) (No. C-974), box 1404, American Civil Liberties Union Records, Series 4, Subseries 4A, Princeton ACLU Papers; Plaintiff's Brief on Unconstitutionality at 8–44, Wheeler v. Goodman, box 1831, American Civil Liberties Union Records, Series 4, Subseries 4A, Princeton ACLU Papers.

73. Broughton v. Brewer, 298 F. Supp. 260, 266–67 (S.D. Ala. 1969); Complaint for Declaratory Judgment at 4, Gallant v. Barlow (W.D. Tex.), n.d., roll 180, Series 4, ACLU Archives, microfilm ; Affidavit of Nancy McFarland Phillips, Chairman, San Antonio chapter, ACLU, Barlow v. Gallant, 401 U.S. 986 (1971), roll 180, Series 4, ACLU Archives, microfilm ; see also Wheeler v. Goodman, 306 F. Supp. 58, 60 (W.D.N.C. 1969).

74. Dombrowski v. Pfister, 380 U.S. 479, 489 (1965).

75. See, e.g., "Leftists and War Foes Set Up Center in Capital," *New York Times*, February 16, 1968, 20; First Amended Complaint at 4, Gallant v. Barlow (No. SA-69-CA-158), box K18, David Richards Papers; Robert Bruce Miller, telephone interview with author, October 9, 2012; Memorandum on Permanent Injunction at 4, Goldman v. Knecht, 295 F.Supp. 897 (D. Colo. 1969) (No. C-974), box 1404, American Civil Liberties Union Records, Series 4, Subseries 4A, Princeton ACLU Papers.

76. Prior to that time, courts occasionally used "life style" in conjunction with child custody cases and a few other contexts involving children, occasionally conscientious objectors, and sometimes other types of lifestyles (like living the lifestyle of an Alaskan native). It was not until the popularity of the counterculture that the language of lifestyle exploded. See, e.g., *In re* Robles, 84 N.Y.S.2d 827, 831 (N.Y. Dom. Rel. Ct. 1948); *In re* Kingsley, 49 N.Y.S.2d 947, 952 (N.Y. Dom. Rel. Ct. 1944); Marks v. City of Anchorage, 500 P.2d 644, 655 (Alaska 1972); Coates v. City of Cincinnati, 402 U.S. 611, 616 (1971). On Reich, see Charles Reich, "Police Questioning of Law Abiding Citizens," *Yale Law Journal* 75, no. 7 (1966): 1161; Charles Reich, *The Sorcerer of Bolinas Reef* (New York: Random House, 1976); Charles Reich, *The Greening of America* (New York: Crown Trade Paperbacks, 1995); Rodger Citron, "Charles Reich's Journey from the Yale Law Journal to the New York Times Best-Seller List: The Personal History of the Greening of America," *New York Law School Law Review* 52, no. 3 (2007–8): 387, 396; Philip Nobile, ed. *The Con III Controversy: The Critics Look at the Greening of America* (New York: Pocket Books, 1971). See generally Sarah A. Seo, "The New Public," *Yale Law Journal* 125 (forthcoming 2016); Sarah A. Seo, "The Fourth Amendment, Cars, and Freedom in Twentieth-Century America" (PhD diss., Princeton University, 2015).

77. "The Legitimate Scope of Police Discretion to Restrict Ordinary Public Activity," *Harvard Civil Rights-Civil Liberties Law Review* 4, no. 2 (1968): 233, 292–97; Carol Barner Barry and Donald D. Barry, "A Tale of Two Laws and Two Poets," *Maxwell Review* 3, no. 1 (1967): 1–6.

78. Robinson v. California, 370 U.S. 660, 667 (1962); Powell v. Texas, 392 U.S. 514, 536 (1968); Plaintiff's Brief on Unconstitutionality at 8–44, Wheeler v. Goodman, box 1831, American Civil Liberties Union Records, Series 4, Subseries 4A, Princeton ACLU Papers; see also Trial Memorandum at 14–15, Gallant v. Barlow (E.D. Tex.), n.d., roll 180, Series 4, ACLU Archives, microfilm.

79. Oral Argument Notes, Sparrow v. Goodman, n.d., George Daly Papers, provided to author; see also "Hippies' Arrest Brings Protest," 1; "ACLU Challenges Arrest of Hippies," 9; "Youth Nabbed in Police Drive on Hippies Draws Acquittal," 18; Trial Memorandum at 8, Gallant v. Barlow (E.D. Tex.), n.d., roll 180, Series 4, ACLU Archives, microfilm.

80. Louis Henkin, "Foreword: On Drawing Lines," *Harvard Law Review* 82, no. 1 (1968): 63–92; Plaintiff's Brief on Unconstitutionality at 8–44, 57, 62, 74, Wheeler v. Goodman, box 1831, American Civil Liberties Union Records, Series 4, Subseries 4A, Princeton ACLU Papers' see also Memorandum on Permanent Injunction at 8, Goldman v. Knecht, 295 F.Supp. 897 (D. Colo. 1969) (No. C-974), box 1404, American Civil Liberties Union Records, Series 4, Subseries 4A, Princeton ACLU Papers; Trial Memorandum at 12, Gallant v. Barlow (E.D. Tex.), n.d., roll 180, Series 4, ACLU Archives, microfilm.

81. Fenster v. Leary, 229 N.E.2d 426 (N.Y. 1967); Ricks v. District of Columbia, 414 F.2d 1097 (D.C. Cir. 1968); Baker v. Binder, 274 F. Supp. 658 (W.D. Ky. 1967); Alegata v. Com. 231 N.E.2d 201 (Mass. 1967). See, e.g., Plaintiff's Brief on Unconstitutionality at 2, 70, Wheeler v. Goodman, box 1831, American Civil Liberties Union Records, Series 4, Subseries

4A, Princeton ACLU Papers; Broughton, 298 F. Supp. at 271 and n. 24; Complaint for Declaratory Judgment at 8, Gallant v. Barlow (W.D. Tex.), n.d., roll 180, Series 4, ACLU Archives, microfilm.

82. Trial Memorandum at 8–9, Gallant v. Barlow (E.D. Tex.), n.d., roll 180, Series 4, ACLU Archives, microfilm.

83. "If addiction to narcotics is a status which the legislature cannot validly declare to be a crime under Robinson, it follows that the Colorado attempt to declare idleness or indigency coupled with being able-bodied must also (indeed even more) be held beyond the power of the state legislative body." Goldman, 295 F. Supp. at 908; "But to punish them for maintaining and habitual lifestyle 'below' a predetermined level, for being social inferiors (if such they are), is to impose cruel and unusual punishment." Plaintiff's Brief on Unconstitutionality at 72, 76, Wheeler v. Goodman, box 1831, American Civil Liberties Union Records, Series 4, Subseries 4A, Princeton ACLU Papers. See also Hicks, 383 U.S. at 257 (Douglas, J., dissenting) ("I do not see how economic or social status can be made a crime any more than being a drug addict can be") (citing *Robinson*); Trial Memorandum at 13, Gallant v. Barlow (E.D. Tex.), n.d., roll 180, Series 4, ACLU Archives, microfilm; see also " Legitimate Scope of Police Discretion," 233, 294–95.

84. Memorandum on Permanent Injunction at 5, Goldman v. Knecht, 295 F.Supp. 897 (D. Colo. 1969) (No. C-974), box 1404, American Civil Liberties Union Records, Series 4, Subseries 4A, Princeton ACLU Papers; see also Trial Memorandum at 17, Gallant v. Barlow (E.D. Tex.), n.d., roll 180, Series 4, ACLU Archives, microfilm; Complaint for Temporary Injuction [*sic*], Declaratory Judgment, and Permanent Injuction [*sic*], Goldman v. Knecht, 295 F. Supp. 897 (D. Colo. 1969) (No. C-974), box 1404, American Civil Liberties Union Records, Series 4, Subseries 4A, Princeton ACLU Papers; see also First Amended Complaint at 6, Gallant v. Barlow (No. SA-69-CA-158), box K18, David Richards Papers.

85. Sanford Jay Rosen to David R. Richards, Barlow v. Gallant, October 19, 1971, box K18, David Richards Papers; Plaintiff's Brief on Unconstitutionality at 45, 54–55, Wheeler v. Goodman, box 1831, American Civil Liberties Union Records, Series 4, Subseries 4A, Princeton ACLU Papers.

86. Memorandum on Permanent Injunction at 6, Goldman v. Knecht, 295 F.Supp. 897 (D. Colo. 1969) (No. C-974), box 1404, American Civil Liberties Union Records, Series 4, Subseries 4A, Princeton ACLU Papers; United States v. W. Peachtree Tenth Corp., 437 F.2d 221 (5th Cir. 1971).

87. Appellant's Opening Brief at 6, Parr v. Mun. Ct. Monterey-Carmel Jud. Dist., 85 Cal. Rptr. 779 (Ct. App. 1970) (No. 26,594), folder 57.29, container 111, Meiklejohn Civil Liberties Institute Collections, BANC MS 991281 c, The Bancroft Library, University of California, Berkeley (hereafter Bancroft Library); Petition for Rehearing, Parr v. Mun. Ct. Monterey-Carmel Jud. Dist., 85 Cal. Rptr. 779 (Ct. App. 1970) (No. 26,594), folder 57.29, container 111, Meiklejohn Civil Liberties Institute Collections, BANC MS 991281 c, Bancroft Library; Maniwoff, "Hippie House Arrest Erasures Upheld," 14C; Grace Elizabeth Hale, *A Nation of Outsiders: How the White Middle Class Fell in Love with Rebellion in Postwar America* (New York: Oxford University Press, 2011), 224–36; see also Richard Maschal and Dwayne E. Walls, "Arrest Still Puzzles Youth," *Charlotte Observer*, n.d., Charlotte Observer Clipping Files; Abraham Fortas, draft concurrence at 2, Hicks v. D.C. (No. 51), December 6, 1965, box 1365, Douglas Papers.

88. Complaint for Declaratory Judgment at 7, Gallant v. Barlow (W.D. Tex.), n.d., roll 180, Series 4, ACLU Archives, microfilm; see Affidavit of Nancy McFarland Phillips, Chairman, San Antonio chapter, ACLU, Barlow v. Gallant, 401 U.S. 986 (1971), roll 180, Series 4, ACLU Archives, microfilm; Ala. Code § 14–437 (1940); Steve Suitts, telephone interview with author, September 14, 2012. Other lawyers included Jonathan Shapiro of New York, who was working for the NAACP LDF and had previously worked with the Lawyers' Committee for Civil Rights under Law in Mississippi. Shapiro was involved in more cases in Mobile stemming from official suppression of demonstrations and protests. Jonathan Shapiro, e-mail message to author, August 30, 2012; see also LeFlore v. Robinson, 434 F.2d 933 (5th Cir. 1970).

89. Complaint for Declaratory Judgment at 2–4, Gallant v. Barlow (W.D. Tex.), n.d., roll 180, Series 4, ACLU Archives, microfilm; J. Dan Struve to Melvin L. Wulf, August 4, 1969, roll

180, Series 4, ACLU Archives, microfilm; First Amended Complaint at 4, Gallant v. Barlow (No. SA-69-CA-15), n.d., roll 180, Series 4, ACLU Archives, microfilm. Barlow was also consolidated with a challenge from Amarillo, Texas, involving a variety of defendants arrested for vagrancy sixty-six times. See Jurisdictional Statement at 41, Barlow v. Gallant, 401 U.S. 986 (1971) (No. 90), box 1395, American Civil Liberties Union Records, Series 4, Subseries 4A, Princeton ACLU Papers; John Broadfoot, telephone interview with author, February 5, 2013.

90. In Aspen, Joe Edwards and the ACLU brought a lawsuit to stop police harassment and declare the city's vagrancy and loitering ordinances unconstitutional in a class-action lawsuit. According to some reports, though the federal court refused to decide the case, the city repealed the vagrancy ordinance a few months later. Park and Pellow, *The Slums of Aspen*, 86. On Tuscaloosa and Shelby, see Steve Suitts, e-mail message to author, September 14, 2012; Steve Suitts, telephone interview with author, September 14, 2012.

91. Memorandum of Points and Authorities in Support of Plaintiff's Motion for Allowance of Costs and to Tax Counsel Fees as Costs, Wheeler v. Goodman (No. 2431), n.d., box 1831, American Civil Liberties Union Records, Series 4, Subseries 4A, Princeton ACLU Papers; David Richards to Melvin L. Wulf, August 29, 1969, roll 180, Series 4, ACLU Archives, microfilm; Jurisdictional Statement App'x C at 25–26, Barlow v. Gallant, 401 U.S. 986 (1970), roll 180, Series 4, ACLU Archives, microfilm; Brief in Support of Defendant's Answer at 1–3, Gallant v. Barlow (W.D. Tex.) (No. SA69CA158), n.d., 1968, box K18, David Richards Papers. The court found standing because defendants were charged generically with "vagrancy" rather than under specific sections of the law. Jurisdictional Statement at 30–35, Barlow v. Gallant, 401 U.S. 986 (1971) (No. 90), box 1395, American Civil Liberties Union Records, Series 4, Subseries 4A, Princeton ACLU Papers.

92. Wheeler, 298 F. Supp. 943; George Daly, telephone interview with author, September 18, 2012; Robert Morgan to George Daly, May 11, 1972, George Daly Papers (provided to author).

93. Guy Harris, WOAI vice president and general manager, editorial broadcast, November 13–November 15, 1968 (plaintiff exhibit No. 3), Barlow v. Gallant, roll 180, Series 4, ACLU Archives, microfilm; Sam Kindrik, "Hippy Field Meet Proposed," *San Antonio Express*, February 28, 1969, 7-B; Dick West, "Tell Me a Tale of Hippies," *New York Times*, September 2, 1967, 11; see also Brown, "Condemnation and Persecution of Hippies," 33 (quoting San Francisco Police Chief); "Murderous Flower Children," *Chicago Tribune*, December 13, 1969, N12.

94. In re Sealy, 218 So.2d at 765; see also Broughton, 298 F. Supp. at 266; Wheeler, 298 F. Supp. 935; Hughes, 282 F. Supp 881.

95. Wheeler, 306 F. Supp. at 60, 63, 65; Goldman, 295 F. Supp. at 899, 902–3, 906; Wheeler, 298 F. Supp. at 936–37; Dombrowski, 380 U.S. 479; Zwickler v. Koota, 389 U.S. 241 (1967).

96. Wheeler, 298 F. Supp. at 936.

97. Wheeler, 306 F. Supp. at 61–62, 64. Broughton used vagueness but noted the many other constitutional claims the plaintiffs presented. Broughton, 298 F. Supp. at 275 n. 25; see also Goldman, 295 F. Supp. at 903–4, 907–98; Wheeler, 298 F. Supp. at 937, 941–42 (quoting Hughes, 282 F. Supp at 884). Even in cases that were not specifically vagrancy cases, like Philadelphia's *Hughes v. Rizzo*, vagrancy often provided the backdrop. The police in *Hughes* never got around to charging the hippies with a crime before releasing them. But when the federal judge discussed what was wrong with the arrests in the first place, he more than once used vagrancy and loitering cases as his reference point. He condemned the arrests for the same reasons he would likely have used had vagrancy been charged: "our criminal laws are directed toward actions, not status;" "there can be no limitation of the freedom of persons to move interstate;" the "right of free speech and assembly may not be abridged"; and the law may not "suppress one class of idlers in order to make a place more attractive to other idlers of a more desirable class," Hughes, 282 F. Supp at 884–85; Appendix B to Jurisdictional Statement at 37–38, Barlow v. Gallant, 401 U.S. 986 (1971) (No. 90), box 1395, American Civil Liberties Union Records, Series 4, Subseries 4A, Princeton ACLU Papers; Parr, 479 P.2d 353; see also Wheeler, 306 F. Supp. at 61–62; Broughton, 298 F. Supp. at 267; Wheeler, 306 F. Supp. at 62 (quoting Hughes, 282 F. Supp 881); In re Cox, 474 P.2d at 1000.

98. Broughton, 298 F. Supp. at 271; Wheeler, 306 F. Supp. at 64; Goldman, 295 F. Supp. 897; Barlow v. Gallant, 401 U.S. 986 (1971); Lawhorn, "Diligent Young Attorney Knocks Down Vagrancy Law," 61; see also "Around the Nation," *Washington Post*, November 15, 1969, A3; "Haight Hut Raid Plays Major Role in Vagrancy Ruling," 1; J. R. Rosenberry, "Court Voids District Law on Vagrancy," *Washington Post*, December. 24, 1968, A1; "Vagrancy Law Held Invalid," *Washington Post*, March 8, 1969, B2; "In Defense of Idleness," *Wall Street Journal*, July 13, 1967, 16. But see Alford E. Lewis and Paul W. Valentine, "Prostitutes Expand Territory: Police Say Ruling on Vagrancy Hinders Arrests," *Washington Post*, March 3 1969, A20; Guy Harris, WOAI vice president and general manager, editorial broadcast, November 13–November 15, 1968 (plaintiff exhibit No. 3), Barlow v. Gallant, roll 180, Series 4, ACLU Archives, microfilm; Kindrik, "Hippy Field Meet Proposed," 7-B, in plaintiff exhibit No. 3, Barlow v. Gallant, roll 180, Series 4, ACLU Archives, microfilm.

99. Robert Bruce Miller, telephone interview with author, October 9, 2012; Lawhorn, "Diligent Young Attorney Knocks Down Vagrancy Law," 61.

100. Thomas Belden, "Police Erred in Hippie Case," *Charlotte Observer*, August 2, 1969, Charlotte Observer Clipping Files; Nick Taylor, "Vagrancy Law Invalid, Says Police Lawyer," *Charlotte Observer*, August 2, 1969, Charlotte Observer Clipping Files.

101. Vivian Monts, "Sparrow Ruling Being Appealed," *Charlotte Observer*, n.d., Charlotte Observer Clipping Files; see Sparrow, 173 S.E.2d 897; State v. Sparrow, 171 S.E.2d 321 (N.C. Ct. App. 1969); Vivian Monts, "Suit Wants Under-18 Law Killed," *Charlotte Observer*, n.d., Charlotte Observer Clipping Files. Sparrow v. Goodman, 361 F. Supp. 566, 584; Sparrow v. Goodman, 376 F. Supp. 1268 (W.D.N.C. 1974); George Daly, telephone interview with author, September 18, 2012.

102. In re Cox, 474 P.2d at 1004 n.21; "Law Violations by 'Hippies' Up in Country," *Redlands* (CA) *Daily Facts*, October 26, 1968, 4; "Challenge Set to Anti-Hippie Loitering Law," *Van Nuys* (CA) *Valley News*, September 6, 1968, 8; Jim Parks, "Move against Loiter Bugs Dies in Council," *Charlotte Observer*, n.d., Charlotte Observer Clipping Files; Wheeler, 298 F. Supp. at 942.

103. Wheeler, 298 F. Supp. at 936–37. The judge in Wheeler, for example, found that several of the plaintiffs displayed "a high degree of intelligence, clarity of speech, frankness and sense of relevance." Ibid.

Chapter 8

1. Niki Schwartz, phone interview with author, January 18, 2013.

2. ACLU Suspicious Persons Law Case to Be Heard by U.S. Supreme Court on Monday, January 11, 1971, Palmer v. City of Euclid, 1968, Box 1608, American Civil Liberties Union Records, Series 4, Subseries 4A, Department of Rare Books and Special Collections, Princeton University Library (hereafter Princeton ACLU Papers).

3. "Loitering-Law Cases to Supreme Court," *Hutchinson News* (Hutchinson, KS), January 11, 1971, 31; see also Drew Von Bergen, "Supreme Court Studies Ohio Cities Ordinances," *Bryan* (OH) *Times*, January, 12, 1971, 3; "Loitering Laws Face Test," *Sarasota* (FL) *Herald-Tribune*, January 11, 1971, 4.

4. See Wainwright v. New Orleans, 392 U.S. 598 (1968); Sibron v. New York, 392 U.S. 40; Terry v. Ohio, 392 U.S. 1 (1968); Johnson v. Florida, 391 U.S. 596 (1968); see generally Chapter 6, this volume.

5. Niki Schwartz, phone interview with author, January 18, 2013; "Moritz to Honor Niki Z. Schwartz '64 on May 13 in Cleveland," *This Month @ Moritz*, last modified May 2004, http://moritzlaw.osu.edu/alumni-old/newsletter/2004/may/niki.html.

6. Niki Schwartz, phone interview with author, January 18, 2013; Charles Fabrikant, memorandum, n.d., Palmer v. City of Euclid, Box 126, Harry A. Blackmun Papers, Library of Congress (hereafter Blackmun Papers).

7. Brief for Appellant at 21, 23–24, Palmer v. City of Euclid, 402 U.S. 544 (1971) (No. 70–143); David H. Gilston and Lawrence Podell, *The Practical Patrolman* (Springfield, IL: C. C. Thomas, 1959), 43 quoted in ibid. 22 n. 26; Arthur Niederhoffer, *Behind the Shield—The*

Police in Urban Society (Garden City, NY: Doubleday, 1967), 108; Jerome Skolnik, *Justice without Trial: Law Enforcement in Democratic Society* (Garden City, NY: Doubleday, 1965), 44–48, cited in Brief for Appellee at 22 n.25, Palmer v. City of Euclid, 402 U.S. 544 (1971) (No. 70–143); see, e.g., Melvin L. Wulf to Niki Z. Schwartz, June 16, 1970, Box 1831, Wheeler v. Goodman, 1969–1971, American Civil Liberties Union Records, Series 4, Subseries 4A, Princeton ACLU Papers. Schwartz cited the following in his brief: Ricks v. District of Columbia, 414 F.2d 1097 (D.C. Cir. 1968); Scott v. District Attorney, Jefferson Parish, State of Louisiana, 309 F. Supp. 833 (1970); Landry v. Daley, 280 F. Supp. 968 (N.D. Ill. 1968); Baker v. Bindner, 274 F. Supp. 658 (W.D. Ky. 1967); United States v. Margeson, 259 F. Supp. 256 (E.D. Pa. 1966); Arnold v. City and County of Denver, 171 Colo. 1, 464 P.2d 515 (1970); Headley v. Selkowitz, 171 So. 2d 368 (Fla. 1965); Alegata v. Commonwealth, 353 Mass. 287, 231 N.E. 2d 201 (1967); City of Seattle v. Drew, 70 Wash, 2d 405, 423 P.2d 522 (1967); Brief for Appellant at 15 n. 11, Palmer.

8. Niki Schwartz, phone interview with author, January 18, 2013.
9. Ambler Realty Co. v. Village of Euclid, 297 F. 307, 316 (N.D. Ohio 1924), rev'd, 272 U.S. 365 (1926); U.S. Bureau of Census, Census of Population 1960, 1: 37–266, table 72, cited in Brief for Appellant at 20–21, 21 n. 23, Palmer. In 1970, the numbers were fewer than 300 African Americans and more than 70,000 whites. U.S. Bureau of Census, Census of Population 1970, 1: 37–95, Table 23.
10. City of Euclid, Ohio, Ordinance § 583.01(e), reprinted in Brief for Appellant at 2–3, Palmer.
11. Federal Bureau of Investigation, *Uniform Crime Reports* (Washington, DC, 1968), 120, Table 30, cited in Brief for Appellant at 17, Palmer.
12. See, e.g., Swann v. Charlotte-Mecklenburg Bd. of Educ., 402 U.S. 1 (1971); see also Jones v. Alfred H. Mayer Co., 392 U.S. 409 (1968); Shelley v. Kramer, 334 U.S. 1 (1948); Buchanan v. Warley, 245 U.S. 60 (1917); Brief for Appellant at 7, 20, 21, Palmer; Lawrence P. Tiffany, Donald M. McIntyre, Daniel L. Rotenberg, *Detection of Crime: Stopping and Questioning, Search and Seizure, Encouragement and Entrapment* (Boston: Little Brown, 1967), 20, quoted in ibid., 18 n. 15.
13. Brief for Appellant at 31, Palmer; Terry v. Ohio, 392 U.S. 1 (1968).
14. Brief for Appellant at 31, Palmer.
15. Ibid. at 33.
16. Model Code of Pre-Arraignment Procedure § 2.02 at 31–32, 38–41, 45 (Council Draft No. 2, January 27, 1969).
17. Brief for Appellant at 33, Palmer. See President's Commission on Law Enforcement and the Administration of Justice, *Task Force Report: The Courts* (Washington, DC: Government Printing Office, 1967), 103; Wayne R. LaFave, "Penal Code Revision: Considering the Problems and Practices of Police," *Texas Law Review* 45, no. 3 (1967): 451–52, cited in Brief for Appellant at 30, Palmer; William O. Douglas, "Vagrancy and Arrest on Suspicion," *Yale Law Journal* 70, no. 1 (1960): 1; Caleb Foote, "Vagrancy-Type Law and Its Administration," *University of Pennsylvania Law Review* 104, no. 5 (1956): 628–30.
18. Sally E. Hadden, *Slave Patrols: Law and Violence in Virginia and the Carolinas* (Cambridge, MA: Harvard University Press, 2001); Thomas J. Sugrue, *Sweet Land of Liberty: The Forgotten Struggle for Civil Rights in the North* (New York: Random House, 2008), 327. There were very few black police officers even in cities with large black populations into the 1960s. James Jacobs and Jay Cohen, "The Impact of Racial Integration on the Police," Journal of Police Science and Administration 6, no. 2 (June 1978): 169, 175. On the earlier history of police brutality against African Americans, see, e.g., Martha Biondi, *To Stand and Fight: The Struggle for Civil Rights in Postwar New York City* (Cambridge, MA: Harvard University Press, 2003), 74–78; see also Marilynn Johnson, *Street Justice: A History of Police Violence in New York City* (Boston: Beacon Press, 2003).
19. Sugrue, Sweet Land of Liberty, 328–29, 400; President's Commission on Law Enforcement and Administration of Justice, *Task Force Report: The Police* (Washington, DC: Government Printing Office, 1967), 80, 183–85; see, e.g., August Meier and Elliott Rudwick, *CORE: A Study in the Civil Rights Movement 1942–1968* (Urbana: University of Illinois Press, 1975), 379–80.

20. Gerald Faris, "Venice Police Actions Termed 'Harassment': Minorities Seek Investigation of Community Conditions, Removal of Night Commander Venice Police Actions Described as 'Harassment'; Residents Protest," *Los Angeles Times*, August 3, 1969, WS1; see "Court Finds Lynn Negroes Guilty," *Bay St. Banner* (Boston), September 10, 1966, 8; Arval A. Morris, Philip L. Burton, and Gary D. Gayton to Mayor Braman, August 4, 1967, folder 4, box 1872, American Civil Liberties Union Records, Series 4, Subseries 4B, Princeton ACLU Papers; see, e.g., NAACP, "55th Annual Convention Resolutions," June 22–27, 1965, p. 10, folder 001417-006-0875, Series A, Group 3, Papers of the NAACP, Library of Congress, ProQuest History Vault.

21. See, e.g., William L. Van Deburg, ed., *Modern Black Nationalism: From Marcus Garvey to Louis Farrakhan* (New York: New York University Press, 1997), 99–105; Richard Newman, *Black Power and Black Religion: Essays and Reviews* (West Cornwall, CT: Locust Hill Press, 1987); Cedric Johnson, *Revolutionaries to Race Leaders: Black Power and the Making of African American Politics* (Minneapolis: University of Minnesota Press, 2007); Peniel Joseph, *Dark Days, Bright Nights: From Black Power to Barack Obama* (New York: Basic Civitas Books, 2010); Devin Fergus, *Liberalism, Black Power, and the Making of American Politics, 1965–1980* (Athens: University of Georgia Press, 2009); Peniel E. Joseph, ed., *The Black Power Movement: Re-thinking the Civil Rights-Black Power Era* (New York: Routledge, 2006); Peniel Joseph, *Waiting 'Til the Midnight Hour: A Narrative History of Black Power in America* (New York: Henry Holt, 2006); Jeffrey O. G. Ogbar, *Black Power: Radical Politics and African American Identity* (Baltimore, MD: Johns Hopkins University Press, 2004).

22. Sugrue, *Sweet Land of Liberty*, 343–44; Martha Biondi, *The Black Revolution on Campus* (Berkeley: University of California Press, 2012), 55–56; Ibram Rogers, *The Black Campus Movement: Black Students and the Racial Reconstitution of Higher Education* (New York: Palgrave Macmillan, 2012); Diane Brody: *Fraternity* (New York: Spiegel and Grau, 2012); Rollins v. Shannon, 292 F. Supp. 580, 592–93 (E.D. Mo., 1968).

23. Sugrue, *Sweet Land of Liberty*, 303–5, 334; see Robert M. Fogelson, *Violence as Protest: A Study of Riots and Ghettos* (Westport, CT: Greenwood Press, 1980); United States National Advisory Commission on Civil Disobedience, *Report of the National Advisory Commission on Civil Disorders* (New York: Bantham Books, 1968) (hereafter *Kerner Report*); Bryan T. Downes, "A Critical Reexamination of the Social and Political Characteristics of Riot Cities," *Social Science Quarterly* 51, no. 2 (1970): 349–60; Hugh Davis Graham, "On Riots and Riot Commissions: Civil Disorders in the 1960s," *Public Historian* 2, no. 4 (1980), 7–27. The Lemberg Center for the Study of Violence at Brandeis University had larger numbers. Jane A. Baskin, *Race-related Civil Disorders: 1967–1969* (Waltman, MA: Lemberg Center for the Study of Violence, 1971).

24. Robert M. Fogelson, "From Resentment to Confrontation: The Police, the Negroes, and the Outbreak of the Nineteen-Sixties Riots," *Political Science Quarterly* 83, no. 2 (1968): 217; Sugrue, *Sweet Land of Liberty*, 325, 328; Lemberg Center, Summary of an Interview by the Lemberg Center with a Leader of Mothers for Adequate Welfare, quoted in Anthony David Perez, Kimberly M. Berg, and Daniel J. Myers, "Police and Riots, 1967–1969," *Journal of Black Studies* 34, no. 2 (2003): 167, 169; *Kerner Report*, 93.

25. United States National Advisory Commission on Civil Disorders, *Kerner Report*, 26–27; Thomas J. Sugrue, *The Origins of the Urban Crisis: Race and Inequality in Postwar Detroit* (Princeton, NJ: Princeton University Press, 1996), 119–21; Elijah Anderson, *A Place on the Corner* (Chicago: University of Chicago Press, 1978); Elliot Liebow, *Tally's Corner: A Study of Negro Streetcorner Men* (Boston: Little, Brown, 1967).

26. Sugrue, *Sweet Land of Liberty*, 332; Robert B. Watts, "Disorderly Conduct Statutes in Our Changing Society," *William & Mary Law Review* 9, no. 2 (1967); 355.

27. President's Commission on Law Enforcement, *Task Force Report: The Police*, 187, 188; see also President's Commission on Law Enforcement, *Task Force Report: The Courts*, 104; Paul L. Montgomery, "Outbreak of Riots No Surprise to Puerto Ricans in Hartford: Long-Standing Grievances Include High Rents in Slum Buildings—Relations with the Police Are Strained," *New York Times*, September 4, 1969, 38; Walter Rugaber, "Carmichael Found Guilty of Loitering in Atlanta: He Is Ordered to Pay Fine of $53 or serve 50 Days—Appeal Is Planned," *New York Times*, June 23, 1967, 18; "200 Negroes Protest to Paterson Police on Arrest of

Boy, 16," *New York Times*, May 11, 1968, 69; "Cops Battle Youths in Michigan City," *Chicago Daily Defender*, August 31, 1966, 6; "Detroit Policemen Rout Negro Crowds," *New York Times*, August 10, 1966, 28; Martin Gansberg, "Violence Afflicts Englewood Again: Gunfire by Snipers Reported as Well as Looting and Two Supermarket Fires," *New York Times*, July 23, 1967, 1; D. J. R Bruckner, "Getting Respect for the Police," *Los Angeles Times*, January 9, 1970, C6.

28. David R. Farber, *Chicago '68* (Chicago: University of Chicago Press, 1988), 129; N. L. Zaroulis and Gerald Sullivan, *Who Spoke Up? American Protests against the War in Vietnam, 1963–1975* (Garden City, NJ: Doubleday, 1984), 180.

29. Robert M. Fogelson, *Big-City Police* (Cambridge, MA: Harvard University Press, 1977), 239; William Serrin, "God Help our City," *Atlantic*, March 1969, 115; see also Bruckner, "Getting Respect for the Police," C6; Farber, *Chicago '68*, 129–32.

30. Douglas Robinson, "Many Arrested in Racial Riots Get Light Sentences: Stiff Penalty in Cambridge 28 Convicted in Tampa," *New York Times*, November 27, 1967, 52; United States National Advisory Commission on Civil Disorders, *Report of the National Advisory Commission on Civil Disorders* (1971), 323–25, 337–57.

31. *Kerner Report* (1968), 186; Farber, *Chicago '68*,146–47; "Quell School Fight," *Chicago Defender*, October 27, 1973, 1; Martin Waldron, "Black Militant Slain by Houston Police; Gun Fight Injures 4," *New York Times*, July 28, 1970, 1; John D. Vasilopulos and Donald Mosby, "Disorders Erupt at Other Schools: Arrest 24 in Race Clashes at Austin," *Chicago Daily Defender*, September 24, 1969, 1; John Darnton, "Hartford Imposes Curfew," *New York Times*, September 3, 1969, 1; "Negro Teens Smash Coney Island Shops: Disorders Spread to Subway Trains," *Chicago Tribune*, April 15, 1968, 19; Robinson, "Many Arrested in Racial Riots Get Light Sentences: Stiff Penalty in Cambridge 28 Convicted in Tampa," 52; Gansberg, "Violence Afflicts Englewood Again: Gunfire by Snipers Reported as well as Looting and Two Supermarket Fires," 1; "A Ghetto Panty Raid," *Chicago Daily Defender*, July 27, 1970, 9; "Racial Unrest Rips Schools in Las Vegas," *Los Angeles Times*, September 18, 1970, 31; "Part of Paratroopers Withdrawn from Detroit Riot Zones: Romney Removes Ban on Sale of Liquor," *Chicago Tribune*, August 1, 1967, 7; "Detroit Policemen Rout Negro Crowds," 28; "Des Moines Negro Park Flares Up," *Chicago Defender*, July 9, 1966, 2; Michael Rosen to Board of Directors, memorandum, August 30, 1967, Miscellaneous, Lawyers Conference, 1965–1968, folder 4, box 1872, American Civil Liberties Union Records, Series 4, Subseries 4B, Princeton ACLU Papers.

32. City of Cincinnati, Ohio Ordinance § 901-L6 (Loitering at Street Corners) cited in Jurisdictional Statement for Petitioner at 2, Coates v. City of Cincinnati, 402 U.S. 611 (1969) (No. 1370); *Kerner Report* (1968), 26–27.

33. "Welfare Recipients Plan March on Capitol," *Cincinnati Enquirer*, April 29, 1966, 6, http://www.thehistorymakers.com/biography/sokoni-karanja-40; Margaret Joston, "Speaker Urges Negro Control of West End Agencies," *Cincinnati Enquirer*, May 26, 1967, 37.

34. Sokoni Karanja (formerly Lathan Johnson), interview by author, February 5, 2013.

35. Sokoni Karanja (formerly Lathan Johnson), interview by author, February 5, 2013; article, *Cincinnati Post & Times Star*, August 19, 1968, reprinted in Jurisdictional Statement for Petitioner at 38–39, Coates v. City of Cincinnati, 402 U.S. 611 (1971) (No. 1370).

36. Article, *Cincinnati Post & Times Star*, August 19, 1968, reprinted in Jurisdictional Statement for Petitioner at 38–39, Coates v. City of Cincinnati, 402 U.S. 611 (1971)(No. 1370); City of Cincinnati v. Lathan Johnson, No. 10532, Court of Appeals, First Appellate District of Ohio (1968), reprinted in Brief for Petitioner at 16, Coates v. City of Cincinnati, 402 U.S. 611 (1969) (69–117).

37. Jurisdictional Statement for Petitioner at 7, Coates v. City of Cincinnati, 402 U.S. 611 (1969) (No. 1370); *Report on the National Advisory Commission on Civil Disorders* (New York Times edition), 47–50, cited in ibid., 7.

38. Jack Greenberg, *Crusader in the Courts: Legal Battles of the Civil Rights Movement*, ann. ed. (New York: Twelve Tables Press, 2004); Robert Jerome Glennon, "The Jurisdictional Legacy of the Civil Rights Movement," *Tennessee Law Review* 61, no. 3 (1994): 870; see, e.g., Gregory v. City of Chicago, 394 U.S. 111 (1969); Street v. New York, 394 U.S. 576 (1969); Bond v. Floyd, 386 U.S. 116 (1966).

39. Jack Greenberg, "The Supreme Court, Civil Rights, and Civil Dissonance," *Yale Law Journal* 77, no. 8 (1968): 1533–39; see Ford v. Tennessee, 377 U.S. 994 (1964); Jones v. Georgia, 379 U.S. 935 (1964); Diamond v. Louisiana, 376 U.S. 201 (1964); see Anders Walker, "'To Corral and Control the Ghetto': Stop, Frisk, and the Geography of Freedom," *University of Richmond Law Review* 48, no. 4 (2014): 1253, 1256; Cox v. Louisiana, 379 U.S. 536, 555 (1965).

40. Greenberg, "The Supreme Court, Civil Rights, and Civil Dissonance," 1537–38; see Roger K. Newman, *Hugo Black: A Biography* (New York: Pantheon Books, 1994), 548–51; A. E. Dick Howard, "Mr. Justice Black: The Negro Protest Movement and the Rule of Law," *Virginia Law Review* 53, no. 5 (1967): 1030; Michael R. Belknap, "The Warren Court and the Vietnam War: The Limits of Legal Liberalism," *Georgia Law Review* 33, no. 1 (1998): 100; Walker v. City of Birmingham, 388 U.S. 307 (1967); Glenn T. Eskew, *But for Birmingham: The Local and National Movements in the Civil Rights Struggle* (Chapel Hill: University of North Carolina Press, 1997), 238.

41. Sugrue, *Sweet Land of Liberty*; Mark Brilliant, *The Color of America Has Changed: How Racial Diversity Shaped Civil Rights Reform in California, 1941–1978* (New York: Oxford University Press, 2010); Risa L. Goluboff, *The Lost Promise of Civil Rights* (Cambridge, MA: Harvard University Press, 2007).

42. Michael W. Flamm, *Law and Order: Street Crime, Civil Unrest, and the Crisis of Liberalism in the 1960s* (New York: Columbia University Press, 2005). For an argument that blackness was associated with criminality even earlier, see Khalil Gibran Muhammad, *The Condemnation of Blackness: Race, Crime, and the Making of Modern Urban America* (Cambridge, MA: Harvard University Press, 2010); Sugrue, *Sweet Land of Liberty*, 337–46. For an example of the Court's insistence that African American activists comply with the law, see, e.g., Walker, 388 U.S. 307.

43. See, e.g., Broughton v. Brewer, 298 F.Supp. 260, 263–65, 271 (S.D. Ala. 1969); Judge Robert Merhige, Eastern District of Virginia, Memorandum Opinion in Oliver v. Button, June 18, 1969, box 1603, American Civil Liberties Union Records, Series 4, Subseries 4A, Princeton ACLU Papers; 1971 Va. Acts 420; "Vagrancy Laws Make Poverty Crime, 3 Virginians Charge," *Baltimore Afro-American*, July 27, 1968, 18; 1971 Va. Acts 420; Achtenberg v. Mississippi, 393 F.2d 468, 475 (5th Cir. 1968); Eleanor Jackson Piel, interview by author, February 14, 2013; see also Edward Ranzal, "Civil Rights Worker Sues Kress for Arrest at Mississippi Store," *New York Times*, November 14, 1964, 16.

44. Transcript of Oral Argument at 24, 27, 36, 42, 43, Adickes v. S.H. Kress & Co., 398 U.S. 144 (1970) (No. 79).

45. Transcript of Oral Argument at 4, Adickes; William O. Douglas, conference notes, January 15, 1971, Palmer v. City of Euclid, box 1490, William O. Douglas Papers, Library of Congress (hereafter Douglas Papers).

46. Transcript of Oral Argument at 2, Palmer v. City of Euclid, 402 U.S. 544 (1971) (No. 143); Charles Fabrikant, memorandum, n.d., Palmer v. City of Euclid, box 126, Blackmun Papers; Brief for Appellant at 6–8, Palmer.

47. Transcript of Oral Argument at 12, Palmer.

48. Linda Greenhouse, *Becoming Justice Blackmun: Harry Blackmun's Supreme Court Journey* (New York: Times Books/Henry Holt, 2005); Tinsley E. Yarbrough, *Harry A. Blackmun: The Outsider Justice* (Oxford: Oxford University Press, 2008); MAL (Michael A. LaFond, clerk), bench memorandum (handwritten notations by Justice Blackmun), December 12, 1970, Palmer v. City of Euclid, box 126, Blackmun Papers.

49. Justice Harry A. Blackmun, handwritten notes of oral argument, January 11, 1971, Palmer v. City of Euclid, box 126, Blackmun Papers; Justice Harry A. Blackmun, unsigned memorandum, March 5, 1971, Palmer v. City of Euclid, box 126, Blackmun Papers.

50. Justice William O. Douglas, conference notes, January 15, 1971, Palmer v. City of Euclid, box 1490, Douglas Papers.

51. Justice Byron R. White to Chief Justice Warren E. Burger, memorandum, January 21, 1971, Palmer v. City of Euclid, box I-241, William J. Brennan Papers, Library of Congress (hereafter Brennan Papers); Palmer v. City of Euclid, 402 U.S. 544–46 (1971).

52. Palmer v. City of Euclid, 402 U.S. 544, at 546 (Stewart, J., concurring); Justice John M. Harlan to Justice Byron R. White, memorandum, April 8, 1971, Palmer v. City of Euclid Box I-241, Brennan Papers; Justice John M. Harlan to Justice Byron R. White, memorandum, May 13,

1971, Palmer v. City of Euclid, box I-241, Brennan Papers; Justice Harry A. Blackmun to Justice Byron R. White, memorandum, April 9, 1971, Palmer v. City of Euclid, box 70, Papers of Thurgood Marshall, Library of Congress (hereafter Marshall Papers). The limited, as-applied reasoning might have resulted from a new Burger Court resolve to jettison the Warren Court's recent and somewhat novel use of facial void for vagueness invalidations and return to the historically more common as-applied form. See Christina M. Burkholder, "Recent Supreme Court Developments of the Vagueness Doctrine: Four Cases Involving the Vagueness Attack on Statutes during the 1972–73 Term," *Connecticut Law Review* 7, no. 1 (1974): 94, 110–15; cf. "The First Amendment Overbreadth Doctrine," *Harvard Law Review* 83, no. 4 (1970): 844–927. It might also have resulted from fears that eliminating crime control vagrancy law uses would result in the freeing of murderers; see, e.g. Justice William O. Douglas, memorandum, December 25, 1970, Ricehill v. Iowa, box 1498, Douglas Papers; Ricehill v. Iowa, 401 U.S. 942 (1971) (denying certiorari without any noted dissent from Justice Douglas).

53. Thompson v. Louisville, 362 U.S. 199 (1960).
54. Jurisdictional Statement for Petitioner at 18–20, 23–24, Coates v. City of Cincinnati, 402 U.S. 611 (1969) (No. 117) (reproducing trial transcripts).
55. Jurisdictional Statement for Petitioner at 25–28, Coates v. City of Cincinnati, 402 U.S. 611 (1969) (No. 117) (reproducing the trial transcripts in Cincinnati v. Hastings, et al., Nos. 7857, 7858, 7859, 7860, Hamilton County Municipal Court (1968)).
56. Brief for Appellant at 3, 4, 6, Coates v. City of Cincinnati, 402 U.S. 611 (1969) (No. 117).
57. Columbus v. Becher, 180 N.E.2d 836, 838 (Ohio 1962); Jurisdictional Statement for Petitioner at 4, Coates v. City of Cincinnati, 402 U.S. 611 (1969) (No. 117); Brief for Appellant at 8, Coates.
58. TCA (Thomas C. Armitage, clerk), memorandum, May 12, 1970, Coates v. City of Cincinnati, box 1490, Douglas Papers; Jurisdictional Statement for Petitioner at 9–12, Coates v. City of Cincinnati, 402 U.S. 611 (1969) (No. 117) (reproducing the opinion of the Supreme Court of Ohio).
59. Brief for Appellant at 7–8, Coates.
60. TAC (Thomas C. Armitage, clerk), memorandum, May 12, 1970, Coates v. City of Cincinnati, box 1490, Douglas Papers; MAL (Michael A. LaFond, clerk), memorandum, December 12, 1970, Coates v. City of Euclid, box 125, Blackmun Papers; see also Jurisdictional Statement for Petitioner at 11, Coates v. City of Cincinnati, 402 U.S. 611 (1969) (No. 117) (reproducing the opinion of the Supreme Court of Ohio).
61. Justice Harry A. Blackmun, memorandum, n.d., Coates v. City of Cincinnati, box 125, Blackmun Papers. On labor's decline, see, e.g., Melvyn Dubofsky, *The State and Labor in Modern America* (Chapel Hill: University of North Carolina Press, 1994); Nelson Lichtenstein, *State of the Union: A Century of American Labor* (Princeton, NJ: Princeton University Press, 2002); Kim Moody, *An Injury to All: The Decline of American Unionism* (New York: Verso, 1988); Robert H. Zieger, *American Workers, American Unions*, 2nd ed. (Baltimore, MD: Johns Hopkins University Press, 1994).
62. Zaroulis and Sullivan, *Who Spoke Up?* 12–13; Marilyn Blatt Young, *The Vietnam Wars, 1945–1990* (New York: Harper Collins, 1991), 197–200. On desertion, see Frank Kusch, *All American Boys: Draft Dodgers in Canada from the Vietnam War* (Westport, CT: Praeger, 2001), 91. On the size and makeup of the anti-war movement, see Charles DeBenedetti, "On the Significance of Citizen Peace Activism: America, 1961–1975," in *The Vietnam Antiwar Movement*, ed. Walter L. Hixson (New York: Garland, 2000), 41–43; Charles DeBenedetti, "A CIA Analysis of the Anti-Vietnam War Movement: October 1967," in *The Vietnam Antiwar Movement*, ed. Walter L. Hixson (New York: Garland, 2000), 115–22.
63. Zaroulis Sullivan, *Who Spoke Up?*; Students for a Democratic Society, *Port Huron Statement of the Students for a Democratic Society*, http://coursesa.matrix.msu.edu/~hst306/documents/huron.html (last visited June 22, 2013). See also James Miller, *Democracy is in the Streets: From Port Huron to the Siege of Chicago* (Cambridge, MA: Harvard University Press, 1994); Leroy F. Aarons, "'Don't Trust Anybody over 30': Phrasemaker, at 30, Still Radical," *Washington Post*, March 23, 1970, A1; Brief of Youth Franchise Coalition et al. Amicus Curiae at 11, Oregon v. Mitchell, 400 U.S. 112 (1970) (No. 46); Hal Draper, *Berkeley: The New Student Revolt* (New York: Grove Press, 1965); David Lance Goines, *The Free Speech*

Movement: Coming of Age in the 1960s (Berkeley: Ten Speed Press, 1993); W. J. Rorabaugh, *Berkeley at War, the 1960s* (New York: Oxford, 1989).

64. Maurice Isserman and Michael Kazin, "The Failure and Success of the New Radicalism," in *Rise and Fall of New Deal Order, 1930–1980,* ed. Steve Fraser and Gary Gerstle (Princeton, NJ: Princeton University Press, 1989); see David Steigerwald, "The Liberal-Radical Debates of the 1960s," in *Debating the 1960s: Liberal, Conservative, and Radical Perspectives,* ed. Michael W. Flamm and David Steigerwald (Lanham, MD: Rowman and Littlefield, 2008), 68–69.

65. See, e.g., Lawrence E. Davies, "Shotguns and Tear Gas Disperse Rioters near the Berkeley Campus," *New York Times,* May 16, 1969, 1 (showing a disturbing photo with students on buildings and tear gas exploding).

66. "Rebels Seize Office at Buffalo University," *Washington Post,* March 20, 1969, 4; see also Isserman and Kazin, "The Failure and Success of the New Radicalism"; Harold Jacobs, *Weatherman* (Berkeley, CA: Ramparts Press, 1970), 51–53.

67. See, e.g., Morris Kaplan, "25 Are Arraigned in Protest Here: 40 More Will be Charged in Anti-Nixon Demonstration," *New York Times,* December 11, 1969, 24; Howard LaCasa, to Miss Peggy Kerry, December 11, 1969, folder R-W, Paul Chevigny Papers, New York Civil Liberties Union Headquarters (made available to author) (hereafter "Chevigny Papers"); Thomas P. Ronan, "2 Arrested at Anti-Nixon Protest Say They Were Beaten by Police," *New York Times,* December 14, 1969, 41; Homer Bigart, "48 Arrested, 7 Policemen Hurt as 3,000 Protest Nixon's Visit," clipping, folder R-W, Paul Chevigny Papers; Kristen Bachler to Paul Chevigny, December 29, 1969, folder R-W, Paul Chevigny Papers; Report on Police Brutality at Waldorf-Astoria December 9, December 11, 1969, folder R-W, Paul Chevigny Papers; Abel Silver and Mary Connelly, "Mayor Backs Police on Clash," *New York Post,* December 10, 1969, 5; Joan Morrison and Robert K. Morrison, *From Camelot to Kent State: The Sixties Experience in the Words of Those Who Lived It* (New York: Times Books, 1987), 330–31; see Ron Hahne, Ben Morea, and Jacques Vaché, *Black Mask and Up Against the Wall Motherfucker: The Incomplete Works of Ron Hahne, Ben Morea, and the Black Mask Group* (London: Unpopular Books, 1993); Ben Morea, interview by Iain McIntyre, 2006, posted by Red Marriott, March 24, 2012, http://libcom.org/history/against-wall-motherfucker-interview-ben-morea;Leaflet, folder R-W, Paul Chevigny Papers.

68. Samuel Walker, *In Defense of American Liberties: A History of the ACLU* (New York: Oxford University Press, 1990), 279–81; Alan H. Levine to Franklin A. Thomas, March 31, 1967, Police Files, Paul Chevigny Papers; Alan H. Levine, Memorandum Regarding *Press v. Leary,* August 10, 1967, Police Files, Paul Chevigny Papers; "Handbill Arrests Protested in Suit," *New York Times,* June 22, 1967, 19; compare Plaintiff's Brief in Strother v. Thompson, September 20, 1965, Police Files, Paul Chevigny Papers, with Complaint in Press v. Leary, Police Files, Paul Chevigny Papers; Burt Neuborne, interview with author, November 8, 2008.

69. Watts, "Disorderly Conduct Statutes," 357; see, e.g., Gunn v. Univ. Comm.to End the War in Viet Nam, 399 U.S. 383 (1970); Sellers v. Laird, 395 U.S. 950 (1969) (Douglas, J., dissenting); O'Brien v. United States, 391 U.S. 367 (1968); see generally Belknap, "The Warren Court and the Vietnam War," 150–51; Frank R. Strong, "Fifty Years of 'Clear and Present Danger': From *Schenk* to *Brandenburg*—and Beyond," *Supreme Court Review* 1969: 41; Michael J. Klarman, "Rethinking the Civil Rights and Civil Liberties Revolution," *Virginia Law Review* 82, no. 1 (1996): 1; John F. Wirenius, "The Road to *Brandenburg*: A Look at the Evolving Understanding of the First Amendment," *Drake Law Review* 43, no. 1 (1993): 1; Tinker v. Des Moines Indep. Cmty. Sch. Dist., 393 U.S. 503 (1969); Cohen v. California, 403 U.S. 15 (1971); see also Bachellar v. Maryland, 397 US 564 (1970); Bond, 385 U.S. 116. On free speech doctrine in the early 1970s, see, e.g., Paul L. Murphy, *The Meaning of Freedom of Speech: First Amendment Freedoms from Wilson to FDR* (Westport, CT: Greenwood, 1972); Paul L. Murphy, *The Constitution in Crisis Times: 1918–1969* (New York: Harper & Row, 1971); Thomas Irwin Emerson, *The System of Freedom of Expression* (New York: Random House, 1970).

70. See Marjorie Heins, "Viewpoint Discrimination," *Hastings Constitutional Law Quarterly* 24, no. 1 (1996): 99; see also, e.g., West Virginia State Bd. of Educ. v. Barnette, 319 U.S. 624 (1943); Hague v. CIO, 307 U.S. 496 (1939).

71. William Shumann, "Last of 682 Demonstrators Arraigned," *Washington Post,* October 25, 1967, A11; Douglas Robinson, "Violence Breaks Out in Several Communities—Pickets

Arrested," *New York Times*, October 17, 1965, 1; John H. Fenton, "7 War Protestors Beaten in Boston; Draft Card Burning Sparks Attack by 50 School Boys," *New York Times*, April 1, 1966, 5; Stuart Auerbach, "2 Protesters Continue Hunger Strike: 'I Think My Daughter's Wonderful,' Says Mother of Jailed Pacifist, 17," *Washington Post*, May 17, 1967, B1; Schumann v. State of New York, 270 F. Supp 730, 730–32 (S.D.N.Y. 1967); "Reagan Raps Shutdown by State College: Deplores 'Surrender' to Black Militants," *Chicago Tribune*, November 15, 1968, A5; "Six Seized in Protest at Pentagon," *Washington Post*, July 11, 1969, A6; Anne Hebald, "36 Arrested during Catholic Mass at Pentagon," *Washington Post*, August 15, 1969, A14.

72. Jeffrey Kahn, "Ronald Reagan Launched Political Career Using the Berkeley Campus as a Target," *UC Berkeley News Center*, June 8, 2004; Rick Perlstein, *The Invisible Bridge: The Fall of Nixon and the Rise of Reagan* (New York: Simon and Schuster, 2014); Robert Kistler, "Guardsmen Seal Off Riot Area: Riot Area Put under Tight Guard," *Los Angeles Times*, February 28, 1970, 1; Dial Torgerson, "Guard Called In: Santa Barbara Streets Quiet," *Los Angeles Times*, February 28, 1970, 1.

73. "Berkeley Violence Brings Declaration of Civil Disaster," *Los Angeles Times*, September 3, 1968, 3; "March Permit Is Canceled by Berkeley," *Chicago Tribune*, September 4, 1968; Davies, "Shotguns and Tear Gas Disperse Rioters Near the Berkeley Campus: Police and Guard Rout Coast Rioters," 1; Todd Gitlin, "White Watts," *Hard Times*, May 26–June 2, 1969, container 7, Mieklejohn Civil Liberties Institute Collections, BANC MS 991281 c, Bancroft Library, University of California, Berkeley (hereafter Berkeley Mieklejohn Papers); Louise Brown, ed., *ACLU Alert*, July 13, 1969, container 7, Berkeley Mieklejohn Papers; W. J. Rorabaugh, *Berkeley at War, the 1960s* (New York: Oxford University Press, 1989), 164; "UC Prisoners Protest—Judge Curbs Sheriff," news clipping, May 25, 1969, container 7, Berkeley Mieklejohn Papers; James Yandell, *Neither Law nor Order: The People's Park and the People's Police* at 64–65, container 7, Berkeley Mieklejohn Papers.

74. Baker v. Bindner, 274 F.Supp. 658 (W.D.K.Y. 1967); United States v. Cassiagnol, 420 F.2d 868, 872–75 (4th Cir., 1970); see also United States v. Sroka, 307 F. Supp. 400 (E.D. Wisc, 1969); Maurine McLaughlin, "Jurist Frees Viet Protesters," *Washington Post*, September 27, 1969, B6; 34 Fed. Reg. 17954 (Nov. 6, 1969) (codified at 41 C.F.R. 101–19.304 (1970)); see TAC (Thomas C. Armitage, clerk), memorandum, April 14, 1970, Cassiagnol v. United States, box 1461, Douglas Papers.

75. "Students Freed in Denver Sit-In," *Washington Post*, September 25, 1968, A5; People v. Sprowal, 218 N.E.2d 343 (NY 1966); but see People v. Manuel, 356 N.Y.S.2d 248 (N.Y. App. Div. 1974); People v. Sprowal, 268 N.Y.S. 2d 444 (N.Y. App. Div.1966); State v. Oyen, 480 P.2d 766 (Wash. 1971); cf. Seattle v. Drew, 423 P.2d 522 (Wash. 1967); cf. also State v. Fisk, 485 P.2d 81 (Wash. 1971).

76. People v. Deutsch, 172 N.W.2d 392 (Mich. Ct. App. 1969); see, e.g., Gordon v. Schiro, 310 F.Supp. 884 (E.D. La. 1970).

77. Watts, "Disorderly Conduct Statutes," 349, 350–51; Md. Code Ann. § 27–123 (1957) cited in ibid. 350; J. V. Henry, "Breach of the Peace and Disorderly Conduct Laws: Void for Vagueness?" *Howard Law Journal* 12, no. 2 (1966): 318; Sheila Mahoney, "Comment: Disorderly Conduct Statistics," *Harvard Civil Rights-Civil Liberties Law Review* 1 (1966): 152; Alan H. Levine, "Disorderly Conduct: Catch-all Device for New York City's Undesirables," *Civil Liberties in New York*, June 1966, at 2; see also Griffin v. Smith, 193 S.E. 777 (Ga. 1937); Kahalley v. State, 48 So. 2d 794 (Ala. 1950); Original Fayette County Civic and Welfare League, Inc., v. Ellington, 309 F.Supp. 89 (W.D. Tenn. 1970); Landry v. Daley, 280 F.Supp. 938 (N.D. Ill. 1968), rev'd Boyle v. Landry, 401 U.S. 77 (1971); see also Model Penal Code § 250.1 (Tentative Draft No. 13, 1961); Ralph A. Kottke, "Riot and Disorderly Conduct," *Oregon Law Review* 51, no. 3 (1972): 618.

78. Anthony Amsterdam, interview with author, April 2009.

79. Young, *Vietnam Wars, 1945–1990*, 200–202; see Aryeh Neier, *Taking Liberties: Four Decades in the Struggle for Rights* (New York: Public Affairs, 2003).

80. Abe Fortas, *Concerning Dissent and Civil Disobedience* (New York: World, 1968), 108. See also Burke Marshall, "The Protest Movement and the Law," *Virginia Law Review* 51, no. 5 (1965): 785; "How to Heal a Violent Society," *Time*, December 19, 1969, 38; see also Norton J. Cohen, Letter to Mel Wulf, January 9, 1968, folder 4, Box 1872, American Civil Liberties Union Records: Subgroup 2, Legal Case Files Series, 1947–1995: Miscellaneous,

Lawyers Conference, 1965–1968, Subseries 4B, Series 4, Princeton ACLU Papers (hereafter Lawyers Conference, 1965–68, Princeton ACLU Papers); Edward Mosk, letter to Melvin L. Wulf, January 5, 1968, Lawyers Conference, 1965–68, Princeton ACLU Papers; Laurence H. Sperber, letter to Mel Wulf, December 26, 1967, Lawyers Conference, 1965–68, Princeton ACLU Papers; Mel Wulf, letter to Staff Counsel and General Counsel, December 11, 1967, Lawyers Conference, 1965–68, Princeton ACLU Papers.

81. Transcript of Oral Argument, Coates v. City of Cincinnati, 402 U.S. 611 (1971) (No. 117), http://www.oyez.org/cases/1970-1979/1970/1970_117 (hereafter Oyez Project).

82. Under Supreme Court Rule 32.3, nonrecord evidence can't be lodged without submitting a letter describing the material and why it can and the reasons why it may properly be considered by the court, and then the Clerk can request it. Sup Ct. R. 32.3; Transcript of Oral Argument, Coates, Oyez Project; Brief of Appellee at 4–5, Coates v. City of Cincinnati, 402 U.S. 611 (1971) (No. 117).

83. Chief Justice Warren Burger, memorandum to the conference, January 11, 1971, Coates v. Cincinnati, Brennan Papers; Chief Justice Warren Burger, memorandum to the conference, February 8, 1971, Coates v. Cincinnati, Hugo LaFayette Black Papers, Library of Congress (hereafter Black Papers).

84. Paul W. Valentine and William L. Claiborne, "Vets Leave; Mass March Slated Today," *Washington Post*, April 24, 1971, A1; William L. Claiborne, "Protest Planned Near Capitol," *Washington Post*, March 17, 1971, A13; William L. Claiborne and Sanford J. Ungar, "Judge Lifts Ban on Vets, Scolds U.S.," *Washington Post*, April 23, 1971, A1; Paul W. Valentine, "Spirit of Militancy Rises," *Washington Post*, May 2, 1971, 1; Young, *Vietnam Wars, 1945–1990*, 257–59; Richard Halloran, "People's Lobby" Begs for End of War," *New York Times*, April 27, 1971, 8; see Noam Chomsky, "A Special Supplement: Mayday: The Case for Civil Disobedience, " *New York Review of Books*, June 17, 1971; Emanuel John Kalina, "The 1971 Mayday Arrests: A Factual and Legal Analysis," *Maryland Law Forum* 2, no. 1 (1971): 25–30; "Self-Defeat for the Army of Peace," *Time*, May 17, 1971, 13; Lucy G. Barber, *Marching on Washington: The Forging of an American Political Tradition* (Berkeley: University of California Press, 2002), 211–13; Melvin Small, William D. Hoover, and Charles DeBenedetti, *Give Peace a Chance: Exploring the Vietnam Antiwar Movement, Essays from the Charles Debenedetti Memorial Conference* (Syracuse, NY: Syracuse University Press, 1992), 71–90; Melvin Small, *Antiwarriors: The Vietnam War and the Battle for America's Hearts and Minds* (Wilmington, DE: Scholarly Resources, 2002), 119–38; Tom Wells, *The War Within: America's Battle over Vietnam* (Berkeley: University of California Press, 1994), 471–514; Michael Linfield, *Freedom under Fire: U.S. Civil Liberties in Times of War* (Boston: South End Press, 1990), 120; Fredrik Logevall, *Embers of War: The Fall of an Empire and the Making of America's Vietnam* (New York: Random House, 2012); Edward Miller, *Misalliance: Ngo Dinh Diem, the United States, and the Fate of South Vietnam* (Cambridge, MA: Harvard University Press, 2013); Jessica M. Chapman, *Cauldron of Resistance: Ngo Dinh Diem, the United States, and 1950s Southern Vietnam* (Ithaca, NY: Cornell University Press, 2013).

85. "Vets' History: Operation 'Dewey Canyon III,' " *Veteran* 7, no. 2 (April 1977): 16, http://www.vvaw.org/veteran/article/?id=1656; Young, *Vietnam Wars, 1945–1990*, 257. On Resurrection City, see Amy Wright, "Civil Rights' 'Unfinished Business': Poverty, Race, and the 1968 Poor People's Campaign" (Ph.D. diss. University of Texas, 2007). On the Bonus Army, see Roger Daniels, *The Bonus March: An Episode of the Great Depression* (Westport, CT: Greenwood, 1971); Paul Dickson and Thomas B. Allen, *The Bonus Army: An American Epic* (New York: Walker, 2004). The tradition went back even further, to the nineteenth century. See, e.g., Donald Le Crone McMurry, *Coxey's Army: A Study of the Industrial Army Movement of 1894* (Seattle: University of Washington Press, 1968); Carlos A. Schwantes, *Coxey's Army: An American Odyssey* (Lincoln: University of Nebraska Press, 1985); Henry Vincent, *The Story of the Commonweal* (1894; repr., New York: Arno Press, 1969).

86. Sanford J. Ungar, "Vets Can Use Mall, Court Quickly Rules," *Washington Post*, April 20, 1971, A12; Vietnam Veterans against the War/Winter Soldier Organization v. Morton, 506 F.2d 53 n. 9 (D.C. Cir. 1974); "Vets Disobey Court Order, Sleep on Mall," *Washington Post*, April 22, 1971, A1.

87. "Vets Disobey Court Order, Sleep on Mall," A1; Claiborne and Ungar, "Judge Lifts Ban on Vets, Scolds U.S.," A1; "Drumbeat in Washington," *New York Times*, April 24, 1971, 28.

88. "Vets Disobey Court Order, Sleep on Mall," A1; William L. Claiborne, "Police Move Quickly, Gently in Arresting Protesting Vets," *Washington Post*, April 23, 1971, A6; "Drumbeat in Washington," 28.

89. Justice William O. Douglas to William H. Alsup et al. (law clerks), memorandum, April 22, 1971, Law clerks summer Projects, folder 8, box 1121, Douglas Papers.

90. Chief Justice Warren E. Burger, memorandum to conference, May 10, 1971, Coates v. Cincinnati, box 430, Black Papers; Justice Potter Stewart, 4th draft of dissent, recirculated February 4, 1971, Coates v. City of Cincinnati, box 430, Black Papers.

91. Laurence H. Tribe, "Justice Stewart: A Tale of Two Portraits," *Yale Law Journal* 95, no. 7 (1986): 1328; the Supreme Court of Ohio & the Ohio Judicial System, "Potter Stewart," accessed 9 March 2015, http://www.supremecourt.ohio.gov/MJC/places/pStewart.asp; Shuttlesworth v. Birmingham, 382 U.S. 87 (1965). In Hicks, Stewart had agreed that the law was unconstitutional but found the procedural problems determinative for dismissal, and he voted to DIG in Wainwright as well. Justice William O. Douglas, conference notes, October 22, 1965, Hicks v. District of Columbia, box 1365, Douglas Papers; Chief Justice Earl Warren, Vote Tally, n.d., Wainwright v. New Orleans, box 650, Earl Warren Papers, Library of Congress; see also e.g., Mora v. McNamara, 389 U.S. 934, 934–35 (1967) (Stewart, J., dissenting) (dissenting from the denial for petition of writ of certiorari and presenting four questions for the Court to answer, including whether the Vietnam War was a war within the meaning of the Constitution).

92. Justice Potter Stewart, 5th Draft of Dissent, recirculated May 14, 1971, Coates v. City of Cincinnati, box I-240, Brennan Papers. See 28 U.S.C. § 1257 (describing appeals as matter of right until 1988); Times Film Corp. v. Chicago, 365 U.S. 43 (1961).

93. TCA (Thomas C. Armitage, clerk) to Justice William O. Douglas, memorandum, March 26, 1970, Barlow v. Gallant, box 1493, Douglas Papers; TAC (Thomas C. Armitage, clerk) to Justice William O. Douglas, memorandum, March 2, 1971, Barlow v. Gallant, box 1493, Douglas Papers; TAC (Thomas C. Armitage, clerk) to Justice William O. Douglas, memorandum, April 12, 1970, Wheeler v. Goodman, box 1493, Douglas Papers; Barlow v. Gallant, 401 U.S. 986 (1971); Wheeler v. Goodman, 401 U.S. 987 (1971); Justice Potter Stewart, 5th Draft of Dissent, recirculated May 14, 1971, Coates v. City of Cincinnati, box I-240, Brennan Papers; Justice John Marshall Harlan to Justice Potter Stewart, May 27, 1971, Coates v. City of Cincinnati, box I-240, Brennan Papers.

94. Coates v. City of Cincinnati, 402 U.S. 611, 613, 614, 616 (1971).

95. Fred P. Graham, "High Court Upsets Anti-Loitering Law in a 5–4 Decision," *New York Times*, June 2, 1971, 1, 19. There was, and remains, considerable confusion about overbreadth doctrine that led to conflicts among the justices in Coates and other cases. See, e.g., United States v. Salerno, 481 U.S. 739 (1987); Washington State Grange v. Washington State Republican Party, 552 U.S. 442 (2008); Richard H. Fallon Jr., "Making Sense of Overbreadth," *Yale Law Journal* 100, no. 4 (January 1991): 853–908; "The First Amendment Overbreadth Doctrine," 844–927. For the substantive view, see, e.g., Bd. of Trs. v. Fox, 492 U.S. 469, 484–85 (1989); Charles Alan Wright, Arthur R. Miller, and Edward H. Cooper, *Federal Practice and Procedure* § 3531.94, vol. 13A, 3rd ed. (Eagan, MN: Thomson/West, 2008). For the standing view, see, e.g., Members of City Council v. Taxpayers for Vincent, 466 U.S. 789, 800 n. 19 (1984); Coates, 402 U.S. at 615 n. 5.

96. Coates, 402 U.S. at 616, 616 n.6; Graham, "High Court Upsets Ant-Loitering Law in a 5–4 Decision," 1; John P. MacKenzie, "Loitering Law Upset by Court as Too Vague," *Washington Post*, June 2, 1971, A1.

97. Transcript of Oral Argument, Coates, Oyez Project; see Sophia Rosenfeld, *Common Sense: A Political History* (Cambridge, MA: Harvard University Press, 2011) (noting the various, sometimes contradictory, ways that "common sense" has been used by political actors throughout American history).

98. See, e.g., Cox, 379 U.S. 536; Coates, 402 U.S. at 619–21.

99. Coates, 402 U.S. at 617 (Black, J., separate opinion). This was an unusual suggestion. See Kennedy v. Silas Mason Co., 334 U.S. 249, 256–57 (1948).

100. Coates, 402 U.S. at 616.
101. Justice Harry A. Blackmun, memorandum, n.d., Palmer v. City of Euclid, box 126, Blackmun Papers; Appellant's Brief at 3, Coates v. City of Cincinnati, 402 U.S. 611 (1971) (No. 117); see ACLU Suspicious Persons Law Case to be Heard by U.S. Supreme Court on Monday, January 11, January 9, 1971, Palmer v. City of Euclid, box 1608, American Civil Liberties Union Records, Subseries 4A, Series 4, Princeton ACLU Papers; Transcript of Oral Argument, Palmer, Oyez Project.
102. Compare Miscellaneous Docket Sheet, n.d., Palmer v. Euclid, box 1454, Douglas Papers, with Notes Regarding, n.d., Coates v. City of Cincinnati, box 1484, and Justice William O. Douglas, Conference Notes, January 15, 1971, Coates v. City of Cincinnati, box 1490, Douglas Papers; Justice Harry A. Blackmun, memorandum, n.d., Palmer v. City of Euclid, box 126, Blackmun Papers.
103. Graham, "High Court Upsets Anti-Loitering Law in a 5–4 Decision," 1; MacKenzie, "Loitering Law Upset by Court as Too Vague," A1; Glen Elsasser, "Supreme Court Issues Warning on Suspicious Persons Laws," *Chicago Tribune*, May 25, 1971, 3; Fred P. Graham, "Loitering: It's Not Enough that Someone Is Annoyed," *New York Times*, June 6, 1971, E7; Ronald J. Ostrow, "High Court Restricts Accident Bonding Rule," *Los Angeles Times*, May 25, 1971, 14.
104. Graham, "High Court Upsets Anti-Loitering Law in a 5–4 Decision," 1; Elsasser, "Supreme Court Issues Warning on Suspicious Persons Law," 3; see also "Court Rejects Appeal of N.Y. Redistricting," *Washington Post*, May 19, 1970, A7 ("The law, similar to many which are said to give police excessive discretion . . ."); MacKenzie, "Loitering Law Upset by Court as Too Vague," A1; Ostrow, "Court Upsets Vaguely Worded Law to Control Demonstrators," 1.
105. Graham, "Loitering: It's Not Enough That Someone Is Annoyed," E7.
106. Ibid.

Chapter 9

1. See, e.g., Robin Yeamans, "Constitutional Attacks on Vagrancy Laws," *Stanford Law Review* 20, no. 4 (1968): 782; Christopher Smith, "Symposium: Kansas Criminal Code: Vagrancy," *University of Kansas Law Review* 19, no. 4 (1970–71): 772; Gary V. Dubin and Richard H. Robinson, "The Vagrancy Concept Reconsidered: Problems and Abuses of Status Criminality," *New York University Law Review* 37, no. 1 (1962): 102; Charles Ares to Justice William O. Douglas, February 6, 1968, Vagrancy folder, box 666, William O. Douglas Papers, Library of Congress (hereafter Douglas Papers) (describing "in house" recommendation from city attorney to police chief not to use vagrancy law and noting decrease in vagrancy arrests in Tuscon, Arizona); Sidney C. Levine to Justice William O. Douglas, September 5, 1961, Vagrancy folder, box 666, Douglas Papers (local court in Des Moines, Iowa, invalidated loitering law); "Va. Arrests Vagrants Despite End of Law," *Washington Post*, November 10, 1968, A31; 1971 Va. Acts 420. See, e.g., Mark Budnitz, "Criminal Law—Statutory Offences—Vagrancy Laws Invalid as Too Vague and as Improper Exercise of Police Power," *Harvard Civil Rights-Civil Liberties Law Review* 3, no. 2 (1968): 439–49; Joel R. Campbell, "Criminal Law—Suspicious Person Ordinances— Due Process Standards," *Akron Law Review* 4, no. 2 (1971): 231; Ronald W. Crenshaw, "Vagrancy Statute: To Be or Not to Be," *South Dakota Law Review* 15, no. 2 (1970): 351; Alan M. Dershowitz, "On 'Preventative Detention,'" *New York Review of Books*, March 13, 1969, 22; James R. Dirmann, "Constitutional Law—Georgia Vagrancy Statute—An Analysis of Statutes' Criminality," *Mercer Law Review* 20, no. 1 (1969): 294; Gregory Foote, "The Unconstitutionality of Oregon's Loitering Statute," *Oregon Law Review* 51, no. 3 (1972): 624; H. Bruce Hamilton, "Constitutional Law—Vagrancy, Loitering and Related Offenses Held Unconstitutional because of Vagueness and Overbreadth," *Nebraska Law Review* 48, no. 1 (1968): 284; P. Bruce Harper, "Locomotion, Liberty and Legislation," *Montana Law Review* 32, no. 2 (1971): 279; John E. Hauge, "Vagrancy—A Crime of Status," *Wake Forest Intramural Law Review* 6, no. 2 (1970): 307; William A. Kurtz, "Two More Strikes against Vague Vagrancy Ordinances: Palmer v. Euclid and

Coates v. Cincinnati," *Ohio State Law Journal* 32, no. 4 (1971): 902; P. Michael Lahan, "Trends in the Law of Vagrancy," *Connecticut Law Review* 1, no. 2 (1968): 350; William F. Maher and William E. Williams, "Vagrancy—A Study in Constitutional Absolescence," *University of Florida Law Review* 22, no. 3 (1970): 384; Harold G. Melville, "Florida Vagrancy Statute: Here Today, Gone Tomorrow—Hopefully," *University of Miami Law Review* 25, no. 2 (1971): 345; Beverly C. Moore, "Vagrancy and Related Offenses," *Harvard Civil Rights-Civil Liberties Law Review* 4, no. 2 (1969): 291; John M. Murtagh, "Status Offenses and Due Process of Law," *Fordham Law Review* 36 (1967–68): 51; Cliff Nelson and Ray Steele, "Vagrancy Dilemma: An Empirical Study," *Osgoode Hall Law Journal* 7, no. 2 (1970): 177; Raymond Nimmer, "Court-Directed Reform of Vagrancy-type Laws," *Judicature* 54, no. 2 (1970): 50; Smith, "Vagrancy," 771; Joseph Van Walraven, "Vagrancy: Loitering as Definitional Conduct in Oklahoma," *Tulsa Law Journal* 8, no. 1 (1972): 74; John T. Walsh, "Vagrancy: A Crime of Status," *Suffolk University Law Review* 2, no. 2 (1968): 156; Harry M. Zimmerman, "Louisiana Vagrancy Law—Constitutionally Unsound," *Louisiana Law Review* 29, no. 2 (1969): 361. But see William Sidney Davis, "Vagrancy—Loitering Laws: An Antithesis to Recent Jurisprudential Trends," *Tennessee Law Review* 35, no. 4 (1968): 617.

2. Goldman v. Knecht, 295 F. Supp. 897 (D. Colo. 1969); Robert Bruce Miller, telephone interview with author, October 2012; Brief for Petitioner at 22–23, Hicks v. United States, 383 U.S. 252 (1965) (No. 51); Monroe Freedman, telephone interview with author, August 13, 2012; Niki Schwartz, telephone interview with author, January 18, 2013; see also Doran Williams (Executive Director, Texas Civil Liberties Union) to Melvin Wulf, April 8, 1969, Gallant v. Barlow, box 1395, American Civil Liberties Union Records, Series 4, Subseries 4A, Department of Rare Books and Special Collections, Princeton University.

3. Lazarus v. Fairclough, 301 F. Supp. 266 (S.D. Fla. 1969). The Court also denied cert in Odom v. Pensacola. Miscellaneous Docket Sheet, n.d., Odom v. City of Pensacola (No. 6009 IFP), box 1486, Douglas Papers; see also REG (Robert E. Gooding Jr.) to Justice Harry A. Blackmun, memorandum, January 4, 1971, Papachristou v. City of Jacksonville, box 143, Harry A. Blackmun Papers, Library of Congress (hereafter Blackmun Papers).

4. Fla. Stat. § 856.02 (1965); see also Jacksonville, Fla., Ord. Code § 26–57; West Palm Beach, Fla., Ord. § 33.63.

5. Brief for Petitioner at 3 n. 3, Papachristou v. City of Jacksonville, 405 U.S. 156 (1972) (No. 70–5030). See Comprehensive Alcoholism Prevention, Control and Treatment Act, 1971 Fla. Laws 375 (c. 71–132). Minor changes had also been made in 1869 and 1905. Brief for Petitioner at 16, Smith v. Florida, 405 U.S. 172 (1972) (No. 70-5055); United States v. Kilgen, 431 F.2d 627, 628 (5th Cir. 1970) (quoting appellant's brief); see also GTF (George T. Frampton) to Justice Harry A. Blackmun, bench memorandum, December 4, 1971, Smith v. Florida (No. 70-5055), box 144, Blackmun Papers.

6. J. Francis Paschal, "Douglas Blount Maggs," *Duke Law Journal*, no. 1 (1963): i–iv; Howard E. Covington Jr. and Marion A. Ellis, *Terry Sanford: Politics, Progress, and Outrageous Ambitions* (Durham, NC: Duke University Press, 1999), 171.

7. Sam Jacobson, telephone interview with author, May 2013.

8. Johnson v. Florida, 391 U.S. 596 (1968); Johnson v. Florida, 216 So. 2d 7 (Fla. 1968); Johnson v. Florida, 202 So. 2d 852 (Fla. 1967); Phillip Hubbart, telephone interview with author, May 23, 2013; see also Snow v. Florida, 179 So. 2d 99 (Fla. Dist. Ct. App. 1965); Reeves v. Florida, 187 SO. 2d 403 (Fla. Dist. Ct. App. 966).

9. Phillip Hubbart, telephone interview with author, May 23, 2013; Second Draft Opinion, Smith v. Florida, December 27, 1971, box 1559, Douglas Papers; Appendix at 5–6, Smith v. Florida, 405 U.S. 172 (1971) (No. 70-5055).

10. Sam Jacobson, telephone interview with author, May 2013.

11. Ibid.

12. Ibid.

13. Papachristou v. City of Jacksonville, 405 U.S. 156 (1972); Sam Jacobson, telephone interview with author, May 2013. Heath's record indicated that he was also "loitering."

14. Brief for Petitioner at 10, 28 n. 14, Papachristou; Sam Jacobson, in discussion with author, May 2013.

15. Papachristou, 405 U.S. at 159; Brief for Petitioner at 7–8, Papachristou.
16. Brief for Petitioner at 6, Papachristou.
17. Papachristou, 405 U.S. at 159 (1972); Sam Jacobson, telephone interview with author, May 2013.
18. Sam Jacobson, telephone interview with author, May 2013; Brief for Petitioner at 7, Papachristou.
19. Sam Jacobson, telephone interview with author, May 2013.
20. Ibid.
21. Terry v. Ohio, 392 U.S. 1, 5 (1968); President's Commission on Law Enforcement and Administration of Justice, *Task Force Report: The Police* (Washington, DC: Government Printing Office, 1967), 184.
22. Kenneth Rexroth, "The Fuzz," *Playboy*, July 1967, 76; Wayne R. LaFave, *Arrest: The Decision to Take a Suspect into Custody* (New York: Little, Brown, 1965), 455; President's Commission on Law Enforcement and Administration of Justice, *Task Force Report: The Police*, 187; see, e.g., State v. Hall 52 A.2d 845, 846 (N.J. Ct. Spec. Sess. 1947).
23. Brief for Petitioner at 24, Papachristou. On the legal suppression of interracial sex, see Hannah Rosen, *Terror in the Heart of Freedom: Citizenship, Sexual Violence, and the Meaning of Race in the Postemancipation South* (Chapel Hill: University of North Carolina Press, 2009), 74–75, 172–73, 194–202; Crystal Nicole Feimster, *Southern Horrors: Women and the Politics of Rape and Lynching* (Cambridge, MA: Harvard University Press, 2009), 50–51, 91–92, 98, 165, 177; Grace Hale, *Making Whiteness: The Culture of Segregation in the South, 1890–1940* (New York: Vintage Books, 1999), 199–239; Martha Elizabeth Hodes, *White Women, Black Men: Illicit Sex in the Nineteenth-Century South* (New Haven, CT: Yale University Press, 1997), 176–208; Ida B. Wells, *On Lynchings: Southern Horrors, a Red Record, Mob Rule in New Orleans* (New York: Arno Press, 1969); Andrew B. Leiter, *In the Shadow of the Black Beast: African American Masculinity in the Harlem and Southern Renaissances* (Baton Rouge: Louisiana State University Press, 2010), 17–50; Joy James, *Resisting State Violence: Radicalism, Gender, and Race in U.S. Culture* (Minneapolis: University of Minnesota Press, 1996); James Goodman, *Stories of Scottsboro* (London: Vintage, 1994); Peggy Pascoe, *What Comes Naturally: Miscegenation Law and the Making of Race in America* (Oxford: Oxford University Press, 2009), 19–21; Walter Wadlington, "The Loving Case: Virginia's Anti-Miscegenation Statute in Historical Perspective," *Virginia Law Review* 52, no. 7 (1966): 1191; Randall Kennedy, *Race, Crime, and the Law* (London: Vintage, 1998); Barbara Meil Hobson, *Uneasy Virtue* (Chicago: University of Chicago Press, 1987), 31, 36.
24. For miscegenation laws, see Pace v. Alabama, 106 U.S. 583 (1883); Perez v. Sharp, 198 P.2d 17 (Cal. 1948); see generally Pascoe, *What Comes Naturally*, 200–45; Wadlington, "The Loving Case," 1212. A Baltimore criminal court also held a related law unconstitutional, but it remained on the books in Maryland. Wadlington, "The Loving Case," 1212 n. 146; cf. Naim v. Naim, 350 U.S. 891 (1955), 350 U.S. 985 (1956). For the Florida case, see McLaughlin v. Florida, 379 U.S. 184, 198 (1964) (Stewart, J., concurring). On *Loving*, see Pascoe, *What Comes Naturally*, 253; Loving v. Virginia, 388 U.S. 1 (1967). Maryland repealed its law in 1967 while the Loving litigation was pending. See Loving, 388 U.S. at 6, n. 5; Wadlington, "The Loving Case."
25. Ed Cray, *Big Blue Line: Police Power vs. Human Rights* (New York: Coward, McCann and Geoghegan, 1967), 31–32, 227 n.3; Brief for the N.A.A.C.P. Legal Defense and Educational Fund, Inc., as Amicus Curiae at 45, Sibron v. New York, 392 U.S. 40 (1968) (No. 63); see American Civil Liberties Union of Southern California, *Report, Police Malpractice and the Watts Riot* (1965), 15–16, reproduced in Cray, *Big Blue Line*, 31; Pascoe, *What Comes Naturally*, 254.
26. Jackson v. Denver, 124 P.2d 240, 243 (Colo. 1942) (Bock, J., dissenting); "In Love? You're a 'Vagrant,'" *New Journal and Guide* (Norfolk, VA), May 24, 1958, 1.
27. "Dixie Police Spur Jim Crow," *Baltimore Afro-American*, August 25, 1951, 2.
28. "Porter, 42, Weds White Girl, 19," *Baltimore Afro-American*, September 8, 1951, 18; Lou Adams, "The Right to Love, N," *New York Amsterdam News*, April 16, 1955, 1.
29. Arletta Claire, "Arletta's Advice," *Chicago Daily Defender*, January 17, 1966, 19; "Survey Shows Negroes Still Harassed for Fraternizing with White Women," *Chicago Defender*, June 11, 1966, 4.

30. On Jacksonville and Jim Crow, see Robert Casanello, *To Render Invisible: Jim Crow and Public Life in New South Jacksonville* (Gainesville: University of Florida Press, 2013); Jessica R. Pliley, *Policing Sexuality: The Mann Act and the Making of the FBI* (Cambridge, MA: Harvard University Press, 2014); Beth L. Baily, *From Front Porch to Back Seat: Courtship in Twentieth-Century America* (Baltimore, MD: Johns Hopkins University Press, 1988).

31. See Shevin v. Lazarus, 301 F. Supp 266 (S.D. Fla. 1969), cert. denied 401 U.S. 987 (1971); Goldman, 295 F. Supp. 897; Goodman v. Wheeler, 306 F.Supp. 58 (W.D.N.C. 1969), cert. denied 401 U.S. 987 (1971); Barlow v. Gallant, No. SA-69-CA-158 (W.D.Tex.1969), cert. denied 401 U.S. 986 (1971); see also Kugler v. Karp, 310 F. Supp. 627 (D.N.J. 1970), cert. denied 401 U.S. 930 (1971); Wright v. City of Montgomery, 282 F. Supp. 291 (M.D. Ala. 1968), cert. denied 401 U.S. 989 (1971); Buchanan v. Wade, 308 F. Supp. 729 (N.D. Tex. 1970), cert. denied 401 U.S. 989 (1971); Koen v. Long, 302 F. Supp. 1383 (E.D. Mo. 1969), cert. denied 401 U.S. 923 (1971); Justice Hugo Black, Memorandum on Cases Held for Dombrowsi Group, n.d., box 1486, Douglas Papers; Justice William J. Brennan to Justice Hugo Black, memorandum (cases held for Dombrowski Group), March 9, 1971, box 1486, Douglas Papers.

32. LAP (Lucas A. Powe), memorandum, March 25, 1971, Smith v. Florida (70–5055), box 1559, Douglas Papers; REG (Robert E. Gooding Jr.) to Justice Harry A. Blackmun, memorandum, January 4, 1971, Papachristou v. City of Jacksonville, box 143, Blackmun Papers; REG (Robert E. Gooding Jr.), memorandum, March 29, 1971, Smith v. Florida, box 144, Blackmun Papers.

33. Cert. granted June 14, 1971; LAP (Lucas A. Powe), memorandum, December 26, 1970, Papachristou v. City of Jacksonville (No. 70-5030), box 1558, Douglas Papers; Docket Sheet, Papachristou v. City of Jacksonville (No. 70-5030), box 1523, Douglas Papers; Johnson, 216 So.2d at 8; "Vagrancy Conviction Changed," *Panama City* (FL) *News*, November 21, 1968. On resumed police enforcement, see LAP (Lucas A. Powe), memorandum, December 26, 1970, Papachristou v. City of Jacksonville (No. 70-5030), box 1558, Douglas Papers; Kilgen, 431 F.2d at 631; see, e.g., Schuster v. Florida, 235 So. 2d 30 (Fla. Dist. Ct. App. 1970); Newbold v. Florida, 229 So. 2d 876 (Fla. Dist. Ct. App. 1969); see also Cantrell v. Folsom, 332 F. Supp. 767 (M.D. Fla. 1971); Mills v. Wainwright, 415 F.2d 787 (5th Cir. 1969); Fairclough, 301 F. Supp. 266; Smith v. State, 239 So. 2d 250 (Fla. 1970); see also REG (Robert E. Gooding Jr.), memorandum, February 10, 1971, Smith v. Florida (No. 70–5055), box 144, Blackmun Papers; LAP (Lucas A Powe), memorandum, November 16, 1970, Shevin v. Lazarus (No. 43), Cert Memos O.T. 1970 folder, box 1493, Douglas Papers; LAP (Lucas A. Powe), memorandum, March 2, 1971, Barlow v. Gallant (No. 90), Cert Memos O.T. 1970 folder, box 1493, Douglas Papers; TCA (Thomas C. Armitage), supplemental memorandum, June 24, 1970, Faircloth v. Lazarus (No. 43), Cert Memos O.T. 1970 folder, box 1493, Douglas Papers; MAL (Michel A. LaFond), memorandum, November 13, 1970, Faircloth v. Lazarus (No. 43), Certiorari Memorandum, box 762, Blackmun Papers; DCB (Dennis C. Brown), memorandum, n.d., Faircloth v. Lazarus (No. 43), Cert Memos O.T. 1970 folder, box 1493, Douglas Papers; TCA (Thomas C. Armitage), memorandum, December 6, 1969, Faircloth v. Lazarus (No. 630), Cert Memos O.T. 1970 folder, box 1493, Douglas Papers. The judgment was vacated and remanded for reconsideration in light of *Younger v. Harris*, with only Justice Douglas voting to note probable jurisdiction and affirm. Lazarus, WOD, LOC, box 1484, Administrative Docket Book, Orig. #41–47/#1–160.

34. "Vagrancy Law Expected to Be Ruled Out," *Sarasota* (FL) *Herald-Tribune*, September 26, 1971, 13-A; "Jacksonville Attorney Challenges State's Vagrancy Law," *Ocala* (FL) *Star-Banner*, September 26, 1971, 7A.

35. Brief for Petitioner at 2, 19, 24, 29–31, Papachristou; Brief for Petitioner at 9–10, Smith.

36. See, e.g., Brief for Petitioner at 27–28, Smith; Brief for Petitioner at 22, 24, Papachristou.

37. Brief for Respondent at 21, Papachristou; Transcript of Oral Argument at 36, Papachristou v. City of Jacksonville, 405 U.S. 156 (1972) (No. 70–5030).

38. Brief for Respondent at 15–17, Smith v. Florida, 405 U.S. 156 (1972) (No. 70-5055).

39. Brief for Petitioner at 26, 28, Papachristou; "Feedback," WJCT-TV, Jacksonville, March 7, 1969, quoted in ibid. at 27; see also Brief for Petitioner at 21, Smith (discussing attorney general's comments); "Vagrancy Law Expected to Be Ruled Out," 13-A; "Jacksonville Attorney Challenges State's Vagrancy Law," 7A.

40. Transcript of Oral Argument at 5–6, Papachristou.
41. Ibid. at 16–17; Phillip Hubbart, telephone interview with author, May 23, 2013.
42. Phillip Hubbart, telephone interview with author, May 23, 2013; GTF (George T. Frampton) to Justice Harry A. Blackmun, bench memorandum, December 4, 1971, Smith v. Florida (No. 70–5055), box 144, Blackmun Papers; DCB (Dennis C. Brown), memorandum, June 2, 1971, and LAP (Lucas A. Powe), handwritten notes on memo, June 8, 1971, Papachristou v. Jacksonville (No. 70–5030), box 1558, Douglas Papers; LAP (Lucas A. Powe), memorandum, n.d., Papachristou v. City of Jacksonville (No. 70–5030), box 1558, Douglas Papers; Palmer v. City of Euclid, 402 U.S. 544 (1971); Wainwright v. City of New Orleans, 392 U.S. 598 (1968); Terry, 392 U.S. 1; Johnson, 391 U.S. 596.
43. Transcript of Oral Argument, Smith v. Florida, 405 U.S. 172 (1972) (No. 70–5055); ibid. at 42.
44. Reply Brief at 5, Papachristou v. City of Jacksonville, 405 U.S. 156 (1972) (No. 70–5030).
45. Justice William O. Douglas, Conference Notes, December 10, 1971, Papachristou v. Jacksonville (No. 70-5030), box 1558, Douglas Papers.
46. GTF (George T. Frampton), bench memorandum, December 2, 1971, Papachristou v. City of Jacksonville (No. 70-5030), box 143, Blackmun Papers; Justice Harry A. Blackmun, memorandum, December 7, 1971, Smith v. Florida (No. 70–5055), box 144, Blackmun Papers.
47. GTF (George T. Frampton), bench memorandum, December 4, 1971, Papachristou v. City of Jacksonville (No. 70-5030), box 143, Blackmun Papers; Justice Harry A. Blackmun, memorandum, December 7, 1971, Smith v. Florida (No. 70–5055), box 144, Blackmun Papers.
48. Chief Justice Warren E. Burger, memorandum to conference, December 20, 1971, Smith v. Florida (No. 70-5055), box 92, Thurgood Marshall Papers, 1949–1991, Library of Congress; Justice William O. Douglas, Conference Notes, December 10, 1971, Smith v. Florida (No. 70–5055), box 1559, Douglas Papers.
49. Second Draft Opinion, p. 2, December 27, 1971, Smith v. Florida (No. 70-5055), box 1559, Douglas Papers (quoting Hanks v. State, 195 So. 2d 49 (Fla. Dist. Ct. App. 1966)); Fifth Draft Opinion, January 31, 1972, Smith v. Florida (No. 70-5055), box 1559, Douglas Papers; Fourth Draft Opinion, recirculated January 3, 1972, Smith v. Florida (No. 70-5055), box 1559, Douglas Papers.
50. Brief for Petitioner at 19, Papachristou; see also Transcript of Oral Argument at 3, 10, Papachristou; on Lusky, see Chapter 3, this volume; see also Paul G. Flynn, "Vagrancy Laws and the Right to Privacy," *University of San Francisco Law Review* 2 (1968): 337–54.
51. Draft Opinion, n.d., Papachristou v. City of Jacksonville (No. 70–5030), box 1558, Douglas Papers.
52. Bruce Murphy, *Wild Bill: The Legend and Life of William O. Douglas* (New York: Random House, 2003); Edwards v. California, 314 U.S. 160, 178 (1941) (Douglas, J., concurring) (citation omitted); Shuttlesworth v. Birmingham, 382 U.S. 87, 96 (1965) (Douglas, J., concurring) (citation omitted); Hicks v. District of Columbia, 383 U.S. 252, 256–57 (1966) (Douglas, J., dissenting). Douglas's commitment to the freedom of locomotion was also implicated in *Terry v. Ohio*, 392 U.S. 1 (1968), where he dissented alone. Justice Byron R. White to Justice William O. Douglas, memorandum, February 8, 1972, Papachristou v. City of Jacksonville (No. 70-5030), box 1558, Douglas Papers; see generally William O. Douglas, *Go East, Young Man: The Early Years: The Autobiography of William O. Douglas* (New York: Random House, 1974), 76–79; William O. Douglas, *Of Men and Mountains* (New York: Harper, 1950), 9–16; William O. Douglas to Edward L. R. Elson, December 7, 1977, in *The Douglas Letters: Selections from the Private Papers of Justice William O. Douglas*, ed. Melvin I. Urofsky (Bethesda, MD: Adler and Adler, 1987), 425–26; William O. Douglas, "Vagrancy and Arrest on Suspicion," *Yale Law Journal* 70, no. 1 (1960): 4. For the argument that Douglas lacked credibility as a storyteller, see Murphy, *Wild Bill*, 118–23. On physical mobility as long central to the Anglo-American conception of liberty, see St. George Tucker, *Blackstone's Commentaries: With Notes of Reference, to the Constitution and Laws, of the Federal Government of the United States; and of the Commonwealth of Virginia* (Philadelphia: William Young Birch and Abraham Small, 1803), 2: 134; Thomas M. Cooley, *A Treatise on the Constitutional Limitations Which Rest upon the Legislative Power of the State of the American Union* (Boston: Little, Brown, 1868), 339.

53. Papachristou, 405 U.S. at 164 n. 7; Nicolas N. Kittrie, *The Right to Be Different: Deviance and Enforced Therapy* (London: Penguin Books, 1973): Mary Douglas, *Natural Symbols: Explorations in Cosmology* (London: Barrie and Rockliff, 1970); see also Gerald N. Grob, *Mental Illness and American Society, 1875–1940* (Princeton, NJ: Princeton University Press, 1983).

54. See Papachristou, 405 U.S. at 164 n.6 (quoting Reich); Charles A. Reich, *The Sorcerer of Bolinas Reef* (New York: Random House, 1976); Charles Reich, *The Greening of America* (New York: Random House, 1970); Philip Nobile, ed., *The Con III Controversy: The Critics Look at the Greening of America* (New York: Pocket Books, 1971); see also Rodger D. Citron, "Charles Reich's Journey from the *Yale Law Journal* to the *New York Times* Best-Seller List: The Personal History of the Greening of America," *New York Law School Law Review* 52, no. 3 (2008): 387–418; Sarah A. Seo, "The New Public," *Yale Law Journal* 125 (forthcoming 2016); Sarah A. Seo, "The Right to Privacy in Public," in *The Fourth Amendment, Cars, and Freedom in Twentieth-Century America* (Ph.D. diss., Princeton University, 2015).

55. On the preferred status of speech and assembly rights, see Saia v. New York, 334 U.S. 558, 562 (1948); see also West Virginia State Bd. of Educ. v. Barnette, 319 U.S. 624, 639 (1943); Thornhill v. Alabama, 310 U.S. 88, 95–96 (1940); Schneider v. State, 308 U.S. 147, 161 (1939); see G. Edward White, "The First Amendment Comes of Age," *Michigan Law Review* 95, no. 2 (1996): 299–391; Michael Klarman, "An Interpretive History of Modern Equal Protection," *Michigan Law Review* 90, no. 2 (1991): 213–318; Second Draft Opinion, December 28, 1971, Papachristou v. City of Jacksonville (No. 70-5030), box 1558, Douglas Papers. Justice Douglas cites *Shelton v. Tucker*, 364 U.S. 479 (1960), *Harper v. Virginia Board of Elections*, 383 U.S. 663 (1966), and *Kramer v. Union Free School District*, 395 U.S. 621 (1969), and *Cantwell v. Connecticut*, 310 U.S. 296 (1940). RLJ (Richard L. Jacobson) to Justice William O. Douglas, memorandum, January 10, 1972, Papachristou v. City of Jacksonville (No. 70-5030), box 1558, Douglas Papers; cf. Louis Henkin, "Foreword: On Drawing Lines," *Harvard Law Review* 82, no. 1 (1968): 63 n. 92; William N. Eskridge Jr., "Some Effects of Identity-Based Social Movements on Constitutional Law in the Twentieth Century," *Michigan Law Review* 100, no. 8 (2002): 2230–31.

56. For examples of Douglas's resistance to using substantive due process, see Griswold v. Connecticut, 381 U.S. 479 (1965); Skinner v. Oklahoma, 316 U.S. 535 (1942).

57. Fourth Draft Opinion, December 30, 1971, Papachristou v. City of Jacksonville (No. 70-5030), box 1558, Douglas Papers.

58. Eisenstadt v. Baird, 405 U.S. 438 (1972); Roe v. Wade, 410 U.S. 113 (1973); see also Doe v. Bolton, 410 U.S. 179 (1973).

59. Ricks v. District of Columbia, 414 F.2d 1097 (D.C. Cir.1968); Kirkwood v. Ellington, 298 F. Supp. 461 (W.D. Tenn., 1969).

60. See, e.g., H. L. A. Hart, *Law, Liberty and Morality* (Palo Alto, CA: Stanford University Press, 1963); see also Herbert L. Packer, "The Aims of the Criminal Law Revisited: A Plea for a New Look at 'Substantive Due Process,'" *Southern California Law Review* 44, no. 2 (1971): 493 (describing abortion as a victimless crime).

61. Justice Harry A. Blackmun, memorandum to the conference, May 18, 1972, Roe v. Wade (No. 70-18), box 151, Blackmun Papers; Justice Harry A. Blackmun, memorandum to the conference, May 25, 1972, Doe v. Bolton (No. 70-40), box 152, Blackmun Papers; see Linda Greenhouse, *Becoming Justice Blackmun: Harry Blackmun's Supreme Court Journey* (New York: Macmillan, 2005).

62. Justice William J. Brennan to Justice William O. Douglas, December 30, 1971, Roe v. Wade (No. 70-18), William J. Brennan Papers, 1945–1998, Library of Congress; see, e.g., United States v. Vuitch, 402 U.S. 62, 78 (1971) (Douglas, J., dissenting in part); Poe v. Ullman, 67 U.S. 497, 517, 539 (1961) (Douglas, J., dissenting, Harlan, J., dissenting).

63. Olmstead v. United States, 77 U.S. 438, 478 (1928) (Brandeis, J., dissenting).

64. Justice William J. Brennan to Justice William O. Douglas, December 30, 1971, Papachristou v. City of Jacksonville (No. 70-5030), box I-274, William J. Brennan Papers, 1945–1998, Library of Congress.

65. Rider 8, Papachristou v. City of Jacksonville (No. 70-5030), box 1558, Douglas Papers; see also Fifth Draft Opinion, December 30, 1971, Papachristou v. City of Jacksonville (No. 70-5030), box 1558, Douglas Papers.

66. Stewart also asked Douglas to delete a later reference to the Bill of Rights. Justice William O. Douglas to Justice Potter Stewart, January 28, 1972, Papachristou v. City of Jacksonville (No. 70-5030), box 1558, Douglas Papers; handwritten note from Justice Potter Stewart to Justice William O. Douglas, January 28, 1872, Papachristou v. City of Jacksonville (No. 70-5030), box 1558, Douglas Papers; see Edited draft, January 28, 1972, Papchristou v. City of Jacksonville (No. 70-5030), box 1558, Douglas Papers (showing deletion of paragraph with the Bill of Rights reference).

67. Justice William O. Douglas, Conference Notes, December 10, 1971, Papachristou v. Jacksonville (No. 70-5030), box 1558, Douglas Papers; Griswold, 381 U.S. at 527–28 (Stewart, J., dissenting); Katz v. United States, 389 U.S. 347, 350–51 (1967); see also Henkin, "Forward: On Drawing Lines," 71 n. 25; "The Void-for-Vagueness Doctrine in the Supreme Court," *University of Pennsylvania Law Review* 109, no. 1 (1960): 67; John Calvin Jeffries Jr., "Legality, Vagueness, and the Construction of Penal Statutes," *Virginia Law Review* 71, no. 2 (1985): 189, 212.

68. Roe, 410 U.S. at 153 (1973); Moore v. City of East Cleveland, 431 U.S. 494, 499 (plurality opinion); ibid. at 531 (Stewart, J., dissenting); Papachristou, 405 U.S. at 164.

69. Papachristou, 405 U.S. at 162.

70. Roe, 410 U.S. at 152–54 (1973); ibid. at 169 (Stewart, J., concurring).

71. Bolton, 410 U.S. at 213 (Douglas, J., concurring).

72. Sam Jacobson, phone interview with author, July 2013; Fred P. Graham, "A Vagrancy Law in Florida Upset by Supreme Court: Jacksonville Ordinance Held Too Vague—Broad Ruling Expected to Void Many Similar Statutes across the Nation," *New York Times*, February 25, 1972, 1; Ronald J. Ostrow, "Supreme Court Voids Ordinance on Vagrancy: Ruling on Jacksonville, Fla. Law Appears Broad Enough to Apply to Entire Nation," *Los Angeles Times*, February 25, 1972, A4. But see "Court Overrules Vagrancy Law, Bans Secret Immunity: Says Jury Must Know of Deals by Prosecution," *Los Angeles Times*, February 23, 1972, A2; Anthony Lewis, "The Divided Court," *New York Times*, July 1, 1972, 21 (discussing the broad application of Papachristou).

73. "Rogues and Vagabonds," *Washington Post*, February 26, 1972, A14; see also Philip B. Kurland, "1971 Term: The Year of the Stewart-White Court," *Supreme Court Review*, 1972, 181.

74. Edelman v. California, 344 U.S. 357, 366 (1953) (Black, J., dissenting); Anthony Amsterdam, "Federal Constitutional Restrictions on the Punishment of Crimes of Status, Crimes of General Obnoxiousness, Crimes of Displeasing Police Officers, and the Like," *Criminal Law Bulletin* 3, no. 4 (1967): 205.

75. Papachristou, 405 U.S. at 169 n. 15.

76. Papachristou, 405 U.S. at 159; Thornhill, 310 U.S at 97–98 (1940), quoted in ibid. at 170; Shuttlesworth, 382 U.S. at 90, quoted in ibid. at 170. With the exception of Cold War cases involving communists or alleged communists. On the Court's less protective stance toward alleged communists in the 1950s, see Chapter One, this volume.

77. Justice Harry A. Blackmun, memorandum, December 7, 1971, Papachristou v. City of Jacksonville (No. 70-5030), box 143, Blackmun Papers.

78. Edwards, 314 U.S. at 174, quoted in ibid. at 162; Amsterdam, "Federal Constitutional Restrictions on the Punishment of Crimes of Status," 226, quoted in ibid. at 170–71. For examples of the Court's protection of the poor in other contexts, see, e.g., Fuentes v. Shevin, 407 U.S. 67, 90 (1972); Boddie v. Connecticut, 401 U.S. 371 (1971); Goldberg v. Kelly, 397 U.S. 254 (1970); Shapiro v. Thompson, 394 U.S. 618 (1969); King v. Smith, 392 U.S. 309 (1968); Arceneaux v. Louisiana, 376 U.S. 336 (1964); Shevin v. Lazarus, 401 U.S. 987 (1971); Wallace v. State, 161 S.E.2d 288 (Ga. 1968) cert. denied 393 U.S. 1123 (1969); Fenster v. Leary, 229 N.E.2d 426 (N.Y. 1967). On the rise of the free market, see Daniel T. Rodgers, *Age of Fracture* (Cambridge, MA: Harvard University Press, 2011) For the quote, see Papachristou, 405 U.S. at 161–62 n. 4, 162–63 (1972).

79. Papachristou, 405 U.S. at 164, 170. For examples of Burger Court protection of the right to travel, see, e.g., Dunn v. Blumstein, 405 U.S. 330, 338–43 (1972) (voting); Shapiro, 396 U.S. at 638 (welfare benefits); see also Kurland, "1971 Term," 181. For other Burger Court protections of nonconformity, see Conclusion, this volume.

80. Papachristou, 405 U.S. at 162, 169.

81. Papachristou, 405 U.S. at 167 (quoting Caleb Foote, "Vagrancy-Type Law and Its Administration," *University of Pennsylvania Law Review* 104, no. 5 (1956): 631). For Burger Court intervention in local court procedure, see, e.g., Argersinger v. Hamlin, 407 U.S. 25, 33 (1972); Ward v. Village of Monroeville, Ohio, 409 U.S. 57 (1972); Niki Schwartz, telephone interview with author, January 2013; Papachristou, 405 U.S. at 168; Adams v. Williams, 407 US 143 (1972). For the quotes, see Gooding v. Wilson, 405 U.S. 518, 528, (1972); Lewis v. City of New Orleans, 415 U.S. 130, 136 (1974).

82. Papachristou, 405 U.S. at 168 (quoting Foote); Papachristou, 405 U.S. at 162, 166, 170–71.

83. Powell v. Texas, 392 U.S. 514 (1968).

84. See Reed v. Reed, 404 U.S. 71 (1971). See, e.g., Michael J. Klarman, *From the Closet to the Altar: Courts, Backlash, and the Struggle for Same-Sex Marriage* (New York: Oxford, 2013); Marc Stein, *Sexual Injustice: Supreme Court Decisions from Griswold to Roe* (Chapel Hill: University of North Carolina Press, 2010).

85. On the Burger Court's increased conservatism, see, e.g., Washington v. Davis, 426 U.S. 229 (1976); Matthews v. Eldridge, 424 U.S. 319 (1976); Milliken v. Bradley, 418 U.S. 717 (1974); San Antonio Indep. Sch. Dist. v. Rodriguez, 411 U.S. 1 (1973); United States v. Kras, 409 U.S. 434, (1973); Moose Lodge No. 107 v. Irvis, 407 U.S. 163 (1972); Lloyd Corp. v. Tanner, 407 U.S. 551 (1972); Lindsey v. Normet, 405 U.S. 56 (1972); Dandridge v. Williams, 397 U.S. 471 (1970). But see Boddie v. Connecticut, 401 U.S. 371 (1971). For cases protecting lifestyles, see, e.g., Doe v. Bolton, 410 U.S. 179, 214 (1973) (Douglas, J., concurring); Ham v. South Carolina, 409 U.S. 524, 530 (1973) (Douglas, J., concurring in part and dissenting in part); Ham v. South Carolina, 409 U.S. 524, 530–31 (1973) (Marshall, J., concurring in part and dissenting in part); Wisconsin v. Yoder, 406 US 205, 217 (1972); cf. U.S. Dep't of Agriculture v. Moreno, 413 U.S. 528, 534 (1973). On the Burger Court as less conservative than the conventional wisdom, see, e.g., Vincent Blasi, ed., *The Burger Court: The Counter-Revolution That Wasn't* (New Haven, CT: Yale University Press, 1983); Bernard Schwartz, ed., *The Burger Court: Counter Revolution or Confirmation?* (New York: Oxford University Press, 1998); Jerold H. Israel, "Criminal Procedure, the Burger Court, and the Legacy of the Warren Court," *Michigan Law Review* 75 (June 1977): 1319–1425. On victimless crimes, see Richard Nixon, "Remarks at the Opening Session of the National Conference on the Judiciary in Williamsburg, Virginia, March 11, 1971," *Public Papers of the Presidents of the United States: Richard Nixon 1971* (Washington, DC: Government Printing Office, 1972), 420; "Williamsburg Cradles Another Revolution," *American Bar Association Journal* 57, no. 5 (1971): 422 (quoting Nixon's address); Allen Wiggins, "Judge Says Antivice Laws Serve No Useful Purpose," *Plain Dealer* (Cleveland), May 8, 1973, 19-B; National Advisory Commission on Criminal Justice Standards and Goals, *A National Strategy to Reduce Crime* (Washington, DC: Government Printing Office, 1973), 205.

86. See, e.g., "States Warned on Decriminalizing Victimless Crimes," *New York Times*, December 26, 1976, 39; Tom Goldstein, "Rethinking Victimless Crimes," *New York Times*, February 6, 1977, E5; "Shoot the Messenger," *Wall Street Journal*, November 13, 1978, 24; Anthony G. Amsterdam, "A Selective Survey of Supreme Court Decisions in Criminal Law and Procedure," *Criminal Law Bulletin* 9, no. 5 (1973): 389, 390.

87. J. Harvie Wilkinson III and G. Edward White, "Constitutional Protection for Personal Lifestyles," *Cornell Law Review* 62, no. 3 (1977): 564, 612, 613; see also Thomas C. Grey, "Do We Have an Unwritten Constitution?" *Stanford Law Review* 27, no. 3 (1975): 703; "On Privacy: Constitutional Protection for Personal Liberty," *New York University Law Review* 48, no. 4 (1973): 670. But cf. William Safire, "The Way We Live Now: On Language," *New York Times Magazine*, July 20, 2003, 20 (quoting Vice President Spiro Agnew on those "lifestyles that have neither life nor style"). See generally Ruthann Robson, *Dressing Constitutionally: Hierarchy, Sexuality, and Democracy from Our Hairstyles to Our Shoes* (New York: Cambridge University Press, 2013).

88. See, e.g., Stanley v. Illinois, 405 U.S. 645 (1972) (unmarried father); Reed v. Reed, 404 U.S. 71 (1971) (woman); U.S. Dept. of Agriculture v. Moreno, 413 U.S. 528 (1973) (hippies); Frontiero v. Richardson, 411 U.S. 677 (1973) (women); Weber v. Aetna Cas. & Sur. Co., 406 U.S. 164 (1972) (illegitimate children); Levy v. Louisiana, 391 U.S. 68 (1968) (illegitimate children); Harper v. Va. Bd. of Elections, 383 U.S. 663 (1966) (poor people); Griffin v. Illinois,

351 U.S. 12 (1956) (poor people); cf. Craig v. Boren, 429 U.S. 190 (1976) (announcing inter-
mediate scrutiny standard for women). See generally Gerald Gunther, "Foreword: In Search
of Evolving Doctrine on a Changing Court: A Model for a Newer Equal Protection," *Harvard
Law Review* 86, no. 1 (1972): 1–48.

89. See Bolton, 410 U.S. at 210–15 (Douglas, J., concurring); Laird v. Tatum, 408 U.S. 1, 28–29
(1972) (Douglas, J., dissenting); Eisenstadt, 405 U.S. at 460 (Douglas, J., concurring);
Reverend Edward L. R. Elson, "Funeral Remarks in Tribute to William O. Douglas, January
23, 1980," *American University Law Review* 29, no. 1 (1980): 3; see also Douglas, *Go East,
Young Man*, 75–86 (Douglas enlarging his discussion, two years after *Papachristou*, of his own
vagrant past, as well as hoboes more generally).

90. Kurland, "1971 Term," 181.

91. Section 856.021, Fla. Stat. § 856.021 (West Supp. 1975).

92. State v. Ecker, 311 So.2d 104, 110 (Fla. 1975); see also Hamrick v. Wainwright, 465 F.2d 940
(5th Cir.1972); Wilt v. State, 333 So. 2d 556 (Fla. Dist. Ct. App. 1976); B.A.A. v. State, 333
So. 2d 552 (Fla. Dist. Ct. App. 1976).

93. D.A. v. State, 471 So. 2d 147, 153 (Fla. Dist. Ct. App. 1985) (internal citation and quotations
omitted); see also S.F. v. State, 354 So. 2d 474, 476 (3rd Dist. Ct. App. Fla., 1978).

94. Sam Jacobson, telephone interview with author, July 2013.

Conclusion

1. See, e.g., William Cohen, Jonathan D. Varat, and Vikram Amar, *Constitutional Law: Cases and
Materials*, 13th ed. (New York: Foundation Press, 2009); Peter W. Low, John Calvin Jeffries
Jr., and Richard J. Bonnie, *Criminal Law: Cases and Materials* (New York: Foundation Press,
1982); Russell L. Weaver et al., *Constitutional Law: Materials, and Problems*, 2nd. ed. (New
York: Aspen, 2011). For law review articles, see, e.g., William N. Eskridge, "Some Effects of
Identity-Based Social Movements on Constitutional Law in the Twentieth Century," *Michigan
Law Review* 100 (2002): 2062; John C. Jeffries Jr., "Legality, Vagueness, and the Construction
of Penal Statutes," *Virginia Law Review* 71 (1985): 189; Robert C. Post, "Reconceptualizing
Vagueness: Legal Rules and Social Orders," *California Law Review* 82 (1994): 491; Debra
Livingston, "Police Discretion and the Quality of Life in Public Places: Courts, Communities,
and the New Policing," *Columbia Law Review* 97 (1997): 551.

2. Scholars have recently emphasized state and local legislative and administrative organs
as potential agencies for reform. See Rachel Harmon, "Promoting Civil Rights through
Proactive Policing Reform," *Stanford Law Review* 62, no. 1 (2009): 1; Rachel Harmon, "The
Problem of Policing," *Michigan Law Review* 110, no. 5 (2012): 761; Barry Friedman and Maria
Ponomarenko, "Governing Policing," *New York University Law Review* 90 (forthcoming).

3. Van Gosse, *Rethinking the New Left: An Interpretive History* (New York: Palgrave Macmillan, 2005);
Van Gosse, "A Movement of Movements: The Definition and Periodization of the New Left," in *A
Companion to Post-1945 America*, ed. Roy Rosenzweig and Jean-Christophe Agnew (Hoboken,
NJ: Wiley-Blackwell, 2002). Other efforts at historical integration include Jacqueline Castledine,
Cold War Progressives: Women's Interracial Organizing for Peace and Freedom (Urbana-Champaign:
University of Illinois Press, 2012); Lisa Phillips, *A Renegade Union: Interracial Organizing and
Labor Radicalism* (Urbana-Champaign: University of Illinois Press, 2013); Gordon K. Mantler,
Power to the Poor: Black-Brown Coalition and the Fight for Economic Justice, 1960–1974 (Chapel
Hill: University of North Carolina Press, 2013); Jakobi Williams, *From the Bullet to the Ballot:
The Illinois Chapter of the Black Panther Party and Racial Coalition Politics in Chicago* (Chapel Hill:
University of North Carolina Press, 2013). See generally Catherine A. Conner, "Coalitions and
the Long Civil Rights Movement," *Reviews in American History* 42, no. 4 (2014): 730–38.

4. For notable exceptions, see, e.g., Mark Brilliant, *The Color of American Has Changed: How
Racial Diversity Has Shaped Civil Rights Reform in California* (New York: Oxford University
Press, 2010); Tomiko Brown-Nagin, *Courage to Dissent: Atlanta and the Long History of the Civil
Rights Movement* (New York: Oxford University Press, 2011); Sophia Z. Lee, *The Workplace
Constitution from the New Deal to the New Right* (New York: Cambridge University Press,
2014); Serena Mayeri, *Reasoning from Race: Feminism, Law, and the Civil Rights Movement*
(Cambridge, MA: Harvard University Press, 2011); Laura Kalman, *Yale Law School and the
Sixties: Revolt and Reverberations* (Chapel Hill: University of North Carolina Press, 2005).

5. See, e.g., Nelson Lichtenstein, *State of the Union: A Century of American Labor* (Princeton, NJ: Princeton University Press, 2002).
6. On enforcing invalidated laws, see, e.g., William Glaberson, "Long Fight Ends over Arrests for Loitering," *New York Times*, February 7, 2012. On evading litigation, see, e.g., Govt. of the Canal Zone v. Castillo L., 568 F.2d 405 (5th Cir. 1978); People v. Solomon, 108 Cal. Rptr. 867 (Cal. Ct. App. 1973); State v. Williams, 315 So.2d 449 (Fla. Dist. Ct. App. 1975); Dinitz v. Christensen, 577 P.2d 873 (Nev. 1978); State v. Jones, 511 P.2d 74 (Wash. Ct. App. 1973).
7. Anthony G. Amsterdam, "A Selective Survey of Supreme Court Decisions in Criminal Law and Procedure," *Criminal Law Bulletin* 9, no. 5 (1973): 389, 390, 396.
8. For lower court cases taking the doctrine seriously, see, e.g., State v. Rackle, 523 P.2d 299, 301 (1974). For invalidations of vagrancy laws, see, e.g., Lawson v. Kolender, 658 F.2d 1362 (9th Cir. 1981); Powell v. Stone, 507 F.2d 93 (9th Cir. 1974), rev'd on other grounds, Stone v. Powell, 428 U.S. 465 (1976); United States ex rel. Newsome v. Malcolm, 492 F.2d 1166 (2d Cir. 1974); Anderson v. Nemetz, 474 F.2d 814 (9th Cir. 1973); Timmons v. City of Montgomery, 658 F. Supp. 1086 (M.D. Ala. 1987); Russo v. State, 270 So.2d 428 (Fla. Dist. Ct. App. 1972); Baker v. State, 478 S.W.2d 445 (Tex. Crim App. 1972); State v. Martinez, 538 P.2d 521 (Wash. 1971), overruled by State v. Smith, 610 P.2d 869 (1980); see supra note 5 for cases upholding vagrancy laws.
9. Thomas J. Sugrue, *Origins of the Urban Crisis: Race and Inequality in Postwar Detroit* (Princeton, NJ: Princeton University Press, 1996). On the 1970s generally, see, e.g., Edward D. Berkowitz, *Something Happened: A Political and Cultural Overview of the Seventies* (New York: Columbia University Press, 2006); Jefferson Cowie, *Stayin' Alive: The 1970s and the Last Days of the Working Class* (New York: New Press, 2010); David Frum, *How We Got Here: The 70's, the Decade That Brought You Modern Life (for Better or Worse)* (New York: Basic Books, 2000); Dan Berger, ed., *The Hidden 1970s: Histories of Radicalism* (New Brunswick, NJ: Rutgers University Press, 2010). On changes in ideas about criminal justice, see, e.g., National Advisory Committee on Criminal Justice Standards and Goals, *Organized Crime: Report of the Task Force on Organized Crime* (Washington, DC: Government Printing Office, 1976), 65; "Shoot the Messenger," *Wall Street Journal*, November 13, 1978, 24.
10. To some extent the racial politics of criminal justice had changed, as was apparent in the commentary on City of Chicago v. Morales, 527 U.S. 41 (1999). See, e.g., Randall Kennedy, *Race, Crime, and the Law* (New York: Pantheon Books, 1997); Dan M. Kahan and Tracey L. Meares, "The Coming Crisis in Criminal Procedure," *Georgetown Law Journal* 86, no. 2 (1998): 1153–84; Dorothy E. Roberts, "Foreword: Race, Vagueness, and the Social Meaning of Order-Maintenance Policing," *Journal of Criminal Law & Criminology* 89, no. 3 (1999); 775; Richard C. Schragger, "The Limits of Localism," *Michigan Law Review* 100, no. 2 (2001): 371–472. For veteran lawyers' involvement, see Commonwealth v. Sefranka, 414 N.E.2d 602 (Mass. 1980); People v. Weger, 59 Cal. Rptr. 661 (Cal. Ct. App. 1967), *cert. denied*, 389 U.S. 1047 (1968).
11. Notes for Conference, November 10, 1982, Kolender v. Lawson (No. 81–1320), box I: 609, William J. Brennan Papers, 1945–1998, Library of Congress.
12. Hibel v. Sixth Judicial Dist. Court of Nevada, 542 U.S. 177 (2004); City of Chicago v. Morales, 527 U.S. 41 (1999); Kolender v. Lawson, 461 U.S. 352 (1983); see Richard C. Schragger, "The Limits of Localism," *Michigan Law Review* 100, no. 2 (2001): 371–472. But see City of Chicago v. Morales, 527 U.S. 41, 73, 98 (1999) (Scalia, J., dissenting and Thomas, J., dissenting).
13. On displacement to disorderly conduct, see David Thacher, "Policing after Papachristou: A Case Study of the Impact of Legal Change on the Police," presented at the Law and Society Association Annual Conference, Boston, Massachusetts, May 30, 2013. On lingering, see, e.g., J. David Goodman, "Police Patrols in New York Public Housing Draw Scrutiny," *New York Times*, December 15, 2014, A1; cf. Peter Ramsay, *The Insecurity State: Vulnerable Autonomy and the Right to Security in the Criminal Law* (Oxford: Oxford University Press, 2013).
14. On order maintenance and the like, see Robert C. Ellickson, "Controlling Chronic Misconduct in City Spaces: Of Panhandlers, Skid Rows, and Public-Space Zoning," *Yale Law Journal* 105, no. 5 (1996): 1165–248; James Q. Wilson and George L. Kelling, "Broken Windows," *Atlantic*, March 1, 1982; see also Debra Livingston, "Police Discretion and the Quality of Life in Public Places: Courts, Communities, and the New Policing," *Columbia Law Review* 97 (1997): 551. For the liberals, see, e.g., Bernard Harcourt, *Illusion of Order:*

The False Promise of Broken Windows Policing (Cambridge, MA: Harvard University Press, 2001); David Alan Sklansky, *Democracy and the Police* (Stanford, CA: Stanford University Press, 2007). On pretext, see, e.g., Eric Citron, "Police Pretext as a Democracy Problem," *Yale Law Journal Pocket Part* 116 (2007): 364; Markus Dirk Dubber, "Policing Possession: The War on Crime and the End of Criminal Law," *Journal of Criminal Law & Criminology* 91, no. 4 (2001): 908; Amanda Geller and Jeffrey Fagan, "Pot as Pretext: Marijuana, Race and the New Disorder in New York City Street Policing," *Journal of Empirical Legal Studies* 7, no. 4 (2010): 596; Steve Herbert and Katherine Beckett, "Zoning Out Disorder: Assessing Contemporary Practices of Urban Social Control," *Studies in Law, Politics, & Society* 47 (2009): 3; Lisa Weil, "Drug-Related Evictions in Public Housing: Congress' Addiction to a Quick Fix," *Yale Law & Policy Review* 9, no. 1 (1991): 161. On the racial aspect, see, e.g., Michelle Alexander, *The New Jim Crow: Mass Incarceration in the Age of Colorblindness*, rev. ed. (New York: New Press, 2010), 28–29; Jerome Miller, *Search and Destroy: African-American Males in the Criminal Justice System* (New York: Cambridge University Press, 1996); Randall Kennedy, *Race, Crime, and the Law* (New York: Pantheon Books, 1997), 86, 91; Michael Tonry, *Punishing Race* (New York: Oxford University Press, 2011); Amy E. Lerman and Vesla M. Weaver, *Arresting Citizenship: The Democratic Consequences of American Crime Control* (Chicago: University of Chicago Press, 2014); David A. Harris, " 'Driving While Black' and All Other Traffic Offenses: The Supreme Court and Pretextual Traffic Stops," *Journal of Criminal Law & Criminology* 87, no. 2 (1997): 550; Tracey Maclin, "*Terry v. Ohio's* Fourth Amendment Legacy: Black Men and Police Discretion," *St. John's Law Review* 72, no. 3–4 (1998): 1271–322; Dorothy E. Roberts, "Constructing a Criminal Justice System Free of Racial Bias: An Abolitionist Framework," *Columbia Human Rights Law Review* 39, no. 1 (2007): 261; Dorothy E. Roberts, "Foreword: Race, Vagueness, and the Social Meaning of Order-Maintenance Policing," *Journal of Criminal Law & Criminology* 89, no. 3 (1999); 775.

15. On deinstitutionalization, see Erving Goffman, *Asylums: Essays on the Social Situation of Mental Patients and Other Inmates* (Garden City, NY: Anchor Books, 1961); Nicholas N. Kittrie, *The Right to Be Different: Deviance and Enforced Therapy* (Baltimore, MD: Johns Hopkins University Press: 1971); Thomas Szasz, *The Myth of Mental Illness: Foundations of a Theory of Personal Conduct* (New York: Hoeber-Harper, 1961); see also Gerald N. Grob, *Mental Illness and American Society, 1875–1940* (Princeton, NJ: Princeton University Press, 1983). On officials' response, see, e.g., Richard Lamb, ed., *The Homeless Mentally Ill: A Task Force Report of the American Psychiatric Association* (Washington, DC: American Psychiatric Association, 1984); Andrew T. Scull, *Decarceration: Community Treatment and the Deviant: A Radical View* (Englewood Cliffs, NJ: Prentice-Hall, 1977); Pranay Gupte, "The Derelict Population Is Declining, but the Whole City Is Its 'Flophouse,' " *New York Times*, October 23, 1973, 49. On new techniques of control, see, e.g., Katherine Beckett and Steve Herbert, *Banished: The New Social Control in Urban America* (Oxford: Oxford University Press, 2010); Teresa Gowan, *Hobos, Hustlers, and Backsliders: Homeless in San Francisco* (Minneapolis: University of Minnesota Press, 2010); National Law Center on Homelessness and Poverty, *No Homeless People Allowed: A Report on Anti-Homeless Laws, Litigation, and Alternatives in 49 United States Cities* (Washington, DC: National Law Center on Homelessness & Poverty, 1994), 10–12, 16–21, 36–39; National Law Center on Homelessness and Poverty, *The Right to Remain Nowhere: A Report on Anti-Homeless Laws and Litigation in 16 United States Cities* (Washington, DC: National Center on Homelessness & Poverty, 1993), 2; Harry Simon, "Towns without Pity: A Constitutional and Historical Analysis of Official Efforts to Drive Homeless Persons from American Cities," *Tulane Law Review* 66, no. 4 (1992): 650–51; Donald E. Baker, Comment, " 'Anti-Homeless' Legislation: Unconstitutional Efforts to Punish the Homeless," *University of Miami Law Review* 45, no. 2–3 (1991): 417–66; Helen Hershkoff and Adam Cohen, "Begging to Differ: The First Amendment and the Right to Beg," *Harvard Law Review* 105 (1991): 896; Bernard E. Harcourt, "From the Asylum to the Prison: Rethinking the Incarceration Revolution," *Texas Law Review* 84 (2006): 1751–86; Jonathan Simon, *Governing through Crime: How the War on Crime Transformed American Democracy and Created a Culture of Fear* (New York: Oxford University Press, 2007).

16. On child support, see, e.g., Charlotte Libov, "State Enforcing Child Support Payments," *New York Times*, January 3, 1988, CN1; Tamar Lewin, "New Tools for States Bolster Collection

of Child Support," *New York Times*, June 15, 1991, 1. On transwomen, see, e.g., Patricia A. Cain, "Litigating for Lesbian and Gay Rights: A Legal History," *Virginia Law Review* 79, no. 7 (1993): 1551–642; Richard Symanski, *The Immoral Landscape: Female Prostitution in Western Societies* (Toronto: Butterworths, 1981). On migrant workers, see, e.g., State v. Shack, 277 A.2d 369 (N.J. 1971); Michael Holley, "Disadvantaged by Design: How the Law Inhibits Agricultural Guest Workers from Enforcing Their Rights," *Hofstra Labor and Employment Law Journal* 18, no. 2 (2001): 574–624; Wayne King, "Florida Peonage Charges Reflect Plight of Migrant," *New York Times*, March 17, 1973, 12. On free speakers, see, e.g., Timothy Zick, "Property, Place, and Public Discourse," *Washington University Journal of Law and Policy* 21 (2006): 173–224; Niemotko v. Maryland, 340 U.S. 268 (1951). On day laborers, see, e.g., Comite de Jornaleros de Redondo Beach v. City of Redondo Beach, 657 F.3d 936 (9th Cir. 2011); "Day Labor and Free Speech," *New York Times*, June 14, 2010, A22. On minority teen dress, see, e.g., State v. Miglavs, 337 Or. 1, 90 P.3d 607 (2007); Niko Koppel, "Are Your Jeans Sagging? Go Directly to Jail," *New York Times*, August 30, 2007. On sex offenders, see, e.g., Laura Bauer, "Georgia Ruling on Sex Offenders Prompts Other States, Including Missouri, to Re-Examine Laws," *Kansas City Star*, November 28, 2007; Michael Schwirtz, "In 2 Trailers, the Neighbors Nobody Wants," *New York Times*, February 4, 2013. On juveniles, see, e.g., David R. Barrett, William J. T. Brown, and John M. Cramer, "Juvenile Delinquents: The Police, State Courts, and Individualized Justice," *Harvard Law Review* 79, no. 4 (1966): 775–810; Lois A. Weithorn, "Envisioning Second-Order Change in America's Responses to Troubled and Troublesome Youth," *Hofstra Law Review* 33, no. 4 (2005): 1305–506. On undocumented workers, see, e.g., Eric Bailey, "2 Cities Find Alien Battle Bigger than Both of Them," *Los Angeles Times*, November 22, 1987, A1; Cara Tonucci, "Legalizing the Immigration Posse," *National Lawyers Guild Review* 68, no. 1 (2011): 1–31; Transcript of Oral Argument at 40, Thompson v. City of Louisville, 362 U.S. 199 (1960) (No. 59); Phillip Hubbart, interview with author, May 2013; Anthony Amsterdam, interview with author, April 2009.

17. See, e.g., Floyd v. City of New York, 959 F. Supp. 2d 540 (S.D.N.Y. 2013); Daniels v. City of New York, No. 99 CIV 1695, 2001 WL 228091 (S.D.N.Y. Mar. 8, 2001); Issa Kohler-Hausmann, "Managerial Justice & Mass Misdemeanors," *Stanford Law Review* 66, no. 3 (2014): 614; Issa Kohler-Hausmann, "Misdemeanor Justice: Control without Conviction," *American Journal of Sociology* 119, no. 2 (2013): 351.

INDEX

Page numbers in *italics* indicate illustrations.